CUSTOMIZED DERIVATIVES

ALL ROYALTIES
FROM THE SALE OF THIS BOOK
WILL BE DONATED TO

United Nations Children's Fund

CUSTOMIZED DERIVATIVES

A Step-by-Step Guide to Using Exotic Options, Swaps, and Other Customized Derivatives

K. RAVINDRAN

McGraw-Hill

New York San Francisco Washington, D.C. Auckland Bogotá
Caracas Lisbon London Madrid Mexico City Milan
Montreal New Delhi San Juan Singapore
Sydney Tokyo Toronto

Library of Congress Cataloging-in-Publication Data

Ravindran, K., date.
   Customized derivatives : a step-by-step guide to using exotic
options, swaps, and other customized derivatives / K. Ravindran.
     p.   cm.
   ISBN 0-7863-0556-8
   1. Derivative securities. I. Title.
HG6024.A3R38 1998
332.84'5—dc21   97-9623
                                          CIP

McGraw-Hill

A Division of The McGraw·Hill Companies

The sponsoring editor for this book was Stephen Isaacs and the production
supervisor was Suzanne W. B. Rapcavage. This book was set in ITCCentury Light
by Jana Fisher and Lisa Mellott through the services of Barry E. Brown
(Broker—Editing, Design and Production).

Printed and bound by R.R. Donnelley & Sons Company.

This publication is designed to provide accurate and authoritative information in
regard to the subject matter covered. It is sold with the understanding that neither
the author nor the publisher is engaged in rendering legal, accounting, or other
professional service. If legal advice or other expert assistance is required, the
services of a competent professional person should be sought.

      —From a Declaration of Principles jointly adopted by a Committee of the
                American Bar Association and a Committee of Publishers.

Dedicated to
my family and the future of children of the world

C O N T E N T S

Chapter 4

Intuitive Methods for Pricing Options   203

E X H I B I T S

Chapter 3

Chapter 4

E X A M P L E S

METHODOLOGIES

COMMONLY USED NOTATIONS

0	=	current time
S_t	=	price of underlying asset at time t
$S_{i,t}$	=	price of asset i at time t
X	=	strike price of option
r_d	=	continuously compounded domestic risk-free rate
r_f	=	continuously compounded foreign risk-free rate of underlying asset (In the context of an equity market, this represents the continuously compounded dividend rate of asset, and in the context of a commodity market, this represents the continuously compounded convenience yield of asset.)
$r_{i,f}$	=	continuously compounded foreign risk-free rate of asset i.
q	=	continuously compounded dividend rate of a foreign currency denominated asset
ef	=	exercise frequency of underlying option
fc	=	frequency associated with the payment of the second installment in a compound option
sf	=	sampling frequency associated with underlying option
T	=	life of derivative
σ	=	annualized volatility of underlying asset
σ_i	=	annualized volatility of asset i
σ_s	=	annualized volatity of foreign currency denominated asset
σ_{FX}	=	annualized volatility of foreign currency
$\rho_{FX,S}$	=	correlation between continuously compounded returns of currency (denominated in domestic per foreign) and foreign currency denominated asset
$\rho_{i,j}$	=	correlation between continuously compounded returns of assets i and j
$\Sigma_{n,n}$	=	variance-covariance matrix of the continuously compounded returns of the n assets and is given by the n × n matrix where $\rho_{i,j} = \rho_{j,i}$ for i ≠ j

$$
\left[
\begin{array}{ccccccc}
\sigma_1^2 & \rho_{1,2}\sigma_1\sigma_2 & \cdots & \rho_{1,r}\sigma_1\sigma_r & \rho_{1,r+1}\sigma_1\sigma_{r+1} & \cdots & \rho_{1,n}\sigma_1\sigma_n \\
\rho_{2,1}\sigma_2\sigma_1 & \sigma_2^2 & \cdots & \rho_{2,r}\sigma_2\sigma_r & \rho_{2,r+1}\sigma_2\sigma_{r+1} & \cdots & \rho_{2,n}\sigma_2\sigma_n \\
\bullet & \bullet & & \bullet & \bullet & & \bullet \\
\bullet & \bullet & & \bullet & \bullet & & \bullet \\
\bullet & \bullet & & \bullet & \bullet & & \bullet \\
\rho_{r,1}\sigma_r\sigma_1 & \rho_{r,2}\sigma_r\sigma_2 & \cdots & \sigma_r^2 & \rho_{r,r+1}\sigma_r\sigma_{r+1} & \cdots & \rho_{r,n}\sigma_r\sigma_n \\
\hline
\rho_{r+1,1}\sigma_{r+1}\sigma_1 & \rho_{r+1,2}\sigma_{r+1}\sigma_2 & \cdots & \rho_{r+1,r}\sigma_{r+1}\sigma_r & \sigma_{r+1}^2 & \cdots & \rho_{r+1,n}\sigma_{r+1}\sigma_n \\
\bullet & \bullet & & \bullet & \bullet & & \bullet \\
\bullet & \bullet & & \bullet & \bullet & & \bullet \\
\bullet & \bullet & & \bullet & \bullet & & \bullet \\
\rho_{n,1}\sigma_n\sigma_1 & \rho_{n,2}\sigma_n\sigma_2 & \cdots & \rho_{n,r}\sigma_n\sigma_r & \rho_{n,r+1}\sigma_n\sigma_{r+1} & \cdots & \sigma_n^2
\end{array}
\right]
$$

$\Sigma_{11,r,r}$ = variance-covariance matrix of the continuously compounded returns of the first r of the n assets, which is extracted from $\Sigma_{n,n}$ and is given by the r × r matrix

$$
\left[
\begin{array}{ccc}
\sigma_1^2 & \cdots & \rho_{1,r}\sigma_1\sigma_r \\
\bullet & \cdots & \bullet \\
\bullet & \cdots & \bullet \\
\rho_{r,1}\sigma_r\sigma_1 & \cdots & \sigma_r^2
\end{array}
\right]
$$

$\Sigma_{22,n-r,n-r}$ = variance-covariance matrix of the continuously compounded returns of the last n–r of the n assets, which is extracted from $\Sigma_{n,n}$ and is given by the (n–r) × (n–r) matrix

$$
\left[
\begin{array}{ccc}
\sigma_{r+1}^2 & \cdots & \rho_{r+1,n}\sigma_{r+1}\sigma_n \\
\bullet & \cdots & \bullet \\
\bullet & \cdots & \bullet \\
\rho_{n,r+1}\sigma_n\sigma_{r+1} & \cdots & \sigma_n^2
\end{array}
\right]
$$

$\Sigma_{12,r,n-r}$ = variance-covariance matrix of the continuously compounded returns, which is extracted from $\Sigma_{n,n}$ and is given by the r × (n–r) matrix

$$
\left[
\begin{array}{ccc}
\rho_{1,r+1}\sigma_1\sigma_{r+1} & \cdots & \rho_{1,n}\sigma_1\sigma_n \\
\bullet & \cdots & \bullet \\
\bullet & \cdots & \bullet \\
\rho_{r,r+1}\sigma_r\sigma_{r+1} & \cdots & \rho_{r,n}\sigma_r\sigma_n
\end{array}
\right]
$$

$\Sigma_{21,n-r,r}$ = variance-covariance matrix of the continuously compounded returns, which is extracted from $\Sigma_{n,n}$ and is given by the (n–r) × r matrix

$$\begin{bmatrix} \rho_{r+1,1}\sigma_{r+1}\sigma_1 & \cdots & \rho_{r+1,r}\sigma_{r+1}\sigma_r \\ \bullet & \cdots & \bullet \\ \bullet & \cdots & \bullet \\ \rho_{n,1}\sigma_n\sigma_1 & \cdots & \rho_{n,r}\sigma_n\sigma_r \end{bmatrix}$$

$\Sigma^{-1}_{22,n-r,n-r}$ = inverse of the matrix $\Sigma_{22,n-r,n-r}$

$\hat{\Sigma}_{n,n}$ = standardized variance-covariance matrix of the continuously compounded returns of the n assets and is given by the n $\times$ n matrix where $\rho_{i,j} = \rho_{j,i}$ for $i \neq j$

$$\begin{bmatrix} 1 & \rho_{1,2} & \cdots & \rho_{1,r} & \cdots & \rho_{1,n-1} & \vdots & \rho_{1,n} \\ \rho_{2,1} & 1 & \cdots & \rho_{2,r} & \cdots & \rho_{2,n-1} & \vdots & \rho_{2,n} \\ \bullet & \bullet & & \bullet & & \bullet & \vdots & \bullet \\ \bullet & \bullet & & \bullet & & \bullet & \vdots & \bullet \\ \bullet & \bullet & & \bullet & & \bullet & \vdots & \bullet \\ \rho_{r,1} & \rho_{r,2} & \cdots & 1 & \cdots & \rho_{r,n-1} & \vdots & \rho_{r,n} \\ \bullet & \bullet & & \bullet & & \bullet & \vdots & \bullet \\ \bullet & \bullet & & \bullet & & \bullet & \vdots & \bullet \\ \bullet & \bullet & & \bullet & & \bullet & \vdots & \bullet \\ \rho_{n-1,1} & \rho_{n-1,2} & \cdots & \rho_{n-1,r} & \cdots & 1 & \vdots & \rho_{n-1,n} \\ \hdashline \rho_{n,1} & \rho_{n,2} & \cdots & \rho_{n,r} & \cdots & \rho_{n,n-1} & \vdots & 1 \end{bmatrix}$$

$\hat{\Sigma}_{11,n-1,n-1}$ = standardized variance-covariance matrix of the continuously compounded returns of the first (n–1) of the n assets, which is extracted from $\hat{\Sigma}_{n,n}$ and is given by the (n–1) $\times$ (n–1) matrix

$$\begin{bmatrix} 1 & \cdots & \rho_{1,n-1} \\ \bullet & \cdots & \bullet \\ \bullet & \cdots & \bullet \\ \rho_{n-1,1} & \cdots & 1 \end{bmatrix}$$

$\hat{\Sigma}_{22,1,1}$ = standardized variance-covariance matrix of the continuously compounded returns of the last asset, which is extracted from $\hat{\Sigma}_{n,n}$ and is given by the number 1

$\hat{\Sigma}_{12,n-1,1}$ = standardized variance-covariance matrix of the continuously compounded returns, which is extracted from $\hat{\Sigma}_{n,n}$ and is given by the (n–1) $\times$ 1 matrix

$$\begin{bmatrix} \rho_{1,n} \\ \bullet \\ \bullet \\ \rho_{n-1,n} \end{bmatrix}$$

$\hat{\Sigma}_{21,1,n-1}$ = standardized variance-covariance matrix of the continuously compounded returns, which is extracted from $\hat{\Sigma}_{n,n}$ and is given by the $1 \times (n-1)$ matrix

$$\begin{bmatrix} \rho_{n,1} & \cdots & \rho_{n,n-1} \end{bmatrix}$$

$\hat{\Sigma}^{-1}_{11,n-1,n-1}$ = inverse of the matrix $\hat{\Sigma}_{11,n-1,n-1}$

PREFACE

While the reader is assumed to have some general understanding of basic derivatives as well as first-year calculus, this book is appropriate for any student, academic, and practitioner (which would include everyone from end user to market maker and from back-office to front-office employee) who is interested in looking at the bigger picture of derivatives and exotic derivatives. Since derivative products proliferate at warp speed, it is difficult to keep abreast of all products transacted in the marketplace and be intimate with all the bells and whistles attached to each new product. The fact that each creation is simply some permutation of the basic underlying building blocks, makes it imperative to define the building blocks in a finite yet robust sense such that all new products become permutations and combinations of these building blocks. To do this, I have adapted in this book a building block approach in which all the blocks are created in a manner that each block has its own unique payoff profile. By understanding these blocks well, I have found from my experience that almost all (if not all) new products encountered can be easily understood using the building blocks. I believe that these building blocks can help one develop a timeless thinking concept that can be effectively used to understand, intuit, and even analyze any market-driven flavor-of-the-day product.

Although many articles provide an overview to the universe of exotic derivatives, there are very few books on the subject, and nearly all of them have been written from a product-focused point of view with a heavy emphasis on mathematics. While mathematics is crucial to the process of quantifying the risks associated with any product, it is only a tool to help one understand the behavior of financial markets. In my experience as a trader (risk manager), marketer, quant, teacher, academic, and consultant, I have found that at least 90 percent of the derivatives and exotic derivatives that trade in the marketplace across any asset class can be valued using permutations and combinations of certain mathematical tools, identities, and relationships. I have provided these tools in the Appendix of this book in the hope that a technically/quantitatively bent reader would be able to use these tools effectively to value many of these derivatives. For readers who are not technically/quantitatively inclined, I have also provided in a step-by-step fashion the binomial and Monte Carlo methodologies. Using numerical examples, I show how these recipes are applied to value the building blocks.

ACKNOWLEDGMENTS

In my quest to savor and enjoy every minute of life, I have met many beautiful people who have helped in some way. In the realm of mathematics and finance, two special people have played a crucial role in my life.

The first is Ernest Enns of the University of Calgary. Ernest has influenced the way I now think about and teach mathematics in that one should think of mathematics as a problem-solving tool and not shy away from borrowing ideas from other disciplines as long as they help solve the problem.

The second individual is David Matthews of the University of Waterloo. David was instrumental in introducing me to the idea of applying my varied skills to financial markets, in particular derivatives. Since I had never seen a trading room before, he was kind enough to take time from his busy schedule to bring me to one. It is a day I will always remember.

This book would have not been possible without the feedback from many of my colleagues. I appreciate the time they have taken out of their tight schedules to comment on earlier drafts of this manuscript. These people include Bob Carbrey, Simon Chan, Shaun Cumby, Jim Darling, Cindy Forbes, Craig Fowler, Houben Huang, Adrian Hussey, Harry Kat, Adam Kolkiewicz, Ari Levy, Josephine Marks, Stephen Orlich, Catherine Reimer, Frederick Shen, Alex Wei, and Jennifer Weir. However, they are by no means responsible for any errors present in this book.

Finally, I would like to thank the staff at McGraw-Hill, particularly Kevin Thornton and Stephen Isaacs, for being patient and understanding during the course of this project.

ABOUT THE AUTHOR

Dr. K. Ravindran is a principal of Consolidated Risk-Management Solutions Inc. (CRMS), an independent risk-management consulting firm that specializes in advising corporations and institutions (financial/nonfinancial) in holistic risk-quantification and risk-management techniques, unique approaches developed by CRMS. Using his experience at major financial institutions, he also consults on product development, portfolio management, financial engineering, building benchmark solutions, developing risk-management platforms, developing pricing models, and hedging strategies for vanilla and exotic derivatives across all asset classes.

Dr. Ravindran is also an adjunct professor in both the Department of Statistics and Actuarial Science at the University of Waterloo and the Department of Mathematics and Statistics at the Universityof Calgary. In addition to regular business and teaching duties, he is the founding editor of the *Canadian Derivatives Strategies* newsletter, a member of the editorial board of the *Journal of Derivatives Use, Trading and Regulation*, and an associate editor of the book *The Handbook of Derivative Instruments: Products, Pricing, Portfolio Applications, and Risk Management (Rev. ed.)*. He holds a Ph.D. in probability and teaches various short courses on exotic and customized derivatives, as well as contributing numerous articles to professional journals and books.

1

SETTING THE STAGE

INTRODUCTION

The word *derivative* as defined in most dictionaries means "derived from" or "not primitive." As such, a derivative, in the context of financial markets, is a financial instrument whose value or price can be derived from the value(s) of other underlying instruments that can be observed in the marketplace. It should come as no surprise to the reader that this definition does not preclude instruments whose values can be derived from the values of other underlying derivative instruments. While the cash market instruments across any asset class would include the likes of a bond, stock, T-bill, currency and so on, the simplest form of a derivative that is linked to these underlying assets would be an instrument such as a futures contract, a forward contract, a swap contract, and an option contract. The value of any of these four contracts in its simplest form, depends on the price and/or rate of only one underlying cash instrument at a prespecified time in the future.

Since their inception, derivative instruments have slowly gained acceptance as useful risk-management and yield-enhancement tools. In doing so, derivatives have grown to become a part of any treasurer's or portfolio manager's standard arsenal for mitigating the increasing level of sophisticated and complex risks inherent in the financial markets. Due to this widely growing acceptance, the derivatives market has flourished exponentially over the decade, with financial institutions constantly providing creative and innovative solutions to institutional, governmental, corporate, and commerical end users to more effectively and efficiently manage risks, enhance yields and borrow funds. This rapid forging ahead of the innovative boundary causes many newly created derivatives to quickly become mainstream or outdated.

The desire to remain competitive in a dynamically changing market forced many financial institutions in the late 1970s and early 1980s to start hiring mathematicians, physicists, and engineers as their in-house "rocket scientists" or "quants" to develop more sophisticated over-the-counter derivative contracts for their clients. As the level of complexity in the derivative instruments increased, risk management of these contracts became more of a science than an art. For those with an aversion to mathematics, derivatives trading and marketing became more mystical and magical than ever.

In addition to this, the disasters and scandals linked with derivatives trading have been catalysts for people who do not fully understand the derivatives business to perceive the derivatives market as a minefield. The following are some of the factors leading to these disastrous occurrences:

1. A trader who wants to trade a new product does not or cannot get his trading models verified by an independent party before trading.
2. A trader takes a view on the underlying market movements using his trading portfolio without completely understanding the risks embedded in the portfolio.
3. A marketer sells a product without completely understanding the risks embedded in the product.
4. A hedger decides to speculate in financial markets to make up for the losses incurred in the day-to-day business.
5. An end user purchases a "windfall" generating derivative without fully understanding the risks embedded in the product and without being able to independently value the product.
6. An internal control system that is not in place to ensure that the risks, profits, and losses reported by a trader is accurate and independently verified. Furthermore, even if this system were in place, it may not be powerful enough to have a quick response time if the total market risks the firm is exposed to need to be known immediately during volatile market conditions.

Although the above reasons have been and will continue to be key factors leading to disastrous occurences, they are by no means exhaustive or restricted to derivatives.[1] Whatever the reasons for derivatives-related disasters, a bad aura surrounds these financial instruments. Despite the value that derivatives add to many users, the misuse and abuse of derivatives, suffered at the hands of a few users, fueled by the media, have contributed to the bad stigma attached to the name *derivatives*.

One positive thing that has come out of all the bad publicity is that both the market-makers and end users have been forced to put tighter controls in place and share information with one another. On the flip side, there are some end users who have completely refrained from using derivatives as risk-management tools. This, as any rational *practitioner* would appreciate, contradicts the notion of prudent risk-management practice[2]. It is even scarier to sometimes see end users who

---

[1] An important reading for any user of derivatives is the renowned Global Derivatives Study Group
     Report (1993), also known as the G-30 Report. It addresses these issues and states the
     recommendations.

just do not want to do anything about risk-management because they have been and continue to be of the mind-set that anything to do with risk-management implies taking on market risks.

The irony of the bad press about derivatives is that many ardent skeptics themselves do not fully understand the meaning or the uses of derivatives. Without realizing that all derivatives can be synthetically replicated with the underlying cash markets, some skeptics have even commented that trading in the underlying cash markets is less risky than trading in the derivatives market. Little do these skeptics realize that in their everyday life, they are faced with choices about buying derivatives (for example, life/fire insurance policies, airline tickets, houses). In their pursuit of skepticism, they fail to recognize that a financial derivative is no different from a derivative that they are exposed to and accept in their everyday life as a normal thing.[3]

Whatever the reason for shying away from derivatives, it is true that derivatives are no different from fire, in the sense that derivatives can be good servants but bad masters. Consequently, when using derivatives, in addition to completely understanding the trades, any end user should also fully comprehend the tax, accounting, and legal implications arising from these trades. Furthermore, the end user should ensure that any trades put on do indeed help achieve the risk–reward objectives set out by the board of directors or senior management. While it is imperative for the end user to be able to independently mark-to-market his or her entire portfolio, it is just as important for suitable internal controls to be put in place so as to protect the organization from unforseen disasters.

OBJECTIVES OF THE BOOK

There has been and continues to be a lot of material written on the theoretical, applied, and control aspects of derivatives. While many books on this subject have focused on vanilla derivatives, only a few have been written on the subject of nontraditional and/or customized derivatives. Furthermore, the focus of these materials has been the theory underlying the pricing of derivative products with

---

[2] The word *practitioner* in the context of this book refers to both a market maker and an end user.

[3] A mutual fund manager came up to me during one of my seminars and told me that in his business there is no room for derivatives and that he personally finds derivatives very complex and confusing. This comment prompted me to ask him if he knew that he was already using derivatives in his daily life. He quickly replied no. When I asked him if he loved eating pizzas, he immediately responded with a yes. I then told him that the basic ingredients that go into making a pizza are flour, cheese, and tomato sauce. Thus, if the price of either the flour, cheese, or tomato sauce rises, I would expect the price of pizza to rise. Therefore, the pizza can be thought of as a derivative of the flour, cheese, and tomato sauce, which in turn can be thought of as the underlying variables. After hearing this analogy, he told me that he never knew derivatives could be so easily explained and was rather surprised at how omnipresent derivatives are in everyone's daily life.

very little attention paid to the application of these products and the intuition underlying them. Although there have been many articles written by academicians and practitioners on the valuation and the hedging methods of exotic derivatives, little has been published on the applications and the intuition underlying the behavior of these complex instruments without the use of mathematics. Furthermore, as almost no material has been written about viewing these complex instruments using a systematic building-block approach, practitioners lacking a good quantitative background often get intimidated by these products, and students fail to get a better appreciation of how these derivatives are applied.

This book has been written to bridge this information gap. More precisely, instead of focusing on derivative products, which can make such a book outdated quickly, this book breaks the universe of derivatives into basic building blocks. Using practical examples, the book provides the intuition underlying each building block and illustrates a step-by-step approach to valuing these building blocks. In addition, for each example, subtleties that any practitioner should be aware of and observations that offer greater insights to the example and/or building block are also provided. It is my intent to create a framework in which all derivative products can be categorized and understood in a systematic and coherent manner. In the process, I hope to lay to rest the thought that exotic derivatives is essentially a rocket science and dispel the myth that one needs a Ph.D. to understand exotic derivatives. Thus, the book achieves the following three objectives:

1. Illustrates the building blocks of vanilla derivatives and the 11 building blocks of exotic derivatives.
2. Illustrates the uses and the risk characteristics associated with these building blocks in an intuitive manner.
3. Illustrates how the intuitively appealing binomial and Monte Carlo methods can be methodically applied in a step-by-step fashion to value any derivative.

The reader of this book is assumed to have a basic knowledge of derivatives. The intended audience is end users (corporates, governments, institutions), derivatives marketing/trading professionals, accountants, risk-management consultants, back- and middle-office personnel, senior management, and boards of directors. This book is designed to provide the reader with a better grasp of the intuition instead of turning the reader into a "quant."

A TOUR OF THE BOOK

After defining a *vanilla derivative*, Chapter 2 describes the use of vanilla derivatives across all the asset classes with the aid of practical examples. In the process, the chapter addresses the question of why options are better suited as vehicles for discussing the whole gamut of derivatives. In addition to explaining the traditional European-style and American-style options, the chapter goes on to show why a certain type of exotic option fits nicely into the category of a vanilla option. The chapter concludes with examples of the limitations of vanilla derivatives and how exotic derivatives better address the sophistication and complexity of modern risk exposure.

In Chapter 3, the entire gamut of exotic options is broken down into 11 building blocks that can be used to understand any complex or sophisticated derivative. Keeping mathematics to a bare minimum, the use of each block is described in detail, with plenty of intuition provided in the explanation of the effects of the parameters underlying the option on the premium of the option.

Chapter 4 shows, in a step-by-step fashion, how the intuitively appealing binomial method and Monte Carlo method can be applied to value the building blocks discussed in earlier chapters. In addition to walking through the steps for each example, by breaking down each valuation method into four categories, the chapter provides a generic how-to description of each valuation method. To be able to understand and use these generic methodologies, I would encourage the reader to go through each methodology in conjunction with the accompanying examples.

Due to the frequent mathematical and probabilistic questions I get from fellow practitioners, I have stated without proofs various probabilistic, statistical, and mathematical results that I deem relevant for the use in options or derivatives pricing. Since I have personally used these results time and time again to value all sorts of exotic derivatives, I hope that the results given are general enough for the quantitatively bent readers to use this part of the book as a valuable derivatives modelling tool. I have also included a glossary of the traded derivatives and strategies in the financial markets.

SOME PARTING THOUGHTS

Risk, which is inherent in any type of business, can be essentially split into the following two components:

1. Financial or market risk.
2. Non-financial or business risk.

While the first type of risk can be very often hedged by the appropriate financial instruments, the second is usually thought to be unhedgeable and hence is accepted as a part of doing business.

About a decade ago, most financial institutions offered products that only mitigated risks in a particular asset class. As such, a commodity producer who is exposed to interest rate, oil price, and gas price risk could only hedge the interest-rate risk, oil price risk, and gas price risk separately and independently. With the increase in competition, in order to distinguish themselves as the leading market makers, more derivatives dealers have started offering customized hedging solutions that would span at least one asset class. The implication of this is that the commodity producer can now hedge his firm's total loss against the interest-rate risk, oil price risk, and gas price risk and hence protect his profit by purchasing a single customized solution as opposed to a strip of more expensive traditional alternatives.

Although the development of financial risk management described in the previous paragraph was only applicable to the market-risk component, the next dimension of risk management in my opinion lies in the fact that market risks must be considered in tandem with business or operational risks. This notion of considering both the financial and non-financial risks in tandem is the heart and soul of holistic risk management. In this form of risk management, the day-to-day operation of a business or physical assets is optimally designed to take into consideration the fluctuations in the liabilities and the costs/prices of both resources and raw materials. More succintly, instead of considering risk management as an aftermath of a business strategy, risk management should form the basis of a business strategy. Once the operations are designed to work at an optimal level, the market risks arising from this type of operation would typically be minimized. It is to this minimized level of market risks that one would apply the notion of customized solutions to protect a company's profit. Hence, it is crucial for one to completely understand how the appropriate businesses are run before trying to make sure that the operations are working at an optimal level and deciding what customized solution is the most appropriate to the organization.

Furthermore, even if a customized solution has been identified, it is not sufficient to just understand and be able to value the solution. One should weigh all the pros and cons associated with a transaction and get into one only if adds value to the bottom line of the organization. I have found that for anyone to be comfortable with the risk characteristics, behavior, and the price of a product, time has to be spent with the valuation tool. There is no shortcut to achieving this objective. Thus, the more familiar one is with the tools, the less uncomfortable one will be with the product. This is my primary reason for presenting the use of the binomial method and the Monte Carlo method in a step-by-step fashion. Consequently, it may be the case that given the nature of the trade size and the user's risk/reward objectives, the best way to hedge the identified market risks components would be to actively buy and sell the underlying assets. Thus, insisting on the use of derivatives to hedge all market risks may not necessarily be a prudent form of risk management. Whatever the implementation strategy, it is important for one to first be able to decompose the customized solution into its building-block components. In doing so, the user can arrive at a rule-of-thumb premium associated with the strategy and often imply the risk-characteristics of the strategy using factors influencing the values of all the underlying building blocks. To help the reader understand all the building blocks, I will start with a discussion on the applications of vanilla derivatives and arrive at the building blocks of these type of derivatives in the next chapter.

2

ⓖ DESCRIPTION AND USES OF VANILLA DERIVATIVES

INTRODUCTION

Due to the globalization of economies and deregulation in financial markets, the market risks faced by any corporation or instituition, regardless of its size or domain of operation, easily span at least one asset class. Whatever the nature of business, any financial risk can more often than not be categorized into at least one of the six following major tradeable asset classes: currency[1], interest rate, equity, commodity, credit, and catastrophe. In this book, although the use of derivatives is focused in the first four asset classes, examples of use in the remaining two asset classes will be briefly mentioned.

To set the platform for the discussion of exotic derivatives strategies, this chapter will provide the reader with an overview of the vanilla derivatives used in the currency, interest-rate, equity, and commodity asset classes. In providing this overview, I hope to get the reader warmed up to the way I think about products and strategies that they are already comfortable with. This will make it easier for the reader to understand my train of thought when discussing the more complex products in the later chapters. At the end of this overview, I hope to convince the reader that the universe of derivatives can indeed be constructed by using only options on the appropriate underlying assets. In addition, I will introduce a new product to the vanilla derivatives family, which despite being a logical and natural member of the traditional derivative family, is still considered an exotic or a non-vanilla derivative by many.

---

[1] Some people classify a currency asset class under the umbrella of a commodity asset class. I will for the purposes of our discussion treat currency as an asset class by itself.

What is a vanilla derivative? It is tempting to say that a vanilla derivative is simply an ordinary or plain derivative. However, with the financial markets progressing at a very fast pace, it is of little surprise that what was new and exotic a short while ago may quickly become a dinosaur. This, coupled with the fact that "vanilla derivative" means different things to different people, makes defining it a daunting task. Thus, I feel that the best way to define a vanilla derivative is to provide examples of these derivatives across the four asset classes.

VANILLA DERIVATIVES IN THE FOUR ASSET CLASSES

In any of the four asset classes, all vanilla derivative contracts can be generally categorized into futures contracts, forward contracts, swap contracts, and option contracts, whose underlying assets themselves are the appropriate futures, forward, spot, and swap contracts. These decompositions are summarized in Exhibit 1.

EXHIBIT 1   Examples of Vanilla Derivatives

Asset Class	Underlying Derivative Contracts			
	Spot[2]	Futures	Forward	Swap
Currency	O[3]	O, D[4]	O, D	O, D
Interest rate	O	O, D	O, D	O, D
Equity	O	O, D	O, D	O, D
Commodity	O	O, D	O, D	O, D

2 Represents cash instruments such as stocks, bonds, and T-bills.
3 Represents an option contract.
4 Represents both an option contract and a nonoption-related derivative contract.

To interpret Exhibit 1, take for example O, D in the cell corresponding to the Currency row and the Futures column. This implies that both the currency futures contract and the option on the currency futures contract are examples of vanilla derivatives. Similarly, O in the cell corresponding to the Equity row and the Spot column indicates that the option on an equity spot (or stock) contract is an example of a vanilla derivative.

With Exhibit 1 summarizing all the vanilla derivatives across the four asset classes, I will now illustrate the use of each of these contracts.

THE FUTURES CONTRACT

Introduction

A futures contract is essentially an agreement between two parties in which (1) the seller guarantees the asset price at a prespecified time in the future to the buyer for no up-front cost and (2) the buyer guarantees the seller that a purchase will be made at the agreed-upon price at the prespecified time. The asset price is agreed to at the inception of the contract, and both parties have to fulfill the contract regardless of the market conditions on the contract expiration date. More succintly, both the buyer and the seller of a futures contract are obligated to perform their ends of the contract regardless of the market conditions on the expiry date. Thus, on the maturity date of the futures contract, the buyer (seller) of the futures contract will purchase (sell) the asset regardless of whether the price of the asset at that time is lower or higher than the guaranteed price.

Since a futures contract trades only on the exchange, the buyer or short-seller[5] of such a contract must deposit a fraction of the price as a margin amount, as required by the exchange. As the margin amount set aside for the contract typically changes daily due to fluctuations in the futures price, the margin can be equivalently viewed as a mark-to-market position that is required by the exchange. Furthermore, because the exchange acts as an intermediary between the buyer and the seller, the counterparty to both the buyer and the seller of the contract is essentially the exchange. However, because the exchange is a well-capitalized clearinghouse, the assumption that any transactor of an exchange-traded contract would not be exposed to counterparty risk is not far fetched.

A Futures Contract Example

Although the settlement procedures for the futures transactions vary with each product, the mechanics presented in Example 1 illustrate the use of a currency futures contract. For examples detailing the mechanics underlying the uses of other types of futures contracts, the reader is advised to consult both the exchanges and other books on the futures contracts (for example, Schwager [1984] and Stoll and Whaley [1993]).

---

[5] A short-seller of a contract is a person who sells a contract that he or she does not own. An example of short-selling in everyday life happens when a magazine subscription is made to a publisher by an individual. By selling to the individual, issues of the subscription that is not already in existence, the publisher can be viewed as a short-seller of the magazine.

EXAMPLE 1   A Currency Futures Transaction

A U.K. exporter sells his goods in the United States for a total amount of US$ 10 mm[6]. Every time the exporter bills his clients, it takes exactly three months before he gets reimbursed.

To hedge himself, he buys 94 lots of three-month futures contracts from the Chicago Mercantile Exchange at 1.7000 US/£, where the size of each futures contract lot is £62,500[7].

Time (months)	Impact of Futures Contract on the Hedger
0 3	☞ No premium is paid by hedger[8] ☞ Hedger pays US$ 9.987 mm to receive £ 5.874 mm

6 mm in the context of this book represents one million.

7 Since the size of a contract lot is £62,500, the hedger would have to pay US$ 106,250 on the expiry of the futures contract to receive £62,500. See also Observation 1.

8 In practice, the hedger has to put up a margin amount for the purchase at the inception of the contract. As mentioned in Observation 4, the use of margins is neglected in this example.

It is important for the reader to make the following six observations about Example 1:

OBSERVATION 1   As shown in Example 1, 94 lots of the currency futures contracts are bought by the exporter. To arrive at this number, one has to first calculate the price of a currency futures contract in U.S. funds. Since the size of a lot is £62,500 and the three-month currency futures are trading at 1.7000 *US/£*, the size of one lot in U.S. funds is £62,500 • 1.7000 *US/£* = *US*$ 106,250. The number of futures contracts that need to be purchased can now be obtained by dividing US$ 10 mm by US$ 106,250. This results in approximately 94 lots (or contracts).

OBSERVATION 2   In purchasing the 94 futures contracts, the exporter has effectively converted an amount of US$ 9.987 mm (= 1.7000 *US/£* • £62,500 • 94 contracts), which is less than the billed amount of US$ 10 mm. The reason for this inexactness is the fact that it is impossible for the exporter to buy fractional lots of the futures contracts. Thus, by the nature of the futures contracts, one should not be surprised to see residual U.S. funds left unhedged.

OBSERVATION 3 In buying the futures contracts, the exporter has assumed that his cash inflow takes place on the day the futures contract gets settled. In the event that he does not receive his cash flow on this day, he is exposed to the risk arising from the mismatch in the timing of the cash flows, which is known as a *basis risk*[9]. Futhermore, even if the exporter knew the timing of his incoming cash flows exactly, it would very often be impossible for him to purchase a futures contract that would settle on this date. This follows from the fact that the currency futures contract only expires on specific dates, for example, the second business day preceding the third Wednesday of the month.

OBSERVATION 4 The margin regulations imposed by the exchange have been ignored in the above example. Since the exporter is buying the futures contract, he has to put up a margin for this purchase. As mentioned earlier, because this margin amount is adjusted every day using the closing futures price, in practice the example will reflect the fact there is a daily flow of cash between the exporter and the exchange. This margin, which can be viewed as a mark-to-market procedure put in place by the exchange, protects the exchange from the buyer defaulting on his contract.

OBSERVATION 5 If the exporter wanted to purchase a futures contract, barring the margin that has to be deposited, the exporter would not have to pay or receive any money for the purchase at the inception of the contract. In the context of our example, by setting aside an appropriate margin, the exporter could have purchased a futures contract that would have allowed him to sell the U.S. dollars at a rate of 1.7000 US/£. Since this rate is defined by the market, by the nature of the futures contract it would not be possible for the exporter to sell the U.S. dollars at an off-market rate (that is, any rate that is different from the market rate). Thus, if the market rate itself is unfavorable to the exporter, the futures contract can only be used to transact at this unfavorable rate.

---

[9] The term *basis risk* is also used to describe the risk that arises from hedging a market exposure with a closely related asset. An example of this would be the hedging of the exposure to mortgage rates with either bond yields or swap rates.

OBSERVATION 6 When the exchange rate on the expiry of the contract is 1.6800 US/£, a profit of £ $\left(\dfrac{9.987}{1.6800} - \dfrac{9.987}{1.7000} \right)$ = £0.07 mm can be realized if the hedger, instead of purchasing a futures contract, chooses to convert his U.S. dollars to sterling using the spot exchange-rate market. On the other hand, if the exchange rate on the expiry of the contract is 1.7200 US/£, a loss of £ $\left(\dfrac{9.987}{1.7200} - \dfrac{9.987}{1.7000} \right)$ = –£0.068 mm can be realized if the hedger, instead of purchasing a futures contract, chooses to convert his U.S. dollars to sterling using the spot exchange-rate market. This profit and loss profile is illustrated in Exhibit 2 for various exchange-rate levels on the contract maturity date, where the number 0.5882 is given by the quotient $\dfrac{1}{1.7000}$. Although the hedged position appears insensitive in Exhibit 2 for various changes in the underlying spot rate, this appearance is due more to the scaling of the graph. Since, only US\$ 9.987 mm was hedged using the futures contract, a residual amount of US\$ 0.013 mm is subject to market risk. Thus, in reality, the hedged position would indicate a very gentle positively sloped line just like

EXHIBIT 2   Risks with and without Hedging

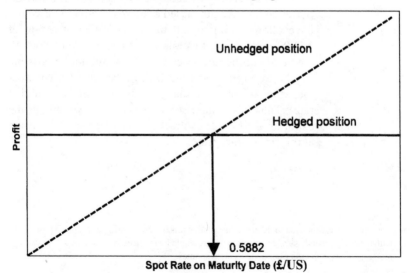

Spot Rate on Maturity Date (£/US)

the positively sloped line representing the unhedged position in Exhibit 2.

Given the fact that the exporter's objective was to hedge or equivalently eradicate the volatility of the incoming cash flow, he should not be concerned about the upside given away due to potential favorable market movements. More precisely, he should not worry about the profit potential foregone if the U.S. dollar strengthens on the contract maturity date, as shown in Exhibit 2, to exceed a level of 0.5882 £/US. If the ability to participate in potential favorable movements in the market is just as important as hedging, the exporter would be better off using other, more efficient option-related strategies discussed later in this book.

Characteristics of the Futures Contract

The profits associated with the purchase of a futures contract are more succinctly written in Exhibit 3 and graphed as in Exhibit 4. The profit graph illustrated in Exhibit 4 refers to potential profit and loss that can be realized by both the purchaser and the seller of the contract. As can be seen, the seller's profit position is simply the mirror image of the buyer's position, indicating that the buyer's gain is the seller's loss and vice versa.

Knowing how a futures contract works and what the profit and loss associated with the contract is, the next logical step would be to identify the factors influencing the price of a futures contract. Before doing this, it is imperative to first understand that pricing a futures contract implies finding a guaranteed price/rate at which the buyer (seller) could purchase (sell) the underlying asset on the contract maturity date for no up-front cost. Depending on the type of futures contract, there are various factors that influence the price. These factors have been summarized and tabulated in Exhibit 5 for the four asset classes.

EXHIBIT 3 Profits to the Buyer of a Futures Contract

Type of Contract	Profit at Time T
$F_{UT}(0,T,X)$	$S_T - X$

where

0	= Current time
T	= Time of futures maturity
X	= Guaranteed price
S_T	= Price of the underlying asset at time T
$F_{UT}(0,T,X)$	= Futures contract purchased at time 0 with parameters T and X

EXHIBIT 4 Futures Profit as Maturity

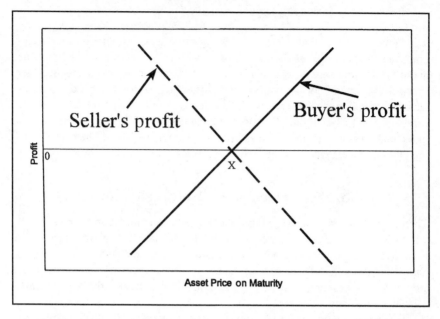

Exhibit 5 can be easily interpreted once the factors of influence are properly understood. While the factors dividend rate, foreign risk-free rate, underlying asset price, and life of contract are self-explanatory, convenience yield is used to describe both the storage and transportation costs associated with the underlying commodity and is couched in terms of a yield. The reader is referred to Hull (1997) for an in-depth explanation of this terminology.

It should come as no surprise to the reader that while only three factors affect the price of an interest-rate futures contract, four factors are crucial in deter-

EXHIBIT 5 Factors Influencing the Price of a Futures Contract

	Types of Contracts			
Factors	**Interest Rate Futures**	**Currency Futures**	**Equity Futures**	**Commodity Futures**
Convenience yield				✔
Dividend rate			✔	
Foreign risk-free rate		✔		
Domestic risk-free rate	✔	✔	✔	✔
Underlying asset price	✔	✔	✔	✔
Life of contract	✔	✔	✔	✔

mining the price of futures contracts from the remaining three asset classes, where the fourth factor reduces the growth rate of the asset. Furthermore, in identifying these factors, the effect of economic conditions, political environment, transactions cost and so on will not be considered in this book.

To understand how these factors affect the price of a futures contract, one has to first derive a no-arbitrage relationship between the futures contract and the asset underlying the futures contract. The reader is referred to Stoll and Whaley (1993) and Hull (1997) for these relationships. Once these relationships are identified, it is easy to determine the effect of these factors on the futures contract, which is summarized in Exhibit 6.

EXHIBIT 6 Effect of Increase in Value of Underlying Factors on Futures Price

Factors	Effect on Futures Price
r_f	$\Downarrow$
r_d	$\Uparrow$
S_0	$\Uparrow$
T when i) $r_d \geq r_f$	$\Uparrow$
ii) $r_d < r_f$	$\Downarrow$

To intuit the above results, consider the effect of r_f in the context of an equity market. Increasing this factor reduces the growth rate of the underlying asset since a dividend paid on a stock can reduce the stock price. Thus, the higher the dividend rate, the lower the stock price, resulting in a lower future expected price of the stock. Since the futures price is in essence the future expected price of the stock, increasing r_f while keeping other factors constant would result in a lower futures price. Similar reasoning can be used to intuit the effect of this factor in both the currency and the commodity asset class.

As r_d represents the risk-free rate of the economy, all assets in the economy would grow at this rate. Clearly, the higher the value of r_d, the greater the growth of the asset; resulting in a higher future expected price of the asset. Because the futures price is in essence the future expected price of the asset, increasing r_d and keeping all the other factors constant would result in a higher futures price. Similarly, since an increase in S_0 results in a higher future expected price of the asset, increasing S_0 also leads to an increase in the futures price.

To intuit the effect of T on the futures price, consider, for example, the equity-asset class. Since r_d has a positive effect on the growth rate of the asset and r_f has a negative effect on the growth rate of the asset, if $r_d \geq r_f$, the net effect on the asset's growth rate is still nonnegative. As long as this growth rate is nonnegative, the future price of the asset is expected to increase, causing an increase in the futures price. Similar reasoning can be used to intuit the effect of T when $r_d < r_f$.

THE FORWARD CONTRACT
Introduction

Like a futures contract, a forward contract is an agreement between two parties where the seller guarantees the asset price at a prespecified time out in the future to the buyer for no up-front cost, and the buyer guarantees the seller that a purchase will be made at the agreed-upon price regardless of the market conditions. Thus, although a forward contract helps achieve the same objective as a futures contract in terms of application, there are some differences between these contracts.[10]

Since the interest-rate forwards, equity forwards, and commodity forwards are just special cases of the interest-rate swaps, equity swaps, and commodity swaps respectively, this section will only focus on currency forward contracts.

A Forward Contract Example

The mechanics underlying the transaction of a currency forward contract are illustrated in Example 2 on page 17.

It is important for the reader to make the following seven observations about Example 2.

OBSERVATION 1 Instead of using a 2½-month forward contract, the exporter could have used either a two-month futures contract or a three-month futures contract. In the event he uses a two-month futures contract, he would buy 94 lots of currency futures at 1.6920 US/£, while using a three-month futures contract would result in a purchase of 94 lots of currency futures at 1.7000 US/£.

OBSERVATION 2 Regardless of the type of futures contract, using the futures contracts results in the exporter buying 94 lots of the contracts. This implicitly means a small proportion of the U.S. funds have been left unhedged using the futures contracts. By using the forward contract as illustrated in Example 2, the exporter would end up with no unhedged U.S. funds. More precisely, with the forward contract, he would be completely hedged.

OBSERVATION 3 With the forward contract, the exporter has the luxury of purchasing a hedge to mitigate his risk on the day of the in-

---

[10] These differences have been summarized in Exhibit 8.

EXAMPLE 2   A Currency Forward Transaction

A U.K. exporter sells his goods in the United States for a total amount of US$ 10 mm. Every time the exporter bills his clients, it takes exactly 2½ months before he gets reimbursed.

To hedge himself, he uses a 2½-month forward contract that would allow him to sell the U.S. dollar at 0.5896 £/US.[11] The U.S. dollar is currently trading at 0.5970 £/US, and the 2-month and 3-month futures contracts are trading at 1.6920 US/£ and 1.7000 US/£ respectively.

Time (months)	Impact of Forward Contract on the Hedger
0	☛ No premium is paid by hedger
2½	☛ Hedger pays US$ 10 mm to receive £5.896 mm

11 While the spot rate and the forward rate are quoted in £/US, the futures rates are quoted in US/£. This observation is generally true for the way all spot, futures, and forward currency contracts are quoted in the marketplace. As another example, consider the Canadian dollar/U.S. dollar exchange rate. In the spot and forward contracts, this is quoted in Cad/U.S.; whereas, in the futures contract it is quoted as U.S./Cad.

coming cash flows. If the futures contracts are used as alternatives, because the futures contracts do not expire in exactly 2½ months, the exporter would be exposed to the basis risk. Hence, futures contracts cannot be used effectively if customized contract expiry dates are required.

OBSERVATION 4   In the purchase of the futures contracts that was illustrated in Example 1, the exporter had to set aside margin deposits that are imposed by the exchange. In entering into a forward contract, no mark-to-market provision is needed, and hence no margin is required. This implies that the exporter would be exposed to the credit risk of his counterparty, and the counterparty is exposed to his credit risk. In practice, to be able to transact in an over-the-counter trade, his counterparty would usually be a financial institution, which would require him to have a minimum credit rating.[12]

12 Even if the forward contract were constructed to identically replicate the settlement date underlying the expiry of the futures contract, both the forward contract and the futures contract would still, in practice, differ in price. This difference arises from the fact that while the mark-to-market mechanism underlying a futures contract is done daily, it is only done on the contract expiration date for a forward contract.

OBSERVATION 5 To purchase the futures contracts in Example 1, the exporter could only transact in contracts whose rates were implied by the markets. As in the futures contract, Example 2 also shows that to sell the U.S. dollar 2½-month forward, the exporter could similarly use a market-implied rate of 1.6960 US/£. However, unlike the futures contract, a forward contract allows the exporter to alternatively sell his U.S. dollars at an off-market rate for an up-front payment. More precisely, if the exporter enters into a 2½-month forward contract that obligates him to sell US$ 10 mm at a favorable rate of 1.6850 US/£ when the market rate is 1.6960 US/£, he would end up making a payment of £0.038 mm to his counterparty at the inception of the forward contract. On the other hand, if the exporter enters into a structurally similar contract that obligates him to sell US$ 10 mm at an unfavorable rate of 1.7000 US/£ when the market rate is 1.6960 US/£, he would receive a payment of £0.014 mm from his counterparty at the inception of the contract.

OBSERVATION 6 Like Example 1, when the exchange rates on the maturity of the contract are 1.6800 US/£ and 1.7200 US/£, the profit and loss respectively that would be realized from using the forward contract are

$$£\left(\frac{10}{1.6800} - \frac{10}{1.6960}\right) = £0.056 \text{ mm}$$

and

$$£\left(\frac{10}{1.7200} - \frac{10}{1.6960}\right) = -£0.082 \text{ mm.}$$

Although the profit and loss profile with and without the hedge would be philosophically no different from that illustrated in Exhibit 2, unlike the line depicting the hedged position, the line arising from the use of a forward contract as a hedge would be perfectly horizontal. This is because the entire amount of US$ 10 mm has been hedged.

OBSERVATION 7 Like the futures contract example, Example 2 showed the hedger receiving an amount of £5.896 mm and paying an amount of US$ 10 mm on the maturity of the contract. In practice, this forward contract will cash settle as the hedger converts his U.S. dollars to British pounds using the exchange rate prevailing on the contract maturity date.

More precisely, if the exchange rate on maturity date turns out to be 0.5750 £/US, the hedger would receive an amount of £5.75 mm for his US$ 10 mm using the spot market. From his forward contract, he would receive an additional amount of £10 • (0.5896 − 0.5750) = £0.146 mm. This will result in the hedger receiving a total amount of £(5.75 + 0.146) = £5.896 mm.

On the other hand, if the exchange rate on maturity date turns out to be 0.5950 £/US, the hedger would receive an amount of £5.95 mm for his US$ 10 mm using the spot market. From his forward contract, he would pay an amount of £10 • (0.5950 − 0.5896) = £0.0540 mm. This will result in the hedger receiving a total amount of £(5.95 − 0.054) = £5.896 mm.

Characteristics of the Forward Contract

The profits associated with the purchase of a forward contract are more succintly written as Exhibit 7. Its graph is no different from Exhibit 4.

EXHIBIT 7 Profits to the Buyer of a Forward Contract

	Type of Contract	Profit at Time T
	$F_{OR}(0,T,X)$	$S_T - X - P_T^{*}$[13]
where		
0	= Current time	
T	= Time of forward maturity	
X	= Guaranteed price	
S_T	= Price of the underlying asset at time T	
$F_{OR}(0,T,X)$	= Forward contract purchased at time 0 with parameters T and X	
P_T^{*}	= Payment paid/received by purchaser and the interest accrued until time T on this payment	

[13] When X is a market rate, no cash flow gets exchanged at the inception of the contract. On the other hand, if X is an off-market rate, cash flows get exchanged at the inception of the contract. When cash flows do get exchanged, the interest accruing on this cash flow amount during the life of the contract is also foregone by the party making the payment. As such, P_T^{*}, which represents both the payment and interest paid or received in the forward contract transaction, has a zero value if X is a market rate and has a nonzero value if X is an off-market rate.

Pricing a forward contract is no different from valuing a futures contract in that one has to find the guaranteed price at which both the buyer and seller will fulfill their obligations on the contract maturity date for either no up-front cost or a prespecified up-front payment.

The factors that influence the price of a forward contract are no different from those presented in Exhibit 5, and the effect of these factors is identical to those presented in Exhibit 6. The similarities and differences between a futures and a forward contract are summarized in Exhibit 8.

EXHIBIT 8 Comparison between a Futures and a Forward Contract

	Futures Contract	Forward Contract
Differences	Exchange traded	Over-the-counter traded
	Margin required	No margin required
	No counterparty credit exposure	Counterparty credit exposure
	Expiry dates cannot be customized	Expiry dates can be customized
	Guaranteed off-market prices/ rates not possible	Guaranteed off-market prices/rates possible
	Contracts sold as lots	Contracts sold as total dollar amounts
	Physical settlement at most times	Cash settlement at most times
Similarities	Identical payoffs on expiry date	
	Prices of the contracts are affected by the variables given in Exhibit 5 in a manner similar to Exhibit 6	

THE VANILLA SWAP CONTRACT

Introduction

A swap contract, like a forward contract, is an over-the-counter agreement between two parties who obligate themselves to fulfill their parts of the contract on prespecified dates in the future. More precisely, the obligation is made by both parties to exchange cash flows based on the movements linked to the prices, values, or returns of the underlying assets. Although many variations of swaps have been created and traded in the derivatives markets, depending on the asset class, a swap in its simplest form is usually of the fixed-floating form although sometimes it can be of the fixed-fixed form.

To understand how a swap works, this section will describe a currency swap, an interest-rate swap, an equity swap, and a commodity swap and then present examples illustrating the use of each of these swaps.

- **Currency swap:** A currency swap is an agreement between two parties where the cash flows are exchanged in two different currencies based on the appropriate interest rates. Unlike the swaps in the other asset classes, a fixed-fixed currency coupon swap, which is illustrated in Example 3, is the simplest form of a currency swap contract. Regardless of the type of currency swap contract, the counterparties typically exchange the interest cash flows and the notional principal amounts of the swap. While the former gets exchanged at prespecified periods during the life of the swap, the latter only gets exchanged at both the inception and the maturity of the swap contract.

- **Interest-rate swap:** An interest-rate swap is an agreement between two parties where cash flows are exchanged in a single currency based on the appropriate interest rates. Unlike a currency swap, only the interest cash flows get exchanged by both parties at prespecified periods during the life of an interest-rate swap. Furthermore, a fixed-floating interest-rate swap, which is illustrated in Example 6, is the simplest form of an interest-rate swap contract.

- **Equity Swap:** An equity swap is an agreement between two parties where cash flows are exchanged in a single currency based on the capital appreciation of the equity index. Like an interest-rate swap, in addition to both parties not exchanging the notional principal amounts of the contract, the simplest form of an equity swap is the fixed-floating swap. The mechanics underlying the purchase of a fixed-floating equity swap are illustrated in Example 7.

- **Commodity Swap:** A commodity swap is an agreement between two parties where cash flows are exchanged in a single currency based on the price differentials between the fixed and floating prices of the underlying commodity and no exchange of principal underlying the swap is done. Like the interest-rate and equity swap, the notional principal amounts of the swap do not get exchanged by both parties in the contract. The simplest form of a commodity swap is the fixed-floating swap. The mechanics underlying the purchase of a fixed-floating commodity swap is illustrated in Example 8.

Swap Contract Examples

Currency Swap Contracts

The mechanics underlying the transaction of a currency fixed-fixed coupon swap is illustrated in Example 3.

EXAMPLE 3 A Fixed-Fixed Currency Coupon Swap Transaction

A Canadian insurance company issues US$ 100 mm worth of fixed-rate annuities in the U.S. market. Each annuity has a life of two years, a face value of US$ 100, and pays out a fixed-rate coupon of 6.5 percent semiannually to the investors. It wants to invest the US$ 100 mm in fixed-rate Canadian assets.

To meets its obligations to the investors in the United States, the insurance company decides to get into a two-year fixed-fixed currency coupon swap with a counterparty. In this two-year semiannually reset swap, it would receive interest payments based on a fixed rate of 6.5 percent on a notional amount of US$ 100 mm in U.S. funds and pay interest payments on a fixed rate of 7 percent on a notional amount of Cad$ 138 mm in Canadian funds.

Time (months)	Impact of Currency Coupon Swap Contract on the Hedger
0	☛ US$ 10 mm paid by hedger ☛ Cad$ 138 mm received by hedger
6	☛ Cad$ (138 • 0.5 • 0.07) = Cad$ 4.83 mm paid by hedger ☛ US$ (100 • 0.5 • 0.065) = US$ 3.25 mm received by hedger
12	☛ Cad$ (138 • 0.5 • 0.07) = Cad$ 4.83 mm paid by hedger ☛ US$ (100 • 0.5 • 0.065) = US$ 3.25 mm received by hedger
18	☛ Cad$ (138 • 0.5 • 0.07) = Cad$ 4.83 mm paid by hedger ☛ US$ (100 • 0.5 • 0.065) = US$ 3.25 mm received by hedger
24	☛ Cad$ (138 • 0.5 • 0.07) = Cad$ 4.83 mm paid by hedger ☛ Cad$ 138 mm paid by hedger ☛ US$ (100 • 0.5 • 0.065) = US$ 3.25 mm received by hedger ☛ US$ 100 mm received by hedger

It is important for the reader to make the following four observations about Example 3.

OBSERVATION 1 The interest paid and received by the insurance company on each settlement date are calculated using the simple interest formula *Interest = Principal • Time • Rate*. More precisely, the Canadian interest amount out by the insurance company is based on a notional principal of Cad$

138 mm, a fixed rate of 7 percent, and a time of 0.5 years, and the U.S. interest amount received by the insurance company is based on a notional principal of US$ 100 mm, a fixed rate of 6.5 percent, and a time of 0.5 years.

OBSERVATION 2 In calculating the interest that was paid and received by the insurance company, the assumption that there is exactly 0.5 years between each cash flow period was made. Depending on the risks managed, it is possible for the interest calculated in either currency to be based on the actual number of days between each cash flow period or any other day-count convention.

OBSERVATION 3 Instead of transacting in a currency swap to hedge itself, the insurance company could alternatively use the currency forwards to purchase U.S. dollars. More precisely, the insurance company would purchase four forward contracts so that the first would expire in 6 months, the second would expire in 12 months, the third would expire in 18 months, and the last would expire in 24 months. In practice, since the 6-month, 12-month, 18-month, and 24-month currency forward rates typically vary from each other, an average forward rate is used to convert the Canadian dollar denominated cash flow to a U.S. dollar denominated one. As transacting in a currency forward contract is less credit intensive than transacting in a currency swap contract, by getting into a sequence of currency forwards, the insurance company's credit exposure to its counterparty is drastically reduced.[14] Despite this advantage, the liquidity in the currency forward contract diminishes as the maturity of the contract increases (usually past five years), whereas the liquidity in a currency swap contract would still be good for a 10- to 15-year term.

OBSERVATION 4 The fixed-fixed currency coupon swap discussed in Example 3 can also be thought of as a cross-currency loan in which the interest amounts are paid on the fixed rates. More precisely, the insurance company can be thought of

---

[14] In a forward contract, it was seen via Observation 7 in Example 2 that the settlement made on the contract maturity date was based on the difference between what was paid and what was received. Thus, the party owing the larger amount paid out the netted difference. In a currency swap, however, there is a physical exchange of the U.S. dollar cash flows for the Canadian dollar cash flows that result in no netting of the difference. Due to the lack of cash flow netting, the exposure to a counterparty's credit is greater in a currency swap.

as borrowing from its counterparty for two years an amount of Cad$ 138 mm at a semiannual interest rate of 7 percent. The counterparty, on the other hand, can be viewed as borrowing from the insurance company for two years an amount of US$ 100 mm at a semiannual interest rate of 6.5 percent.

Example 3 is more succintly represented in Exhibit 9, where the dotted (bold) lines indicate the flow of cash from the insurance company (counterparty) to the counterparty (insurance company).

EXHIBIT 9 Fixed-Fixed Currency Coupon Swap

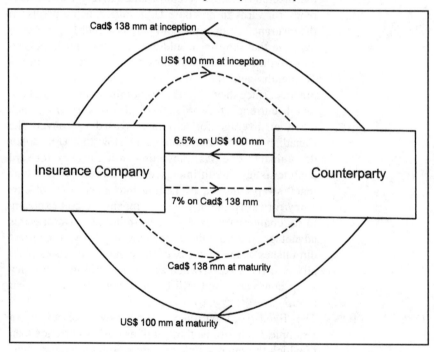

Although the fixed-fixed vanilla currency coupon swap illustrated in Example 3 may be the simplest form of currency coupon swap, it is not as widely used as a fixed-floating currency coupon swap. In this variation, in addition to the regular exchange of principals, one party while paying interest on a fixed rate in one currency receives interest on a floating rate index in another currency.

The mechanics illustrated in Example 4 on page 26 better exemplify the use of a fixed-floating currency coupon swap.

It is important for the reader to make the following two observations about Example 4.

OBSERVATION 1 As in Example 3, the insurance company in Example 4 could have alternatively tried to use the currency forward market to hedge its risks faced in converting its Canadian floating rate asset to its U.S. fixed-rate liability. In addition to the illiquidity issue mentioned in Observation 3 of Example 3, there is one other disadvantage associated with this strategy. This disadvantage arises from the fact that since the insurance company owns a floating rate asset, it would not know with precision at the inception of the contract how many Canadian dollars this asset would be generating. As a result, the notional principal amount of the forward contracts are not known at the time of contract inception.[15]

OBSERVATION 2 The fixed-floating currency coupon swap in Example 4, which can be represented in Exhibit 10, can be easily converted to a fixed-fixed currency coupon swap by swapping the floating leg for a fixed leg using an interest-rate swap. More precisely, the insurance company could enter into a two-year interest-rate swap of notional size Cad$ 138 mm with another counterparty (say, Counterparty Z) in which the company would receive the interest on the floating BA rate and pay the interest on the fixed rate. By doing this, the insurance company would have effectively exchanged its floating-rate exposure for a fixed-rate exposure. This is illustrated in Exhibit 11, which shows only the exchange of interest cash flows.

Although the two variations of the currency coupon swaps presented in Examples 3 and 4 started today and expired at a prespecified time in the future, it is important for the reader to realize that depending on the risks being managed, the insurance company may decide to get into a swap that starts out at

---

[15] Since the insurance company knows with precision what its U.S. liabilities are at the inception of the contract, it could in fact create a string of currency forwards such that its liabilities are matched exactly. This would mean that the company would know right up front what its Canadian-denominated obligations are to its counterparty. The setback, however, arises from the fact that the company would not know at the time of contract inception whether the Canadian floating-rate assets would generate enough revenue to meet its Canadian dollar obligations.

EXAMPLE 4 A Fixed-Floating Currency Coupon Swap Transaction

A Canadian insurance company issues US$ 100 mm worth of fixed-rate annuities in the United States. Each annuity has a life of two years, a face value of US$ 100, and pays out a fixed-rate coupon of 6.5 percent semiannually to the investors. It wants to invest the US$ 100 mm in floating-rate Canadian assets.

To meet its obligations to the investors in the United States, it decides to hedge itself with a two-year fixed-floating currency coupon semiannual swap. In this two-year semi-annually reset swap, it would receive a fixed rate of 6.5 percent in U.S. funds on a notional amount of US$ 100 mm and pay a six-month BA floating rate on a notional amount of Cad$ 138 mm in Canadian funds. The current value of the six-month BA rate is 6.35 percent.

Time (months)	BA rates (%)	Impact of Currency Coupon Swap Contract on the Hedger
0	6.35	☞ US$ 10 mm paid by hedger ☞ Cad$ 138 mm received by hedger
6	5.00	☞ Cad$ $(138 \cdot 0.5 \cdot 0.0635) = $ Cad$ 4.3815 mm paid by hedger ☞ US$ $(100 \cdot 0.5 \cdot 0.065) = $ US$ 3.25 mm received by hedger
12	5.50	☞ Cad$ $(138 \cdot 0.5 \cdot 0.05) = $ Cad$ 3.45 mm paid by hedger ☞ US$ $(100 \cdot 0.5 \cdot 0.065) = $ US$ 3.25 mm received by hedger
18	6.00	☞ Cad$ $(138 \cdot 0.5 \cdot 0.055) = $ Cad$ 3.795 mm paid by hedger ☞ US$ $(100 \cdot 0.5 \cdot 0.065) = $ US$ 3.25 mm received by hedger
24		☞ Cad$ $(138 \cdot 0.5 \cdot 0.06) = $ Cad$ 4.14 mm paid by hedger ☞ Cad$ 138 mm paid by hedger ☞ US$ $(100 \cdot 0.5 \cdot 0.065) = $ US$ 3.25 mm received by hedger ☞ US$ 100 mm received by hedger

EXHIBIT 10   Fixed-Floating Currency Coupon Swap

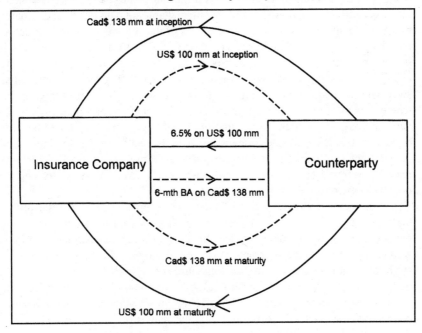

EXHIBIT 11   Fixing the Floating Interest Rate Component in Example 4

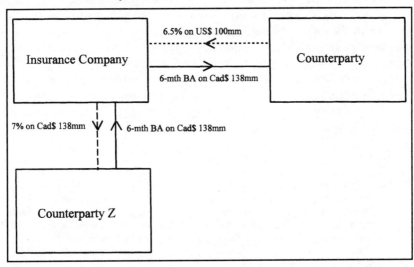

some prespecified time in the future.[16] Furthermore, the cash flows in the examples were settled semiannually, and the interest amount paid out on each floating rate settlement date was dependent on the value of the interest rate set six months prior and calculated using a constant notional principal throughout the life of the swap. Depending on the type of risks to be mitigated, it is possible, for example, for the company to get into a five-year fixed-floating currency coupon swap whose floating rate is indexed to the then-prevailing 10-year swap rate where the cash flows are settled monthly using a notional principal amount that varies across each settlement calculation. In addition, this swap could be structured such that there was no time lag between the setting of the floating-rate index and the settlement of the cash flow arising from this setting. The interested reader is referred to Dattatreya, Venkatesh, and Venkatesh (1994) for applications of some of these swaps.

Another variation on the vanilla currency coupon swap theme that still remains to be discussed is the zero-coupon currency swap. Like the traditional currency coupon swap discussed earlier, this type of swap can be classified into a zero-coupon fixed-fixed currency swap, a zero-coupon floating-fixed currency swap, or a zero-coupon floating-floating currency swap. Whatever the classification, a zero-coupon currency swap is exactly the same as a traditional currency coupon swap with the major difference being the way the interest cash flows are compounded and settled. To illustrate the mechanics of a zero-coupon currency swap, Example 5 on page 29 illustrates a zero-coupon fixed-floating currency swap.

The various permutations and combinations on the vanilla currency swap theme are summarized in Exhibit 12.

To interpret Exhibit 12, the reader should first observe that any vanilla currency swap has two legs. In a fixed-fixed and floating-floating type swap, both legs are of the fixed type and the floating type, respectively; while in a fixed-floating type swap, one leg is of the fixed type and the other leg is of the floating type. Whenever a category is applicable, only one entry must be used from each category to describe the two legs of the swap. The exception to this rule is the last category, where each entry can only be applied to a floating leg component.

As an example, consider the following entries from each category: At-Market Coupon, Spot, one-year, Constant, Cad – US, Monthly – Monthly,

---

[16] Known as forward start swaps, these type of swaps can be easily replicated using the previously discussed spot start swaps. As an example, consider the two-year fixed-floating swap in Example 4 and assume that the insurance company wants this swap to start in a year's time. To replicate this forward start swap, the insurance company would enter into a three-year spot start fixed-floating swap in which the company would be paying a six-month BA rate and a one-year spot start floating-fixed swap in which the company would be receiving a six-month BA rate, where the principals exchanged would be identical to those in a forward start swap. The fixed rate of the forward start swap can be calculated by using the prevailing fixed rates in both the three-year and one-year swaps and then finding the value of the fixed rate such that the sum of the present values of the two underlying swap transactions is zero.

EXAMPLE 5 A Fixed-Floating Currency Zero-Coupon Swap Transaction

A Canadian insurance company issues US$ 100 mm worth of fixed rate annuities in the United States. Each annuity has a life of a year, a face value of US $100, and pays both the interest and the principal out at the end of the year to the investors. The interest paid out is a fixed rate of 6 percent that is compounded semiannually.

Since the company wants to invest the US$ 100 mm in zero-coupon floating rate Canadian assets, it uses a one-year zero-coupon fixed-floating currency swap to hedge itself. The swap entered into allows the insurance company to receive a semiannually compounded fixed rate of 6.5 percent in U.S. funds on a notional amount of US$ 100 mm and pay a floating rate of (BA − 10) bps reset and compounded semiannually on a notional amount of Cad$ 138 mm in Canadian funds. The current value of the six-month BA rate is 6.5 percent.

Time (months)	BA rates (%)	Impact of Currency Zero-Coupon Swap Contract on the Hedger
0	6.50	☛ US$ 10 mm paid by hedger ☛ Cad$ 138 mm received by hedger
6	5.00	
12		☛ Cad$ {138 • [1+((0.065 − 0.0010)•0.5)] • [1+((0.05−0.0010)•0.5)]} − Cad$ 138 = Cad$ 7.9052 mm paid by hedger ☛ Cad$ 138 mm paid by hedger ☛ US$ {100 • [1+(0.06•0.5)] • [1+(0.06•05.)]} − US$ 100 = US$ 6.09 mm received by hedger ☛ US$ 100 mm received by hedger

$\frac{Actual}{365} - \frac{Actual}{365}$, and Fixed − Fixed.[17] These cell entries can be combined to be intepreted as an at-market coupon spot start one-year monthly-settled fixed-fixed swap on a constant notional principal amount where the day-count basis used for both the Canadian and U.S. legs of the swap are $\frac{Actual}{365}$. As another example, consider the swap whose entries from each category are At-Market Coupon, Spot, one-year, Constant, Cad − US, Monthly − Quarterly, $\frac{Actual}{365} - \frac{Actual}{360}$, Fixed −

---

[17] Since the settlement process in a fixed-fixed swap is standard, no term from the last category, Type of Settlement, is present. This is consistent with footnote 19.

EXHIBIT12 Variations on the Vanilla Currency Swap

Type of Swap[18]	Start Time of Swap	Term of Swap	Principal	Underlying Currencies	Frequency of Settlement	Day-count Basis	Underlying Rates	Type of Settlement[19]
At-Market Coupon	Spot	1 year	Constant	Cad - US	Monthly - Monthly	$\frac{\text{Actual}}{365} - \frac{\text{Actual}}{365}$ [20]	Fixed - Fixed	Arrears[24]
Off-Market Coupon	Forward	2 years	Accreting	Cad - DM	Monthly - Quarterly		Fixed - 1-mth rate[21]	Regular[25]
At-Market Zero Coupon		3.5 years	Ammortizing	US - DM	Quarterly - Yearly	$\frac{\text{Actual}}{365} - \frac{\text{Actual}}{360}$	Fixed - 3-mth rate[22]	Advance[26]
Off-Market Zero Coupon		etc.	Rollercoaster	etc.	etc.	etc.	3-mth rate - 10-yr swap rate[23]	
etc.							etc.	

18 The items in this category are defined in the Glossary.

19 These entries are only applicable to the floating-rate entries in the Underlying Rates category.

20 The number of calendar days between each cash flow period that is used to calculate the interest on both legs of the swap.

21 The floating-rate component of the swap is linked to the one-month LIBOR.

22 The floating-rate component of the swap is linked to the three-month LIBOR.

23 The floating-rate components of the swap are linked to the three-month LIBOR and the 10-year swap rate.

24 There is no time lag between the setting of the floating-rate component and the settlement arising from this setting.

25 There is a time lag between the setting of the floating-rate component and the settlement arising from this setting. Typically, this time lag is reflected by the Frequency of Settlement category.

26 There is an additional time lag imposed between the setting of the floating-rate component and the settlement arising from this setting. Consider, for example, footnote 22. If the regular time lag is three months, the time lag under this type of settlement is (2•3 = 6) months.

one-month LIBOR, and Arrears. These cell entries can be intepreted as an at-market coupon spot start one-year fixed-floating swap on a constant notional principal amount, where the rate and the day-count basis used for the Canadian leg of the swap are the fixed rate and $\dfrac{Actual}{365}$ respectively, the rate and the day-count basis used for the U.S. leg of the swap are the one-month LIBOR and $\dfrac{Actual}{360}$ respectively, with the floating rate being set in arrears. Furthermore, while the Canadian leg of the swap will be settled monthly, the U.S. leg of the swap will be compounded every month and settled quarterly.

Interest-Rate Swap Contracts

The mechanics underlying the transaction of a fixed-floating interest rate swap are illustrated in Example 6 on page 32.

It is important for the reader to make the following three observations about Example 6:

OBSERVATION 1 As with the currency coupon swap presented in Example 4, the reader will realize that the fixed-floating interest-rate swap presented in Example 6 can also be represented as two loans denominated in the same currency. The first is a US$ 200 mm loan taken by the corporation from the counterparty at a semiannual rate of 5 percent, while the second is a US$ 200 mm loan taken by the counterparty from the corporation at a six-month floating rate.

OBSERVATION 2 Although Example 6 illustrates the payment of the interest cash flows from one party to the other, in practice, the interest payments are netted out with the differential payment being made by the party owing the larger amount. In Example 6, at the six-month time period, instead of the corporation paying its counterparty US$ 5 mm and receiving US$ 4.5 mm; the corporation would make a net payment of US$ 0.5 mm to the counterparty. Similarly, at the 12-month time period, the corporation would pay its counterparty US$ 5 mm and receive US$ 5.2 mm; resulting in the corporation receiving a net payment of US$ 0.2 mm from the counterparty.

OBSERVATION 3 Since an interest-rate swap can be treated as two loans, it is not unreasonable to expect the counterparties to exchange the notional principal amounts at both the inception and the maturity of the swap contract. However, because the loans are denominated in the same currency and are of the same magnitude, the exchange of principals would have no effect on the swap, making the exchange a redundant exercise. Thus, it should

EXAMPLE 6   A Fixed-Floating Interest-Rate Swap Transaction

A U.S. corporation has a two-year floating rate liability on a notional principal of US$ 200 mm that is linked to the six-month US$ LIBOR. Afraid that the six-month rates over the next two years are going to increase, the corporate treasurer decides to swap the floating-rate liabilities for a fixed-rate one.

To hedge itself, the corporation gets into a two-year semiannually reset fixed-floating interest swap on a notional size of US$ 200 mm. With this swap, the treasurer would effectively receive a six-month LIBOR and pay a fixed rate of 5 percent. The current six-month US$ LIBOR is 4.5 percent.

Time (months)	BA rates (%)	Impact of Interest Rate Swap Contract on the Hedger
0	4.50	
6	5.20	☛ US$ (200 • 0.5 • 0.05) = US$ 5 mm paid by hedger ☛ US$ (200 • 0.5 • 0.045) = US$ 4.5 mm received by hedger
12	5.50	☛ US$ (200 • 0.5 • 0.05) = US$ 5 mm paid by hedger ☛ US$ (200 • 0.5 • 0.052) = US$ 5.2 mm received by hedger
18	4.70	☛ US$ (200 • 0.5 • 0.05) = US$ 5 mm paid by hedger ☛ US$ (200 • 0.5 • 0.055) = US$ 5.5 mm received by hedger
24		☛ US$ (200 • 0.5 • 0.05) = US$ 5 mm paid by hedger ☛ US$ (200 • 0.5 • 0.047) = US$ 4.7 mm received by hedger

come as no surprise to the reader that no principals get exchanged in an interest-rate swap contract, which is consistent with the mechanics presented in Example 6.[27]

---

[27] The ability to net out these payments such that
  • No principals get exchanged in the swap.
  • The party owing the larger amount pays the difference in the interest amounts,
making this type of swap less credit-intensive than a currency coupon swap. However, it is important for the reader to note that the credit-intensiveness of an interest-rate swap increases when the transaction involves a zero-coupon interest-rate swap.

OBSERVATION 4 If the swap presented in Example 6 were a 6-month swap starting in six months, then the 5.20 percent LIBOR value at the six-month period would be the only applicable rate, and the fixed rate of the swap would be 4.75 percent.[28] This rate would result in a net cash inflow of US$ 0.45 mm to the hedger at the 12-month period. If this amount is present-valued to the six-month period using the rate of 5.20 percent, this one-period forward start swap is also called a forward rate agreement (FRA) and is an example of a forward contract in the interest-rate asset class.[29]

Example 6 is more succinctly represented in Exhibit 13.

EXHIBIT 13   Fixed-Floating Interest-Rate Swap

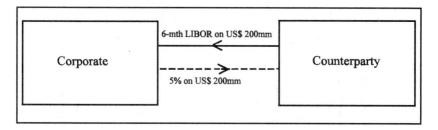

The fixed-floating vanilla interest-rate swap in Exhibit 13 is the simplest form of interest-rate swap. Depending on the types of risk the user wants to mitigate, the zero-coupon interest-rate swap and other variations can be easily constructed. All the variations on the vanilla interest-rate swap theme are summarized in Exhibit 14.

Since the nine categories in Exhibit 14 are no different from those in Exhibit 12, the reader should refer to the explanation accompanying Exhibit 12.

Equity Swap Contracts

The mechanics underlying the transaction of an equity fixed-floating swap are illustrated in Example 7 on page 35.

---

[28] Just because the 4.75 percent represents the fixed rate of a six-month swap starting in six months, it does not necessarily mean that the six-month forward starting swap rate must always be less than the two-year swap rate. While the longer-term swap rates are higher than the shorter-term rates in an upward sloping yield-curve environment, an inversion in the curve can cause the reverse to be true.

[29] The interest-rate forward contract is essentially a one-period or single-period swap contract. Although it is usual to settle this type of contract in a manner described in Observation 4, it is not unusual to settle this type of contract at the 12-month period, like a 6-month swap contract forward starting in six months, instead of settling it at the 6-month period.

EXHIBIT 14   Variations on the Vanilla Interest Rate Swap

Type of Swap[30]	Start Time of Swap	Term of Swap	Principal[30]	Underlying Currencies	Frequency of Settlement	Day-Count Basis	Underlying Rates	Type of Settlement[31]
At-Market Coupon	Spot	1 year	Constant	Cad	Monthly - Monthly	$\frac{\text{Actual}}{365} - \frac{\text{Actual}}{365}$ [32]	Fixed - 1-mth rate[33]	Arrears[36]
Off-Market Coupon	Forward	2 years	Accreting	US	Monthly - Quarterly	$\frac{\text{Actual}}{365} - \frac{\text{Actual}}{360}$	Fixed - 3-mth rate[34]	Regular[37]
At-Market Zero Coupon		3.5 years	Ammortizing	DM	Quarterly - Yearly		3-mth rate - 10-yr swap rate[35]	Advance[38]
Off-Market Zero Coupon		etc.	Rollercoaster	etc.	etc.	etc.	etc	
etc.								

30 The items in this category are defined in the Glossary.

31 These entries are only applicable to the floating-rate entries in Underlying Rates category.

32 The number of calendar days between each cash flow period that is used to calculate the interest on both legs of the swap.

33 The floating-rate component of the swap is linked to the one-month LIBOR.

34 The floating-rate component of the swap is linked to the three-month LIBOR.

35 The floating-rate components of the swap are linked to the three-month LIBOR and the 10-year swap rate.

36 There is no time lag between the setting of the floating rate component and the settlement arising from this setting.

37 There is a time lag imposed between the setting of the floating rate component and the settlement arising from this setting. Typically, this time lag is reflected in the Frequency of Settlement category.

38 There is an additional time lag imposed between the setting of the floating rate component and the setting of the floating rate and the settlement arising from this setting. Consider, for example, footnote 34. If the regular time lag three months, the time lag under this type of settlement is (2*3 = 6) months.

EXAMPLE 7 A Fixed-Floating Equity Swap Transaction

A U.K. investor has a large portfolio of equities that is used to track or mirror the FTSE-100 index. Because of the view that the equity market is going to drop, the manager wants to convert a portion of the portfolio without any liquidation to an asset that pays off a fixed rate of return.

To do this, she gets into a one-year equity swap on a notional size of £300 mm with a counterparty. In this swap, she would pay the semiannual return on the FTSE-100 index for receiving a fixed rate of 10 percent. The current value of the FTSE-100 index is 3,500 points.

Time (months)	FTSE-100 (points)	Impact of Interest-Rate Swap Contract on the investor
0	3,500	
6	3,750	☞ $£300 \cdot \dfrac{3750 - 3500}{3500} = £21.42$ mm paid by investor ☞ $£(300 \cdot 0.5 \cdot 0.1) = £15$ mm received by investor
12	3,680	☞ $£300 \cdot \dfrac{3680 - 3750}{3750} = -£5.61$ mm paid by investor ☞ $£(300 \cdot 0.5 \cdot 0.1) = £15$ mm received by investor

It is important for the reader to make the following five observations about Example 7:

OBSERVATION 1 As with the interest-rate swap presented in Example 6, the reader will realize that the fixed-floating equity swap presented in Example 7 can also be represented as two loans denominated in the same currency. The first is a £300 mm loan taken by the investor from the counterparty at a floating rate that is equal to the six-month return on the FTSE-100 index, while the second is a £300 mm loan taken by the counterparty from the investor at a semiannual fixed rate of 10 percent.

OBSERVATION 2 Like the interest-rate swap, since the loans in the equity swap are denominated in the same currency and are of the same magnitude, exchanging the principals has no effect on the swapping, making it a redundant exercise. Thus, no principals get exchanged in an equity swap contract. Furthermore, the interest payments are netted out on each payment date, with the differential payment being made by the party owing the larger amount.[39]

OBSERVATION 3 In the above example, the interest calculated using the return on the equity index is based on a different formula. More precisely, to calculate the simple interest in both the currency and interest-rate swaps, the formula *Interest = Principal • Time • Rate* is used. On the other hand, to calculate the interest based on the return of the index, the formula

$$Interest = Principal \bullet \frac{New\ index\ level - Old\ index\ level}{Old\ index\ level}$$

is used. Typically, the type of index used in calculating the return is the total return index value (TRIV) as opposed to the spot price index value (SPIV).

OBSERVATION 4 It is possible for the new index level to be smaller than the old index level in the formula given in Observation 3 that is used to calculate the interest on the index. This implies that there is a potential for this interest amount to be negative. Consequently, a party that would ordinarily pay interest using the positive return on the equity index to its counterparty will now instead receive interest from its counterparty. This characteristic of the equity swap is captured in Example 7 at the 12-month time period, where the return to the counterparty is shown to be –£5.61 mm, which results in the portfolio manager getting a total of £(5.61 + 15) = £20.61 mm.

OBSERVATION 5 If the swap presented in Example 7 were a six-month swap that starts today and ends in six months, in addition to the 3,500 points, the 3,750 points of FTSE-100 at the six-month period would be the only other applicable index value. When these are the only values used in the calculation of the return on the equity index, the fixed rate of the swap would be 8 percent[40]. This rate would result in a net cash outflow of £9.42 mm from the investor at the six-month period. This one-period swap is also called a forward equity contract and is an example of a forward contract in the equity asset class.

Example 7 is more succinctly represented in Exhibit 15.

---

[39] See footnote 27.

[40] Just because the 8 percent represents the fixed rate of a six-month swap starting today, it does not necessarily mean that the six-month equity spot starting swap rate must always be less than the one-year swap rate. See also footnote 28.

EXHIBIT 15 Fixed-Floating Equity Swap

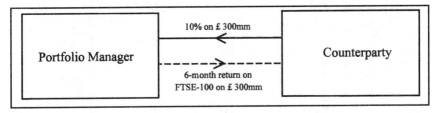

The fixed-floating vanilla equity swap in Exhibit 15 is the simplest form of equity swap. Depending on the types of risks the user wants to mitigate, a floating-floating equity swap, a zero-coupon fixed-floating equity swap, and other variations can be easily constructed. Furthermore, despite its simplicity, a fixed-floating equity swap is not as common as a floating-floating equity swap, which is typically used by a portfolio manager.

A floating-floating equity swap can be used to effectively convert an equity portfolio to an interest-rate portfolio without incurring extensive transaction costs from the actual liquidation of the equity portfolio and the actual acquisition of the interest-rate portfolio. An example of this transaction would be to swap the returns on a FTSE-100 index for the interest payments linked to £ LIBOR. Another useful floating-floating swap structure is the swapping of the returns on the FTSE-100 index for the returns on the utility-sector component of the index. With this type of swap, the portfolio manager can effectively take a view on the utility component of the FTSE-100 index without liquidating any portion of her portfolio.

All the variations on the vanilla equity swap theme are summarized in Exhibit 16.

Since the variations on the vanilla equity swap theme are no different from those of the vanilla currency and interest-rate swap themes, the reader is referred to the explanation accompanying Exhibit 12 for the interpretation of Exhibit 16.

Commodity Swap Contracts

The mechanics underlying the transaction of a commodity fixed-floating swap are illustrated in Example 8 on page 39.

It is important for the reader to make the following two observations about Example 8:

OBSERVATION 1 Unlike the currency, interest-rate, and equity swaps presented in the earlier examples, the fixed-floating commodity swap presented in Example 8 cannot be easily intuited as two loans denominated in the same currency. However, the swap can be thought of as a contract that would allow the producer to lock in the price of the crude oil.

EXHIBIT 16 Variations on the Vanilla Equity Swap

Type of Swap[41]	Start Time of Swap	Term of Swap	Principal[30]	Underlying Currencies	Frequency of Settlement	Day-count Basis	Underlying Rates	Type of Settlement[42]
At-Market Coupon	Spot	1 year	Constant	Cad	Monthly - Monthly	$\frac{\text{Actual}}{365} - \frac{\text{Actual}}{365}$ [43]	Fixed - TSE-100	Arrears[44]
Off-Market Coupon	Forward	2 years	Accreting	US	Monthly - Quarterly	$\frac{\text{Actual}}{365} - \frac{\text{Actual}}{360}$	Fixed - FTSE-100	Regular[45]
At-Market Zero Coupon		3.5 years	Ammortizing	DM	Quarterly - Yearly	etc.	TSE-100 - S&P-100	Advance[46]
Off-Market Zero Coupon		etc.	Rollercoaster	etc.	etc.		etc.	
etc.								

41 The items in this category are defined in the Glossary.
42 These entries are only applicable to the floating-rate entries in the Underlying Rates Category.
43 The number of calendar days between each cash flow period that is used to calculate the interest of the swap.
44 There is no time lag between the setting of the floating-rate component and the settlement arising from this setting.
45 There is a time lag between the setting of the floating-rate component and the settlement arising from this setting. Typically, this time lag is reflected by the Frequency of Settlement category.
46 There is an additional time lag imposed between the setting of the floating rate and the settlement arising from this setting.

OBSERVATION 2 If the swap presented in Example 8 were a one-month swap starting today, the average price of US$ 18 per barrel for the one-month period would be the only applicable price, and the fixed price of the swap would be US$ 18.50[47]. This price would result in a net cash inflow of US$ 0.03 mm to the hedger at the one-month period. This one-period swap is also called a commodity forward contract and is an example of a forward contract in the commodity asset class.

Example 8 is more succintly represented in Exhibit 17.

EXAMPLE 8   A Fixed-Floating Commodity Swap Transaction

A producer of WTI crude oil is afraid of the drop in price of the WTI contract and wishes to hedge his production for the next quarter. He gets into a monthly-settled three-month swap contract with a counterparty in which he would receive an average fixed price of US$ 20 per barrel for an amount of 60,000 barrels per month.

Time (months)	Monthly Average WTI Price (US$)	Impact of Commodity Swap Contract on the Hedger
0		
1	18.00	☛ US$ (60,000 • 20) = US$ 1.2 mm received by hedger ☛ US$ (60,000 • 18) = US$ 1.08 mm paid by hedger
2	20.50	☛ US$ (60,000 • 20) = US$ 1.2 mm received by hedger ☛ US$ (60,000 • 20.50) = US$ 1.23 mm paid by hedger
3	18.75	☛ US$ (60,000 • 20) = US$ 1.2 mm received by hedger ☛ US$ (60,000 • 18.75) = US$ 1.125 mm paid by hedger

---

[47] Just because the US$ 18.50 represents the fixed price of a one-month swap starting today, it does not necessarily mean that the one-month spot starting swap price must always be less than the three-month swap price. See footnote 28.

EXHIBIT 17 Fixed-Floating Commodity Swap

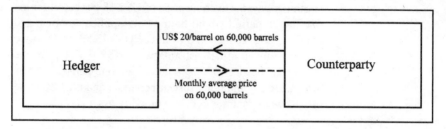

The fixed-floating vanilla commodity swap in Exhibit 17 is the simplest form of commodity swap. Depending on the types of risks the user wants to mitigate, other variations can be easily constructed. Like fixed-floating commodity swaps, floating-floating commodity swaps are used by the producers and end users to swap from one type of exposure to another. These types of swaps are also being increasingly used by portfolio managers seeking diversification in their portfolio and higher returns from the prices of the underlying commodities, which the commodity markets offer. Consequently, it is not unusual for portfolio managers to transact into a swap where they would receive the return on the price of a commodity or a commodity index for the return on another commodity index or an equity index.

All the variations on the vanilla commodity swap theme are summarized in Exhibit 18.

Since the variations on the vanilla commodity swap theme are no different from those of the vanilla currency and interest-rate swap themes, the reader is referred to the explanations acccompanying Exhibit 12 for the interpretation of Exhibit 18.

Characteristics of the Swap Contracts

As was discussed in the previous section, while a fixed-fixed swap is only prevalent in the currency asset class, a fixed-floating swap and a floating-floating swap are generally available in all four asset classes. Whatever the type of swap, each swap can be alternatively thought of as a string of agreements that allow the hedger to exchange cash flows linked to one index for cash flows linked to another index. Thus, as mentioned earlier, each swap contract can equivalently be thought of as a chain of forward contracts, where the swap rate underlying the chained contract can be obtained by blending the rates of the individual forward contracts.[48] Consequently, the profit or loss on each settlement date underlying the purchased swap contract would be no different from that of a forward contract and can be succintly written, as in Exhibit 7, and graphed as in Exhibit 4.

---

[48] It is this motivation that is used to value swaps. See, for example Dattatreya, Venkatesh and Venkatesh (1994), Jarrow and Turnbull (1996), Hull (1997), and Ravindran (1997a).

EXHIBIT 18 Variations on the Vanilla Commodity Swap

Type of Swap[48]	Start Time of Swap	Term of Swap	Principal[48]	Underlying Currencies	Frequency of Settlement	Day-Count Basis	Underlying Rates	Type of Settlement[49]
At-Market Coupon	Spot	1 year	Constant	Cad	Monthly - Monthly	$\frac{\text{Actual}}{365} - \frac{\text{Actual}}{365}$ [50]	Fixed - Gas Price	Arrears[51]
Off-Market Coupon	Forward	2 years	Accreting	US	Monthly - Quarterly	$\frac{\text{Actual}}{365} - \frac{\text{Actual}}{360}$	Fixed - WTI Price	Regular[52]
At-Market Zero Coupon		3.5 years	Ammortizing		Quarterly - Yearly		Gas Price - WTI Price	Advance[53]
Off-Market Zero Coupon		etc.	Rollercoaster	etc.	etc.	etc.	etc.	
etc.								

49 The items in this category are defined in the Glossary.

50 These entries are only applicable to the floating-rate entries in the Underlying Rates Category.

51 The number of calendar days between each cash flow period that is used to calculate the interest of the swap.

52 There is no time lag between the setting of the floating-rate component and the settlement arising from this setting.

53 There is a time lag between the setting of the floating-rate component and the settlement arising from this setting. Typically, this time lag is reflected by the Frequency of Settlement category.

54 There is an additional time lag imposed between the setting of the floating rate and the settlement arising from this setting.

Pricing a swap contract is no different from valuing a forward and futures contract in that to value it, one has to find the guaranteed rate or price at which both the buyer and seller will fulfill their obligations on each settlement date during the life of the contract for no up-front cost. Exhibit 19 illustrates the meaning of pricing each type of swap that has been presented in Examples 3, 4, 5, 6, 7, and 8.

Many more factors influence the price of a swap contract than a futures or forward contract. These factors are summarized in Exhibit 20 across the various asset classes.

As can be observed from Exhibit 20, while eight factors influence the value of an interest-rate swap, nine factors influence the value of a currency swap, equity swap, and commodity swap.[55]

THE VANILLA OPTION CONTRACT
Introduction

Like a futures, forward, or swap contract, an option contract is an agreement between any two parties where the seller guarantees the asset price at a prespecified time in the future to the buyer for an up-front premium. However, unlike the previous contracts, only the seller of this contract is obligated to perform his end of the contract.

The two common types of option contracts in the financial marketplace are European-style options and American-style options. Buyers of both a European-style call option and an American-style call option pay a premium at the inception of the option contract for the right to buy the underlying asset at a specified price (also known as the strike price). However, the buyer of the European-style option can only do so (also known as exercise) on the option expiry date, while the purchaser of the latter can exercise at any time until and inclusive of the option expiry date. Similarly, while the buyers of both a European-style put option and an American-style put option pay a premium at the inception of the option contract for the right to sell the underlying asset at a strike price, the purchaser of the for-

---

[55] One other factor that sometimes plays a role in the value of an interest-rate swap contract and a currency swap contract but has been ommitted in the discussion is the volatility of the floating rate underlying the interest-rate swap. More precisely, when the term of the floating-rate component underlying the interest-rate swap is not equal to the time between the setting of this rate and the settlement arising from this settlement (i.e., tenor), the volatility of the underlying interest-rate index can be shown to play a crucial role in the pricing of the swap. Known as a constant maturity swap (CMS) , an example of this type of swap would be a spot start monthly reset fixed-floating swap, where the floating rate is indexed to then-prevailing 10-year swap rate. The greater the discrepancy in time between the term of the floating-rate index and the tenor, the greater the effect of the volatility in the swap value. The reader is referred to Brotherton-Ratcliffe and Iben (1993) and Hull (1997) for an in-depth discussion on this adjustment, known as the convexity adjustment. See Ravindran (1997a) for the intuition underlying the valuation of regular swaps and the implicit assumptions made in valuing these instruments. See also constant maturity treasuries (CMTs) in the Glossary section.

EXHIBIT 19   Meaning of Pricing At-Market Vanilla Swap Contracts

Example 3	A 2-year semiannually reset currency swap in which the hedger swaps 6.5% fixed rate on a notional amount of US$ 100 mm for a 7% fixed rate on a notional amount of Cad$ 138 mm. Pricing ➡ Finding a 7% fixed rate on a notional amount of Cad$ 138 mm such that the present value of the swap contract is zero.
Example 4	A 2-year semiannually reset currency swap in which the hedger swaps 6.5% fixed rate on a notional amount of US$ 100 mm for a 6-month BA floating rate on a notional amount of Cad$ 138 mm. Pricing ➡ Finding a 0% spread in addition to the 6-month BA floating rate on a notional amount of Cad$ 138 mm such that the present value of the swap contract is zero.
Example 5	A 1-year semiannually reset zero-coupon currency swap in which the hedger swaps 6.5% fixed rate on a notional amount of US$ 100 mm for a (6-month BA floating rate - 10 basis points) on a notional amount of Cad$ 138 mm. Pricing ➡ Finding a –0.1% spread in addition to the 6-month BA floating rate on a notional amount of Cad$ 138 mm such that the present value of the swap contract is zero.
Example 6	A 2-year semiannually reset interest-rate swap on a notional amount of US$ 200 mm in which the hedger swaps 6-month LIBOR floating rate for a 5% fixed rate. Pricing ➡ Finding a 5% fixed rate on a notional amount of US$ 200 mm such that the present value of the swap contract is zero.
Example 7	A 1-year semiannually reset equity swap on a notional amount of £ 300 mm in which the investor swaps the 6-month return on the FTSE-100 index for a 10% fixed rate. Pricing ➡ Finding a 10% fixed rate on a notional amount of £ 300 mm such that the present value of the swap contract is zero.
Example 8	A 3-month monthly reset commodity swap on a notional amount of 60,000 barrels in which the hedger swaps the monthly average crude oil price for US$ 20 per barrel. Pricing ➡ Finding an average of US$ 20 per barrel price on a notional amount of 60,000 barrels such that the present value of the swap contract is zero.

EXHIBIT 20   Factors Influencing the Price of a Swap Contract

Factors	Interest-Rate Swap	Currency Swap	Equity Swap	Commodity Swap
Convenience yield				✔
Dividend rate			✔	
Foreign yield curve		✔		
Underlying floating-rate index	✔	✔	✔	✔
Domestic yield curve	✔	✔	✔	✔
Type of swap	✔	✔	✔	✔
Start date of swap	✔	✔	✔	✔
Term of swap	✔	✔	✔	✔
Principal	✔	✔	✔	✔
Underlying currency(ies)	✔	✔	✔	✔
Frequency of settlement[56]	✔	✔	✔	✔
Day-count basis	✔	✔	✔	✔
Type of settlement	✔	✔	✔	✔

56 This is sometimes also known as the tenor of a swap. Each swap would typically have a minimum of one tenor (if both legs of the swap settle at the same frequency) and a maximum of two tenors (if both legs of the swap settle at different frequencies).

mer can only do so (or exercise) on the option expiry date, while the purchaser of the latter can exercise at any time until and inclusive of the option expiry date.

Despite the fact that the only philosophical difference between the European-style option and the American-style option lies in the number of exercise points, the reality is that the behavior of a rational purchaser could be different for each type of option. Consequently, it would be easier to first discuss European-style options in this section and the next, followed by the American-style options.

Although not obligated to fulfill his part of the contract, a rational buyer[57] of a European-style call (put) option would exercise his option and purchase (sell) the underlying asset only if the option finishes in-the-money and not exercise otherwise. Exhibit 21 defines both an in-the-money finishing option and an out-of-the-money finishing option.

---

[57] For tax or accounting reasons, sometimes it is rational to exercise an option even if it finishes out-of-the-money. For ease of illustration, in my definition of a rational buyer, I will not consider the tax and accounting implications arising from the exercise of the option.

EXHIBIT 21 Definition of Finishing In-the-Money and Finishing Out-of-the-Money

Type of Option	Finishing In-the-Money[58]	Finishing Out-of-the-Money
Call option	Asset price on option maturity is greater than strike price	Asset price on option maturity is lesser than strike price
Put option	Asset price on option maturity is less than strike price	Asset price on option maturity is greater than strike price

58 In practice, if the term *in-the-money option* is used, it refers to the fact that the current price (or rate) of the underlying asset is greater than the strike price (or rate) for a call option and less than the strike price (or rate) for a put option. Similarly, when the term *out-of-the-money option* is used, it refers to the fact that the current price (or rate) of the underlying asset is less than the strike price (or rate) for a call option and greater than the strike price (or rate) for a put option.

An option can thus be alternatively thought of as an insurance contract that allows the purchaser to be protected against unfavorable movements in the price (or rate) of the underlying asset.

In Exhibit 1, it was shown that regardless of the asset class, the asset underlying an option contract is either a spot contract, futures contract, forward contract, or swap contract. While an option on a futures contract trades in the same exchange as the underlying futures contract, an option whose underlying asset is either the spot, forward, or swap contract would usually trade in the over-the-counter market.[59] Regardless of the nature of the underlying asset, as long as the buyer of the option chooses not to exercise the option, the parties involved in the contract can walk away from the contract with no cash or physical transaction arising from the settlement of the option. On the other hand, if the buyer of the option chooses to exercise the option, the transaction that would take place upon exercise could either be in the form of a cash settlement or physical settlement. In the event of a physical settlement upon exercise, the dynamics underlying the asset following the option settlement would be no different from any of the underlying instruments discussed earlier in the chapter.

As an illustration, consider the producer described in Example 8 who pays an up-front premium to purchase a two-month option that would give him the right to receive an average fixed price of US$ 20 per barrel for 60,000 barrels on a fixed-floating monthly reset three-month swap upon option expiry. If

---

[59] An example of this exception would be stocks and stock options that trade on the exchange.

this option gets exercised by the purchaser on the expiry date, the transaction ensuing the physical settlement of the option would be the oil swap described in Example 8.

Hence, barring market conventions, the philosophy underlying the mechanics of the use of an option is no different across any underlying asset. Consequently, for the purposes of illustration, only the use of a European-style currency option and an interest-rate cap will be discussed.

Option Contract Examples

Example 9 on page 47 illustrates the use of a European-style currency put option.

It is important for the reader to make the following three important observations about Example 9.

OBSERVATION 1 When the option finishes in-the-money, the exporter will in practice convert his U.S. dollars into Canadian ones, using the exchange rate 1.3450 Cad/US, resulting in a total of Cad$ 134.5 mm. Since the option finished in-the-money, the option seller (or writer) will pay the exporter an additional amount of Cad$ $100 \cdot (1.3600 - 1.3450) =$ Cad$ 1.5 mm, as illustrated in Example 9. This would result in a total revenue of Cad$ $(134.5 + 1.5)$ mm = Cad$ 136 mm to the exporter.[60]

OBSERVATION 2 In the context of Example 9, the put option on the U.S. dollar that was purchased by the buyer would serve as a protection when the U.S. dollar weakens. Since the value of the U.S. dollar is an inverse reciprocal of the Canadian dollar, the weakening of the U.S. dollar implies the strengthening of the Canadian dollar. Consequently, the purchase of a put option on the U.S. dollar is analogous to the purchase of a call option on the Canadian dollar, and the purchase of a call option on the U.S. dollar is similarly equivalent to the purchase of a put option on the Canadian dollar. This feature, which is only inherent in currency options, does not extend to options in other asset classes.

---

[60] This is an example of a cash-settled currency option and is analogous to Observation 7 of Example 2. In practice, if a physical delivery of the asset underlying the option is required, the option writer usually has to be informed at the inception of the contract, especially if the asset underlying the option is a gas contract, oil contract, grain contract, and so on.

EXAMPLE 9 A Vanilla European-Style Currency Option Transaction

A Canadian exporter sells his goods in the United States. Every time the exporter bills his clients, it takes exactly 2½ months before he gets reimbursed. He bills his clients a total amount of US$ 100 mm. To hedge himself completely, he contemplates using a forward contract. Since the 2½-month currency forward is currently trading at 1.3600 Cad/US, the exporter feels that in 2½ months the U.S. dollar will definitely get stronger. He decides to convert the incoming cash flow using the currency spot market in 2½ months.

However, because he is afraid of being wrong about the U.S. dollar, he is prepared to pay a premium of Cad$ 1.351mm to purchase a 2½-month put option on US$ 100 mm struck at 1.3600 Cad/US.

Time (months)	Exchange Rate (Cad/US)	Impact of Option on the Hedger
0		☞ Cad$ 1.351 mm premium paid by exporter
2½	Case A: Put Option is Exercised at the End of 2½ Months	
	1.3450	☞ Payoff of Cad$ [100 • (1.3600 − 1.3450)] = Cad$ 1.5 mm paid to exporter ☞ Cad$ 1.351 mm of premium and Cad$ 0.015[60] mm of interest on this premium foregone by exporter ☞ Profit to investor: Cad$ [1.5 − (1.351 + 0.015)] = Cad$ 0.134 mm
	Case B: Put Option is Not Exercised at the End of 2½ Months	
	1.3650	☞ Cad$ 1.351 mm of premium and Cad$ 0.015 mm of interest on this premium foregone by exporter ☞ Profit to investor: −Cad$ (1.351 + 0.015) = − Cad$ 1.366 mm

60 This is the 2½-month interest calculated on the option premium of Cad$ 1.351 mm that was paid at the inception of the option contract by the option buyer.

OBSERVATION 3 Although the hedger can theoretically make an infinite amount of money from purchasing the option in Example 9, the maximum amount he can lose is the option premium paid at the inception of the contract and the accrued interest on this premium. Consequently, the hedger's downside is restricted to the premium paid for the insurance, resulting in the hedger knowing full well his maximum downside risk at the time he enters into the transaction.

Example 10 discusses the use of an interest-rate cap.

EXAMPLE 10   A Vanilla European-Style Cap Transaction

A U.S. corporate treasurer is exposed to floating-rate liabilities that are linked to the three-month US$ LIBOR. Afraid of the increase in these rates over the next year, the treasurer wants to hedge herself.

To hedge herself, she purchases a one-year quarterly reset cap that is struck at 6 percent on a notional amount of US$ 200 mm for 16 basis points; where the first caplet expires in three months and the third caplet expires in nine months.

Time (months)	US$ LIBOR (%)	Impact of Option on the Treasurer
0		☛ US$ 0.16 mm premium paid by treasuer
1st Caplet Expires Out-of-the-Money		
3	5.75	
2nd Caplet Expires In-the-Money and Treasurer is Given Payoff from 1st Caplet		
6	6.40	☛ No payoff from 1st caplet paid to treasurer
3rd Caplet Expires In-the-Money and Treasurer is Given Payoff from 2nd Caplet		
9	8.10	☛ Payoff of US$ [200 • (0.064 − 0.060) • 0.25] = US$ 0.2 mm from 2nd caplet paid to treasurer
Treasurer is Given Payoff from 3rd Caplet		
12		☛ Payoff of US$ [200 • (0.081 − 0.060) • 0.25] = US$ 1.05 mm from 3rd caplet paid to treasurer

It is important for the reader to make the following three observations from Example 10.

OBSERVATION 1 The one-year cap contract is comprised of three individual call options, called caplets, on the three-month US$ LIBOR.[62] Each caplet is in essence an option on a three-month interest rate forward contract that allows the purchaser the right to pay a fixed rate on a three-month US$ LIBOR. This type of forward contract, which is mentioned in Observation 4 of Example 6, is a single-period swap contract.

Furthermore, with the purchase of the three caplets, the total borrowing cost to the treasurer for each quarter will never exceed $US\$ (200 \bullet 0.06 \bullet 0.25) = US\$ 3$ mm.

OBSERVATION 2 Although only one strike rate and one constant notional principal amount was applied to the three individual caplets, due to the types of risks managed, the treasurer could have just as well entered into a one-year cap contract comprised of varying strike rates and notional amounts across each caplet.

OBSERVATION 3 Like the earlier examples on the swap rates, this example also assumed that the time between each option expiry and the settlement arising from the expiry[63] is always constant, more precisely 0.25 years. In practice, to calculate this settlement, the actual number of calendar days in a tenor is used.

Furthermore, as in a currency or interest-rate swap, the term of the floating-rate index underlying a caplet does not have to necessarily equal the tenor of the caplet. Caps of this type are called constant maturity swap caps (CMS caps) or constant maturity treasury caps (CMT caps).

Characteristics of the Option Contracts

The profits associated with the purchase of a European-style option contract are more succintly written in Exhibit 22 and graphed in Exhibit 23 and 24.

The formulae that are used to price the European-style options were first developed by Black and Scholes (1973) for nondividend paying stocks. Instead

---

[62] A floor is similarly defined as a collection of floorlets, where each floorlet is a put option on an interest rate. See Glossary.

[63] This is also known as the tenor of the caplet. See also Footnote 56.

EXHIBIT 22 Profits to the Buyer of a European-Style Vanilla Option

Type of Contract	Profit at Expiry Time T
$C_E(0,T,X)$	$\max[-P^*_{T,C}, S_T - X - P^*_{T,C}]$
$P_E(0,T,X)$	$\max[-P^*_{T,P}, X - S_T - P^*_{T,P}]$

where

0	=	Current time or time today
T	=	Maturity of the contract
X	=	Strike value
S_T	=	Value of the underlying asset at time T
$C_E(0,T,X)$	=	Call option purchased at time 0 with parameters T and X
$P_E(0,T,X)$	=	Put option purchased at time 0 with parameters T and X
$P^*_{T,C}$	=	Amount foregone by purchaser of call option due to premium and the interest accured until time T on this premium
$P^*_{T,P}$	=	Amount foregone by purchaser of put option due to premium and the interest accrued until time T on this premium

EXHIBIT 23 Call Option Buyer's Profit at Maturity

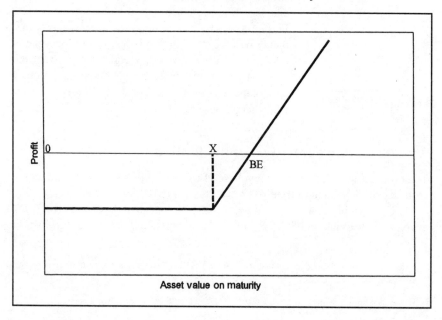

EXHIBIT 24 Put Option Buyer's Profit at Maturity

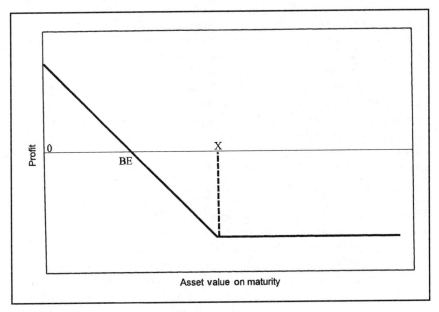

of using these formulae to price the options, one can use a binomial tree or Monte Carlo simulations for valuation[64]. The application of the binomial tree method and the Monte Carlo method, which were initially proposed by Cox, Ross, and Rubinstein (1979) and Boyle (1977) respectively, are described with numerical examples in Chapter 4. The reader is referred to Hull (1997), Jarrow and Turnbull (1996) and Stoll and Whaley (1993) for excellent introductions to the mathematics underlying the fundamentals of futures/forward/swap/option pricing and to Ravindran (1993a) for the relationship between option pricing and a recreational problem in the field of probability maximization called the "secretary problem."

Whatever the methodology used in valuing an option, any option price can be intuitively split into two components known as the intrinsic value component and the time or extrinsic value component. The intrinsic value, which characterizes the amount of in-the-moneyness of the option if exercised immediately[65], is calculated by subtracting the strike (underlying asset) price from the underlying asset (strike) price for a call (put) option. If this difference turns out to be negative, a value of zero is assigned to the intrinsic value. The implication of this is that an option's intrinsic value can never be negative. The time value, on the other hand, characterizes the effect of volatility and time on the option price. It is cal-

---

[64] These methods are discussed in great depth in Chapter 4, using very little mathematics.

[65] In reality, a European-style option cannot be exercised until the maturity of the option. The terminology "if exercised immediately" is an artificial device created to break the option premium down into components a trader can easily intuit.

culated by subtracting the intrinsic value from the option premium and as a result could be negative. Thus, for any given option price, the higher the intrinsic-value component, the lower the time-value component; and the lower the intrinsic-value component, the higher the time-value component.

The figures given in Exhibits 23 and 24 represent the profit and loss on the option maturity date to the purchaser of a European-style call and put option, respectively. As can be seen from Exhibit 23 and recalled from our earlier discussions, as long as the asset value exceeds the strike value on the option maturity date, the rational buyer would exercise the call option. However, since an option premium was paid at the inception of the contract, the buyer would only break even (denoted by BE) when the value of the asset reaches $BE = X + P^*_{T,C}$; both X and $P^*_{T,C}$ have been defined in Exhibit 22 and BE is illustrated in Exhibit 23. Similarly, the buyer of a put option would only break even when the value of the asset reaches $BE = X - P^*_{T,P}$; where both X and $P^*_{T,P}$ have again been defined in Exhibit 22, while BE is the point shown in Exhibit 24. Clearly, the higher the premium paid for the option, the greater the movement in the underlying asset value that is required before the buyer of the option can break even.[66]

As mentioned earlier, in addition to possessing the properties of a European-style option, an American-style option allows the buyer to exercise at any time during the life of the option. Because of this, it would be intuitively reasonable to expect the value of an American option to be at least as large as that of its European counterpart. The profits associated with the purchase of an American-style option are more succintly written in Exhibit 25.

Unlike the European-style option, no closed-form formulae can be used to value an American-style option. Consequently, one has to use a binomial tree to value such an option. Using Monte Carlo simulations to value American-style options is somewhat tricky; until Tilley's 1993 paper, it was generally assumed that American-style options could not be valued using this method. Both the binomial tree method and Monte Carlo method are used in Chapter 4 to illustrate the valuation of American-style options.

As discussed earlier, the rational behavior of a European-style option buyer is different from that of an American-style option buyer. This difference, as illustrated in Exhibits 22 and 25, shows that as long as the American-style option is not exercised before the option maturity date, the rational behavior on the maturity date of the buyer is no different from that of the buyer of a European-style option. More precisely, ignoring the option premium paid at the inception of the contract, the option will be exercised by the rational purchaser as long as the op-

---

[66] The buyer of the option should apply this type of analysis before purchasing an option. It is only by going through this analysis that the buyer can realize if it is actually possible for the transaction to break even or know the likelihood that the option hedge will be used. If the behavior of the underlying market makes it difficult to realize such a movement in practice, then purchasing an option on that underlying may not be the most effective or efficient strategy.

EXHIBIT 25 Profits to the Buyer of an American-Style Vanilla Option

Type of Option	Profit at Time t	Profit at Expiry Time T
$C_A(0,T,X)$	$\max[S_t - X - P^*_{t,C}, C_{A,t} - P^*_{t,C}]$	$\max[-P^*_{T,C}, S_T - X - P^*_{T,C}]$
$P_A(0,T,X)$	$\max[X - S_t - P^*_{t,P}, P_{A,t} - P^*_{t,P}]$	$\max[-P^*_{T,P}, X - S_T - P^*_{T,P}]$

where

0	=	Current time or time today
t	=	Time of exercise, where $0 \le t \le T$
T	=	Maturity of the Contract
X	=	Strike value
S_t	=	Value of the underlying asset at time t
$C_A(0,T,X)$	=	Call option purchased at time 0 with parameters T and X
$P_A(0,T,X)$	=	Put option purchased at time 0 with parameters T and X
$C_{A,t}$	=	Call option premium at time t, when purchased at time t with parameters T and X
$P_{A,t}$	=	Put option premium at time t, when purchased at time t with parameters T and X
$P^*_{t,C}$	=	Amount foregone by purchaser of call option due to premium and the interest accrued until time t on this premium
$P^*_{t,P}$	=	Amount foregone by purchaser of put option due to premium and the interest accrued until time t on this premium

tion finishes in-the-money. However, with the ability to exercise anytime during the life of the option, the buyer of an American-style option, as indicated in Exhibit 25, will not readily exercise as soon as the intrinsic value is positive. Instead, the buyer will only exercise the option if the expected payoff that can be obtained by not exercising the option is less than that obtained by exercising the option. Thus, unlike the behavior of the buyer on the option maturity date, it would be reasonable to expect the buyer of an American-style option to exercise early if the option is deeply in-the-money. This implies that for the buyer of an American-style option to exercise at any time prior to the option maturity date, the price of the underlying asset has to surpass some optimal threshold. Furthermore, this optimal threshold for each day in the life of the option, in practice, can only be realized on that day itself. As a result, at the inception of the option contract, the series of optimal threshold levels for varying times in the option life can be only estimated. By stringing all these levels together, one can arrive at an expected optimal exercise boundary associated with an American-style option.

This expected optimal exercise boundary[67] is illustrated in Exhibit 26 for both the American-style call and put options. As can be seen from the exhibit, although the buyer of the option will exercise his option initially only if the option is very highly in-the-money, this behavior is relaxed as the maturity of the option draws near. Furthermore, as the maturity of the option draws near, the expected optimal exercise boundary would converge to the strike value of the option.

EXHIBIT 26 Expected Optimal Exercise Boundaries for American-Style Options

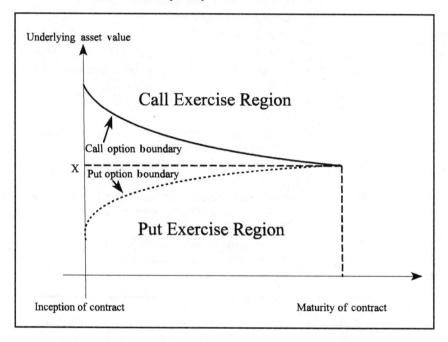

To be able to value an option, one has to first identify the factors that would influence an option price. These factors are summarized in Exhibit 27 for all four asset classes:

As can be seen from Exhibit 27, seven factors contribute to the value of a currency, equity, and commodity option contract, whereas only six factors contribute to the value of an interest-rate option contract. The factor labeled "exercise type" in the exhibit refers to the fact that the option could either have a European-style or an American-style exercise feature.

---

[67] This expected boundary is only an expectation of what the exercise boundary would look like in the future given the current market conditions and is not a "true" exercise boundary. Thus, it is only good or valid at the time the option is priced. As soon as market conditions change or the option life decays, the expected boundary will also change.

EXHIBIT 27 Factors Influencing the Value of a Traditional Vanilla Option Contract

Factors	Interest-Rate Option	Currency Option	Equity Option	Commodity Option
Convenience yield				✔
Dividend rate			✔	
Foreign risk-free rate		✔		
Domestic risk-free rate	✔	✔	✔	✔
Underlying asset value	✔	✔	✔	✔
Strike value	✔	✔	✔	✔
Volatility of asset value	✔	✔	✔	✔
Exercise type	✔	✔	✔	✔
Life of contract	✔	✔	✔	✔

One observation a reader should make from Exhibit 27 is that whenever any of the foreign risk-free rate or dividend or convenience yield is set equal to zero, the price of a European-style vanilla call option on that asset can be shown to be the same as that of its American counterpart. To intuit this, consider a stock option with no dividend as an example. By exercising an American-style call option early, the buyer of the option has to pay up a strike price of X for a stock that does not pay any dividend. Due to the accrued interest on the strike price that is foregone if the option is exercised before time T, it is optimal for the buyer of the option to delay exercising as much as possible. Since the early exercise feature has not provided any additional benefit to the buyer, it would be reasonable to expect the American-style option premium to be the same as the European-style option premium in this instance.

Option Contracts As Building Blocks

One key distinction between an option contract and all other derivative contracts discussed so far is that while both the buyer and seller of the latter contracts are obligated to perform their ends of the contract, only the seller of the former contract is obligated to perform his end of the contract. Due to the way that the call option contracts and put option contracts are specified, all assets underlying an option contract can be synthetically created using the call and put option contracts on the same underlying asset. As a result, even though the asset underlying an option contract could be either the underlying cash instrument, futures contract, forward contract, or swap contract, these contracts can usually be easily replicated using the appropriate option contracts.

As an illustration, consider Example 2 in which the U.K. exporter sold the U.S. dollar using the forward contract at 0.5896 £/US. Instead of buying the forward contract, the exporter could have alternatively bought a call option on the U.S. dollar on a notional amount of US$ 10 mm and sold a put option on the U.S. dollar on the same notional amount, where both the options are struck at 0.5896 £/US and expire on the same day as the forward contract. For no arbitrage to occur, the exporter should be indifferent between buying a forward contract and buying a synthetic contract that is created using the call and put options. This replication is illustrated in Exhibit 28.

EXHIBIT 28 Replicating a Long Forward Position with Call and Put Options

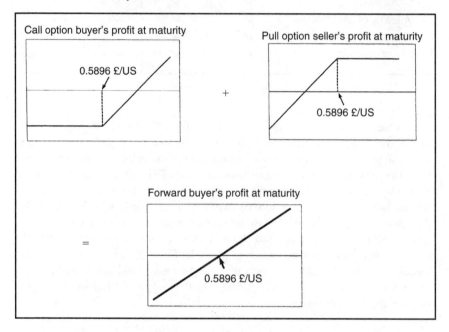

While any long position in the forward contract can be synthetically created by going long a call option on the forward contract and going short a put option on the forward contract, any short position in the forward contract can be similarly synthetically created by going short a call option on the forward contract and going long a put option on the forward contract, where the options are struck at the forward rate and expire on the contract maturity date. This synthetic replication strategy can easily be extended to encompass forward-start swap contracts[68].

---

[68] Theoretically, one can similarly replicate a long (short) position on the futures contract by going long (short) a call option on the futures contract and going short (long) a put option on the futures contract. However, since the exchange requires a mark-to-market to be done daily, it becomes difficult to replicate a futures contract with call and put options on the futures contract.

Although only the synthetic replication strategies for the derivatives expiring at some time in the future has been discussed, it is important for the reader to realize that these replication strategies can be extended to encompass contracts that start today. Consider as an illustration the hedger in Example 6. Since the hedger is paying a fixed rate of 5 percent and receiving a floating rate of six-month US$ LIBOR, he is in fact long a swap contract[69]. This long position in the swap can be replicated by a long position in the call option on the swap rate (also called a right-to-pay swaption) and a short position in the put option on the swap rate (also called a right-to-receive swaption), where both the options are struck at 5 percent and expire immediately (i.e., life of option is zero).

Since the above replication strategy holds true for any underlying asset, one can conclude that regardless of the asset class, any spot, forward, or swap contract can be synthetically replicated using both the European-style call and put option contracts on the appropriate underlying instruments. Thus, instead of using a forward contract, a swap contract, and an option contract to discuss the use of derivatives, only option contracts will be used as a platform for the basis of this discussion.

The above-mentioned European- and American-style call and put options, in addition to serving as useful building blocks for the vanilla derivatives, also serve as a valuable platform upon which one can build other strategies and instruments such as the *bull spread, bear spread, strangle*, and *straddle*. The reader is referred to the Glossary for definitions of many of the strategies that can be constructed using these options.

THE NEW VANILLA OPTION CONTRACT

Introduction

In the previous section, I split the vanilla options into two categories known as the European- and American-style options and showed how any derivative contract can be replicated using the European-style call and put options. These European- and American-style option contracts can be more succinctly summarized as follows:

A European-style option allows the purchaser to exercise the contract only on the option maturity date, while an American-style option allows the purchaser to exercise the contract at any time from option inception date to option maturity date.

---

[69] Since the hedger is paying a fixed rate of 5 percent on the swap, the price of the hedge increases if the swap rate increases (e.g., to 7 percent). The reason for this follows from the fact that the hedger is paying a rate that is 2 percent below the market rate and hence benefits by paying the lower rate. Similarly, when the swap rate drops to a level that is less than 5 percent, the price of the hedge decreases.

Furthermore, being long an asset typically implies an increase in the price of the held asset as the value of the asset increases. Since the price of the swap increases as the value of the swap rate increases, the hedger by definition is long the swap. On the other hand, if the hedger is instead receiving a fix rate on a swap, he is short the swap.

From the above summary, the reader will realize that moving from one exercise point (in the case of a European-style option) to infinite exercise points (in the case of an American-style option) defines the two extremities of the number of exercise points. Consequently, it is only natural to try to construct an option that is an intermediary of these extremities.

An example of such an option is the Mid-Atlantic, Bermudan, or quasi-American-style option. The purchaser of a Mid-Atlantic-style option would be allowed to exercise the option only on prespecified discrete dates, although there are some variations, which include the possibility of the purchaser exercising the option anytime during a prespecified time interval in the life of the option. Due to the frequency of exercise in a Mid-Atlantic-style option, it would be intuitively reasonable to expect the value of a Mid-Atlantic option to be no less expensive than that of a structurally similar European-style option and no more expensive than a structurally similar American-style option.

Despite the fact that a Mid-Atlantic-style option is an intermediary between a European-style and an American-style option, many consider a Mid-Atlantic-style option exotic. For the purposes of presenting a unified approach to the reader, I prefer to label a Mid-Atlantic-style option a vanilla option.

A Mid-Atlantic-Style Option Contract Example

The case study in Example 11 on page 59 better illustrates the use of a Mid-Atlantic-style option in the interest-rate asset class.

It is important for the reader to make the following three observations about Example 11.

OBSERVATION 1 The note in the example was only recalled by the issuer when the intrinsic value of the note was positive. For accounting or tax reasons, it is not uncommon for the issued notes to be recalled even when the intrinsic value is zero.[70]

OBSERVATION 2 It was assumed that the investor in the above example exercises her option as soon as the note gets called. This implicitly means that the investor exercises into the underlying swap regardless of whether the mark-to-market value of the swap to the investor is positive. In practice, when the note gets called, the investor would exercise the option only if the mark-to-market value of the swap to the investor is positive. However, if the mark-to-market value of the swap to the investor is negative, the investor would choose to get into the swap at the then-prevailing favorable market rate and sell off the option. This characteristic is no different

---

[70] This is analogous to the reason given in footnote 57.

EXAMPLE 11 A Mid-Atlantic-style Option Transaction

A U.S. investor owns a large amount of semiannual 6.5 percent coupon callable notes that were issued by a corporation at US$ 100. The issued note has a two-year life and can be recalled by the issuer for US$ 101 on the second or third coupon date.

To hedge against this recall, the investor purchases a Mid-Atlantic option on a swap from a financial institution that would allow her to exercise either in one year or 1½ years into a one-year or a six-month swap, respectively. The swap when exercised into by the investor would allow her to receive a semiannual fixed rate of 6.5 percent and pay the six-month US$ LIBOR rate. The cost of the hedge is US$ 0.41 for every US$ 100 of face amount.

Time (months)	Bond Price (US $)	Amount Paid by Investor to Issuer (US $)	Amount Paid by Issuer to Investor (US $)	How the Mid-Atlantic Option Impacts the Investor
0	100	100		☛ Premium of US$ 0.41 is paid for hedge by the investor.
6	99.5		$100 \cdot \dfrac{0.065}{2} = 3.25$	

Case 1: Note Is Called at the End of 1 Year

12	102.5		$[100 \cdot \dfrac{0.065}{2}] + 101$ $= 104.25$	☛ Investor exercises her option to receive a fixed rate of 6.5% on the 1-year swap.

Case 2: Note is Called at the End of 1½ Years

12	99.75		$100 \cdot \dfrac{0.065}{2} = 3.25$	
18	102		$[100 \cdot \dfrac{0.065}{2}] + 101$ $= 104.25$	☛ Investor exercises her option to receive a fixed rate of 6.5% on the ½-year swap

EXAMPLE 11   A Mid-Atlantic-style Option Transaction (Continued)

Case 3: Note is Not Called

12	99.75		$100 \cdot \dfrac{0.065}{2} = 3.25$	
18	101		$100 \cdot \dfrac{0.065}{2} = 3.25$	
24	100		$[100 \cdot \dfrac{0.065}{2}] + 100$ $= 103.25$	

from the discussion on exercise feature underlying the purchase of an American-style option.

OBSERVATION 3 Instead of purchasing the Mid-Atlantic option as in the example, the investor could have purchased two European-style swaptions[71]. These swaptions would allow the investor the right to receive a semiannual rate of 6.5 percent, where the first swaption would expire in one year and be exercised into a one-year swap and the second swaption would expire in 1½ years and be exercised into a six-month swap. The total cost of this strategy to the investor is US$ 0.62 for every US$ 100 of face amount. Since this is more expensive than the value of the Mid-Atlantic option, the Mid-Atlantic option provides a cheaper and a more effective form of hedge.[72]

Characteristics of the Mid-Atlantic-Style Option Contracts

The profits associated with the purchase of a Mid-Atlantic-style option contract are more succinctly written in Exhibit 29.

---

[71] A swaption is an option whose underlying asset is a swap. The swaptions mentioned in Observation 3 are sometimes also known as right-to-receive swaptions. See Glossary.

[72] In purchasing two European-style swaptions, if the note gets recalled at the end of one year, only the one-year swaption gets exercised. Thus, in addition to the one-year swaption, the hedger would have also paid for the 1½-year swaption, which she would not have ended up using. To avoid this form of over-hedging, some investors would probability-weigh the notional amount on each of the two swaption contracts and dynamically manage the notional amounts on these contracts using these probabilistic weights throughout the life of the note.

EXHIBIT 29 Profits to the Buyer of a Mid-Atlantic-Style Vanilla Option

Type of Option	Profit at Time t	Profit at Expiry Time T
$C_{MA}(0,T,X)$	$\max[S_t - X - P^*_{t,C}, C_{MA,t} - P^*_{t,C}]$	$\max[-P^*_{T,C}, S_T - X - P^*_{T,C}]$
$P_{MA}(0,T,X)$	$\max[X - S_t - P^*_{t,P}, P_{MA,t} - P^*_{t,P}]$	$\max[-P^*_{T,P}, X - S_T - P^*_{T,P}]$

where		
0	=	Current time or time today
t	=	Time of exercise, where t is a subset of time interval $[0,T]$
T	=	Maturity of the Contract
X	=	Strike value
S_t	=	Value of the underlying asset at time t
$C_{MA}(0,T,X)$	=	Call option purchased at time 0, struck at X and maturing at time T
$P_{MA}(0,T,X)$	=	Put option purchased at time 0, struck at X and maturing at time T
$C_{MA,t}$	=	Call option premium at time t, when purchased at time t, strike is X and maturity is time T
$P_{MA,t}$	=	Put option premium at time t, when purchased at time t, strike is X and maturity is time T
$P^*_{t,C}$	=	Amount foregone by purchaser of call option due to premium and the interest accrued until time t on this premium
$P^*_{t,P}$	=	Amount foregone by purchaser of put option due to premium and the interest accrued until time t on this premium

As with the American-style option, there is generally no analytical formula that can be used to value a Mid-Atlantic-style option. This results in one using the binomial tree approach or the Monte Carlo approach to value a Mid-Atlantic option.

Since the factors determining the value of a Mid-Atlantic-style option are no different from those affecting the value of a structurally similar European or American-style option, Exhibit 30 summarizes the list of factors that influence the value of any option across any asset class.

Besides replacing the factor "exercise type" in Exhibit 27 by the factor "frequency of exercise", Exhibit 30 is no different than Exhibit 27. While the term *exercise type* referred to either a European-style exercise or an American-style exercise, *frequency of exercise*, a self-explanatory term, can range anywhere from one (for European-style options) to infinity (for American-style options).

EXHIBIT 30 Factors Influencing the Value of a Vanilla Option Contract

Factors	Interest-Rate Option	Currency Option	Equity Option	Commodity Option
Convenience yield				✔
Dividend rate			✔	
Foreign risk-free rate		✔		
Domestic risk-free rate	✔	✔	✔	✔
Underlying asset value	✔	✔	✔	✔
Strike value	✔	✔	✔	✔
Volatility of asset value	✔	✔	✔	✔
Frequency of exercise	✔	✔	✔	✔
Life of contract	✔	✔	✔	✔

Now that the factors influencing the value of an option contract have been identified, it will be useful to understand how these factors actually affect the value of the contract. To do this, one has to first derive a no-arbitrage relationship between the option contract and the asset underlying the option contract[73], after which the results summarized in Exhibit 31 can be arrived at.

It is important for the reader to note that although Exhibit 31 illustrates the case when the underlying factors increase in value, one can use the results from the same exhibit to obtain the effect of the underlying factors decreasing by simply reversing the direction of the effects. In the case of the factor T, this makes no difference, of course.

The effect of the above seven factors on a call option premium can be intuited as follows:

r_f: Because this factor has the effect of reducing the growth rate of the asset, with all the other variables remaining the same, increasing the value of r_f results in the asset growing at a slower rate and hence a lower expected asset value on the option maturity date. Since the value of a call option will only increase if the value of the asset increases, this lower expected value of the asset leads to a lower option premium.

---

[73] This is equivalent to taking the expectation of the payoffs given in Exhibits 22, 25, and 29 with respect to the future movements in the asset price underlying the option and then present-valuing at the continuously compounded risk-free rate r_d. Footnote 38 in Chapter 4 contains the mathematical formulation for a European-style put option.

EXHIBIT 31   Effect of Increase in Value of Underlying Factors on Option Premium

	Type of Option Contracts	
Factors	Call	Put
r_f	⇓	⇑
r_d	⇑	⇓
S_0	⇑	⇓
X	⇓	⇑
σ	⇑	⇑
ef	⇑	⇑
T	⇕	⇕

r_d: This factor has the effect of increasing the growth rate of the asset, resulting in a higher expected asset value and hence a higher future value of the option premium. Since increasing r_d has a smaller effect on the present valuing of the option premium as compared with the growth rate of the asset, the net result would still be an increase in the option premium.

S_0: Increasing the underlying asset value implies increasing the intrinsic value of the call option. Since the intrinsic value is one component of the option premium, an increase in the intrinsic value, with all the other factors remaining the same, would lead to an increase in the option premium.

X: Increasing the strike value implies decreasing the intrinsic value of the call option. Since the intrinsic value is one component of the option premium, a decrease in the intrinsic value, with all the other factors remaining the same, would lead to a decrease in the option premium.

σ: Increasing the volatility implies increasing the chances of the call option finishing in-the-money. Similarly, an increase in volatility implies an increase in the probability of the option finishing out-of-the-money. Since the buyer of the option would have lost only his premium if the option finishes out-of-the-money, the upside potential due to a volatility increase is greater than the downside potential, hence the increase in the option premium.

ef: Increasing the frequency of exercise implies increasing the chances of exercising the call when it is highly in-the-money during the life of the option. This would never lead to a decrease in the option premium.

The intuition presented can be similarly extended to reason the behavior of a put option premium when the underlying factors change.

CONCLUSION

Thus far, the chapter has discussed and illustrated some examples of how vanilla derivatives get used across all four asset classes. Although these examples are by no means exhaustive, they provide the reader with the framework and platform necessary to discuss exotic derivatives. Whatever the uses, it is important for the reader to know that any underlying asset or nonoption-related derivative in the marketplace can usually be synthetically created using European-style call and put options on an appropriate underlying asset.[74] Furthermore, in addition to the European-style options, it was shown that the Mid-Atlantic-style options and American-style options form the backbone of the class of vanilla derivatives. Henceforth, I will use these options as a platform to discuss the exotic derivatives across all four asset classes in the next chapter.

---

[74] The ability to synthetically replicate becomes difficult for a futures contract. See footnote 68.

◎ DESCRIPTION AND
USES OF EXOTIC
OPTIONS

INTRODUCTION

In Chapter 2, I provided an overview of vanilla derivatives for each asset class and discussed the application of a futures contract, a forward contract, a swap contract and an option contract. Despite the type of insurance or yield-enhancing opportunities that vanilla derivatives provide, end users, more often than not, require solutions that manage their risk or monetize their market view more effectively, if possible, at a lower cost. As examples, consider the following two cases:

A. A Canadian energy producer wants to hedge his exposure to the oil, gas, interest-rate and currency markets, to the extent that he wants to meet expense budget set for the next three months. What can he do for his company?

Strategy 1: Buy an interest-rate option, a currency option, an oil option, and a gas option, each of which mitigates the individual risks arising from the corresponding asset class, where all these instruments would expire in three months.

Strategy 2: Buy an integrated risk-management solution expiring in three months that hedges the total budgeted amount in Canadian funds.

The second solution provides a cheaper and more effective means of hedging. The rationale behind the lower cost is that it uses the notion of correlation between all different financial markets and avoids overhedging. This idea is discussed in this chapter in the context of a basket option, which is the third building block of the exotic options.

B. Based on the current shape of the yield curve, an asset manager believes that the spread between the five-year bond yield and the three-year bond yield would widen in three months (that is, the yield curve would get steeper). How can the asset manager effectively take a view on the curve?

Strategy 1: Buy a duration-weighted amount of the underlying bonds and then unwind the positions in three months. This strategy could involve huge cash positions and a large possible downside.

Strategy 2: Buy a European-style option that pays off the maximum of the difference of the two bond yields (that is, five-year bond yield less three-year bond yield) and zero at the end of three months. To enter into such an option, the asset manager only needs to pay an up-front premium to monetize his view.

The second solution again provides a cheaper and more effective means of monetizing a view and is described in this chapter in the context of a spread option, which is the first building block of the exotic options. The rationale behind the lower price is that it uses the notion of correlation between two underlying bonds, and if the market moves against the asset manager, the asset manager would have only lost the premium.

The above examples describe just two of the numerous single and multifactor path-dependent risks that investor and risk managers may wish to speculate upon or hedge. In each instance, the vanilla options are totally inefficient, thereby clearly demonstrating the need for the use of nontraditional derivatives.

Since the derivatives market is continually evolving, new products are created frequently. While a few of them have never-before-seen risk profiles, many of them are just packages or twists of the old products that may potentially result in a new risk profile. Thus, instead of providing the reader with a list of exotic products that could quickly become extinct, I prefer to break the whole gamut of exotic derivative products into 11 building blocks[1]. This, I feel, will help the reader to better understand any type of twisted complex product and to intuit its value.

The objective of this chapter is to provide examples of the 11 building blocks underpinning the nonvanilla or exotic derivatives across all asset classes through the use of options. The blocks are discussed in alphabetical order[2], and

---

[1] These building blocks have been carved out in a manner such that each building block describes a unique way in which the payoff underlying a derivative is calculated (e.g., the payoff on the settlement date is linked to the average of the prices/values realized by an asset during the life of the contract, the payoff on the settlement date is linked to the difference between the prices/values realized by two assets on the maturity of the contract, and so on). Thus, if a derivative contract has a payoff on the settlement date that is linked to the difference between the average of the prices/values realized during the life of the contract by two assets, the price of this derivative will not necessarily be equal to the sum of the individual prices paid for each building block.

[2] The exception to this is the spread option building block. Since the intuition provided for the other building blocks is sometimes dependent on the results of this building block, the chapter starts off with this block and then discusses the remaining 10 building blocks alphabetically.

the pricing and risk characteristics underlying each building block are intuited and explained as much as possible. These building blocks, the backbone of understanding existing exotic derivatives, can also be used to understand and decompose or build more customized derivative-driven solutions.

THE BUILDING BLOCKS OF EXOTIC OPTIONS

Just as vanilla options were categorized into European-style options, Mid-Atlantic-style options, and American-style options, exotic options can be similarly categorized. However, unlike vanilla options, for each exercise type in an exotic option, there are an additional 11 basic building blocks. More precisely, each European-style exotic option, Mid-Atlantic-style exotic option, and American-style exotic option can be further decomposed into 11 building blocks, which are summarized in Exhibit 32.

As can be seen in Exhibit 32, any option can be categorized as a vanilla option or an exotic option. Furthermore, while both the vanilla and the exotic option can be categorized as a European-style option, a Mid-Atlantic-style option, or an American-style option, only the exotic option can be categorized further as a spread option, an average option, a basket option, and so on.

EXHIBIT 32 Building Blocks of the Options World

Option Type	Exercise Type	Payoff Type
Vanilla	European-style Mid-Atlantic-style American-style	
Exotic	European-style Mid-Atlantic-style American-style	Spread Average Basket Cash-or-nothing Choice Compound Deferred strike Lookback Nonlinear payoff Product Sudden birth/death

Since the entries presented in Exhibit 32 are the basic building blocks of the options world and almost any derivative can be replicated using options, one can conclude that any derivative instrument, regardless of whether it is vanilla or exotic, can be created using only these building blocks. Furthermore, as the risk characteristics of a structurally similar European-style option, Mid-Atlantic-style option, and American-style option are the same,[3] I will only discuss exotic options in the context of European-style options.

THE SPREAD OPTION CONTRACT

Introduction

Spread options are options that can be used to monetize a view on the relative movement between any two asset prices or values in the same economy. Suppose, for example, that a fund manager feels that the current yield differential of 100 basis points between the 10-year Government of Canada (GOC) bond and the 2-year GOC bond is too narrow based on historical data and thinks that this difference in yield will widen in a month. To monetize her view, she would like to put on a trading strategy that would pay her Cad\$ 10,000 for every basis point the spread between the 10-year GOC bond yield and the 2-year GOC bond yield widens beyond 100 basis points in one month's time. As her first strategy, she could purchase the underlying bonds by going long and short the appropriate notional amount of the bonds.[4] With this strategy, if she is wrong in a month's time,

---

[3] Although the factors underlying the European-style, Mid-Atlantic-style, and American-style options have similar directional impacts on the option premiums, the magnitude of the impact may be different.

[4] The dollar duration of a 2-year bond and a 10-year bond is approximately Cad\$ 164 per basis point per million and Cad\$ 610 per basis point per million, respectively, where the dollar duration of a bond is defined as a dollar value change in the bond price of a million-dollar face value when the yield of the bond changes by one basis point. Since, the investor wants to be paid an amount of Cad\$ 10,000 for every basis point the spread between the bond yields increases beyond 100 basis points, this is equivalent to the investor requiring for every basis point move in each underlying bond yield a Cad\$ 10,000 change in the price of the corresponding bond.

As the dollar duration of a 2-year bond is Cad\$ 164 per basis point per million, to see a Cad\$ 10,000 change in the price of this bond, she would have to purchase a notional amount of Cad\$ $\frac{10,000}{164}$ = Cad\$ 61 mm of 2-year bonds. Similarly, since the dollar duration of the 10-year bond is Cad\$ 610, she would have to sell a notional amount of Cad\$ 16.4 mm of 10-year bonds to see a Cad\$ 10,000 change in the bond price for every basis point change in the bond yield. Thus, her first strategy would be to purchase Cad\$ 61 mm of 2-year bonds and sell Cad\$ 16.4 mm of 10-year bonds today and liquidate this position in a month's time.

It is important for the reader to realize that the investor is taking on some yield-curve risk by assuming that the dollar durations of the bonds calculated today would be the same in a month's time. More precisely, although the dollar-duration values are calculated today, as the bond lives get shortened by a month in a month's time, these values would change. Furthermore, for any bond, as the time horizon of the view increases and the life of the bond gets shorter, the risk arising from using this constant dollar-duration assumption would increase drastically.

she has the potential for large losses when liquidating the position. Thus, the downside of replicating the spread using the underlying bonds can be costly and sometimes disastrous. See Ravindran (1995a) for a discussion.

An alternative way to monetize her view would be to buy a spread option that pays at the end of one month the difference between the 10-year bond yield, the 2-year bond yield and an offset of 100 basis points if her view is right and nothing if her view is wrong. More precisely, her in-the-money payoff at the end of one month is the 10-year yield minus the 2-year yield minus the 0.01. Thus, if the market view of the fund manager turns out to be wrong, her maximum downside in using this spread option will be limited to the option premium that was paid at the inception of the contract.[5]

The spread option can also be used to bet on the movement of the swap spreads (that is, swap rate minus bond yield).[6] As another example, suppose that current market conditions are such that the three-year swap spread (that is, the difference between the three-year swap rate and the three-year on-the-run bond yield) is 18 basis points. An investor feels that this spread will narrow in two months' time by at least five basis points. To monetize her view, she can purchase a spread option on the three-year swap spread with an offset of 13 basis points that expires in two months. With this option, she would get an in-the-money payoff of [0.0013 − (3-year swap rate − 3-year bond yield)] on the option maturity date.

A Spread Option Contract Example

The sequence of events in Example 12 on page 71 better illustrates the nature of a spread option transaction.

It is important for the reader to make the following two observations about Example 12:

OBSERVATION 1 Although the investor in Example 12 monetized a view on the difference between a swap rate and a bond yield, it is not compulsory for the two underlying assets to be tradeable assets. For example, the investor could have alternatively monetized a view on the difference between the five-year swap spread rate and the two-year swap spread rate; neither of which is a tradeable asset by itself.

OBSERVATION 2 Instead of purchasing an option on the swap spread, the investor could have alternatively purchased a two-month put option on the three-year swap rate and a two-month call op-

---

[5] This is analogous to Observation 3 of Example 9 (Chapter 2).

[6] Since a swap spread measures the spread over the government bonds at which a financial institution can borrow money, a swap spread reflects the creditworthiness of the financial institution. Consequently, an option whose underlying asset is a swap spread can also be viewed as a credit option.

tion on the three-year bond yield.[7] More precisely, she would purchase a two-month at-the-money right-to-receive swaption on the three-year swap and a two-month at-the-money call option on the three-year bond yield. This strategy would cost her Cad\$ 0.0952 mm, which is more expensive than the purchase of an option on the swap spread by 19 percent.

Characteristics of Spread Option Contracts

The profit profile associated with the purchase of spread options can be more generally written, as detailed in Exhibit 33 and graphed in Exhibits 34 and 35, where I have defined spread in the graphs to represent the quantity $aS_{1,T} - bS_{2,T}$.

Although closed-form solutions due to Margrabe (1978) and Hull (1997) exist when $a = b = 1$ and the strike value X (called an offset in the context of a spread option) is zero, the spread option has to be generally evaluated numerically.[8] Furthermore, instead of employing a two-dimensional integral to value the spread option for a nonzero strike, Ravindran (1993b) shows how to reduce the valuation problem to an option on a single asset so as to apply intuition and quicker numerical methods. However, as before, one can alternatively apply the binomial method and the Monte Carlo method to value this type of option, as shown in chapter 4.

The reader should observe that the profit and loss graphs to the buyer of a vanilla option that are presented in Exhibits 23 and 24 are philosophically no different from those in Exhibits 34 and 35. Furthermore, as discussed on page 52, the break-even analysis is crucial in determining whether this type of view-monetizing strategy is cost-effective.[9]

---

[7] Since the investor is of the view that the swap spread will narrow in the future, this narrowing of the swap spread can be achieved if any one of the following happens at the end of two months:

1. The rate of decrease in three-year swap rate is greater than that in three-year bond yield.
2. A decrease in three-year swap rate and no change in three-year bond yield.
3. A decrease in three-year swap rate and an increase in three-year bond yield.
4. No change in three-year swap rate and an increase in three-year bond yield.
5. The rate of increase in three-year swap rate is slower than that in three-year bond yield.

   Consequently, buying a two-month put option on the three-year swap rate would help monetize (2) and (3), and buying a two-month call option on the 3-year bond yield would help monetize (3) and (4). Furthermore, although both the put and call option do somewhat capture the effects in (1) and (5), respectively, they do so only in an absolute sense. More precisely, they do not capture the relative movements between the two bond yields as required in (1) and (5).

[8] Since this type of option can be viewed as an option to exchange asset 1 for asset 2 it is sometimes also known as the exchange or the Magrabe option.

[9] From Example 12, it can be seen that for the option buyer to break even, the swap spread has to be lower than 4.9 basis points on the option maturity date. Based on where the market had been historically, the chances of the swap spread going down this low is negligible. Consequently, the purchase of the option on the swap spread is not money well-spent.

EXAMPLE 12   A European-Style Spread Option Transaction

The investor feels that in two months, the Canadian three-year swap spread will narrow by at least five basis points. She pays a premium of Cad$ 0.08 mm for a spread option on a Cad$ 100 mm notional amount with an offset of 13 basis points that allows her to monetize this view. Thus, for every basis point the option finishes in-the-money, the investor gets paid $10,000. The current swap spread is 18 basis points.

Time (months)	Swap Spread (basis points)	Impact of Option on the Investor
0	18	☞ Cad$ 0.080 mm premium paid by investor
2	*Case A: Call Option Is Exercised at the End of 2 Months*	
	9	☞ Payoff of Cad$ [100 • (0.0013 – 0.0009)] = Cad$ 0.04 mm paid to investor ☞ Cad$ 0.08 mm of premium and Cad$ 0.001 mm of interest on this premium foregone by investor ☞ Profit to investor: Cad$ [0.04 – (0.08 – 0.001)] = –Cad$ 0.041 mm
	Case B: Call Option Is Not Exercised at the End of 2 Months	
	17	☞ Cad$ 0.08 mm of premium and Cad$ 0.001 mm of interest on this premium foregone by investor ☞ Profit to investor: –Cad$ (0.08 + 0.001) = – Cad$ 0.081 mm

To be able to value an option, one has to first identify the factors that would influence an option price. These factors are summarized in Exhibit 36 for all four asset classes.

As can be seen in Exhibit 36, while nine factors contribute to the value of a currency, equity, and commodity option contract, only eight factors contribute to the value of an interest-rate option contract. Compared to the factors influencing the value of a vanilla option in Exhibit 30, in addition to each asset having its own set of parameters, two additional factors influence the value of a spread option. These two factors, which are given in the last two rows of Exhibit 36, are as follows:

1. **Correlation between asset values.** Correlation between the continuously compounded returns of the two underlying asset values
2. **Coefficients associated with asset values.** Scale factor associated with each asset underlying the spread option

EXHIBIT 33 Profits to the Buyer of a European-Style Spread Option

Type of Spread Option	Profit at Expiry Time T
$C_E(0,T,a,b,X)$	$\max[-P^*_{T,C},(aS_{1,T} - bS_{2,T}) - X - P^*_{T,C}]$
$P_E(0,T,a,b,X)$	$\max[-P^*_{T,P},X - (aS_{1,T} - bS_{2,T}) - P^*_{T,P}]$

where

$\quad\quad 0 =$ Current time or time today

$\quad\quad T =$ Time of option maturity

$\quad S_{i,T} =$ Value of underlying asset i at time T, where i = 1, 2

$\quad\quad a =$ Coefficient of asset 1

$\quad\quad b =$ Coefficient of asset 2

$\quad\quad X =$ Strike value of option

$C_E(0,T,a,b,X) =$ European call spread option purchased at time 0 with parameters T, a, b, and X

$P_E(0,T,a,b,X) =$ European put spread option purchased at time 0 with parameters T, a, b, and X

$\quad P^*_{T,C} =$ Amount foregone by purchaser of call option due to premium and the interest accrued until time T on this premium

$\quad P^*_{T,P} =$ Amount foregone by purchaser of put option due to premium and the interest accrued until time T on this premium

EXHIBIT 34 Spread Call Option Buyer's Profit at Maturity

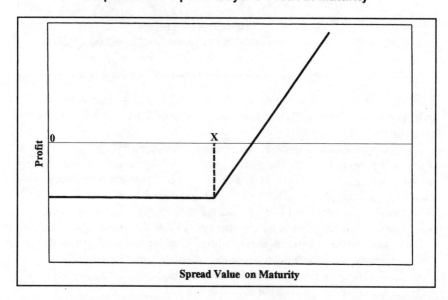

Spread Value on Maturity

EXHIBIT 35 Spread Put Option Buyer's Profit at Maturity

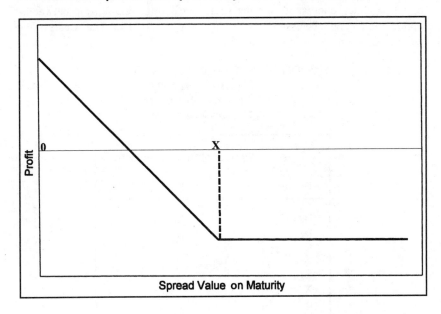

EXHIBIT 36 Factors Influencing the Value of a Spread Option Contract

Factors	Interest-Rate Option	Currency Option	Equity Option	Commodity Option
Convenience yields				✔
Dividend rates		✔	✔	
Foreign risk-free rate		✔		
Domestic risk-free rate	✔	✔	✔	✔
Underlying asset values	✔	✔	✔	✔
Strike value	✔	✔	✔	✔
Volatilities of asset values	✔	✔	✔	✔
Frequency of exercise	✔	✔	✔	✔
Life of contract	✔	✔	✔	✔
Correlation between asset values	✔	✔	✔	✔
Coefficients associated with asset values	✔	✔	✔	✔

To understand how the above-mentioned factors influence the value of an option contract, one has to first derive a no-aribitrage relationship between the option contract and the assets underlying the option contract. The effects of these factors are summarized in Exhibit 37.

EXHIBIT 37 Effect of Increase in Value of Underlying Factors on Spread Option Premium

	Type of Option Contracts	
Factors	**Call**	**Put**
$r_{1,f}$	⇓	⇑
$r_{2,f}$	⇑	⇓
r_d	⇑	⇓
$S_{1,0}$	⇑	⇓
$S_{2,0}$	⇓	⇑
X	⇓	⇑
σ_1	⇕	⇕
σ_2	⇕	⇕
ef	⇑	⇑
T	⇕	⇕
$\rho_{1,2}$	⇓	⇓
a	⇑	⇓
b	⇓	⇑

Since the effects of T, X, and ef are obvious and no different from those in Exhibit 31, the effects of the remaining 10 factors will now be intuited. From the profit profile of a call option in Exhibit 33, if one thinks of the spread (that is, $aS_{1,T} - bS_{2,T}$) as an asset, it is obvious that the value of the spread call option will increase as the value of the asset increases. Furthermore, the value of the asset $aS_{1,T} - bS_{2,T}$ will only increase if either the value of a or $S_{1,T}$ increases, or the value of b or $S_{2,T}$ decreases. As the reader will realize, while a and b are direct inputs, the values of $S_{1,T}$ and $S_{2,T}$ are dependent on other underlying variables. More precisely, an increase in $S_{1,0}$ or a decrease in $r_{1,f}$ would lead to an increase in the value of $S_{1,T}$ while a decrease in $S_{2,0}$ or an increase in $r_{2,f}$ would lead to a decrease in the value of $S_{2,T}$. Thus, increasing a, $r_{2,f}$ or $S_{1,0}$ would lead to an increase in the call option premium, while increasing the value of b, $r_{1,f}$ and $S_{2,0}$ would lead to a decrease in the option premium.

The effects of $\rho_{1,2}$ are easily intuited by again viewing the spread $aS_{1,T} - bS_{2,T}$ as an asset and realizing that $\rho_{1,2}$ represents the correlation between the continuously compounded returns of the two underlying assets[10] and not the correlation between the natural logarithms of the underlying asset values.[11] As is well known, the variance of the difference between any two asset values is the sum of

---

[10] A statistical implication of the statement "$\rho_{1,2}$ represents the correlation between the continuously compounded returns of the two underlying assets" is that the natural logarithm of the future first asset value and the natural logarithm of the future second asset value given the current values of these assets have a joint distribution that is a bivariate normal distribution, with $\rho_{1,2}$ representing the correlation between the natural logarithm of the future first asset value and the natural logarithm of the future second asset value, where the term *natural logarithm* is defined in footnote 3, Chapter 4. The reader is referred to Assumptions 1 and 2 in the Appendix for the mathematics underpinning these statements. Despite this, to calculate $\rho_{1,2}$ from historical data, it is not correct to simply take the natural logarithms of the set of historical numbers and then calculate the correlation between these sets. See footnote 11 of this chapter. Relationship 18 of the Appendix provides the formula that should be used in the calculation of $\rho_{1,2}$ from historical asset prices/values.

Furthermore, if one assumed that the natural logarithm of the future first asset value and the natural logarithm of the future second asset value given the current values of these assets have a joint distribution that is a bivariate normal distribution, with $\rho^*_{1,2}$ representing the correlation between the future first asset value and the future second asset value, the value of $\rho_{1,2}$ will not necessarily be the same as that of $\rho^*_{1,2}$. More precisely, the relationship between $\rho_{1,2}$ and $\rho^*_{1,2}$ is given in Relationship 6 of the Appendix.

[11] As discussed in footnote 10, despite the statistical equivalence, $\rho_{1,2}$ cannot be calculated from the historical data by computing the correlation between the natural logarithms of the future asset values. This can be better understood if we considered the sets of numbers $\{1, 2, 3, 4, 5, 6, 7\}$ and $\{1.1, 1.2, 1.4, 1.7, 1.95, 2, 2.2\}$.

1. Calculating the correlation between continuously compounded returns
   A. For each set, calculate the second observation divided by the first observation, the third observation divided by the second observation, . . ., the seventh observation divided by the sixth observation. This transforms the first set of numbers into $\{2, 1.5, 1.333, 1.25, 1.2, 1.167\}$ and the second set of numbers into $\{1.091, 1.167, 1.214, 1.147, 1.026, 1.1\}$.
   B. Take the natural logarithm of all the numbers in each set (this can be done using the Microsoft Excel spreadsheet command "=ln( )"). The first and second set obtained from (1A.) will now be transformed into the sets $\{0.693, 0.405, 0.288, 0.223, 0.182, 0.154\}$ and $\{0.087, 0.154, 0.194, 0.137, 0.025, 0.095\}$, respectively.
   C. Find the correlation between the sets of numbers obtained in (1B.) (this can be done using the Microsoft Excel spreadsheet command "=correl()"). The correlation number obtained is 0.064 and is denoted by $\rho_{1,2}$ in footnote 10.
2. Calculating correlation between the natural logarithms of the underlying asset values
   A. For each set, calculate the natural logarithm of each number. This transforms the first set into $\{0, 0.693, 1.099, 1.386, 1.609, 1.792, 1.946\}$ and the second set into $\{0.095, 0.182, 0.336, 0.531, 0.668, 0.693, 0.788\}$.
   B. Find the correlation between the sets of numbers obtained in (2A.). The correlation number obtained is 0.968 and is denoted by $\rho^*_{1,2}$ in footnote 10.

As can be seen above, the correlation value calculated using the continuously compounded returns of the two underlying assets can be different from that calculated using only the values of the assets. The reason for this stems from the fact that although the values of both assets move in the same direction, the day-to-day change in the values of the assets can be uncorrelated.

the variances of these asset values minus the covariance between these asset values.[12] Thus, as the value of the correlation between the asset values increase, the variance of the spread decreases, causing the volatility of the spread to decrease and hence the option premium to decrease.[13] However, since the correlation[14] between the asset values only increases as $\rho_{1,2}$ increases, an increase in $\rho_{1,2}$ results in a decrease in the option premium.

To illustrate the effect of volatilities of the underlying assets, consider σ_1. Since an increase in σ_1 results in an increase in the variance of the first asset, when $\rho_{1,2}$ is negative, increasing the value σ_1 results in the increase of the variance of the spread $aS_{1,T} - bS_{2,T}$, as can be seen from footnote 12. Furthermore, as the increase in this variance results in an increase in the option premium, an increase in σ_1 increases the option premium when $\rho_{1,2}$ is negative. Alternatively, when $\rho_{1,2}$ is positive, although an increase in σ_1 results in an increase in the variance of the first asset, depending on the size of σ_2 and given the fact that the covariance between the two assets is subtracted to obtain the variance of the spread $aS_{1,T} - bS_{2,T}$, the variance of the spread may decrease. Thus, when $\rho_{1,2}$ is positive, an increase in σ_1 may result in a decrease in the option premium, leaving one to conclude that as σ_1 increases, the option premium may not necessarily increase. The same sort of reasoning can be applied to intuit the effect of σ_2 on the option premium and the effect of all the underlying factors on the put option premium.

Like the effects of $\rho_{1,2}$, the effects of r_d are easily intuited by again viewing the spread $aS_{1,T} - bS_{2,T}$ as an asset. To intuit the effects of r_d, I will first assume that $a = b = 1$ and $X = 0$. In this instance, a spread option can be viewed as a call exchange option whose in-the-money payoff is $S_{1,T} - S_{2,T}$. Furthermore, this option can be thought of as a vanilla call option which is struck at the second asset's underlying rate $S_{2,0}$; where the asset underlying the option is the first asset with volatility $\sqrt{\sigma_1^2 - 2\rho_{1,2}\sigma_1\sigma_2 + \sigma_2^2}$, and dividend rate $r_{1,f}$ in an environment where the risk-free rate is $r_{2,f}$. This would readily imply that the option premium would be independent of r_d.

To intuit this result, observe that the first asset grows at a rate of r_d while paying a dividend rate of $r_{1,f}$ and the second asset grows at a rate of r_d while paying a dividend rate of $r_{2,f}$. Thus, the first asset can be thought of as growing at a rate of $r_d - r_{1,f}$ in an environment where the risk-free rate is r_d, and the second as-

---

[12] This is illustrated in the equation

$$Var(A1 - A2) = Var(A1) + Var(A2) - 2 \cdot Cov(A1,A2)$$
$$= Var(A1) + Var(A2) - 2 \cdot Corr(A1,A2) \cdot \sqrt{Var(A1) \cdot Var(A1)}$$

where the terms *Var*, *Cov*, and *Corr* represent the words *variance*, *covariance*, and *correlation*, respectively.

[13] The relationship between the variance and the volatility of an asset is given in footnote 19 of the Appendix.

[14] This is denoted by $\rho*_{1,2}$ in footnote 10.

set can be thought of as growing at a rate of $r_d - r_{2,f}$ in an environment where the risk-free rate is r_d. The first asset relative to the second asset (or equivalently in the environment of the second asset) will grow at a rate of $(r_d - r_{1,f}) - (r_d - r_{2,f})$, which simplies to $r_{2,f} - r_{1,f}$. Hence, this relative growth rate can be alternatively interpreted as the first asset growing in the second environment at a rate of $r_{2,f}$ and paying a dividend at a rate of $r_{1,f}$. Furthermore, since one is in the environment of the second asset, the second asset value, which plays the role of a strike value in the payoff formula, will have a zero growth rate.[15]

Although each of the assets would have its own volatility, it would be easier to intuit the effects if one artificially sets the second asset's volatility to zero and the first asset's volatility to the volatility of the spread between the two assets. In doing so, $S_{2,0}$ the value of the second asset at the inception of the contract, will still be $S_{2,0}$ on the maturity of the contract when observed in its own environment. In addition, the volatility of the first asset relative to the second asset can be obtained using footnote 12. All these results are summarized in Exhibit 38, where $S_{1,T_{S_{2,T}}}$ represents the first asset in the environment of the second asset.

EXHIBIT 38 Distributional Characteristics of the First Asset in the Environment of the Second Asset

Variables	Risk-Free Rate	Dividend Rate	Volatility
$S_{1,T}$	r_d	$r_{1,f}$	σ_1
$S_{2,T}$	r_d	$r_{2,f}$	σ_2
$S_{1,T_{S_{2,T}}}$	$r_{2,f}$	$r_{1,f}$	$\sqrt{\sigma_1^2 - 2\rho_{1,2}\sigma_1\sigma_2 + \sigma_2^2}$

To intuit the effects of r_d when $X \neq 0$, it is easier to use the argument that relative to the second asset $bS_{2,T}$, the growth rate of the spread $aS_{1,T} - bS_{2,T}$ is independent of the risk-free rate r_d. Furthermore, since X can be viewed as growing at a zero rate in a risk-neutral world, it grows at a rate of $-(r_d - r_{2,f})$ relative to the second asset. Thus, as the value of r_d increases, the growth rate of X becomes more negative, resulting in the value of X becoming smaller. This, coupled with the fact that a lower X leads to a greater option premium, results in the increase

---

[15] An example of this is given by Kolkiewicz and Ravindran (1994). A bird flying from east to west at x m/s in a train that is also moving from east to west at the same speed. As long as both the bird and the train are moving at the same speed in the same direction, the speed of the bird relative to that of the train (or as observed by someone in the train) will be independent of x and have a value of 0. By thinking of the first asset as the bird and the second asset as the train, they reason that it is not surprising that the growth rate of one asset relative to the other is independent of the risk-free rate.

in the option premium when r_d is increased. The results for the put option can be similarly intuited.

Unlike volatilities, which can be easily traded, there is no market for correlation trading. Thus, the only means of getting a good estimate for the correlation number would be to use the methodology illustrated in footnote 11 on the historical asset values. Hence, correlation estimation is crucial to both the pricing and the hedging of a spread option. Like a vanilla option, the spread option can be hedged using the delta-hedging technique on each of the variables. Here, however, the deltas obtained for a spread option will be a function of the correlation between the continuously compounded returns of the underlying assets.

As in the basket option, purchasing an option on a spread between two assets is usually cheaper than purchasing two individual options on each of the underlying assets[16] for the following two reasons[17]:

1. Higher correlation implies greater savings.
2. Option on a portfolio is cheaper than a portfolio of options.

Since the first reason is already intuited on page 74, I will just intuit the second reason. The second reason can be easily explained by assuming that $a = b = 1$ and looking at the regions in Exhibits 39 and 40 where the spread option and the vanilla options would pay off on the maturity of the contracts.

EXHIBIT 39   Call Spread Payoff Region to Buyer on Option Maturity Date

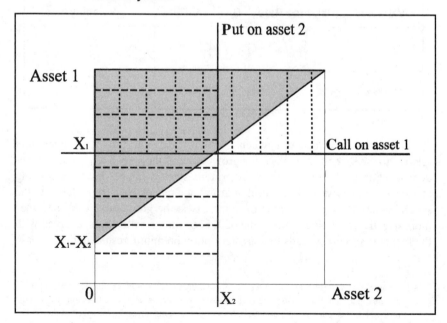

---

[16] An example of this was seen in Observation 2 accompanying Example 12.

[17] People generally tend to attribute the cheapness of the spread option to only the first reason.

**EXHIBIT 40   Put Spread Payoff Region to Buyer on Option
                Maturity Date**

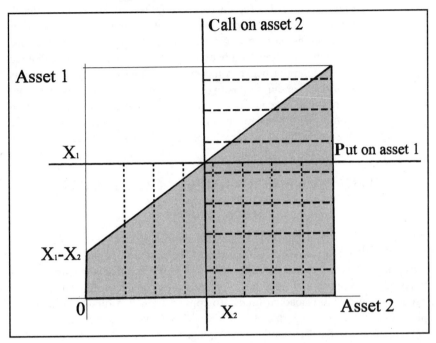

Ignoring the option premiums that were paid at the inception of the contracts and assuming that the options expire at the same time, Exhibit 39 illustrates the in-the-money payoff region on option maturity date to the purchaser of

1. A spread option that is struck at $X_1 - X_2$ and is denoted by the shaded area.
2. A vanilla call option on asset 1 that is struck at X_1 and is denoted by the vertical dotted lines that lie above the horizontal line passing through X_1.
3. A vanilla put option on asset 2 that is struck at X_2 and is denoted by the horizontal dotted lines that lie to the left of the vertical line passing through X_2.

As can be seen from the exhibit, the in-the-money payoff region from the purchase of a call spread option is smaller than the sum of the regions due to the purchase of the two vanilla options; which would obviously result in the spread option costing less. A similar reasoning could be used on Exhibit 40 to conclude that the purchase of a put spread option would be cheaper than the purchase of the two appropriate vanilla options.

Other Applications

Spread options can also be effectively used by liability managers to manage their risks. The following example, which is by no means exhaustive, illustrates such a use of a spread option.

Application An insurance company launches a new guaranteed investment cer-
tifificate (GIC) issue into the retail market that offers a three-year
rate to its investors for a two-year term deposit. Using the feedback
from its marketing department, it launches this GIC campaign for
two months, hoping to attract a total of $50 million in deposits.
Since the insurance company would be exposed to the risk that the
rate differential between the three-year and two-year instruments
would widen during this two-month period, it purchases an at-the-
money call spread option on this notional amount. This option
would pay the insurance company only if the spread between the
three-year and two-year widens beyond the strike rate.

THE AVERAGE OPTION CONTRACT

Introduction

A Canadian exporter is exposed to the exchange-rate risk between the Canadian
and U.S. dollar every week. The treasurer of the company, in preparing a quarterly budget, has to forecast the cash inflows and outflows from the existing contracts of the company and state the company's expected net profit or loss for the
upcoming quarter in Canadian funds. To convert Canadian funds, the treasurer
picks an average exchange rate of 1.3250 Cad/US. Clearly, the treasurer does not
have to worry if the U.S. dollar gets stronger and the average of the weekly
Cad/US exchange rates over the next quarter exceeds the 1.3250 Cad/US level.
However, if the Canadian dollar gets stronger over the next quarter, he will not be
able to meet his budget. In order to hedge himself, or more precisely his budget,
he would need a three-month currency put option on the U.S. dollar that is based
on the weekly averaging of exchange rates for the next quarter and struck at
1.3250 Cad/US. This type of option is called an averaging rate put option.

An Average Option Contract Example

Example 13 on page 81 illustrates the sequence of events depicting the nature of the transaction.

It is important for the reader to make the following six observations about
Example 13:

OBSERVATION 1 In dealing with the average rate option in Example 13, to
compute the in-the-money payoff on the option maturity
date, the realized average was calculated using the spot rates
that were expressed in Cad/US[18]. Should the treasurer instead calculate the realized average using the spot rates expressed in US/Cad and then take the reciprocal of the

---

[18] See Observation 2 accompanying Example 9.

EXAMPLE 13 A European-Style Average Rate Option Transaction

The Canadian dollar is currently trading at 1.3250 Cad/US. A treasurer who has just submitted his quarterly budget wants to hedge against the strengthening of the Canadian dollar.

He pays a premium of Cad$ 1.0699 mm to buy an averaging put option on the U.S. dollar that is struck at 1.3250 Cad/US and matures in three months on a notional amount of US$ 140 mm. To do the averaging, the exchange rates are monitored once a week (also called a weekly sampling period) at noon starting from today's spot rate of 1.3250 Cad/US until and including the exchange rate at the expiry date of the option. An arithmetic average is calculated for all 14 observed rates and then compared with a strike rate of 1.3250 Cad/US.

Time (months)	Average Exchange Rate (Cad/US)	Impact of Option on the Treasurer
0	1.3250	☞ Cad$ 1.0699 mm premium paid by treasurer
3	*Case A: Put Option Is Exercised at the End of 3 Months*	
	1.3150	☞ Payoff of Cad$ [140 • (1.3250 – 1.3150)] = Cad$ 1.4 mm paid to treasurer ☞ Cad$ 1.0699 mm of premium and Cad$ 0.015 mm of interest on this premium foregone by treasurer ☞ Profit to treasurer: Cad$ [1.4 – (1.0699 + 0.015)] = Cad$ 0.3151 mm
	Case B: Put Option Is Not Exercised at the End of 3 Months	
	1.3300	☞ Cad$ 1.0699 mm of premium and Cad$ 0.015 mm of interest on this premium foregone by treasurer ☞ Profit to treasurer: –Cad$ (1.0699 + 0.015) = –Cad$ 1.0849 mm

computed average, he could possibly get a drastically different answer. This is because the reciprocal of an average may
not necessarily be equal to the average of the reciprocal.[19]

OBSERVATION 2 The type of averaging discussed in the above example is
arithmetic in nature. The treasurer could have alternatively
bought a put option, whose payoff on the option maturity date
is based on a geometric average of the weekly observed
rates.[20] Since a geometric average is always less than an arithmetic average, it can be concluded in general that an arithmetic average rate put option can never be more expensive
than a structurally similar geometric average rate put option.[21]
The converse is, however, true for an average rate call option.

OBSERVATION 3 If the notional sizes of the currency exposure vary over the
weekly observed periods, the treasurer would be better off
purchasing a weighted averaging option on the currency rates.
This can be further customized to entertain either a regular averaging frequency or an irregular averaging frequency, where
an example of an irregular averaging frequency would be the
observing of the daily exchange rates for the first month and
the biweekly exchange rates over the next two months. This
level of customization will depend totally on the risk profile
and the cash flow projection of the company.

OBSERVATION 4 Although the sampling period for computing the average in
the above example starts on the inception of the option contract and ends on the option maturity date, nothing prohibits
the transacting of an average rate option whose sampling
period is not a subset of the option life. To illustrate, suppose the hedger decides to sell the average rate option back
into the marketplace at the end of two months. In doing so,
the average rate option would still be left with a one-month
averaging life that would need to be blended with the run-

---

[19] To understand this statement better, consider, for example, the exchange-rate triplet
(1.2800,1.2900,1.3000) Cad/US, whose arithmetic average can be easily shown to be 1.2900
Cad/US (i.e., the arithmetic average of the numbers 1.2800, 1.2900, 1.3000 is
$\frac{1.2800 + 1.2900 + 1.3000}{3} = 1.2900$). When these exchange rates are expressed in US/Cad,
the triplet (1.2800,1.2900,1.3000) becomes $\left(\frac{1}{1.2800}, \frac{1}{1.2900}, \frac{1}{1.3000}\right)$, whose arithmetic
average of 0.7752 US/Cad is not a reciprocal of the average 1.2900 Cad/US.

[20] The geometric average of the numbers 1.2800, 1.2900, 1.3000 is defined as $(1.2800 \cdot 1.2900 \cdot 1.3000)^{1/3} = 1.2899$.

[21] Although this is the only reason that people generally give to intuit the reason for the arithmetic
average rate put option being cheaper than the geometric average rate put option, in reality,
the volatility of these types of averages plays a role.

ning average calculated over the previous two months. Thus, the option life of one month is a subset of the averaging period of three months.

OBSERVATION 5 In addition to purchasing a three-month hedge, the treasurer will in practice also convert his U.S. dollars to Canadian ones, using the weekly exchange rates. More precisely, the treasurer will actually go to the currency market weekly to convert his cash inflow of US$ 10 mm. Thus, when the average exchange rate at the end of three months, as pointed out in Case 1 of Example 13, turns out to be 1.3150 Cad/US, the treasurer would have effectively converted his US$ 140 mm notional amount to Cad$ 184.1 mm. Because the option finished in-the-money, the option seller will pay the treasurer an amount of US$ 140 mm • (1.3250 – 1.3150) Cad/US, which is equivalent to Cad$ 1.4 mm. This would result in a total revenue of Cad$ (184.1 + 1.4) mm = Cad$ 185.5 mm, which, as expected, would be the same as the total budgeted amount of Cad$ (140 • 1.3250) mm = Cad$ 185.5 mm.

OBSERVATION 6 Instead of purchasing an average rate option as in the above example, the treasurer could have alternatively bought US$ 10 mm worth of Canadian dollars using the spot market and a strip of 13 European-style put options on the U.S. dollar ranging in maturity from 1 to 13 weeks. While each option contract would be struck at 1.3250 Cad/US and based on a notional amount of US$ 10 mm, the first option contract would expire in 1 week and the 13th option contract would expire in 13 weeks. This strategy would cost the treasurer Cad$ 1.2460 mm, which is about 15 percent more expensive than the average rate put option in the example. The intuition underlying this is discussed on page 92.

Characteristics of the Average Option Contracts

The profit profile associated with the purchase of the average options can be more generally written, as illustrated in Exhibit 41. The graphs associated with the purchase of Category I and III options are presented in Exhibits 42 and 43, and those associated with the purchase of Category II and IV options are presented in Exhibits 44 and 45.

The reader should note that in Exhibit 41, while Categories II and IV represent the arithmetic average options and the geometric average options, respectively, Categories I and III represent the floating arithmetic average strike options and the floating geometric average strike options, respectively. When the weights associated with the sampled values of the asset are set equal to each other, the formulae for valuing a European-style geometric average option is given in Kemna and Vorst (1990), while that for a European-style arithmetic average option is

EXHIBIT 41   Profits to Buyer of a European-Style Average Option

Type of Average Option	Profit at Expiry Time T
$C_{E,I}(0,T,RA,w_{i+1},...,w_n,t_{i+1},...,t_n)$	$\max\left[-P^*_{T,CI},S_T - RA - \sum_{j=i+1}^{n} w_jS_{t_j} - P^*_{T,CI}\right]$
$P_{E,I}(0,T,RA,w_{i+1},...,w_n,t_{i+1},...,t_n)$	$\max\left[-P^*_{T,PI},RA + \sum_{j=i+1}^{n} w_jS_{t_j} - S_T - P^*_{T,PI}\right]$
$C_{E,II}(0,T,X,RA,w_{i+1},...,w_n,t_{i+1},...,t_n)$	$\max\left[-P^*_{T,CII},RA + \sum_{j=i+1}^{n} w_jS_{t_j} - X - P^*_{T,CII}\right]$
$P_{E,II}(0,T,X,RA,w_{i+1},...,w_n,t_{i+1},...,t_n)$	$\max\left[-P^*_{T,PII},X - RA - \sum_{j=i+1}^{n} w_jS_{t_j} - P^*_{T,PII}\right]$
$C_{E,III}(0,T,RA,w_{i+1},...,w_n,t_{i+1},...,t_n)$	$\max\left[-P^*_{T,CIII},S_T - RA \prod_{j=i+1}^{n} S_{t_j}^{w_j} - P^*_{T,CIII}\right]$
$P_{E,III}(0,T,RA,w_{i+1},...,w_n,t_{i+1},...,t_n)$	$\max\left[-P^*_{T,PIII},RA \prod_{j=i+1}^{n} S_{t_j}^{w_j} - S_T - P^*_{T,PIII}\right]$
$C_{E,IV}(0,T,X,RA,w_{i+1},...,w_n,t_{i+1},...,t_n)$	$\max\left[-P^*_{T,CIV},RA \prod_{j=i+1}^{n} S_{t_j}^{w_j} - X - P^*_{T,CIV}\right]$
$P_{E,IV}(0,T,X,RA,w_{i+1},...,w_n,t_{i+1},...,t_n)$	$\max\left[-P^*_{T,PIV},X - RA \prod_{j=i+1}^{n} S_{t_j}^{w_j} - P^*_{T,PIV}\right]$

where

0 = Current time or time today

T = Time of option maturity

t_j = Times at which the asset values are sampled, where $j = 1,2,...,n$; $t_{i+1} \geq 0$; and $t_n \leq T$

S_{t_j} = Asset value sampled at time t_j

RA = Running arithmetic (geometric) average realized for the first i observations for Category I and II (Category III and IV) options and is

given by $\sum_{j=1}^{i} w_jS_{t_j}(\prod_{j=i+1}^{n} S_{t_j}^{w_j})$

w_j = Weight associated with asset value S_{t_j},

where $\sum_{j=1}^{n} w_j = 1$

S_T = Asset value on option maturity

X = Strike value of option

$C_{E,k}(0,T,RA,w_{i+1},...,w_n,t_{i+1},...,t_n)$ = European average call option purchased at time 0 with parameters $T,RA,w_{i+1},...,w_n,t_{i+1},...,t_n$, where $k = I, III$

EXHIBIT 41 Profits to a Buyer of a European-Style Average Option (Continued)

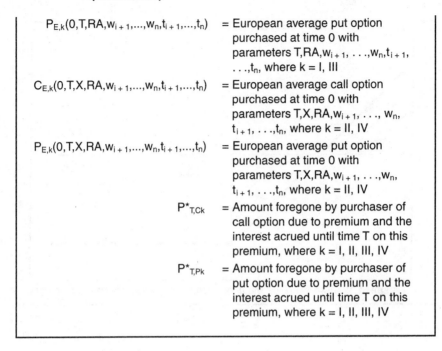

$P_{E,k}(0,T,RA,w_{i+1},...,w_n,t_{i+1},...,t_n)$ = European average put option purchased at time 0 with parameters $T,RA,w_{i+1}, ...,w_n,t_{i+1}, ...,t_n$, where k = I, III

$C_{E,k}(0,T,X,RA,w_{i+1},...,w_n,t_{i+1},...,t_n)$ = European average call option purchased at time 0 with parameters $T,X,RA,w_{i+1}, ..., w_n, t_{i+1}, ...,t_n$, where k = II, IV

$P_{E,k}(0,T,X,RA,w_{i+1},...,w_n,t_{i+1},...,t_n)$ = European average put option purchased at time 0 with parameters $T,X,RA,w_{i+1}, ...,w_n, t_{i+1}, ...,t_n$, where k = II, IV

$P^*_{T,Ck}$ = Amount foregone by purchaser of call option due to premium and the interest acrued until time T on this premium, where k = I, II, III, IV

$P^*_{T,Pk}$ = Amount foregone by purchaser of put option due to premium and the interest acrued until time T on this premium, where k = I, II, III, IV

EXHIBIT 42 Category I & III Average Call Option Buyer's Profit at Maturity

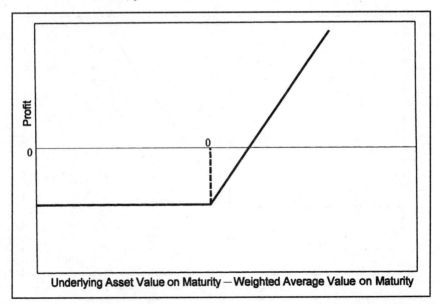

EXHIBIT 43   Category I & III Average Put Option Buyer's Profit at Maturity

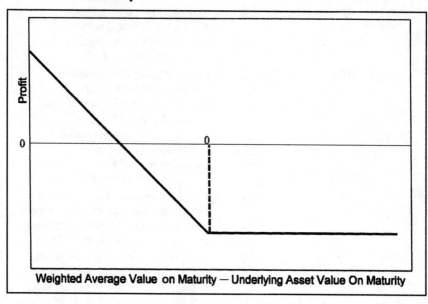

EXHIBIT 44   Category II & IV Average Call Option Buyer's Profit at Maturity

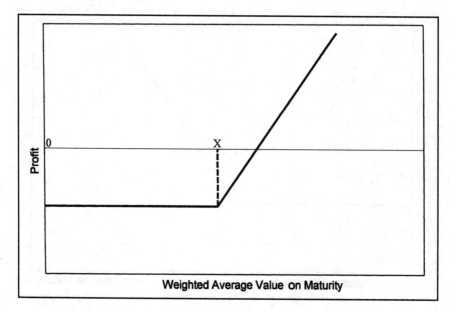

EXHIBIT 45   Category II & IV Average Put Option Buyer's Profit at Maturity

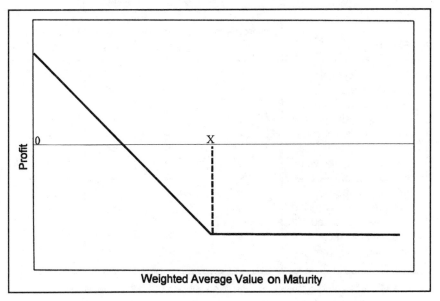

given in Levy (1992). New accurate results for valuing European-style arithmetic average options have been published by several researchers since Levy's work. However, the simplicity and robustness associated with Levy's method still makes it an attractive valuation tool for practitioners. The valuation formulae for both the European-style geometric and arithmetic average options have been extended to entertain the possibility of nonuniform weights in Ravindran (1995b) and Zhang (1995). Bouaziz, Briys, and Crouhy (1994) provide valuation formulae for the floating strike arithmetic average options when the continuously sampled points are equally weighted using an exponential approximation. As stated in Vorst (1995), the method developed by Levy can also be used to value floating strike options. The premiums obtained using all these sophisticated formulae can be alternatively calculated using the intuitively appealing binomial method and the Monte Carlo method presented in chapter 4.

As can be easily observed, the profit and loss graphs to the buyer of an average option that are presented in Exhibits 42, 43, 44, and 45 are philosophically no different from those in Exhibits 23 and 24. Thus, as discussed on page 52, the break-even analysis is crucial in determining whether this type of hedging strategy is cost-effective.

To be able to value an option, one has to first identify the factors that would influence an option price. These factors are summarized in Exhibit 46 for all four asset classes.

As can be seen in Exhibit 46, while 10 factors contribute to the value of a currency, equity, and commodity option contract; only 9 factors contribute to the

EXHIBIT 46   Factors Influencing the Value of an Average Option Contract

Factors	Interest-Rate Option	Currency Option	Equity Option	Commodity Option
Convenience yield				✔
Dividend rate			✔	
Foreign risk-free rate		✔		
Domestic risk-free rate	✔	✔	✔	✔
Underlying asset value	✔	✔	✔	✔
Strike value	✔	✔	✔	✔
Volatility of asset value	✔	✔	✔	✔
Frequency of exercise	✔	✔	✔	✔
Life of contract	✔	✔	✔	✔
Frequency of sampling	✔	✔	✔	✔
Weights associated with sampled values	✔	✔	✔	✔
Running average[22]	✔	✔	✔	✔

22 Only applicable if the averaging process is already underway at the time the option is purchased.

value of an interest-rate option contract. When compared to the factors influencing the value of a vanilla option in Exhibit 30, three additional factors influence the value of an average rate option. These three factors, which are given in the last three rows of the above exhibit, are as follows

1. **Frequency of sampling.** Frequency at which the value of asset is monitored for the averaging.
2. **Weights associated with sampled values.** Weights attached with each sampled asset value.
3. **Running average.** Sum (product) of the weighted realized values of the asset in the context of an arithmetic (geometric) average option contract.

To understand how the above-mentioned factors influence the value of an option contract, one has to first derive a no-arbitrage relationship between the option contract and the asset underlying the option contract. The effects of these factors are summarized in Exhibit 47.

The effects of ef and T on all the options and those of r_f, r_d, S_0, σ and X on Category II and IV options are obvious and no different from Exhibit 31. Furthermore, the effects of r_f, r_d, S_0, σ, sf, w, and RA on Category I and III options are not straightforward and hence need to be intuited.[23]

_____

[23] The effects of sf, w, and RA on Category II and IV option premiums can be easily intuited using the arguments presented for options from the other categories.

EXHIBIT 47 Effect of Increase in Value of Underlying Factors on Average Option Premium

	Type of Option Contracts							
	Category I		Category II		Category III		Category IV	
Factors	**Call**	**Put**	**Call**	**Put**	**Call**	**Put**	**Call**	**Put**
r_f	⇓	⇑	⇓	⇑	⇓	⇑	⇓	⇑
r_d	⇑	⇓	⇑	⇓	⇑	⇓	⇑	⇓
S_0	⇑	⇓	⇑	⇓	⇑	⇓	⇑	⇓
X			⇓	⇑			⇓	⇑
σ	⇕	⇕	⇑	⇑	⇕	⇕	⇑	⇑
ef	⇑	⇑	⇑	⇑	⇑	⇑	⇑	⇑
T	⇕	⇕	⇕	⇕	⇕	⇕	⇕	⇕
sf [24]	⇕	⇕	⇕	⇕	⇕	⇕	⇕	⇕
w [25]	⇕	⇕	⇕	⇕	⇕	⇕	⇕	⇕
RA	⇓	⇑	⇑	⇓	⇓	⇑	⇑	⇓

24 Increase in sf implies increase in the number of points used for averaging.

25 If the averaging is done over n points, w has n components. Since $\sum_{i=1}^{n} w_i = 1$, all the n components of w cannot be simultaneously increased. More precisely, increasing one component of w would lead to a reduction in at least one of the other of $n - 1$ components.

To intuit the effect of S_0 on the Category I and III options, I will consider as an example the Category III call option. With a running weighted average of RA, this can be viewed as a spread option with parameters a = 1, b = RA, and X = 0. Furthermore, as discussed on page 74, by thinking of the spread $S_T - (RA \cdot \prod_{j=i+1}^{n} S_{t_j}^{w_j})$ as an asset, the value of the option premium will increase if value of the spread increases. Since the expected future value of this spread can be shown to be directly proportional to the underlying asset value, the value of the spread would increase as S_0 increases. Similar intuition can be applied to arrive at the results for the remaining of the options in Categories I and III.

As with S_0, to understand the intuition underlying the effect of σ on Category I and III options, I will discuss again the Category III call option. With a running product value of RA, this can again be viewed as a spread option with parameters a = 1, b = RA and X = 0. By thinking of the spread $S_T - (RA \cdot \prod_{j=i+1}^{n} S_{t_j}^{w_j})$ as an asset, it would be reasonable to expect the option premium to increase if the volatility of the spread increases. Because the value of an asset is observed at various points in time, given the current asset value, the correlation between the continuously compounded returns of the asset at two different points in time will always be positively correlated.[26] This would imply that the correlation between the continuously compounded return of S_T and the continuously compounded return of

$RA \cdot \prod_{j=i+1}^{n} S_{t_j}{}^{w_j}$ will never be negative. Furthermore, when σ increases, it would

be reasonable to expect the volatility of S_T to increase at a faster rate than the

volatility of $RA \cdot \prod_{j=i+1}^{n} S_{t_j}{}^{w_j}$ because the weighting would tend to cause the volatil-

ity of $RA \cdot \prod_{j=i+1}^{n} S_{t_j}{}^{w_j}$ to dampen. As discussed on page 76, because of the posi-

tive correlation, the volatility of the spread will not necessarily increase; resulting sometimes in an increase and other times in a decrease of the option premium. Similar intuition can be applied to arrive at the results for the remaining options in Categories I and III.

It was stated in footnote 24 that for a fixed option life, increasing sf implies increasing the number of points used to calculate the average value of the asset. To intuit the results shown in Exhibit 47, I will consider the Category II call option and assume that the asset values used for the averaging process are all

equally weighted (i.e., $w_1 = w_2 = \ldots = w_n = \dfrac{1}{n}$). Since the notion of averaging an

asset value has the effect of dampening the volatility of the asset value, it may at first glance seem reasonable to expect a continuously averaged option to be cheaper than a structurally similar but less frequently averaged option. More precisely, one would tend to think that as sf increases, the option premium would decrease. Exhibit 48 shows this effect of varying the sampling (averaging) frequency of a simple arithmetic averaging call option on the premium of such an option.

Despite the figure in Exhibit 48, it is not necessarily true that the greater the sampling frequency, the cheaper the options. To illustrate this, assume that the averaging period underlying the call option starts today and ends in exactly 365 days. If only two asset values are used in calculating this average and these are monitored at the inception and the maturity of the contract, each of these values would contribute 50 percent to the calcuation of the average. While the asset value today has no volatility, the asset value monitored on option maturity has a volatility associated with it. Futhermore, the distribution of the average of these two values on the option maturity date will be centered around the average of today's asset value and the expected value of the asset in 365 days.

Suppose now that the averaging was done over three asset values, where the third asset value is monitored one day from now. In this instance, in addition to the asset value on the option maturity, the asset value one day from today will have a volatility component attached to it. Since each of the asset values con-

---

[26] This is given in Relationship 6A of the Appendix.

EXHIBIT 48 Effect of Averaging Frequency on Call Premium

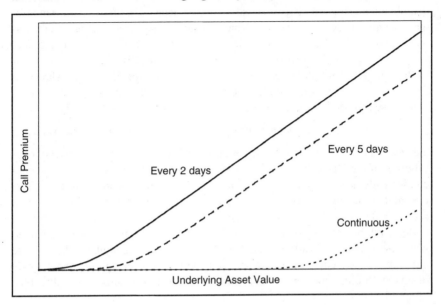

tributes about 33 percent towards the calculation of the average, the distribution of the average of these three values on the option maturity date will be centered around the average of today's asset value, the expected value of the asset one day from now, and the expected value of the asset 365 days from now. Given that the weights are now more concentrated around the inception of the contract, the center of the distribution obtained in this case will be lower than that obtained when only two points were averaged. Furthermore, despite the fact that there is an additional volatility contribution of the asset value one day from now, it is not enough to increase the total volatility of the distribution. Thus, with a lower center of the future average value distribution and a lower volatility of this distribution, the call premium obtained using three averaged asset values would be lower than that obtained using only two asset values.

The third asset value is instead monitored 364 days from today. In addition to the asset value on the option maturity date, the third asset value will also have a volatility component attached to it. Since each of the asset values contribute about 33 percent towards the calculation of the average, the distribution of the average of these three values on the option maturity date will be centered around the average of today's asset value, the expected value of the asset in 364 days, and the expected value of the asset in 365 days. Given that the weights are now more concentrated around the maturity of the contract, the center of the distribution obtained in this case will be higher than that obtained when only two points were averaged. Furthermore, the additional volatility contribution of the asset value 364 days from now would increase the total volatility of the distribution. Thus, with a higher center of the distribution and a higher volatility of this distribution, the call premium obtained using three averaged asset values would be higher than that obtained using only two asset values. Thus, depending on when the values of the asset are sampled, increasing sf may sometimes lead to an increase in the option premium. The results for the other types of options can be similarly intuited.

The effect of the weights can be intuited using the discussion that is similar to the one given for the effect of sf. As earlier, to intuit the results shown in Exhibit 47, I will consider the Category II call option and assume that the asset values used for the averaging process are all equally weighted (i.e., $w_1 = w_2 = ...$ = $w_n = \frac{1}{n}$). As long as an average rate option is not weighted in a manner such that the weights increase as the maturity of the option draws closer, the impact of contribution of a realized spot rate towards the averaging of the sampled points decreases with the passage of time. Furthermore, if the weights are created such that the value of the last observation has a 100 percent contribution (i.e., $w_1 = w_2 = ...$ = $w_{n-1} = 0$ and $w_n = 1$), the average call option is no different from a vanilla call option, and the option premium in this instance will be higher than that obtained when the weights were all set equal to each other. Thus, depending on how all the individual weight components are changed, the effect on the option premium may be mixed. Similar intuition can be applied to arrive at the results for the other type of options.

Like all vanilla options, increasing the value of the strike of the call (put) option leads to a decrease (increase) in the option premium. Since RA represents the running weighted average for the observed values, for Category I and II options, RA plays the role of a strike value in these type of options. Increasing RA in the context of the Category I call option will increase the strike value, which in turn will lead to a decrease in the option premium. Furthermore, increasing RA in the context of the Category I put option will increase the strike value, which in turn will lead to an increase in the option premium. The effects of RA on the Category II options can similarly be intuited to arrive at the results shown in Exhibit 47.

To intuit the effect of RA on Category III and IV options, the reader should first observe that unlike the arithmetic sum, RA has a multiplicative effect on the geometric average. Consequently, the purchaser of a Category III call option can be alternatively thought of as someone who has the option to exchange S_T for

$$RA \cdot \prod_{j=i+1}^{n} S_{t_j}^{w_j}.$$ Since this is analogous to the purchase of an exchange option or a spread option with $a = 1$, $b = RA$ and $X = 0$; the reader is referred to Exhibit 37 for the effect of RA on a spread option premium. This intuition can similarly be applied to arrive at the results in Exhibit 47 for the remaining options in Category III and IV.

In Observation 6 of Example 13, I commented that the cost of an average-rate option is lower than that of a strip of individual European-style options. More precisely, when the averaging process in an average option starts either today or sometime in the future, the cost of an average option is lower than the cost of a sequence of European-style vanilla options, each of which expires on the dates the asset values get sampled.

To intuit this, consider the purchase of a Category II one-year arithmetic average option in which the asset values are sampled every day for 360 days starting tomorrow on a notional amount of US$ 360 mm. An alternative to this strategy would be to purchase 360 European-style options on a notional amount of US$ 1 mm, each of which is struck at the same level as the average rate option; where the first option would expire in one day, the second in two days, the third in three days, and so on. If one ignored the time value captured while future valuing the in-the-money payoffs of the 360 vanilla options, the total in-the-money payoff from the second strategy would be no different from that obtained using the first strategy. However, because each of these 360 options settles independently and there is no netting-out effect from the realized values of the asset, it is possible for some of the 360 options to finish in-the-money and for the average rate option to finish out-of-the-money, resulting in a greater payoff to the buyer of the second strategy. This observation, in conjunction with the fact that there is less of a dampening effect in the volatility of each of the 360 options, naturally implies that an option on a portfolio of correlated assets is cheaper than a portfolio of options, as illustrated in Observation 6 of Example 13. In particular, when $n = 2$, that is, the averaging is done over two asset values—one can use the discussion presented on page 101 to intuit the reason why the option on a basket of correlated assets is cheaper than a portfolio of options.

At first glance, it may seem to appear that the exception to the discussion in the above paragraph occurs when one sells the average option after 10 months where the running sum is greater than the strike value. In this case, although the purchaser of this two-month average option could alternatively buy 60 vanilla options on a notional amount of US$ 6 mm, depending on the in-the-moneyness of the option, the value of this average option may not necessarily be lower than the total cost of the 60 vanilla options. The reason for this stems from the fact that since the average option is already in-the-money, it would be highly unlikely that another 60 observations would have enough impact to make the average option become out-of-the-money. However, as mentioned earlier, since all 60 options would expire independently, it is the possibility of these options expiring out-of-the-money that would determine the relative cheapness of the second strategy.

This apparent relative cheapness of the 60 vanilla options over the two-month average option exists by virtue of the fact that one is not exactly comparing apples with apples. More precisely, by rewriting $\dfrac{1}{360}\displaystyle\sum_{i=1}^{360} S_{t_i}$ as $\dfrac{1}{360}\displaystyle\sum_{i=1}^{300} S_{t_i} +$ $\dfrac{1}{360}\displaystyle\sum_{i=301}^{360} S_{t_i}$, it can be seen that this simplifies to $RA + \dfrac{1}{360}\displaystyle\sum_{i=301}^{360} S_{t_i}$. Because RA is a known constant value at the end of 10 months, one can adjust the strike value of the average option X to $X - RA$. Thus, it is indeed more appropriate to compare this two-month average option with a sequence of 60 vanilla options, each of which is struck at $X - RA$ instead of X. Doing this will lead us to the conclusion arrived at two paragraphs earlier.

Regardless of the weights associated with each sampled asset value, the market risks associated with an average option decrease as the option approaches its maturity. This is because as the number of points used in the averaging process increases, the contribution from each future unrealized asset value decreases; resulting in well-behaved Greeks (delta, gamma, etc.).[27]

Other Applications

Although I discussed the use of an average option in the context of a currency transaction, treasurers can effectively use the concept of averaging options to cap their total annual borrowing costs.

In instances where an underlying asset class trades like an average, the average option is essentially a vanilla option in that asset class. For example, consider the trading of WTI or Brent contracts, whose prices trade as arithmetic averages. In this instance, transacting in a vanilla European-style option on a WTI or a Brent contract is actually equivalent to transacting in an arithmetic average European-style option, where the underlying asset is an averaged price. Thus, depending on the way an underlying asset class trades, an average rate option may not necessarily be construed as an exotic option.

THE BASKET OPTION CONTRACT

Introduction

Although the TSE 35, TSE 100, and TSE 300 represent three of the major equity market indexes in Canada, none of the industries represented in these indexes are weighted in a biased fashion in specific sectors (e.g., oil, utilities, forest). To illustrate, consider the forest sector component of the TSE 100 index, which has 18 forest sector stocks that contribute only a total of 4.82 percent to the index.

Due to economic fundamentals and cyclic trends, suppose, for example, that the investor feels the paper and forest sector stocks are in general going to increase in value over the next month. To monetize her view, she could purchase a call option on the TSE 100 index. As mentioned earlier, the setback of this strategy is the fact that the paper and forest sector constitute only a meager 4.82 percent of the TSE 100 index. A more effective way to achieve the same objective would be to purchase a one-month at-the-money call option on the basket of 18 stocks.[28] Options of this sort are known as basket or portfolio options.

---

[27] It is for these reasons that it is safer and easier to manage the risks on average options than their vanilla counterparts.

[28] As in the spread option, the investor could alternatively monetize her view by purchasing the underlying stocks and holding them to maturity. Should the investor's view turn out wrong, she would be faced with potentially large losses when liquidating the position.

A Basket Option Contract Example

Example 14 on page 96 better illustrates the sequence of events depicting the nature of the transaction.

It is important for the reader to make the following three observations about Example 14.

OBSERVATION 1 Example 14 is just one of the many variations that could be structured to suit the client's objective. Due to the liquidity constraints or the view on the performance of the stocks relative to each other, the investor could have alternatively monetized her view by requesting instead that the stocks IPL, TRP, and W have contributing weights of 50 percent, 30 percent, and 20 percent, respectively, to the basket. Since the at-the-money strike value under this scenario works out to be Cad\$ [(0.5 • 28) + (0.3 • 18) + (0.2 • 23)] = Cad\$ 24, it would make sense for the investor to have an in-the-money payoff equal to the amount of the in-the-moneyness of the option multiplied by the number of option contracts, instead of simply multiplying the amount of the in-the-moneyness of the option by the notional principal amount of the trade, as illustrated in Example 14.

OBSERVATION 2 Although Example 14 describes the use of an option on a basket of three stocks, nothing prevents the investor from transacting into an option whose underlying basket has two, four, five, or more stocks. Furthermore, if the investor in our example had a view on all 300 stocks underlying the TSE 300 index whose weights mirror the index, she could have alternatively purchased an option on the index directly.

OBSERVATION 3 Instead of purchasing a one-month call basket option, the investor could alternatively purchase three one-month at-the-money call options on the individual stocks. The notional principal on each stock option would be approximately Cad\$ 0.7246 mm $\left(= \dfrac{50}{69} \right)$. This strategy, which is analogous to the strategy put forth in Observation 6 of Example 13, would cost the investor Cad\$ 1.21 mm; an increase of 10 percent in premium.

Characteristics of Basket Option Contracts

Although Example 14 illustrates the use of an option on a basket of three stocks, the profit and loss to the buyer of an option on a basket of n stocks, where $n \geq 2$, can be more generally written, as detailed in Exhibit 49 and graphed in Exhibit 50 and 51.

EXAMPLE 14 A European-Style Basket Option Transaction

Since the pipeline sector of the TSE 300 index has good economic fundamentals, an investor feels that the three stocks in this sector, symbolized by IPL, TRP, and W, should increase in value in a month. IPL, TRP, and W are currently trading at Cad$ 28, Cad$ 18 and Cad$ 23, respectively.

To monetize her view, the investor pays a premium of Cad$ 1.1 mm to purchase 50 million dollars worth of call option on a basket of three stocks that expire in one month. In purchasing this basket option, the investor desires each stock to be weighted by an amount that is proportional to the value of the stock. More precisely, each stock price would be weighted by an amount of $\frac{1}{28 + 18 + 23} = \frac{1}{69}$, and the strike value of the at-the-money option would be $\left(\frac{1}{69} \cdot 28\right) + \left(\frac{1}{69} \cdot 18\right) + \left(\frac{1}{69} \cdot 23\right) = 1$.

Time (months)	(Stock 1, Stock 2, Stock 3); Basket Value	How the Option Impacts the Investor
0	(28,18,23);1[29]	☛ Cad$ 1.1 mm premium paid by the investor
1	**Case 1: Call Option Is Exercised at the End of 1 Month**	
	(35,16,25);1.1	☛ Payoff of Cad$ [50 • (1.1 – 1.0)] = Cad$ 5 mm. ☛ Cad$ 1.1 mm of premium and Cad$ 0.004 mm of interest on this premium foregone by investor ☛ Profit to investor: Cad$ [5 – (1.1 + 0.004)] = Cad$ 3.896 mm
	Case 2: Call Option Is Not Exercised at the End of 1 Month	
	(30,16,20);0.95	☛ Cad$ 1.1 mm of premium and Cad$ 0.004 mm of interest on this premium foregone by investor ☛ Profit to investor: –Cad$ (1.1 + 0.004) = –Cad$ 1.104 mm

29 The triplet (29,18,23) represents the information that the values of the IPL stock, TRP stock, and W stock are Cad$ 28, Cad$ 18, and Cad$ 23 respectively; the number 1 refers to the value of the basket obtained using the formul a $\left(\frac{1}{69} \cdot 28\right) + \left(\frac{1}{69} \cdot 18\right) + \left(\frac{1}{69} \cdot 23\right) = 1$.

EXHIBIT 49 Profits to the Buyer of a European-Style Basket Option

Type of Basket Option	Profit at Expiry Time T
$C_E(0,T,X,w_1,...,w_n)$	$\max\left[-P^*_{T,C}, \sum_{i=1}^{n} w_i S_{i,T} - X - P^*_{T,C}\right]$
$P_E(0,T,X,w_1,...,w_n)$	$\max\left[-P^*_{T,P}, X - \sum_{i=1}^{n} w_i S_{i,T} - P^*_{T,P}\right]$

where

0 = Current time or time today

T = Time of option maturity

$S_{i,T}$ = Asset value i at time T, where i = 1,2,...,n

w_i = Weight associated with asset value $S_{i,T}$, where

$$\sum_{i=1}^{n} w_i = 1$$

X = Strike value of option

$C_E(0,T,X,w_1,...,w_n)$ = European basket call option purchased at time 0, with parameters T, X, $w_1,...,w_n$

$P_E(0,T,X,w_1,...,w_n)$ = European basket put option purchased at time 0, with parameters T, X, $w_1,...,w_n$

$P^*_{T,C}$ = Amount foregone by purchaser of call option due to premium and the interest accrued until time T on this premium

$P^*_{T,P}$ = Amount foregone by purchaser of put option due to premium and the interest accrued until time T on this premium

EXHIBIT 50 Basket Call Option Buyer's Profit at Maturity

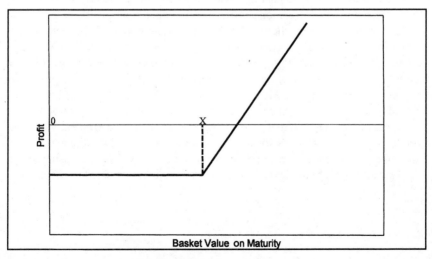

EXHIBIT 51 Basket Put Option Buyer's Profit at Maturity

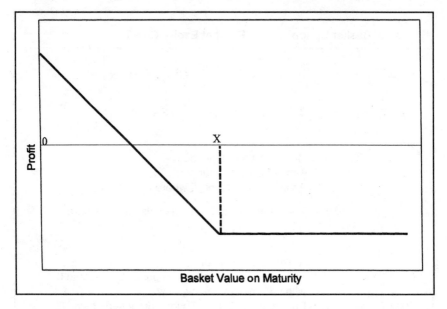

From Exhibits 41 and 49, it can be seen that the profits of a basket option closely resemble those of a Category II arithmetic average option. The only distinguishing feature between the profit profiles is that for an arithmetic average option, the value of one asset is monitored n times during the life of the option while for a basket option, the values of n assets are monitored simultaneously on the expiry date of the option. As a result, unlike the average option, there is no notion of running average present in a basket option.

Furthermore, one can think of the average option as an option on a basket of n auto-correlated assets that are monitored sequentially at different points in time, where the autocorrelation coefficient can either be implicitly calculated or closely approximated,[30] whereas, unlike an average option, the correlation between the values of the n assets comprising the basket can only be historically calculated. The ability to think of an arithmetic average option as a basket option allows us to value a basket option using the methods developed for pricing an arithmetic average option. Although this was the spirit of the methodology discussed by Huynh (1994), there is a simpler variation of the pricing formula. One could modify the algorithm of Levy (1992) to effectively and efficiently arrive at good approximate solutions for many practical situations. Like the average options, the premiums for these options can be alternatively obtained using the intuitively appealing binomial and Monte Carlo methods presented in chapter 4.

---

[30] This is given by Relationship 6A in the Appendix.

As can be easily observed, the profit and loss graphs to the buyer of an average option that are presented in Exhibits 23 and 24 are philosophically no different from those given in Exhibits 50 and 51. Thus, as discussed on page 52, the break-even analysis is crucial in determining whether this type of view-monetizing strategy is cost-effective.

To be able to value an option, one has to first identify the factors that would influence an option price. These factors are summarized in Exhibit 52 for all four asset classes.

EXHIBIT 52 Factors Influencing the Value of a Basket Option Contract

Factors	Interest-Rate Option	Currency Option	Equity Option	Commodity Option
Convenience yields				✔
Dividend rates			✔	
Foreign risk-free rates		✔		
Domestic risk-free rates	✔	✔	✔	✔
Underlying asset values	✔	✔	✔	✔
Strike value	✔	✔	✔	✔
Volatilities of asset values	✔	✔	✔	✔
Frequency of exercise	✔	✔	✔	✔
Life of contract	✔	✔	✔	✔
Weights associated with asset values	✔	✔	✔	✔
Correlations between asset values	✔	✔	✔	✔

As can be seen from Exhibit 52, while nine factors contribute to the value of a currency, equity, and commodity option contract; only eight factors contribute to the value of an interest-rate option contract. When compared to the factors influencing the value of a vanilla option in Exhibit 30, two additional factors influence the value of a basket option. These two factors, which are given in the last two rows of Exhibit 52, are as follows:

1. **Correlations between asset values.** Correlations between the continuously compounded returns of any two underlying asset values.
2. **Weights associated with asset values.** Contributing weight of each underlying asset to the basket.

To understand how the above-mentioned factors influence the value of an option contract, one has to first derive a no-arbitrage relationship between the option contract and the assets underlying the option contract. The effects of these factors are summarized in Exhibit 53.

EXHIBIT 53   Effect of Increase in Value of Underlying Factors on Basket Option Premium

Factors	Type of Option Contracts	
	Call	Put
r_f [31]	⇓	⇑
r_d	⇑	⇓
S_0 [31]	⇑	⇓
X	⇓	⇑
σ [31]	⇕	⇕
ef	⇑	⇑
T	⇕	⇕
w [32]	⇕	⇕
ρ [33]	⇑	⇑

31 If the basket is made up of n assets, this factor has n components. As a result, an increase in the factor implies the increase in at least one of the n components of the factor. For example, r_f is in fact $r_{1,f}, r_{2,f}, \ldots, r_{n,f}$.

32 If the basket is made up of n assets, this factor has n components. Since $\sum_{i=1}^{n} w_i = 1$, all the n components of w cannot be simultaneously increased. More precisely, increasing one component of w would lead to a reduction in at least one of the other of $n - 1$ components.

33 If the basket is made up of n assets, this factor is a $n \times n$ matrix. Although only $\dfrac{n(n-1)}{2}$ correlations are calculated from the n underlying assets, the correlation matrix has n^2 components. Since this is a symmetric matrix, an increase in this factor implies an increase in at least one of the $\dfrac{n(n-1)}{2}$ components of the factor. For example, when $n = 3$ this factor is a 3×3 matrix with the following $3^2 (= 9)$ components:

$$\begin{bmatrix} 1 & \rho_{1,2} & \rho_{1,3} \\ \rho_{1,2} & 1 & \rho_{2,3} \\ \rho_{1,3} & \rho_{2,3} & 1 \end{bmatrix}$$

where $\rho_{i,j}$ is the correlation between the continuously compounded returns of asset i and asset j. Since there are three correlations, increasing ρ implies increasing at least one of $\rho_{1,2}, \rho_{1,3}$, and $\rho_{2,3}$.

Since seven out of the nine factors are the same as those in Exhibit 31, it is tempting to say that one can easily use these effects to intuit the results in Exhibit 45. While the effects of r_f, r_d, S_0, X, ef, and T are obvious and no different from those in Exhibit 31, the effects of σ, w, and ρ on the option premiums are not straightforward and hence need to be intuited. To do this, I will for the sake of clarity, assume that our basket is comprised of two indexes; although the arguments presented can be extended to intuit the results for a general n.

The effects of $\rho_{1,2}$ are easily intuited by considering the call basket option and viewing $w_1S_{1,T} + w_2S_{2,T}$ as an asset; where $\rho_{1,2}$ represents the correlation between the continuously compounded returns of the two underlying assets.[34] As is well known, the variance of the sum of any two asset values is the sum of the variances of these asset values plus the covariance between these asset values.[35]

Like the spread option, when $\rho_{1,2}$ increases, the correlation between the values of the underlying assets also increases.[36] Thus, as the value of the correlation between the asset values increase, the variance of the basket increases, causing the volatility of the basket to increase and hence the option premium to increase.[37] Since the correlation between the asset values only increases as $\rho_{1,2}$ increases, an increase in $\rho_{1,2}$ results in an increase in the option premium. The same philosophy can be applied to arrive at the results for the basket put option.

To intuit the effect of the volatilities of the underlying assets, consider the volatility of the first asset. Since an increase in this volatility results in an increase in the variance of the first asset, when $\rho_{1,2}$ is positive, this leads to an increase in the variance of the basket $w_1S_{1,T} + w_2S_{2,T}$, as can be seen from footnote 35. Furthermore, as the increase in this variance results in an increase in the option premium, an increase in the volatility of the first asset increases the option premium when $\rho_{1,2}$ is positive. Alternatively, when $\rho_{1,2}$ is negative, although an increase in the volatility of the first asset results in an increase in the variance of the first asset, depending on the size of the volatility of the second asset and given the fact that one is now subtracting the covariance between the two assets to obtain the variance of the basket $w_1S_{1,T} + w_2S_{2,T}$, the variance of the basket may decrease. Thus, when ρ is negative, an increase in the volatiity of the first asset may result in a decrease in the option premium. The same sort of reasoning can be applied to intuit the effect of σ_1 and σ_2 on the basket put option premium and the effect of w_1 and w_2 on the basket option premium.

Although basket options can be valued by modifying the arithmetic average rate option pricing formulae, the risk characteristics of a basket option are totally different from those of an averaging option. The reader should recall that for an average option, in addition to the risk characteristics diminishing in magnitude as the option nears its maturity date, there is only one asset underlying the option, resulting in no correlation risk present in an averaging option. Unlike the averag-

---

[34] See footnotes 10 and 11.

[35] This is illustrated in the equation

$$Var(w_1S_{1,T} + w_2S_{2,T}) = w_1{}^2Var(S_{1,T}) + w_2{}^2Var(S_{2,T}) + 2w_1w_2Cov(S_{1,T},S_{2,T})$$
$$= w_1{}^2Var(S_{1,T}) + w_2{}^2Var(S_{2,T}) + 2w_1w_2Corr(S_{1,T},S_{2,T})\sqrt{Var(S_{1,T})Var(S_{2,T})}$$

where the terms *Var*, *Cov* and *Corr* represent the words *variance*, *covariance*, and *correlation*, respectively.

[36] See footnote 14.

[37] See footnote 13.

ing option, the risk characteristics of a basket option do not diminish as the option nears its maturity date, and the historical correlation coefficients between the underlying assets are crucial inputs to valuing the option. Furthermore, for an option written on a basket of n assets, the value of the option will depend on $\dfrac{n(n-1)}{2}$ historical correlation coefficients. Among these coefficients, it is intuitively reasonable to expect the correlation coefficient contribution from any two assets to be high as long as their individual contributing weights to the basket is large. Thus, in addition to delta hedging a basket option, the correlation risk component should be carefully managed, with special consideration given to heavily weighted assets.

It is crucial for the reader to note from the discussion given earlier that the effect of correlations on the valuation and hedging of a basket option can be totally avoided if a basket trades as an asset by itself. To illustrate, suppose that the investor had a view on the TSE 100 index, which trades like an asset by itself, and the investor wants to create a basket using these 100 stocks whose weights mirror the composition of the TSE 100 index. When valuing or hedging an option on a basket of these 100 stocks, because the index trades like an asset, this basket option can alternatively be viewed as a vanilla European-style option on the TSE 100 index.[38] By viewing the basket option in this light, the laborious task of calculating $\dfrac{100 \cdot (100-1)}{2} = 4{,}950$ correlations and 100 volatilities arising from the 100 assets is erradicated and replaced by the simple task of calculating the volatility of the TSE 100 index. Furthermore, to hedge the sale of the option, the seller has to only buy or sell the appropriate amounts of TSE 100 units.

It may be tempting for the reader to apply this argument to our illustration using three stocks, which was presented in Example 14. More precisely, it may at first glance be reasonable to think that since the values of the historical values of the basket can be calculated, one can treat the index of three stocks as if it were trading like a single asset and calculate its historical volatility. By doing this, one can treat the basket option like a vanilla option on this index and get around the problem of dealing with the correlations between the three underlying stocks. The setback of this thought process is that to hedge the position arising from the sale of the option, the seller has to buy a unit of the index. Because the index does not trade by itself, the seller is left with hedging the option position using the three underlying stocks, which implicitly implies the need to know the correlation coefficients between these three stocks. Thus, as long as the basket underlying the option trades as an asset, the valuation and the hedging of a basket option become no different than that of a vanilla option on that asset, resulting in the avoidance of the correlation philosophy.

As discussed in Observation 3 accompanying Example 14, an option on a basket of n assets is usually cheaper than purchasing n individual options on each of the underlying assets. Exhibit 54 illustrates this fact when n = 2 for various correlation levels for a call basket option whose underlying assets are equally weighted.

---

[38] This is analogous to the comments on pg. 94 regarding the WTI contracts and average options.

EXHIBIT 54 Effect of Correlation on Call Premium

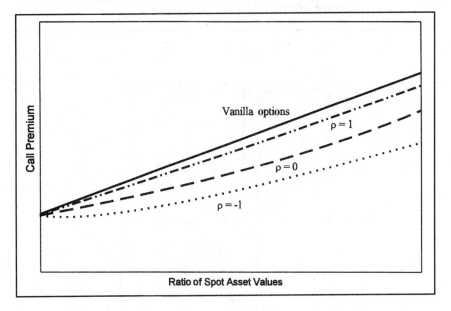

As was discussed earlier and can be seen in Exhibit 54, regardless of the correlation level and whether the option is a call or a put, the value of a basket option is always cheaper than the purchase of the two individual options, for the following two reasons:

1. Lower correlation implies greater savings.[39]
2. Option on a portfolio is cheaper than a portfolio of options,

Nevertheless, many people generally try to intuit the cheapness of the basket option using only the first reason.

As an astute reader will realize, using the first reason is equivalent to concluding that an increase in the correlation implies an increase in option premium; which was discussed on page 101. The second reason can be more easily intuited by looking at the regions in Exhibits 55 and 56 where the basket option and the vanilla options would pay off upon the maturity of the contracts.

Ignoring the option premiums that were paid at the inception of the contracts and assuming that the options expire at the same time, Exhibit 55 illustrates the payoff region on option maturity date to the purchaser of

1. A basket option that is struck at $X_1 + X_2$ and is denoted by the shaded area.
2. A vanilla call option on asset 1 that is struck at X_1 and is denoted by the vertical dotted lines that lie above the horizontal line passing through X_1.
3. A vanilla call option on asset 2 that is struck at X_2 and is denoted by the horizontal dotted lines that lie to the right of the vertical line passing through X_2.

---

[39] This effect is in contrast to that in a spread option.

**EXHIBIT 55   Call Basket Payoff Region to Buyer on Option
Maturity Date**

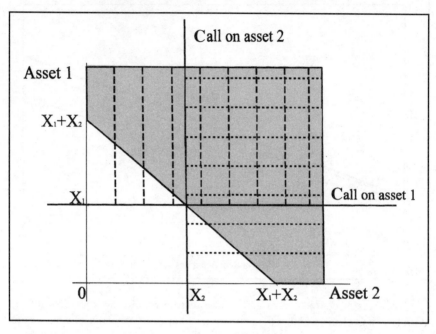

As can be seen from Exhibit 55, the payoff region due to the purchase of a call basket option is smaller than the sum of the regions due to the purchase of the two call vanilla options; which would obviously result in the basket option costing less, regardless of the level of correlation. A similar reasoning could be used on Exhibit 56 to conclude that the purchase of a put basket option would be cheaper than the purchase of the two put vanilla options.

Other Applications

Basket options can also be effectively used by foreign investors with views on specific sectors. Suppose, for example, that a Japanese investor has a view that the utility component of the TSE 100 index is going to drop in value over the next two weeks with no view on the movements of the Yen/Cad exchange rate. As in the above example, one can structure a put option on a basket of stocks that make up the utility component of the TSE 100 index, where the option would be a Yen-denominated put on a basket of Canadian utility stocks. More precisely, if the option finishes in-the-money, the investor would receive the option payoff in Yen. For his ability to monetize a view, the investor would pay a Yen-denominated premium at the inception of the option contract. Options of this sort allow the investor to take a view on a subindex of any foreign market without being subjected to the currency risk.

**EXHIBIT 56   Put Basket Payoff Region to Buyer on Option
Maturity Date**

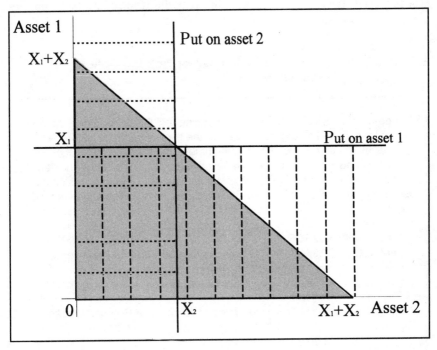

As in the average option, there are many situations where the underlying basket trades as an asset by itself. In these instances, the basket option is essentially a vanilla option on that basket. Furthermore, since there is no notion of correlation between the underlying assets, a basket option may not necessarily be construed as an exotic option.

THE CASH-OR-NOTHING OPTION CONTRACT

Introduction

Based on current market conditions, an asset manager feels that the forward three-month US$ LIBOR is at its all-time low. She thinks that the index will go up in a week after the announcement of the government budget but does not have a feel for the magnitude of the increase. Clearly, a vanilla call option is not going to be helpful in strictly reflecting the direction of a market movement. Cash-or-nothing options are instruments that allow the buyer to target the directional movement of the market. More precisely, if an investor has a view that the market will not be trading below a certain level in a week and wants to receive a pre-specified dollar amount if she is right, she could buy a cash-or-nothing option that will help monetize her view.

A Cash-or-Nothing Option Contract Example

The sequence of events in Example 15 illustrates the nature of the transaction underlying a cash-or-nothing option.

EXAMPLE 15 A European-Style Cash-or-Nothing Option Transaction

Three-month US$ LIBOR is currently trading at 5.6 percent. Despite the steepness of the forward yield curve on the short end, the investor feels that given the current economic environment, the three-month LIBOR will never exceed 5.5 percent over the next two weeks. To monetize her view, she pays a premium of US$ 4.76 mm to buy a cash-or-nothing option that would pay her US$ 100 mm if LIBOR trades below 5.5 percent at the end of two weeks.

Time (weeks)	US$ LIBOR (%)	How the Option Impacts the Investor
0	5.60	☞ US$ 4.76 mm premium paid by investor
2		*Case 1: Put Option Is Exercised at the End of 2 Weeks*
	3.80	☞ Payoff of 100 mm ☞ US$ 4.76 mm of premium and US$ 0.01 mm of interest on this premium foregone by investor ☞ Profit to investor: US$[100 − (4.76 + 0.01)] mm = US$ 95.23 mm
		Case 2: Put Option Is Not Exercised at the End of 2 Weeks
	5.80	☞ US$ 4.76 mm of premium and US$ 0.01 mm of interest on this premium foregone by investor ☞ Profit to investor: −US$ (4.76 + 0.01) mm = −US$ 4.77 mm

It is important for the reader to make the following observation about Example 15.

OBSERVATION Regardless of how much in-the-money the option finishes, the investor only gets a constant payoff of US$ 100 mm.

Characteristics of Cash-or-Nothing Option Contracts

The profit and loss to the buyer of a European-style cash-or-nothing option is summarized in Exhibit 57 and graphed in Exhibits 58 and 59.

EXHIBIT 57 Profits to the Buyer of a European-Style Cash-or-Nothing Option

Type of Cash-or-Nothing Option	Profit at Expiry Time T
$C_E(0,T,X,B)$	$-P^*_{T,C}$ if $S_T < X$ $B - P^*_{T,C}$ if $S_T \geq X$
$P_E(0,T,X,B)$	$-P^*_{T,P}$ if $S_T > X$ $B - P^*_{T,P}$ if $S_T \leq X$

where

0 = Current time or time today
T = Time of option maturity
S_T = Asset value on option maturity
X = Strike value of option
B = In-the-money payoff in dollar amount
$C_E(0,T,X,B)$ = European cash-or-nothing call option purchased at time 0, with parameters T, X, B
$P_E(0,T,X,B)$ = European cash-or-nothing put option purchased at time 0, with parameters T, X, B
$P^*_{T,C}$ = Amount foregone by purchaser of call option due to premium and the interest accrued until time T on this premium
$P^*_{T,P}$ = Amount foregone by purchaser of put option due to premium and the interest accrued until time T on this premium

As can be easily observed, unlike the profit profiles seen for the options discussed thus far, the profit profile associated with the purchase of a cash-or-nothing option is discontinuous. Furthermore, because of this discontinuous profile, there is no notion of a break-even level for the buyer of this option. This should come as no surprise to the reader given the fact that when the option finishes in-the-money, the buyer would receive a bet amount that is independent of the in-the-moneyness of the option. Thus, to calculate the cost-effectiveness of the cash-or-nothing option, the purchaser should determine the likelihood of the option finishing in-the-money instead of calculating the chances of breaking even.

EXHIBIT 58   Cash-or-Nothing Call Option Buyer's Profit at Maturity

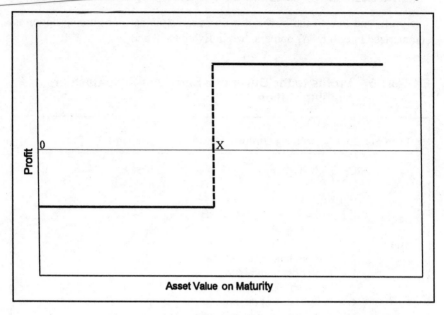

EXHIBIT 59   Cash-or-Nothing Put Option Buyer's Profit at Maturity

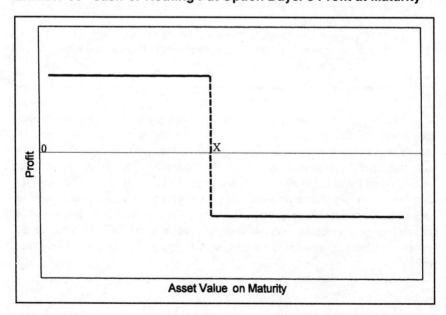

Since the cash-or-nothing option has a payoff that is inherently a bet that is independent of the in-the-moneyness of the option, it is easy to value this product. More precisely, it would be intuitively reasonable to expect the option premium to be equal to the present value of the product of the bet payoff and probability that the option would finish in-the-money. The premium for such an option can be obtained, as shown in chapter 4, using either the binomial method or the Monte Carlo method.

To be able to value an option, one has to first identify the factors that would influence an option price. These factors are summarized in Exhibit 60 for all four asset classes.

EXHIBIT 60   Factors Influencing the Value of a Cash-or-Nothing Option Contract

Factors	Interest-Rate Option	Currency Option	Equity Option	Commodity Option
Convenience yield				✔
Dividend rate			✔	
Foreign risk-free rate		✔		
Domestic risk-free rate	✔	✔	✔	✔
Underlying asset value	✔	✔	✔	✔
Strike value	✔	✔	✔	✔
Volatility of asset value	✔	✔	✔	✔
Frequency of exercise	✔	✔	✔	✔
Life of contract	✔	✔	✔	✔
Size of bet	✔	✔	✔	✔

As can be seen in Exhibit 60, while eight factors contribute to the value of a currency, equity, and commodity option contract; only seven factors contribute to the value of an interest-rate option contract. When compared to the factors influencing the value of a vanilla option in Exhibit 60, one additional factor influences the value of a cash-or-nothing option. This factor, which is given in the last row of Exhibit 60, is the "size of bet," which refers to the bet amount that the purchaser of the option stands to receive if the option finishes in-the-money.

To understand how the above-mentioned factors influence the value of an option contract, I will as before, have to first derive a no-aribitrage relationship between the option contract and the asset underlying the option contract. The effects of these factors are summarized in Exhibit 61.

Since seven out of the eight factors are the same as those in Exhibit 31, it is tempting to say that one could easily use these effects to intuit the results in Exhibit 61. While the effects of r_f, r_d, S_0, X, ef, and T are obvious and no different from those in Exhibit 31, the effect of B on the option premium needs to be intuited.

EXHIBIT 61 Effect of Increase in Value of Underlying Factors on Cash-or-Nothing Option Premium

	Type of Option Contracts	
Factors	**Call**	**Put**
r_f	⇓	⇑
r_d	⇑	⇓
S_0	⇑	⇓
X	⇓	⇑
σ	⇑	⇑
ef	⇑	⇑
T	⇕	⇕
B	⇑	⇑

The effect of B is easily intuited by considering the call cash-or-nothing option. Exhibit 62 shows the difference in the premiums of a cash-or-nothing call option for a varying B. As shown in the figure, the option premium increases when the size of the bet payoff increases and all the other factors are kept constant. To intuit this, the reader should first recall from earlier discussion that the premium of a cash-or-nothing option is calculated by present valuing the product of the bet size and the probability of the option finishing in-the-money. Since the probability of the option finishing in-the-money is independent of the bet size, in-

EXHIBIT 62 Effect of Bet Size on Call Premium

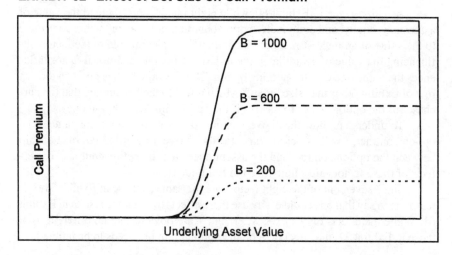

creasing the bet amount would increase the value of the product; which in turn would lead to an increase in the cash-or-nothing option premium.

Unlike the pricing, the hedging of this product is not easy. In practice, the sale of a cash-or-nothing call option is usually hedged by buying call options at a lower strike value and selling the same amount of call options at a higher strike value, which an astute reader will realize is the purchase of a bull spread. This hedging strategy is illustrated in Exhibit 63.

EXHIBIT 63   Convergence of a Bull Spread to a Cash-or-Nothing Call Option

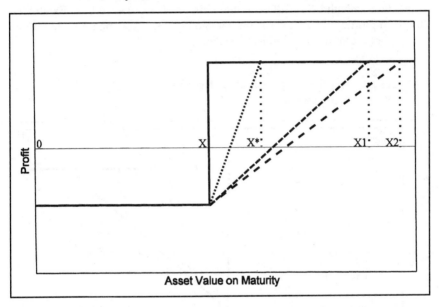

By comparing Exhibit 63 to Exhibit 58, it can be easily seen that the solid line depicts the profit profile to the purchaser of a cash-or-nothing call option that is struck at a level of X. To replicate this profile, as shown in the exhibit, the purchaser could buy a bull spread struck at levels X and X2 on some notional amount such that profit profiles are identically matched. Alternatively, as shown in the exhibit, the purchaser could buy a bull spread struck at levels X and X1 on a greater notional amount such that profit profiles are identically matched. Thus, to exactly replicate the profit profile of a cash-or-nothing call option, the seller has to buy an infinite number of vanilla call options struck at X and sell another infinite number of vanilla call options struck at X, where X* would be only infinitesimally larger than X. It is important to note that because this cannot be done in practice, the above-mentioned static hedge strategy cannot be used to perfectly replicate the profit profile of a cash-or-nothing option. As a result, the hedge amounts put in place at the inception of the contract may have to be rebalanced as required during the life of the option. The above methodology can be used to similarly hedge the sale of a cash-or-nothing put option with the purchase of a bear spread.

It is crucial for the reader to realize that although philosophically it may be easy to think about replicating a cash-or-nothing option with a vertical spread, the details involved in carrying out the transaction are fundamentally dependent on the following two factors:

1. The settlement process for the asset underlying the option.
2. The denomination of the bet payoff.

Since the relevance of the second factor is obvious, I will only discuss the first factor. To illustrate this point, I will discuss the hedging of the sale of a cash-or-nothing call option in a commodity framework when one is dealing with the price of an ounce of gold, and in an interest-rate framework when one is dealing with a three-month US$ LIBOR. While Exhibit 64 is extracted from Exhibit 63; the profit profiles of the trades in the commodity framework and the interest-rate framework are shown in Exhibits 65 and 66, respectively.

EXHIBIT 64   Replicating a Cash-or-Nothing Call Option with a Bull Spread

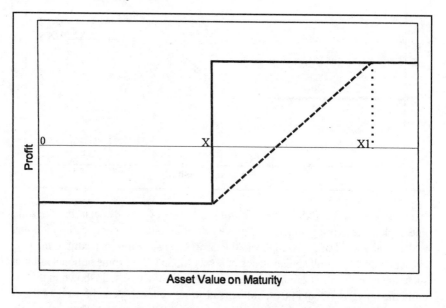

I will first consider Exhibit 65. The first column in the exhibit, "Spot Gold Price Interval," refers to the price intervals of an ounce of gold on option maturity date, which are partitioned, as seen in Exhibit 64. The first column contains as its entries the price intervals '0 – X', 'X – X1', and 'X1 – ∞'. The second column, "Profit to Purchaser of Cash-or-Nothing Option," refers to the profit profile to the cash-or-nothing option buyer as the price of gold ranges from 0 to ∞. From Exhibits 64 and 65, it can be seen that as long as the option finishes in-the-money, the buyer gets a profit of $B - P^*_{T,C1}$. The third column, "Profit to Purchaser of Bull Spread," refers to the fact that the buyer of the cash-or-nothing option wants

EXHIBIT 65   Replicating a Cash-or-Nothing Call Option with a Bull Spread in a Commodity Framework

Spot Gold Price Interval	Profit to Purchaser of Cash-or-Nothing Option	Profit to Purchaser of Bull Spread		
		Buy N_G of $C_E(0,T,X)$	Sell N_G of $C_E(0,T,X1)$	Net Profit
$0 - X$	$-P^*_{T,C1}$	$-N_G \cdot P^*_{T,C2}$	$N_G \cdot P^*_{T,C3}$	$N_G \cdot [P^*_{T,C3} - P^*_{T,C2}]$
$X - X1$	$B - P^*_{T,C1}$	$N_G \cdot [S_T - X - P^*_{T,C2}]$	$N_G \cdot P^*_{T,C3}$	$N_G \cdot [S_T - X + P^*_{T,C3} - P^*_{T,C2}]$
$X1 - \infty$	$B - P^*_{T,C1}$	$N_G \cdot [S_T - X - P^*_{T,C2}]$	$-N_G \cdot [S_T - X1 - P^*_{T,C3}]$	$N_G \cdot [X1 - X + P^*_{T,C3} - P^*_{T,C2}]$

EXHIBIT 66　Replicating a Cash-or-Nothing Call Option with a Bull Spread in an Interest-Rate Framework

Spot† Three-Month LIBOR Interval	Profit to Purchaser of Cash-or-Nothing Option	Profit to Purchaser of Bull Spread		
		Buy N_I of $C_E(0,T,X)$	Sell N_I of $C_E(0,T,X1)$	Net Profit
$0 - X$	$-P^*_{T,C1}$	$-N_I \cdot P^*_{T,C2}$	$N_I \cdot P^*_{T,C3}$	$N_I \cdot [P^*_{T,C3} - P^*_{T,C2}]$
$X - X1$	$B - P^*_{T,C1}$	$N_I \cdot [(S_T - X)L - P^*_{T,C2}]$	$N_I \cdot P^*_{T,C3}$	$N_I \cdot [(S_T - X)L + P^*_{T,C3} - P^*_{T,C2}]$
$X1 - \infty$	$B - P^*_{T,C1}$	$N_I \cdot [(S_T - X)L - P^*_{T,C2}]$	$-N_I \cdot [(S_T - X1)L - P^*_{T,C3}]$	$N_I \cdot [(X1 - X)L + P^*_{T,C3} - P^*_{T,C2}]$

to replicate the cash-or-nothing profit profile by purchasing and selling N_G vanilla gold call options that expire at the same time, where these options are struck at X and X1, respectively. While the first column of this category refers to the profit profile when N_G vanilla call options struck at X are purchased and the second column of this category refers to the profit profile when N_G vanilla call options struck at X1 are sold, the third column of the same category refers to net position of the bull spread buyer.

The interpretation of Exhibit 66 is generally no different from that of Exhibit 65 since the underlying asset is now a three-month US$ LIBOR as compared to the price of gold and the number of interest-rate caplet contracts purchased and sold is N_I. This exception stems from the fact that the in-the-money payoff for a single vanilla option is now $(S_T - X)L$ instead of $S_T - X$. The reason for this exception is that when purchasing a caplet on a three-month LIBOR, S_T and X would represent the three-month LIBOR and the strike rate, respectively. As in Example 10, the in-the-money payoff would be settled three months later, and the amount settled on per dollar of notional amount would be calculated by multiplying the in-the-money payoff with the time required to settle on the contract. Thus, the in-the-money rate payoff of $S_T - X$ is multiplied by the following factor L:

$$L = 0.25 \cdot \frac{\$1 \text{ present valued from } (T + 0.25) \text{ years}}{\$1 \text{ present valued from T years}}$$

where the number 0.25 represents the three months converted to years, and the ratio of discount factors represents the present valuing from the date of cash flow settlement to the time of option maturity. Although this ratio will simply be the three-month discount factor on the option maturity date, the reader should realize that the ratio can only be estimated at the inception of the contract using the then-prevailing yield curve. This ratio will change as the shape of the yield curve changes.

Thus, from Exhibit 65, to determine N_G, the number of gold call options that should be bought and sold, one has to equate the cash-or-nothing profit profile to the net profit profile for each of the price intervals. Doing this allows one to arrive at the following expression for N_G:

$$N_G = \frac{B}{X1 - X}$$

One can similarly equate the profit profiles in Exhibit 66, to determine N_I. Doing this gives the following expression for N_I:

$$N_I = \frac{B}{(X1 - X)L}$$

From these expressions for N_G and N_I, it can be seen that the amount of option contracts bought or sold in order to replicate the sale of a cash-or-nothing call option is dependent on the way the underlying asset gets settled since the meanings of X and X1 may vary across asset classes. Futhermore, it is important for the reader to realize that since N_I is dependent on L and L changes as the shape of the yield curve changes, the value of N_I would change as the shape of the yield curve changes; unlike N_G.

Other Applications

Note Structures

Cash-or-nothing options can also be effectively used in note structures. For example, an investor who thinks that the three-month US$ LIBOR at the end of six months will be trading above 5.25 percent can purchase a six-month note that pays off a coupon of 6.5 percent if he is right and no coupon if he is wrong. An astute reader will realize that instead of purchasing this six-month note, the investor could achieve his objective by alternatively purchasing a six-month cash-or-nothing call option that is struck at 5.25 percent. Despite this fact, the legal, tax, and accounting hurdles put before the fund managers in some countries prevent the direct purchase of these options for view monetization.

Another popular note structure that protects the investor against a last-minute spike in LIBOR is called a range note or fairway note. In this type of note, the purchaser receives a coupon size that is less than 6.5 percent for taking on less risk. Suppose, for example, that there are 120 business days during this six-month period. The investor would receive a coupon of at most 5 percent only if the three-month LIBOR exceeds a strike level of 5.25 percent on every business day for 120 such days. However, should the strike level be breached on only 90 of these business days, the investor would receive a coupon size of $\frac{90}{120} \cdot 5\% = 3.75\%$ at the end of six months. As an astute reader will realize, the investor in this structure has in fact purchased a sequence of 120 cash-or-nothing call options, all of which are struck at 5.25 and have a bet size of $\frac{1}{120} \cdot 5\%$, which would get settled on the day the note matures; where the first option would expire in 1 business day, the second in 2 business days and so on, until the last option which would expire in 120 business days. The reader is referred to Ravindran (1993c), Peng and Dattatreya (1995), and Das (1996) for further examples of such structures.

Although the two examples discussed above looked at view-monetizing strategies on only the absolute movements of interest rates, nothing stops one from extending the same philosophy to encompass view-monetizing strategies on the relative movements of interest rates. To illustrate, suppose that the difference between the current 10-year forward U.S. Treasury yield and the current 2-year forward U.S. Treasury yield is about 100 basis points. The investor feels that based on the current market conditions, this difference in yields will widen further in a month. Not having a good feel for how much the widening is going to be, he is only interested in betting that the difference between the 10-year and 2-year U.S. Treasury yields in a month will surpass the 100 basis-point mark. To monetize his views, he could buy a cash-or-nothing spread option, which will pay him US$ 100 mm if his view is right.

The notion of betting on relative movements of interest rates can be easily extended to entertain the possibility of betting on relative interest-rate movements across different yield-curve environments.

Contingent Premium Options

Cash-or-nothing options also lend themselves naturally to liability management in the form of contingent premium or pay-later options. In this variation, instead of paying a premium at the inception of the contract, the purchaser of the product pays the premium only if the option finishes in-the-money. Because the premium is only conditionally paid, the amount of premium paid for this type of option would be larger than that paid for a structurally similar vanilla option. Example 16 better illustrates the use of a contingent premium option.

EXAMPLE 16   A European-Style Contingent Premium Option Transaction

Three-month crude oil futures are currently trading at US$ 20.50 per barrel. An energy producer who expects to sell his 100,000 barrels of production in three months feels the price over the next three months should increase due to some uncertainties in the energy markets.

Afraid of being wrong with his market prediction, he decides to purchase a three-month contingent premium put option on crude oil. In the event the option finishes in-the-money, he would end up paying a premium of US$ 0.29 mm on option maturity.

Time (months)	Oil Price (US$)	How the Hedge Impacts the Producer
0		
3		*Case 1: Option Is Not Exercised at the End of 3 Months*
	21.00	
		Case 2: Option Is Exercised at the End of 3 Months
	17.00	☛ Payoff of US$ [100,000 • (20.50 – 17.00)] = US$ 0.35 mm ☛ Premium of US$ 0.29 mm paid by producer ☛ Profit to hedger: US$ (0.35 – 0.29) = US$ 0.06 mm

It is important for the reader to make the following three observations about Example 16.

OBSERVATION 1 The purchaser must pay a conditional premium of US$ 0.29 mm at the end of three months even if the option goes in-the-money by US$ 0.01. Thus, it is not beneficial to the purchaser of the option when the option finishes only slightly in-the-money, as illustrated in Exhibit 67.

EXHIBIT 67 Contingent Premium Put Option Buyer's Profit at Maturity

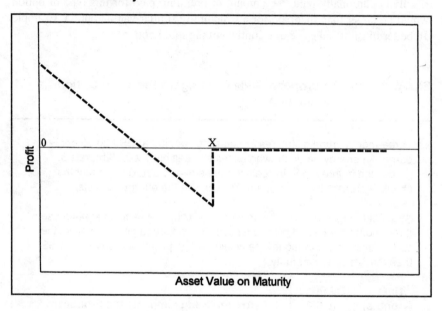

OBSERVATION 2 The conditional premium paid for this type of option is greater than that paid for a structually similar vanilla option. Although Example 16 illustrates the use of a conditional premium option when no up-front premium is paid, to reduce the amount of conditional premium that needs to be paid when the option finishes in-the-money the hedger could pay some premium up-front. Hence, whenever the amount of premium paid up-front is equal to that required to purchase a structurally similar vanilla option, it would be intuitively reasonable to expect no conditional premium to be required if the option finished in-the-money. This would imply that under this circumstance, a contingent premium op-

tion is indeed a vanilla option; which in the context of our example turns out to be US$ 0.15 mm.

OBSERVATION 3 The purchase of a conditional premium call (put) option can be replicated by purchasing a structurally similar vanilla call (put) option and selling a cash-or-nothing call (put) option. The bet size associated with the cash-or-nothing option would be exactly the same as the conditional premium that must be paid if the contingent premium option finished in-the-money. In the context of Example 16, the purchase of the contingent premium put option is equivalent to the purchase of a vanilla put option and the sale of the cash-or-nothing put option whose bet size is US$ 0.29 mm.

THE CHOICE OPTION CONTRACT
Introduction

It is common for someone with a view about the impact of a major event (election results, referendum, and so on,) on a financial market to buy an option (for example, a vanilla call option) that will help monetize the view. Come the event date, it is also common for that person to realize that the view was totally wrong and wish that a vanilla put option had been purchased instead. For such a person, an option that gives the opportunity to choose between a vanilla call option and a vanilla put option on the event date would serve as a useful and valuable instrument. The chooser option, also known as the pay-now-choose-later option, allows the buyer to choose between a vanilla call option and a vanilla put option at a prespecified time in the future. More precisely, the investor pays an up-front premium to make a choice between a call and a put option, both of which are struck at the same level and expire on the same day.

A Choice Option Contract Example

The sequence of events in Example 17 on page 120 illustrates the nature of the transaction underlying a chooser option.

It is important for the reader to make the following six observations about Example 17.

OBSERVATION 1 The investor was assumed to hold on to the option for another two months upon exercising into the underlying vanilla option at the end of the three months. In practice, upon making a choice, he could have opted to sell the underlying vanilla option in the market instead of holding it until the option expiry date.

EXAMPLE 17   A European-Style Choice Option Transaction

The Canadian dollar is currently trading at 1.3200 Cad/US, and the federal election is in three months. An investor who has no view about the impact of election results wants the ability to buy an instrument that will enable him to make a choice between a vanilla call option and a vanilla put option at the end of three months.

The investor pays a premium of Cad$ 1.86 mm to buy a European-style chooser option (i.e., an option to choose three months from now between a European-style call option and a European-style put option on U.S. dollars with both the options being struck at 1.3200 Cad/US and expiring two months after the choice date) on a notional amount of US$ 50 mm.

Time (months)	Exchange Rate (Cad/US)	How the Hedge Impacts the Investor
0	1.3200	☛ Cad$ 1.86 mm premium is paid by the investor
Case 1: Chooser Option Is Exercised into a Call Option at the End of 3 Months		
3	1.3300	☛ Vanilla call option on the U.S. dollar is chosen by investor.
5	*Case 1A: Call Option Is Exercised at the End of 5 Months*	
	1.3600	☛ Payoff of Cad$ [50 • (1.3600 − 1.3200)] = Cad$ 2 mm paid to investor ☛ Cad$ 1.86 mm of premium and Cad$ 0.04 mm of interest on this premium foregone by investor ☛ Profit to investor: Cad$ [2 − (1.86 + 0.04)] = Cad$ 0.1 mm
	Case 1B: Call Option Is Not Exercised at the End of 5 Months	
	1.3150	☛ Cad$ 1.86 mm of premium and Cad$ 0.04 mm of interest on this premium foregone by investor ☛ Profit to investor: −Cad$ (1.86 + 0.04) = −Cad$ 1.9 mm
Case 2: Chooser Option Is Exercised into a Put Option at the End of 3 Months		
3	1.3100	☛ Vanilla put option on the U.S. dollar is chosen by investor.

EXAMPLE 17   A European-Style Choice Option Transaction

5	**Case 2A: Put Option Is Exercised at the End of 5 Months**	
	1.3150	☞ Payoff of Cad$ [50 • (1.3200 – 1.3150)] = Cad$ 0.1 mm paid to investor ☞ Cad$ 1.86 mm of premium and Cad$ 0.04 mm of interest on this premium foregone by investor ☞ Profit to investor: Cad$ [0.1 – (1.86 + 0.04)] = Cad$ 1.8 mm
	Case 2B: Put Option Is Not Exercised at the End of 5 Months	
	1.3250	☞ Cad$ 1.86 mm of premium and Cad$ 0.04 mm of interest on this premium foregone by investor ☞ Profit to investor: –Cad$ (1.86 + 0.04) = –Cad$ 1.9 mm

OBSERVATION 2   The investor purchased a simple chooser option, whereby he made a choice between a vanilla call option and a vanilla put option struck at the same level and expiring at the same time. Depending on the view, the investor could have alternatively bought a complex chooser option that would have allowed him a choice between a vanilla call option with strike X_1 and time to maturity T_1, and a vanilla put option with strike X_2 and time to maturity T_2, where X_1 need not necessarily be equal to X_2 and T_1 need not necessarily be equal to T_2.

OBSERVATION 3   If the choice date in the above example of a simple chooser option was set to five months, which in our example is the maturity date of the option, the investor would have effectively bought himself a five-month straddle that is struck at 1.3200 Cad/US. Because of the ability to choose at the end of five months, with this strategy the investor will always get a positive payoff. Thus, the closer the choice date is to the option maturity date, the more expensive the chooser option becomes, which is exactly what Exhibit 68 illustrates.

To interpret Exhibit 68, first note that t represents the choice time. Thus, t = 0 implies that the choice is made today, while t = T implies that the choice is made on the maturity date of the vanilla options. To intuit the results of Exhibit 68, observe that in delaying the time of choice there is more certainty about the chosen option finishing in-the-money, which in turn implies that the value of the choice option should increase.

EXHIBIT 68   Effect of Choice Times on a Simple Chooser Option

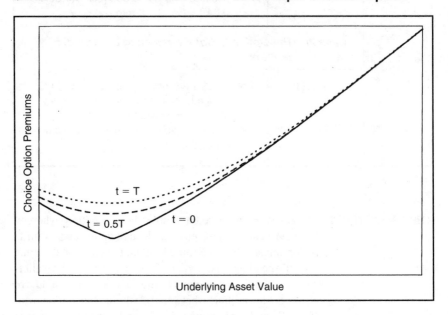

OBSERVATION 4   Although Example 17 illustrates the choice between a vanilla European-style call option and a vanilla European-style put option, the investor could have just as well been given the ability to choose between a vanilla American-style call option and a vanilla American-style put option. Furthermore, the added twist of offering the investor the ability to make a choice at any moment from the inception of the contract until the final choice time *t* has no value. This stems from the fact that market information increases as time decays, and, as illustrated in Exhibit 68, it is always beneficial for the investor to delay his decision of choice.

OBSERVATION 5   Despite the fact that I have only discussed the investor's ability to choose between options whose values are obtained using only one asset, one could have just as well offered the investor the ability to choose between options whose values are obtained using more than one asset spanning different asset classes. Consider, for example, the currency asset class. The investor could have instead bought an option that would have allowed him to make a choice in this asset class between five currency call options expiring at the same time, where each option would be struck at a different level. In particular, when the choice date is set to the option expiry date, this type of option is also called an alternative currency option.

OBSERVATION 6   Another variation that could be added to the above example is that the investor could have alternatively purchased or sold an option that would have allowed for the choice of an option that was lower in value. Thus, on the choice date, the purchaser of the option would choose among the instruments the lowest value of the option as opposed to the highest value of the option. The reader is referred to page 190 for an application of this type of option. Furthermore, when there are more than two options to choose from, it is possible for the purchaser to be allowed a choice between the maximum of a set of options and a minimum of another set of options or any other combination.

Characteristics of Choice Option Contracts

The profit profile of the buyer of a European-style choice option is summarized in Exhibit 69. As the reader will realize, as long as the choice is made before the underlying option expires, the graph of the profit profile to the buyer once a choice is made is no different from those presented in Exhibits 23 and 24.

The formulae required to value both a simple and a complex chooser option, which were discussed in the previous section, have been given by Rubenstein (1991a). Like all other options discussed thus far, the choice options can be alternatively valued using the binomial and Monte Carlo methods described in Chapter 4.

To be able to value an option, one has to first identify the factors that would influence an option price. These factors are summarized in Exhibit 70 for all four asset classes.

As can be seen from Exhibit 70, while 10 factors contribute to the value of a currency, equity, and commodity option contract, only 9 factors contribute to the value of an interest-rate option contract. When compared to the factors influencing the value of a vanilla option in Exhibit 30, there are three additional factors that influence the value of a choice option. These three factors, which are given in the last three rows of Exhibit 70, are as follows:

1. **Correlations between asset values.**   Correlations between the continuously compounded returns of any two assets if there is more than one asset underlying the option.

EXHIBIT 69   Profits to the Buyer of a European-Style Choice Option

Type of Choice Option	Profit at Choice Time t
$Ch_E(0,t,O_1,O_2,...,O_n)$	$max[-P^*_{t,Ch},max(O_1,O_2,...,O_i) - P^*_{t,Ch},$ $min(O_{i+1},O_{i+2},...,O_n)-P^*_{t,Ch}]$

where

0 = Current time or time today

t = Time of choice between options, where $t <$ $max(T_1,T_2,...,T_n)$

O_i = Value of European-style option i that is struck at X_i and maturing at time T_i, where $i = 1,2,...,n$

$Ch_E(0,t,O_1,O_2,...,O_n)$ = European choice option purchased at time 0 with parameters t, O_1, O_2, ..., O_n

$P^*_{t,Ch}$ = Amount foregone by purchaser of choice option due to premium and the interest accrued until time t on this premium

EXHIBIT 70   Factors Influencing the Value of a Choice Option Contract

Factors	Interest-Rate Option	Currency Option	Equity Option	Commodity Option
Convenience yields				✔
Dividend rates			✔	
Foreign risk-free rates		✔		
Domestic risk-free rates	✔	✔	✔	✔
Underlying asset values	✔	✔	✔	✔
Strike values	✔	✔	✔	✔
Volatilities of asset values	✔	✔	✔	✔
Frequency of exercise	✔	✔	✔	✔
Life of contracts	✔	✔	✔	✔
Correlations between asset values[40]	✔	✔	✔	✔
Choice time	✔	✔	✔	✔
Type of extrema	✔	✔	✔	✔

40 This factor is only applicable when there are at least two assets underlying the option.

2. **Choice time.** Time at which the choice is made between all the underlying options.
3. **Type of Extrema.** Nature of extrema embedded within the option that would allow the purchaser to choose either the highest, the lowest, or a combination thereof at the time of the choice.

To understand how the above-mentioned factors influence the value of an option contract, one will first derive a no-aribitrage relationship between the option contract and the assets underlying the option contract. The effects of these factors are be summarized in Exhibit 71.

It is easy to observe that 7 of the 10 factors are the same as those in Exhibit 31. Despite this, the reality is that with the exception of the factors ef, t, and ET, the factors r_f, r_d, S_0, X, σ, T, and ρ have mixed effects on the option premium depending on what exactly ET is, the type of options (call or put) underlying the choice, and the correlation between the underlying assets.

EXHIBIT 71   Effect of Increase in Value of Underlying Factors on Choice Option Premium

Factors	Choice Option Contract
r_f [41]	⇕
r_d	⇕
S_0 [41]	⇕
X [41]	⇕
σ [41]	⇕
ef	⇑
T [41]	⇕
ρ [42]	⇕
t	⇑
ET [43]	⇑

41 If there are n options underlying the choice, this factor has n components. An increase in the factor implies an increase in at least one of the n components of the factor. For example, r_f is in fact $r_{1,f}, r_{2,f}, \ldots, r_{n,f}$.

42 If the choice is made between n options, this factor is a n × n matrix with n^2 components, where $\rho_{i,j}$ (for i,j = 1, 2,...,n) represents the correlation between the continuously compounded returns of assets underlying the options. See also footnote 33.

43 Increasing this factor implies the ability to choose the most expensive option from a greater number of underlying options. Suppose, for example, that the purchaser is allowed to make a choice at time t between a maximum of five options (i.e., A, B, C, D, and E) and a minimum of three options (i.e., F, G, and H). Then increasing this factor would imply the ability to choose between the maximum of six or more options (e.g., A, B, C, D, E, and F; A, B, C, D, E, and G; A, B, C, D, E, F, and G, etc.) and the minimum of the remaining (i.e., two or fewer) options.

While the effect of ef is obvious, the effects of t can be easily intuited by realizing that the greater t gets, the more certain the purchaser can be that the choice made will end up providing the best profit potential. This effect, which was exemplified in Observation 3, implies that an increase in t results in an increase in the option premium. To intuit the effect of ET, the reader should observe that increasing ET implies increasing the subpool of options from which the purchaser of the option can select the highest of the option values.[44] Since increasing the pool size increases the chances of the purchaser realizing a higher profit potential, the amount of premium paid to participate in a larger subpool size should increase. Thus, an increase in ET results in an increase in the option premium.

A choice option is usually bought by someone who does not want to be affected by the uncertainty towards the run-up to a major event (elections, referendum, etc.). Buyers who want to avoid paying for the volatility caused by the event and are uncertain about the direction of the market should buy a choice option, with the choice date being set about one day after the event. Whatever the available choices to the purchaser of a choice option, it is intuitively reasonable to expect the value of a choice option to get larger as the time of choice is delayed, which was illustrated in Exhibit 68. The exception to this intuition occurs when the short-end volatility spikes up, in which case the ability to make a choice further out in time may cost less. This can be explained by observing the fact that as the event date draws closer and the outcome of the event becomes more uncertain (or equally split), the volatility of the market to the event date increases. Furthermore, since the outcome of the event will be realized on the event date, the volatility of the market out to a day past the event date becomes less, making an option that allows a choice further out in time cheaper.

Other Applications

Suppose, for example, that the payoffs in Exhibit 69 are defined in a manner so that the buyer is allowed to choose the highest value at time T between n call options, where all the n options are struck at X and expire at time T. Thus, at time T, the purchaser's profit will be

$$max[-P^*_{T,C}, max[(S_{1,T} - X), (S_{2,T} - X), ..., (S_{n,T} - X)] - P^*_{T,C}]$$

which can be simplified into

$$max[-P^*_{T,C}, max(S_{1,T}, S_{2,T}, ..., S_{n,T}) - X - P^*_{T,C}]$$

Similarly, if the buyer is allowed to choose the lowest value at time T between n put options, where all the n options are struck at X and expire at time T, the purchaser's profit profile will be

$$max[-P^*_{T,P}, min[(X - S_{1,T}), (X - S_{2,T}), ..., (X - S_{n,T})] - P^*_{T,P}]$$

---

[44] See footnote 43.

which can be simplified into

$$\max[-P^*_{T,P}, X + \min(-S_{1,T}, -S_{2,T}, ..., -S_{n,T}) - P^*_{T,P}] =$$
$$\max[-P^*_{T,P}, X - \max(S_{1,T}, S_{2,T}, ..., S_{n,T}) - P^*_{T,P}]^{45}$$

These profit profiles, which are special cases of those in Exhibit 69, are more succinctly rewritten in Exhibit 72.

EXHIBIT 72   Profits to the Buyer of a European-Style Maxima Option

Type of Maxima Option	Profit at Expiry Time T
$C_E(0,T,X,n)$	$\max[-P^*_{T,C}, \max(S_{1,T}, S_{2,T}, ..., S_{n,T}) - X - P^*_{T,C}]$
$P_E(0,T,X,n)$	$\max[-P^*_{T,P}, X - \max(S_{1,T}, S_{2,T}, ..., S_{n,T}) - P^*_{T,P}]$

where

0 = Current time or time today
T = Time of choice and option maturity
$S_{i,T}$ = Asset value i at time T, where i = 1, 2, ..., n
X = Strike value of option
n = Number of assets underlying option
$C_E(0,T,X,n)$ = European maxima call option purchased at time 0 with parameters T, X, and n
$P_E(0,T,X,n)$ = European maxima put option purchased at time 0 with parameters T, X, and n
$P^*_{T,C}$ = Amount foregone by purchaser of call option due to premium and the interest accrued until time T on this premium
$P^*_{T,P}$ = Amount foregone by purchaser of put option due to premium and the interest accrued until time T on this premium

Suppose now that the buyer is allowed to choose the lowest value at time T between n call options, where all the n options are struck at X and expire at time T. At time T, the purchaser of this option will receive a profit of

$$\max[-P^*_{T,C}, \min[(S_{1,T} - X), (S_{2,T} - X), ..., (S_{n,T} - X)] - P^*_{T,C}]$$

which can be simplified into

$$\max[-P^*_{T,C}, \min(S_{1,T}, S_{2,T}, ..., S_{n,T}) - X - P^*_{T,C}]$$

---

[45] This can be obtained using the result in Relationship 1 of the Appendix.

Similarly, if the buyer is allowed to choose the highest value at time T between n put options, where all the n options are struck at X and expire at time T, the purchaser's profit will be

$$max[-P^*_{T,P}, max[(X - S_{1,T}),(X - S_{2,T}),...,(X - S_{n,T})] - P^*_{T,P}]$$

which can be simplified into

$$max[-P^*_{T,P}, X + max(-S_{1,T} - S_{2,T},...,-S_{n,T}) - P^*_{T,P}] =$$
$$max[-P^*_{T,P}, X - min(S_{1,T},S_{2,T},...,S_{n,T}) - P^*_{T,P}]^{46}$$

These profit profiles, which are again special cases of those in Exhibit 69, are more succinctly rewritten in Exhibit 73.

EXHIBIT 73 Profits to the Buyer of a European-Style Minima Option

Type of Minima Option	Profit at Expiry Time T
$C_E(0,T,X,n)$	$max[-P^*_{T,C}, min(S_{1,T},S_{2,T},...,S_{n,T}) - X - P^*_{T,C}]$
$P_E(0,T,X,n)$	$max[-P^*_{T,P}, X - min(S_{1,T},S_{2,T},...,S_{n,T}) - P^*_{T,P}]$

where

0 = Current time or time today
T = Time of choice and option maturity
$S_{i,T}$ = Asset value i at time T, where i = 1, 2, ..., n
X = Strike value of option
n = Number of assets underlying option
$C_E(0,T,X,n)$ = European minima call option purchased at time 0 with parameters T, X, and n
$P_E(0,T,X,n)$ = European minima put option purchased at time 0 with parameters T, X, and n
$P^*_{T,C}$ = Amount foregone by purchaser of call option due to premium and the interest accrued until time T on this premium
$P^*_{T,P}$ = Amount foregone by purchaser of put option due to premium and the interest accrued until time T on this premium

The profit profiles illustrated in Exhibits 72 and 73 depict those of the maxima and minima options, respectively, which collectively belong to a class of options known as the extrema options. Although the extrema options are indeed special cases of the choice options, what are the applications of these options?

---
46 See footnote 45.

1. In selling a bond futures contract in either the Montreal or the Chicago Mercantile Exchange, the seller must typically deliver the cheapest of a basket of 25 bonds. An option on this futures contract is an example of a use of an extrema option.

    Stulz (1982) provided analytical expressions for valuing the extrema options when n = 2. Furthermore, when X in Exhibit 72 is set to zero, the call maxima option, for example, simplifies to a function of the exchange options. More precisely, when X = 0 and n = 2, the purchase of a call maxima option is equivalent to the purchase of an option that allows the second asset to be exchanged for the first asset at expiry time T and the purchase of the second asset. Similarly, when X = 0 and n = 2, the purchase of a call minima option is equivalent to the purchase of the second asset and the sale of an option that allows the buyer to exchange the first asset for the second asset at time T.[47]

    Finally, the reader should realize that when X = 0, the maxima and the minima put options will be worthless. This follows from the trivial observation that an asset price cannot be negative.

2. Extrema structures can also be embedded into binary quanto options in the structuring of notes. A Canadian investor, for example, could buy a one-month note that pays off a coupon that is a fraction of 5 percent, where this fraction represents the proportion of business days in the six-month period during which the maximum of three-month BA and (1.15 • three-month US$ LIBOR) exceeds a level of 4 percent, where all the transactions are carried out in Canadian funds. Such a note can be similarly structured to pay out in U.S. funds.

THE COMPOUND OPTION CONTRACT

Introduction

A manufacturer is bidding for a contract to manufacture a certain set of goods. If she is awarded the contract a month after the bid is submitted, she is required to manufacture the goods at the bidded price. However, if she decides to wait until the date of award to purchase the raw materials required for manufacturing, she is exposed to the potential increase in the cost of materials. To hedge herself, she wants to buy a call option on the price of the materials that is struck at the level of her tendered bid only if she is awarded the contract. Due to the hedging difficulties arising from nonmarket related risk, it is usually difficult for an investment house to sell an option that is contingent on the buyer being awarded a contract. Consequently, the manufacturer's best alternative would be to buy an option that would allow her to receive a call option at the award date for an extra premium. This option, also known as a compound option, option-on-option, or

---

[47] This is discussed in footnote 8.

split payment option, is a derivative that allows the buyer to pay an initial up-front premium for an option that she may need later. The buyer then pays an additional premium only if she decides that she needs this option.

A Compound Option Contract Example

The sequence of events in Example 18 on page 131 illustrates the nature of a compound option transaction.

It is important for the reader to make the following six observations about Example 18.

OBSERVATION 1 It was assumed that the hedger, upon being awarded the contract at the end of one month, exercised into a six-month vanilla call option on the pound by paying a premium of £ 0.87 mm. In reality, despite being awarded the contract, the hedger will only pay a premium of £ 0.87 mm if the then-prevailing market value of the six-month call option is greater than £ 0.87 mm. However, in the event that the call value is less than £ 0.87 mm, the hedger would instead choose to purchase this option from the market.

OBSERVATION 2 It was assumed that the hedger did not exercise the underlying option if she was not awarded the contract. In practice, even if she is not awarded the contract, it may still be optimal for her to exercise her compound option and sell the underlying call option to the market as long as the premium obtained by selling the option is greater than £ 0.87 mm.

OBSERVATION 3 The hedger was assumed to have purchased an option whereby the option premium was paid in two installments: the first, a compulsory one, at the inception of the contract and the second, an optional one, one month later. The sizes of these premiums are totally arbitrary in the sense that the hedger could have instead chosen to pay an amount £ 1 mm as a second installment, in which case she would end up paying a compulsory initial premium of £ 0.77 mm. The dynamics between these premiums are discussed in detail in the next section.

OBSERVATION 4 Depending on the type of risks the hedger is trying to mitigate, it is possible for her to purchase an option whereby the option premium is paid in more than two installments. More precisely, in the context of Example 18, suppose that the announcement of the awarding of the contract is done in two stages. The first stage, which is one week after the submission of the bid, will be used to identify and isolate a handful of serious bidders. The second stage, which is one month after the submission of the bid, will be used to select

EXAMPLE 18   A European-Style Compound Option Transaction

The U.S. dollar is currently trading at 1.7250 US/£. A U.K. manufacturer bids on a U.S. contract using today's exchange rate and will only know the outcome of the bidding one month from now. If the outcome is successful, she would be faced with a currency exposure six months after the results of the bidding and consequently wants to protect herself from the weakening of the dollar.

To hedge herself, she purchases a six-month vanilla call option on the pound that is struck at 1.7250 US/£ and conditionally starting one month from now on a notional amount of US$ 100 mm. For this, she pays an initial premium of £ 0.87 mm to purchase a compound option so that she can receive her call option by paying an additional premium of £ 0.87 mm.

Time (months)	Exchange Rate (US/£)	Impact of Option on the Hedger
0	1.7250	☛ £ 0.87 mm premium paid by hedger
Case 1: Contract Gets Awarded at the End of 1 Month		
1	1.7100	☛ £ 0.87 mm premium paid by hedger
7	*Case 1A: Call Option Is Exercised at the End of 7 Months*	
	1.7500	☛ Payoff of £ [100 • (1.7500 − 1.7250)] = £ 2.5 mm paid to hedger ☛ £ 1.74 mm of total premium and £ 0.06 mm of interest on this premium foregone by hedger ☛ Profit to hedger: £ [2.5 − (1.74 + 0.06)] = £ 0.7 mm
	Case 1B: Call Option Is Not Exercised at the End of 7 Months	
	1.7150	☛ £ 1.74 mm of total premium and £ 0.06 mm of interest on this premium foregone by hedger ☛ Profit to hedger: −£ [1.74 + 0.06] = −£ 1.8 mm
Case 2: Contract Does Not Get Awarded at the End of 1 Month		
1	1.7300	☛ £ 0.87 mm of premium and £ 0.005 mm of interest on this premium foregone by hedger ☛ Profit to hedger: −£ [0.87 + 0.005] = −£ 0.875 mm

the winner of the contract from the previously identified pool of serious bidders. In such an instance, the hedger could purchase a call-on-call-on-call option, in which she would pay a compulsory initial premium of £ 0.6 mm and two optional installments of £ 0.6 mm. The first optional installment would be paid in a week , and the second optional installment would be paid in a month. The dynamics between the three premiums will be discussed in detail in the next section, and another example of an application of a compound option in which the premium is paid for in more than two installments will be given on later in this section.

OBSERVATION 5 Instead of purchasing a call-on-call option, the hedger could have alternatively purchased a seven-month vanilla call option on the pound for £ 1.69 mm at the time of bidding. This option would hedge her exposure should she be awarded the contract. However, in the event she does not get awarded the contract, she can sell the purchased option back into the market one month later. By comparing the premiums, it can be seen that in purchasing a call-on-call option, the hedger only foregoes a fraction of the premium up-front. In our example, the hedger ended up paying an up-front premium of £ 0.87 mm for the call-on-call option, which is only about 51 percent of that required for the seven-month call option.

OBSERVATION 6 The hedger, in the context of our example, purchased a call-on-call option, in which a call option was exercised into another call option. Similarly, due to the nature of risks mitigated, the hedger could have alternatively purchased either a call-on-put option, a put-on-call option, or a put-on-put option, all of which are described in the next section.

Characteristics of Compound Option Contracts

The profit profile associated with the purchase of these compound options can be more generally written, as in Exhibit 74. While the profit profiles at the time of the second installment are graphed in Exhibit 75 and 76, the graphs on the option maturity date upon the payment of the second installment are no different from those presented in Exhibits 23 and 24.

Although Geske (1979) and Rubinstein (1991b) provided analytical expressions for valuing European-style compound options, the binomial and the Monte Carlo method can also be used to value these options. The use of these methods will be illustrated in chapter 4.

As can be easily observed, the profit and loss graphs to the buyer of a compound option on the second installment date that are presented in Exhibits 75 and 76 are philosophically no different from those given in Exhibits 23 and 24. Thus,

EXHIBIT 74   Profits to the Buyer of a European-Style Compound Option

Type of Compound Option	Profit at Time t	Profit at Expiry Time T if Compound Option is Exercised at Time t
$C_E C_E$ (0,t,T,X_t,X)	$\max[-P^*_{t,CC}, C_{E,t} - X_t - P^*_{t,CC}]$	$\max[-P^*_{T,CC}, S_T - X - P^*_{T,CC}]$
$C_E P_E$ (0,t,T,X_t,X)	$\max[-P^*_{t,CP}, P_{E,t} - X_t - P^*_{t,CP}]$	$\max[-P^*_{T,CP}, X - S_T - P^*_{T,CP}]$
$P_E C_E$ (0,t,T,X_t,X)	$\max[-P^*_{t,PC}, X_t - C_{E,t} - P^*_{t,PC}]$	$\max[-P^*_{T,PC}, S_T - X - P^*_{T,PC}]$
$P_E P_E$ (0,t,T,X_t,X)	$\max[-P^*_{t,PP}, X_t - P_{E,t} - P^*_{t,PP}]$	$\max[-P^*_{T,PP}, X - S_T - P^*_{T,PP}]$

where

0 = Current time or time today
t = Time of optional second installment
T = Time of option maturity
S_T = Asset value on option maturity
X_t = Size of optional second installment
X = Strike value of underlying option
$C_E C_E(0,t,T,X_t,X)$ = European call-on-call option purchased at time 0 with parameters t, T, X_t, and X
$C_E P_E(0,t,T,X_t,X)$ = European call-on-put option purchased at time 0 with parameters t, T, X_t, and X
$P_E C_E(0,t,T,X_t,X)$ = European put-on-call option purchased at time 0 with parameters t, T, X_t, and X
$P_E P_E(0,t,T,X_t,X)$ = European put-on-put option purchased at time 0 with parameters t, T, X_t, and X
$C_{E,t}$ = European call option purchased at time t with parameters T and X
$P_{E,t}$ = European put option purchased at time t with parameters T and X
$P^*_{t,CC}$ = Amount foregone by purchaser of call-on-call option due to initial premium and the interest accrued until time t on this premium
$P^*_{t,CP}$ = Amount foregone by purchaser of call-on-put option due to initial premium and the interest accrued until time t on this premium
$P^*_{t,PC}$ = Amount foregone by purchaser of put-on-call option due to initial premium and the interest accrued until time t on this premium
$P^*_{t,PP}$ = Amount foregone by purchaser of put-on-put option due to initial premium and the interest accrued until time t on this premium
$P^*_{T,CC}$ = Amount foregone by purchaser of call-on-call option due to initial and optional premiums and the interest accrued until time T on this premium
$P^*_{T,CP}$ = Amount foregone by purchaser of call-on-put option due to initial and optional premiums and the interest accrued until time T on this premium
$P^*_{T,PC}$ = Amount foregone by purchaser of put-on-call option due to initial and optional premiums and the interest accrued until time T on this premium
$P^*_{T,PP}$ = Amount foregone by purchaser of put-on-put option due to initial and optional premiums and the interest accrued until time T on this premium

as discussed on page 52, the break-even analysis is crucial in determining whether this type of hedging strategy would make any sense.[48]

To be able to value an option, one has to first identify the factors that would influence an option price. These factors are summarized in Exhibit 77 for all four asset classes.

As can be seen in Exhibit 77, 10 factors contribute to the value of a currency, equity, and commodity option contract, whereas only nine factors con-

---

[48] It is more precise to say that there are two break-even levels associated with this option. The first is to determine whether the initial compulsory premium is worth paying, and the second is to determine whether the second optional premium is worth paying.

**EXHIBIT 75   Call-on-Call and Call-on Put Option Buyer's Profit
at Second Installment**

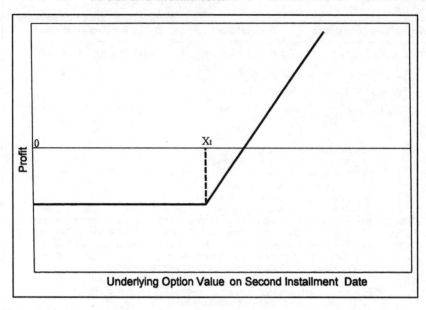

**EXHIBIT 76   Put-on-Call and Put-on-Put Option Buyer's Profit
at Second Installment**

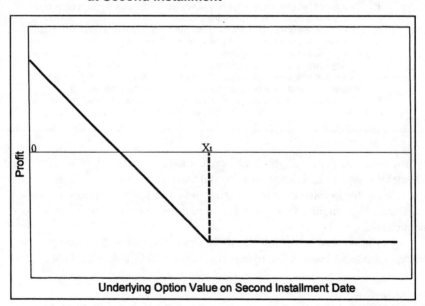

EXHIBIT 77   Factors Influencing the Value of a Compound Option Contract

Factors	Interest-Rate Option	Currency Option	Equity Option	Commodity Option
Convenience yield				✔
Dividend rate			✔	
Foreign risk-free rate		✔		
Domestic risk-free rate	✔	✔	✔	✔
Underlying asset value	✔	✔	✔	✔
Strike value	✔	✔	✔	✔
Volatility of asset value	✔	✔	✔	✔
Frequency of exercise	✔	✔	✔	✔
Life of contract	✔	✔	✔	✔
Frequency of exercise in compound option	✔	✔	✔	✔
Size of installment	✔	✔	✔	✔
Time between payments	✔	✔	✔	✔

tribute to the value of an interest-rate option contract. When compared to the factors influencing the value of a vanilla option in Exhibit 30, three additional factors influence the value of a compound option. These factors, which are given in the last three rows of Exhibit 77, are as follows:

1. **Frequency of exercise in compound option.** Frequency at which the installment component can be paid (e.g., the ability to pay the second installment weekly during the one-month period in the context of Example 18); and is analogous to the "Frequency Of Exercise" category.
2. **Size of installment.** Magnitude of the optional installment.
3. **Time between payments.** Time between the compulsory payment and the optional installment.

To understand how the above-mentioned factors influence the value of an option contract, one would have to first derive a no-aribitrage relationship between the option contract and the asset underlying the option contract. The effects of these factors are summarized in Exhibit 78.

One can obtain the effects on the value of a vanilla option for the factors in common with those in Exhibit 31. In addition to using these effects to intuit the results in Exhibit 78, I will also provide the intuition underlying the effect of the four new factors on the option premium.

The call-on-call option in Example 18 was viewed as the purchase of a vanilla call option in which the buyer paid the premium in two installments: a

EXHIBIT 78 Effect of Increase in Value of Underlying Factors on Compound Option Premium

Factors	Type of Contracts			
	Call-on-Call Option	Call-on-Put Option	Put-on-Call Option	Put-on-Put Option
r_f	⇓	⇑	⇑	⇓
r_d	⇑	⇓	⇓	⇑
S_0	⇑	⇓	⇓	⇑
X	⇓	⇑	⇑	⇓
σ	⇑	⇑	⇓	⇓
ef	⇑	⇑	⇑	⇑
T	⇕	⇕	⇕	⇕
fc	⇑	⇑	⇑	⇑
X_t	⇓	⇓	⇑	⇑
t	⇕	⇕	⇕	⇕

first, compulsory, payment and a second, optional, payment. The reader will realize that a call-on-call option can be alternatively viewed as an option that would allow the purchaser to buy a call option on the second installment date for a strike value that is equal to the second optional payment. More precisely, a call-on-call option can be viewed as a European-style call option that is struck at the second optional premium and maturing on the second installment date, where the asset underlying the option is another European-style call option. Similarly, while a call-on-put option can be viewed as an option that would allow the purchaser to buy a put option on the second installment date for the second optional amount, a put-on-call option can be viewed as an option that would allow the purchaser to sell a call option on the second installment date for the second optional amount, and a put-on-put option can be viewed as an option that would allow the purchaser to sell a put option on the second installment date for the second optional amount. The characteristics of the four types of compound options are summarized in Exhibit 79.

In any compound option where the purchaser of the option pays the premium in two installments, the initial compulsory payment for the option is determined by the size of the second optional payment. More precisely, the dynamics between the premiums for a call-on-call option and a call-on-put option are such that the lower the initial compulsory payment, the higher the second optional payment; and the higher the initial compulsory payment, the lower the second optional payment. To intuit this, consider a call-on-call option and recall that the purchase of a call-on-call option is equivalent to the purchase of a European-style vanilla call option whose underlying asset is another European-style vanilla call option that is struck at the second optional installment and matures on the second

EXHIBIT 79 Summary of European-Style Compound Options

What the Purchaser of the Option Does	Call-on-Call	Call-on-Put	Put-on-Call	Put-on-Put
Pays 1st compulsory premium	✓	✓	✓	✓
Pays 2nd optional premium	✓	✓		
Receives 2nd optional premium			✓	✓
Receives vanilla call after paying 2nd premium	✓			
Receives vanilla put after paying 2nd premium		✓		
Pays vanilla call after receiving 2nd premium			✓	
Pays vanilla put after receiving 2nd premium				✓

installment date. Thus, the higher the strike level (or the second optional premium), the more out-of-the-money the first option gets and hence the smaller the premium on the first option (or initial compulsory premium). Alternatively, the lower the strike level (or the second optional premium), the more in-the-money the first option gets and hence the larger the premium on the first option (or initial compulsory premium). It can similarly be concluded that the lower the initial compulsory payment for a put-on-call option and a put-on-put option, the lower the second optional payment; and the higher the initial compulsory payment, the higher the second optional payment, all of which can be intuited in a manner that is similar to that for a call-on-call option.

Furthermore, by thinking of a compound option as a vanilla option whose underlying asset is another option, it becomes easier to intuit the effect of the factors presented in the first eight rows of Exhibit 79. Take for example, a call-on-call option and a call-on-put option, which are essentially call options whose respective underlying assets are the call and put options. As long as the value of the underlying call option and the put option increases, the value of the first call option will increase, causing the initial compulsory premium to increase. Similarly, a put-on-call option and a put-on-put option are both put options whose respective underlying assets are the call and put options. Here, as long as the value of the underlying call option and the put option decreases, the value of the first put option would increase. Since the effects of the first eight factors on a vanilla option can be easily observed from Exhibit 31, one can use these results to intuit the effect of the same parameters on the compound option.

As an example, consider the factor r_d, which has the capability of increasing the value of a vanilla call option and decreasing the value of vanilla put option when it increases. Since an increase in the underlying call option value increases the value of a call-on-call option and decreases the value of a put-on-call option, increasing r_d leads to an increase in the premium of a call-on-call option and a decrease in the premium of a put-on-call option, as shown in Exhibit 79. Similarly, one can conclude that increasing r_d leads to a decrease in the premium of a put-on-call option and an increase in the premium of a put-on-put option, as shown in Exhibit 79.

In the case of a call-on-call option, when the size of the second optional payment X_t, is zero the initial compulsory payment for the option will be equal to the premium of a structurally similar vanilla call option. This can be intuited by considering the call-on-call option that was discussed in Example 18, in which the second installment was paid in a month's time and the underlying call option expired six months thereafter. If the second optional payment is zero, since the purchaser of the option can acquire the underlying call option at no extra cost, the purchaser will always exercise into the underlying call option. Thus, it would be reasonable to conclude that after paying the initial compulsory premium, the purchaser of a call-on-call option would have acquired a seven-month vanilla call option at no additional cost. Since the purchaser can alternatively acquire this option by buying a seven-month vanilla call option at the inception of the contract, for no arbitrage to be maintained the initial compulsory payment on this call-on-call option must be the same as that of the vanilla call option premium. It can be similarly concluded that when the second installment in the purchase of a call-on-put option is zero, the initial compulsory premium will be the same as that of a structurally similar vanilla put option.

Unlike the call-on-call option and the call-on-put option, setting the second optional installment for the purchase of either a put-on-call option or a put-on-put option to zero implies that the initial compulsory premium is zero. To intuit this, consider for example, a put-on-call option in which the second installment is paid in a month's time and the underlying call option expires six months thereafter. When the second optional payment is zero, the purchaser of the option would have the right to sell the underlying six-month call option at no cost, which implies that the purchaser will never exercise into the call option. Because the purchaser will never exercise the option, there is no value in the option and hence the initial compulsory premium must be zero. It can be similarly concluded that when the second installment in the purchase of a put-on-put option is zero, the initial compulsory premium will also be zero.

Exhibit 80 illustrates the effect of varying the second optional premium on the initial compulsory premium for a call-on-call option.

The curve $X_t = 0\%$ represents the premium (or the first compulsory payment) of a call-on-call option when there is no second installment. As discussed above, this curve also represents the premium of a structurally similar European-style vanilla call option premium. While the curve $X_t = 20\%$ represents the initial compulsory payment required for the purchase of a call-on-call option when 20

EXHIBIT 80   Effect of X_t on the Premium of a Call-on-Call Option

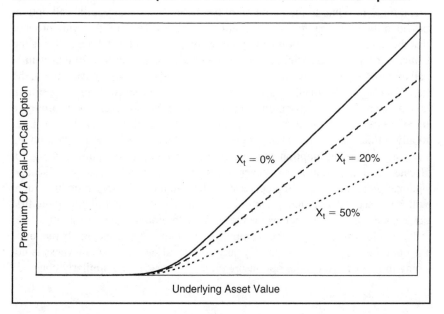

percent of a structurally similar vanilla call option premium has been paid as a second installment, the curve $X_t = 50\%$ represents the initial compulsory payment required for the purchase of a call-on-call option when 50 percent of a structurally similar vanilla call option premium has been paid as a second installment. As explained and intuited earlier, Exhibit 80 shows that the higher the second optional premium for a call-on-call option, the lower the initial compulsory premium.

From the exhibit, it can be seen that regardless of the size of the second optional premium, the sum of the two premiums for the call-on-call option can never be less than the premium required for the purchase of a structurally similar vanilla call option. Furthermore, as the number of installments increases, the sum of the premiums paid by the purchaser to acquire the underlying call option also increases. To illustrate, consider Observation 5 in Example 18, which shows that when the premium of the option is paid in one installment, a call-on-call option that is indeed a vanilla call option costs the purchaser £ 1.69 mm. For the same option, Example 18 shows that the total premium paid by the purchaser in two installments amounts to £ 1.74 mm, and Observation 4 in the same example shows that the total premium paid by the purchaser in three installments amounts to £ 1.8 mm. The philosophy of relating the number of installments to the total amount of premium paid can also be extended to encompass the call-on-put, put-on-call option, and put-on put option.

As is well known, an increase in the life of a European-style call or put option typically leads to an increase in the premium of the option. Similarly, as the time between payments, t, in a compound option increases, it is intuitively reasonable to expect the initial compulsory premium to also increase. Furthermore, when the second installment date is the contract inception date, one would expect the sum of the initial compulsory premium and the second optional installment premium to be equal to the premium of a structurally similar vanilla call option, provided the initial compulsory premium is not zero. To intuit this, first observe that the purchase of a call-on-call option when the second installment date is the contract inception date is equivalent to purchasing a structurally similar vanilla call option. Consequently, in order to exercise into the underlying call option, the purchaser of a call-on-call option has to pay both the initial compulsory premium and the second optional premium at the inception of the contract. For no arbitrage to be in effect, the sum of these premiums must be equal to the value of a structurally similar call option. At this stage, the reader may be tempted to question the necessity of the assumption that the initial compulsory premium is not zero. Because option premiums can never be less than zero and increasing the second optional premium results in a decrease in the initial compulsory premium, there will be a second optional premium level at which the initial premium first achieves a zero value. Increasing the optional premium beyond this threshold value would still result in a zero compulsory premium. More succinctly put, once the option is way out-of-the-money, any additional out-of-the-moneyness is not going to further reduce the option premium. The reader can similarly conclude that for a call-on-put option, when the second installment date is the contract inception date, the sum of the initial compulsory premium and the second optional installment premium will be equal to the premium of a structurally similar vanilla put option, provided the initial compulsory premium is not zero.

Unlike the call-on-call option and the call-on-put option, the observation in the above paragraph cannot be generalized to the put-on-call option and the put-on-put option. To come up with an analogous observation for these options, consider a put-on-call option when the second installment date is set to the contract inception date. First observe that the purchase of a put-on-call option when the second installment date is the contract inception date is equivalent to selling a structurally similar vanilla call option. In order to exercise into the underlying call option, the purchaser of a put-on-call option has to pay the initial compulsory premium and receive the second optional premium at the inception of the contract. For no arbitrage to be in effect, the net amount received by the purchaser of a put-on-call option must be equal to the premium received from the sale of a structurally similar call option. It can similarly be concluded that for a put-on-put option, when the second installment date is the contract inception date, the difference between the second optional installment premium and the initial compulsory premium must be equal to the premium obtained from the sale of a structurally similar vanilla put option, provided the initial compulsory premium is not zero.

Other Applications

Although the discussion so far has been based on the use of compound options in the currency asset class, these types of options have been and will continue to be used heavily in the other asset classes with minor variations. As an illustration, I will give another example, which is by no means exhaustive.

A liability manager wants to purchase a one-year monthly reset interest-rate cap to manage his floating-rate exposure. Since the forward yield curve is steeply upward sloping, purchasing such a cap (or 11 one-month caplets) becomes quite expensive. To cheapen the premium, the liability manager decides to purchase an interest-rate cap by paying the premiums in 11 installments. Thus, in addition to paying the initial compulsory premium today, the purchaser would pay the second optional installment in a month's time, the third optional installment in two month's time, and so on. Furthermore, unlike previous examples of compound options, upon the payment of each optional installment, the purchaser has the right to exercise only the next immediate caplet. Thus, while the last cash flow settlement in a one-year monthly resettable cap occurs at the end of 12 months and the last caplet gets exercised at the end of 11 months, the last optional installment would be paid at the end of 10 months. A cap of this sort, which is also known as a rent-a-cap, is a popular hedge instrument among corporate treasurers.

THE DEFERRED STRIKE OPTION CONTRACT
Introduction

Given that the current forward yield curve is steeply upward sloping and the volatility levels are low, a Canadian corporate whose floating-rate liability is linked to the three-month BA rate wants to protect itself from the increase in short rates. To ensure itself, it could purchase a quarterly resetting interest-rate cap, which could prove to be costly. The liability manager feels that this steepness in the forward yield curve is based only on where the market participants expect the three-month BA rates to trade in the future and gives no indication of the levels at which the three-month BA rates will actually trade. Furthermore, based on the historical three-month BA rates, the liability manager feels that the actual values of the three-month BA rate will be around where it is right now and will never be as high as implied by the forward curve. To monetize his view and ensure himself simultaneously, the manager's best alternative is to purchase a quarterly resetting one-year periodic cap that in addition to monetizing his view would provide a cheaper form of protection.

The periodic cap mentioned above is an example of a deferred strike option. Although the premium of a deferred strike option is paid for today, the strike value associated with this type of option is either completely or partially unknown at the inception of the contract. This strike value, however, becomes completely specified before the maturity of the option.

A DEFERRED STRIKE OPTION
CONTRACT EXAMPLE

The sequence of events in Example 19 on page 143 illustrates the nature of a periodic cap transaction.

It is important for the reader to make the following four observations about Example 19.

OBSERVATION 1 It is assumed that the strike rate of each periodic caplet was always set three months prior to the expiry of the caplet when the underlying index was a three-month BA rate. Due to the nature of the liabilities and the timing of the cash flows in the asset/liability portfolio, the hedger could have alternatively purchased a periodic cap where the tenor of the underlying rate would have no relation to the frequency at which the strike rate underlying each caplet is set. For example, the hedger could have purchased a semiannually reset periodic cap in which the index underlying the settlement of a cap is the then-prevailing on-the-run, five-year Government of Canada bond yield, and the floating strike rate of the cap is set three months prior to the expiry of each caplet.

EXAMPLE 19   A European-Style Periodic Cap Transaction

The liability manager pays Cad$ 0.16 mm to buy a one-year periodic cap on a notional amount of Cad$ 100 mm that is reset quarterly. In this cap, there are three caplets, the first of which expires in three months and the last of which expires in nine months. Furthermore, the strike rate of each caplet will be set equal to the sum of the previous three-month BA setting and 50 basis points. The current three-month BA is 5.5 percent.

Time (months)	BA Rate (%)	Impact of Option on the Hedger
0	5.5	☛ Cad$ 0.16 mm premium paid by hedger ☛ Strike rate of 1st caplet is (5.5 + 0.5)% = 6%
1st Caplet Expires out-of-the-money		
3	5.8	☛ Strike rate of 2nd caplet is (5.8 + 0.5)% = 6.3%
2nd Caplet Expires in-the-money and Hedger Is Given Payoff from 1st Caplet		
6	6.4	☛ No payoff from 1st caplet paid to hedger ☛ Strike rate of 3rd caplet is (6.4 + 0.5)% = 6.9%
3rd Caplet Expires in-the-money and Hedger Is Given Payoff from 2nd Caplet		
9	8.1	☛ Payoff of Cad$ [100 • (0.064 − 0.063) • 0.25] = Cad$ 0.025 mm from 2nd caplet paid to hedger
Hedger Is Given Payoff from 3rd Caplet		
12		☛ Payoff of Cad$ [100 • (0.081 − 0.069) • 0.25] = Cad$ 0.03 mm from 3rd caplet paid to hedger

OBSERVATION 2   The floating component of the strike rate in Example 19 was dependent on only the value of the underlying three-month BA rate at a certain point in time. Due to the types of risks managed, it is not inconceivable for the hedger to purchase a cap in which the strike rate is set using some path-

dependent feature of the underlying rate. More precisely, the hedger in Example 19 could have purchased a periodic cap in which the floating strike rate for each caplet is set as follows:

> The lowest value of the three-month BA rate monitored during a one-month period, commencing three months prior to expiry of the caplet, and concluding two months prior to the expiry of the same caplet.

This type of caplet is also an example of a partial look-back option, which will be discussed further in the next building block.

OBSERVATION 3 In Example 19, the maximum strike level achieved during the life of the cap was 6.9 percent. If the hedger had instead bought a structurally similar cap that was struck at 6.9 percent, he would have ended up paying a premium of Cad$ 0.2 mm. This premium is 10 percent greater than what he paid for the periodic cap. Of course with the periodic cap, one could argue that the short rates could have spiked up, causing the strike level to be much higher and hence lessen the amount of insurance provided to the hedger. This argument, however, would only be valid if the liability manager's view taken at the inception of the contract proves to be wrong during the life of the cap.

OBSERVATION 4 In the application of a periodic cap, the strike rate for each underlying caplet was composed of two components: a floating-rate component and a fixed-rate component. Depending on the type of risks managed, it is possible for either one of the components to be absent from the structure. As the reader will realize, when the floating-rate component is absent from the strike rate of a periodic caplet, each periodic caplet becomes a vanilla caplet. Furthermore, when the fixed-rate component is absent from the strike rate of a periodic caplet, a periodic caplet becomes a vanilla caplet forward starting at a time at which the floating strike rate is fixed.

Characteristics of Deferred Strike Option Contracts

The profit profile associated with the purchase of these deferred strike options can be more generally written, as detailed in Exhibit 81, and the graph upon the maturity of the underlying options are no different from those illustrated in Exhibits 23 and 24.

When Z in Exhibit 81 is set to the value of the underlying asset at time t (where t < T), the pricing formulae for both the call and put options are given in Hull (1997). As before, the numerical methods illustrated in Chapter 4 can be used to value these options. Furthermore, the break-even analysis discussion on

EXHIBIT 81   Profits to the Buyer of a European-Style Deferred Strike Option

Type of Deferred Strike Option	Profit at Expiry Time T
$C_E(0,T,Z)$	$\max[-P^*_{T,C}, S_T - Z - P^*_{T,C}]$
$P_E(0,T,Z)$	$\max[-P^*_{T,P}, Z - S_T - P^*_{T,P}]$

where

0 = Current time or time today
T = Time of option maturity
S_T = Asset value at time T
Z = Function used to set the strike value of option
$C_E(0,T,Z)$ = European call option purchased at time 0 with parameters T, Z
$P_E(0,T,Z)$ = European put option purchased at time 0 with parameters T, Z
$P^*_{T,C}$ = Amount foregone by purchaser of call option due to premium and the interest accrued until time T on this premium
$P^*_{T,P}$ = Amount foregone by purchaser of put option due to premium and the interest accrued until time T on this premium

page 52 should be applied in order to make sure that the hedging strategy employed is indeed cost-effective.

To be able to value a deferred strike option, one would have to first identify the factors that would influence an option price, which are summarized in Exhibit 82 for all four asset classes:

EXHIBIT 82   Factors Influencing the Value of a Deferred Strike Option Contract

Factors	Interest-Rate Option	Currency Option	Equity Option	Commodity Option
Convenience yield				✔
Dividend rate			✔	
Foreign risk-free rate		✔		
Domestic risk-free rate	✔	✔	✔	✔
Underlying asset value	✔	✔	✔	✔
Volatility of asset value	✔	✔	✔	✔
Frequency of exercise	✔	✔	✔	✔
Life of contract	✔	✔	✔	✔
Method used to calculate strike	✔	✔	✔	✔

As can be seen in Exhibit 82, seven factors contribute to the value of a currency, equity, and commodity option contract, whereas only six factors contribute to the value of an interest-rate option contract. When compared to the factors influencing the value of a vanilla option in Exhibit 30, although the total number of factors is still the same, there is one new factor in Exhibit 82 that has replaced the strike value in Exhibit 27. This factor, which is given in the last row of Exhibit 82, is the "method used to calculate strike," which refers to the function used to specify the strike level, for example, the average of all the daily observed asset values, the maximum of all the weekly observed asset values, the value of the asset at a specified time minus a constant value, and so on.

To understand how the above-mentioned factors influence the value of an option contract, one would have to first derive a no-aribitrage relationship between the option contract and the asset underlying the option contract. The effects of these factors are summarized in Exhibit 83.

EXHIBIT 83   Effect of Increase in Value of Underlying Factors on Deferred Strike Option Premium

Factors	Type of Contracts	
	Call Option	Put Option
r_f	⇕	⇕
r_d	⇕	⇕
S_0	⇕	⇕
σ	⇕	⇕
ef	⇑	⇑
T	⇕	⇕
Z	⇕	⇕

Since nearly all the factors are the same as those in Exhibit 31, it is tempting to say that one could easily use these effects to intuit the results in Exhibit 83. However, because the effect of these variables are highly dependent on the nature of the strike function, it is difficult to pinpoint the effects accurately without knowing the exact form of Z.

When Z in Exhibit 83 is set to the value of the underlying asset at time t, it can be shown that the premium of a deferred strike option is proportional to the premium of a vanilla at-the-money option with life T − t. Furthermore, if the underlying asset does not pay any dividend, it can be shown that the purchase of a deferred strike option is equivalent to the purchase of a T − t year vanilla option. The reader is referred to Hull (1997) for the mathematics underlying these conclusions, which can be intuited as follows:

By purchasing a deferred strike option whose underlying asset does not pay any dividend, the buyer has effectively bought an option that expires at time T and allows the strike price to be set at time t. Since the value of this option is solely based on the difference in prices of the same asset at times T and t, this option can be thought of as one that would allow the purchaser to exchange one asset for another, where the two assets in addition to being identical to each other are also autocorrelated. Because these are identical assets prior to the fixing of the floating rate, the growth rate of one asset relative to the other will always be zero, making the option on the difference valueless until the value of one asset gets fixed. Since this fixing takes place only at time t, the option will start having a value only after time t; making the effective life of the option T – t. Thus, as long as the asset does not pay any dividend, this is equivalent to the buyer purchasing an at-the-money option today with a life of T – t.

A deferred strike option can also be thought of as a spread option that allows the purchaser to exchange at time T the value of one asset for the value of another asset, where the first asset value is the value of the asset at time T, and the second asset value would be Z in Exhibit 81, which could be some function of the same asset value at various points in time and some cash. Unlike a typical spread option where the correlation coefficient can only be historically calculated, the autocorrelation between these two can usually be implicitly calculated because one is actually monitoring a single variable at various points in time.[49]

Since a deferred strike option becomes a vanilla European-style option once the strike component has been set, risk management on a deferred strike option is identical to that of a vanilla option only after the floating strike component is specified. Prior to the fixing of the floating strike component, one can still delta hedge a deferred strike option because the correlation coefficient between continuously compounded returns in S_T and the function used to set the strike component can often be implicitly calculated.

By purchasing a vanilla interest-rate cap, a hedger is in fact mitigating the market risks arising from the movements in absolute rate levels and the volatility of these levels. If the absolute rate level turns out to be unfavorable and the volatility of the absolute rate level turns out to be favorable at the inception of the contract, a hedger cannot use an interest-rate cap effectively to lock in a favorable volatility level before locking in a favorable absolute rate level. In situations like these, a deferred strike option can be effectively used by a hedger to isolate the timing of the hedging of the absolute rate levels from that of the volatility of these levels. More precisely, by alternatively purchasing a periodic cap, the hedger can hedge away the volatility component of the risk at the inception of the contract and the absolute levels of the rates at the times at which the floating strike rates get fixed.

---

[49] This is similar in philosophy to the discussion given earlier when an average option was compared to a basket option.

Other Applications

Although the discussion so far has been based on the use of deferred strike options in the interest-rate asset class, these types of options have been and will continue to be used heavily in the other asset classes with minor variations. As illustrations, I will give two other examples.

Application 1   A liability manager is afraid of the increase in the short-term LIBOR and wants to lock in the lowest possible fixed rate in a two-year swap. To do this, he could enter into a two-year quarterly reset fixed-floating interest swap in which he would pay a fixed rate of 5.20 percent and receive the floating three-month LIBOR. Due to the upward sloping nature of the yield curve, his view is that the three-month LIBOR would increase. As a result, he could enter into a look-back swap in which he would end up paying a fixed rate of 5.10 percent and receiving the lower of the LIBOR or LIBOR-in-arrears. By entering into such a swap, the liability manager has in fact entered into a two-year vanilla fixed-floating swap and sold a periodic floor to lower the fixed rate of 5.20 percent by 10 basis points.

Application 2   A portfolio manager wants to monetize his view that the election in a week's time will impact the FTSE 100 market negatively, which is contrary to what other market participants believe. To monetize the view that this negative effect will carry on until about a week after the elections, he could either sell a two-week call option or purchase a two-week put option on the FTSE 100 index. However, because he is unsure about the height the index will reach just prior to elections, he is unable to define a strike level in the purchase of the two-week vanilla options. To monetize his view more effectively, he could either sell a deferred strike two-week call option or buy a deferred strike two-week put option, where the floating strike rate component would be set immediately after the elections.

THE LOOKBACK OPTION CONTRACT

Introduction

A U.S. manufacturer receives his raw materials from Canada, and upon the receipt of his bills, he has until the end of the month to settle his accounts. Since he knows the total currency risk he is exposed to at the end of every month and has no view of the currency market, he wants to protect himself against a weakening U.S. dollar. Purchasing a one-month vanilla European-style put option on the U.S. dollar is not going to be useful, as the manufacturer would only be protected against the weakening of the U.S. dollar at the end of the month. A better alternative for the manufacturer would be to purchase a one-month European-style put option on the U.S. dollar that would allow him to lock in a better rate should the U.S. dollar strengthen during the life of the option. More precisely, to address his concerns, he would need to buy a European-style put option on the U.S. dollar that would give him a maximum protection. This type of option, which is known as a look-back or no-regret option, gives the purchaser maximum protection for an initial up-front premium that is paid at the inception of the contract.

A LOOKBACK OPTION CONTRACT EXAMPLE

The sequence of events in Example 20 on page 150 illustrates the nature of a lookback option transaction.

It is important for the reader to make the following three observations about Example 20.

OBSERVATION 1   This type of option, which is also called a regular lookback option, is not really an option in that it can never finish out-of-the-money on the option maturity date. To intuit this, observe that the sampling period that contains the exchange rates encountered during the life of the option also includes as its sample point the spot exchange rate on the option maturity date. Consequently, the purchaser of the option cannot do any worse than the spot rate on the option maturity date. Furthermore, depending on the type of risks mitigated, one could have alternatively structured an option that would pay the buyer on the option maturity date an in-the-money payoff that is the difference between a prespecified strike rate and the lowest (or the highest) exchange rate realized during the life of the option. Since it is possible for this type of option to finish out-of-the-money, these types of options are called modified lookback options or look-forward options.[50]

OBSERVATION 2   It was assumed that the manufacturer in purchasing the lookback option was satisfied with sampling the exchange rates daily. Depending on the type of risks being managed, it is possible for the purchaser to specify a sampling period that may be of any frequency (for example, once every 5 days, once every 5 days for the first 2 weeks and once every 10 days for the last 2 weeks, etc.). The effect of increasing the sampling frequency on the option premium is discussed in detail in the next section.

---

[50] This is analogous to the Category I and II arithmetic average options or the Category III and IV geometric average options. See footnote 51.

EXAMPLE 20   A European-Style Look-back Option Transaction

The U.S. dollar is currently trading at 0.7195 US/Cad. A U.S. manufacturer who receives a bill of Cad$ 25 mm has until 30 days after the receipt of the bill to pay for the goods received from his Canadian suppliers. Because of the inversion in the forward yield curves between these two economies, he decides not to use the 30-day forward and to use the currency spot market 30 days later.

To enable him to lock-in future strengthening of the U.S. dollar from the current spot level over the next 30-day period, he purchases a 30-day Eurpoean-style look-back call option on the U.S. dollar for an up-front premium of US$ 0.23 mm on a notional amount of Cad$ 25 mm. If the option finishes in-the-money, it would pay the manufacturer the difference between the spot rate on the option maturity date and the lowest value the US/Cad exchange-rate exhibits during the life of the option (inclusive of the spot rates at both the inception of the contract and the maturity of the option). The spot rates are observed at noon on each business day and are denominated in US/Cad.

Time (months)	Exchange Rate (US/Cad)	Impact of Option on the Hedger
0	0.7195	☞ US$ 0.23 mm premium paid by hedger
1	Case A: Call Option Is Exercised at the End of 1 Month	
	0.7250	☞ Lowest value of U.S. dollar realized during the one-month period is 0.7150 US/Cad ☞ Payoff of US$ [25 • (0.7250 − 0.7150)] = US$ 0.25 mm paid to hedger ☞ US$ 0.23 mm of premium and US$ 0.001 mm of interest in this premium foregone by hedger ☞ Profit to hedger: US$ [0.25 − (0.23 + 0.001)] = US$ 0.019 mm
	Case B: Call Option Is Not Exercised at the End of 1 Month	
	0.7100	☞ Lowest value of U.S. dollar realized during the one-month period is 0.7100 US/Cad ☞ US$ 0.23 mm of premium and US$ 0.001 mm of interest on this premium foregone by hedger ☞ Profit to hedger: −US$ (0.23 + 0.001) = −US$ 0.231 mm

OBSERVATION 3 The lookback option that was purchased in Example 20 had a sampling or a lookback period that started at the inception of the contract and ended on the option maturity date. If the purchaser of the option had a view about the movements of the exchange rate either during the first week or any subperiod of the month, this view can be effectively embedded into the lookback option. More precisely, suppose that the manufacturer in our example had a view that the Canadian dollar will get weaker in two weeks time and so only needs the lookback period to commence in two weeks. To hedge himself, he could purchase a partial lookback option that will have its lookback period starting in two weeks and ending two weeks thereafter.

As long as the partial lookback period does not include the option maturity date as one of its sampling points, the partial lookback option cannot always be in-the-money, unlike the typical lookback option. Thus, the discussion in Observation 1 only holds true for a partial lookback option when the option maturity date is used as a sampling point in the partial lookback period.

CHARACTERISTICS OF LOOKBACK OPTION CONTRACTS

The profit profile associated with the purchase of these lookback options can be more generally written, as detailed in Exhibit 84. While the graphs associated with the purchase of the Category I and II options are presented in Exhibits 85, 86, and 87, those associated with the purchase of Category III and IV options are presented in Exhibits 88 and 89, when $RV = S_0$.

The reader should note that in Exhibit 84, while Categories I and II represent both partial and full lookback options, Categories III and IV represent both the partial and full modified lookback options. Although both the European and American-style lookback options can be priced using the binomial method regardless of the sampling frequency, Goldman, Sosin, and Gatto (1979) have provided closed-form solutions to price European-style full lookback options on nondividend paying stocks when the assumption of a continuous time-sampling period is used. These assumptions have also been used by Garman (1987) and Conze and Viswanathan (1991) to value European-style full lookback options on dividend paying stocks and European-style modified lookback options on nondividend paying stocks, respectively. Heynen and Kat (1994) extended these results to value a partial lookback option on nondividend paying stocks. Chan (1996) extended nearly all these results to entertain dividend paying stocks with partial lookback features.

Exhibit 85 illustrates the profit profile of the buyer of a Category I lookback call option when the value of the underlying asset on option maturity date is used

EXHIBIT 84   Profits to the Buyer of a European-Style Lookback Option

Type of Look-back Option	Profit at Expiry Time T
$C_{E,I}(0,T,RV,t_{i+1},...,t_n)$	$\max[-P^*_{T,CI}, S_T - \min(\min[S_{t_j}],RV) - P^*_{T,CI}]$
$P_{E,I}(0,T,RV,t_{i+1},...,t_n)$	$\max[-P^*_{T,PI}, \min(\min[S_{t_j}],RV) - S_T - P^*_{T,PI}]$
$C_{E,II}(0,T,RV,t_{i+1},...,t_n)$	$\max[-P^*_{T,CII}, S_T - \max(\max[S_{t_j}],RV) - P^*_{T,CII}]$
$P_{E,II}(0,T,RV,t_{i+1},...,t_n)$	$\max[-P^*_{T,PII}, \max(\max[S_{t_j}],RV) - S_T - P^*_{T,PII}]$
$C_{E,III}(0,T,X,RV,t_{i+1},...,t_n)$	$\max[-P^*_{T,CIII}, \max(\max[S_{t_j}],RV) - X - P^*_{T,CIII}]$
$P_{E,III}(0,T,X,RV,t_{i+1},...,t_n)$	$\max[-P^*_{T,PIII}, X - \max(\max[S_{t_j}],RV) - P^*_{T,PIII}]$
$C_{E,IV}(0,T,X,RV,t_{i+1},...,t_n)$	$\max[-P^*_{T,CIV}, \min(\min[S_{t_j}],RV) - X - P^*_{T,CIV}]$
$P_{E,IV}(0,T,X,RV,t_{i+1},...,t_n)$	$\max[-P^*_{T,PIV}, X - \min(\min[S_{t_j}],RV) - P^*_{T,PIV}]$

where

0 = Current time or time today

T = Time of option maturity

t_i = Times at which the asset values are sampled, where $i = 1,2,...,n$; $t_{i+1} \geq 0$, and $t_n \leq T$

$\min[S_{t_j}]$ = Minimum of asset values sampled at times $t_{i+1},...,t_n$

$\max[S_{t_j}]$ = Maximum of asset values sampled at times $t_{i+1}, ...,t_n$

RV = Running maximum (minimum) value realized until and inclusive of time 0 for Category II and III (Category I and IV) options for the first i observations and is given by $\max_{j=1,...,i} S_{t_j}$ ($\min_{j=1,...,i} S_{t_j}$)

S_T = Asset value on option maturity

X = Strike value of option

$C_{E,k}(0,T,RV,t_{i+1},...,t_n)$ = European lookback Category k call option purchased at time 0 with parameters T, RV, $t_{i+1},...,t_n$, where $k = I, II$

$P_{E,k}(0,T,RV,t_{i+1},...,t_n)$ = European lookback Category k put option purchased at time 0 with parameters T, RV, $t_{i+1},...,t_n$, where $k = I, II$

$C_{E,k}(0,T,X,RV,t_{i+1},...,t_n)$ = European lookback Category k call option purchased at time 0 with parameters T, X, RV, $t_{i+1}, ...,t_n$, where $k = III, IV$

$P_{E,k}(0,T,X,RV,t_{i+1},...,t_n)$ = European lookback Category k call option purchased at time 0 with parameters T, X, RV, $t_{i+1}, ...,t_n$, where $k = III, IV$

$P^*_{T,Ck}$ = Amount foregone by purchaser of call option due to premium and the interest accrued until time T on this premium, where $k = I, II, II, IV$

$P^*_{T,Pk}$ = Amount foregone by purchaser of put option due to premium and the interest accrued until time T on this premium, where $k = I, II, II, IV$

EXHIBIT 85   Category I Lookback Call Option Buyer's Profit at Maturity When Time T Included

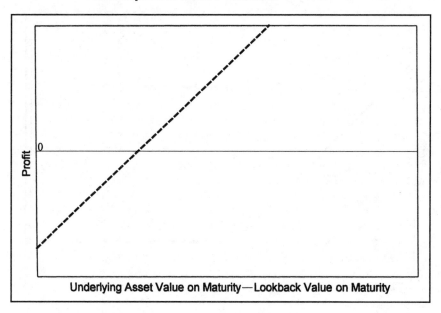

Underlying Asset Value on Maturity—Lookback Value on Maturity

EXHIBIT 86   Category I & II Lookback Call Option Buyer's Profit at Maturity When Time T Excluded

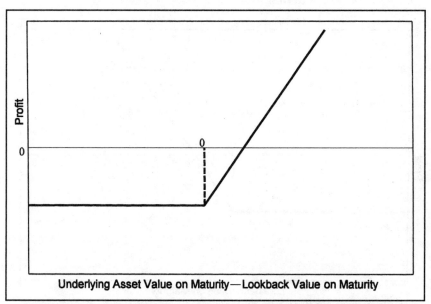

Underlying Asset Value on Maturity—Lookback Value on Maturity

EXHIBIT 87   Category I & II Lookback Put Option Buyer's Profit at Maturity When Time T Excluded

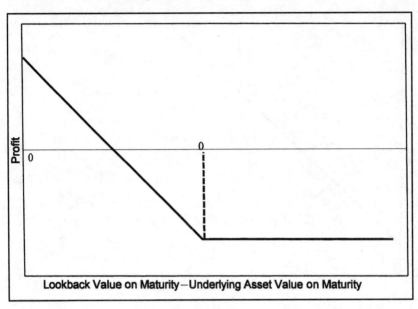

Lookback Value on Maturity—Underlying Asset Value on Maturity

EXHIBIT 88   Category III & IV Lookback Call Option Buyer's Profit at Maturity

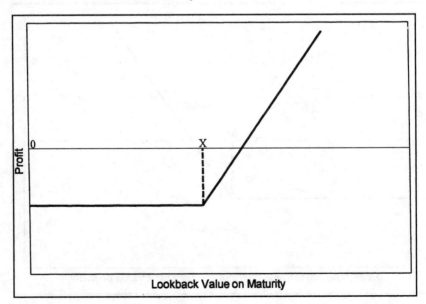

Lookback Value on Maturity

**EXHIBIT 89   Category III & IV Lookback Put Option Buyer's
Profit at Maturity**

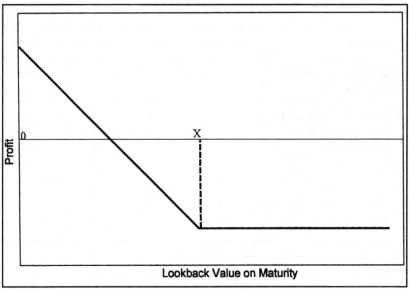

as one of the sampling points. Since the Category I call options always finish in-the-money, the spread value in this exhibit, which represents the in-the-money payoff from these options, is always nonnegative. The graph in Exhibit 85 can also be used to illustrate a Category II Put Option buyer's profit profile at maturity when time T is included. Hence, as indicated in the exhibit, there is no notion of optionality to the purchaser, and the profit profile is similar to that obtained by purchasing a futures contract, which was shown in Exhibit 4. Only when the sampling of the asset value on option maturity is removed can there be a notion of option embedded into the contract, as illustrated in Exhibits 86 and 87.[51] Regardless of the type of lookback option, the break-even analysis discussed on page 52 is crucial in determining whether this type of view-monetizing or hedging strategy is cost-effective.

To be able to value an option, one has to first identify the factors that would influence an option price, which are summarized in Exhibit 90 for all four asset classes.

As can be seen in Exhibit 90, nine factors contribute to the value of a currency, equity, and commodity option contract, whereas only eight factors contribute to the value of an interest-rate option contract. When compared to the

---

[51] This is unlike the feature of a Category I or Category III average option in which, regardless of the sampling of the asset value on option maturity date, the option is not necessarily in-the-money.

**EXHIBIT 90   Factors Influencing the Value of a Look-back Option
             Contract**

Factors	Interest-Rate Option	Currency Option	Equity Option	Commodity Option
Convenience yield				✔
Dividend rate			✔	
Foreign risk-free rate		✔		
Domestic risk-free rate	✔	✔	✔	✔
Underlying asset value	✔	✔	✔	✔
Strike value[52]	✔	✔	✔	✔
Volatility of asset value	✔	✔	✔	✔
Frequency of exercise	✔	✔	✔	✔
Life of contract	✔	✔	✔	✔
Dates of sampling	✔	✔	✔	✔
Running value[53]	✔	✔	✔	✔

52 Only applicable for the modified look-back options (i.e., Categories III and IV).

53 Only applicable if the sampling process is already underway at the time the option is purchased, as in the average options.

factors influencing the value of a vanilla option in Exhibit 30, two additional factors influence the value of a lookback option. These factors are as follows:

1. **Frequency of sampling.** Frequency at which the asset values are monitored in order to calculate the appropriate maximum or minimum value.

2. **Running value.** Realized maximum value in the case of a Category II and III option and realized minimum value in the case of a Category I and IV option.

To understand how the above-mentioned factors influence the value of an option contract, one will have to first derive a no-aribitrage relationship between the option contract and the asset underlying the option contract. The effects of these factors are summarized in Exhibit 91.

Since nearly all the factors are the same as those given in Exhibit 31, it is tempting to say that one could easily use these effects to intuit the results in Exhibit 91. While the effects of X, ef, and T are obvious and no different from those in Exhibits 31, the effect of r_f, r_d, σ, S_0, sf, and RV on the option premiums need to be intuited.

Like all vanilla call and put options, increasing the value of S_0 leads to an increase and a decrease of the option premiums, respectively. Similarly, in the Category III and Category IV options, it can be intuited that an increase in S_0 leads to an increase in the call option premiums and a decrease in the put option premiums. To intuit this, the reader has to realize that since the maximum and the minimum values in the profit profiles in Exhibit 91 are increasing functions of S_0, increasing S_0 implies increasing both the maximum and minimum value. Similar

EXHIBIT 91 Effect of Increase in Value of Underlying Factors on Lookback Option Premium

Factors	Type of Option Contracts							
	Category I Options		Category II Options		Category III Options		Category IV Options	
	Call	Put	Call	Put	Call	Put	Call	Put
r_f	⇒	⇐	⇒	⇐	⇒	⇐	⇒	⇐
r_d	⇐	⇒	⇐	⇒	⇐	⇒	⇐	⇒
S_0	⇐	⇔	⇐	⇔	⇐	⇒	⇐	⇒
X					⇒	⇐	⇒	⇐
σ	⇐	⇐	⇐	⇐	⇐	⇐	⇐	⇐
ef	⇐	⇐	⇐	⇐	⇐	⇐	⇐	⇐
T	⇔	⇔	⇔	⇔	⇔	⇔	⇔	⇔
sf [54]	⇐	⇒	⇒	⇐	⇐	⇒	⇒	⇐
RV [55]	⇒	⇐	⇒	⇐	⇐	⇒	⇐	⇒

[54] See footnote 23.

[55] For the Category II and III (Category I and IV) options, increasing RV implies increasing the running maximum (minimum) value, which cannot be less (greater) than the current asset value S_0. Furthermore, this running value is only applicable if the sampling process is already underway. If the sampling process starts at the inception of the option contract, then RV is S_0.

reasoning can be applied to intuit the results of r_f, r_d, and σ for the Category III and Category IV options.

In order to intuit the effect of S_0, r_f, r_d, and σ on the Category I and II options, I will, as an example, consider the Category I call and put options when the asset values at the inception of the contract and time t are sampled, where $t < T$ and the running minimum is RV. From Exhibit 84, the in-the-money payoff on option maturity to the purchaser of the call and put options can be more succinctly written as $S_T - \min[RV,S_t]$ and $\min[RV,S_t] - S_T$, respectively. These payoffs can be alternatively rewritten, as shown in Exhibit 92.

EXHIBIT 92   In-the-Money
Payoffs of the
Category I Look-
back Call and Put
Options

	$S_t < RV$	$S_t \geq RV$
Call option	$S_T - S_t$	$S_T - RV$
Put option	$S_t - S_T$	$RV - S_T$

From page 146, an astute reader will realize that when $S_t < RV$, the call option payoff is $S_T - S_t$ which is roughly similar to the purchase of an at-the-money vanilla call option with life $T - t$. Since I have already illustrated the effects of S_0, r_f, r_d, and σ on the vanilla call option premium in Exhibit 31, I can use these results to intuit the effect of these factors, as shown in Exhibit 91. Furthermore, when $S_t \geq RV$, the call option payoff of is $S_T - RV$ is similar to the purchase of a vanilla call option with life T and strike value RV. One can similarly apply the results of Exhibit 31 to intuit the effects of S_0, r_f, r_d, and σ, as shown in Exhibit 91. To intuit the effects of S_0, r_f, r_d, and σ on a Category I put option, one can go through a similar exercise of first examining the payoffs when $S_t < RV$ and $S_t \geq RV$ and then using the results of Exhibit 31 to arrive at the effects illustrated in Exhibit 91.

Due to the high level of insurance provided by a lookback option, depending on the category, it would be reasonable to expect a lookback option to be either costly or cheap. Whatever the type of option, the cost of a lookback option is directly proportional to sf, the frequency of sampling. To intuit this, observe first from Exhibit 84 that each profit profile is a function of either the maximum lookback value or a minimum lookback value. Regardless of the profile, sampling an additional asset value enhances the ability to make the maximum value bigger or the minimum value smaller. This follows from the fact that

1. If one samples an additional asset value, this value can either be bigger than the existing maximum value (in which case the maximum value is now set to the asset value) or smaller than the existing maximum value (in which case the maximum value remains unchanged).

2. If one samples an additional asset value, this value can either be bigger than the existing minimum value (in which case the minimum value remains unchanged) or smaller than the existing minimum value (in which case the minimum value gets set to the new asset value).

Thus, increasing the frequency of sampling has the potential of increasing the maximum value and decreasing the minimum value. By the nature of the profit profile, this readily implies that a Category I call option will increase in value every time sf is increased, which concurs with the summary in Exhibit 91. One can similarly intuit the effect of this factor on the other types of options.

Increasing RV for a Category I call option results in increasing the running minimum value, which the reader will recall cannot exceed the current asset value S_0. By increasing this running minimum value, the intrinsic value of the option is decreased. Since this intrinsic value is nonnegative and an option value can be partitioned into its intrinsic value and time-value components, a decrease in the intrinsic value would lead to a decrease in the option premium, as illustrated in Exhibit 91. The effect of RV on the other types of options can be similarly intuited.

Exhibit 93 shows the difference in premiums between a modified lookback call option with continuous sampling frequency, a modified lookback call option with discrete sampling frequency, and a vanilla call option when the strikes and the times to maturity of the options are identical.

EXHIBIT 93 Effect of Sampling on Category IV Lookback Call Option Premiums

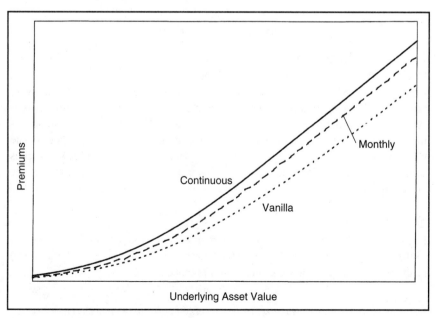

Due to the similarity in the payoff profile, a lookback option can be alternatively viewed as some of the options discussed earlier in this chapter. Take, for example, the Category III and Category IV lookback options, which can alternatively be viewed as an extrema option that was discussed in Exhibits 72 and 73. As with the similarity between an arithmetic average option and a basket option, a similar relation exists between an extrema option and a modified lookback option. As the reader may recall, an extrema option is an option whose underlying asset could either be the maximum or the minimum of n correlated assets, whereas a modified lookback option is an option whose underlying asset could be the maximum or the minimum value realized by one asset during the life of the option. While the correlation in an extrema option as in the basket option can only be historically calculated, the correlation as in the average rate option can many times be implicitly calculated for the lookback option.

The reader should realize that, if only the option maturity date were sampled, both the Category III and Category IV lookback options become vanilla options. In addition, if the sampling were done only on the contract inception date, both the Category I and II lookback options would become vanilla options struck at RV. Furthermore, as long as the asset value on the option maturity date is not sampled for a Category I and Category II lookback option, these options can also be alternatively viewed as a deferred strike option, where the strike value is set using the maximum and minimum function.[56]

The risk associated with a lookback option can be easily managed using delta hedging. Like any other exotic option, the risk can also be alternatively managed by appropriately replicating the payoffs using European-style vanilla options.

Other Applications

Liability Management

Based on the current yield curve, the three-year swap rate starting six months from now is 6.5 percent, which is higher than the current three-year spot swap rate of 4.73 percent. Suppose that a client who wants to pay fix in a three-year swap thinks that the realized three-year swap rate in six months is going to be less than 4.73 percent. To monetize her view, she could get into a swap whereby she would receive on each coupon date a floating rate of the six-month LIBOR plus some spread and pay a fixed rate on the swap that will be the maximum of the current three-year swap rate and the three-year swap rate realized in six months.

Shout Options

Regardless of the option category, the purchaser of a lookback option receives an in-the-money payoff that is linked to the extremum (i.e., maximum or minimum) of the n asset values that are sampled at n prespecified times. A lookback option

---

[56] Z, in the context of the deferred strike function, is either the maxima or the minima function.

can alternatively be thought of as an option that would allow the purchaser the ability to choose at most n values from the asset values prevailing on each of the n prespecified dates "as they occur" so that the extremum can be calculated on the option expiry date using these n selected values. The words as they occur should emphasize to the reader that every time an asset value is sampled, the purchaser has to make a decision about accepting the value, knowing fully well that any rejected value cannot be accepted at a later time. Since the purchaser can choose every presented value from each of the n prespecified dates and still not violate the condition of choosing at most n values, the rational purchaser would select all the n asset values from which the extremum would be calculated.[57]

Clearly, by keeping the number of prespecified dates unchanged and reducing the number of available choices to the purchaser from n to n* where n > n*, the purchaser's decision is no longer as trivial as when he had n choices. This follows from the fact that because the purchaser does not have the luxury of accepting all the n presented values, he has to optimally allocate his n*choices so as to maximize (minimize) the expected maximum (minimum) value calculated on the option expiry date using his accepted values. Since the purchaser is only allowed at most n* choices, the maximum (minimum) value calculated on the option expiry date using these selected values will never be greater (smaller) than those calculated using the n selected values. The intuition underlying this statement is no different from that presented on page 158.

In particular, when n* = 2 and one of the accepted values must be the asset value on the option maturity date, a lookback option becomes a shout option. More precisely, the four categories of lookback options presented in Exhibit 84 now collapses to the four categories of shout options. Furthermore, using the reason given earlier, one can conclude that while Category I and III call lookback options and Category II and IV put lookback options will be more expensive than Category I and III call shout options and Category II and IV put shout options, respectively, Category I and III put lookback options and Category II and IV call lookback options will be cheaper than Category I and III put shout options and Category II and IV call shout options, respectively.

In practice, although the purchaser of a shout option has the ability to make at most two selections (the first being the optional one that is done anytime prior to the option maturity and the second being the compulsory one that is done on the option maturity date), it is possible that the purchaser may not be able to make his first selection due to market conditions. If this happens, the extreme value is calculated using only the asset value on the option maturity date, resulting in the extreme value being this asset value.

To illustrate, consider Category III call lookback and shout options. Based on our earlier discussions, one would expect the lookback option to be more expensive than the shout option. Furthermore, if no shouting is done during the life

---

[57] The selection problem described above is an offshoot of the recreational secretary problem discussed in Rose (1982), Ferguson (1989), and Ravindran (1993a).

of the option, as mentioned earlier, the maximum value is calculated using only the asset value on the option maturity date, making the shout call option a vanilla call option. Consequently, it would be intuitively reasonable to expect the premium for this type of shout option to be no less than that of a structurally similar vanilla option. This observation is demonstrated in Exhibit 94, which illustrates the difference in premiums between a vanilla call option and Category II call lookback and shout options when the strike values and option maturity times are identical.

EXHIBIT 94   European-Style Call Option Premiums

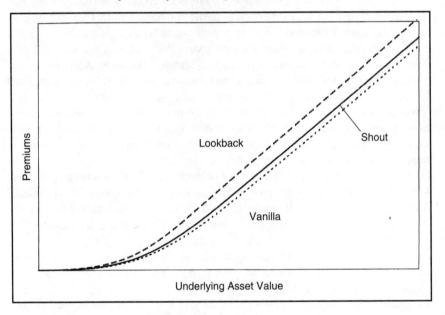

The sequence of events in Example 21 on page 163 illustrates the mechanics underlying a shout option transaction.

It is important for the reader to make the following three observations about Example 21.

OBSERVATION 1   It can be seen from Example 21 that when the hedger did not shout, the option expired worthless. This stems from the convention that with no shouting, the minimum of the asset value at the time of shout and at the option maturity is set to the value of the asset at option maturity. On the other hand, if the hedger had shouted at a level that proved to be the strongest realized level of the Canadian dollar during the life of the option, the payoff to the hedger would be similar to that of a look-back option.

EXAMPLE 21   A European-Style Shout Option Transaction

The Canadian dollar is currently trading at 1.3850 Cad/US. Due to an expected currency exposure in two months, a treasurer wants to be protected against a weakening Canadian dollar. Based on the current market conditions and his views that the Canadian dollar will get stronger, he feels he is better off using the spot market in two months. In order to monetize his view, he inquires about the purchase of a two-month Category I look-back call option on the U.S. dollar and finds that the cost is Cad$ 0.97 mm on a notional amount of US$ 50 mm, which is prohibitive.

Because of his confidence in his market-calling abilities, he is not prepared to pay a high premium for such an option. To lower the cost and incorporate his market-calling abilities, he purchases a two-month European-style shout call option on the U.S. dollar for Cad$ 0.47 mm on the same notional amount, with which he could potentially achieve the same payoff as the look-back option. The purchase of this option would allow him to shout (select) at 12 noon on any business day.

Time (months)	Exchange Rate (US/£)	Impact of Option on the Hedger
0	1.3850	☛ Cad$ 0.47 mm premium paid by hedger
Case 1: Hedger Shouts at the End of 1 Month		
1	1.3750	☛ Strongest showing of the Canadian dollar in the last month ☛ Hedger shouts at this level
2	**Case 1A: Call Option Is Exercised at the End of 2 Months**	
	1.3870	☛ Payoff of Cad$ [50 • (1.3870 − min(1.3870,1.3750))] = Cad$ 0.6 mm paid to hedger ☛ Cad$ 0.47 mm of premium and Cad$ 0.003 mm of interest on this premium foregone by hedger ☛ Profit to hedger: Cad$ [0.6 − (0.47 + 0.003)] = Cad$ 0.127 mm
	Case 1B: Call Option Is Not Exercised at the End of 2 Months	
	1.3700	☛ Cad$ 0.47 mm of premium and Cad$ 0.003 mm of interest on this premium foregone by hedger

EXAMPLE 21   A European-Style Shout Option (Continued)

		☛ Profit to hedger: –Cad$ (0.47 + 0.003) = –Cad$ 0.473 mm

Case 2: Hedger Does Not Shout in the 2-Month Period		
2	1.3870	☛ Cad$ 0.47 mm of premium and Cad$ 0.003 mm of interest on this premium foregone by hedger ☛ Profit to hedger: –Cad$ (0.47 + 0.003) = –Cad$ 0.473 mm

OBSERVATION 2   Although the purchaser has the ability to shout daily, it would be intuitively reasonable to expect the buyer to shout at any time during the life of the option, only if the expected value of the option obtained by shouting is greater than the expected value of the option obtained without shouting. As the reader will realize, this type of rational behavior is analogous to the exercising of a vanilla American-style or Mid-Atlantic-style option that was discussed in the previous chapter.[58]

OBSERVATION 3   As seen in Example 21, the purchaser of the shout option had the opportunity to shout on any business day at 12 noon. Depending on the type of risks managed, nothing prohibits the purchaser of the option from wanting to have the ability to shout only once a week or once every two weeks. Because of this, it should be obvious to the reader that, like the lookback option, the price of a shout option is directly proportional to the frequency of shouting.

THE NONLINEAR PAYOFF OPTION CONTRACT

Introduction

As is well known, a vanilla option has a linear payoff when the option finishes in-the-money. More precisely, if S_T represents the value of the asset on the option maturity date and X represents the strike value of the option, ignoring the option premium paid at the inception of the contract, the purchaser of a European-style vanilla call (put) option would receive a payoff of $S_T - X$ $(X - S_T)$ when the op-

---

[58] Thomas (1993) uses this philosophy to value a shout option with the aid of a binomial tree.

EXHIBIT 95   Nonlinear Call Option In-the-Money Payoffs

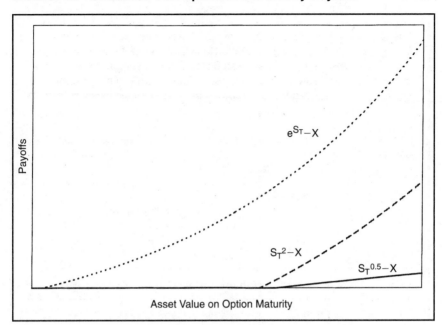

tion goes in-the-money. Thus, the in-the-money payoff is a linear function of the asset value at the time of exercise.

By the same token, a European-style nonlinear payoff option has an in-the-money payoff that is a nonlinear function of the value of the asset at the time of exercise. Some examples of these in-the-money payoffs on the option maturity date, which have been illustrated in Exhibit 95, are $e^{S_T} - X$, $S_T^2 - X$, $S_T^{0.5} - X$.

Nonlinear payoff options that have payoffs where S_T appears as a base rather than a power (e.g., $S_T^2 - X$ and $S_T^{0.5} - X$) are also called power or turbo options. The following example, although applied to a power option, can be easily modified for any nonlinear payoff option.

A Nonlinear Payoff Option Contract Example

The sequence of events in Example 22 on page 166 illustrates the nature of a non-linear payoff option transaction.

It is important for the reader to make the following three observations about Example 22.

OBSERVATION 1 Neglecting the premiums paid out for the options at the inception of the contract, if the investor had bought a vanilla call option instead, the in-the-money payoff to the investor would have been *Cad*$ [30 • (1.3900 − 1.3800)] = *Cad*$

EXAMPLE 22   A European-Style Nonlinear Payoff Option Transaction

The U.S. dollar is currently trading at 1.3850 Cad/US and the one-week forward is trading at a level of 1.3900 Cad/US. A hedge fund manager feels that in one week, the Canadian dollar is never going to be weaker than the 1.3900 Cad/US level. Because of the certainty in his view, he wants to take a leveraged view, knowing up-front what his loss would be if his view turns out to be wrong.

To monetize his view effectively, he purchases a one-week power put option on the U.S. dollar that is struck at a level 1.3900^2 on a notional amount of US\$ 30 mm for Cad\$ 0.54 mm.

Time (weeks)	Exchange Rate (Cad/US)	Impact of Option on the Investor
0	1.3850	☞ Cad\$ 0.54 mm premium paid by investor
1	*Case A: Call Option Is Exercised at the End of 1 Week*	
	1.3800	☞ Payoff of Cad\$ [30 • $(1.3900^2 - 1.3800^2)$] = Cad\$ 0.831 mm paid to investor ☞ Cad\$ 0.54 mm of premium and Cad\$ 0.001 mm of interest on this premium foregone by investor ☞ Profit to investor: Cad\$ [0.831 − (0.54 + 0.0001)] = Cad\$ 0.2909 mm
	Case B: Call Option Is Not Exercised at the End of 1 Week	
	1.3950	☞ Cad\$ 0.54 mm of premium and Cad\$ 0.001 mm of interest on this premium foregone by investor ☞ Profit to investor: −Cad\$ (0.54 + 0.001) = − Cad\$ 0.5401 mm

0.3 mm, which is only approximately 36 percent of the in-the-money payoff obtained from the purchase of the power option. It is important for the reader to observe that this percentage will increase as long as the U.S. dollar weakens further from a level of 1.3800 Cad/US. It should be obvious to the reader that the fact that the option in the example offers a higher payoff than a vanilla option implies that the power option is going to be more expensive than the vanilla option. In the context of the example, a vanilla call option that is struck at 1.3900 Cad/US would cost about 35 percent of a power option.

OBSERVATION 2 The investor purchased a power put option on the U.S. dollar. Depending on the risk appetite of the investor, the investor could have alternatively purchased an option whose in-the-money payoff could either be more leveraged in the form of $1.3900^4 - S_T^4$ or less leveraged in the form of $1.3900^{0.5} - S_T^{0.5}$.

OBSERVATION 3 It may be tempting to argue that instead of purchasing the power put option, the investor could have just as well purchased a vanilla put option on a higher notional amount. However, simply increasing the notional amount of the entire option contract does not necessarily have the same effect as a power option. As shown in Exhibit 96, the scaling of the notional amount on the vanilla option contract does not allow the curvature inherent in the power option payoff to be captured; making the vanilla option a poor instrument when it comes to monetizing this view.

EXHIBIT 96 European-Style Option In-the-Money Payoffs

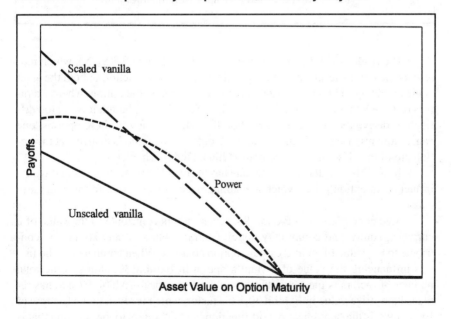

Characteristics of Nonlinear Payoff Option Contracts

Although the discussion thus far has been centered around power options, a power option as mentioned in the beginning of this section is just an example of a nonlinear payoff option. The profit profile associated with the purchase of these nonlinear payoff options can be more generally written, as detailed in Exhibit 97.

EXHIBIT 97   Profits to the Buyer of a European-Style Nonlinear Payoff Option

Type of Nonlinear Payoff Option	Profit at Expiry Time T
$O_E(0,T,X)$	$\max[-P^*_{T,O}, f(S_T,X) - P^*_{T,O}]$

where

$$0 = \text{Current time or time today}$$
$$T = \text{Time of option maturity}$$
$$S_T = \text{Asset value on option maturity}$$
$$X = \text{Strike value of option}$$
$$f(S_T,X) = \text{In-the-money nonlinear payoff function}$$
$O_E(0,T,X) = $ European nonlinear payoff option purchased at time 0 with parameters T, X
$P^*_{T,O} = $ Amount foregone by purchaser of option due to premium and the interest accrued until time T on this premium

The reader should note that in Exhibit 97, the function $f(S_T,X)$, which represents the nonlinear in-the-money payoff function, is a function of both the asset value on the option maturity date and the strike value of the option; where examples of $f(S_T,X)$ include $e^{S_T} - X$, $X^3 - S_T^3$, $(S_T - X)^2$. Although it is not too difficult to derive the closed-form solution for valuing many of these options, one can, as always, use the binomial and the Monte Carlo methods to arrive at the option premiums. Use of these methods is illustrated in Chapter 4.

To be able to value an option, one has to first identify the factors that would influence an option price, which are summarized in Exhibit 98 for all four asset classes.

As can be seen from Exhibit 98, seven factors contribute to the value of a currency, equity, and commodity option contract, whereas only six factors contribute to the value of an interest-rate option contract. When compared to the factors influencing the value of a vanilla option in Exhibit 30, although the total number of factors is the same, there is one new factor in Exhibit 97 that has replaced the strike value in Exhibit 30. This factor, which is given in the last row of Exhibit 98, is the "nonlinear payoff function," which refers to the function that is

**EXHIBIT 98   Factors Influencing the Value of a Nonlinear Payoff
Option Contract**

Factors	Interest-Rate Option	Currency Option	Equity Option	Commodity Option
Convenience yield				✔
Dividend rate			✔	
Foreign risk-free rate		✔		
Domestic risk-free rate	✔	✔	✔	✔
Underlying asset value	✔	✔	✔	✔
Volatility of asset value	✔	✔	✔	✔
Frequency of exercise	✔	✔	✔	✔
Life of contract	✔	✔	✔	✔
Nonlinear payoff function	✔	✔	✔	✔

used to determine the in-the-money payoff, which also includes the strike level of the option.

To understand how the above-mentioned factors influence the value of an option contract, one has to first derive a no-arbitrage relationship between the option contract and the asset underlying the option contract. The effects of these factors are summarized in Exhibit 99.

Since nearly all the factors are the same as those in Exhibit 31, it is tempting to say that one could easily use these effects to intuit the results in Exhibit 99. While the effects of σ and ef are obvious, as with the deferred strike option it is

**EXHIBIT 99   Effect of Increase
in Value of
Underlying
Factors on
Nonlinear Payoff
Option Premium**

Factors	Type of Contracts
r_f	$\Updownarrow$
r_d	$\Updownarrow$
S_0	$\Updownarrow$
σ	$\Uparrow$
ef	$\Uparrow$
T	$\Updownarrow$
$f(S_T, X)$	$\Updownarrow$

difficult to pinpoint accurately the effects of the other factors on a nonlinear pay-off option without knowing the form of $f(S_T,X)$, the in-the-money payoff.

The risk-management of a nonlinear payoff option is tricky in the sense that unlike a vanilla option, delta hedging the sale of a nonlinear payoff option may be costly. This can be intuited by observing that the leveraging that is inherent in a nonlinear payoff option results in the option having a high gamma risk profile. As any trader would appreciate, provided this effect of gamma is favorable (that is, the position makes money as long as there is a move in the market), a high gamma can be trader's nightmare. The route of delta-hedging can therefore be avoided altogether if the hedger instead hedges a nonlinear payoff option using vanilla options just as the cash-or-nothing option was replicated using vanilla options. This can be illustrated by considering the sale of a call option whose non-linear payoff is of the form $(S_T - X)^2$, that is, a power option.

As shown in Exhibit 100, the curvilinear profit profile to the buyer of this type of option can be replicated by buying a number of call options struck at X and an additional number of call options struck at X_1. Like the replication of the cash-or-nothing options, since the number of call option contracts purchased at strikes X and X_1 would depend on the settlement process of the asset underlying the option, for the purposes of this illustration it will be assumed that the asset underlying the option is the price of an ounce of gold.

Assuming that the seller of the nonlinear payoff option replicates the hedge by purchasing N_1 call option contracts struck at X and N_2 call option contracts struck at X_1, the associated profit profiles are summarized in Exhibit 101.

EXHIBIT 100   Call Power Option Buyer's Profit at Maturity

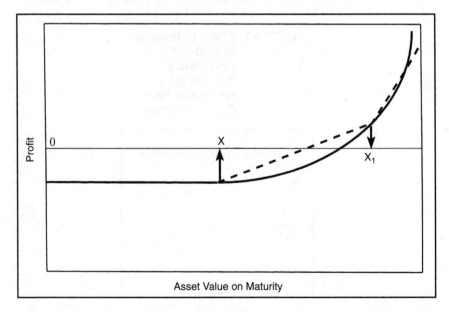

EXHIBIT 101 Replicating a Power Call Option with Vanilla Call Options in a Commodity Framework

Spot Gold Price Interval	Profit To Purchaser of Power Option	Profit to Purchaser of Vanilla Options		
		Buy N of $C_E(0,T,X)$	Buy N_1 of $C_E(0,T_1,X_1)$	Net Profit
$0 - X$	$-P^*_{T,C1}$	$-N \cdot P^*_{T,C2}$	$-N_1 \cdot P^*_{T,C3}$	$-[(N \cdot P^*_{T,C2}) + (N_1 \cdot P^*_{T,C3})]$
$X - X_1$	$(S_T - X)^2 - P^*_{T,C1}$	$N \cdot [S_T - X - P^*_{T,C2}]$	$-N_1 \cdot P^*_{T,C3}$	$[N \cdot (S_T - X - P^*_{T,C2})] - (N_1 \cdot P^*_{T,C3})$
$X_1 - \infty$	$(S_T - X)^2 - P^*_{T,C1}$	$N \cdot [S_T - X - P^*_{T,C2}]$	$N_1 \cdot [S_T - X_1 - P^*_{T,C3}]$	$[N \cdot (S_T - X - P^*_{T,C2})] + [N_1 \cdot (S_T - X_1 - P^*_{T,C3})]$

It is important for the reader to note that in replicating the profit profile of a cash-or-nothing option with a bull spread in Exhibits 65 and 66, I matched the profit profiles of the two strategies with each other in all the three price intervals $0 - X, X - X_1$, and $X_1 - \infty$. Unlike the cash-or-nothing option, due to the curvilinear nature of the profit profile of a power option, as shown in Exhibit 100, it is not possible to replicate the profit profiles in each of the price intervals $0 - X, X - X_1$, and $X_1 - \infty$. Consequently, one has to resort to matching the profit profiles when the price of the gold is X and X_1. At these prices, the profit profile can be rewritten, as summarized in Exhibit 102.

By equating the profit profile of the power option with that of the net profit from the vanilla option for each price of gold (that is, X and X_1), one can arrive at the following expressions for N and N_1 once the value of X_1 is known:

$$N = X_1 - X$$

$$N_1 = \frac{P^*_{T,C1} - (N \bullet P^*_{T,C2})}{P^*_{T,C3}}$$

It is important for the reader to note that as long as any one of N, N_1, and X_1 is known, the remaining two variables can be easily solved for using the above equations.[59] Furthermore, this hedging strategy can be fine-tuned by adding more strike levels and going through a similar analysis to determine the appropriate notional amount of call option contracts that need to be purchased. As would be expected, by buying the appropriate number of vanilla call options at infinite distinct strike-price levels, one would be able to exactly replicate the profit profile of a power option. Furthermore, this would be analogous to the buying and the selling of infinite call options at the appropriate strike levels to perfectly replicate a cash-or-nothing option. This type of hedging strategy can also be effectively employed to hedge other types of curvilinear profit-profile options.

Other Applications

Although the discussion so far has been based on the use of power options for monetizing views on markets, nonlinear payoff options can also be very effectively used for liability or risk management. The following example, which is by no means exhaustive, illustrates such a use of a nonlinear payoff option.

Application Any insurance company typically has its assets and liabilities in its portfolios behaving in a manner such that as interest rates rise, the total value of the assets decreases more quickly than that of the liabilities, and when interest rates fall, the total value of the assets increases more slowly than that of the liabilities. This phenomena is

---

[59] Like the cash-or-nothing option, the values for N, N_1, and X_1 are dependent on the settlement process of the asset underlying the option.

EXHIBIT 102 Replicating a Power Call Option with Vanilla Call Options at Specified Prices

Spot Gold Price	Profit to Purchaser of Power Option	Profit to Purchaser of Vanilla Options		
		Buy N of $C_E(0,T,X)$	Buy N_1 of $C_E(0,T,X_1)$	Net Profit
X	$-P^*_{T,C1}$	$-N \cdot P^*_{T,C2}$	$-N_1 \cdot P^*_{T,C3}$	$-[(N \cdot P^*_{T,C2}) + (N_1 \cdot P^*_{T,C3})]$
X_1	$(X_1 - X)^2 - P^*_{T,C1}$	$N \cdot [X_1 - X - P^*_{T,C2}]$	$-N_1 \cdot P^*_{T,C3}$	$[N \cdot (X_1 - X - P^*_{T,C2})] - (N_1 \cdot P^*_{T,C3})$

often caused by a convexity mismatch arising from the short-dated assets and long-dated liabilities and can be corrected using a non-linear payoff option. More precisely, the insurance company would run a scenario analysis of interest rates to see where these mismatches occur and determine the boundaries within which these risks would be tolerable. Once the intolerable risk in dollar amount is quantified for each scenario, an interest-rate option can then be customized such that it compensates the purchaser the appropriate quantified amount once a scenario is realized. Purchasing this type of hedge would usually be more effective than simply purchasing and/or selling vanilla options to arrive at the required convexity adjustments.

THE PRODUCT OPTION CONTRACT

Introduction

A Canadian investor observes the current five-year Government of Canada (GOC) bond yield and the current five-year U.S. Treasury bond yield to be 5.53 percent and 5.10 percent, respectively. Based on the historical data, the investor notices that the current spread between these yields is relatively small compared to the historical values of this difference, which she feels will widen in a week. To monetize her view, she wants to buy an instrument to achieve her objective without being exposed to the currency risk. More precisely, she wants her payoff to strictly be the product of the notional amount of the contract and the difference in the bond yields if she is right. The instrument she actually needs is called a quanto-spread option.[60] To understand a quanto-spread option better, we will first discuss a simple quanto option.

A quanto option, also known as a guaranteed exchange-rate option, is a member of the product option family that allows the buyer to pay an initial upfront premium in domestic currency for an option that trades in a foreign country and to receive the payoff at a guaranteed exchange rate.

A Product Option Contract Example

The sequence of events in Example 23 on page 175 illustrates the nature of a product option transaction.

It is important for the reader to make the following three observations about Example 23.

---

[60] This definition of a quanto is a loose one that is used to describe this type of instrument. A more precise definition of quanto is given in the Glossary.

EXAMPLE 23   A European-Style Product Option Transaction

The current five-year U.S. Treasury forward yield is trading at 7.01 percent. A Canadian fund manager has a view that the five-year spot bond yield will definitely be higher than 7.10 percent in a week. To monetize her view, she wants to buy an option that will pay her the difference between the five-year bond yield in a week and 7.10 percent if she is right. However, she wants to pay the premium and receive her payoff in Canadian funds, if the option is in-the-money, and does not want to be exposed to the currency risk.

To monetize her view effectively, she purchases a one-week product call option on the bond yield that is struck at a level 7.10 percent on a notional amount of Cad$ 100 mm for Cad$ 0.043 mm.

Time (weeks)	Bond Yield (%)	Impact of Option on the Investor
0	6.95	☛ Cad$ 0.043 mm premium paid by investor
1	*Case A: Call Option Is Exercised at the End of 1 Week*	
	7.15	☛ Payoff of Cad$ [100 • (0.0715 − 0.0710)] = Cad$ 0.05 mm paid to investor ☛ Cad$ 0.043 mm of premium and Cad$ 0.001 mm of interest on this premium foregone by investor ☛ Profit to investor: Cad$ [0.05 − (0.043 + 0.0001)] = Cad$ 0.0069 mm
	Case B: Call Option Is Not Exercised at the End of 1 Week	
	7.00	☛ Cad$ 0.043 mm of premium and Cad$ 0.0001 mm of interest on this premium foregone by investor ☛ Profit to investor: −Cad$ (0.043 + 0.0001) = −Cad$ 0.0431 mm

OBSERVATION 1 Although the investor did not have to undergo any currency exposure, she had implicitly bought an option guaranteeing her an exchange rate of 1 Cad/US. Depending on the type of view of the investor, she could have just as easily structured an instrument where she would receive an in-the-money payoff at any other guaranteed exchange rate (for example, 2 Cad/US) or the exchange rate prevailing on the option maturity date.

OBSERVATION 2 Instead of being paid Cad$ 10,000 for every basis point the option finishes in-the-money, the investor could have alternatively purchased an option whose settlement was dependent on the bond price. More precisely, if the current yield of 7.10 percent corresponds to a price of US$ 102.125 for a par bond, and a yield of 7.15 percent one week later corresponds to a price of US$ 101.875 for the same bond, then the in-the-money payoff received by the investor would be *Cad*$ (102.125 − 101.875) per par bond.

Although, philosophically, a price-based option seems to achieve the objective of a yield-based option, there is still one fundamental difference. This difference arises from the fact that a yield-based option does not have the effect of the duration of the bonds, unlike that of a price-based option.[61]

OBSERVATION 3 In Example 23, as mentioned in Observation 1, the option's payoff is linked to the product of two assets: The first is the U.S. Treasury yield, and the second is the guaranteed exchange rate of 1 Cad/US. Depending on the type of risks managed, it is possible for the investor to purchase an option whose underlying asset is created by multiplying three or more assets. To illustrate, consider an example where an asset is created by multiplying three assets, in which a Canadian investor has a view on the Singapore Straits Times Index and would like to monetize his view in Canadian funds. Since the Straits Times Index trades in Singapore dollars and there is virtually no market for Cad/Sgd dollar, the payoff has to be first translated to U.S. dollars using the US/Sgd exchange rate and then converted to Canadian dollars using the Cad/US exchange rate. Thus, the asset is created by multiplying the foreign asset value with two other currency assets so as to denominate the payoff in the domestic currency.

Characteristics of Product Option Contracts

Although the discussion thus far has been centered around quanto options, quanto options only form a subset of the product options family. The profit profile associated with the purchase of these product options is summarized in Exhibit 103 and graphed in Exhibits 104, 105, 106, 107, 108, 109, 110, and 111.

---

[61] See also footnote 4 on the effect of a bond life on its dollar duration.

EXHIBIT 103 Profits to the Buyer of a European-Style Product Option

Type of Product Option	Profit at Expiry Time T
$C_{E,I}(0,T,X)$	$\max[-P^*_{T,CI},(S_T - X)F_T - P^*_{T,CI}]$
$P_{E,I}(0,T,X)$	$\max[-P^*_{T,PI},(X - S_T)F_T - P^*_{T,PI}]$
$C_{E,II}(0,T,X,\hat{F})$	$\max[-P^*_{T,CII},(S_T - X)\hat{F} - P^*_{T,CII}]$
$P_{E,II}(0,T,X,\hat{F})$	$\max[-P^*_{T,PII},(X - S_T)\hat{F} - P^*_{T,PII}]$
$C_{E,III}(0,T,X,\hat{F})$	$\max[-P^*_{T,CIII},S_T\hat{F} - XF_T - P^*_{T,CIII}]$
$P_{E,III}(0,T,X,\hat{F})$	$\max[-P^*_{T,PIII},XF_T - S_T\hat{F} - P^*_{T,PIII}]$
$C_{E,IV}(0,T,X,\hat{F})$	$\max[-P^*_{T,CIV},S_TF_T - X\hat{F} - P^*_{T,CIV}]$
$P_{E,IV}(0,T,X,\hat{F})$	$\max[-P^*_{T,PIV},X\hat{F} - S_TF_T - P^*_{T,PIV}]$
$C_{E,V}(0,T,K)$	$\max[-P^*_{T,CV},(F_T - K)S_T - P^*_{T,CV}]$
$P_{E,V}(0,T,K)$	$\max[-P^*_{T,PV},(K - F_T)S_T - P^*_{T,PV}]$

where

0 = Current time or time today

T = Time of option maturity

S_T = Foreign asset value on option maturity

F_T = Exchange-rate value (in domestic/foreign units) on option maturity

$\hat{F}$ = Guaranteed exchange-rate value (in domestic/foreign units)

X = Strike value of option in foreign currency

K = Strike rate of option (in domestic/foreign units)

$C_{E,I}(0,T,X)$ = European Category I product call option purchased at time 0 with parameters T and X

$P_{E,I}(0,T,X)$ = European Category I product put option purchased at time 0 with parameters T and X

$C_{E,i}(0,T,X,\hat{F})$ = European Category i product call option purchased at time 0 with parameters T, and X, and $\hat{F}$, where i = II, III, and IV

$P_{E,i}(0,T,X,\hat{F})$ = European Category i product put option purchased at time 0 with parameters T, and X, and $\hat{F}$, where i = II, III, and IV

$C_{E,V}(0,T,K)$ = European Category V product call option purchased at time 0 with parameters T and K

$P_{E,V}(0,T,K)$ = European Category V product put option purchased at time 0 with parameters T and K

$P^*_{T,Ci}$ = Amount foregone by purchaser of call option Category i due to premium and the interest accrued until time T on this premium, where i = I, II, . . ., V

$P^*_{T,Pi}$ = Amount foregone by purchaser of put option Category i due to premium and the interest accrued until time T on this premium, where i = I, ii, . . ., V

**EXHIBIT 104   Category I & II Product Call Option Buyer's Profit
at Maturity**

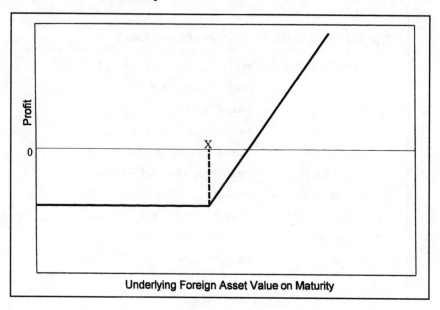

Underlying Foreign Asset Value on Maturity

**EXHIBIT 105   Category I & II Product Put Option Buyer's Profit
at Maturity**

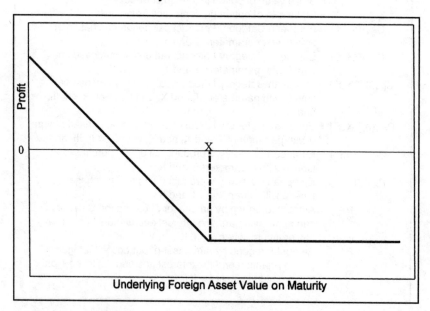

Underlying Foreign Asset Value on Maturity

**EXHIBIT 106 Category III Product Call Option Buyer's Profit
at Maturity**

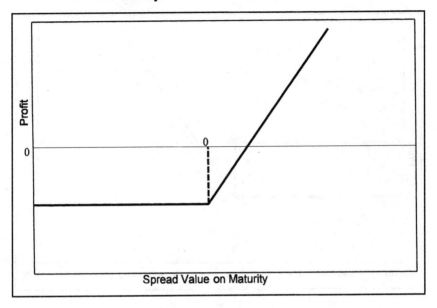

**EXHIBIT 107 Category III Product Put Option Buyer's Profit
at Maturity**

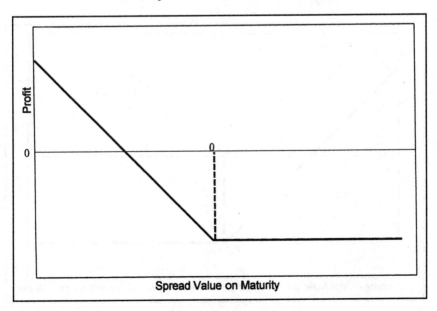

**EXHIBIT 108   Category IV Product Call Option Buyer's Profit
at Maturity**

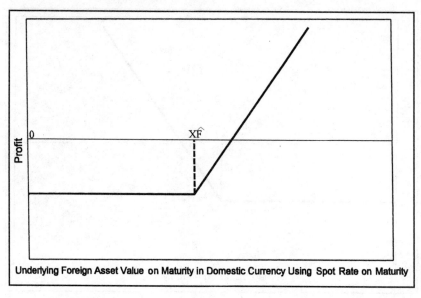

**EXHIBIT 109   Category IV Product Put Option Buyer's Profit
at Maturity**

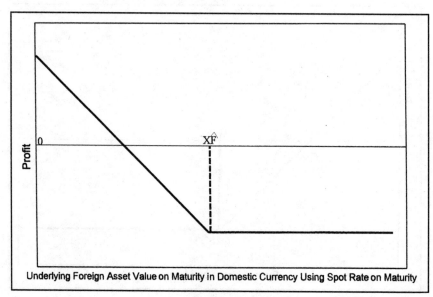

EXHIBIT 110 Category V Product Call Option Buyer's Profit at Maturity

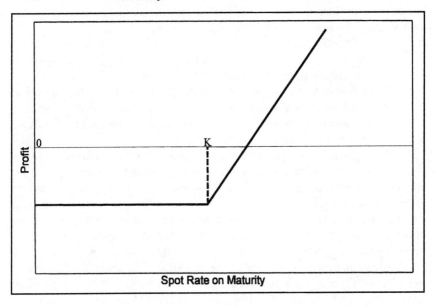

EXHIBIT 111 Category V Product Put Option Buyer's Profit at Maturity

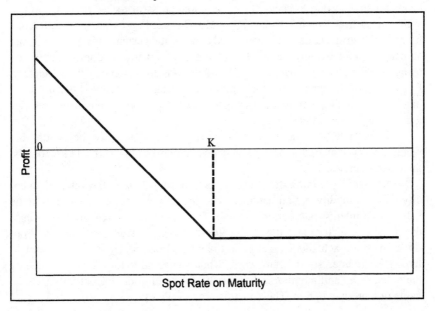

Since I used the term *product* to describe the options in this building block, the reader should obviously expect some sort of multiplication between underlying assets in the option payoff. From Exhibit 103, the reader can observe that the two assets in this regard would be as follows:

1. The foreign asset.
2. The currency that is required to convert this foreign asset into a domestically denominated one.

It is important for the reader to understand that the multiplication of the foreign asset and its appropriate currency is just one example of a product. Depending on the views monetized or the risks managed, the product could also possibly involve two noncurrency-related assets.

Pricing product options can be tricky when one of the underlying assets is currency. To avoid arbitrage across different economies and receive a payout in the domestic currency, the center of the distribution of the foreign asset value may have to be readjusted. This readjustment would be a function of the volatilites of the underlying assets and the correlation between the returns on the assets. Once this readjustment is made, the technique used to price these options is no different from any regular option pricing technique. This is discussed in detail in Chapter 4.

Although both the European and the American-style product options can be priced using the binomial method once the center of the distribution of the future asset values is adjusted, Reiner (1992) and Wei (1996) have provided analytical expressions for pricing the product options illustrated in Exhibit 95. In addition to these methods, one can also use the binomial and the Monte Carlo methods to value these options.

Exhibits 104 and 105 illustrate the profit profile of the buyer of a Category I and II product option when the underlying foreign asset value is compared against a strike value to check the in-the-moneyness of these types of options. While the term *spread* in Exhibits 106 and 107 is used to represent the difference between the strike value that is converted to domestic currency using the spot rate at maturity and the foreign asset value at maturity converted to domestic currency using a guaranteed exchange rate, Exhibits 108 to 111 are self-explanatory. Regardless of the type of product option, the break-even analysis discussed on page 52 is crucial in determining whether this type of view-monetizing or hedging strategy is cost-effective.

To be able to value an option, we have to first identify the factors that would influence an option price, which are summarized in Exhibit 112 across the three asset classes.

As can be seen in Exhibit 112, 13 factors contribute to the value of an equity and commodity option contract, whereas only 12 factors contribute to the value of an interest-rate option contract. The reader should realize that because the strike rate factor plays the role of the strike value factor for Category V options, there are actually 12 factors in the equity/commodity framework and 11 factors in the interest-rate framework. When compared to the factors influencing the value of a vanilla option in Exhibit 30, four additional factors influence the value of a product option. These factors are as follows:

EXHIBIT 112   Factors Influencing the Value of a Product Option Contract[62]

Factors	Interest-Rate Option	Equity Option	Commodity Option
Convenience yield			✔
Dividend rate		✔	
Foreign risk-free rate	✔	✔	✔
Domestic risk-free rate	✔	✔	✔
Underlying asset value	✔	✔	✔
Strike value	✔	✔	✔
Strike rate[63]	✔	✔	✔
Volatility of asset value	✔	✔	✔
Frequency of exercise	✔	✔	✔
Life of contract	✔	✔	✔
Underlying exchange rate[64]	✔	✔	✔
Guaranteed exchange rate[65]	✔	✔	✔
Volatility of exchange rate	✔	✔	✔
Correlation between asset value and exchange rate	✔	✔	✔

[62] It is assumed that the factors underlying the product are (1) a foreign-denominated asset and (2) the currency that is required to convert the foreign denominated asset into a domestic denominated one. With this assumption, it is presumed that the foreign-denominated asset was either equity-linked, commodity-linked, or interest-rate-linked, which is often the case in the transactions executed in the financial marketplace. However, it is important for the reader to note that it is possible for both the underlying assets to be from the same asset class (e.g., currency-related).

[63] This factor is only related to the currency component and hence applicable only to Category V options.

[64] This factor is only applicable to Category I, III, IV, and V options.

[65] This factor is only applicable to Category II, III, and IV options.

1. **Underlying exchange rate** The second asset underlying the conversion of the foreign-denominated asset into a domestic-denominated one.
2. **Guaranteed exchange rate** The fixed exchange rate that is applied to convert a foreign-denominated asset into a domestic-denominated one.
3. **Volatility of exchange rate** Volatility of the exchange-rate.
4. **Correlation between asset value and exchange rate** Correlation between the continuously compounded returns of the underlying asset and the exchange rate.

To understand how the above-mentioned factors influence the value of an option contract, one has to first derive a no-aribitrage relationship between the option contract and the asset underlying the option contract. The effects of these factors are summarized in Exhibit 113.

While the effects of X, K, ef, and T are obvious and no different from those in Exhibits 31, the intuition underlying the effects of the remaining eight factors can be made by categorizing these factors into the following two groups:

1. Factors whose effects are obvious from the profit profiles given in Exhibit 103 and need no further knowledge of the distribution of the assets underlying the option. Examples of these factors are S_0, F_0, and $\hat{F}$.

   Take, for example, the Category IV put option. From the profit profile in Exhibit 103, it can be seen that increasing $\hat{F}$ leads to an increase in product of X and $\hat{F}$. Since the product X $\hat{F}$ is a constant that plays the role of a strike value, increasing the strike value of a put option results in the increase in the option premium; as shown in Exhibit 113. To intuit the effect of S_0 and F_0, it can be observed from Exhibit 113 that the product $S_T F_T$ can be thought of as a single asset. As long as the underlying value of this asset increases, the value of the put option decreases. Since this asset is comprised of multiplying two assets, the value of this asset can be increased by either an increase in the foreign denominated asset value or an increase in the exchange-rate value. Thus, an increase in either S_0 and F_0 leads to a decrease in the put option premiums, as shown in Exhibit 113. This approach can be easily applied to intuit the effects of the factors on the other category options.

2. Factors whose effects cannot be intuited by simply looking at the profit profiles in Exhibit 103 need the knowledge of the distribution of the assets underlying the option. Examples of these factors are r_f, q, r_d, σ_S, σ_F, and $\rho_{FX,S}$.

Before trying to intuit the effect of the underlying factors on the option premiums, it is important for the reader to realize that in order to value a product option, it can be shown that both the underlying currency F_T, and the underlying foreign asset S_T have the domestic risk-free rates, foreign risk-free/dividend rates, and volatilities, as summarized in Exhibit 114.

While the risk-free rate, dividend rate, and the volatility F_T of that is given in Exhibit 114 is no different from that discussed in Chapter 2, the same cannot be said about S_T. More precisely, although the risk-free rate and the volatility seem to be no different from that discussed in Chapter 2, the dividend rate that was shown in Chapter 2 to be q is drastically different from that given in Exhibit 114[66]. Furthermore, the reader should also realize that although S_T is a foreign asset, the risk-free rate associated with it is indeed a domestic risk-free rate. The rationale and the intuition for this and the fact that the dividend is not q is given in Chapter 4.

Once the risk-free rates, dividend rates, and volatilities of F_T and S_T are specified, one can arrive at the corresponding risk-free rate, dividend rate, and volatility for the product $F_T S_T$.[67]

Category I Options

To intuit the effect of the six factors, r_f, q, r_d, σ_S, σ_F, and $\rho_{FX,S}$ on the put option premium, one has to first rewrite the in-the-money payoff of the put option (X −

---

[66] More precisely, the dividend is of the form $q + (r_d - r_f + \rho_{FX,S}\sigma_S\sigma_F)$.

[67] This can be done using Relationship 8i in the Appendix.

EXHIBIT 113 Effect of Increase in Value of Underlying Factors on Product Option Premium

Factors	Type of Option Contracts									
	Category I		Category II		Category III		Category IV		Category V	
	Call	Put	Call	Put	Call	Put	Call	Put	Call	Put
r_f	⇑	⇓	⇑	⇓	⇑	⇓			⇓	⇑
q^{68}	⇓	⇑	⇓	⇑	⇓	⇑	⇓	⇑	⇓	⇓
r_d			⇓	⇓	⇓	⇑	⇑	⇓	⇑	⇓
S_0	⇑	⇓	⇑	⇓	⇑	⇓	⇑	⇓	⇑	⇑
X	⇓	⇑	⇓	⇑	⇓	⇑	⇓	⇑		
K									⇓	⇑
σ_S	⇑	⇑	⇕	⇕	⇕	⇕	⇕	⇕	⇕	⇕
ef	⇑	⇑	⇑	⇑	⇑	⇑	⇑	⇑	⇑	⇑
T	⇕	⇕	⇕	⇕	⇕	⇕	⇕	⇕	⇕	⇕
F_0^{69}	⇑	⇑			⇓	⇑	⇑	⇓	⇑	⇓
$\hat{F}$			⇑	⇑	⇑	⇓	⇓	⇑		
σ_F			⇕	⇕	⇕	⇕	⇕	⇕	⇕	⇕
$\rho_{FX,S}$			⇓	⇑	⇓	⇕	⇑ .	⇑	⇑	⇓

68 This factor is only applicable to the equity and commodity asset class.

69 Increase in both the underlying exchange rate and the guaranteed exchange rate implies that the foreign currency unit is getting stronger relative to the domestic currency unit. For example, suppose that the underlying foreign index trades in Canada and that the domestic country is the United States, then the currency would be denominated in US/Cad, and an example of increase in the exchange rate would imply currency trading from a level of 0.7550 US/Cad to a level of 0.7750 US/Cad.

$S_T)F_T$ as $XF_T - S_TF_T$. Since this in-the-money payoff is analogous to that of an option that allows S_TF_T to be exchanged for XF_T, once the distributional forms of both XF_T and S_TF_T are known, the results on Exhibit 38 can be used to intuit the summary given in Exhibit 113 for options from this category.

Exhibit 115 illustrates the fact that while XF_T can be thought of as a single asset that trades in the domestic country, grows at a risk-free rate r_d, pays a dividend rate of r_f, and has a volatility of σ_F, S_TF_T can be thought of as a single asset that trades in the domestic country, grows at a risk-free rate r_f, pays a dividend rate of q, and has a volatility of $\sqrt{\sigma_S^2 + 2\rho_{FX,S}\sigma_S\sigma_F + \sigma_F^2}$. Using the results in Exhibit 38, it can be shown that $XF_{T_{S_TF_T}}$, in Exhibit 115, represents asset XF_T in the environment of S_TF_T, which would grow at a risk-free rate of q, pay a dividend rate of r_f, and have a volatility of σ_S.[70] Since this is independent of r_d, $\rho_{FX,S}$,

---

70 The volatility of $XF_{T_{S_TF_T}}$ can be obtained by setting $\sigma_1 = \sigma_F$, $\sigma_2 = \sqrt{\sigma_S^2 + 2\rho_{FX,S}\sigma_S\sigma_F + \sigma_F^2}$ and

$$\rho_{1,2} = \frac{\sigma_F^2 + \rho_{FX,S}\sigma_S\sigma_F}{\sigma_F\sqrt{\sigma_S^2 + 2\rho_{FX,S}\sigma_S\sigma_F + \sigma_F^2}}.$$

EXHIBIT 114 Distributional Characteristics of F_T, S_T, and $S_T F_T$

Variables	Risk-Free Rate	Dividend Rate	Volatility
F_T	r_d	r_f	σ_F
S_T	r_d	$r_d - (r_f - \rho_{FX,S}\sigma_F\sigma_S - q)$	σ_S
$S_T F_T$	r_d	q	$\sqrt{\sigma_S^2 + 2\rho_{FX,S}\sigma_S\sigma_F + \sigma_F^2}$

EXHIBIT 115 Distributional Characteristics of Variables in Category I

Variables	Risk-Free Rate	Dividend Rate	Volatility
XF_T $S_T F_T$	r_d r_d	r_f q	σ_F $\sqrt{\sigma_S^2 + 2\rho_{FX,S}\sigma_S\sigma_F + \sigma_F^2}$
$XF_{T_{S_T F_T}}$	q	r_f	σ_S

and σ_F, these three factors do not affect the option premium, as summarized in Exhibit 113.

Furthermore, as discussed in the section on spread options, the in-the-money put option payoff of $XF_T - S_T F_T$ can be equivalently thought of as a call option on XF_T whose strike value is $S_T F_T$. While the increase in the dividend rate of r_f would lead to a decrease in the option premium, the increase in the risk-free rate of q and a volatility of σ_S would lead to an increase in the option premium. A similar form of reasoning can be used to arrive at the results in Exhibit 113 for the call option.

Category II Options

To intuit the effect of the six factors, r_f, q, r_d, σ_S, σ_F, and $\rho_{FX,S}$, on the put option premium, one has to first observe that $\hat{F}$ is a constant. Thus, the put option can be thought of as an option contract with an in-the-money payoff of $X - S_T$ on a notional amount of $\hat{F}$. Since this in-the-money payoff is analogous to that of a vanilla put option with an underlying asset of S_T and strike of X, once one knows the distributional form of S_T, one can easily use the results in Exhibit 31 to intuit the summary given in Exhibit 113 for options from this category.

Exhibit 116, which is extracted from Exhibit 114, illustrates the fact that S_T is a foreign asset that is going to be denominated to the domestic currency, which grows at a risk-free rate r_d, pays a dividend rate of $r_d - (r_f - \rho_{FX,S}\sigma_S\sigma_F - q)$, and has a volatility of σ_S. Since this is a single-asset put option, one can use the results of Exhibit 116 and Exhibit 31 to intuit the effects of r_f, r_d, q, σ_S, σ_F, and $\rho_{FX,S}$.

EXHIBIT 116 Distributional Characteristics of Variables in Category II

Variables	Risk-Free Rate	Dividend Rate	Volatility
S_T	r_d	$r_d - (r_f - \rho_{FX,S}\sigma_S\sigma_F - q)$	σ_S

Increasing r_f would lead to a decrease in the dividend rate, which in turn results in a decrease in the put option premium. On the other hand, since an increase in both q and $\rho_{FX,S}$ results in an increase in the dividend rate, increasing the values of these factors would lead to an increase in the put option premium. Unlike r_f, q, and $\rho_{FX,S}$, however, increasing r_d leads to both an increase in the risk-free rate and the dividend rate simultaneously. While the effects end up cancelling each other out, in present valuing the domestic currency-denominated option value from the option maturity date, one would end up using a higher value of r_d, which would lead to a reduction in the option premium.

The intuition underlying the effect of σ_S and σ_F is not as straightforward as the previous three factors in that the effect depends on whether $\rho_{FX,S}$ is positive or negative. More precisely, if $\rho_{FX,S}$ is positive, increasing either σ_S or σ_F would increase the put option premium since the value of the dividend rate $r_d - (r_f - \rho_{FX,S}\sigma_S\sigma_F - q)$ would be increased.

However, if $\rho_{FX,S}$ were negative, while increasing either σ_S or σ_F would decrease the dividend rate and hence the put option premium, increasing σ_S would also result in an increase in the option volatility and hence the option premium.

As a result, increasing either σ_S or σ_F may have mixed effects on the option premium, as summarized in Exhibit 113. The reader can similarly intuit the results for the call option.

Category III Options

To intuit the effect of the six factors on the put option premium, one has to first observe that the in-the-money payoff of the put option $XF_T - S_T\hat{F}$ is analogous to that of an option that allows $S_T\hat{F}$ to be exchanged for XF_T. As with the Category I options, once the distributional form of both XF_T and $S_T\hat{F}$ are known, one can easily use the results on Exhibit 38 to intuit the summary given in Exhibit 113 for options from this category.

As shown in Exhibit 117, which is a combination of Exhibits 115 and 116, $XF_{T_{S_T\hat{F}}}$ would grow at a risk-free rate of $r_d - (r_f - \rho_{FX,S}\sigma_S\sigma_F - q)$ a dividend rate of r_f and have a volatility of $\sqrt{\sigma_S^2 - 2\rho_{FX,S}\sigma_S\sigma_F + \sigma_F^2}$.[71] As with Category I, the in-the-money put option payoff of $XF_T - S_T\hat{F}$ can be equivalently thought of as a call option on XF_T whose strike value is $S_T\hat{F}$. Consequently, an increase in r_f leads to both an increase in the dividend rate and a decrease in the risk-free rate, both of which can only reduce the option premium. An increase in r_d or q, however, leads to an increase in the risk-free rate, which in turn increases the option premium.

The intuition underlying the effect of σ_S, σ_F and $\rho_{FX,S}$ is not as straightforward as the previous three factors in that the effect depends on whether $\rho_{FX,S}$ is positive or negative. More precisely, if $\rho_{FX,S}$ is positive, increasing either σ_S or

---

[71] The volatility of $XF_{T_{S_T\hat{F}}}$ can be obtained by setting $\sigma_1 = \sigma_F$, $\sigma_2 = \sigma_S$, and $\rho_{1,2} = \rho_{FX,S}$.

EXHIBIT 117 Distributional Characteristics of Variables in Category III

Variables	Risk-Free Rate	Dividend Rate	Volatility
XF_T	r_d	r_f	σ_F
$S_T\hat{F}$	r_d	$r_d - (r_f - \rho_{FX,S}\sigma_S\sigma_F - q)$	σ_S
$XF_{T_{S_T\hat{F}}}$	$r_d - (r_f - \rho_{FX,S}\sigma_S\sigma_F - q)$	r_f	$\sqrt{\sigma_S^2 - 2\rho_{FX,S}\sigma_S\sigma_F + \sigma_F^2}$

σ_F would increase the risk-free rate $r_d - (r_f - \rho_{FX,S}\sigma_S\sigma_F - q)$ and may increase the volatility $\sqrt{\sigma_S^2 - 2\rho_{FX,S}\sigma_S\sigma_F. + \sigma_F^2}$. However, if $\rho_{FX,S}$ is negative, increasing either σ_S or σ_F would decrease the risk-free rate while increasing the volatility, again resulting in a possible increase in the option premium. Furthermore, increasing $\rho_{FX,S}$ would, in addition to increasing the risk-free rate, result in a decrease in the option volatility, producing a possible increase in the option premium. Thus, increasing either σ_S, σ_F or $\rho_{FX,S}$ would result in a possible increase in the option premium, as summarized in Exhibit 113. The reader can similarly intuit the results for the call option.

Category IV Options

To intuit the effect of the six factors on the put option premium, it is necessary to know the distributional form of $S_T F_T$. Once this is known, one can easily use the results in Exhibit 31 to intuit the summary given in Exhibit 113 for options from this category when the payoff is of the form $X\hat{F} - S_T F_T$.

EXHIBIT 118 Distributional Characteristics of Variables in Category IV

Variables	Risk-Free Rate	Dividend Rate	Volatility
$S_T F_T$	r_d	q	$\sqrt{\sigma_S^2 + 2\rho_{FX,S}\sigma_S\sigma_F + \sigma_F^2}$

Exhibit 118, which is extracted from Exhibit 114, illustrates the fact that $S_T F_T$ is a foreign asset that is denominated to the domestic currency that grows at a risk-free rate r_d, pays a dividend rate of q, and has a volatility of $\sqrt{\sigma_S^2 + 2\rho_{FX,S}\sigma_S\sigma_F + \sigma_F^2}$. Since this is a single-asset put option, one can now use the results of Exhibit 118 and Exhibit 31 to intuit the effects of r_f, r_d, q, σ_S, σ_F, and $\rho_{FX,S}$.

The absence of r_f in Exhibit 118 indicates that this factor does not play any role in affecting the value of the put option premium. Increasing r_d would lead to an increase in the risk-free rate, which in turn results in a decrease in the put option premium. On the other hand, an increase in q results in an increase in the dividend rate, which can only cause the put option premium to increase. Futhermore, as an increase in $\rho_{FX,S}$ results in an increase in volatility, increasing $\rho_{FX,S}$ would lead to an increase in the put option premium.

The intuition underlying the effect of σ_S and σ_F is similar to the one presented for the Category III in that the effect depends on whether $\rho_{FX,S}$ is positive or negative. More precisely, if $\rho_{FX,S}$ is positive, increasing either σ_S or σ_F will increase the put option premium since the value of the volatility will be increased. However, if $\rho_{FX,S}$ is negative, increasing either σ_S or σ_F would result in a possible increase in the option volatility and hence the option premium. Consequently, increasing either σ_S or σ_F may have mixed effects on the option premium, as summarized in Exhibit 113. The reader can similarly intuit the results for the call option.

Category V Options

To intuit the effect of the six factors on the put option premium, as with Category I one has to first rewrite the in-the-money payoff $(K - F_T)S_T$ as $KS_T - S_TF_T$. Since this in-the-money payoff is analogous to that of an option that allows S_TF_T to be exchanged for KS_T, once the distributional forms of both KS_T and S_TF_T are known, one can easily use the results in Exhibit 38 to intuit the summary given in Exhibit 113.

EXHIBIT 119 Distributional Characteristics of Variables in Category V

Variables	Risk-Free Rate	Dividend Rate	Volatility
KS_T	r_d	$r_d - (r_f - \rho_{FX,S}\sigma_S\sigma_F - q)$	σ_S
S_TF_T	r_d	q	$\sqrt{\sigma_S^2 + 2\rho_{FX,S}\sigma_S\sigma_F + \sigma_F^2}$
$KS_{T_{S_TF_T}}$	q	$r_d - (r_f - \rho_{FX,S}\sigma_S\sigma_F - q)$	σ_F

As shown in Exhibit 119, using the results in Exhibit 38 it can be seen that $XS_{T_{S_TF_T}}$ grows at a risk-free rate of q, pays a dividend rate of $r_d - (r_f - \rho_{FX,S}\sigma_S\sigma_F - q)$, and has a volatility of σ_F.[72] As with Category I, the in-the-money put option payoff of $KS_T - S_TF_T$ can be equivalently thought of as a call option on KS_T whose strike value is S_TF_T. As a result, an increase in r_f leads to a decrease in the dividend rate, which in turn increases the option premium. An increase in either r_d or $\rho_{FX,S}$, however, leads to an increase in the dividend rate, which in turn decreases the option premium. Increasing q leads to both an increase in the risk-free rate and the dividend rate, simultaneously. Although both the effects end up neutralizing each other, in present-valuing the option premium using q as a domestic risk-free rate, a lower discount factor would be used. Hence, an increase in q would lead to a lower option premium.

---

[72] The volatility of $XF_{T_{S_TF_T}}$ can be obtained by setting $\sigma_1 = \sigma_F$, $\sigma_2 = \sqrt{\sigma_S^2 + 2\rho_{FX,S}\sigma_S\sigma_F + \sigma_F^2}$ and

$$\rho_{1,2} = \frac{\sigma_S^2 + \rho_{FX,S}\sigma_S\sigma_F}{\sigma_F\sqrt{\sigma_S^2 + 2\rho_{FX,S}\sigma_S\sigma_F + \sigma_F^2}}.$$

The intuition underlying the effect of σ_S and σ_F is similar to the one presented for the Category III in that the effect depends on whether $\rho_{FX,S}$ is positive or negative. More precisely, if $\rho_{FX,S}$ is positive, increasing either σ_S or σ_F would increase the dividend rate and hence decrease the option premium. However, if $\rho_{FX,S}$ is negative, increasing either σ_S or σ_F would result in a possible decrease in the dividend rate and hence increase the option premium. Furthermore, an increase in σ_F also leads to an increase in the option volatility and hence the option premium. Increasing either σ_S or σ_F may have mixed effects on the option premium, as summarized in Exhibit 113. The reader can similarly intuit the results for the call option.

Depending on the category, the hedging of certain product options can sometimes be quite complicated. Whatever the level of complication, hedging any product option would imply hedging the risk due to the movements in the foreign asset values and the appropriate underlying currency unit. The static hedge parameters for almost all the categories have been given in Wei (1996) and are briefly discussed in Chapter 4.

As in the basket, choice, and spread options, the correlation between the two underlying assets is a necessary input for valuing product options. In the context of our example, this will be the correlation between the five-year Treasury bond price and the Cad/US exchange rate. This correlation usually has about a 10 to 15 percent contribution to the price of a product option.

Other Applications

Although the discussion so far has been based on the use of product options for monetizing views on markets, these options can also be very effectively used for liability or risk management. The following example, which is by no means exhaustive, illustrates such a use of a product option.

Application   Due to the nature of the assets and liabilities in different environments, liability managers can also exploit the cheap borrowing cost in one environment (for example, the United States) to fund the activities in the other environment (for example, Canada) by using a differential swap to swap from a BA to a LIBOR plus some spread without undergoing any currency risk or exchange of principal.

THE SUDDEN BIRTH/DEATH OPTION CONTRACT

Introduction

When transacting in any option, it is important to specify the life of the option, which has thus far been assumed to be a known constant that is prespecified at the inception of the contract. An option that violates this assumption by allowing the maturity date to be a random variable is called a sudden birth/death option.

Although the class of sudden birth/death options may at the first glance appear to be somewhat impractical, on careful examination it can be seen that variations on the sudden birth/death theme have been and will continue to be widely used. An example of a sudden death option that has been and still is quite popular in the insurance industry is the guaranteed minimum death benefit (GMDB). Succinctly put, a GMDB is essentially a principal guaranteed note whose coupon is linked to an index (for example, TSE 35, S&P 500). The fundamental distinction between this note and any other structured note is that a GMDB expires only at the time of the purchaser's death. The interested reader is referred to Bernard (1993), Gootzeit et. al. (1994), Mitchell (1994), Mueller (1992), and Ravindran and Edelist (1996) for in-depth discussions on valuing GMDBs and variations on GMDBs.

Another variation of the sudden birth/death option that is widely used in the financial markets is the barrier option. Although vanilla options serve as good disaster insurance, prevailing market conditions sometimes make such insurance costly. In these circumstances, the premium can be effectively reduced by using barrier options. A barrier option, alternatively known as a trigger or a knock-in/knock-out option, is an option that serves as a conditional insurance that may suddenly come into effect (or cease to exist) upon the occurence of an event. Although the investor pays a premium for such an instrument at the inception of the contract, the option would only come into existence (or cease to exist) if a pre-specified barrier or level is triggered during the life of the option. Despite the fact that we will only discuss barrier options, the reader should keep in mind that these type of options are indeed special cases of the much broader sudden birth/death option spectrum.

A Barrier Option Contract Example

The sequence of events in Example 24 on page 194 illustrates the nature of a barrier option transaction that is an example of a sudden death option.

It is important for the reader to make the following four observations about Example 24:

OBSERVATION 1 The option discussed in Example 24 is also called the up-and-out option (where the term *up* refers to the fact that the current spot level must transverse up towards the barrier, and the term *out* refers to the option being extinguished upon hitting the barrier). Depending on the type of risks managed, the hedger could have just as well used other variations of this option, which include the up-and-in option, the down-and-out option, and the down-and-in option.[73]

---

[73] Because a call on the Canadian dollar is the same as the put on the U.S. dollar, the up-and-out put option on the U.S. dollar is the same as the down-and-out call option on the Canadian dollar. This type of symmetry only holds for the currency asset class.

EXAMPLE 24   A European-Style Barrier Option Transaction

The Canadian dollar is currently trading at 1.3300 Cad/US. Because of expected currency exposure in one month, the client is worried about the U.S. dollar weakening below the 1.3100 Cad/US level. Buying a one-month put option on the U.S. dollar with a strike rate of 1.3100 Cad/US would be an ideal solution. Current market conditions, however, make this insurance costly.

To overcome the cost, the put option can be purchased with an added feature that if the exchange rate during the life of the option exceeds a 1.3600 Cad/US barrier, the put option would cease to exist. Presumably, if the U.S. dollar can strengthen to a level of 1.3600 Cad/US, it is unlikely to weaken below a level of 1.3100 Cad/US by the time the option expires. The cost of the put option on a notional amount of US$ 50 mm is Cad$ 0.691 mm.

Time (months)	Exchange Rate (Cad/US)	Impact of Option on the Hedger
0	1.3300	☞ Cad$ 0.691 mm premium paid by hedger
Case 1: Barrier Is Not Breached during the Life of Option		
1	*Case A: Put Option Is Exercised at the End of 1 Month*	
	1.2900	☞ Payoff of Cad$ [50 • (1.3100 – 1.2900)] = Cad$ 1 mm paid to hedger ☞ Cad$ 0.691 mm of premium and Cad$ 0.003 mm of interest on this premium foregone by hedger ☞ Profit to hedger: Cad$ [1 – (0.691 + 0.003)] = Cad$ 0.306 mm
	Case B: Put Option Is Not Exercised at the End of 1 Month	
	1.3200	☞ Cad$ 0.691 mm of premium and Cad$ 0.003 mm of interest on this premium foregone by hedger ☞ Profit to hedger: –Cad$ (0.691 + 0.003) = –Cad$ 0.694 mm
Case 2: Barrier Is Breached during the Life of Option		
1		☞ Cad$ 0.691 mm of premium and Cad$ 0.003 mm of interest on this premium foregone by hedger ☞ Profit to hedger: –Cad$ (0.691 + 0.003) = –Cad$ 0.694 mm

OBSERVATION 2 Unlike a GMDB, which has a completely random time of expiry, the knock-out option that was discussed above has a random time of expiry for only one month. Thus, if the option does not get extinguished during the one-month period, it will be forced to mature at the end of the one-month period.

OBSERVATION 3 The premium of the option discussed above is a function of the barrier level chosen. More precisely, the farther the barrier from the current exchange rate level, the more expensive the up-and-out option. This is because the probability of the option extinguishing diminishes as the level of the barrier is raised.

OBSERVATION 4 Instead of purchasing a down-and-out put option, the hedger could alternatively purchase a one-month vanilla put option at the inception of the contract. Once the exchange rate breaches a barrier level of 1.3600 Cad/US the investor could sell the option back in the marketplace. Despite the fact that this strategy achieves the same objective, there are three disadvantages associated with this strategy:

1. The investor has to cough up a higher initial premium for the vanilla put option.
2. The market has to be constantly monitored by the investor so as to unwind the position appropriately. This type of disciplined mind-set may be difficult for some traders to follow.
3. Once the barrier is breached, the put option will be highly out-of-the-money. As a result, the sale of this put option back into the marketplace may not necessarily be a lucrative trade since the option may essentially be only left with the time-value component.

Characteristics of Barrier Option Contracts

The profit profile associated with the purchase of barrier options can be more generally written, as detailed in Exhibit 120. As the reader will realize, as long as the barrier is (is not) breached for an in-option (out-option), the graph of the profit profile to the buyer on the option maturity date will be no different from those presented in Exhibits 23 and 24.

It is important to note that each of the above profit profiles can be decomposed further into the up and down options, depending on whether $S_0 < H$. Assuming a continuous trading market, the pricing formulae for the barrier options corresponding to the above payoffs have been given by Rubinstein and Reiner (1991). If a barrier option is bought on an underlying index that is trading in an illiquid market, the exact times of monitoring the breaching of the barrier by the index must be specified in the contract in advance. Furthermore, when the monitoring of the index is done at discrete times, no analytical expressions exist for the pricing of the barrier options and, consequently, the prices can only be evaluated numerically (for example, multivariate integrals, binomial method,

EXHIBIT 120   Profits to the Buyer of a European-Style
Barrier Option

Type of Barrier Option	Profit at Expiry Time T If Barrier Is Breached	Profit at Expiry Time T If Barrier Is Not Breached
$C_{E,In}(0,T,X,H)$	$\max[-P^*_{T,CI}, S_T - X - P^*_{T,CI}]$	$-P^*_{T,CI}$
$C_{E,Out}(0,T,X,H)$	$-P^*_{T,CO}$	$\max[-P^*_{T,CO}, S_T - X - P^*_{T,CO}]$
$P_{E,In}(0,T,X,H)$	$\max[-P^*_{T,PI}, X - S_T - P^*_{T,PI}]$	$-P^*_{T,PI}$
$P_{E,Out}(0,T,X,H)$	$-P^*_{T,PO}$	$\max[-P^*_{T,PO}, X - S_T - P^*_{T,PO}]$

where

0 = Current time or time today
T = Time of option maturity
S_T = Value of underlying asset at time T
H = Barrier level of the option
$C_{E,In}(0,T,X,H)$ = European in-call barrier option purchased at time 0 with parameters T, X, and H
$C_{E,Out}(0,T,X,H)$ = European out-call barrier option purchased at time 0 with parameters T, X, and H
$P_{E,In}(0,T,X,H)$ = European in-put barrier option purchased at time 0 with parameters T, X, and H
$P_{E,Out}(0,T,X,H)$ = European out-put barrier option purchased at time 0 with parameters T, X, and H
$P^*_{T,CI}$ = Amount foregone by purchaser of in-call option due to premium and the interest accrued until time T on this premium
$P^*_{T,CO}$ = Amount foregone by purchaser of out-call option due to premium and the interest accrued until time T on this premium
$P^*_{T,PI}$ = Amount foregone by purchaser of in-put option due to premium and the interest accrued until time T on this premium
$P^*_{T,PO}$ = Amount foregone by purchaser of out-put option due to premium and the interest accrued until time T on this premium

Monte Carlo method. The use of both the binomial and Monte Carlo methods to value this option will be illustrated in Chapter 4.

As mentioned earlier, it should come as no surprise to the reader that the profit profiles associated with the purchase of the barrier options are no different from that of the vanilla options. To illustrate, consider for example, the in-option. Upon hitting the barrier, a vanilla option comes alive, resulting in a vanilla option profit profile on maturity, while no breaching of the barrier implies the loss of the premium paid at the inception of the contract. Thus, although the profit and loss graphs to the buyer of a barrier option are no different from that of a vanilla option, the break-even analysis discussed on page 52 is still crucial in determining whether this type of view monetizing strategy is cost-effective.

To be able to value an option, one has to first identify the factors that would influence an option price. These factors are summarized in Exhibit 121 for all four asset classes.

EXHIBIT 121 Factors Influencing the Value of a Barrier Option Contract

Factors	Interest-Rate Option	Currency Option	Equity Option	Commodity Option
Convenience yield				✔
Dividend rate			✔	
Foreign risk-free rate		✔		
Domestic risk-free rate	✔	✔	✔	✔
Underlying asset value	✔	✔	✔	✔
Strike value	✔	✔	✔	✔
Volatility of asset value	✔	✔	✔	✔
Frequency of exercise	✔	✔	✔	✔
Life of contract	✔	✔	✔	✔
Barrier level	✔	✔	✔	✔
Times at which asset values are sampled	✔	✔	✔	✔

As can be seen in Exhibit 121, while nine factors contribute to the value of a currency, equity, and commodity option contract, only eight factors contribute to the value of an interest-rate option contract. When compared to the factors influencing the value of a vanilla option in Exhibit 30, two additional factors influence the value of a barrier option. These factors, which are given in the last row of Exhibit 121, are as follows:

1. **Barrier Level.** Level of the barrier.
2. **Times at which asset values are sampled.** Times at which breaching of the barrier is monitored.

To understand how the above-mentioned factors influence the value of an option contract, one must first derive a no-arbitrage relationship between the option contract and the asset underlying the option contract. The effects of these factors are summarized in Exhibit 122.

While the effects of X, ef, and T are obvious and no different from those in Exhibit 31, the effects of the remaining six factors will now be intuited. To intuit the effect of these factors, I will first consider each of the four types of options.

Down-and-In Options

In this instance, the option starts off at the inception of the contract with $S_0 > H$. To intuit the effect of the six factors r_f, r_d, σ, S_0, H, and sf, I will consider the down-

EXHIBIT 122   Effect of Increase in Value of Underlying Factors on Barrier Option Premium

	Type of Option Contracts							
	Down-and-In		Down-and-Out		Up-and-In		Up-and-Out	
Factors	Call	Put	Call	Put	Call	Put	Call	Put
r_f	⇕	⇑	⇓	⇕	⇓	⇕	⇕	⇑
r_d	⇕	⇓	⇑	⇕	⇑	⇕	⇕	⇓
S_0	⇓	⇓	⇑	⇑	⇑	⇑	⇓	⇓
X	⇓	⇑	⇓	⇑	⇓	⇑	⇓	⇑
σ	⇑	⇑	⇕	⇕	⇑	⇑	⇕	⇕
ef	⇑	⇑	⇑	⇑	⇑	⇑	⇑	⇑
T	⇕	⇕	⇕	⇕	⇕	⇕	⇕	⇕
H	⇑	⇑	⇓	⇓	⇓	⇓	⇑	⇑
sf[74]	⇑	⇑	⇓	⇓	⇑	⇑	⇓	⇓

74 See footnote 24.

and-in call option. When the level of H increases, the probability of the underlying option coming alive also increases since H will now be closer to S_0. This increase in probability will in turn lead to an increase in the barrier option premium.

Similarly, increasing sf implies an increase in the frequency of sampling at which the breaching of the barrier is monitored. The greater this frequency of monitoring, the greater the chances of hitting the barrier, leading to a higher probability of the underlying option coming alive. Thus, increasing sf would lead to an increase in the option premium.

Intuiting the effects of S_0 is somewhat trickier in the sense that increasing S_0 leads to an increase in the underlying vanilla call option premium. Furthermore, increasing S_0 also leads to a decrease in the probability of the underlying option coming alive since S_0 would now be further away from H. Thus, although the vanilla option premium increases, this vanilla option would only come alive if the asset value breaches the barrier. Since it can be shown that the effect of this probability value is greater than that of the vanilla option premium, the option premium would decrease as S_0 increases.

As shown in Exhibit 31, increasing σ would result in an increase in the call option premium. Furthermore, increasing σ would result in an increase in the probability of hitting the barrier. Since the call option would only come alive once the barrier has been hit, increasing σ would result in an increase in the down-and-in call option premium, as illustrated in Exhibit 122.

Like σ, an increase in r_d would result in an increase in the call option premium, as illustrated in Exhibit 31. However, increasing r_d would increase the growth rate of the underlying asset and hence decrease the chance of the asset transversing downwards to hit the barrier. This would of course lead to a decrease in the option premium. Thus, depending on the other underlying factors, an increase in r_d would not necessarily increase in the down-and-in call option premium, as shown in Exhibit 122. Similar reasoning can be applied to intuit the effect of r_f on the call option premium.

The intuition underlying the effects of these factors on the down-and-in put option is similar to that presented for an up-an-in call option.

Down-and-Out Options

In this instance, the option starts off at the inception of the contract with $S_0 > H$. To intuit the effect of the six factors r_f, r_d, σ, S_0, H, and sf, I will consider the down-and-out call option. When the level of H increases, the probability of the underlying option extinguishing also increases since H will now be closer to S_0. This increase in probability will in turn lead to a decrease in the barrier option premium.

Similarly, increasing sf implies the increase in the frequency of sampling at which the breaching of the barrier is monitored. The greater this frequency of monitoring, the greater the chances of hitting the barrier leading to a higher probability of the underlying option being extinguished. Thus, increasing sf would lead to a decrease in the option premium.

Unlike that for a down-and-in option, the effects of r_f, r_d, and S_0 are somewhat similar and easier to intuit. Consequently, I will just consider the effect of S_0 on the down-and-out call option premium. It was shown in Exhibit 31 that an increase in S_0 would lead to an increase in the underlying vanilla call option premium. Furthermore, since S_0 would now be further away from H, increasing S_0 would also lead to a decrease in the probability of the underlying call option being extinguished. Thus, as both the vanilla option premium increases and probability of the vanilla option extinguishing decreases, the option premium would increase as S_0 increases.

The effect of σ can be intuited by observing that as σ increases, the vanilla call option premium increases. Furthermore, as discussed for the down-and-in call option premium, increasing σ would also lead to an increase in the probability of the underlying asset hitting the barrier. Since the option would cease to exist once the barrier is breached, an increase σ in would lead to the demise of the call option. As a result, depending on the other factors, an increase in may not necessarily lead to an increase in the down-and-out call option premium.

The intuition underlying the effects of these factors on the down-and-out put option is similar to that presented for an up-an-out call option.

Up-and-In Options

In this instance, the option starts off at the inception of the contract with $S_0 < H$. To intuit the effect of the six factors r_f, r_d, σ, S_0, H, and sf, I will consider the up-and-in call option. When the level of H increases, the probability of the underlying option coming alive decreases since H will now be further away from S_0. This decrease in probability will in turn lead to a decrease in the barrier option premium.

Increasing sf implies an increase in the frequency of sampling at which the breaching of the barrier is monitored. The greater this frequency of monitoring, the greater the chances of hitting the barrier, leading to a higher probability of the underlying option coming alive. Thus, increasing sf would lead to an increase in the option premium.

Since the effects of r_f, r_d, σ, and S_0 are somewhat similar and easier to intuit, I will just consider the effect of S_0 on the up-and-in call option premium. As shown in Exhibit 31, increasing S_0 leads to an increase in the underlying vanilla call option premium. Furthermore, since S_0 would now be closer to H, an increase in S_0 would also lead to an increase in the probability of the underlying option coming alive. As both the vanilla option premium and the probability of the vanilla option coming alive increases when S_0 increases, the up-and-in call option premium would be increased as S_0 is increased.

The intuition underlying the effects of these factors on the up-and-in put option is similar to that presented for a down-and-in call option.

Up-and-Out Options

In this instance, the option starts off at the inception of the contract with $S_0 < H$. To intuit the effect of the six factors r_f, r_d, σ, S_0, H, and sf, I will consider the up-and-out call option. When the level of H increases, the probability of the underlying option extinguishing decreases since H will now be further away from S_0. This decrease in probability will in turn lead to an increase in the barrier option premium.

Increasing sf implies the increase in the frequency of sampling at which the breaching of the barrier is monitored. The greater this frequency of monitoring, the greater the chances of hitting the barrier leading to a higher probability of the underlying option extinguishing. Thus, increasing sf would lead to a decrease in the option premium.

Like the down-and-in options, the effect of S_0 is somewhat trickier to intuit since increasing S_0 leads to an increase in the underlying vanilla call option premium and an increase in the probability of the underlying option extinguishing as S_0 would now be closer to H. As in the down-and-in call option, since the effect of the latter is greater than the former, the option premium would decrease as S_0 increases.

An increase in r_d would result in an increase in the call option premium, as illustrated in Exhibit 31. However, increasing r_d would increase the growth rate of the underlying asset and hence the chances of the asset transversing upwards to hit the barrier so as to kill the existing option. This would of course lead to a decrease in the option premium. Thus, depending on the other underlying factors, an increase in r_d would not necessarily increase in the up-and-out call option premium, as shown in Exhibit 122. Similar reasoning can be applied to intuit the effect of r_f and σ on the call option premium.

The intuition underlying the effects of these factors on the up-and-out put option is similar to that presented for a down-an-out call option.

Although the barrier options are usually hedged using the classic delta-hedging methodology, the effect of gamma is eminent in these options. To overcome this, a static hedging strategy that is philosophically motivated by the ability to replicate the payoff profile of a barrier option could be used. It should be noted that with the profit profile structures given in Exhibit 120, going long a vanilla call option is equivalent to going long an up-and-in and an up-and-out call option if $S_0 < H$ or going long a down-and-in and a down-and-out call option if $S_0 > H$. This relationship holds true regardless of the barrier level, where I have implicitly assumed that all the options are struck at the same level and have the same time to maturity. Hence, one can conclude that the premium of any barrier option can never be greater than that of a corresponding vanilla option. Exhibit 123 illustrates this fact for a structurally similar vanilla call option, up-and-in call option, and up-and-out call option.

EXHIBIT 123   In, Out, and Vanilla Option Premiums

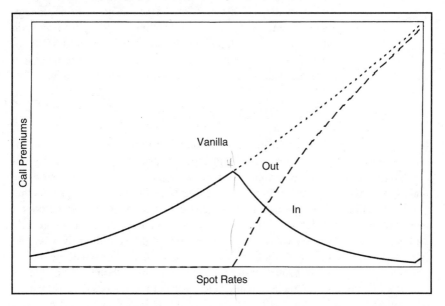

Other Applications

Although the discussion so far has been based on the use of barrier options in which the breaching of the barrier was done during the life of the option, one could have just as well only monitored the breaching of the barrier on the option maturity date. The following example, which is by no means exhaustive, illustrates another variation on the barrier option theme in addition to the effective use of barrier options in the convertible warrants and technical trading, just to name a few.

Application Instead of monitoring the breaching of the barrier during the life of the option, one can monitor this breaching on the option expiry date itself. Unlike Example 24, if the barrier level of 1.3600 Cad/US is set on the expiry date, there is no cheapening effect from the use of a barrier. To have a cheapening effect, one would have to set the barrier to a level that is less than 1.3100 Cad/US, which is the strike rate of the option. As an example, the barrier could be set at 1.1000 Cad/US on the expiry date such that if the exchange rate at the end of one month is above 1.3100 Cad/US or less than 1.1000 Cad/US, the option expires worthless and the client loses his premium. In the range 1.1000 Cad/US to 1.3100 Cad/US, in addition to losing the premium, the client's payoff will be the difference between the strike rate and the exchange rate at maturity. It is important to note that this type of one-point barrier strategy amounts to the client giving up some of the upside due to the view that in the event the U.S. dollar weakens below 1.3100 Cad/US in a month, it will never weaken below the 1.1000 Cad/US level. Consequently, this strategy is different from simply buying and selling vanilla European-style put options on the U.S. dollar at strike levels 1.3100 and 1.1000, respectively. One can similarly create an example where the client buys a vanilla call option and gives away part of the upside.

CONCLUSION

It was described in Chapter 2 how all vanilla derivatives can be built using the options framework as a platform. This replication philsophy can be similarly extended to the universe of exotic derivatives, which can be built using the underlying exotic options. In this chapter, I discussed the 11 building blocks that I believe can be effectively used to create any exotic product. Because products are continually created in the derivatives market, given the fact that there are only 24 hours in a day and individuals have other reponsibilities in their lives, knowing every product intimately both by name and payoff profile would be an impossible task. Instead, it is much easier for a person to think about building blocks and how any product can be built using at least one of these blocks. Thus, instead of providing a product knowledge that can quickly become outdated, I prefer to provide ageless tools with which readers can dissect any product.

Although the discussion in this chapter is built around the use of each building block, there are many other uses that have not been discussed. Thus, for every risk-management problem, it is very important to first understand the nature of the risks before prescribing any product as a solution. While being able to intuit the effect of the underlying factors on the option premiums is quite important, it is just as important to be able to at least have an idea of how to go about valuing these options. To teach the reader this, in the next chapter, I will present the intuitively appealing binomial method and the Monte Carlo method, which the reader can use without much sophistication.

4

⑥ INTUITIVE METHODS FOR PRICING OPTIONS

INTRODUCTION

In the previous two chapters, when discussing the characteristics of vanilla and exotic options, I alluded to the issue of valuing these derivatives. While the ability to intuit the effect of the factors underlying a derivative is important, it is just as important to be able to price a product using the market parameters. Without the ability to value a product, it becomes impossible to mark-to-market a portfolio and quantify the dollar value impact on the portfolio caused by a change in any one of the underlying factors.

The valuation of a derivative can basically be split into the following two steps:

Step 1: Modeling the asset-value movements underlying the derivative.

Step 2: Using the model developed in Step 1 to value the derivative of interest.

Although one standard model is widely used to model the behavior of currency, equity, and commodity markets, more than one model is widely used to describe interest-rate movements. Regardless of the model used in Step 1, the methodolgy(ies) employed in Step 2 revolves philsophically around the issue of using the model generated in the earlier step to arrive at the required value. These methodologies, which can generally be categorized into four groups, range in sophistication from heavy-duty mathematics to intuitive, applied probabilistic methods. While the heavy-duty mathematics is prevalent in nearly all published research articles and books, the simple, intuititive methods are usually not given the same level of exposure, due to their inefficiency. By providing the reader with ageless intuitive tools that can be applied across any model and asset class with very little mathematical sophistication, it is precisely this void that I am trying to fill in this chapter.

Since an option can be used to construct any derivative, I will provide a step-by-step approach to using two intuitive option-valuation techniques: the binomial method and the Monte Carlo method. Instead of focusing on the programming efficiency and the speed at which these valuation algorithms converge, I will concentrate on employing the above methodologies to value examples of options that were discussed in the previous chapters and address some of the issues a practitioner has to keep in mind when applying these methods.

ASSUMPTIONS UNDERLYING ASSET VALUE MOVEMENTS

As stated in the beginning of this chapter, in the currency, equity, and commodity asset classes, the assumption underlying the movement of a spot price/rate process is pretty much standard. Using the notation in Exhibit 31, this assumption[1], can be written as follows:

At a prespecified time T in the future, $\ln(S_T)$ has a normal distribution with mean $\ln S_0 + \left(r_d - r_f - \dfrac{\sigma^2}{2}\right)T$ and variance $\sigma^2 T$, where $r_d - r_f$ is known as the drift (or growth) rate of the underlying spot exchange rate (or stock price or spot commodity price) process[2,3,4].

The implication of the above assumption is demonstrated in Exhibit 124, and the mathematical representation of the distribution of future asset value(s) is given in Relationship 2 of the Appendix.

In Chapter 2, it was seen that in addition to the underlying cash market contracts, there is also a futures and/or forward contract that trades in each of the currency, interest-rate, equity, and commodity asset class. Using a forward contract to also represent a futures contract, a standard assumption underlying the movement of a forward price/rate is as follows:

---

[1] See Assumption 1 of the Appendix.

[2] For readers who are familiar with the diffusion equation notation, this assumption is usually written as $dS/S = (r_d - r_f)dt + \sigma dz$, where dz is a standard Weiner process.

[3] The natural logarithm of the number 5, for example, is written as $\ln 5$ and is defined as the value of x that satisfies the equation $2.718^x = 5$.

[4] This implicitly assumes that one is a risk-neutral investor living in a risk-neutral world. To a risk-adverse or a risk-prone investor, the definition of "risk-neutrality" is different, and hence the growth rate of the asset is different. Furthermore, present valuing in this different "risk-neutral" environment neutralizes this growth rate, and the net effect is hence the same as in the risk-neutral world. The option premiums derived using this assumption are also valid for both a risk-adverse and a risk-prone investor.

EXHIBIT 124   Graph of the Future Asset Value Distribution

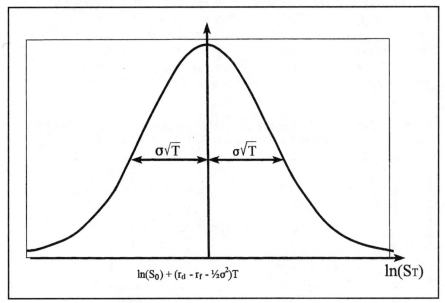

$$\ln(S_0) + (r_d - r_f - \tfrac{1}{2}\sigma^2)T \qquad\qquad \ln(S_T)$$

At a prespecified time T in the future, $\ln(F_T)$ has a normal distribution with mean $\ln F_0 - \left(\dfrac{\sigma^2}{2}\right)T$ and variance $\sigma^2 T$, where the drift rate associated with a forward price or rate is 0[5].

While F_0 in the above assumption represents the current forward price (rate) of a contract maturing at time T, F_T, represents the forward price (rate) at the end of time T. As an astute reader will realize, F_T can be thought of equivalently as representing S_T, the spot price (rate) at time T. Furthermore, it is important to note that this convergence to the spot price (rate) happens only at time T and not before or after time T; provided the settlement mechanisms underlying the spot and the forward contract are identical to each other. The graph depicting the distribution of the movement in the forward price (rate) is no different in shape from that given in Exhibit 124, and the reader is again referred to Relationship 2 of the Appendix for the mathematical representation of the distribution.

The philosophical difference between the spot-rate drift process and the forward-rate drift process is that in the former, the market has not factored in

---

[5] For readers who are familiar with the diffusion equation notation, this assumption is usually written as $dF/F = \sigma dz$, where dz is a standard Weiner process.

the expected growth rate of the asset, while in the latter, it is already factored in.[6] This is illustrated in Exhibit 125, which also shows that although the initial starting points of the processes may be different, both the processes converge to the spot rate at time T when the settlement mechanisms underlying these processes are identical. As can be seen in the exhibit, one can alternatively intuit the growth rate of the process to measure the steepness of the growth-rate line/curve.

**EXHIBIT 125 The Difference Between the Spot Rate Drift Process
and the Forward Rate Drift Process When $r_d > r_f$ [7]**

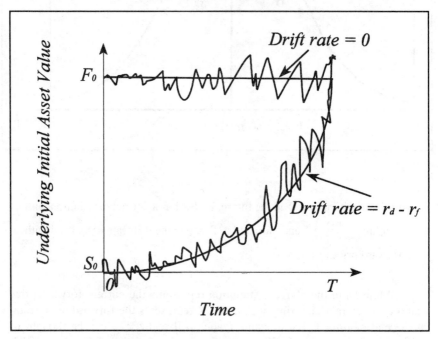

[7] When $r_d < r_f$, the curve depicting the growth of the spot-rate process would now be pointing downwards. More precisely, it will be a mirror image of the case when $r_d > r_f$, with the mirror placed on the horizontal axis. Similarly, when $r_d < r_f$, the line depicting the forward-rate process will be a mirror image of the line given in the exhibit. As in the exhibit, both the curve and line will converge at time T when $r_d < r_f$.

Because of the similarity in spot price (rate) and forward price (rate) distributions across the various asset classes, for the remainder of this chapter, unless otherwise stated, I will assume the spot-rate process in the currency asset class.

---

[6] The fact that a forward-rate process has zero drift makes the forward-rate process more appealing to model than a spot-rate process.

Types Of Valuation Techniques

Using a lognormal assumption that was discussed in the previous section to represent future stock price movements, Black and Scholes in their celebrated 1973 seminal paper developed analytical expressions to price European-style vanilla options on a nondividend-paying stock.[8] Since then, various researchers have developed both numerical techniques and closed-form solutions to value all types of options across the asset classes. These methods can be essentially categorized as follows:

I. Tree Method

The binomial method due to Cox, Ross, and Rubinstein (1979) and the trinomial method due to Boyle (1986) are the two most popular versions among practitioners. The idea underlying these methods involves

A. Creating the future asset-value movements starting from the current asset value in some probability weighted fashion using the model developed in Stage 1.

B. Using the asset-value tree created in (A) and employing the notion of backward induction or dynamic programming to value the option.

While the binomial method only allows an asset value to move upwards or downwards in the future, the trinomial method allows the asset value to move upwards, downwards, or remain unchanged in the future. Furthermore, although the binomial method may be more intuitive and easier to implement than the trinomial method, it is less efficient (that is, it converges more slowly).

The tree method can be used to value the European-style, Mid-Atlantic-style, and American-style options across any asset class. Despite its versatility, practitioners typically use this method to value only Mid-Atlantic-style and American-style options.

II. Finite-Difference Method

This popular method describes a category of numerical procedures (for example, implicit finite difference method, explicit finite difference method, and hopscotch method) used to solve the process (that is, partial differential equation) satisfied by both the option payoff and its underlying asset-value movements developed in Stage 1. Like the tree method, this versatile method can be used to value the European-style, Mid-Atlantic-style, and American-style options. The trinomial method discussed earlier is very similar to the explicit finite-

---

[8] Black (1976) used the futures model described in footnote 5 to value options on futures contracts. This model has since become very popular with practitioners who use it to model options or derivatives whose underlying assets are either forward or futures contracts.

difference method. The reader is referred to Hull (1997) for the details of the relationship. The reader is also referred to Wilmott, Dewynne, and Howison (1993) for details on implementing efficient finite-difference algorithms.

III. Monte Carlo Method

With the low cost of computer hardware and the increasing speed of computer chips, this intuitive method is becoming increasingly popular. Introduced by Boyle in 1977 to value European-style options, this versatile method involves

A. Simulating the future asset-value paths originating from the current asset value using the model developed in Stage 1 and the calculation of the option value along each simulated path.

B. Averaging the results obtained in (A) over the number of paths generated.

Despite its popular use in European-style option valuation, until Tilley's 1993 paper, it was generally believed that a Monte Carlo Method cannot be used to value Mid-Atlantic-style options and American-style options.

IV. Closed-Form Solutions

This method of approach, if feasible, offers the best possible solution to valuing options in terms of implementation and efficiency. Despite its speed and ease of implementation, the problem with this approach is its inability to find closed-form expressions that would allow us to value the options using the model developed in Stage 1. Although this approach does not work for Mid-Atlantic-style options and American-style options, it works very frequently for all types of European-style options.

When closed-form solutions are not available, depending on the number of assets or the nature of the path-dependence in the final payoff of the option, one may end up doing a multidimensional integral[9]. Like the Monte Carlo Method, due to the availability and cheapness of computer hardware, the use of numerical integration techniques in evaluating these multidimensional integrals has increased in popularity.

It should come as no surprise to the reader that a Monte Carlo method is just another way of performing a numerical integration. More precisely, while a numerical integration involves defined divisions of the region that needs to be integrated, a Monte Carlo method involves random (or undefined) divisions of the region that needs to be integrated.[10]

---

[9] This may sometimes be done under the guise of a quasi-Monte Carlo simulation.

[10] This is discussed in Observation 4 of Example 38.

THE BINOMIAL METHOD

As mentioned earlier, the Cox-Ross-Rubinstein method in essence says that given the current value of an exchange rate, there are only two possible states (an up-state and a down-state) that the exchange-rate process can occupy at time T in the future. Using this idea and the assumption underlying the movement of a spot exchange-rate process, an exchange-rate tree is first generated for the entire option period by partitioning the life of the option into small time intervals. This tree is then used to generate a corresponding tree of option prices that is used to value any European-style, Mid-Atlantic-style, and American-style option.

To value a currency option that expires at time T, one would first divide the time T into n equal subtime intervals of length $\frac{T}{n}$ each. Denoting the current exchange-rate level by S_0, the exchange rate at time $\frac{T}{n}$ (denoted henceforth by Δt) later is assumed to move either up to a level of $S_0 u$ with probability p or down to a level of $S_0 d$ with complimentary probability 1-p, where u and p represent the magnitude and probability of an upward jump, respectively and d and 1-p represent the magnitude and probability of the downward jump, respectively. Assuming that the current time is 0, Exhibit 126 shows the generation of the exchange-rate tree at the first four times 0, Δt, $2\Delta t$, and $3\Delta t$.

From Exhibit 126, one can see that every node in the tree generates an upward node and a downward node time Δt later. Partitioning the life of the option into n sub-time intervals would lead to exactly 2^n nodes at time T (or $n\Delta t$). Since an accurate option value can only be obtained by shortening the length of the sub-time interval Δt (or equivalently increasing the value of n), in the pursuit of accuracy one could potentially end up with a massive and messy tree as n gets large. This is because an increase in n would lead to an exponential increase in the number of nodes.

By assuming that the nodes of the tree recombine (that is, an upward move in the exchange rate followed by a downward one or a downward move in the exchange rate followed by an upward one is the same as no movement in the exchange rate), one can reduce the number of nodes at time T from 2^n to n + 1. The mathematical relationship that allows for this reduction in the number of nodes is the equation $u = \frac{1}{d}$. Exhibit 127 illustrates this recombining exchange-rate tree for the times 0, Δt, $2\Delta t$, and $3\Delta t$.

Although the size of the tree may have been reduced using the relationship u = 1/d, one would still need to find the value of u and p. This can be done by first recalling from the model assumption given earlier that at time Δt in the future, $\ln(S_{\Delta t})$ has a normal distribution with mean:

$$\ln S_0 + \left(r_d - r_f - \frac{\sigma^2}{2}\right)\Delta t$$

**EXHIBIT 126   Binomial Tree of Spot Exchange Rates
for the First Four Times**

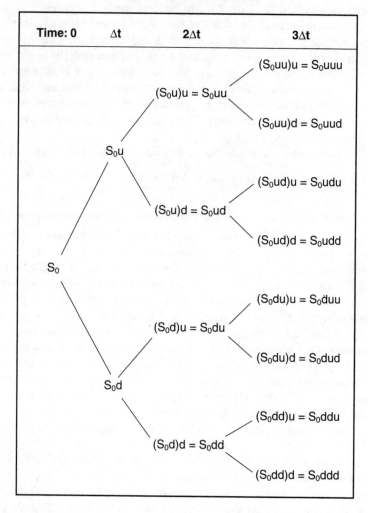

and variance $\sigma^2 \Delta t$. To obtain the values of u and p, one would assume that Δt is small enough[11] and then find the mean and the variance of $S_{\Delta t}$ using the properties given in Relationship 7 of the Appendix.[12] These are then equated to the mean and variance of the future exchange-rate movement using the one-

---

[11] It is possible for the probabilities to be negative when Δt is not small enough. To ensure non-negative probabilities, σ must be greater than $|r_d - r_f| \sqrt{\Delta t}$, where $|r_d - r_f|$ represents the absolute value of the difference $r_d - r_f$.

[12] This method is also known as the "method of moments" in statistics. See, for example, Hogg and Craig (1989).

EXHIBIT 127   Recombining the Exchange-Rate Tree Using the Binomial Method

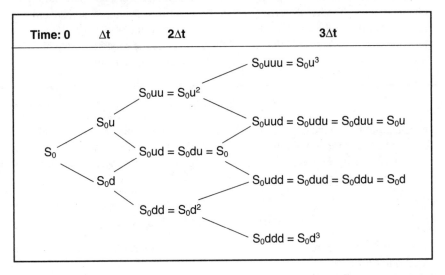

step tree shown in Exhibit 128, to give rise to the following expressions for u^{13}, d, and p:

$$u = e^{\sigma\sqrt{\Delta t}},\ d = \frac{1}{u},\ \text{and}\ p = \frac{e^{(r_d - r_f)\Delta t} - d}{u - d}$$

EXHIBIT 128   One-Step Binomial Tree for One Underlying Asset

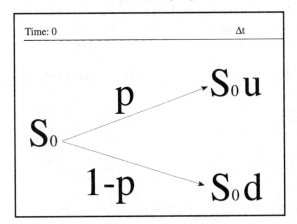

---

[13] It is more precise to use the expression $u = \dfrac{B + \sqrt{B^2 - 4A^2}}{2A}$, where $A = e^{(r_d - r_f)\Delta t}$ and $B = A^2 e^{\sigma^2 \Delta t} + 1$.

With this expression for u, one does not need to worry about the negative probabilities mentioned in footnote 11. By applying Taylor's theorem (see Relationship 15 of the Appendix) to this exact expression of u and assuming that Δt is small enough, one can arrive at the expression $u = e^{\sigma\sqrt{\Delta t}}$.

As can be seen from the formulae and exhibit, the greater the exchange-rate volatility, the greater the distance between S_0u and S_0d. This, as one would intuitively expect, implies that the greater the volatility, the more spread out the branches of the exchange-rate tree. Furthermore, the value of p can be intuited by looking at it as a measure of the ratio of the distance of the expected value of $S_{\Delta t}$ (= $S_0e^{(r_d - r_f)\Delta t}$) from S_0d to the distance between S_0u and S_0d. This results in p being:

$$\frac{S_0e^{(r_d - r_f)\Delta t} - S_0d}{S_0u - S_0d}$$

which simplifies to the expression of p that was given earlier. Thus, the closer the center of the distribution of future exchange rates is to S_0u, the higher the value of p.

Using these expressions, one can now generate an exchange-rate tree that would allow us to price currency options.

Valuing Vanilla Options

The steps that are required to value a currency option are summarized in Methodology 1.

The use of a binomial method to value a European-style, Mid-Atlantic style, and American-Style vanilla put option is illustrated in Example 25 on page 214.

It is important for the reader to make the following five important observations about Example 25.

OBSERVATION 1 To obtain a more accurate value for the three types of options valued in Example 25, one would have to reduce the value of Δt (or equivalently increase the value of n). A rule-of-thumb number for Δt that is reasonable for most instances is 0.01. In the context of the example, increasing n results in the American-style option premium converging

METHODOLOGY 1 Using The Binomial Method to Value Vanilla Options

Stage 1
Determine S_0, X, r_d, r_f, σ, T, n
Stage 2
Calculate the values of Δt, u, d and p using the formulae: $\Delta t = \dfrac{T}{n}$, $u = e^{\sigma\sqrt{\Delta t}}$; $d = \dfrac{1}{u}$, and $p = \dfrac{e^{(r_d - r_f)\Delta t} - d}{u - d}$
Stage 3
Generate a tree for the underlying asset starting from the current asset price today and ending on the option maturity, as shown below:

METHODOLOGY 1 Using The Binomial Method to Value Vanilla Options (Continued)

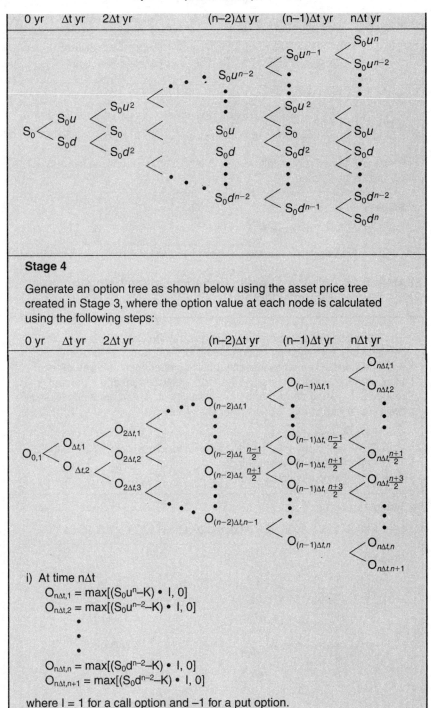

0 yr	Δt yr	2Δt yr	(n–2)Δt yr	(n–1)Δt yr	nΔt yr

Stage 4

Generate an option tree as shown below using the asset price tree created in Stage 3, where the option value at each node is calculated using the following steps:

i) At time $n\Delta t$

$$O_{n\Delta t,1} = \max[(S_0 u^n - K) \cdot I, 0]$$
$$O_{n\Delta t,2} = \max[(S_0 u^{n-2} - K) \cdot I, 0]$$
$$\vdots$$
$$O_{n\Delta t,n} = \max[(S_0 d^{n-2} - K) \cdot I, 0]$$
$$O_{n\Delta t,n+1} = \max[(S_0 d^{n-2} - K) \cdot I, 0]$$

where $I = 1$ for a call option and -1 for a put option.

METHODOLOGY 1   Using The Binomial Method to Value Vanilla Options (Continued)

ii) At time $i\Delta t$ (for $i = n-1, n-2, n-3] \ldots, 2, 1, 0$)

$O_{i\Delta t,1} = \max\{(S_0u^i-K) \cdot I \cdot E, [p \cdot O_{(i+1)\Delta t,1} + (1-p) \cdot O_{(i+1)\Delta t,2}]e^{-r_d\Delta t}\}$

$O_{i\Delta t,2} = \max\{(S_0u^{i-2}-K) \cdot I \cdot E, [p \cdot O_{(i+1)\Delta t,2} + (1-p) \cdot O_{(i+1)\Delta t,3}]e^{-r_d\Delta t}\}$

$\bullet$

$\bullet$

$\bullet$

$O_{i\Delta t,i} = \max\{(S_0d^{i-2}-K) \cdot I \cdot E, [p \cdot O_{(i+1)\Delta t,i} + (1-p) \cdot O_{(i+1)\Delta t,i+1}]e^{-r_d\Delta t}\}$

$O_{i\Delta t,i+1} = \max\{(S_0d^i-K) \cdot I \cdot E, [p \cdot O_{(i+1)\Delta t,i+1} + (1-p) \cdot O_{(i+1)\Delta t,i+2}]e^{-r_d\Delta t}\}$

where E = 1 if exercise is allowed at $i\Delta t$ and 0 if no exercise is allowed at $i\Delta t$ and I is as defined in i).

Stage 5

The option premium is given by $O_{0,1}$.

EXAMPLE 25   Valuing a Vanilla Currency Option Using the Binomial Method

The Canadian dollar is currently trading at 1.3000 Cad/US. An investor wants to buy a 4½-year put option on the U.S. dollar that is struck at 1.3000 Cad/US. The current continuously compounded risk-free rates of interest in the United States and Canada are 6 percent and 8 percent, respectively. Using an exchange-rate volatility of 10 percent, and dividing the 4½-year period into four subintervals, value

1. An American put option.
2. A Mid-Atlantic put option when the investor can only exercise at the 2¼-year period and 4½-year period.
3. A European put option.

Stage 1

$S_0 = 1.3000$, $X = 1.3000$, $r_d = 0.08$, $r_f = 0.06$, $\sigma = 0.1$, $T = 4.5$, $n = 4$

Stage 2

$$\Delta t = \frac{T}{n} = \frac{4.5}{4} = 1.125$$

$$u = e^{\sigma\sqrt{\Delta t}} = e^{0.1\sqrt{1.125}} = 1.1119$$

$$d = \frac{1}{u} = \frac{1}{1.1119} = 0.8994$$

$$p = \frac{e^{(r_d-r_f)\Delta t} - d}{u - d} = \frac{e^{(0.08-0.06)(1.125)} - 0.8994}{1.1119 - 0.8994} = 0.5805$$

EXAMPLE 25   Valuing a Vanilla Currency Option Using the Binomial Method (Continued)

Stage 3

0 yr	1(1.125) yr	2(1.125) yr	3(1.125) yr	4(1.125) yr

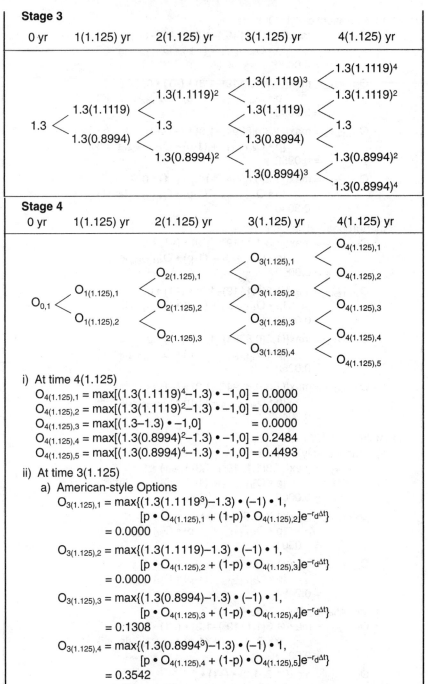

Stage 4

0 yr	1(1.125) yr	2(1.125) yr	3(1.125) yr	4(1.125) yr

i) At time 4(1.125)

$O_{4(1.125),1} = \max[(1.3(1.1119)^4 - 1.3) \bullet -1, 0] = 0.0000$
$O_{4(1.125),2} = \max[(1.3(1.1119)^2 - 1.3) \bullet -1, 0] = 0.0000$
$O_{4(1.125),3} = \max[(1.3 - 1.3) \bullet -1, 0] \qquad\qquad = 0.0000$
$O_{4(1.125),4} = \max[(1.3(0.8994)^2 - 1.3) \bullet -1, 0] = 0.2484$
$O_{4(1.125),5} = \max[(1.3(0.8994)^4 - 1.3) \bullet -1, 0] = 0.4493$

ii) At time 3(1.125)

   a) American-style Options

$O_{3(1.125),1} = \max\{(1.3(1.1119^3) - 1.3) \bullet (-1) \bullet 1,$
$$[p \bullet O_{4(1.125),1} + (1-p) \bullet O_{4(1.125),2}]e^{-r_d\Delta t}\}$$
$$= 0.0000$$

$O_{3(1.125),2} = \max\{(1.3(1.1119) - 1.3) \bullet (-1) \bullet 1,$
$$[p \bullet O_{4(1.125),2} + (1-p) \bullet O_{4(1.125),3}]e^{-r_d\Delta t}\}$$
$$= 0.0000$$

$O_{3(1.125),3} = \max\{(1.3(0.8994) - 1.3) \bullet (-1) \bullet 1,$
$$[p \bullet O_{4(1.125),3} + (1-p) \bullet O_{4(1.125),4}]e^{-r_d\Delta t}\}$$
$$= 0.1308$$

$O_{3(1.125),4} = \max\{(1.3(0.8994^3) - 1.3) \bullet (-1) \bullet 1,$
$$[p \bullet O_{4(1.125),4} + (1-p) \bullet O_{4(1.125),5}]e^{-r_d\Delta t}\}$$
$$= 0.3542$$

EXAMPLE 25   Valuing a Vanilla Currency Option Using the Binomial Method (Continued)

b) Mid-Atlantic-style Options

$O_{3(1.125),1} = \max\{(1.3(1.1119^3)-1.3) \cdot (-1) \cdot 0,$
$$[p \cdot O_{4(1.125),1} + (1-p) \cdot O_{4(1.125),2}]e^{-r_d\Delta t}\}$$
$$= 0.0000$$

$O_{3(1.125),2} = \max\{(1.3(1.1119)-1.3) \cdot (-1) \cdot 0,$
$$[p \cdot O_{4(1.125),2} + (1-p) \cdot O_{4(1.125),3}]e^{-r_d\Delta t}\}$$
$$= 0.0000$$

$O_{3(1.125),3} = \max\{(1.3(0.8994)-1.3) \cdot (-1) \cdot 0,$
$$[p \cdot O_{4(1.125),3} + (1-p) \cdot O_{4(1.125),4}]e^{-r_d\Delta t}\}$$
$$= 0.0952$$

$O_{3(1.125),4} = \max\{(1.3(0.8994^3)-1.3) \cdot (-1) \cdot 0,$
$$[p \cdot O_{4(1.125),4} + (1-p) \cdot O_{4(1.125),5}]e^{-r_d\Delta t}\}$$
$$= 0.3040$$

c) European-style Options

$O_{3(1.125),1} = \max\{(1.3(1.1119^3)-1.3) \cdot (-1) \cdot 0,$
$$[p \cdot O_{4(1.125),1} + (1-p) \cdot O_{4(1.125),2}]e^{-r_d\Delta t}\}$$
$$= 0.0000$$

$O_{3(1.125),2} = \max\{(1.3(1.1119)-1.3) \cdot (-1) \cdot 0,$
$$[p \cdot O_{4(1.125),2} + (1-p) \cdot O_{4(1.125),3}]e^{-r_d\Delta t}\}$$
$$= 0.0000$$

$O_{3(1.125),3} = \max\{(1.3(0.8994)-1.3) \cdot (-1) \cdot 0,$
$$[p \cdot O_{4(1.125),3} + (1-p) \cdot O_{4(1.125),4}]e^{-r_d\Delta t}\}$$
$$= 0.0952$$

$O_{3(1.125),4} = \max\{(1.3(0.8994^3)-1.3) \cdot (-1) \cdot 0,$
$$[p \cdot O_{4(1.125),4} + (1-p) \cdot O_{4(1.125),5}]e^{-r_d\Delta t}\}$$
$$= 0.3040$$

iii) At time 2(1.125)

a) American-style Options

$O_{2(1.125),1} = \max\{(1.3(1.1119^2)-1.3) \cdot (-1) \cdot 1,$
$$[p \cdot O_{3(1.125),1} + (1-p) \cdot O_{3(1.125),2}]e^{-r_d\Delta t}\}$$
$$= 0.0000$$

$O_{2(1.125),2} = \max\{(1.3-1.3) \cdot (-1) \cdot 1,$
$$[p \cdot O_{3(1.125),2} + (1-p) \cdot O_{3(1.125),3}]e^{-r_d\Delta t}\}$$
$$= 0.0501$$

$O_{2(1.125),3} = \max\{(1.3(0.8994^2)-1.3) \cdot (-1) \cdot 1,$
$$[p \cdot O_{3(1.125),3} + (1-p) \cdot O_{3(1.125),4}]e^{-r_d\Delta t}\}$$
$$= 0.2484$$

b) Mid-Atlantic-style Options

$O_{2(1.125),1} = \max\{(1.3(1.1119^2)-1.3) \cdot (-1) \cdot 1,$
$$[p \cdot O_{3(1.125),1} + (1-p) \cdot O_{3(1.125),2}]e^{-r_d\Delta t}\}$$
$$= 0.0000$$

$O_{2(1.125),2} = \max\{(1.3-1.3) \cdot (-1) \cdot 1,$
$$[p \cdot O_{3(1.125),2} + (1-p) \cdot O_{3(1.125),3}]e^{-r_d\Delta t}\}$$
$$= 0.0365$$

EXAMPLE 25   Valuing a Vanilla Currency Option Using the Binomial Method (Continued)

$O_{2(1.125),3}$ = max{(1.3(0.8994^2)–1.3) • (–1) • 1,

$\qquad\qquad$ [p • $O_{3(1.125),3}$ + (1-p) • $O_{3(1.125),4}$]e$^{-r_d\Delta t}$}

$\qquad$ = 0.2484

c) European-style Options

$\qquad O_{2(1.125),1}$ = max{(1.3(1.1119^2)–1.3) • (–1) • 0,

$\qquad\qquad$ [p • $O_{3(1.125),1}$ + (1-p) • $O_{3(1.125),2}$]e$^{-r_d\Delta t}$}

$\qquad\qquad$ = 0.0000

$\qquad O_{2(1.125),2}$ = max{(1.3–1.3) • (–1) • 0,

$\qquad\qquad$ [p • $O_{3(1.125),2}$ + (1-p) • $O_{3(1.125),3}$]e$^{-r_d\Delta t}$}

$\qquad\qquad$ = 0.0365

$\qquad O_{2(1.125),3}$ = max{(1.3(0.8994^2)–1.3) • (–1) • 0,

$\qquad\qquad$ [p • $O_{3(1.125),3}$ + (1-p) • $O_{3(1.125),4}$]e$^{-r_d\Delta t}$}

$\qquad\qquad$ = 0.1671

iv) At time 1(1.125)

a) American-style Options

$\qquad O_{1(1.125),1}$ = max{(1.3(1.1119)–1.3) • (–1) • 1,

$\qquad\qquad$ [p • $O_{2(1.125),1}$ + (1-p) • $O_{2(1.125),2}$]e$^{-r_d\Delta t}$}

$\qquad\qquad$ = 0.0192

$\qquad O_{1(1.125),2}$ = max{(1.3(0.8994)–1.3) • (–1) • 1,

$\qquad\qquad$ [p • $O_{2(1.125),2}$ + (1-p) • $O_{2(1.125),3}$]e$^{-r_d\Delta t}$}

$\qquad\qquad$ = 0.1308

b) Mid-Atlantic-style Options

$\qquad O_{1(1.125),1}$ = max{(1.3(1.1119)–1.3) • (–1) • 0,

$\qquad\qquad$ [p • $O_{2(1.125),1}$ + (1-p) • $O_{2(1.125),2}$]e$^{-r_d\Delta t}$}

$\qquad\qquad$ = 0.0140

$\qquad O_{1(1.125),2}$ = max{(1.3(0.8994)–1.3) • (–1) • 0,

$\qquad\qquad$ [p • $O_{2(1.125),2}$ + (1-p) • $O_{2(1.125),3}$]e$^{-r_d\Delta t}$}

$\qquad\qquad$ = 0.1146

c) European-style Options

$\qquad O_{1(1.125),1}$ = max{(1.3(1.1119)–1.3) • (–1) • 0,

$\qquad\qquad$ [p • $O_{2(1.125),1}$ + (1-p) • $O_{2(1.125),2}$]e$^{-r_d\Delta t}$}

$\qquad\qquad$ = 0.0140

$\qquad O_{1(1.125),2}$ = max{(1.3(0.8994)–1.3) • (–1) • 0,

$\qquad\qquad$ [p • $O_{2(1.125),2}$ + (1-p) • $O_{2(1.125),3}$]e$^{-r_d\Delta t}$}

$\qquad\qquad$ = 0.0834

v) At time 0

a) American-style Options

$\qquad O_{0,1}$ = max{(1.3–1.3) • (–1) • 0,

$\qquad\qquad$ [p • $O_{2(1.125),1}$ + (1-p) • $O_{2(1.125),2}$]e$^{-r_d\Delta t}$}

$\qquad\qquad$ = 0.0603

b) Mid-Atlantic-style Options

$\qquad O_{0,1}$ = max{(1.3–1.3) • (–1) • 0,

$\qquad\qquad$ [p • $O_{2(1.125),1}$ + (1-p) • $O_{2(1.125),2}$]e$^{-r_d\Delta t}$}

$\qquad\qquad$ = 0.0514

EXAMPLE 25   Valuing a Vanilla Currency Option Using the Binomial Method (Continued)

c) European-style Options

$$O_{0,1} = \max\{(1.3–1.3) \bullet (–1) \bullet 0,$$
$$[p \bullet O_{2(1.125),1} + (1-p) \bullet O_{2(1.125),2}]e^{-r_d\Delta t}\}$$
$$= 0.0394$$

Stage 5

i) The value of the American-style put option is given by 0.0603 Cad/US.
ii) The value of the Mid-Atlantic-style put option is given by 0.0514 Cad/US.
iii) The value of the European-style put option is given by 0.0394 Cad/US.

to 0.0634 Cad/US, the Mid-Atlantic-style option premium converging to 0.0547 Cad/US, and the European-style option premium converging to 0.0445 Cad/US.

OBSERVATION 2   Although the premiums would converge to the true option value when Δt is decreased, as shown in Exhibit 129, they do not necessarily converge smoothly.

More precisely, when changes from an odd (even) number to an even (odd) number, the premiums obtained tend to oscillate. This is because as n changes from an odd number to an even number and back, the center of the tree also shifts

EXHIBIT 129   Convergence of Option Premiums Using a Binomial Method

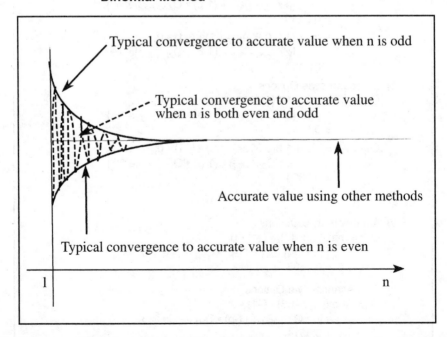

from $\dfrac{S_0 e^{\sigma \sqrt{\Delta t}} + S_0 e^{-\sigma \sqrt{\Delta t}}}{2}$ to S_0 and back, causing a change in the exchange-rate values that contribute to the in-the-money payoff of the option. Although this oscillation causes a small variation in the option premiums in many cases, the magnitude of the discrepancy can be serious if the notional amount of the option contract is very large. As can be seen from the exhibit, to avoid this oscillation, one could either make n large (for example, n > 100) or restrict n to either the set of even integers or the set of odd integers.

OBSERVATION 3 Since an exercise is only permissable for a European-style option on the maturity of the option, there is an alternative way of calculating the European-style option premium. To do this, one has to first compute the payoffs on the option maturity, as illustrated in *Stage 4 i*. The total number of possible paths that can lead to a particular payoff and the probability of getting such a payoff using exactly one of these possible paths is then calculated. The option premium is then obtained by present-valuing the sum of each product obtained by multiplying an option payoff with the total number paths landing to the payoff and the corresponding probability associated with each path.

At time $n\Delta t$, the product of the total number of paths leading to the node $u^\alpha d^\beta$ and the corresponding probability associated with each path is given by the coefficients of $u^\alpha d^\beta$ in the expansion $[pu + (1 - p)d]^n$, where $\alpha, \beta = 0, 1, 2, \ldots, n$ and $\alpha + \beta = n$.

In the context of the example, since $n = 4$, one would have to first expand $[pu + (1 - p)d]^4$. Doing this would result in

$$[pu+(1 - p)d]^4 = p^4 u^4 + 4p^3(1 - p)u^2 +$$
$$6p^2(1 - p)^2 + 4p(1 - p)^3 d^2 + (1 - p)^4 d^4$$

Exhibit 130 illustrates the extracted coefficients from the above equation for each of the five option payoffs given in *Stage 4 i* and the calculation of the option premium using these coefficients.

Summing up the weighted payoffs and discounting[14] by $e^{-(0.08)4.5}$ results in a value of 0.0394, which agrees with the value obtained using the tree.

As before, increasing the value of n results in a more accurate value. This alternative method, although easier to implement, is only useful when computing premiums for European-style options with uncomplicated path-dependent features.

---

[14] Since the option payoffs at time $4\Delta t$ are discounted to time 0, the discount factor is $e^{-r_d(4\Delta t)} = e^{-0.08(4.5)}$

EXHIBIT 130   Calculation of Vanilla Option
Premium Using Alternative Method

Nodes	Coefficients	Option Payoff	Weighted Payoff
S_0u^4	p^4	0.0000	0.0000
S_0u^2	$4p^3(1-p)$	0.0000	0.0000
S_0	$6p^2(1-p)^2$	0.0000	0.0000
S_0d^2	$4p(1-p)^3$	0.2484	0.0426
S_0d^4	$(1-p)^4$	0.4493	0.0139

OBSERVATION 4   The delta (sensitivity of the option premium to a change in the underlying exchange rate), gamma (sensitivity of the option delta to a change in the underlying exchange rate), and theta (sensitivity of the option premium to a decay in the option life) can be obtained using the value of the nodes in both the exchange-rate tree and the option-premium tree. More precisely,

$$\text{delta} = \frac{O_{\Delta t,1} - O_{\Delta t,2}}{S_0u - S_0d}$$

$$\text{gamma} = \frac{\dfrac{O_{2\Delta t,1} - O_{2\Delta t,2}}{S_0u^2 - S_0} - \dfrac{O_{2\Delta t,2} - O_{2\Delta t,3}}{S_0 - S_0d^2}}{0.5(S_0u^2 - S_0d^2)}$$

$$\text{theta} = \frac{O_{2\Delta t,2} - O_{0,1}}{2\Delta t}$$

Unlike the above sensitivities, vega (sensitivity of the option premium to a change in volatility), domestic rho (sensitivity of the option premium to a change in the domestic risk-free rate), and foreign rho (sensitivity of the option premium to a change in the foreign risk-free rate) cannot be calculated from the nodes of the tree. To calculate these sensitivities, one has to revalue the option with an increase in the underlying parameters and then compute the rate of change in the option premium[15]. Thus,

---

[15] This methodology can also be used to calculate delta, gamma, and theta of the option. In this context, $\text{delta} = \dfrac{O_{0,1}(S_0 + \varepsilon) - O_{0,1}}{\varepsilon}$, $\text{gamma} = \dfrac{\dfrac{O_{0,1}(S_0 + \varepsilon) - O_{0,1}}{\varepsilon} - \dfrac{O_{0,1} - O_{0,1}(S_0 - \varepsilon)}{\varepsilon}}{\varepsilon}$, and

$\text{theta} = \dfrac{O_{0,1} - O_{0,1}(T - \varepsilon)}{\varepsilon}$.

$$vega = \frac{O_{0,1}(\sigma + \varepsilon) - O_{0,1}}{\varepsilon}$$

$$domestic\ rho = \frac{O_{0,1}(r_d + \varepsilon) - O_{0,1}}{\varepsilon}$$

$$foreign\ rho = \frac{O_{0,1}(r_f + \varepsilon) - O_{0,1}}{\varepsilon}$$

where $O_{0,1}(\sigma + \varepsilon)$, $O_{0,1}(r_d + \varepsilon)$ and $O_{0,1}(r_f + \varepsilon)$ represent the value of the option when the volatility, domestic risk-free rate, and foreign risk-free rate are each increased by an infinitesimal amount ε.

In the context of the European-style option example, when n = 4 and $\varepsilon = 0.01$, it can be shown that

$$delta = \frac{0.0140 - 0.0834}{1.3(1.1119) - 1.3(0.8994)} = -0.2512$$

$$gamma = \frac{\dfrac{0.0000 - 0.0365}{1.3(1.1119)^2 - 1.3} - \dfrac{0.0365 - 0.1671}{1.3 - 1.3(0.8994)^2}}{0.5[1.3(1.1119)^2 - 1.3(0.8994)^2]} = 1.4648$$

$$theta = \frac{0.0365 - 0.0394}{2(1.125)} = -0.0013$$

$$vega = \frac{0.0464 - 0.0394}{0.01} = 0.7000$$

$$domestic\ rho = \frac{0.0258 - 0.0394}{0.01} = -1.3600$$

$$foreign\ rho = \frac{0.0544 - 0.0394}{0.01} = 1.5000$$

OBSERVATION 5 To value the above option using a forward exchange-rate model that was described on page 205, one would still use the approach described in Methodology 1 by modifying the expression for p. This stems from the fact that, the probability of an upward move, would now be defined as:

$$\frac{1 - d}{u - d}$$

The reason for this can be intuited by observing that since the forward-rate process would have already factored in the market expectation of the future (see page 205), the expected value of $F_{\Delta t}$ is F_0. Furthermore, since p can be equivalently thought of as the ratio of distances, as discussed on page 212, it is straightforward to see why the expression for p should be given as above.

As long as the initial forward rate, F_0, is the forward exchange rate that is applied to time T, and the settlement mechanism underlying this contract is identical to that of a spot contract, the value of the European-style option should be independent of the underlying asset. More precisely, regardless of whether the underlying asset is a spot contract or a forward contract, the value of the European-style option will be the same. Furthermore, since the forward rate converges to the spot rate only on the maturity date, blindly using a forward-rate model to value either the American-style or Mid-Atlantic-style options can be disastrous. This is because the exercise features embedded in the early-exercise options would almost always entail the comparison of a spot exchange rate with a strike rate. Because of the nature of convergence of the forward rate to the spot rate at time $n\Delta t$, it is not the case that this forward rate would also converge to the spot rates at earlier times Δt, $2\Delta t$, . . . , $(n-1)\Delta t$. Thus, depending on market conditions and terms of the option, an option premium calculated by comparing a forward rate with the strike rate at any node during these times can be drastically different from the premium calculated by comparing the spot exchange rate with the strike rate at these times.

There are, however, two ways of overcoming this deficiency in the forward rate model:

A. **Redefining the settlement process.** Instead of comparing the spot exchange rate with the strike rate at each node, one could compare the forward rate (expiring at time T) with the strike rate at each node. Since the user would typically be exposed to the spot exchange-rate risk, this approach may expose the user to basis risk; rendering it unfavorable for use.

B. **Using a multifactor forward-rate model.** In this approach, one would start with n initial forward rates applied to times Δt, $2\Delta t$, . . ., $n\Delta t$ and create a $(n + 1)$-dimensional tree that would incorporate both the absolute and relative movements between all the n forward rates.[16] This method, which is described in Methodology 3, is similar to the process used to value options on multiple assets.

[16] This is in a sense the modeling of the entire yield curve. Models of this sort are also called term structure (or integrated yield curve) models

Valuing Exotic Options

In this section, I use the binomial method, which was discussed earlier, to value the 11 option building blocks presented in Chapter 3. Instead of addressing these options in the same sequence as in Chapter 3, I will for the purposes of clarity first decompose the building blocks into the following two categories:

1. Domestic-currency-denominated option on domestic-currency-denominated asset/s.
2. Domestic-currency-denominated option on foreign-currency-denominated asset/s.

Each of these categories will then be subdivided into an option on a single asset and an option on multiple assets. This decomposition is illustrated in Exhibit 131.

EXHIBIT 131   Categorization of the 11 Exotic Option Building Blocks

Exotic Options			
Domestic-Currency-Denominated Option on Domestic-Currency-Denominated Asset/s		**Domestic-Currency-Denominated Option on Foreign-Currency-Denominated Asset/s**	
Payoff Linked to Single Asset	**Payoff Linked to Multiple Assets**	**Payoff Linked to Single Asset**	**Payoff Linked to Multiple Assets**
e.g.[17] Average option Cash-or-nothing option Choice option Compound option Deferred-start option Lookback option Nonlinear payoff option Sudden birth/death option	e.g. Basket option Spread option	e.g. Product option (Category II)	e.g. Product option (Category I, III, IV and V)

17 The options categorized in this group are in their simplest forms. For example, while the choice option described on page 120 has a payoff that is linked to one underlying asset value, the variations discussed on page 126 have their payoffs linked to more than one underlying asset value; making it possible for the choice option to also fall into the category of "payoff linked to multiple assets."

Domestic-Currency-Denominated Option on a Single Domestic-Currency-Denominated Asset

The valuation methods for these types of options are very similar to those used when valuing vanilla options. The steps required to value these options are summarized in Methodology 2.

METHODOLOGY 2 Using the Binomial Method to Value a Domestic-Currency-Denominated Option on a Single Domestic-Currency Denominated Asset

Stage 1

Determine S_0, r_d, r_f, σ, T, n and other necessary parameters[18]

Stage 2

Calculate the values of Δt, u, d and p using the formulae:

$$\Delta t = \frac{T}{n}, \; u = e^{\sigma \sqrt{\Delta t}}, \; d = \frac{1}{u}, \; \text{and } p = \frac{e^{(r_d - r_f)\Delta t} - d}{u - d}$$

Stage 3

Generate a tree for the underlying asset starting from the current asset price today and ending on the option maturity, as shown below:

0 yr Δt yr $2\Delta t$ yr $(n-2)\Delta t$ yr $(n-1)\Delta t$ yr $n\Delta t$ yr

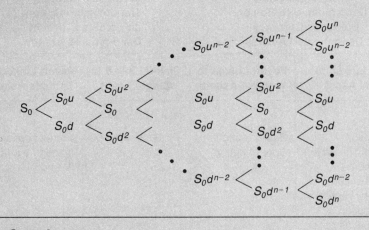

Stage 4

Generate an option tree as shown below using the asset price tree created in Stage 3, where the option value at each node is calculated using the following steps:

---

18 These parameters would be dependent on the type of exotic option priced. An example of such a parameter would be the necessity to know B, the size of the bet payoff, when valuing a cash-or-nothing option.

METHODOLOGY 2 Using the Binomial Method to Value a Domestic-Currency Denominated Option on a Single Domestic-Currency-Denominated Asset (Continued)

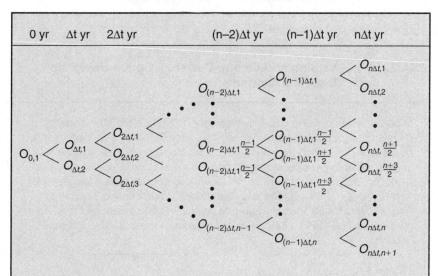

0 yr	Δt yr	2Δt yr		$(n-2)\Delta t$ yr	$(n-1)\Delta t$ yr	$n\Delta t$ yr

i) At time $n\Delta t$ (for $j = 1, 2, 3, \ldots, n-1, n, n+1$)

$$O_{n\Delta t,j} = I_{n\Delta t,j}$$

where $I_{n\Delta t,j}$ represents the intrinsic value of the option when $S_0 u^{n-2(j-1)}$ is used in the calculation of option payoff

ii) At time $i\Delta t$ (for $i = n-1, n-2, n-3, \ldots, 2, 1, 0$)

$$O_{i\Delta t,1} = \max\{I_{i\Delta t,1} \bullet E, [p \bullet O_{(i+1)\Delta t,1} + (1-p) \bullet O_{(i+1)\Delta t,2}]e^{-r_d\Delta t}\}$$
$$O_{i\Delta t,2} = \max\{I_{i\Delta t,2} \bullet E, [p \bullet O_{(i+1)\Delta t,2} + (1-p) \bullet O_{(i+1)\Delta t,3}]e^{-r_d\Delta t}\}$$

$\cdot$

$\cdot$

$$O_{i\Delta t,i} = \max\{I_{i\Delta t,i} \bullet E, [p \bullet O_{(i+1)\Delta t,i} + (1-p) \bullet O_{(i+1)\Delta t,i+1}]e^{-r_d\Delta t}\}$$
$$O_{i\Delta t,i+1} = \max\{I_{i\Delta t,i+1} \bullet E, [p \bullet O_{(i+1)\Delta t,i+1} + (1-p) \bullet O_{(i+1)\Delta t,i+2}]e^{-r_d\Delta t}\}$$

where $E = 1$ if exercise is allowed at $i\Delta t$ and 0 if no exercise is allowed at $i\Delta t$; $I_{i\Delta t,j}$ (for $j = 1, 2, 3, \ldots, i-1, i, i+1$) represents the intrinsic value of the option when $S_0 u^{i-2(j-1)}$ is used in the calculation of the option payoff

Stage 5

The option premium is given by $O_{0,1}$.

Since the methodologies required to value an American-style option, Mid-Atlantic-style option, and European-style option are philosophically no different from each other, in the remainder of this chapter, I will focus on valuing European-style exotic options, unless otherwise specified.

The use of a binomial method to value a European-style average rate put option is illustrated in Example 26.

EXAMPLE 26 Valuing an Average Currency Option Using the Binomial Method

The Canadian dollar is currently trading at 1.3000 Cad/US. An investor wants to buy a continuously averaged 4½-year Category II European-style put option (i.e., the in-the-money payoff on the maturity date is strike rate minus the arithmetically averaged rate) on the U.S. dollar that is struck at 1.3000 Cad/US. The current continuously compounded risk-free rates-of-interest in the United States and Canada are 6 percent and 8 percent respectively. Using an exchange-rate volatility of 10 percent and dividing the 4½-year period into four equal subintervals, I want to value this put option.

Stage 1

$S_0 = 1.3000$, $X = 1.3000$, $r_d = 0.08$, $r_f = 0.06$, $\sigma = 0.1$, $T = 4.5$, $n = 4$

Stage 2

From Example 25, it can be seen that $\Delta t = 1.125$, $u = 1.1119$, $d = 0.8994$, $p = 0.5805$

Stage 3

0 yr	1(1.125) yr	2(1.125) yr	3(1.125) yr	4(1.125) yr

- $1.3(1.1119)^4$
- $1.3(1.1119)^3$
- $1.3(1.1119)^2$
- $1.3(1.1119)^2$
- $1.3(1.1119)$
- $1.3(1.1119)$
- 1.3
- 1.3
- $1.3(0.8994)$
- $1.3(0.8994)$
- $1.3(0.8994)^2$
- $1.3(0.8994)^2$
- $1.3(0.8994)^3$
- $1.3(0.8994)^4$

EXAMPLE 26   Valuing an Average Currency Option Using the Binomial Method (Continued)

Stage 4

0 yr	1(1.125) yr	2(1.125) yr	3(1.125) yr	4(1.125) yr

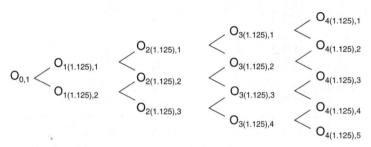

i) At time 4(1.125)

   a) Calculating $O_{4(1.125),1}$

     To calculate the intrinsic value $O_{4(1.125),1}$, I have to first calculate the average realized by this path in order to arrive at a final exchange-rate value of $1.3(1.1119)^4$. From the tree in Stage 3, it can be seen that the path taken to reach $1.3(1.1119)^4$ is [1.3, 1.3(1.1119), $1.3(1.11119)^2$, $1.3(1.1119)^3$, $1.3(1.1119)^4$], whose average is calculated to be 1.6254. Thus,

$$O_{4(1.125),1} = \max[1.3000 - 1.6254, 0] = 0.0000$$

   b) Calculating $O_{4(1.125),2}$

     To calculate the value $O_{4(1.125),2}$, I need to calculate the average realized by this path in order to arrive at a final exchange-rate value of $1.3(1.1119)^2$. From the tree in Stage 3, it can be seen that unlike $O_{4(1.125),1}$, four paths lead to a final value of $1.3(1.1119)^2$:

Path 1:	[1.3, 1.3(1.1119), $1.3(1.1119)^2$, $1.3(1.1119)^3$, $1.3(1.1119)^2$]
Path 2:	[1.3, 1.3(1.1119), $1.3(1.1119)^2$, 1.3(1.1119), $1.3(1.1119)^2$]
Path 3:	[1.3, 1.3(1.1119), 1.3, 1.3(1.1119), $1.3(1.1119)^2$]
Path 4:	[1.3, 1.3(0.8994), 1.3, 1.3(1.1119), $1.3(1.1119)^2$]

Although the averages associated with Paths 1 to 4 are 1.5494, 1.4811, 1.4196, and 1.3644, respectively, because none of the averages are less than 1.3, the intrinsic value associated with each path is zero regardless of the path. Thus,

$$O_{4(1.125),2} = 0.0000$$

   c) Calculating $O_{4(1.125),3}$

     To calculate the value of $O_{4(1.125)3}$, I need to calculate the average realized by this path in order to arrive at a final exchange-rate value

EXAMPLE 26   Valuing an Average Currency Option Using the Binomial Method (Continued)

of 1.3. From the tree in *Stage 3*, it can be seen that, six paths lead to a final value of 1.3:

Path 1:   [1.3, 1.3(1.1119), 1.3(1.1119)^2, 1.3(1.1119), 1.3]
Path 2:   [1.3, 1.3(1.1119), 1.3, 1.3(1.1119), 1.3]
Path 3:   [1.3, 1.3(1.1119), 1.3, 1.3(0.8994), 1.3]
Path 4:   [1.3, 1.3(0.8994), 1.3, 1.3(1.1119), 1.3]
Path 5:   [1.3, 1.3(0.8994), 1.3, 1.3(0.8994), 1.3]
Path 6:   [1.3, 1.3(0.8994), 1.3(0.8994)^2, 1.3(0.8994), 1.3]

The averages associated with Paths 1 to 6 are 1.4196, 1.3582, 1.3029, 1.3029, 1.2477, and 1.1980, respectively. While the intrinsic values associated with Paths 1 to 4 are zero, the intrinsic values associated with Paths 5 and 6 are 0.0523 and 0.1020, respectively. Thus,

$$O_{4(1.125),3} = \begin{array}{ll} 0.0000 & \text{if Paths 1, 2, 3, 4} \\ 0.0523 & \text{if Path 5} \\ 0.1020 & \text{if Path 6} \end{array}$$

d) Calculating $O_{4(1.125),4}$

The following are the four paths that lead to a final exchange-rate value of 1.3(0.8994)^2.

Path 1:   [1.3, 1.3(1.1119), 1.3, 1.3(0.8994), 1.3(0.8994)^2]
Path 2:   [1.3, 1.3(0.8994), 1.3, 1.3(0.8994), 1.3(0.8994)^2]
Path 3:   [1.3, 1.3(0.8994), 1.3(0.8994)^2, 1.3(0.8994), 1.3(0.8994)^2]
Path 4:   [1.3, 1.3(0.8994), 1.3(0.8994)^2, 1.3(0.8994)^3, 1.3(0.8994)^2]

The averages associated with paths 1 to 4 are 1.2533, 1.1980, 1.1483, and 1.1036, respectively. The intrinsic values associated with each of the paths are 0.0468, 0.1020, 0.1517, and 0.1964, respectively. Thus

$$O_{4(1.125),4} = \begin{array}{ll} 0.0467 & \text{if Path 1} \\ 0.1020 & \text{if Path 2} \\ 0.1517 & \text{if Path 3} \\ 0.1964 & \text{if Path 4} \end{array}$$

e) Calculating $O_{4(1.125),5}$

To calculate the average realized by the path transversed to reach a final exchange-rate value of 1.3(0.8994)^4, I first observe that the only path that leads to the final value is [1.3, 1.3(0.8994), 1.3(0.8994)^2, 1.3(0.8994)^3, 1.3(0.8994)^4].

The average associated with this path is 1.0635, which gives an intrinsic value of 0.2365, Thus,

$$O_{4(1.125),5} = 0.2365$$

EXAMPLE 26   Valuing an Average Currency Option Using the Binomial Method (Continued)

ii) At time 3(1.125)

   a) Calculating $O_{3(1.125),1}$

     To calculate the value of $O_{3(1.125),1}$, I have to first calculate the value of the option that can be obtained by exercising at that node and the expected value of the option by carrying on from that node. Since this is a European-style option, the value obtained by exercising the option is zero. Furthermore, the expected value of the option by not exercising is given by

$$\{[p \bullet O_{4(1.125),1}] + [(1 - p) \bullet O_{4(1.125),2}]\}e^{-r_d \Delta t} = 0.0000$$

     Thus, the value of $O_{3(1.125),1}$ is max[0.0000,0.0000] = 0.0000.

   b) Calculating $O_{3(1.125),2}$

     The option value due to exercise is zero. Furthermore, the expected value of the option from not exercising is $\{[p \bullet O_{4(1.125),2}] + [(1-p) \bullet O_{4(1.125),3}]\}e^{-r_d \Delta t}$. However, while $O_{4(1.125),2} = 0$, the value of $O_{4(1.125),3}$ depends on the path transversed by the exchange rate. Thus,

$$O_{3(1.125),2} = \begin{array}{l} 0.0000 \;\; \text{if path is } [1.3, 1.3(1.1119), 1.3(1.1119)^2, 1.3(1.1119)] \\ 0.0000 \;\; \text{if path is } [1.3, 1.3(1.1119), 1.3, 1.3(1.1119)] \\ 0.0000 \;\; \text{if path is } [1.3, 1.3(0.8994), 1.3, 1.3(1.1119)] \end{array}$$

     Hence, $O_{3(1.125),2} = 0$

   c) Calculating $O_{3(1.125),3}$

     The option value due to exercise is zero, and the expected value of the option from not exercising is dependent on the path transversed by the exchange rate and is given by $\{[p \bullet O_{4(1.125),3}] + [(1-p) \bullet O_{4(1.125),4}]\}e^{-r_d \Delta t}$. Thus,

$$O_{3(1.125),3} = \begin{array}{l} 0.0179 \;\; \text{if path is } [1.3, 1.3(1.1119), 1.3, 1.3(0.8994)] \\ 0.0669 \;\; \text{if path is } [1.3, 1.3(1.8994), 1.3, 1.3(0.8994)] \\ 0.1123 \;\; \text{if path is } [1.3, 1.3(0.8994), 1.3(0.8994)^2, 1.3(0.8994)] \end{array}$$

   d) Calculating $O_{3(1.125),4}$

     The option value due to exercise is zero, and the expected value of the option from not exercising is dependent on the path transversed by the exchange rate and is given by $\{[p \bullet O_{4(1.125),4}] + [(1-p) \bullet O_{4(1.125),5}]\}e^{-r_d \Delta t}$. Thus

$$O_{3(1.125),4} = 0.1949 \;\; \text{if path is } [1.3, 1.3(0.8994), 1.3(0.8994)^2, 1.3(0.8994)^3]$$

     which implies that $O_{3(1.125),4} = 0.1949$.

EXAMPLE 26   Valuing an Average Currency Option Using the Binomial Method (Continued)

iii) At time 2(1.125)

   a) Calculating $O_{2(1.125),1}$

   Due to no exercise, $O_{2(1.125),1}$ is given by the formula

   $$\{[p \bullet O_{3(1.125),1}] + [(1-p) \bullet O_{3(1.125),2}]\}e^{-r_d\Delta t}$$

   Thus, the value of $O_{2(1.125),1}$ is 0.0000.

   b) Calculating $O_{2(1.125),2}$

   The option value $O_{2(1.125),2}$ is given by

   $$\{[p \bullet O_{3(1.125),2}] + [(1-p) \bullet O_{3(1.125),3}]\}e^{-r_d\Delta t}$$

   However, while $O_{3(1.125),2} = 0$, the value of $O_{3(1.125),3}$ depends on the path transversed by the exchange rate. Thus,

   $$O_{2(1.125),2} = \begin{array}{ll} 0.0069 & \text{if path is } [1.3, 1.3(1.1119), 1.3] \\ 0.0256 & \text{if path is } [1.3, 1.3(0.8994), 1.3] \end{array}$$

   c) Calculating $O_{2(1.125),3}$

   The option value $O_{2(1.125),3}$ is given by

   $$\{[p \bullet O_{3(1.125),3}] + [(1-p) \bullet O_{3(1.125),4}]\}e^{-r_d\Delta t}$$

   However, while $O_{3(1.125),4} = 0.1949$, the value of $O_{3(1.125),3}$ depends on the path transversed by the exchange rate. Thus,

   $$O_{2(1.125),3} = 0.1343 \quad \text{if path is } [1.3, 1.3(0.8994), 1.3(0.8994)^2].$$

   Hence, $O_{2(1.125),3} = 0.1343$.

iv) At time1(1.125)

   a) Calculating $O_{1(1.125),1}$

   Due to no exercise, $O_{1(1.125),1}$ is given by the formula

   $$\{[p \bullet O_{2(1.125),1}] + [(1-p) \bullet O_{2(1.125),2}]\}e^{-r_d\Delta t}$$

   However, while $O_{2(1.125),1} = 0$, the value of $O_{2(1.125),2}$ depends on the path transversed by the exchange rate. Thus,

   $$O_{1(1.125),1} = 0.0026 \quad \text{if path is } [1.3, 1.3(1.1119)]$$

   Hence, $O_{1(1.125),1} = 0.0026$.

   b) Calculating $O_{1(1.125),2}$

   The option value $O_{1(1.125),2}$ is given by

   $$\{[p \bullet O_{2(1.125),2}] + [(1-p) \bullet O_{2(1.125),3}]\}e^{-r_d\Delta t}$$

   However, while $O_{2(1.125),3} = 0.1343$, the value of $O_{2(1.125),2}$ depends on the path transversed by the exchange rate. Thus,

   $$O_{1(1.125),2} = 0.0651 \quad \text{if path is } [1.3, 1.3(0.8894)]$$

   Hence, $O_{1(1.125),2} = 0.0651$.

EXAMPLE 26   Valuing an Average Currency Option Using the Binomial Method (Continued)

v) At time 0

Due to no exercise, $O_{0,1}$ is given by the formula

$$\{[p \bullet O_{1(1.125),1}] + [(1-p) \bullet O_{1(1.125),2}]\}e^{-r_d\Delta t}$$

Thus, $O_{0,1} = 0.0263$.

Stage 5

The option premium is 0.0263 Cad/US.

It is important for the reader to make the following five observations about Example 26.

OBSERVATION 1 To obtain a more accurate value for the average-rate option valued in Example 26, one has to reduce the value of Δt. If the exchange rates were sampled every Δt-period for the averaging process and the value of Δt simultaneously decreased to improve the accuracy, it can be shown that the value of the continuously averaged rate option is 0.0279 Cad/US.

OBSERVATION 2 As can be observed from the example, although valuing an average-rate option using a binomial tree may be easy to understand and implement when n is small, implementing a 50-step tree can be very tedious and cumbersome due to the nature of the path dependence. Hull and White (1993) provide an efficient way of using the binomial tree to value these types of options. Their method uses the philosophy of computing both upper and lower bounds for the averaging process throughout the nodes of the tree.

OBSERVATION 3 Although a European-style average option can be valued using the methodology described in Observation 2 of Example 25, this method is only useful once the average value (or, equivalently, the intrinsic value of the option) is calculated for each path. Thus, the problem of computing the average along each path remains.

OBSERVATION 4 If the European-style average option is the only option of interest, fortunately for us there is an easier way of using the binomial tree to value the average-rate options. In this approximate and simplified approach, one would model the average rate process instead of trying to calculate the average from the underlying exchange-rate process, as illustrated in Example 26. More precisely, to use a binomial tree to value a continuously averaged rate option, one would need to use the relationship

$$u_* = e^{\sigma_* \sqrt{\Delta t}}; \ d_* = \frac{1}{u_*}, \ p_* = \frac{e^{(r_d - r_*)\Delta t} - d_*}{u_* - d_*}$$

where

$$A = \frac{2e^{[2(r_d - r_f) + \sigma^2]T}}{(r_d - r_f + \sigma^2)[2(r_d - r_f) + \sigma^2]T^2}$$

$$B = \frac{2}{(r_d - r_f)T^2} \left[\frac{1}{2(r_d - r_f) + \sigma^2} - \frac{e^{(r_d - r_f)T}}{r_d - r_f + \sigma^2} \right]$$

$$M_1 = \frac{e^{(r_d - r_f)T} - 1}{(r_d - r_f)T}$$

$$M_2 = A + B$$

$$r_* = r_d - \frac{\ln(M_1)}{T}$$

$$\sigma_* = \sqrt{\frac{\ln(M_2) - 2\ln(M_1)}{T}}$$

With this definition of u_*, d_*, and p_*, one can now create a continuously arithmetically averaged tree, which will be analogous to the underlying exchange-rate tree built in *Stage 4* of Example 26. To value the option using this arithmetic average tree, as in Stage 5 of Example 25, the intrinsic value of the option at each node using the value of the average at that node is calculated. The intrinsic values are then present-valued. In the context of our example, when $\Delta t = 1.125$, the value of u_*, d_*, and p_* can be shown to be 1.0640, 0.9398, and 0.5765, respectively. These parameters, when used, yield an option price of 0.0250 Cad/US. As in Observation 1, by making Δt small enough, I can arrive at an option premium of 0.0279 Cad/US.

To value a European-style continuously and geometrically averaged option, one can still use the above expressions for u_*, d_*, and p_*, where r_* and σ_* would now be defined as follows:

$$r_* = \frac{1}{2}\left(r_d + r_f + \frac{\sigma^2}{6}\right)$$

$$\sigma_* = \frac{\sigma}{\sqrt{3}}$$

The reason for being unable to use the above approximation to value both American-style and Mid-Atlantic-style options arises from the fact that in performing the above approximation one did not in any way monitor the running average throughout the tree. Instead, the tree modeled the average that will be realized at time T. Furthermore, when early exercise is embedded into the option, it is very often the case that the option holder would exercise using the running average as opposed to the expected value of the average at a future time. As an astute reader will realize, this problem is analogous to using the binomial tree to value options whose underlying assets are forward rates, which were discussed in Observation 5 of Example 25.

OBSERVATION 5 Valuing a Category I and III European-style average option (that is, the in-the-money option payoff on the maturity date is the difference between the average rate and the spot rate on the maturity date) using the methodology described in Example 26 is pretty straightforward although tedious. However, applying the philosophy of creating an average-rate tree that was discussed in Observation 4 is a bit trickier. This is because the payoff, upon option maturity, is dependent on both the underlying exchange rate and the realized average exchange rate. Since one would have generated only an average-rate tree, there is still a need for an underlying exchange rate. With these two binomial trees, the ideas underlying Examples 34 and 35 are used to arrive at the option value.

The use of a binomial method to value a European-style cash-or-nothing put option is illustrated in Example 27.

EXAMPLE 27 Valuing a Cash-or-Nothing Currency Option Using the Binomial Method

The Canadian dollar is currently trading at 1.3000 Cad/US. An investor wants to buy a 4½-year cash-or-nothing put option on the U.S. dollar that is struck at 1.3000 Cad/US. The current continuously compounded risk-free rates of interest in the United States and Canada are 6 percent and 8 percent respectively. Using an exchange-rate volatility of 10 percent, a bet payoff of C$ 1,000, and dividing the 4½-year period into four equal subintervals, I want to value a European-style cash-or-nothing put option.

Stage 1

$S_0 = 1.3000$, $X = 1.3000$, $B = 1000$, $r_d = 0.08$, $r_f = 0.06$, $\sigma = 0.1$, $T = 4.5$, $n = 4$

EXAMPLE 27 Valuing a Cash-or-Nothing Currency Option Using the Binomial method (Continued)

Stages 2, 3

Since the exchange-rate tree is no different from that in Example 26, the reader is referred to Example 26 for these stages.

Stage 4

For the diagram of the option tree, the reader is again referred to Example 26.

i) At time $4(1.125)$

    a) Calculating $O_{4(1.125),1}$, $O_{4(1.125),2}$ and $O_{4(1.125),3}$

        Since the exchange-rate values at these nodes are never less than 1.3, the option has finished out-of-the-money at these nodes. Thus,

$$O_{4(1.125),1} = O_{4(1.125),2} = O_{4(1.125),3} = 0.0000$$

    b) Calculating $O_{4(1.125),4}$ and $O_{4(1.125),5}$

        Since the exchange-rate value at these nodes are less than 1.3, the option has finished in-the-money at these nodes. Thus,

$$O_{4(1.125),4} = O_{4(1.125),5} = 1000.$$

ii) At time $3(1.125)$

Because no early exercise is allowed,

$$O_{3(1.125),1} = \max[0, p \bullet O_{4(1.125),1} + (1 - p) \bullet O_{4(1.125),2}]e^{-r_d \Delta t}$$
$$= 0.0000$$

$$O_{3(1.125),2} = \max[0, p \bullet O_{4(1.125),2} + (1 - p) \bullet O_{4(1.125),3}]e^{-r_d \Delta t}$$
$$= 0.0000$$

$$O_{3(1.125),3} = \max[0, p \bullet O_{4(1.125),3} + (1 - p) \bullet O_{4(1.125),4}]e^{-r_d \Delta t}$$
$$= 383.3941$$

$$O_{3(1.125),4} = \max[0, p \bullet O_{4(1.125),4} + (1 - p) \bullet O_{4(1.125),5}]e^{-r_d \Delta t}$$
$$= 913.9312$$

iii) At time $2(1.125)$

Since no early exercise is allowed,

$$O_{2(1.125),1} = \max[0, p \bullet O_{3(1.125),1} + (1-p) \bullet O_{3(1.125),2}]e^{-r_d \Delta t}$$
$$= 0.0000$$

$$O_{2(1.125),2} = \max[0, p \bullet O_{3(1.125),2} + (1-p) \bullet O_{3(1.125),3}]e^{-r_d \Delta t}$$
$$= 146.9910$$

$$O_{2(1.125),3} = \max[0, p \bullet O_{3(1.125),3} + (1-p) \bullet O_{3(1.125),4}]e^{-r_d \Delta t}$$
$$= 553.8006$$

EXAMPLE 27   Valuing a Cash-or-Nothing Currency Option Using the Binomial method (Continued)

iv) At time 1(1.125)

Due to the lack of early exercise,

$$O_{1(1.125),1} = \max[0, p \bullet O_{2(1.125),1} + (1-p) \bullet O_{2(1.125),2}]e^{-r_d \Delta t}$$
$$= 56.3555$$

$$O_{1(1.125),2} = \max[0, p \bullet O_{2(1.125),2} + (1-p) \bullet O_{2(1.125),3}]e^{-r_d \Delta t}$$
$$= 290.3081$$

v) At time 0

$$O_{0,1} = \max[0, p \bullet O_{1(1.125),1} + (1-p) \bullet O_{1(1.125),2}]e^{-r_d \Delta t}$$
$$= 141.2011$$

Stage 5

The cash-or-nothing put option premium is C$ 141.20.

It is important for the reader to make the following four observations about Example 27.

OBSERVATION 1 To obtain a more accurate value for the cash-or-nothing option valued in Example 27, one has to reduce the value of Δt. Unlike the options seen earlier, to see any form of convergence when using a binomial method to value this type of option, n has to be very large (for example, n > 1000) before the premium can converge to C$ 261.75. Furthermore, only when the option is struck at S_0, does the method lead to a well-behaved convergence of the option premium when n is only odd (or only even) like the behavior illustrated in Exhibit 129. At any other strike levels, regardless of whether n is only odd (or only even), there are sudden jumps in the option premium, as illustrated in Exhibits 132 and 133.

The jumps in the out-of-the-money and in-the-money option premiums can be explained by looking closely at the option payoff upon exercise and supposing, for example, that the strike level is 1.3500 Cad/US and n = 4. Since the cash-or-nothing option pays off a constant bet amount only if the option is in-the-money, the put option premium would not change as long as the strike rate lies in

**EXHIBIT 132   Convergence of In-the-Money Option Premium
Using a Binomial Method**

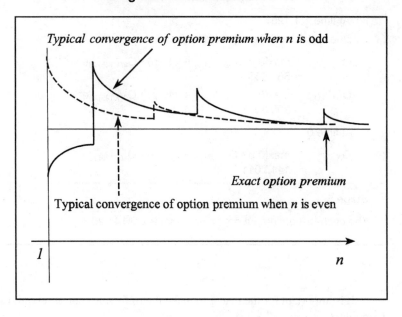

**EXHIBIT 133   Convergence of Out-of-the-Money Option
Premium Using a Binomial Method**

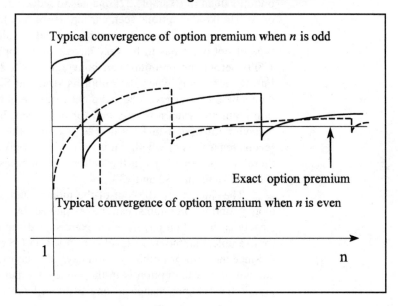

the interval to 1.3 to $1.3(1.1119)^2$. Furthermore, increasing the value of n results in this interval shrinking in length. More precisely, as n gets larger, the upper end of the interval, $1.3e^{2\sigma\sqrt{\Delta t}}$ (which is $1.3(1.1119)^2$ when n = 4) converges to 1.35 at a threshold value of n = n*. Immediately beyond this threshold value, one would get $1.3e^{2\sigma\sqrt{\Delta t^*}} <$ 1.35 and $1.3e^{4\sigma\sqrt{\Delta t^*}} > 1.35$, implying a start of a new interval ranging from $1.3e^{2\sigma\sqrt{\Delta t^*}}$ to $1.3e^{4\sigma\sqrt{\Delta t^*}}$ in which the premium will be insensitive to the strike level. This change in both the upper and lower bounds of the interval results in a jump in the option premium, following which the covergence process is repeated. As n gets larger, the jump in the option premium is dampened, leading to greater accuracy.

Due to the jump in premiums occurring at times immediately after the threshold values of n are reached, in addition to restricting to only odd (or only even) integers for n, it is important to be able to choose an "optimal" value of n just before the jump occurs. This "optimal" value of n can be chosen using a modification of the algorithm put forward by Boyle and Lau (1994) to overcome similar problems when valuing barrier options. More precisely, the value of n is chosen such that

A) n is the largest odd integer satisfying the inequality

$$n < \frac{m^2\sigma^2T}{\left[\ln\left(\dfrac{S_0}{X}\right)\right]^2} \quad \text{when m} = 1, 3, 5, 7, \ldots, \text{or}$$

B) n is the largest even integer satisfying the inequality

$$n < \frac{m^2\sigma^2T}{\left[\ln\left(\dfrac{S_0}{X}\right)\right]^2} \quad \text{when m} = 2, 4, 6, 8, \ldots$$

Since there is a problem with the convergence when valuing options that are not-at-the-money, I will illustrate the application of this technique when valuing an in-the-money option. Assuming $S_0 = 1.3$, X = 1.35, $\sigma = 0.1$, T = 4.5

and using the equation in (A), when m = 1, one would need n to be the largest odd integer that is less than

$$\frac{1^2 \bullet 0.1^2 \bullet 4.5}{\left[\ln\left(\dfrac{1.3}{1.35}\right)\right]^2} = 31.59$$

This would imply that n = 31. To ensure convergence, one should now set m = 3 in the equation and select the next n such that is the largest odd integer that is less than

$$\frac{3^2 \bullet 0.1^2 \bullet 4.5}{\left[\ln\left(\dfrac{1.3}{1.35}\right)\right]^2} = 284.34$$

This would imply that n = 284. If further convergence is required, the process is repeated for higher odd values of m.

OBSERVATION 2 In calculating the cash-or-nothing option premium, it was assumed that even if the exchange rate at expiry was 1.3000 Cad/US, the option finished out-of-the money. Although this would not make any difference when Δt is very small, the difference could be drastic for a larger Δt. To illustrate, suppose I had given a payoff of C$ 1,000 to the purchaser of the option when the exchange rate is 1.3000 Cad/US. When n = 4, it can be shown that the cash-or-nothing put option premium is C$ 389.44, which is more than twice the amount obtained in the above example. Thus, in addition to carefully choosing an "optimal" value of n (or equivalently Δt) as discussed in Observation 1, special attention should be given to computing the in-the-money payoffs when the strike value lies on the node of the tree.

OBSERVATION 3 To overcome the problems mentioned in Observations 1 and 2 and to obtain the convergence of a cash-or-nothing option premium when increasing n, one can use the philosophy of replicating a cash-or-nothing option with vanilla options that was discussed on page 111. More precisely, since a vanilla option premium converges to its true value when n increases, the C$ 1,000 payoff using a bear spread on a notional amount of $\dfrac{US\$\ 1,000}{1.3000 - 1.2999} = US\$\ 10,00,000$ can be replicated, where the lower strike level is 1.2999 Cad/US and the upper strike level is 1.3000 Cad/US. The difference in these option premiums would then equate to the cash-or-nothing option premium.

The use of a binomial method to value a European-style choice option is illustrated in Example 28.

EXAMPLE 28   Valuing a Choice Currency Option Using the Binomial Method

The Canadian dollar is currently trading at 1.3000 Cad/US. An investor wants to buy a 4½-year choice option that would allow him to choose in 2.25 years between a U.S. dollar call and a U.S. dollar put, both of which are struck at 1.3000 Cad/US and expire 2.25 years after the choice time. The current continuously compounded risk-free rates of interest in the United States and Canada are 6 percent and 8 percent respectively. Using an exchange-rate volatility of 10 percent and dividing the 4½-year period into four equal subintervals, I want to value this European-style choice option.

Stage 1

$S_0 = 1.3000$, $X = 1.3000$, $r_d = 0.08$, $r_f = 0.06$, $\sigma = 0.1$, $t = 2.25$, $T = 4.5$, $n = 4$

Stages 2, 3

As with the earlier example, since the exchange-rate tree is no different from that presented in Example 26, the reader is referred to Example 26 for these stages.

Stage 4

For the diagram of the option tree, the reader is again referred to Example 26.

i) At time 4(1.125)

If a call option is chosen at 2.25 years, the intrinsic values of the option at all the nodes are

$\max[1.3(1.1119)^4 - 1.3, 0] = 0.6870$
$\max[1.3(1.1119)^2 - 1.3, 0] = 0.3072$
$\max[1.3 \quad\quad\quad - 1.3, 0] = 0.0000$
$\max[1.3(0.8994)^2 - 1.3, 0] = 0.0000$
$\max[1.3(0.8994)^4 - 1.3, 0] = 0.0000$

**EXAMPLE 28   Valuing a Choice Currency Option Using the
Binomial Method (Continued)**

If a put option is chosen at 2.25 years, the intrinsic values of the option
at all the nodes are

$\max[1.3–1.3(1.1119)^4,0] = 0.0000$
$\max[1.3–1.3(1.1119)^2,0] = 0.0000$
$\max[1.3–1.3,0] \qquad\quad = 0.0000$
$\max[1.3–1.3(0.8994)^2,0] = 0.2484$
$\max[1.3–1.3(0.8994)^4,0] = 0.4493$

Thus,

$O_{4(1.125,1)} = \begin{matrix} 0.6870 & \text{if call is chosen} \\ 0.0000 & \text{if put is chosen} \end{matrix}$

$O_{4(1.125,2)} = \begin{matrix} 0.3072 & \text{if call is chosen} \\ 0.0000 & \text{if put is chosen} \end{matrix}$

$O_{4(1.125,3)} = 0.0000$

$O_{4(1.125,4)} = \begin{matrix} 0.0000 & \text{if call is chosen} \\ 0.2484 & \text{if put is chosen} \end{matrix}$

$O_{4(1.125,5)} = \begin{matrix} 0.0000 & \text{if call is chosen} \\ 0.4493 & \text{if put is chosen} \end{matrix}$

ii) At time 3(1.125)

Due to lack of early exercise, depending on the type of option chosen,
the option values at all the nodes are

$O_{3(1.125),1} = \begin{matrix} [p \bullet 0.6870 + (1–p) \bullet 0.3072]e^{-r_d\Delta t} = 0.4823 & \text{if call is chosen} \\ [p \bullet 0.0000 + (1–p) \bullet 0.0000]e^{-r_d\Delta t} = 0.0000 & \text{if put is chosen} \end{matrix}$

$O_{3(1.125),2} = \begin{matrix} [p \bullet 0.3072 + (1–p) \bullet 0.0000]e^{-r_d\Delta t} = 0.1630 & \text{if call is chosen} \\ [p \bullet 0.0000 + (1–p) \bullet 0.0000]e^{-r_d\Delta t} = 0.0000 & \text{if put is chosen} \end{matrix}$

$O_{3(1.125),3} = \begin{matrix} [p \bullet 0.0000 + (1–p) \bullet 0.0000]e^{-r_d\Delta t} = 0.0000 & \text{if call is chosen} \\ [p \bullet 0.0000 + (1–p) \bullet 0.2484]e^{-r_d\Delta t} = 0.0952 & \text{if put is chosen} \end{matrix}$

$O_{3(1.125),4} = \begin{matrix} [p \bullet 0.0000 + (1–p) \bullet 0.0000]e^{-r_d\Delta t} = 0.0000 & \text{if call is chosen} \\ [p \bullet 0.2484 + (1–p) \bullet 0.4493]e^{-r_d\Delta t} = 0.3040 & \text{if put is chosen} \end{matrix}$

iii) At time 2(1.125)

If no choice/exercise is made at this time, the option values at all the nodes
are

$\text{node 1} = \begin{matrix} [p \bullet 0.4823 + (1–p) \bullet 0.1630]e^{-r_d\Delta t} = 0.3184 & \text{if call is chosen} \\ [p \bullet 0.0000 + (1–p) \bullet 0.0000]e^{-r_d\Delta t} = 0.0000 & \text{if put is chosen} \end{matrix}$

$\text{node 2} = \begin{matrix} [p \bullet 0.1630 + (1–p) \bullet 0.0000]e^{-r_d\Delta t} = 0.0865 & \text{if call is chosen} \\ [p \bullet 0.0000 + (1–p) \bullet 0.0952]e^{-r_d\Delta t} = 0.0365 & \text{if put is chosen} \end{matrix}$

$\text{node 3} = \begin{matrix} [p \bullet 0.0000 + (1–p) \bullet 0.0000]e^{-r_d\Delta t} = 0.0000 & \text{if call is chosen} \\ [p \bullet 0.0952 + (1–p) \bullet 0.3040]e^{-r_d\Delta t} = 0.1671 & \text{if put is chosen} \end{matrix}$

EXAMPLE 28   Valuing a Choice Currency Option Using the Binomial Method (Continued)

Since a choice is made between a call and put option at this time, the holder of the option will only select a call (put) if the value of the call (put) is greater than the value of the put (call). Thus, the option values at all three nodes are

$$O_{2(1.125),1} = \max[0.3184, 0.0000] = 0.3184$$
$$O_{2(1.125),2} = \max[0.0865, 0.0365] = 0.0865$$
$$O_{2(1.125),3} = \max[0.0000, 0.1671] = 0.1671$$

iv) At time 1(1.125)

Since no exercise is made at this time, the option values at all the nodes are

$$O_{1(1.125),1} = [p \cdot O_{2(1.125),1} + (1-p) \cdot O_{2(1.125),2}]e^{-r_d \Delta t} = 0.2021$$
$$O_{1(1.125),2} = [p \cdot O_{2(1.125),2} + (1-p) \cdot O_{2(1.125),3}]e^{-r_d \Delta t} = 0.1100$$

v) At time 0

The option value at this node is

$$O_{0,1} = [p \cdot O_{1(1.125),1} + (1-p) \cdot O_{1(1.125),2}]e^{-r_d \Delta t} = 0.1494$$

Stage 5

The choice option premium is 0.1494 Cad/US.

It is important for the reader to make the following observation about Example 28.

OBSERVATION 1 To obtain a more accurate value for the choice option in Example 28, one has to reduce the value of Δt. Doing this would give us an option value of 0.1540   Cad/US.

The use of a binomial method to value a European-style call-on-put option is illustrated in Example 29 on page 242.

It is important for the reader to make the following two observations about Example 29.

OBSERVATION 1 To obtain a more accurate value for the compound option in Example 29, one has to reduce the value of Δt. Doing this would result in an option value of 0.0408 Cad/US.

OBSERVATION 2 In currency markets, it is the usually the case that the purchaser of a compound option would pay both the first and the second premium in a single currency. In the context of

EXAMPLE 29   Valuing a Compound Currency Option Using the Binomial Method

The Canadian dollar is currently trading at 1.3000 Cad/US. An investor wants to buy a 4½-year call-on-put option that would allow him to pay in 2.25 years 0.0050 Cad/US for a U.S. dollar put that is struck at 1.3000 Cad/US and expiring 2.25 years after the second installment date. The current continuously compounded risk-free rates of interest in the United States and Canada are 6 percent and 8 percent respectively. Using an exchange-rate volatility of 10 percent and dividing the 4½-year period into four equal subintervals, I want to value this European-style compound option.

Stage 1

$S_0 = 1.3000$, $X_1 = 0.0050$, $X_2 = 1.3000$, $r_d = 0.08$, $r_f = 0.06$, $\sigma = 0.1$, $t = 2.25$, $T = 4.5$, $n = 4$

Stages 2, 3

Since the exchange rate tree is no different from that presented in Example 26, the reader is referred to Example 26 for these stages.

Stage 4

For the diagram of the option tree, the reader is again referred to Example 26.

i) At time 4(1.125)

The intrinsic values associated with a put option are

$O_{4(1.125,1)} = \max[1.3 - 1.3(1.1119)^4, 0] = 0.0000$
$O_{4(1.125,2)} = \max[1.3 - 1.3(1.1119)^2, 0] = 0.0000$
$O_{4(1.125,3)} = \max[1.3 - 1.3, 0] \qquad = 0.0000$
$O_{4(1.125,4)} = \max[1.3 - 1.3(0.8994)^2, 0] = 0.2484$
$O_{4(1.125,5)} = \max[1.3 - 1.3(0.8994)^4, 0] = 0.4493$

ii) At time 3(1.125)

Due to lack of early exercise, the option values at all the nodes are

$O_{3(1.125),1} = [p \bullet 0.0000 + (1-p) \bullet 0.0000]e^{-r_d \Delta t} = 0.0000$
$O_{3(1.125),2} = [p \bullet 0.0000 + (1-p) \bullet 0.0000]e^{-r_d \Delta t} = 0.0000$
$O_{3(1.125),3} = [p \bullet 0.0000 + (1-p) \bullet 0.2484]e^{-r_d \Delta t} = 0.0952$
$O_{3(1.125),4} = [p \bullet 0.2484 + (1-p) \bullet 0.4493]e^{-r_d \Delta t} = 0.3040$

iii) At time 2(1.125)

If no exercise is allowed at this time, the option values at all the nodes are

EXAMPLE 29   Valuing a Compound Currency Option Using the Binomial Method (Continued)

node 1 = [p • 0.0000 + (1–p) • 0.0000]$e^{-r_d \Delta t}$ = 0.0000
node 2 = [p • 0.0000 + (1–p) • 0.0952]$e^{-r_d \Delta t}$ = 0.0365
node 3 = [p • 0.0952 + (1–p) • 0.3040]$e^{-r_d \Delta t}$ = 0.1671

Since the holder of the option has the ability to exercise the call option into a put option, the call will only be exercised if the put value is greater than 0.0050 Cad/US. Thus, the option values on these nodes are

$O_{2(1.125),1}$ = max[0.0000–0.0050,0] = 0.0000
$O_{2(1.125),2}$ = max[0.0365–0.0050,0] = 0.0000
$O_{2(1.125),3}$ = max[0.1671–0.0050,0] = 0.1621

iv) At time 1(1.125)

Since no exercise is made at this time, the option values at all the nodes are

$O_{1(1.125),1}$ = [p • $O_{2(1.125),1}$ + (1–p) • $O_{2(1.125),2}$]$e^{-r_d \Delta t}$ = 0.0000
$O_{1(1.125),2}$ = [p • $O_{2(1.125),2}$ + (1–p) • $O_{2(1.125),3}$]$e^{-r_d \Delta t}$ = 0.0621

v) At time 0

The option value at this node is

$O_{0,1}$ = [p • $O_{1(1.125),1}$ + (1–p) • $O_{1(1.125),2}$]$e^{-r_d \Delta t}$ = 0.0238

Stage 5

The compound option premium is 0.0238 Cad/US.

---

the example, this could imply that the investor may wish to pay both the initial compulsory premium and the second optional premium in U.S. dollars. In such an instance, one should be careful when incorporating the exercise feature in the binomial tree at the 2.25-year period. More precisely, at the 2.25-year period, instead of simply comparing the put option premium at each node with 0.0050 Cad/US, as was done in our example, one should first convert the put option premiums at each node to Canadian dollars using the appropriate U.S. notional amount. The Canadian-dollar-denominated option premiums across each node are now converted into U.S.-dollar-denominated ones by multiplying with the corresponding spot rates (in US/Cad) across each node of the tree. These converted premiums in U.S. dollars are now compared with the U.S.-dollar-denominated second installment amount to determine whether the first option finishes in the money. To arrive at an initial up-front premium in U.S. dollars, one would then discount these U.S.-denominated in-the-money payoffs that were calculated at the 2.25-year period using the U.S. risk-free rate.

The use of a binomial method to value a European-style deferred strike option is illustrated in Example 30.

EXAMPLE 30 Valuing a Deferred-Strike Currency Option Using the Binomial Method

The Canadian dollar is currently trading at 1.3000 Cad/US. An investor wants to buy a 4½-year deferred start put option on the U.S. dollar whose strike rate will be set in exactly 2.25 years time. The current continuously compounded risk-free rates of interest in the United States and Canada are 6 percent and 8 percent respectively. Using an exchange-rate volatility of 10 percent and dividing the 4½-year period into four equal subintervals, I want to value this European-style option.

Stage 1

$S_0 = 1.3000$, $r_d = 0.08$, $r_f = 0.06$, $\sigma = 0.1$, $t = 2.25$, T $= 4.5$, n $= 4$

Stages 2, 3

Since the exchange-rate tree is no different from that presented in Example 26, the reader is referred to Example 26 for these stages.

Stage 4

For the diagram of the option tree, the reader is again referred to Example 26.

i) At time 4(1.125)

  a) Calculating $O_{4(1.125),1}$

    To calculate the intrinsic value $O_{4(1.125),1}$, one has to first calculate the strike rate of the option that is applicable to this node. To arrive at a final exchange-rate value of $1.3(1.1119)^4$, it can be seen from the tree in *Stage 3* that the path taken is $[1.3, 1.3(1.1119), 1.3(1.1119)^2, 1.3(1.1119)^3, 1.3(1.1119)^4]$. This implies a strike rate of $1.3(1.1119)^2$ and hence an option value of

$$O_{4(1.125),1} = \max[1.3(1.1119)^2 - 1.3(1.1119)^4, 0]$$
$$= 0.0000$$

  b) Calculating $O_{4(1.125),2}$

    In order to calculate the value of $O_{4(1.125),2}$, one would need to find the strike rate that needs to be applied to this node. From the tree in

EXAMPLE 30 Valuing a Deferred-Strike Currency Option Using the Binomial Method (Continued)

Stage 3, it can be seen that there are four paths that lead to a final value of $1.3(1.1119)^2$:

Path 1: $[1.3, 1.3(1.1119), 1.3(1.1119)^2, 1.3(1.1119)^3, 1.3(1.1119)^2]$
Path 2: $[1.3, 1.3(1.1119), 1.3(1.1119)^2, 1.3(1.1119), 1.3(1.1119)^2]$
Path 3: $[1.3, 1.3(1.1119), 1.3, 1.3(1.1119), 1.3(1.1119)^2]$
Path 4: $[1.3, 1.3(0.8994), 1.3, 1.3(1.1119), 1.3(1.1119)^2]$

Since the strike rates associated with Path 1 to 4 are $1.3(1.1119)^2$, $1.3(1.1119)^2$, 1.3, and 1.3, respectively, because neither of the rates is greater than $1.3(1.1119)^2$, the intrinsic value associated with each path is zero regardless of the path. Thus

$$O_{4(1.125),2} = 0.0000$$

c) Calculating $O_{4(1.125),3}$

In order to calculate the value $O_{4(1.125),3}$, one would need to know the path transversed in order to arrive at a final exchange-rate value of 1.3. From the tree in Stage 3, it can be seen that there are six paths that lead to a final value of 1.3:

Path 1: $[1.3, 1.3(1.1119), 1.3(1.1119)^2, 1.3(1.1119), 1.3]$
Path 2: $[1.3, 1.3(1.1119), 1.3, 1.3(1.1119), 1.3]$
Path 3: $[1.3, 1.3(1.1119), 1.3, 1.3(0.8994), 1.3]$
Path 4: $[1.3, 1.3(0.8994), 1.3, 1.3(1.1119), 1.3]$
Path 5: $[1.3, 1.3(0.8994), 1.3, 1.3(0.8994), 1.3]$
Path 6: $[1.3, 1.3(0.8994), 1.3(0.8994)^2, 1.3(0.8994), 1.3]$

The strike rates associated with Paths 1 to 6 are $1.3(1.1119)^2$, 1.3, 1.3, 1.3, 1.3, and $1.3(0.8994)^2$, respectively. While the intrinsic values associated with Paths 2 to 6 are 0, the intrinsic value associated with Path 1 is 0.3072. Thus,

$$O_{4(1.125),3} = \begin{array}{ll} 0.3072 & \text{if Path 1} \\ 0.0000 & \text{if Paths 2, 3, 4, 5, 6} \end{array}$$

d) Calculating $O_{4(1.125),4}$

The following are the four paths leading to a final exchange rate value of $1.3(0.8994)^2$

Path 1: $[1.3, 1.3(1.1119), 1.3, 1.3(0.8994), 1.3(0.8994)^2]$
Path 2: $[1.3, 1.3(0.8994), 1.3, 1.3(0.8994), 1.3(0.8994)^2]$
Path 3: $[1.3, 1.3(0.8994), 1.3(0.8994)^2, 1.3(0.8994), 1.3(0.8994)^2]$
Path 4: $[1.3, 1.3(0.8994), 1.3(0.8994)^2, 1.3(0.8994)^3, 1.3(0.8994)^2]$

The strike rates associated with Paths 1 to 4 are 1.3, 1.3, $1.3(0.8994)^2$, and $1.3(0.8994)^2$, respectively. The intrinsic values associated with each of the paths are 0.2484, 0.2484, 0, and 0, respectively. Thus

$$O_{4(1.125),4} = \begin{array}{ll} 0.2484 & \text{if Paths 1, 2} \\ 0.0000 & \text{if Paths 3, 4} \end{array}$$

EXAMPLE 30   Valuing a Deferred-Strike Currency Option Using the Binomial Method (Continued)

e) Calculating $O_{4(1.125),5}$

Since $[1.3, 1.3(0.8994), 1.3(0.8994)^2, 1.3(0.8994)^3, 1.3(0.8994)^4]$ is the only path that leads to $1.3(0.8994)^4$, the strike rate at this node is $1.3(0.8994)^2$. Thus the intrinsic value at this node is

$$O_{4(1.125),5} = 0.2009$$

ii) At time 3(1.125)

a) Calculating $O_{3(1.125),1}$

Since this is a European-style option, the value obtained by exercising the option is 0. Furthermore, the expected value of the option by not exercising is given by

$$\{[p \bullet O_{4(1.125),1}] + [(1-p) \bullet O_{4(1.125),2}]\}e^{-r_d\Delta t} = 0.0000$$

Thus, the value of $O_{3(1.125),1}$ is 0.0000.

b) Calculating $O_{3(1.125),2}$

The option value due to exercise is 0. Furthermore, the expected value of the option from not exercising is $\{[p \bullet O_{4(1.125),2}] + [(1-p) \bullet O_{4(1.125),3}]\}e^{-r_d\Delta t}$. However, while $O_{4(1.125),2} = 0$, the value of $O_{4(1.125),3}$ depends on the path tranversed by the exchange rate. Thus,

$$O_{3(1.125),2} = \begin{array}{ll} 0.1178 & \text{if path is } [1.3, 1.3(1.119), 1.3(1.1119)^2, 1.3(1.1119)] \\ 0.0000 & \text{if path is } [1.3, 1.3(1.1119), 1.3, 1.3(1.1119)] \\ 0.0000 & \text{if path is } [1.3, 1.3(0.8994), 1.3, 1.3(1.1119] \end{array}$$

c) Calculating $O_{3(1.125),3}$

The option value due to exercise 0, and the expected value of the option from not exercising is dependent on the path transversed by the exchange rate and is given by $\{p \bullet O_{4(1.125),3}] + [(1-p) \bullet O_{4(1.125),4}]\}e^{-r_d\Delta t}$. Thus,

$$O_{3(1.125),3} = \begin{array}{ll} 0.0952 & \text{if path is } [1.3, 1.3(1.1119), 1.3, 1.3(0.8994)] \\ 0.0952 & \text{if path is } [1.3, 1.3(0.8994), 1.3, 1.3(0.8994)] \\ 0.0000 & \text{if path is } [1.3, 1.3(0.8994), 1.3(0.8994)^2, 1.3(0.8994)] \end{array}$$

d) Calculating $O_{3(1.125),4}$

The option value due to exercise is 0, and the expected value of the option from not exercising is dependent on the path transversed by the exchange rate and is given by $\{[p \bullet O_{4(1.125),4}] + [(1-p) \bullet O_{4(1.125),5}]\}e^{-r_d\Delta t}$. Thus,

$$O_{3(1.125),4} = 0.0770 \quad \text{if path is } [1.3, 1.3(0.8994), 1.3(0.8994)^2, 1.3(0.8994)^3]$$

Hence, $O_{3(1.125)4} = 0.0770$.

EXAMPLE 30 Valuing a Deferred-Strike Currency Option Using the Binomial Method (Continued)

iii) At time 2(1.125)

    a) Calculating $O_{2(1.125),1}$

      Due to no exercise, $O_{2(1.125),1}$ is given by the formula

$$\{[p \bullet O_{3(1.125),1}] + [(1-p) \bullet O_{3(1.125),2}]\}e^{-r_d \Delta t}$$

      While $O_{3(1.125),1} = 0$, the value of $O_{3(1.125),2}$ depends on the path transversed by the exchange rate. Thus,

$$O_{2(1.125),1} = 0.0452 \quad \text{if path is } [1.3, 1.3(1.1119), 1.3(1.1119)2]$$

      Thus, the value of $O_{2(1.125),1}$ is 0.0452.

    b) Calculating $O_{2(1.125),2}$

      The option value $O_{2(1.125),2}$ is given by

$$\{[p \bullet O_{3(1.125),2}] + [(1-p) \bullet O_{3(1.125),3}]\}e^{-r_d \Delta t}$$

      While $O_{3(1.125),2} = 0$, the value of $O_{3(1.125),3}$ depends on the path transversed by the exchange rate. Thus,

$$O_{2(1.125),2} = \begin{array}{ll} 0.0365 & \text{if path is } [1.3, 1.3(1.1119), 1.3] \\ 0.0365 & \text{if path is } [1.3, 1.3(0.8994), 1.3] \end{array}$$

      Hence, $O_{2(1.125),2} = 0.0365$.

    c) Calculating $O_{2(1.125),3}$

      The option value $O_{2(1.125),3}$ is given by

$$\{[p \bullet O_{3(1.125),3}] + [(1-p) \bullet O_{3(1.125),4}]\}e^{-r_d \Delta t}$$

      While $O_{3(1.125),4} = 0.0770$, the value of $O_{3(1.125),3}$ depends on the path transversed by the exchange rate. Thus,

$$O_{2(1.125),3} = 0.0295 \quad \text{if path is } [1.3, 1.3(0.8994), 1.3(0.8994)^2].$$

      Hence, $O_{2(1.125),3} = 0.0295$.

iv) At time 1(1.125)

    a) Calculating $O_{1(1.125),1}$

      Due to no exercise, $O_{1(1.125),1}$ is given by the formula

$$\{[p \bullet O_{2(1.125),1}] + [(1-p) \bullet O_{2(1.125),2}]\}e^{-r_d \Delta t}$$

      Thus,

$$O_{1(1.125),1} = 0.0380$$

    b) Calculating $O_{1(1.125),2}$

      The option value $O_{1(1.125),2}$ is given by

$$\{[p \bullet O_{2(1.125),2}] + [(1-p) \bullet O_{2(1.125),3}]\}e^{-r_d \Delta t}$$

EXAMPLE 30   Valuing a Deferred-Strike Currency Option Using the Binomial Method (Continued)

Thus,

$$O_{1(1.125),2} = 0.0307$$

v) At time 0

Due to no exercise, $O_{0,1}$ is given by the formula

$$\{[p \bullet O_{1(1.125),1} + [(1-p) \bullet O_{1(1.125),2}]\}e^{-r_d \Delta t}$$

Thus, $O_{0,1} = 0.032$.

Stage 5

The deferred-strike option premium is 0.032 Cad/US.

It is important for the reader to make the following observation about Example 30.

OBSERVATION 1 To obtain a more accurate value for the deferred-strike opton in Example 30, one has to reduce the value of Δt. Doing this leads to a value of 0.0388 Cad/US.

The use of a binomial method to value a European-style Lookback option is illustrated in Example 31 on page 249.

It is important for the reader to make the following two observations about Example 31.

OBSERVATION 1 To obtain a more accurate value for the look-back option in Example 31 when continuous sampling is employed, one has to reduce the value of Δt. Doing this gives a value of 0.1124 Cad/US.

OBSERVATION 2 As can be seen from the example, valuing a look-back option using the binomial tree can be laborious. Simon Babbs (1992) suggested an efficient way of using the binomial tree to value such options. Instead of simply generating a tree of the underlying asset price, his method revolved around the philosophy of generating a tree representing the ratio of the maximum (or minimum) price to the underlying asset price.

EXAMPLE 31 Valuing a Lookback Currency Option Using the Binomial Method

The Canadian dollar is currently trading at 1.3000 Cad/US. An investor wants to buy a continuously sampled 4½-year Category IV lookback put option (i.e., the in-the-money option payoff on the maturity date is strike rate minus the lowest sampled rate) on the U.S. dollar that is struck at 1.3000 Cad/US. The current continuously compounded risk-free rates of interest in the United States and Canada are 6 percent and 8 percent respectively. Using an exchange-rate volatility of 10 percent and dividing the 4½-year period into four equal subintervals, I want to value this European-style option.

Stage 1

$S_0 = 1.3000$, $X = 1.3000$, $r_d = 0.08$, $r_f = 0.06$, $\sigma = 0.1$, $T = 4.5$, $n = 4$

Stages 2, 3

Since the exchange-rate tree is no different from that presented in Example 26, the reader is referred to Example 26 for these stages.

Stage 4

For the diagram of the option tree, the reader is again referred to Example 26.

i) At time 4(1.125)

   a) Calculating $O_{4(1.125),1}$

      To calculate the intrinsic value of $O_{4(1.125),1}$, one has to first calculate the lowest value reaching in arriving at a final value of $1.3(1.1119)^4$. To arrive at a final exchange-rate value of $1.3(1.1119)^4$, it can be seen from the tree in Stage 3 that the path taken is [1.3, 1.3(1.1119), $1.3(1.1119)^2$, $1.3(1.1119)^3$, $1.3(1.1119)^4$]. This implies the lowest value reached is 1.3 and hence an option value of

$$O_{4(1.125),1} = \max[1.3 - 1.3, 0] = 0.0000$$

   b) Calculating $O_{4(1.125),2}$

      In order to calculate the value of $O_{4(1.125),2}$, one would need to know the lowest value realized in reaching this node. From the tree in Stage 3, it can be seen that there are four paths that lead to a final value of $1.3(1.1119)^2$:

Path 1: [1.3, 1.3(1.1119), $1.3(1.1119)^2$, $1.3(1.1119)^3$, $1.3(1.1119)^2$]
Path 2: [1.3, 1.3(1.1119), $1.3(1.1119)^2$, 1.3(1.1119), $1.3(1.1119)^2$]
Path 3: [1.3, 1.3(1.1119), 1.3, 1.3(1.1119), $1.3(1.1119)^2$]
Path 4: [1.3, 1.3(0.8994), 1.3, 1.3(1.1119), $1.3(1.1119)^2$]

EXAMPLE 31 Valuing a Lookback Currency Option Using the Binomial Method (Continued)

Since the lowest values associated with Paths 1 to 4 are 1.3, 1.3, 1.3, and 1.3(0.8994), respectively, the intrinsic value associated with each path is

$$O_{4(1.125),2} = \begin{array}{ll} 0.0000 & \text{if Paths 1, 2, 3} \\ 0.1308 & \text{if Path 4} \end{array}$$

c) Calculating $O_{4(1.125),3}$

In order to calculate the value of $O_{4(1.125),2}$, one would need to know the path transversed in order to arrive at a final exchange-rate value of 1.3. From the tree in Stage 3, it can be seen that there are six paths that lead to a final value of 1.3:

Path 1: $[1.3, 1.3(1.1119), 1.3(1.1119)^2, 1.3(1.1119), 1.3]$
Path 2: $[1.3, 1.3(1.1119), 1.3, 1.3(1.1119), 1.3]$
Path 3: $[1.3, 1.3(1.1119), 1.3, 1.3(0.8994), 1.3]$
Path 4: $[1.3, 1.3(0.8994), 1.3, 1.3(1.1119), 1.3]$
Path 5: $[1.3, 1.3(0.8994), 1.3, 1.3(0.8994), 1.3]$
Path 6: $[1.3, 1.3(0.8994), 1.3(0.8994)^2, 1.3(0.8994), 1.3]$

The lowest values associated with Paths 1 to 6 are 1.3, 1.3, 1.3(0.8994), 1.3(0.8994), 1.3(0.8994), and 1.3(0.8994)^2, respectively. The intrinsic values associated with Paths 1 to 6 are

$$O_{4(1.125),3} = \begin{array}{ll} 0.0000 & \text{if Paths 1, 2} \\ 0.1308 & \text{if Paths 3, 4, 5} \\ 0.2484 & \text{if Path 6} \end{array}$$

d) Calculating $O_{4(1.125),4}$

The following are the four paths leading to a final exchange rate value of 1.3(0.8994)^2:

Path 1: $[1.3, 1.3(1.1119), 1.3, 1.3(0.8994), 1.3(0.8994)^2]$
Path 2: $[1.3, 1.3(0.8994), 1.3, 1.3(0.8994), 1.3(0.8994)^2]$
Path 3: $[1.3, 1.3(0.8994), 1.3(0.8994)^2, 1.3(0.8994), 1.3(0.8994)^2]$
Path 4: $[1.3, 1.3(0.8994), 1.3(0.8994)^2, 1.3(0.8994)^3, 1.3(0.8994)^2]$

The lowest values associated with Paths 1 to 4 are 1.3(0.8994)^2, 1.3(0.8994)^2, 1.3(0.8994)^2, and 1.3(0.8994)^3, respectively. The intrinsic values associated with each of the path is

$$O_{4(1.125),4} = \begin{array}{ll} 0.2484 & \text{if Paths 1, 2, 3} \\ 0.3452 & \text{if Paths 3, 4} \end{array}$$

e) Calculating $O_{4(1.125),5}$

Since $[1.3, 1.3(0.8994), 1.3(0.8994)^2, 1.3(0.8994)^3, 1.3(0.8994)^4]$ is the only path that leads to 1.3(0.8994)^4, the lowest value realized is 1.3(0.8994)^4. Thus the intrinsic value at this node is

$$O_{4(1.125),5} = 0.4493$$

EXAMPLE 31 Valuing a Lookback Currency Option Using the Binomial Method (Continued)

ii) At time 3(1.125)

a) Calculating $O_{3(1.125),1}$

Since this is a European-style option, the value obtained by exercising the option is 0. Furthermore, the expected value of the option by not exercising is given by

$$\{[p \bullet O_{4(1.125),1}] + [(1-p) \bullet O_{4(1.125),2}]\}e^{-r_d \Delta t}$$

However, while $O_{4(1.125),2} = 0$, the value of $O_{4(1.125),3}$ depends on the path transversed by the exchange rate. Thus,

$O_{3(1.125),1} = 0.0000$ if path is $[1.3, 1.3(1.1119), 1.3(1.1119)^2, 1.3(1.1119)^3]$

Hence, the value of $O_{3(1.125),1}$ is 0.0000.

b) Calculating $O_{3(1.125),2}$

The option value due to exercise is 0. Furthermore, the expected value of the option from not exercising is $\{[p \bullet O_{4(1.125),2}] + [(1-p) \bullet O_{4(1.125),3}]\}e^{-r_d \Delta t}$. Since both $O_{4(1.125),2}$ and $O_{4(1.125),3}$ depend on the paths transversed by the exchange rate,

$$O_{3(1.125),2} = \begin{matrix} 0.0000 \\ 0.0000 \\ 0.1195 \end{matrix} \quad \begin{matrix} \text{if path is } [1.3, 1.3(1.119), 1.3(1.1119)^2, 1.3(1.1119)] \\ \text{if path is } [1.3, 1.3(1.1119), 1.3, 1.3(1.1119)] \\ \text{if path is } [1.3, 1.3(0.8994), 1.3, 1.3(1.1119] \end{matrix}$$

c) Calculating $O_{3(1.125),3}$

The option value due to exercise is zero, and the expected value of the option from not exercising is dependent on the path transversed by the exchange rate and is given by $\{p \bullet O_{4(1.125),3}] + [(1-p) \bullet O_{4(1.125),4}]\}e^{-r_d \Delta t}$. Thus,

$$O_{3(1.125),3} = \begin{matrix} 0.1646 \\ 0.1646 \\ 0.2270 \end{matrix} \quad \begin{matrix} \text{if path is } [1.3, 1.3(1.1119), 1.3, 1.3(0.8994)] \\ \text{if path is } [1.3, 1.3(0.8994), 1.3, 1.3(0.8994)] \\ \text{if path is } [1.3, 1.3(0.8994), 1.3(0.8994)^2, 1.3(0.8994)] \end{matrix}$$

d) Calculating $O_{3(1.125),4}$

The option value due to exercise is zero, and the expected value of the option from not exercising is dependent on the path transversed by the exchange rate and is given by $\{[p \bullet O_{4(1.125),4}] + [(1-p) \bullet O_{4(1.125),5}]\}e^{-r_d \Delta t}$. Thus,

$O_{3(1.125),4} = 0.3602$ if path is $[1.3, 1.3(0.8994), 1.3(0.8994)^2, 1.3(0.8994)^3]$

Hence, $O_{3(1.125)4} = 0.3602$.

iii) At time 2(1.125)

a) Calculating $O_{2(1.125),1}$

Due to no exercise, $O_{2(1.125),1}$ is given by the formula

$$\{[p \bullet O_{3(1.125),1}] + [(1-p) \bullet O_{3(1.125),2}]\}e^{-r_d \Delta t}$$

EXAMPLE 31   Valuing a Lookback Currency Option Using the Binomial Method (Continued)

While $O_{3(1.125),1} = 0$, the value of $O_{3(1.125),2}$ depends on the path transversed by the exchange rate. Thus,

$O_{2(1.125),1} = 0.0000$ if path is $[1.3, 1.3(1.1119), 1.3(1.1119)^2]$

making the value of $O_{2(1.125),1}$ 0.0000.

b) Calculating $O_{2(1.125),2}$

The option value $O_{2(1.125),2}$ is given by

$$\{[p \bullet O_{3(1.125),2}] + [(1-p) \bullet O_{3(1.125),3}]\}e^{-r_d \Delta t}$$

Since both $O_{3(1.125),2}$ and $O_{3(1.125),3}$ depend on the paths transversed by the exchange rate,

$$O_{2(1.125),2} = \begin{array}{ll} 0.0631 & \text{if path is } [1.3, 1.3(1.1119), 1.3] \\ 0.1265 & \text{if path is } [1.3, 1.3(0.8994), 1.3] \end{array}$$

c) Calculating $O_{2(1.125),3}$

The option value $O_{2(1.125),3}$ is given by

$$\{[p \bullet O_{3(1.125),3}] + [(1-p) \bullet O_{3(1.125),4}]\}e^{-r_d \Delta t}$$

While $O_{3(1.125),4} = 0.3602$, the value of $O_{3(1.125),3}$ depends on the path transversed by the exchange rate. Thus,

$O_{2(1.125),3} = 0.2585$ if path is $[1.3, 1.3(0.8994), 1.3(0.8994)^2]$.

Hence, $O_{2(1.125),3} = 0.2585$.

iv) At time 1(1.125)

a) Calculating $O_{1(1.125),1}$

Due to no exercise, $O_{1(1.125),1}$ is given by the formula

$$\{[p \bullet O_{2(1.125),1}] + [(1-p) \bullet O_{2(1.125),2}]\}e^{-r_d \Delta t}$$

Since $O_{2(1.125),2}$ is dependent on the path transversed,

$O_{1(1.125),1} = 0.0242$ if path is $[1.3, 1.3(1.1119)]$

Thus, $O_{1(1.125),1} = 0.0242$.

b) Calculating $O_{1(1.125),2}$

The option value $O_{1(1.125),2}$ is given by

$$\{[p \bullet O_{2(1.125),2}] + [(1-p) \bullet O_{2(1.125),3}]\}e^{-r_d \Delta t}$$

which simplifies to

$O_{1(1.125),2} = 0.1662$ if path is $[1.3, 1.3(0.8994)]$.

Thus, $O_{1(1.125),1} = 0.1662$.

EXAMPLE 31 Valuing a Lookback Currency Option Using the Binomial Method (Continued)

v) At time 0

Due to no exercise, $O_{0,1}$ is given by the formula

$$\{[p \bullet O_{1(1.125),1} + [(1-p) \bullet O_{1(1.125),2}]\}e^{-r_d \Delta t}$$

Thus, $O_{0,1} = 0.0765$.

Stage 5

The Category IV lookback put option premium is 0.0765 Cad/US.

The use of a binomial method to value a European-style nonlinear payoff option is illustrated in Example 32.

EXAMPLE 32 Valuing a Nonlinear Payoff Currency Option Using the Binomial Method

The Canadian dollar is currently trading at 1.3000 Cad/US. An investor wants to buy a 4½-year nonlinear payoff put option on the U.S. dollar that is struck at 1.3000^2 Cad/US. The current continuously compounded risk-free rates of interest in the United States and Canada are 6 percent and 8 percent respectively. Using an exchange-rate volatility of 10 percent, and dividing the 4½-year period into four equal subintervals, I want to value this European-style option.

Stage 1

$S_0 = 1.3000$, $X = 1.3000$, $r_d = 0.08$, $r_f = 0.06$, $\sigma = 0.1$, $T = 4.5$, $n = 4$

Stages 2, 3

Since the exchange-rate tree is no different from that presented in Example 26, the reader is referred to Example 26 for these stages.

EXAMPLE 32 Valuing a Nonlinear Payoff Currency Option Using the Binomial Method (Continued)

Stage 4

For the diagram of the option tree, the reader is again referred to Example 26.

i) At time 4(1.125)

The intrinsic values of the option at all the nodes are

$\max\{1.3^2-[1.3(1.1119)^4]^2,0\} = 0.0000$
$\max\{1.3^2-[1.3(1.1119)^2]^2,0\} = 0.0000$
$\max\{1.3^2-[1.3]^2 \qquad ,0\} = 0.0000$
$\max\{1.3^2-[1.3(0.8894)^2]^2,0\} = 0.5841$
$\max\{1.3^2-[1.3(0.8994)^4]^2,0\} = 0.9664$

ii) At time 3(1.125)

Due to lack of early exercise, the option values at all the nodes are

$O_{3(1.125),1} = [p \bullet 0.0000 + (1-p) \bullet 0.0000]e^{-r_d \Delta t} = 0.0000$
$O_{3(1.125),2} = [p \bullet 0.0000 + (1-p) \bullet 0.0000]e^{-r_d \Delta t} = 0.0000$
$O_{3(1.125),3} = [p \bullet 0.0000 + (1-p) \bullet 0.5841]e^{-r_d \Delta t} = 0.2239$
$O_{3(1.125),4} = [p \bullet 0.5841 + (1-p) \bullet 0.9664]e^{-r_d \Delta t} = 0.6804$

iii) At time 2(1.125)

Since no exercise is made at this time, the option values at all the nodes are

$O_{2(1.125),1} = [p \bullet 0.0000 + (1-p) \bullet 0.0000]e^{-r_d \Delta t} = 0.0000$
$O_{2(1.125),2} = [p \bullet 0.0000 + (1-p) \bullet 0.2239]e^{-r_d \Delta t} = 0.0858$
$O_{2(1.125),3} = [p \bullet 0.2239 + (1-p) \bullet 0.6804]e^{-r_d \Delta t} = 0.3796$

iv) At time 1(1.25)

Due to the lack of exercise at this time, the option values at all the nodes are

$O_{1(1.125),1} = [p \bullet 0.0000 + (1-p) \bullet 0.0858]e^{-r_d \Delta t} = 0.0329$
$O_{1(1.125),2} = [p \bullet 0.0858 + (1-p) \bullet 0.3796]e^{-r_d \Delta t} = 0.1911$

v At time 0

The option value at this node is

$O_{0,1} = [p \bullet 0.0329 + (1-p) \bullet 0.1911]e^{-r_d \Delta t} = 0.0907$

Stage 5
The nonlinear payoff option premium is 0.0907 Cad/US.

It is important for the reader to make the following two observations about Example 32.

OBSERVATION 1 To obtain a more accurate value for the non-linear option in Example 32, one has to reduce the value of Δt. Doing this gives an option value of 0.1264 Cad/US.

OBSERVATION 2 Instead of using the binomial tree to value a power option directly, it is possible to derive the result of the power option using the premiums derived for vanilla options. This follows from the discussion given on page 170 that any nonlinear payoff option can be replicated using vanilla options. This is analogous to the replication of a cash-or-nothing option using vanilla options, which was discussed in Observation 3 of Example 27.

The use of a binomial method to value a European-style knockout put option is illustrated in Example 33.

EXAMPLE 33 Valuing a Knock-Out Currency Option Using the Binomial Method

The Canadian dollar is currently trading at 1.3000 Cad/US. An investor wants to buy a continuously monitored 4½-year knock-out put option on the U.S. dollar that is struck at 1.3000 Cad/US. The current continuously compounded risk-free rates of interest in the United States and Canada are 6 percent and 8 percent respectively. Using an exchange-rate volatility of 10 percent, a barrier level of 1.1500 Cad/US, and dividing the 4½-year period into four equal subintervals, I want to value this European-style option.

Stage 1

$S_0 = 1.3000$, $X = 1.3000$, $H = 1.1500$, $r_d = 0.08$, $r_f = 0.06$, $\sigma = 0.1$, $T = 4.5$, $n = 4$

Stages 2, 3

Since the exchange-rate tree is no different from that presented in Example 26, the reader is referred to Example 26 for these stages.

Stage 4

For the diagram of the option tree, the reader is again referred to Example 26.

EXAMPLE 33 Valuing a Knock-Out Currency Option Using the Binomial Method

i) At time 4(1.125)

The intrinsic values of the option at all the nodes are

$$max[1.3–1.3(1.1119)^4,0] = 0.0000$$
$$max[1.3–1.3(1.1119)^2,0] = 0.0000$$
$$max[1.3–1.3,0]\qquad\quad = 0.0000$$
$$max[1.3–1.3(0.8894)^2,0] = 0.2484$$
$$max[1.3–1.3(0.8994)^4,0] = 0.4493$$

ii) At time 3(1.125)

Due to lack of early exercise, the option values at all the nodes are

$$node1 = [p \bullet 0.0000 + (1–p) \bullet 0.0000]e^{-r_d\Delta t} = 0.0000$$
$$node2 = [p \bullet 0.0000 + (1–p) \bullet 0.0000]e^{-r_d\Delta t} = 0.0000$$
$$node3 = [p \bullet 0.0000 + (1–p) \bullet 0.2484]e^{-r_d\Delta t} = 0.0952$$
$$node4 = [p \bullet 0.2484 + (1–p) \bullet 0.4493]e^{-r_d\Delta t} = 0.3040$$

However, since the put option is knocked out if the exchange rate falls below 1.1500, the holder of the option gets a zero payoff whenever the exchange rate is less than 1.1500. Forcing the option value at node 4 to be 0, I have,

$$O_{3(1.125),1} = 0.0000$$
$$O_{3(1.125),1} = 0.0000$$
$$O_{3(1.125),3} = 0.0952$$
$$O_{3(1.125),4} = 0.0000$$

iii) At time 2(1.125)

Since no exercise is made at this time, the option values at all the nodes are

$$node\ 1 = [p \bullet 0.0000 + (1–p) \bullet 0.0000]e^{-r_d\Delta t} = 0.0000$$
$$node\ 2 = [p \bullet 0.0000 + (1–p) \bullet 0.0952]e^{-r_d\Delta t} = 0.0365$$
$$node\ 3 = [p \bullet 0.0952 + (1–p) \bullet 0.0000]e^{-r_d\Delta t} = 0.0505$$

Since the put option is knocked out if the exchange rate falls below 1.1500, one would force the option value on node 3 to be zero. Thus,

$$O_{2(1.125),1} = 0.0000$$
$$O_{2(1.125),2} = 0.0365$$
$$O_{2(1.125),3} = 0.0000$$

iv) At time 1(1.125)

Due to the lack of early exercise, the option values at all the nodes are

$$node\ 1 = [p \bullet 0.0000 + (1–p) \bullet 0.0365]e^{-r_d\Delta t} = 0.0140$$
$$node\ 2 = [p \bullet 0.0365 + (1–p) \bullet 0.0000]e^{-r_d\Delta t} = 0.0194$$

Since the put option is knocked out if the exchange rate falls below 1.1500 and none of the exchange rates is less than 1.1500, one would have

EXAMPLE 33   Valuing a Knock-Out Currency Option Using the Binomial Method (Continued)

$$O_{1(1.125),1} = 0.0140$$
$$O_{1(1.125),2} = 0.0194$$

v) At time 0

The option value at this node is

$$O_{0,1} = [p \bullet 0.0140 + (1-p) \bullet 0.0194]e^{-r_d\Delta t} = 0.0149$$

Stage 5
The knock-out option premium is 0.0149 Cad/US.

It is important for the reader to make the following four observations from Example 33.

OBSERVATION 1   To obtain a more accurate value for the knock-out option in Example 33 where the breaching of the barrier would be monitored continuously, one would have to reduce the value of Δt. Doing this gives an option value of 0.0019 Cad/US.

OBSERVATION 2   Like the binary option, the barrier option premium will be insensitive when the barrier lies between nodes. As a result, it is very important to be able to pick out the "optimal" n (or equivalent Δt) in order to arrive at a proper converging process. This value of n can be selected using a modified version of the algorithm employed for the binary option in Observation 1 of Example 27.

To more precisely, the value of n is chosen such that
A. n is the largest odd integer satisfying the inequality

$$n < \frac{m^2\sigma^2 T}{\left[\ln\left(\frac{S_0}{H}\right)\right]^2} \text{ when m} = 1,3,5,7,..., \text{ or}$$

B. n is the largest even integer satisfying the inequality

$$n < \frac{m^2\sigma^2 T}{\left[\ln\left(\frac{S_0}{H}\right)\right]^2} \text{ when m} = 2,4,6,8,...$$

OBSERVATION 3   To value a 4½-year down-and-in option with a strike level of 1.3000 Cad/US and a barrier level 1.1500 Cad/US using the tree, one could use the tree to calculate the payoffs associated with the paths that breach the barrier. However, compared to the down-and-out option example illustrated above, calculating the premium of a down-and-in option would be more laborious, in that every path that would breach the barrier has to be accounted for. Fortunately, by exploiting the relationship between the out-option, in-option, and vanilla option, discussed on page 201, one can arrive at the required option premium. More precisely, in order to calculate the option premium of a down-and-in put option, one would subtract the down-and-out put option premium from the vanilla put option premium.

OBSERVATION 4   Consider a down-and-in option with a strike level of 1.3000 Cad/US and a barrier level of 1.1500 Cad/US. Suppose further that the breaching of the barrier is continuously monitored during the 4½-year period and upon breaching, a 6-month put option comes alive. This type of option is different from that discussed in Observation 3, in that the option discussed earlier had a fixed maturity date (and hence a decreasing option life), whereas this option would have a fixed option life (and hence a variable maturity date).

It is important for the reader to note that the premium for this type of option cannot be computed using the idea discussed in Observation 3, where the in-option premium is computed by first calculating both the out-option premium and the vanilla option premium. This is because there is no relationship between this type of in-option and the vanilla option or even the out-option. Thus, to value this type of option with a fixed option life, one would have to go through the laborious task of monitoring the paths.

Domestic-Currency-Denominated Option on Multiple Domestic-Currency-Denominated Assets

In the previous section, I showed that an option on a single asset can be valued using a binomial tree that mimics the movements of the underlying asset. Similarly, it would be reasonable to expect an option on m mutiple assets to be valued using m binomial trees mimicking the movements of the m underlying assets. Due to the effect of correlated movements between asset values, in addition to generating future movements of each asset value, one has to ensure that all the m trees "communicate" with each other. Since a binomial tree is defined by the parameters p and u, we can use either p or u (or both p and u) to act as communication parameter(s) between the trees. Although a variety of methods[19] use either p or u (or both p and u) to act as a communication parameter(s) between the trees, I will adopt the method proposed by Boyle, Evnine, and Gibbs (1988)[20] for valuing options on multiple assets. For ease of understanding, I will first describe this method when m = 2.

---

[19] See, for example, Ravindran (1994), Rubinstein (1994), and Hull (1997).

[20] This method uses p as the only communication parameter.

Denoting the current exchange-rate levels by $(S_{1,0}, S_{2,0})$, the exchange rates at time Δt later are assumed to move to either $(S_{1,0}u_1, S_{2,0}u_2)$ with probability p_1 or $(S_{1,0}u_1, S_{2,0}d_2)$ with probability p_2, or to $(S_{1,0}d_1, S_{1,0}u_2)$ with probability p_3 or $(S_{1,0}d_1, S_{2,0}d_2)$ with probability $p_4 = 1 - p_1 - p_2 - p_3$, where $u_k = e^{\sigma_k \sqrt{\Delta t}}$ and $u_k = \dfrac{1}{d_k}$ (for $k =$ 1,2). Furthermore, the probabilities[21], which are obtained by matching the characteristic function[22] of the bivariate continuously compounded return distribution with that obtained from the one-step tree shown in Exhibit 134[23], are given by the expressions

$$p_1 = \frac{1}{4}\left[1 + \rho_{1,2} + \left(\frac{\mu_1}{\sigma_1} + \frac{\mu_2}{\sigma_2}\right)\sqrt{\Delta t}\right]$$

$$p_2 = \frac{1}{4}\left[1 - \rho_{1,2} + \left(\frac{\mu_1}{\sigma_1} - \frac{\mu_2}{\sigma_2}\right)\sqrt{\Delta t}\right]$$

$$p_3 = \frac{1}{4}\left[1 - \rho_{1,2} + \left(-\frac{\mu_1}{\sigma_1} + \frac{\mu_2}{\sigma_2}\right)\sqrt{\Delta t}\right]$$

$$p_4 = 1 - p_1 - p_2 - p_3$$

where $\mu_k = r_d - r_{k,f} - \dfrac{\sigma_k^2}{2}$ for $k = 1,2$ and $\rho_{1,2}$ is the correlation between the continuously compounded returns of assets 1 and 2.

EXHIBIT 134   One-Step Binomial Tree for Two Underlying Assets

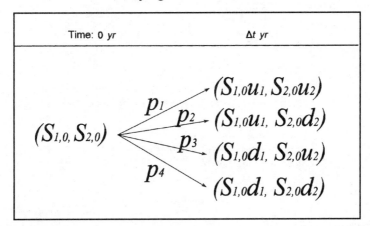

---

[21] It is possible for these probabilities to be negative. Consequently, we have to make sure that Δt is small enough that all the four probabilities are positive.

[22] If R is a random variable, then the characteristic function of R is defined as $E_R(e^{i\theta R})$, where i is the complex number $\sqrt{-1}$, θ is a real number, and $E_R(.)$ represents the expectation of $(.)$ taken with respect to R.

[23] This is similar to the idea of "method of moments" that is mentioned in footnote 12.

Using these expressions, one can now generate two exchange-rate trees that "communicate" with each other. When m = 1, it was seen in the earlier section that the tree had two probabilities, $p_1 = p$ and $p_2 = 1 - p$, and n + 1 nodes at time $n\Delta t$. As can be seen from Exhibit 134, when m = 2, the two-asset tree would have four probabiities, p_1, p_2, p_3, and p_4 (= $1 - p_1 - p_2, -p_3$), and $(n + 1)^2$ nodes at time $n\Delta t$. This increases exponentially with m, and for a general m, the m-asset tree would have 2^m probabilities, $p_1, p_2, \ldots, p_{2m-1}$, and p_{2m} (= $1 - p_1 - p_2, \ldots, p_{2m-1}$), and $(n + 1)^m$ nodes at time $n\Delta t$.

The steps required to value a currency option for a general m are summarized in Methodology 3.

METHODOLOGY 3   Using the Binomial Method to Value a Domestic-Currency-Denominated Option on Multiple Domestic-Currency-Denominated Assets

Stage 1

Determine $S_{k,0}$, r_d, $r_{k,f}$, σ_k, $\rho_{k,l}$, T, n (for k,l = 1,...,m and l > k) and other necessary parameters[24]

Stage 2

Calculate the values of Δt, u_k, d_k (for k = 1,...,m) and p_h (for h = 1, ...,2^m) using the formulae:

$$\Delta t = \frac{T}{n}, \ u_k = e^{\sigma_k \sqrt{\Delta t}}, \ d_k = \frac{1}{u_k}, \text{ and}$$

$$p_h = \frac{1}{2^m}\{1 + \sum_{k=1}^{m-1} \sum_{i=k+1}^{m} J_{k,l}(h)\rho_{k,l} + \sqrt{\Delta t} \sum_{k=1}^{m} \frac{J_k(h)\mu_k}{\sigma_k}\}$$

where

$J_{k,l}(h) = \begin{array}{l} 1 \text{ if asset k and asset l have jumps in the same direction at state h} \\ -1 \text{ if asset k and asset l have jumps in the opposite direction at} \\ \quad \text{state h} \end{array}$

$J_k(h) = \begin{array}{l} 1 \text{ if asset k has an upward jump at state h} \\ -1 \text{ if asset k has a downward jump at state h} \end{array}$

$$\mu_k = r_d - r_{k,f} - \frac{\sigma_k^2}{2}$$

Stage 3

Generate a tree for the kth (for k = 1, ...,m) asset, starting from the current asset price today and ending on the option maturity, as shown below:

METHODOLOGY 3 Using the Binomial Method to Value a Domestic-Currency-Denominated Option on Multiple Domestic-Currency-Denominated Assets (Continued)

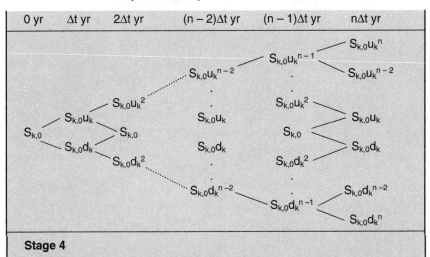

0 yr	Δt yr	$2\Delta t$ yr	$(n-2)\Delta t$ yr	$(n-1)\Delta t$ yr	$n\Delta t$ yr

Stage 4

Generate an option tree as shown below[25], using the m asset price trees created in Stage 3, where the option value at each node is calculated using the following steps:

0 yr	Δt yr	$2\Delta t$ yr	$(n-1)\Delta t$ yr	$n\Delta t$ yr

$O_{n\Delta t,1}$

$O_{n\Delta t,2}$

$O_{2\Delta t,1}$

$O_{\Delta t,1}$

$O_{0,1}$

$O_{\Delta t,2m}$

$O_{2\Delta t,3m}$

$O_{n\Delta t,(n+1)^m - 1}$

$O_{n\Delta t,(n+1)^m}$

i) At time $n\Delta t$ (for $j = 1,2,3,...,(n+1)^m - 1,(n+1)^m$)

$$O_{n\Delta t,j} = I_{n\Delta t,j}$$

where $I_{n\Delta t,j}$ represents the intrinsic value of the option when $(S_{1,0}u_1{}^{c_{n,j,1}}, S_{1,0}u_1{}^{c_{n,j,2}}, ..., S_{m,0}u_m{}^{c_{n,j,m}})$ are used in the calculation of option payoff and

$$c_{\alpha,\lambda,\varphi} = \alpha - 2\left[\frac{(\lambda-1)\mathrm{mod}((\alpha+1)^{m-\varphi+1}) - (\lambda-1)\mathrm{mod}((\alpha+1)^{m-\varphi})}{(\alpha+1)^{m-\varphi}}\right] \text{[26, 27]}$$

METHODOLOGY 3   Using the Binomial Method to Value a Domestic-Currency-Denominated Option on Multiple Domestic-Currency-Denominated Assets (Continued)

ii) At time $i\Delta t$ (for $i = n - 1, n - 2, n - 3, ..., 2, 1, 0$)

$$O_{i\Delta t,1} = \max\left\{ I_{i\Delta t,1} \bullet E, [\sum_{h=1}^{2^m} p_h \bullet O_{(i+1)\Delta t, f(i,1,h)}] e^{-r_d \Delta t} \right\}$$

$$O_{i\Delta t,2} = \max\left\{ I_{i\Delta t,2} \bullet E, [\sum_{h=1}^{2^m} p_h \bullet O_{(i+1)\Delta t, f(i,2,h)}] e^{-r_d \Delta t} \right\}$$

.
.
.

$$O_{i\Delta t,(i+1)^m - 1} = \max\left\{ I_{i\Delta t,(i+1)^m - 1} \bullet E, [\sum_{h=1}^{2^m} p_h \bullet O_{(i+1)\Delta t, f(i,(i+1)^m - 1, h)}] e^{-r_d \Delta t} \right\}$$

$$O_{i\Delta t,(i+1)^m} = \max\left\{ I_{i\Delta t,(i+1)^m} \bullet E, [\sum_{h=1}^{2^m} p_h \bullet O_{(i+1)\Delta t, f(i,(i+1)^m, h)}] e^{-r_d \Delta t} \right\}$$

where $E = 1$ if exercise is allowed at $i\Delta t$ and 0 if no exercise is allowed at $i\Delta t$; $I_{i\Delta t_j}$ (for $j = 1,2,3,...,(I+1)^m - 1,(i+1)^m$) represents the intrinsic value of the option when $(S_{1,0} u_1^{c_i,j,1}, S_{2,0} u_2^{c_i,j,2}, ..., S_{m,0} u_m^{c_i,j,m})$ are used in the calculation of the option payoff, $C_{\alpha,\lambda,\varphi}$ is as defined as above and $f(\beta,\psi,\zeta) = 1 + \dfrac{1}{2}\sum_{k=1}^{m}(\beta + 1 - c_{\beta,\psi,k} - c_{1,\xi,k})(\beta + 2)^{m-k}$.

Stage 5

The option premium is given by $O_{0,1}$.

24 See footnote 18.

25 In the option trees presented in Methodologies 1 and 2, since a node can only lead to a higher or a lower node at time Δt later, it was easy to draw branches connecting the nodes of the option tree. In this methodology, however, to be able to draw these connecting branches, one would have to first determine from any given node where the next four jumps would be at time Δt later. These jumps are in fact determined using the function $f(\beta, \psi, \zeta)$ that is given in Stage 4(ii).

26 A mod(B) is defined as the remainder when A is divided by B. For example, 5 mod(3) = 2. 10 mod(2) = 0 and 21 mod(15) = 6.

27 For any nonnegative integer, A, A mod(1) = 0 and 0 mod(A) = 0.

The use of a binomial method to value a European-style basket option on two underlying assets is illustrated in Example 34 on page 263.

It is important for the reader to make the following four observations about Example 34.

EXAMPLE 34 Valuing a Basket Currency Option Using the Binomial Method

The Canadian dollar is currently trading at 1.3000 Cad/US and 2.2000 Cad/£. A hedger wants to buy a 4½-year European-style call option on the Canadian dollar basket that is struck at Cad$ 480 mm when the notional amounts on the US$ and £ are 200 mm and 100 mm, respectively. More precisely, the payoff on the option maturity date is max[480 − (200 • $S_{1,T}$) − (100 • $S_{2,T}$),0], where $S_{1,T}$ represents the Cad/US rate on option maturity, and $S_{2,T}$ represents the Cad/£ rate on option maturity. The current continuously compounded risk-free rates of interest in the United States, Canada, and the United Kingdom are 6 percent, 8 percent, and 9 percent, respectively. Using a volatility of 10 percent for the Cad/US exchange rate, a volatility of 17 percent for the Cad/£ exchange rate, a correlation of 60 percent, between the continuously compounded returns of these exchange rates, and dividing the 4½-year period into three equal subintervals, I want to value this option.

Stage 1

$S_{1,0} = 1.3000$, $S_{2,0} = 2.2000$, $N_1 = 200$, $N_2 = 100$, $X = 480$, $r_d = 0.08$, $r_{1,f} = 0.06$, $r_{2,f} = 0.09$, $\sigma_1 = 0.1$, $\sigma_2 = 0.17$, $\rho_{1,2} = 0.6$, $T = 4.5$, $n = 3$

Stage 2

$$\Delta t = \frac{T}{n} \qquad = \frac{4.5}{3} \qquad\qquad = 1.5$$

$$u_1 = e^{\sigma_1 \sqrt{\Delta t}} \qquad = e^{0.1\sqrt{1.5}} \qquad\qquad = 1.1303$$

$$d_1 = \frac{1}{u_1} \qquad = \frac{1}{1.1303} \qquad\qquad = 0.8847$$

$$\mu_1 = r_d - r_{1,f} - \frac{\sigma_1^2}{2} = 0.08 - 0.06 - \frac{(0.1)^2}{2} = 0.015$$

$$u_2 = e^{\sigma_2 \sqrt{\Delta t}} \qquad = e^{0.17\sqrt{1.5}} \qquad\qquad = 1.2315$$

$$d_2 = \frac{1}{u_2} \qquad = \frac{1}{1.2315} \qquad\qquad = 0.8120$$

$$\mu_2 = r_d - r_{2,f} - \frac{\sigma_2^2}{2} = 0.08 - 0.09 - \frac{(0.17)^2}{2} = -0.0245$$

$$p_1 = \frac{1}{2^2}\left\{1 + \sum_{k=1}^{1}\sum_{l=k+1}^{2} J_{k,l}(1)\rho_{k,l} + \sqrt{\Delta t}\sum_{k=1}^{2}\frac{J_k(1)\mu_k}{\sigma_k}\right\}$$

$$= \frac{1}{4}\left\{1 + J_{1,2}(1)\rho_{1,2} + \sqrt{\Delta t}\left[\frac{J_1(1)\mu_1}{\sigma_1} + \frac{J_2(1)\mu_2}{\sigma_2}\right]\right\}$$

$$= \frac{1}{4}\left\{1 + [1(0.6)] + \sqrt{1.5}\left[\frac{1(0.015)}{0.1} + \frac{1(-0.0245)}{0.17}\right]\right\}$$

$$= 0.4018$$

EXAMPLE 34   Valuing a Basket Currency Option Using the Binomial Method (Continued)

$$p_2 = \frac{1}{2^2}\left\{1 + \sum_{k=1}^{1}\sum_{l=k+1}^{2} J_{k,l}(2)\rho_{k,l} + \sqrt{\Delta t}\sum_{k=1}^{2}\frac{J_k(2)\mu_k}{\sigma_k}\right\}$$

$$= \frac{1}{4}\left\{1 + J_{1,2}(2)\rho_{1,2} + \sqrt{\Delta t}\left[\frac{J_1(2)\mu_1}{\sigma_1} + \frac{J_2(2)\mu_2}{\sigma_2}\right]\right\}$$

$$= \frac{1}{4}\left\{1 + [-1(0.6)] + \sqrt{1.5}\left[\frac{1(0.015)}{0.1} + \frac{-1(-0.0245)}{0.17}\right]\right\}$$

$$= 0.1901$$

$$p_3 = \frac{1}{2^2}\left\{1 + \sum_{k=1}^{1}\sum_{l=k+1}^{2} J_{k,l}(3)\rho_{k,l} + \sqrt{\Delta t}\sum_{k=1}^{2}\frac{J_k(3)\mu_k}{\sigma_k}\right\}$$

$$= \frac{1}{4}\left\{1 + J_{1,2}(3)\rho_{1,2} + \sqrt{\Delta t}\left[\frac{J_1(3)\mu_1}{\sigma_1} + \frac{J_2(3)\mu_2}{\sigma_2}\right]\right\}$$

$$= \frac{1}{4}\left\{1 + [-1(0.6)] + \sqrt{1.5}\left[\frac{-1(0.015)}{0.1} + \frac{1(-0.0245)}{0.17}\right]\right\}$$

$$= 0.0099$$

$$p_4 = 1 - p_1 - p_2 - p_3$$
$$= 0.3982$$

Stage 3
Asset 1:

0 yr   1(1.5) yr   2(1.5) yr   3(1.5) yr

Asset 2:

0 yr   1(1.5) yr   2(1.5) yr   3(1.5) yr

EXAMPLE 34 Valuing a Basket Currency Option Using the Binomial Method (Continued)

Stage 4

0 yr	1(1.5) yr	2(1.5) yr	3(1.5) yr

$O_{3(1.5),1}$
$O_{3(1.5),2}$
$O_{3(1.5),3}$
$O_{2(1.5),1}$ $O_{3(1.5),4}$
$O_{1(1.5),1}$ $O_{2(1.5),2}$ $O_{3(1.5),5}$
$O_{2(1.5),3}$ $O_{3(1.5),6}$
$O_{1(1.5),2}$ $O_{2(1.5),4}$ $O_{3(1.5),7}$
$O_{0,1}$ $O_{2(1.5),5}$ $O_{3(1.5),8}$
$O_{1(1.5),3}$ $O_{2(1.5),6}$ $O_{3(1.5),9}$
$O_{2(1.5),7}$ $O_{3(1.5),10}$
$O_{1(1.5),4}$ $O_{2(1.5),8}$ $O_{3(1.5),11}$
$O_{2(1.5),9}$ $O_{3(1.5),12}$
$O_{3(1.5),13}$
$O_{3(1.5),14}$
$O_{3(1.5),15}$
$O_{3(1.5),16}$

i) At time 3(1.5)

$O_{3(1.5),1}$ = max{480 − [200 • 1.3(1.1303)^3] − [100 • 2.2(1.2315)^3],0}
= 0.0000

$O_{3(1.5),2}$ = max{480 − [200 • 1.3(1.1303)^3] − [100 • 2.2(1.2315)],0}
= 0.0000

$O_{3(1.5),3}$ = max{480 − [200 • 1.3(1.1303)^3] − [100 • 2.2(0.8120)],0}
= 0.0000

$O_{3(1.5),4}$ = max{480 − [200 • 1.3(1.1303)^3] − [100 • 2.2(0.8120)^3],0}
= 0.0000

$O_{3(1.5),5}$ = max{480 − [200 • 1.3(1.1303)] − [100 • 2.2(1.2315)^3],0}
= 0.0000

$O_{3(1.5),6}$ = max{480 − [200 • 1.3(1.1303)] − [100 • 2.2(1.2315)],0}
= 0.0000

$O_{3(1.5),7}$ = max{480 − [200 • 1.3(1.1303)] − [100 • 2.2(0.8120)],0}
= 7.4820

$O_{3(1.5),8}$ = max{480 − [200 • 1.3(1.1303)] − [100 • 2.2(0.8120)^3],0}
= 68.3368

$O_{3(1.5),9}$ = max{480 − [200 • 1.3(0.8847)] − [100 • 2.2(1.2315)^3],0}
= 0.0000

$O_{3(1.5),10}$ = max{480 − [200 • 1.3(0.8847)] − [100 • 2.2(1.2315)],0}
= 0.0000

$O_{3(1.5),11}$ = max{480 − [200 • 1.3(0.8847)] − [100 • 2.2(0.8120)],0}
= 71.3380

EXAMPLE 34 Valuing a Basket Currency Option Using the Binomial Method (Continued)

$O_{3(1.5),12} = \max\{480 - [200 \cdot 1.3(0.8847)] - [100 \cdot 2.2(0.8120)^3],0\}$
$\qquad = 132.1928$

$O_{3(1.5),13} = \max\{480 - [200 \cdot 1.3(0.8847)^3] - [100 \cdot 2.2(1.2315)^3],0\}$
$\qquad = 0.0000$

$O_{3(1.5),14} = \max\{480 - [200 \cdot 1.3(0.8847)^3] - [100 \cdot 2.2(1.2315)],0\}$
$\qquad = 29.0331$

$O_{3(1.5),15} = \max\{480 - [200 \cdot 1.3(0.8847)^3] - [100 \cdot 2.2(0.8120)],0\}$
$\qquad = 121.3231$

$O_{3(1.5),16} = \max\{480 - [200 \cdot 1.3(0.8847)^3] - [100 \cdot 2.2(0.8120)^3],0\}$
$\qquad = 182.1779$

ii) At time 2(1.5)

a) Calculating $O_{2(1.5),1}$

To calculate the value of $O_{2(1.5),1}$, one has to first observe that due to the lack of early exercise, the value obtained by exercising the option is zero. Furthermore, the expected value of the option obtained by not exercising is

$$O_{2(1.5),1} = [(p_1 \cdot O_{3(1.5),f(2,1,1)}) + (p_2 \cdot O_{3(1.5),f(2,1,2)}) + (p_3 \cdot O_{3(1.5),f(2,1,3)}) + (p_4 \cdot O_{3(1.5),f(2,1,4)})]e^{-r_d \Delta t}$$

Since the values of p_1, p_2, p_3, and p_4, are known, to evaluate the value of $O_{2(1.5),1}$, one would still need to know the values of $O_{3(1.5),f(2,1,1)}$, $O_{3(1.5),f(2,1,2)}$, $O_{3(1.5),f(2,1,3)}$, and $O_{3(1.5),f(2,1,4)}$, which can only be identified once $f(2,1,1)$, $f(2,1,2)$, $f(2,1,3)$ and $f(2,1,4)$ are all known.

$$f(2,1,1) = 1 + \frac{1}{2}\sum_{k=1}^{2}[2 + 1 - c_{2,1,k} - c_{1,1,k}](2 + 2)^{2-k}$$

$$= 1 + \frac{1}{2}[3 - c_{2,1,1} - c_{1,1,1}]4^{2-1} + \frac{1}{2}[3 - c_{2,1,2} - c_{1,1,2}]4^{2-2}$$

$$= \frac{17}{2} - 2c_{2,1,1} - 2c_{1,1,1} - \frac{1}{2}c_{2,1,2} - \frac{1}{2}c_{1,1,2}$$

$$= \frac{17}{2} - 2(2) - 2(1) - \frac{1}{2}(2) - \frac{1}{2}(1)$$

$$= 1$$

Similarly,

$$f(2,1,2) = 1 + \frac{1}{2}\sum_{k=1}^{2}[2 + 1 - c_{2,1,k} - c_{1,2,k}](2 + 2)^{2-k}$$

$$= 1 + \frac{1}{2}[3 - c_{2,1,1} - c_{1,2,1}]4^{2-1} + \frac{1}{2}[3 - c_{2,1,2} - c_{1,2,2}]4^{2-2}$$

$$= \frac{17}{2} - 2c_{2,1,1} - 2c_{1,2,1} - \frac{1}{2}c_{2,1,2} - \frac{1}{2}c_{1,2,2}$$

EXAMPLE 34   Valuing a Basket Currency Option Using the Binomial Method (Continued)

$$= \frac{17}{2} - 2(2) - 2\left\{1 - 2\left[\frac{1\,\text{mod}(2^2) - 1\,\text{mod}(2)}{2}\right]\right\}$$

$$-\frac{1}{2}(2) - \frac{1}{2}\left\{1 - 2\left[\frac{1\,\text{mod}(2) - 1\,\text{mod}(1)}{1}\right]\right\}$$

$$= \frac{17}{2} - 4 - 2(1) - 1 - \frac{1}{2}(-1)$$

$$= 2$$

Furthermore, it can be similarly shown that $f(2,1,3) = 5$ and $f(2,1,4) = 6$. This implies that

$$O_{2(1.5),1} = [(p_1 \bullet O_{3(1.5),1}) + (p_2 \bullet O_{3(1.5),2}) + (p_3 \bullet O_{3(1.5),5})$$
$$+ (p_4 \bullet O_{3(1.5),6})]e^{-r_d\,\Delta t}$$
$$= 0.0000$$

b) Calculating $O_{2(1.5),2}$

To calculate the value of $O_{2(1.5),2}$, one first observes that due to the lack of early exercise, the value obtained by exercising the option is zero. Thus,

$$O_{2(1.5),2} = [(p_1 \bullet O_{3(1.5),f(2,2,1)}) + (p_2 \bullet O_{3(1.5),f(2,2,2)}) + (p_3 \bullet O_{3(1.5),f(2,2,3)})$$
$$+ (p_4 \bullet O_{3(1.5),f(2,2,4)})]e^{-r_d\Delta t}$$
$$= [(p_1 \bullet O_{3(1.5),2}) + (p_2 \bullet O_{3(1.5),3}) + (p_3 \bullet O_{3(1.5),6})$$
$$+ (p_4 \bullet O_{3(1.5),7})]e^{-r_d\Delta t}$$
$$= 2.6424$$

c) Calculating $O_{2(1.5),3}$

Due to the lack of early exercise, the value of $O_{2(1.5),3}$, is given by

$$O_{2(1.5),3} = [(p_1 \bullet O_{3(1.5),f(2,3,1)}) + (p_2 \bullet O_{3(1.5),f(2,3,2)}) + (p_3 \bullet O_{3(1.5),f(2,3,3)})$$
$$+ (p_4 \bullet O_{3(1.5),f(2,3,4)})]e^{-r_d\Delta t}$$
$$= [(p_1 \bullet O_{3(1.5),3}) + (p_2 \bullet O_{3(1.5),4}) + (p_3 \bullet O_{3(1.5),7})$$
$$+ (p_4 \bullet O_{3(1.5),8})]e^{-r_d\Delta t}$$
$$= 24.2003$$

d) Calculating $O_{2(1.5),4}$

Due to the lack of early exercise, the value of $O_{2(1.5),4}$, is given by

$$O_{2(1.5),4} = [(p_1 \bullet O_{3(1.5),f(2,4,1)}) + (p_2 \bullet O_{3(1.5),f(2,4,2)}) + (p_3 \bullet O_{3(1.5),f(2,4,3)})$$
$$+ (p_4 \bullet O_{3(1.5),f(2,4,4)})]e^{-r_d\Delta t}$$
$$= [(p_1 \bullet O_{3(1.5),5}) + (p_2 \bullet O_{3(1.5),6}) + (p_3 \bullet O_{3(1.5),9})$$
$$+ (p_4 \bullet O_{3(1.5),10})]e^{-r_d\Delta t}$$
$$= 0.0000$$

EXAMPLE 34 Valuing a Basket Currency Option Using the Binomial Method (Continued)

e) Calculating $O_{2(1.5),5}$

Due to the lack of early exercise, the value of $O_{2(1.5),5}$, is given by

$$O_{2(1.5),5} = [(p_1 \bullet O_{3(1.5),f(2,5,1)}) + (p_2 \bullet O_{3(1.5),f(2,5,2)}) + (p_3 \bullet O_{3(1.5),f(2,5,3)})$$
$$+ (p_4 \bullet O_{3(1.5),f(2,5,4)})]e^{-r_d \Delta t}$$
$$= [(p_1 \bullet O_{3(1.5),6}) + (p_2 \bullet O_{3(1.5),7}) + (p_3 \bullet O_{3(1.5),10})$$
$$+ (p_4 \bullet O_{3(1.5),11})]e^{-r_d \Delta t}$$
$$= 26.4560$$

f) Calculating $O_{2(1.5),6}$

Due to the lack of early exercise, the value of $O_{2(1.5),6}$, is given by

$$O_{2(1.5),6} = [(p_1 \bullet O_{3(1.5),f(2,6,1)}) + (p_2 \bullet O_{3(1.5),f(2,6,2)}) + (p_3 \bullet O_{3(1.5),f(2,6,3)})$$
$$+ (p_4 \bullet O_{3(1.5),f(2,6,4)})]e^{-r_d \Delta t}$$
$$= [(p_1 \bullet O_{3(1.5),7}) + (p_2 \bullet O_{3(1.5),8}) + (p_3 \bullet O_{3(1.5),11})$$
$$+ (p_4 \bullet O_{3(1.5),12})]e^{-r_d \Delta t}$$
$$= 61.5013$$

g) Calculating $O_{2(1.5),7}$

Due to the lack of early exercise, the value of $O_{2(1.5),7}$, is given by

$$O_{2(1.5),7} = [(p_1 \bullet O_{3(1.5),f(2,7,1)}) + (p_2 \bullet O_{3(1.5),f(2,7,2)}) + (p_3 \bullet O_{3(1.5),f(2,7,3)})$$
$$+ (p_4 \bullet O_{3(1.5),f(2,7,4)})]e^{-r_d \Delta t}$$
$$= [(p_1 \bullet O_{3(1.5),9}) + (p_2 \bullet O_{3(1.5),10}) + (p_3 \bullet O_{3(1.5),13})$$
$$+ (p_4 \bullet O_{3(1.5),14})]e^{-r_d \Delta t}$$
$$= 10.2537$$

h) Calculating $O_{2(1.5),8}$

Due to the lack of early exercise, the value of $O_{2(1.5),8}$, is given by

$$O_{2(1.5),8} = [(p_1 \bullet O_{3(1.5),f(2,8,1)}) + (p_2 \bullet O_{3(1.5),f(2,8,2)}) + (p_3 \bullet O_{3(1.5),f(2,8,3)})$$
$$+ (p_4 \bullet O_{3(1.5),f(2,8,4)})]e^{-r_d \Delta t}$$
$$= [(p_1 \bullet O_{3(1.5),10}) + (p_2 \bullet O_{3(1.5),11}) + (p_3 \bullet O_{3(1.5),14})$$
$$+ (p_4 \bullet O_{3(1.5),15})]e^{-r_d \Delta t}$$
$$= 55.1307$$

i) Calculating $O_{2(1.5),9}$

Due to the lack of early exercise, the value of $O_{2(1.5),9}$, is given by

$$O_{2(1.5),9} = [(p_1 \bullet O_{3(1.5),f(2,9,1)}) + (p_2 \bullet O_{3(1.5),f(2,9,2)}) + (p_3 \bullet O_{3(1.5),f(2,9,3)})$$
$$+ (p_4 \bullet O_{3(1.5),f(2,9,4)})]e^{-r_d \Delta t}$$
$$= [(p_1 \bullet O_{3(1.5),11}) + (p_2 \bullet O_{3(1.5),12}) + (p_3 \bullet O_{3(1.5),15})$$
$$+ (p_4 \bullet O_{3(1.5),16})]e^{-r_d \Delta t}$$
$$= 113.1159$$

iii) At time 1(1.5)

a) Calculating $O_{1(1.5),1}$

Due to the lack of early exercise, the value of $O_{1(1.5),1}$ is given by

$$O_{1(1.5),1} = [(p_1 \bullet O_{2(1.5),f(1,1,1)}) + (p_2 \bullet O_{2(1.5),f(1,1,2)}) + (p_3 \bullet O_{2(1.5),f(1,1,3)})$$
$$+ (p_4 \bullet O_{2(1.5),f(1,1,4)})]e^{-r_d \Delta t}$$
$$= [(p_1 \bullet O_{2(1.5),1}) + (p_2 \bullet O_{2(1.5),2}) + (p_3 \bullet O_{2(1.5),4})$$
$$+ (p_4 \bullet O_{2(1.5),5})]e^{-r_d \Delta t}$$
$$= 9.7890$$

EXAMPLE 34   Valuing a Basket Currency Option Using the Binomial Method (Continued)

b) Calculating $O_{1(1.5),2}$
Due to the lack of early exercise, the value of $O_{1(1.5),2}$ is given by

$$O_{1(1.5),2} = [(p_1 \bullet O_{2(1.5),f(1,2,1)}) + (p_2 \bullet O_{2(1.5),f(1,2,2)}) + (p_3 \bullet O_{2(1.5),f(1,2,3)})$$
$$+ (p_4 \bullet O_{2(1.5),f(1,2,4)})]e^{-r_d \Delta t}$$
$$= [(p_1 \bullet O_{2(1.5),2}) + (p_2 \bullet O_{2(1.5),3}) + (p_3 \bullet O_{2(1.5),5})$$
$$+ (p_4 \bullet O_{2(1.5),6})]e^{-r_d \Delta t}$$
$$= 26.9747$$

c) Calculating $O_{1(1.5),3}$
Due to the lack of early exercise, the value of $O_{1(1.5),3}$ is given by

$$O_{1(1.5),3} = [(p_1 \bullet O_{2(1.5),f(1,3,1)}) + (p_2 \bullet O_{2(1.5),f(1,3,2)}) + (p_3 \bullet O_{2(1.5),f(1,3,3)})$$
$$+ (p_4 \bullet O_{2(1.5),f(1,3,4)})]e^{-r_d \Delta t}$$
$$= [(p_1 \bullet O_{2(1.5),4}) + (p_2 \bullet O_{2(1.5),5}) + (p_3 \bullet O_{2(1.5),7})$$
$$+ (p_4 \bullet O_{2(1.5),8})]e^{-r_d \Delta t}$$
$$= 24.0212$$

d). Calculating $O_{1(1.5),4}$
Due to the lack of early exercise, the value of $O_{1(1.5),4}$ is given by

$$O_{1(1.5),4} = [(p_1 \bullet O_{2(1.5),f(1,4,1)}) + (p_2 \bullet O_{2(1.5),f(1,4,2)}) + (p_3 \bullet O_{2(1.5),f(1,4,3)})$$
$$+ (p_4 \bullet O_{2(1.5),f(1,4,4)})]e^{-r_d \Delta t}$$
$$= [(p_1 \bullet O_{2(1.5),5}) + (p_2 \bullet O_{2(1.5),6}) + (p_3 \bullet O_{2(1.5),8})$$
$$+ (p_4 \bullet O_{2(1.5),9})]e^{-r_d \Delta t}$$
$$= 60.2308$$

iv) At time 0
The option value at this node is given by

$$O_{0,1} = [(p_1 \bullet O_{1(1.5),f(0,1,1)}) + (p_2 \bullet O_{1(1.5),f(0,1,2)}) + (p_3 \bullet O_{1(1.5),f(0,1,3)})$$
$$+ (p_4 \bullet O_{1(1.5),f(0,1,4)})]e^{-r_d \Delta t}$$
$$= [(p_1 \bullet O_{1(1.5),1}) + (p_2 \bullet O_{1(1.5),2}) + (p_3 \bullet O_{1(1.5),3})$$
$$+ (p_4 \bullet O_{1(1.5),4})]e^{-r_d \Delta t}$$
$$= 29.5193$$

Stage 5

The basket option premium is Cad$ 29.52 mm.

OBSERVATION 1 To obtain a more accurate value for the basket option in Example 34, one has to reduce the value of Δt. Doing this gives an option value of Cad$ 29.36 mm.

OBSERVATION 2 A European-style basket option can also be valued using the idea suggested in Observation 3 of Example 25. As before, one has to compute the payoffs on the option maturity as illustrated in Stage 4 i and then multiply each payoff with the total number of paths that lead to the payoff and the corresponding probability associated with each path.

At time $n\Delta t$, for a general m, the product of the total number of paths leading to the node $u_1^{\alpha_1}d_1^{\beta_1}u_2^{\alpha_2}d_2^{\beta_2}$ $...u_m^{\alpha_m}d_m^{\beta_m}$, and the corresponding probability associated with each path is given by the coefficients of $u_1^{\alpha_1}d_1^{\beta_1}u_2^{\alpha_2}$ $d_2^{\beta_2}...u_m^{\alpha_m}d_m^{\beta_m}$ in the expansion

$$[p_1u_1u_2 \ldots u_{m-1}u_m + p_2u_1u_2 \ldots u_{m-1}d_m + \ldots$$
$$+ p_hu_1^{c1,h,1}u_2^{c1,h,2} \ldots u_{m-1}^{c1,h,m-1} u_m^{c1,h,m} + \ldots$$
$$+ p_{2^m}d_1d_2 \ldots d_{m-1}d_m]^n$$

where α_k, $\beta_k = 0, 1, 2, \ldots,$ n and $\alpha_k + \beta_k = n$ (for k = 1, 2, ..., m).

In the context of the example, since m = 2 and n = 3, one would have to first expand $[p_1u_1u_2 + p_2u_1d_2 + p_3d_1u_2 + p_4d_1d_2]^3$. This results in

$$[p_1u_1u_2 + p_2u_1d_2 + p_3d_1u_2 + p_4d_1d_2]^3 = p_1^3u_1^3u_2^3 +$$
$$3p_1^2p_2u_1^3u_2 + 3p_1p_2^2u_1^3d_2 + p_2^3u_1^3d_2^3 + 3p_1^2p_3u_1u_2^3 +$$
$$3p_1(p_1p_4 + 2p_2p_3)u_1u_2 + 3p_2(p_2p_3 + 2p_1p_4)u_1d_2 +$$
$$3p_2^2p_4u_1d_2^3 + 3p_1p_3^2d_1u_2^3 + 3p_3(p_2p_3 + 2p_1p_4)d_1u_2 +$$
$$3p_4(p_1p_4 + 2p_2p_3)d_1d_2 + 3p_2p_4^2d_1d_2^3 + p_3^2p_4d_1^3u_2 +$$
$$3p_3p_4^2d_1^3d_2 + p_4^3d_1^3d_2^3$$

Exhibit 135 illustrates the extracted coefficients from the above equation for each of the 16 option payoffs given in Stage 4 i and the calculation of the option premium using these coefficients.

Summing up the weighted payoffs and discounting[28] the sum by $e^{-(0.08)4.5}$ results in a value of Cad$ 29.52 mm, which agrees with the value obtained using the tree. As before, to obtain a more accurate value of the option premium, one has to increase the value of n.

OBSERVATION 3 When m = 1, it was seen in Observation 4 Example 25 that for a domestic currency-denominated option on a single domestic currency-denominated asset, we had to contend with a total of six risk statistics[29]. The number of risk statistics in-

---

[28] See footnote 14.

EXHIBIT 135   Calculation of Basket Option premium Using Alternative Method

Nodes	Coefficients	Option Payoff	Weighted Payoff
$(S_{1,0}u_1{}^3, S_{2,0}u_2{}^3)$	$p_1{}^3$	0.0000	0.0000
$(S_{1,0}u_1{}^3, S_{2,0}u_2)$	$3p_1{}^2p_2$	0.0000	0.0000
$(S_{1,0}u_1{}^3, S_{2,0}d_2)$	$3p_1p_2{}^2$	0.0000	0.0000
$(S_{1,0}u_1{}^3, S_{2,0}d_2{}^3)$	$p_2{}^3$	0.0000	0.0000
$(S_{1,0}u_1, S_{2,0}u_2{}^3)$	$3p_1{}^2p_3$	0.0000	0.0000
$(S_{1,0}u_1, S_{2,0}u_2)$	$3p_1(p_1p_4 + 2p_2p_3)$	0.0000	0.0000
$(S_{1,0}u_1, S_{2,0}d_2)$	$3p_2(p_2p_3 + 2p_1p_4)$	7.4820	1.3734
$(S_{1,0}u_1, S_{2,0}d_2{}^3)$	$3p_2{}^2p_4$	68.3368	2.9501
$(S_{1,0}d_1, S_{2,0}u_2{}^3)$	$3p_1p_3{}^2$	0.0000	0.0000
$(S_{1,0}d_1, S_{2,0}u_2)$	$3p_3(p_2p_3 + 2p_1p_4)$	0.0000	0.0000
$(S_{1,0}d_1, S_{2,0}d_2)$	$3p_4(p_1p_4 + 2p_2p_3)$	71.3380	13.9558
$(S_{1,0}d_1, S_{2,0}d_2{}^3)$	$3p_2p_4{}^2$	132.1928	11.9540
$(S_{1,0}d_1{}^3, S_{2,0}u_2{}^3)$	$p_3{}^3$	0.0000	0.0000
$(S_{1,0}d_1{}^3, S_{2,0}u_2)$	$3p_3{}^2p_4$	29.0331	0.0034
$(S_{1,0}d_1{}^3, S_{2,0}d_2)$	$3p_3p_4{}^2$	121.3231	0.5714
$(S_{1,0}d_1{}^3, S_{2,0}d_2{}^3)$	$p_4{}^3$	182.1779	11.5027

creases when m increases; in particular, when m = 2, there are 12 risk statistics. Since there will be a delta, gamma, vega, and foreign rho with respect to each underlying asset, this will give rise to a total of eight risk statistics. In addition to the gammas for each of the underlying assets, there will also be a cross gamma (that is, the rate of change in the delta of the first underlying asset when the second underlying asset changes in value), resulting in a total of nine risk statistics. Furthermore, since there is only one time and one

---

[29] These risk statistics were called delta, gamma, theta, vega, domestic rho, and foreign rho.

domestic risk-free rate associated with the option, two additional risk statistics arise from both theta and domestic rho. The final risk statistic, which is due to the risk that is inherent in the correlation estimation, is denoted by varrho. This risk statistics have been summarized in Exhibit 136.

EXHIBIT 136   Risk Statistics for an Option on Two Underlying Assets

Risk Statistics	Computational Formulae[30]
$delta_1$	$$\dfrac{O_{0,1}(S_{1,0} + \varepsilon) - O_{0,1}}{\varepsilon}$$
$delta_2$	$$\dfrac{O_{0,1}(S_{2,0} + \varepsilon) - O_{0,1}}{\varepsilon}$$
$gamma_1$	$$\dfrac{\dfrac{O_{0,1}(S_{1,0} + \varepsilon) - O_{0,1}}{\varepsilon} - \dfrac{O_{0,1} - O_{0,1}(S_{1,0} - \varepsilon)}{\varepsilon}}{\varepsilon}$$
$gamma_2$	$$\dfrac{\dfrac{O_{0,1}(S_{2,0} + \varepsilon) - O_{0,1}}{\varepsilon} - \dfrac{O_{0,1} - O_{0,1}(S_{2,0} - \varepsilon)}{\varepsilon}}{\varepsilon}$$
$gamma_{1,2}$	$$\dfrac{\dfrac{O_{0,1}(S_{1,0} + \varepsilon, S_{2,0} + \delta) - O_{0,1}(S_{1,0}, S_{2,0} + \delta)}{\varepsilon} - \dfrac{O_{0,1}(S_{1,0} + \varepsilon, S_{2,0}) - O_{0,1}(S_{1,0}, S_{2,0})}{\varepsilon}}{\delta}$$
theta	$$\dfrac{O_{0,1} - O_{0,1}(T - \varepsilon)}{\varepsilon}$$
$vega_1$	$$\dfrac{O_{0,1}(\sigma_1 + \varepsilon) - O_{0,1}}{\varepsilon}$$
$vega_2$	$$\dfrac{O_{0,1}(\sigma_2 + \varepsilon) - O_{0,1}}{\varepsilon}$$
varrho	$$\dfrac{O_{0,1}(\rho + \varepsilon) - O_{0,1}}{\varepsilon}$$
domestic rho	$$\dfrac{O_{0,1}(r_d + \varepsilon) - O_{0,1}}{\varepsilon}$$
foreign rho_1	$$\dfrac{O_{0,1}(r_{1,f} + \varepsilon) - O_{0,1}}{\varepsilon}$$
foreign rho_2	$$\dfrac{O_{0,1}(r_{2,f} + \varepsilon) - O_{0,1}}{\varepsilon}$$

30 ε and δ in this exhibit both represent a very small (or infinitiesimal) value.

Using the formulae given in Exhibit 136, one can obtain the risk-statistics for the three-period example discussed earlier.

OBSERVATION 4 Instead of modeling the correlated movements in exchange rates using two binomial trees, one could have alternatively modeled the basket as an asset by itself using only one binomial tree. More precisely, if the basket was of the form $\sum_{k=1}^{m} w_k S_{k,T}$, Methodology 1 can be used to value European-style basket option by setting the initial basket value to $\sum_{k=1}^{m} w_k S_{k,0}$ and

$$u_* = e^{\sigma_* \sqrt{\Delta t}}, \; d_* = \frac{1}{u_*}, \; p_* = \frac{e^{(r_d - r_*)\Delta t} - d_*}{u_* - d_*}$$

where

$$A = \sum_{k=1}^{m} w_k^2 S_{k,0}^2 \, e^{[2(r_d - r_{k,f}) + \sigma_k^2]\Delta t}$$

$$B = 2 \sum_{k=1}^{m-1} \sum_{l=k+1}^{m} w_k w_l S_{k,0} S_{l,0} e^{[2r_d - r_{k,f} - r_{l,f} + \rho_{k,l}\sigma_k\sigma_l]\Delta t}$$

$$M_1 = \sum_{k=1}^{m} w_k S_{k,0} e^{(r_d - r_{k,f})\Delta t}$$

$$M_2 = A + B$$

$$r_* = r_d - \frac{\ln(M_1) - \ln(\sum_{k=1}^{m} w_k S_{k,0})}{\Delta t}$$

$$\sigma_* = \sqrt{\frac{\ln(M_2) - 2\ln(M_1)}{\Delta t}}$$

With this definition of u_*, d_*, and p_*, one can now create a tree whose underlying asset would be a basket of exchange rates. This tree will be analogous to the underlying exchange-rate tree built in Stage 4 of Example 25. To value the option using this tree, as in Stage 5 of Example 25, one can calculate the intrinsic value of the option at each node using the value of the basket at that node and then present value the calculated intrinsic values.

In the context of the example, $m = 2$, $\Delta t = 1.5$, $w_1 = 200$, $w_2 = 100$, and the basket would be of the form $(200 \cdot S_{1,T}) + (100 \cdot S_{2,T})$. Under this circumstance, the initial basket value is 480 and the value of u_*, d_*, and p_* can be shown to be 1.1555, 0.8654, and 0.4973, respectively. These parameters, when used, yield an option price of Cad\$ 31.96. As in Observation 1 making Δt small enough, one can arrive at an option premium of Cad $29.36.

The use of a binomial method to value a European-style spread option is illustrated in Example 35.

EXAMPLE 35 Valuing a Spread Currency Option Using the Binomial Method

The Canadian dollar is currently trading at 1.3000 Cad/US and 2.2000 Cad/£. An investor wants to buy a 4½-year European-style at-the-money call option on the spread between the Cad/US exchange rate and the Cad/£ exchange rate. More precisely, the payoff on maturity is $\max[S_{2,T} - S_{1,T} - 0.9, 0]$, which can be rewritten as $\max[-S_{1,T} + S_{2,T} - 0.9, 0]$, where $S_{1,T}$ represents the Cad/US rate on option maturity and $S_{2,T}$ represents the Cad/£ rate on option maturity. The current continuously compounded risk-free rates of interest in the United States, Canada, and the United Kingdom are 6 percent, 8 percent, and 9 percent, respectively. Using a volatility of 10 percent for the Cad/US exchange rate, a volatility of 17 percent for the Cad/£ exchange rate, a correlation of 60 percent between the continuously compounded returns of these exchange rates, and dividing the 4½-year period into three equal subintervals, I want to value this option.

Stage 1

$S_{1,0} = 1.3000$, $S_{2,0} = 2.2000$, $N_1 = -1$, $N_2 = 1$, $X = -0.9$, $r_d = 0.08$, $r_{1,f} = 0.06$, $r_{2,f} = 0.09$, $\sigma_1 = 0.1$, $\sigma_2 = 0.17$, $\rho_{1,2} = 0.6$, $T = 4.5$, $n = 3$

Stages 2, 3

Since the exchange-rate trees are no different from those presented in Example 34, the reader is referred to Example 34 for these stages.

Stage 4

For the diagram of the option tree, the reader is again referred to Example 34.

i) At time 3(1.5)

$O_{3(1.5),1}$ = $\max[-1.3(1.1303)^3 + 2.2(1.2315)^3 - 0.9, 0]$
  = 1.3317

$O_{3(1.5),2}$ = $\max[-1.3(1.1303)^3 + 2.2(1.2315) - 0.9, 0]$
  = 0.0000

$O_{3(1.5),3}$ = $\max[-1.3(1.1303)^3 + 2.2(0.8120) - 0.9, 0]$
  = 0.0000

$O_{3(1.5),4}$ = $\max[-1.3(1.1303)^3 + 2.2(0.8120)^3 - 0.9, 0]$
  = 0.0000

EXAMPLE 35 Valuing a Spread Currency Option Using the Binomial Method (Continued)

$O_{3(1.5),5}$ = max[−1.3(1.1303) + 2.2(1.2315)^3 − 0.9,0]
= 1.7396

$O_{3(1.5),6}$ = max[−1.3(1.1303) + 2.2(1.2315) − 0.9,0]
=0.3399

$O_{3(1.5),7}$ = max[−1.3(1.1303) + 2.2(0.8120) − 0.9,0]
= 0.0000

$O_{3(1.5),8}$ = max[−1.3(1.1303) + 2.2(0.8120)^3 − 0.9,0]
= 0.0000

$O_{3(1.5),9}$ = max[−1.3(0.8847) + 2.2(1.2315)^3 − 0.9,0]
= 2.0588

$O_{3(1.5),10}$ = max[−1.3(0.8847) + 2.2(1.2315) − 0.9,0]
= 0.6592

$O_{3(1.5),11}$ = max[−1.3(0.8847) + 2.2(0.8120) − 0.9,0]
= 0.0000

$O_{3(1.5),12}$ = max[−1.3(0.8847) + 2.2(0.8120)^3 − 0.9,0]
= 0.0000

$O_{3(1.5),13}$ = max[−1.3(0.8847)^3 + 2.2(1.2315)^3 − 0.9,0]
= 2.3087

$O_{3(1.5),14}$ = max[−1.3(0.8847)^3 + 2.2(1.2315) − 0.9,0]
= 0.9091

$O_{3(1.5),15}$ = max[−1.3(0.8847)^3 + 2.2(0.8120) − 0.9,0]
= 0.0000

$O_{3(1.5),16}$ = max[−1.3(0.8847)^3 + 2.2(0.8120)^3 − 0.9,0]
= 0.0000

ii) At time 2(1.5)

a) Calculating $O_{2(1.5),1}$

Due to the lack of early exercise, the value of $O_{2(1.5),1}$ is given by

$O_{2(1.5),1}$ = [(p_1 • $O_{3(1.5),f(2,1,1)}$) + (p_2 • $O_{3(1.5),f(2,1,2)}$) + (p_3 • $O_{3(1.5),f(2,1,3)}$) + (p_4 • $O_{3(1.5),f(2,1,4)}$)]$e^{-r_d\Delta t}$
= [(p_1 • $O_{3(1.5),1}$) + (p_2 • $O_{3(1.5),2}$) + (p_3 • $O_{3(1.5),5}$) + (p_4 • $O_{3(1.5),6}$)]$e^{-r_d\Delta t}$
= 0.6099

b) Calculating $O_{2(1.5),2}$

Due to the lack of early exercise, the value of $O_{2(1.5),2}$ is given by

$O_{2(1.5),2}$ = [(p_1 • $O_{3(1.5),f(2,2,1)}$) + (p_2 • $O_{3(1.5),f(2,2,2)}$) + (p_3 • $O_{3(1.5),f(2,2,3)}$) + (p_4 • $O_{3(1.5),f(2,2,4)}$)]$e^{-r_d\Delta t}$
= [(p_1 • $O_{3(1.5),2}$) + (p_2 • $O_{3(1.5),3}$) + (p_3 • $O_{3(1.5),6}$) + (p_4 • $O_{3(1.5),7}$)]$e^{-r_d\Delta t}$
= 0.0030

EXAMPLE 35 Valuing a Spread Currency Option Using the Binomial Method (Continued)

c) Calculating $O_{2(1.5),3}$

Due to the lack of early exercise, the value of $O_{2(1.5),3}$ is given by

$$O_{2(1.5),3} = [(p_1 \bullet O_{3(1.5),f(2,3,1)}) + (p_2 \bullet O_{3(1.5),f(2,3,2)}) + (p_3 \bullet O_{3(1.5),f(2,3,3)}) \\ + (p_4 \bullet O_{3(1.5),f(2,3,4)})]e^{-r_d\Delta t}$$
$$= [(p_1 \bullet O_{3(1.5),3}) + (p_2 \bullet O_{3(1.5),4}) + (p_3 \bullet O_{3(1.5),7}) \\ + (p_4 \bullet O_{3(1.5),8})]e^{-r_d\Delta t}$$
$$= 0.0000$$

d) Calculating $O_{2(1.5),4}$

Due to the lack of early exercise, the value of $O_{2(1.5),4}$ is given by

$$O_{2(1.5),4} = [(p_1 \bullet O_{3(1.5),f(2,4,1)}) + (p_2 \bullet O_{3(1.5),f(2,4,2)}) + (p_3 \bullet O_{3(1.5),f(2,4,3)}) \\ + (p_4 \bullet O_{3(1.5),f(2,4,4)})]e^{-r_d\Delta t}$$
$$= [(p_1 \bullet O_{3(1.5),5}) + (p_2 \bullet O_{3(1.5),6}) + (p_3 \bullet O_{3(1.5),9}) \\ + (p_4 \bullet O_{3(1.5),10})]e^{-r_d\Delta t}$$
$$= 0.9281$$

e) Calculating $O_{2(1.5),5}$

Due to the lack of early exercise, the value of $O_{2(1.5),5}$ is given by

$$O_{2(1.5),5} = [(p_1 \bullet O_{3(1.5),f(2,5,1)}) + (p_2 \bullet O_{3(1.5),f(2,5,2)}) + (p_3 \bullet O_{3(1.5),f(2,5,3)}) \\ + (p_4 \bullet O_{3(1.5),f(2,5,4)})]e^{-r_d\Delta t}$$
$$= [(p_1 \bullet O_{3(1.5),6}) + (p_2 \bullet O_{3(1.5),7}) + (p_3 \bullet O_{3(1.5),10}) \\ + (p_4 \bullet O_{3(1.5),11})]e^{-r_d\Delta t}$$
$$= 0.1269$$

f) Calculating $O_{2(1.5),6}$

Due to the lack of early exercise, the value of $O_{2(1.5),6}$ is given by

$$O_{2(1.5),6} = [(p_1 \bullet O_{3(1.5),f(2,6,1)}) + (p_2 \bullet O_{3(1.5),f(2,6,2)}) + (p_3 \bullet O_{3(1.5),f(2,6,3)}) \\ + (p_4 \bullet O_{3(1.5),f(2,6,4)})]e^{-r_d\Delta t}$$
$$= [(p_1 \bullet O_{3(1.5),7}) + (p_2 \bullet O_{3(1.5),8}) + (p_3 \bullet O_{3(1.5),11}) \\ + (p_4 \bullet O_{3(1.5),12})]e^{-r_d\Delta t}$$
$$= 0.0000$$

g) Calculating $O_{2(1.5),7}$

Due to the lack of early exercise, the value of $O_{2(1.5),7}$ is given by

$$O_{2(1.5),7} = [(p_1 \bullet O_{3(1.5),f(2,7,1)}) + (p_2 \bullet O_{3(1.5),f(2,7,2)}) + (p_3 \bullet O_{3(1.5),f(2,7,3)}) \\ + (p_4 \bullet O_{3(1.5),f(2,7,4)})]e^{-r_d\Delta t}$$
$$= [(p_1 \bullet O_{3(1.5),9}) + (p_2 \bullet O_{3(1.5),10}) + (p_3 \bullet O_{3(1.5),13}) \\ + (p_4 \bullet O_{3(1.5),14})]e^{-r_d\Delta t}$$
$$= 1.1862$$

h) Calculating $O_{2(1.5),8}$

Due to the lack of early exercise, the value of $O_{2(1.5),8}$ is given by

$$O_{2(1.5),8} = [(p_1 \bullet O_{3(1.5),f(2,8,1)}) + (p_2 \bullet O_{3(1.5),f(2,8,2)}) + (p_3 \bullet O_{3(1.5),f(2,8,3)}) \\ + (p_4 \bullet O_{3(1.5),f(2,8,4)})]e^{-r_d\Delta t}$$
$$= [(p_1 \bullet O_{3(1.5),10}) + (p_2 \bullet O_{3(1.5),11}) + (p_3 \bullet O_{3(1.5),14}) \\ + (p_4 \bullet O_{3(1.5),15})]e^{-r_d\Delta t}$$
$$= 0.2429$$

EXAMPLE 35 Valuing a Spread Currency Option Using the Binomial Method (Continued)

i) Calculating $O_{2(1.5),9}$

Due to the lack of early exercise, the value of $O_{2(1.5),9}$, is given by

$$O_{2(1.5),9} = [(p_1 \bullet O_{3(1.5),f(2,9,1)}) + (p_2 \bullet O_{3(1.5),f(2,9,2)}) + (p_3 \bullet O_{3(1.5),f(2,9,3)})$$
$$+ (p_4 \bullet O_{3(1.5),f(2,9,4)})]e^{-r_d \Delta t}$$
$$= [(p_1 \bullet O_{3(1.5),11}) + (p_2 \bullet O_{3(1.5),12}) + (p_3 \bullet O_{3(1.5),15})$$
$$+ (p_4 \bullet O_{3(1.5),16})]e^{-r_d \Delta t}$$
$$= 0.0000$$

iii) At time 1(1.5)

a) Calculating $O_{1(1.5),1}$

Due to the lack of early exercise, the value of $O_{1(1.5),1}$ is given by

$$O_{1(1.5),1} = [(p_1 \bullet O_{2(1.5),f(1,1,1)}) + (p_2 \bullet O_{2(1.5),f(1,1,2)}) + (p_3 \bullet O_{2(1.5),f(1,1,3)})$$
$$+ (p_4 \bullet O_{2(1.5),f(1,1,4)})]e^{-r_d \Delta t}$$
$$= [(p_1 \bullet O_{2(1.5),1}) + (p_2 \bullet O_{2(1.5),2}) + (p_3 \bullet O_{2(1.5),4})$$
$$+ (p_4 \bullet O_{2(1.5),5})]e^{-r_d \Delta t}$$
$$= 0.2708$$

b) Calculating $O_{1(1.5),2}$

Due to the lack of early exercise, the value of $O_{1(1.5),2}$ is given by

$$O_{1(1.5),2} = [(p_1 \bullet O_{2(1.5),f(1,2,1)}) + (p_2 \bullet O_{2(1.5),f(1,2,2)}) + (p_3 \bullet O_{2(1.5),f(1,2,3)})$$
$$+ (p_4 \bullet O_{2(1.5),f(1,2,4)})]e^{-r_d \Delta t}$$
$$= [(p_1 \bullet O_{2(1.5),2}) + (p_2 \bullet O_{2(1.5),3}) + (p_3 \bullet O_{2(1.5),5})$$
$$+ (p_4 \bullet O_{2(1.5),6})]e^{-r_d \Delta t}$$
$$= 0.0022$$

c) Calculating $O_{1(1.5),3}$

Due to the lack of early exercise, the value of $O_{1(1.5),3}$ is given by

$$O_{1(1.5),3} = [(p_1 \bullet O_{2(1.5),f(1,3,1)}) + (p_2 \bullet O_{2(1.5),f(1,3,2)}) + (p_3 \bullet O_{2(1.5),f(1,3,3)})$$
$$+ (p_4 \bullet O_{2(1.5),f(1,3,4)})]e^{-r_d \Delta t}$$
$$= [(p_1 \bullet O_{2(1.5),4}) + (p_2 \bullet O_{2(1.5),5}) + (p_3 \bullet O_{2(1.5),7})$$
$$+ (p_4 \bullet O_{2(1.5),8})]e^{-r_d \Delta t}$$
$$= 0.4483$$

d) Calculating $O_{1(1.5),4}$

Due to the lack of early exercise, the value of $O_{1(1.5),4}$ is given by

$$O_{1(1.5),4} = [(p_1 \bullet O_{2(1.5),f(1,4,1)}) + (p_2 \bullet O_{2(1.5),f(1,4,2)}) + (p_3 \bullet O_{2(1.5),f(1,4,3)})$$
$$+ (p_4 \bullet O_{2(1.5),f(1,4,4)})]e^{-r_d \Delta t}$$
$$= [(p_1 \bullet O_{2(1.5),5}) + (p_2 \bullet O_{2(1.5),6}) + (p_3 \bullet O_{2(1.5),8})$$
$$+ (p_4 \bullet O_{2(1.5),9})]e^{-r_d \Delta t}$$
$$= 0.0474$$

iv) At time 0

The option value at this node is given by

$$O_{0,1} = [(p_1 \bullet O_{1(1.5),f(0,1,1)}) + (p_2 \bullet O_{1(1.5),f(0,1,2)}) + (p_3 \bullet O_{1(1.5),f(0,1,3)})$$
$$+ (p_4 \bullet O_{1(1.5),f(0,1,4)})]e^{-r_d \Delta t}$$
$$= [(p_1 \bullet O_{1(1.5),1}) + (p_2 \bullet O_{1(1.5),2}) + (p_3 \bullet O_{1(1.5),3})$$
$$+ (p_4 \bullet O_{1(1.5),4})]e^{-r_d \Delta t}$$
$$= 0.1175$$

EXAMPLE 35   Valuing a Spread Currency Option Using the Binomial Method (Continued)

Stage 5

The spread option premium is Cad$ 0.1175.

It is important for the reader to make the following two observations about Example 35.

OBSERVATION 1 To obtain a more accurate value for the spread option in Example 35, one has to reduce the value of Δt. Doing this gives an option value of Cad$ 0.1169.

OBSERVATION 2 As in the basket option, instead of modeling the correlated movements in exchange rates using two binomial trees, one could have alternatively modeled the spread as an asset by itself using only one binomial tree. More precisely, if the spread payoff on the maturity of the option is of the form $D_T = aS_{1,T} - bS_{2,T}$, we will assume that change in the difference is normally distributed. This arises from the fact that since both $S_{1,T}$ and $S_{2,T}$ are nonegative, $aS_{1,T} - bS_{1,T}$ can range anywhere from $-\infty$ to ∞. As such, it is convenient to assume that this difference is normally distributed. Thus, given the current spread value of D_0, $D_{\Delta t}$, the value of the difference at time Δt in the future can move up (down) to a value of $D_0 + u(D_0 + d)$ with probability $p(1 - p)$, where $d = -u$. The one-step movement of the spread is depicted in Exhibit 137.

EXHIBIT 137   One-Step Binomial Tree for Spread between Two Underlying Assets

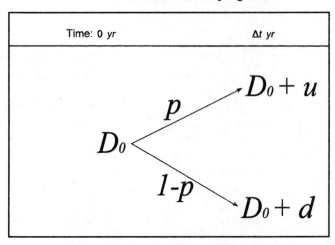

To use the philosophy underlying Methodology 1 to value American-style, Mid-Atlantic-style, and European-style spread options, one has to set the initial spread D_0 value to $aS_{1,0} - bS_{2,0}$ and

$$u_* = \sqrt{(a^2\sigma_1^2 S_{1,0}^2 - 2ab\rho_{1,2}\sigma_1\sigma_2 S_{1,0}S_{2,0} + b^2\sigma_2^2 S_{2,0}^2)\Delta t}$$

$$d_* = -u_*$$

$$p_* = \frac{aS_{1,0}e^{(r_d - r_{1,f})\Delta t} - bS_{2,0}e^{(r_d - r_{2,f})\Delta t} - D_0 - d_*}{u_* - d_*}$$

With this definition of u_*, d_*, and p_*, one can now create a spread tree that is analogous to the underlying exchange-rate tree built in Stage 4 of Example 25. To value the option using this tree, like in Stage 5 of Example 25, one can calcuate the intrinsic value of the option at each node using the value of the spread at that node and then present-value the calculated intrinsic values.

In the context of the example, m = 2, Δt = 1.5, a = 1, b = 1, and the spread would be of the form $S_{2,T} - S_{1,T}$. Under this circumstance, the value of D_0, u_*, d_*, and p_* can be shown to be 0.9, 0.3842, – 0.3842, and 0.4059, respectively. These parameters, when used, yield an option price of Cad $ 0.1325. As in Observation 1, by making Δt small enough, one can arrive at an option premium of Cad $ 0.1169.

Domestic-Currency-Denominated Option on a Single Foreign-Currency-Denominated Asset

I have thus far shown how the binomial method can be used to value a domestic-currency-denominated option on both single and mutiple domestic-currency-denominated assets. As mentioned earlier, these methodologies cannot be readily extended to value a domestic-currency-denominated option on both single and multiple foreign-currency-denominated assets. This is because when a foreign-currency-denominated option on a foreign-currency-denominated asset[31, 32] is valued, one can use the assumption that $\ln S_{for,T}$ is normally distributed with mean

$$\ln S_0 + \left(r_f - q - \frac{\sigma_S^2}{2}\right)T$$ and variance $\sigma_S^2 T$, where S_0, q, r_f, and σ_S have the same representations as those given in Exhibit 113, and $S_{for,T}$ represents the foreign-currency-denominated asset price at time T. However, if a domestic investor is interested in purchasing a structurally similar option that is denominated in the domestic currency, the assumption for the distribution of $\ln S_{for,T}$ (quantified by

---

[31] This will be a "domestic-currency-denominated option" on a "domestic-currency-denominated asset" in the eyes of a foreign investor.

[32] We will assume that this foreign asset is an equity.

$\ln S_{for,T]dom}$) has to somehow reflect the fact that the purchaser does not have to independently use the currency market to convert both the option premium and the in-the-money payoff to the domestic currency.[33] As mentioned at the beginning of this chapter, in the lognormal framework, given the current value of an asset, the two parameters characterizing the potential movements in an asset value are the drift and volatility of the asset. Thus, to be able to quantify the distribution of $\ln S_{for,T]dom}$, one has to define both the volatility and the drift of the foreign asset in the eyes of the domestic investor. Since the volatility measures the annualized standard deviation of the continuously compounded returns of an asset, the volatility of the foreign asset in the eyes of a foreign investor is no different from the volatility of the foreign asset in the eyes of a domestic investor. As a result, the volatility component of $\ln S_{for,T]dom}$ does not need to be adjusted. To correct the drift component of the distribution, it is easier to first assume that the foreign equity does not pay any dividend and intuit the correction using Exhibit 138.

EXHIBIT 138   The No-Arbitrage Condition

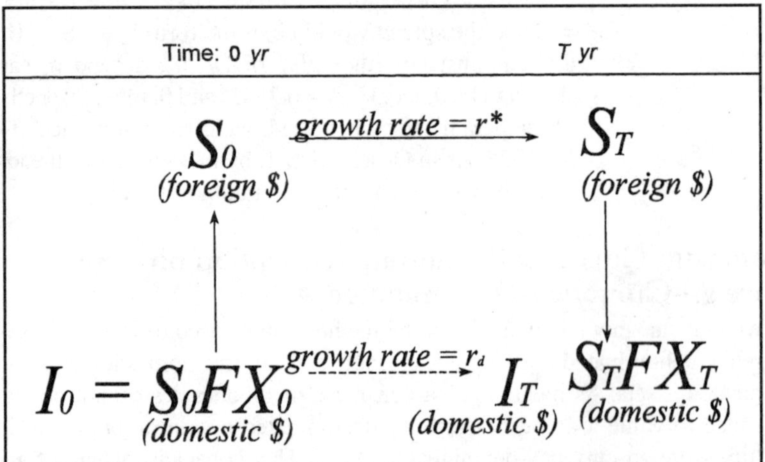

As can be seen from Exhibit 138, an amount of S_0F_0 domestic dollars can be spent today to purchase one unit of foreign equity for a price of S_0 foreign dollars using a current exchange rate of F_0 domestic dollars per foreign dollar. This foreign equity in the eyes of the domestic investor will grow at a rate of r^* (which is what one is trying to determine) and may not necessarily be equal to r_f. The pur-

---

[33] If the domestic investor instead purchases a foreign currency-denominated option on a foreign asset, the investor is exposed to the movements in the currency market. As a result, the premium paid for the option would be no different from the amount paid by the foreign investor.

chased foreign equity then gets sold at time T to realize a value of S_T foreign dollars. The proceeds from this sale get converted to the domestic currency using the then-prevailing exchange rate of F_T domestic dollars per foreign dollar.

As can also be seen from the exhibit, the investor could alternatively use his amount of S_0F_0 domestic dollars (denoted by I_0), to invest in a riskless asset in the domestic economy. Since this is a risk-free asset, it will grow at a continuously compounded risk-free rate of r_d to an amount of I_T which is $S_0F_0e^{r_dT}$. To ensure that no riskless arbitrage is possible, the expected value the investor can get using the first method of investment (that is, the expected value of $S_{for,T]dom}F_T$) should be the same as the expected value obtained using the second method of investment (that is, $S_0F_0e^{r_dT}$).

From the above paragraphs, the following distributional forms can be written for $S_{for,T]dom}$ and F_T:

1. $\ln S_{for,T]dom}$ is normally distributed with mean $\ln S_0 + \left(r^* - \dfrac{\sigma_S^2}{2}\right)T$ and variance σ_S^2T

2. $\ln F_T$ is normally distributed with mean $\ln F_0 + \left(r_d - r_f - \dfrac{\sigma_F^2}{2}\right)T$ and variance σ_F^2T

where the distributional assumption for the exchange-rate movements that is given in (2) is no different from what one has been using to model the exchange rates and value the options on these exchange rates throughout this chapter. To calculate the expected value of $S_{for,T]dom} F_T$ using (1) and (2), one can now use the special case of Relationship 7 in the Appendix when $n = 2$. By setting $A_1 = A_2 = 1$,

$$\mu_1 = \ln S_0 + \left(r^* - \frac{\sigma_S^2}{2}\right)T,\ \mu_2 = \ln F_0 + \left(r_d - r_f - \frac{\sigma_F^2}{2}\right)T,\ \sigma_1 = \sigma_S\sqrt{T},\ \sigma_2 = \sigma_F\sqrt{T},$$

and $\rho_{1,2} = \rho_{FX,S}$, the expected value of $S_{for,T]dom} F_T$ is:

$$e^{\ln S_0 + \left(r^* - \frac{\sigma_S^2}{2}\right)T + \ln F_0 + \left(r_d - r_f - \frac{\sigma_F^2}{2}\right)T + \frac{\sigma_S^2T}{2} + \frac{\sigma_F^2T}{2} + \rho_{FX,S}\sigma_S\sigma_FT}$$

$$= e^{\ln S_0 + \ln F_0 + (r^* + r_d - r_f + \rho_{FX,S}\sigma_S\sigma_F)T}$$

$$= S_0F_0e^{(r^* + r_d - r_f + \rho_{FX,S}\sigma_S\sigma_F)T}$$

Thus, for $S_0F_0e^{(r^* + r_d - r_f + \rho_{FX,S}\sigma_S\sigma_F)T}$ to be equal to $S_0F_0e^{r_dT}$, one needs $r^* = r_f - \rho_{FX,S}\sigma_S\sigma_F$.

Furthermore, for a foreign-currency-denominated asset that pays a continuously compounded dividend rate, it would be intuitively reasonable to expect the correction to be reduced by the dividend rate (i.e., $r^* = r_f - q - \rho_{FX,S}\sigma_S\sigma_F$). Since it is of interest to value an option that has a foreign-denominated underlying asset and is itself denominated in the domestic currency, the present-valuing of the option premium is done using the continuously compounded domestic risk-free rate r_d. As a result, it would be more convenient to rewrite the correction factor r^* as $r_d - q^*$, where $q^* = r_d - r_f + q + \rho_{FX,S}\sigma_S\sigma_F$ and acts like an adjusted dividend rate of the foreign asset. Thus, to value any domestic-currency denominated option on a single foreign-currency denominated asset, one has to first replace q, the continuously compounded dividend rate of the foreign asset by $q^* = r_d - r_f + q +$

$\rho_{FX,S}\sigma_S\sigma_F$ and then proceed with Methodology 2. The steps required to value these type of options are summarized in Methodology 4.

METHODOLOGY 4   Using the Binomial Method to Value a Domestic-Currency-Denominated Option on a Single Foreign-Currency-Denominated Asset

Stage 1
Determine r_d, r_f, q, σ_S, σ_F, $\rho_{FX,S}$, and calculate $q^* = r_d - r_f + q + \rho_{FX,S}\,\sigma_S\,\sigma_F$
Stage 2
Set $r_f = q^*$ and follow Methodology 2.

The use of a binomial method to value a European-style product option on a single asset is illustrated in Example 36.

EXAMPLE 36   Valuing a Category II Product Equity Option Using the Binomial Method

A U.S. stock is currently trading at \$US 20. A Canadian investor wants to buy a 4½-year put option on the stock that is struck at \$US 20. The current continuously compounded risk-free rates of interest in the U.S. and Canada re 6 percent and 8 percent respectively, the volatility of the stock is 30 percent, the continuously compounded dividend rate of the stock is 3 percent, and the correlation between the continuously compounded return of the stock and that of the Cad/US exchange rate is 10 percent. Using a volatility of 10 percent for the exchange rate and dividing the 4½-year period into four equal subintervals, we want to value a European-style Category II product put option (i.e., the in-the-money option payoff on the option maturity date is the product of the guaranteed exchange rate and the difference between the strike value and the stock value on the option maturity date) when the guaranteed exchange rate used in the payoff is 1 Cad/US.
Stage 1
$r_d = 0.08$, $r_f = 0.06$, q = 0.03, $\rho = 0.1$, $\sigma = 0.3$, $\sigma_F = 0.1$, and $q^* = r_d - r_f + q + \rho\sigma\sigma_F = 0.053$
Stage 2
$S_0 = 20$, X = 20, $\hat{F} = 1$, $r_d = 0.08$, $r_f = q^* = 0.053$, $\sigma = 0.3$, T = 4.5, n = 4

EXAMPLE 36 Valuing a Category II Product Equity Option Using the Binomial Method (Continued)

Stage 3

$\Delta t = 1.125$, $u = 1.3746$, $d = 0.7275$, $p = 0.4688$

Stage 4

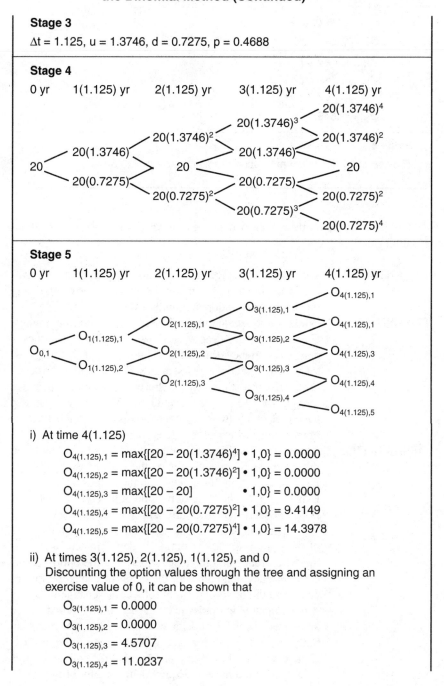

Stage 5

0 yr   1(1.125) yr   2(1.125) yr   3(1.125) yr   4(1.125) yr

i) At time 4(1.125)

$$O_{4(1.125),1} = \max\{[20 - 20(1.3746)^4] \cdot 1, 0\} = 0.0000$$

$$O_{4(1.125),2} = \max\{[20 - 20(1.3746)^2] \cdot 1, 0\} = 0.0000$$

$$O_{4(1.125),3} = \max\{[20 - 20] \qquad\quad \cdot 1, 0\} = 0.0000$$

$$O_{4(1.125),4} = \max\{[20 - 20(0.7275)^2] \cdot 1, 0\} = 9.4149$$

$$O_{4(1.125),5} = \max\{[20 - 20(0.7275)^4] \cdot 1, 0\} = 14.3978$$

ii) At times 3(1.125), 2(1.125), 1(1.125), and 0
Discounting the option values through the tree and assigning an exercise value of 0, it can be shown that

$$O_{3(1.125),1} = 0.0000$$

$$O_{3(1.125),2} = 0.0000$$

$$O_{3(1.125),3} = 4.5707$$

$$O_{3(1.125),4} = 11.0237$$

EXAMPLE 36   Valuing a Category II Product Equity Option Using the Binomial Method (Continued)

$O_{2(1.125),1} = 0.0000$

$O_{2(1.125),2} = 2.2190$

$O_{2(1.125),3} = 7.3101$

$O_{1(1.125),1} = 1.0773$

$O_{1(1.125),2} = 4.4996$

$O_{0,1} = 2.6460$

Stage 6

The Category II product put option premium is Cad$ 2.6460

It is important for the reader to make the following three observations about Example 36.

OBSERVATION 1 To obtain a more accurate value for the product option valued in Example 36, one has to reduce the value of Δt. Doing this gives a put option premium of Cad $ 3.0229.

OBSERVATION 2 While a domestic-currency denominated option on a single domestic currency denominated asset has six risk statistics, a domestic-currency denominated option on a single foreign asset had three additional risk statistics. These additional risk statistics arise from the changes in the continuously compounded foreign risk-free rate, the volatility of the exchange rate, and the correlation between the continuously compounded returns of the foreign asset and the exchange rate.

OBSERVATION 3 As the reader will realize, the value of the option obtained in the example is independent of the current exchange-rate level F_0. Although this agrees with the intuition provided in Exhibit 113, the hedging of the sale of this type of option is in fact dependent on the current exchange-rate level.

This can be better understood if one looks at the delta of the option. Since the option is denominated in the domestic currency and the asset underlying the option is foreign-currency denominated, the delta measures the rate of change in the option premium for a dollar change in S_0 and is denominated in domestic dollar per foreign dollar. To be able to use the value of delta to hedge against movements in both the underlying foreign asset and the underlying exchange rate, one has to first observe that if a call option was sold, one would have to acquire delta amount of the stocks as an initial hedge. Since S_0 trades in foreign dollars, the hedge would amount to a total of (delta • S_0) foreign dollars.

Due to the correlation between the continuously compounded returns of the stock price and the exchange rates, delta will be a function of this correlation. To break down this hedge amount into the number of foreign currency units and the amount of stock in domestic dollars, one can rewrite delta $\cdot S_0$ as $\dfrac{\text{delta} \cdot S_0}{F_0} \cdot F_0$ and $\dfrac{\text{delta}}{F_0} \cdot S_0 F_0$, respectively. This would imply that one would have to hold $\dfrac{\text{delta} \cdot S_0}{F_0}$ units of foreign currency and $\dfrac{\text{delta}}{F_0}$ units of the foreign asset in domestic currency, thus proving the dependence of the hedging requirements on the current exchange rate value F_0.

Domestic-Currency-Denominated Option on Multiple Foreign-Currency-Denominated Assets

As in Methodology 4, to value a domestic-currency-denominated option on multiple foreign assets, one has to first adjust the dividends on any foreign-denominated asset and then apply Methodology 3. These steps are summarized in Methodology 5.

The use of a binomial method to value a European-style product option on multiple assets is illustrated in Example 37.

METHODOLOGY 5 Using the Binomial Method to Value a Domestic-Currency-Denominated Option on Multiple Foreign-Currency-Denominated Assets

Stage 1

Suppose there are m_1 foreign-currency denominated assets that are converted by their respective m_1 exchange rates into the domestic currency and there are an additional m_2 domestic assets such that $m_1 + m_1 + m_2 = m$. Arrange the m assets such that the first m_1 assets are the exchange rates, the next m_1 assets are the foreign-currency denominated assets, and the last m_2 assets are the domestic-currency denominated assets. Furthermore, the m_1 foreign-currency denominated assets are arranged such that the $(m_1 + k)$th foreign asset gets converted into the domestic currency using the kth exchange rate where $k = 1, 2, \ldots, m_1$.

Stage 2

For $k = 1, 2, \ldots, m_1$, determine r_d, $r_{k,f}$, q_{k+m_1}, $\rho_{k,k+m_1}$, σ_k, σ_{k+m_1} and calculate $q^*_{k+m_1} = r_d - r_{k,f} + q_{k+m_1} + \rho_{k,k+m_1}\sigma_k\sigma_{k+m_1}$.

Stage 3

For $k = 1, 2, \ldots, m_1$, set $r_{k+m_1,f} = q^*_{k+m_1}$ and follow Methodology 3.

EXAMPLE 37   Valuing a Category I Product Equity Option Using the Binomial Method

The U.S. stock is currently trading at \$US 20, and the current Cad/US exchange-rate level is at 1.3000 Cad/US. A Canadian investor wants to buy a 4½-year put option on the stock that is struck at \$US 20. The current continuously compounded risk-free rates of interest in the U.S. and Canada are 6 percent and 8 percent, respectively, the volatility of the stock is 30 percent, the continuously compounded dividend rate of the stock is 3 percent, and the correlation between the continuously compounded return of the stock and that of the Cad/US exchange rate is 10 percent. Using a volatility of 10 percent for the exchange rate and dividing the 4½-year period into three equal subintervals, we want to value a European-style Category I product put option (i.e., the in-the-money option payoff on the option maturity date is product of the exchange rate on the option maturity date and the difference between the strike price and stock price on the option maturity date).

Stage 1

$m_1 = 1$, $m_2 = 0$, $m = 2$.

Thus first asset is the foreign exchange rate that is denominated in Cad/US and the second asset is the U.S. stock that is denominated in U.S. dollars.

Stage 2

$r_d = 0.08$, $r_{1,f} = 0.06$, $q_2 = 0.037$, $\rho_{1,2} = 0.1$, $\sigma_1 = 0.1$, $\sigma_2 = 0.3$ and $q_2^* = r_d - r_{1,f} + q_2 + \rho_{1,2}\sigma_1\sigma_2 = 0.053$.

Stage 3

$S_{1,0} = 1.3000$, $S_{2,0} = 20$, $X = 20$, $r_d = 0.08$

$r_{1,f} = 0.06$, $r_{2,f} = q_2^* = 0.053$, $\sigma_1 = 0.1$, $\sigma_2 = 0.3$, $\rho_{1,2} = 0.1$, $T = 4.5$, $n = 3$

Stage 4

$$\Delta t = \frac{T}{n} \qquad = \frac{4.5}{3} \qquad = 1.5$$

$$u_1 = e^{\sigma_1\sqrt{\Delta t}} \qquad = e^{0.1\sqrt{1.5}} \qquad = 1.1303$$

$$d_1 = \frac{1}{u_1} \qquad = \frac{1}{1.1303} \qquad = 0.8847$$

$$\mu_1 = r_d - r_{1,f} - \frac{\sigma_1^2}{2} = 0.08 - 0.06 - \frac{(0.1)^2}{2} = 0.015$$

$$u_2 = e^{\sigma_2\sqrt{\Delta t}} \qquad = e^{0.3\sqrt{1.5}} \qquad = 1.4440$$

$$d_2 = \frac{1}{u_2} \qquad = \frac{1}{1.4440} \qquad = 0.6925$$

$$\mu_2 = r_d - r_{2,f} - \frac{\sigma_2^2}{2} = 0.08 - 0.053 - \frac{(0.3)^2}{2} = -0.018$$

EXAMPLE 37 Valuing a Category I Product Equity Option Using the Binomial Method (Continued)

$$p_1 = \frac{1}{2^2}\left\{1 + \sum_{k=1}^{1}\sum_{l=k+1}^{2} J_{k,l}(1)\rho_{k,l} + \sqrt{\Delta t}\sum_{k=1}^{2}\frac{J_k(1)\mu_k}{\sigma_k}\right\}$$

$$= \frac{1}{4}\left\{1 + J_{1,2}(1)\rho_{1,2} + \sqrt{\Delta t}\left[\frac{J_1(1)\mu_1}{\sigma_1} + \frac{J_2(1)\mu_2}{\sigma_2}\right]\right\}$$

$$= \frac{1}{4}\left\{1 + [1(0.1)] + \sqrt{1.5}\left[\frac{1(0.015)}{0.1} + \frac{1(-0.018)}{0.3}\right]\right\}$$

$$= 0.3026$$

$$p_2 = \frac{1}{2^2}\left\{1 + \sum_{k=1}^{1}\sum_{l=k+1}^{2} J_{k,l}(2)\rho_{k,l} + \sqrt{\Delta t}\sum_{k=1}^{2}\frac{J_k(2)\mu_k}{\sigma_k}\right\}$$

$$= \frac{1}{4}\left\{1 + J_{1,2}(2)\rho_{1,2} + \sqrt{\Delta t}\left[\frac{J_1(2)\mu_1}{\sigma_1} + \frac{J_2(2)\mu_2}{\sigma_2}\right]\right\}$$

$$= \frac{1}{4}\left\{1 + [-1(0.1)] + \sqrt{1.5}\left[\frac{1(0.015)}{0.1} + \frac{-1(-0.018)}{0.3}\right]\right\}$$

$$= 0.2893$$

$$p_3 = \frac{1}{2^2}\left\{1 + \sum_{k=1}^{1}\sum_{l=k+1}^{2} J_{k,l}(3)\rho_{k,l} + \sqrt{\Delta t}\sum_{k=1}^{2}\frac{J_k(3)\mu_k}{\sigma_k}\right\}$$

$$= \frac{1}{4}\left\{1 + J_{1,2}(3)\rho_{1,2} + \sqrt{\Delta t}\left[\frac{J_1(3)\mu_1}{\sigma_1} + \frac{J_2(3)\mu_2}{\sigma_2}\right]\right\}$$

$$= \frac{1}{4}\left\{1 + [-1(0.1)] + \sqrt{1.5}\left[\frac{-1(0.015)}{0.1} + \frac{1(-0.018)}{0.3}\right]\right\}$$

$$= 0.1607$$

$$p_4 = 1 - p_1 - p_2 - p_3$$
$$= 0.2474$$

Stage 5
Asset 1:

0 yr	1(1.5) yr	2(1.5) yr	3(1.5) yr

$$1.3(1.1303)^3$$
$$1.3(1.1303)^2$$
$$1.3(1.1303)$$
$$1.3(1.1303)$$
$$1.3$$ $$1.3$$
$$1.3(0.8847)$$
$$1.3(0.8847)$$
$$1.3(0.8847)^2$$
$$1.3(0.8847)^3$$

EXAMPLE 37   Valuing a Category I Product Equity Option Using the Binomial Method (Continued)

Asset 2:

0 yr   1(1.5) yr   2(1.5) yr   3(1.5) yr

$$
\begin{array}{cccc}
 & & & 20(1.4440)^3 \\
 & & 20(1.4440)^2 & \\
 & 20(1.4440) & & 20(1.4440) \\
20 & & 20 & \\
 & 20(0.6925) & & 20(0.6925) \\
 & & 20(0.6925)^2 & \\
 & & & 20(0.6925)^3
\end{array}
$$

Stage 6

0 yr   1(1.5) yr   2(1.5) yr   3(1.5) yr

$$
\begin{array}{llll}
 & & & O_{3(1.5),1} \\
 & & & O_{3(1.5),2} \\
 & & & O_{3(1.5),3} \\
 & & O_{2(1.5),1} & O_{3(1.5),4} \\
 & O_{1(1.5),1} & O_{2(1.5),2} & O_{3(1.5),5} \\
 & & O_{2(1.5),3} & O_{3(1.5),6} \\
 & O_{1(1.5),2} & O_{2(1.5),4} & O_{3(1.5),7} \\
O_{0,1} & & O_{2(1.5),5} & O_{3(1.5),8} \\
 & O_{1(1.5),3} & O_{2(1.5),6} & O_{3(1.5),9} \\
 & & O_{2(1.5),7} & O_{3(1.5),10} \\
 & O_{1(1.5),4} & O_{2(1.5),8} & O_{3(1.5),11} \\
 & & O_{2(1.5),9} & O_{3(1.5),12} \\
 & & & O_{3(1.5),13} \\
 & & & O_{3(1.5),14} \\
 & & & O_{3(1.5),15} \\
 & & & O_{3(1.5),16}
\end{array}
$$

i) At time $3(1.5)$

$$O_{3(1.5),1} = \max\{1.3(1.1303)^3[20 - 20(1.4440)^3],0\}$$
$$= 0.0000$$

$$O_{3(1.5),2} = \max\{1.3(1.1303)^3[20 - 20(1.4440)],0\}$$
$$= 0.0000$$

$$O_{3(1.5),3} = \max\{1.3(1.1303)^3[20 - 20(0.6925)],0\}$$
$$= 11.5448$$

$$O_{3(1.5),4} = \max\{1.3(1.1303)^3[20 - 20(0.6925)^3],0\}$$
$$= 25.6756$$

$$O_{3(1.5),5} = \max\{1.3(1.1303)[20 - 20(1.4440)^3],0\}$$
$$= 0.0000$$

$$O_{3(1.5),6} = \max\{1.3(1.1303)[20 - 20(1.4440)],0\}$$
$$= 0.0000$$

$$O_{3(1.5),7} = \max\{1.3(1.1303)[20 - 20(0.6925)],0\}$$
$$= 9.0367$$

EXAMPLE 37 Valuing a Category I Product Equity Option Using the Binomial Method (Continued)

$O_{3(1.5),8}$ = max{1.3(1.1303)[20 − 20(0.6925)^3],0}
            = 19.6283

$O_{3(1.5),9}$ = max{1.3(0.8847)[20 − 20(1.4440)^3],0}
            = 0.0000

$O_{3(1.5),10}$ = max{1.3(0.8847)[20 − 20(1.4440)],0}
             = 0.0000

$O_{3(1.5),11}$ = max{1.3(0.8847)[20 − 20(0.6925)],0}
             = 7.0732

$O_{3(1.5),12}$ = max{1.3(0.8847)[20 − 20(0.6925)^3],0}
             = 15.3633

$O_{3(1.5),13}$ = max{1.3(0.8847)^3[20 − 20(1.4440)^3],0}
             = 0.0000

$O_{3(1.5),14}$ = max{1.3(0.8847)^3[20 − 20(1.4440)],0}
             = 0.0000

$O_{3(1.5),15}$ = max{1.3(0.8847)^3[20 − 20(0.6925)],0}
             = 5.5361

$O_{3(1.5),16}$ = max{1.3(0.8847)^3[20 − 20(0.6925)^3],0}
             = 12.0248

ii) At times 2(1.5), 1(1.5) and 0,
Due to the lack of early exercise, it can be shown that

$O_{2(1.5),1}$ = 0.0000

$O_{2(1.5),2}$ = 4.9451

$O_{2(1.5),3}$ = 15.1274

$O_{2(1.5),4}$ = 0.0000

$O_{2(1.5),5}$ = 3.8707

$O_{2(1.5),6}$ = 11.8409

$O_{2(1.5),7}$ = 0.0000

$O_{2(1.5),8}$ = 3.0296

$O_{2(1.5),9}$ = 9.2679

$O_{1(1.5),1}$ = 2.1182

$O_{1(1.5),2}$ = 8.3585

$O_{1(1.5),3}$ = 1.6579

$O_{1(1.5),4}$ = 6.5424

$O_{0,1}$ = 4.3850

Stage 7

The Category I product option premium is Cad$ 4.385.

It is important for the reader to make the following observation about Example 37.

OBSERVATION 1 To obtain a more accurate value for the product option valued in Example 37, one has to reduce the value of Δt. Doing this gives a put option premium of Cad \$ 5.1150.

THE MONTE CARLO METHOD

As mentioned on page 208, the Monte Carlo method in essence says that given the current exchange-rate level, the exchange rate at time T in the future can be obtained by sampling from the distribution of potential exchange-rate movements. Using this idea, one can partition the option life into n time intervals of length Δt each and simulate an exchange-rate path that starts at time 0 and ends at time T. Each simulated path can then be used to compute the option value associated with the path, which is then averaged over all the simulations.

To value a currency option that expires at time T using Monte Carlo simulations, as in the binomial method, I will let each time interval be of length Δt. Assuming that the current time is 0 and the initial exchange rate level is S_0, Exhibit 139 shows the generation of the exchange rates $S_{\Delta t}$, $S_{2\Delta t}$, $S_{3\Delta t}$ at times Δt, $2\Delta t$, and $3\Delta t$, respectively. These simulated rates are connected using the dotted line, illustrating a simulated exchange-rate path starting at time 0 and ending at time $3\Delta t$.

As can be seen from the earlier discussion and Exhibit 139, in order to simulate an exchange rate, one would need the distribution for future exchange-rate movements given the current exchange-rate level. Using the assumption given on page 204, it is obvious that at time Δt in the future $\ln S_{\Delta t}$ has a normal distribution with mean $\ln S_0 + \left(r_d - r_f - \dfrac{\sigma^2}{2} \right)\Delta t$ and variance $\sigma^2 \Delta t$. Hence, to simulate a value of the future spot exchange rate, one has to do the following:

1. Obtain the natural logarithm[34] of the future exchange rate by randomly sampling from a normal distribution with mean $\ln S_0 + \left(r_d - r_f - \dfrac{\sigma^2}{2} \right)\Delta t$ and variance $\sigma^2 \Delta t$.

2. Take the exponential power of the answer that is obtained in step 1 (that is, $e^{\text{answer from i)}}$).

We can alternatively simulate the future spot exchange rate by condensing the above two steps into the formula $S_{\Delta t} = S_0 \bullet e^{(r_d - r_f - \frac{1}{2}\sigma^2)\Delta t} \bullet e^{\sigma z_1 \sqrt{\Delta t}}$ where z_1 is a

---

[34] See footnote 3 for the definition of a natural logarithm.

EXHIBIT 139 Simulated Path of Spot Exchange Rates for the First Four Times

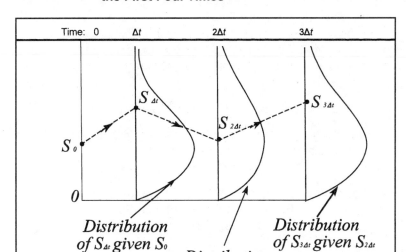

random number that is drawn from the standard normal distribution[35, 36, 37] Now that we can find $S_{\Delta t}$, we can easily generate $S_{2\Delta t}$ by using the formula $S_{2\Delta t} = S_{\Delta t} \bullet$

---

[35] A standard normal distribution is a normal distribution with mean 0 and variance 1.

[36] For a forward-rate process that is given on page 205, the future forward rate can be simulated using the formula $F_{\Delta t} = F_0 \bullet e^{-\frac{1}{2}\sigma^2 \Delta t} \bullet e^{\sigma z_1 \sqrt{\Delta t}}$. Furthermore, if we need $F_{\Delta t}$ to be the spot exchange rate at time Δt, F_0 would be the forward rate that is calculated at the inception of the contract and applied to time Δt. On the other hand, if we were interested in $F_{n\Delta t}$ being the spot exchange rate at time T, F_0, would now be the forward rate that is calculated at the inception of the contract and applied to time T. Furthermore, in the process of converging to the spot rate at time T, $F_{n\Delta t}$ will not converge to a spot rate at any time prior to T. This is consistent with Observation 5 of Example 25.

[37] The generation of a random number from a standard normal distribution, z_1, is done in two steps:
1. Generate a random number in the interval 0 to 1.
2. Use the inverse cumulative standard normal distribution function transformation to convert a randomly sampled number from a uniform distribution in the interval 0 to 1 into a randomly sampled number from a standard normal distribution.
If a Microsoft Excel spreadsheet is used, z_1 can be calculated using the command "=normsinv(rand( ))." Alternatively, if a program/spreadsheet generates only a random number from the interval 0 to 1, z_1 can be calculated using the random number and the approximation given in Relationship 3B of the Appendix. More precisely, z_1 is the solution to the equation $N(z_1) = random\ number$, which can be obtained by setting $a = z_1$ and $p = random\ number$ in this relationship.
Furthermore, if the program/spreadsheet can only generate random integers from the interval {1, 2, 3, ... , M} , the generated random number must be first normalized (or converted into a random number lying in the interval 0 to 1). This can be done by dividing each generated number by M. Using this random normalized number, we can apply Relationship 3ii of the Appendix to solve the equation $N(z_1) = random\ normalized\ number$ for z_1.

$e^{(r_d - r_f - \frac{1}{2}\sigma^2)\Delta t} \cdot e^{\sigma z_2 \sqrt{\Delta t}}$, where z_2 is a random number that is drawn from the standard normal distribution. To generate the spot exchange rates at times $3\Delta t$, $4\Delta t$, . . ., $n\Delta t$ one can recursively apply the formula $S_{i\Delta t} = S_{(i-1)\Delta t} \cdot e^{(r_d - r_f - \frac{1}{2}\sigma^2)\Delta t} \cdot e^{\sigma z_i \sqrt{\Delta t}}$, where z_i is the ith random number that is drawn from the standard normal distribution, and $i = 3, 4, \ldots, n$. With this ability to generate a path of exchange rates starting at time 0 and ending at time $n\Delta t$, one can now value currency options.

Valuing European-Style Vanilla Options

The steps required to value a European-style currency option, which were given in Ravindran (1996a), are summarized in Methodology 6.

METHODOLOGY 6   Using the Monte Carlo Method to Value European-Style Vanilla Options

Stage 1 Determine S_0, X, r_d, r_f, σ, T, n, h (where h represents the total number of paths) and calculate Δt using the formula $\Delta t = \dfrac{T}{n}$
Stage 2 For $j = 1, 2, \ldots, h$, generate $z_{i,j}$, a random number sampled from the standard normal distribution and calculate $S_{i\Delta t,j}$ using the formula $$S_{i\Delta t,j} = S_{(i-1)\Delta t,j} \cdot e^{(r_d - r_f - \frac{1}{2}\sigma^2)\Delta t} \cdot e^{\sigma z_{i,j}\sqrt{\Delta t}}$$ where $i = 1, 2, \ldots, n$ and $S_{0,j} = S_0$.
Stage 3 For $j = 1, 2, \ldots, h$, compute the intrinsic value of the option at time $n\Delta t$ along each path using the formula $$O_j = \max[(S_{n\Delta t,j} - K) \cdot I, 0]$$ where $i = 1, 2, \ldots, n$, and I is as defined in Stage 4i) of Methodology 1.
Stage 4 The option premium is given by the formula $e^{-r_d T}\left[\dfrac{1}{h}\displaystyle\sum_{j=1}^{h} O_j\right]$

It is important for the reader to make the following five observations about Example 38 on page 293.

EXAMPLE 38 Valuing a Vanilla European-Style Currency Option Using the Monte Carlo Simulations

The Canadian dollar is currently trading at 1.3000 Cad/US. An investor wants to buy a 4½-year put option on the U.S. dollar that is struck at 1.3000 Cad/US. The current continuously compounded risk-free rates of interest in the U.S. and Canada are 6 percent and 8 percent respectively. Using an exchange-rate volatility of 10 percent and dividing the 4½-year period into three equal subintervals, I want to value a European-style put option when only nine exchange-rate paths are generated.

Stage 1

$S_0 = 1.3000$, $X = 1.3000$, $r_d = 0.08$, $r_f = 0.06$, $\sigma = 0.1$, $T = 4.5$, $n = 3$, $h = 9$ and $\Delta t = 1.5$.

Stage 2

Paths	0	Δt	2Δt	3Δt
			Time	
1	$S_{0,1} = 1.3000$	$z_{1,1} = -1.2569$ $S_{\Delta t,1} = S_{0,1} \cdot$ $e^{[0.08 - 0.06 - \frac{1}{2}(0.1)^2]1.5} \cdot$ $e^{0.1(z_{1,1})\sqrt{1.5}}$ $= 1.1399$	$z_{2,1} = 1.8482$ $S_{2\Delta t,1} = S_{\Delta t,1} \cdot$ $e^{[0.08 - 0.06 - \frac{1}{2}(0.1)^2]1.5} \cdot$ $e^{0.1(z_{2,1})\sqrt{1.5}}$ $= 1.4620$	$z_{3,1} = 0.9912$ $S_{3\Delta t,1} = S_{2\Delta t,1} \cdot$ $e^{[0.08 - 0.06 - \frac{1}{2}(0.1)^2]1.5} \cdot$ $e^{0.1(z_{3,1})\sqrt{1.5}}$ $= 1.6883$
2	$S_{0,2} = 1.3000$	$z_{1,2} = -0.6072$ $S_{\Delta t,2} = S_{0,2} \cdot$ $e^{[0.08 - 0.06 - \frac{1}{2}(0.1)^2]1.5} \cdot$ $e^{0.1(z_{1,2})\sqrt{1.5}}$ $= 1.2343$	$z_{2,2} = 0.8052$ $S_{2\Delta t,2} = S_{\Delta t,2} \cdot$ $e^{[0.08 - 0.06 - \frac{1}{2}(0.1)^2]1.5} \cdot$ $e^{0.1(z_{2,2})\sqrt{1.5}}$ $= 1.3932$	$z_{3,2} = 0.6095$ $S_{3\Delta t,2} = S_{2\Delta t,2} \cdot$ $e^{[0.08 - 0.06 - \frac{1}{2}(0.1)^2]1.5} \cdot$ $e^{0.1(z_{3,2})\sqrt{1.5}}$ $= 1.5353$

EXAMPLE 38 Valuing a Vanilla European-Style Currency Option Using the Monte Carlo Simulations (Continued)

3	$S_{0,3} = 1.3000$	$z_{1,3} = -0.3867$ $S_{\Delta t,3} = S_{0,3} \cdot$ $e^{[0.08 - 0.06 - \frac{1}{2}(0.1)^2]1.5} \cdot$ $e^{0.1(z_{1,3})\sqrt{1.5}}$ $= 1.2681$	$z_{2,3} = 0.2388$ $S_{2\Delta t,3} = S_{\Delta t,3} \cdot$ $e^{[0.08 - 0.06 - \frac{1}{2}(0.1)^2]1.5} \cdot$ $e^{0.1(z_{2,3})\sqrt{1.5}}$ $= 1.3354$	$z_{3,3} = -0.8018$ $S_{3\Delta t,3} = S_{2\Delta t,3} \cdot$ $e^{[0.08 - 0.06 - \frac{1}{2}(0.1)^2]1.5} \cdot$ $e^{0.1(z_{3,3})\sqrt{1.5}}$ $= 1.2380$
4	$S_{0,4} = 1.3000$	$z_{1,4} = -0.6464$ $S_{\Delta t,4} = S_{0,4} \cdot$ $e^{[0.08 - 0.06 - \frac{1}{2}(0.1)^2]1.5} \cdot$ $e^{0.1(z_{1,4})\sqrt{1.5}}$ $= 1.2284$	$z_{2,4} = 0.1376$ $S_{2\Delta t,4} = S_{\Delta t,4} \cdot$ $e^{[0.08 - 0.06 - \frac{1}{2}(0.1)^2]1.5} \cdot$ $e^{0.1(z_{2,4})\sqrt{1.5}}$ $= 1.2777$	$z_{3,4} = 1.7210$ $S_{3\Delta t,4} = S_{2\Delta t,4} \cdot$ $e^{[0.08 - 0.06 - \frac{1}{2}(0.1)^2]1.5} \cdot$ $e^{0.1(z_{3,4})\sqrt{1.5}}$ $= 1.6134$
5	$S_{0,5} = 1.3000$	$z_{1,5} = -0.4478$ $S_{\Delta t,5} = S_{0,5} \cdot$ $e^{[0.08 - 0.06 - \frac{1}{2}(0.1)^2]1.5} \cdot$ $e^{0.1(z_{1,5})\sqrt{1.5}}$ $= 1.2586$	$z_{2,5} = 0.1930$ $S_{2\Delta t,5} = S_{\Delta t,5} \cdot$ $e^{[0.08 - 0.06 - \frac{1}{2}(0.1)^2]1.5} \cdot$ $e^{0.1(z_{2,5})\sqrt{1.5}}$ $= 1.3180$	$z_{3,5} = -0.6371$ $S_{3\Delta t,5} = S_{2\Delta t,5} \cdot$ $e^{[0.08 - 0.06 - \frac{1}{2}(0.1)^2]1.5} \cdot$ $e^{0.1(z_{3,5})\sqrt{1.5}}$ $= 1.2468$
6	$S_{0,6} = 1.3000$	$z_{1,6} = -0.2770$ $S_{\Delta t,6} = S_{0,6} \cdot$ $e^{[0.08 - 0.06 - \frac{1}{2}(0.1)^2]1.5} \cdot$ $e^{0.1(z_{1,6})\sqrt{1.5}}$ $= 1.2852$	$z_{2,6} = -0.6825$ $S_{2\Delta t,6} = S_{\Delta t,6} \cdot$ $e^{[0.08 - 0.06 - \frac{1}{2}(0.1)^2]1.5} \cdot$ $e^{0.1(z_{2,6})\sqrt{1.5}}$ $= 1.2090$	$z_{3,6} = 2.2871$ $S_{3\Delta t,6} = S_{2\Delta t,6} \cdot$ $e^{[0.08 - 0.06 - \frac{1}{2}(0.1)^2]1.5} \cdot$ $e^{0.1(z_{3,6})\sqrt{1.5}}$ $= 1.6362$

EXAMPLE 38 Valuing a Vanilla European-Style Currency Option Using the Monte Carlo Simulations (Continued)

7	$S_{0,7} = 1.3000$	$z_{1,7} = -1.0825$ $S_{\Delta t,7} = S_{0,7} \cdot$ $e^{[0.08 - 0.06 - \frac{1}{2}(0.1)^2]1.5} \cdot$ $e^{0.1(z_{1,7})\sqrt{1.5}}$ $= 1.1645$	$z_{2,7} = 1.6066$ $S_{2\Delta t,7} = S_{\Delta t,7} \cdot$ $e^{[0.08 - 0.06 - \frac{1}{2}(0.1)^2]1.5} \cdot$ $e^{0.1(z_{2,7})\sqrt{1.5}}$ $= 1.4500$	$z_{3,7} = -0.4808$ $S_{3\Delta t,7} = S_{2\Delta t,7} \cdot$ $e^{[0.08 - 0.06 - \frac{1}{2}(0.1)^2]1.5} \cdot$ $e^{0.1(z_{3,7})\sqrt{1.5}}$ $= 1.3982$
8	$S_{0,8} = 1.3000$	$z_{1,8} = 0.1469$ $S_{\Delta t,8} = S_{0,8} \cdot$ $e^{[0.08 - 0.06 - \frac{1}{2}(0.1)^2]1.5} \cdot$ $e^{0.1(z_{1,8})\sqrt{1.5}}$ $= 1.3537$	$z_{2,8} = 0.6798$ $S_{2\Delta t,8} = S_{\Delta t,8} \cdot$ $e^{[0.08 - 0.06 - \frac{1}{2}(0.1)^2]1.5} \cdot$ $e^{0.1(z_{2,8})\sqrt{1.5}}$ $= 1.5047$	$z_{3,8} = 0.7055$ $S_{3\Delta t,8} = S_{2\Delta t,8} \cdot$ $e^{[0.08 - 0.06 - \frac{1}{2}(0.1)^2]1.5} \cdot$ $e^{0.1(z_{3,8})\sqrt{1.5}}$ $= 1.6778$
9	$S_{0,9} = 1.3000$	$z_{1,9} = -0.1044$ $S_{\Delta t,9} = S_{0,9} \cdot$ $e^{[0.08 - 0.06 - \frac{1}{2}(0.1)^2]1.5} \cdot$ $e^{0.1(z_{1,9})\sqrt{1.5}}$ $= 1.3127$	$z_{2,9} = -0.3169$ $S_{2\Delta t,9} = S_{\Delta t,9} \cdot$ $e^{[0.08 - 0.06 - \frac{1}{2}(0.1)^2]1.5} \cdot$ $e^{0.1(z_{2,9})\sqrt{1.5}}$ $= 1.2915$	$z_{3,9} = 1.8157$ $S_{3\Delta t,9} = S_{2\Delta t,9} \cdot$ $e^{[0.08 - 0.06 - \frac{1}{2}(0.1)^2]1.5} \cdot$ $e^{0.1(z_{3,9})\sqrt{1.5}}$ $= 1.6498$

EXAMPLE 38   Valuing a Vanilla European-Style Currency Option Using the Monte Carlo Simulations (Continued)

Stage 3

Path	Exchange Rate at Time $3\Delta t$	Payoff Option
1	$S_{3\Delta t,1} = 1.6883$	$O_1 = \max[1.3 - 1.6883, 0] = 0.0000$
2	$S_{3\Delta t,2} = 1.5353$	$O_2 = \max[1.3 - 1.5353, 0] = 0.0000$
3	$S_{3\Delta t,3} = 1.2380$	$O_3 = \max[1.3 - 1.2380, 0] = 0.0620$
4	$S_{3\Delta t,4} = 1.6134$	$O_4 = \max[1.3 - 1.6134, 0] = 0.0000$
5	$S_{3\Delta t,5} = 1.2468$	$O_5 = \max[1.3 - 1.2468, 0] = 0.0532$
6	$S_{3\Delta t,6} = 1.6362$	$O_6 = \max[1.3 - 1.6362, 0] = 0.0000$
7	$S_{3\Delta t,7} = 1.3982$	$O_7 = \max[1.3 - 1.3982, 0] = 0.0000$
8	$S_{3\Delta t,8} = 1.6778$	$O_8 = \max[1.3 - 1.6778, 0] = 0.0000$
9	$S_{3\Delta t,9} = 1.6498$	$O_9 = \max[1.3 - 1.6498, 0] = 0.0000$

Stage 4

The option premium is given by $e^{-0.08(4.5)}\left[\dfrac{O_1 + O_2 + O_3 + \ldots + O_9}{9}\right] = 0.0089$ Cad/US.

OBSERVATION 1 To obtain a more accurate value for the European-style option, one would have to reduce the value of Δt and increase h, the number of simulated paths. Rule-of-thumb numbers for Δt and h that are reasonable for most instances are 0.01 years and 4,000 simulations, respectively. Reducing Δt fine enough results in a premium of about 0.0443 Cad/US.

OBSERVATION 2 As observed in the binomial method, if we revalued the option using the same set of parameters or inputs, the option premiums obtained by this method can be identically reproduced. Regardless of the same set of parameters, the premiums obtained using the Monte Carlo simulations cannot be identically reproduced. The weakness of this method arises from the fact that since the option premium is calculated using the random numbers sampled from the standard normal distribution, the premium associated with each random number cannot be replicated unless the same set of random numbers is stored and reused. Although the storing of the random numbers may philosophically sound appealing, as the option life gets longer and more paths are generated, this process would require a computer with a great deal of memory.

OBSERVATION 3 To calculate the risk-statistics associated with this option, it would be easier to revalue the option with an increase in the underlying parameters and then compute the rate of change in the option premium for a change in the value of the underlying parameter. Despite the simplicity of the recalculation of the option premium, one has to be very careful when introducing the change in the underlying parameter. This can be better understood by looking at the calculation of vega as an example.

On page 220, I calculated vega by first using the binomial method to reevaluate the option premium when the volatility is increased by ε. The value of vega is then computed by using the formula given on same page. Given the risk characteristics of the option that was intuited on page 63, it is always the case that $O_{0,1}(\sigma + \varepsilon) > O_{0,1}$ results in a positive value for vega. Although we would use the method that is described above to calculate the value of vega using a Monte Carlo simulation, due to the sampling error that is inherent in the simulations, it is possible that a ε increase in volatility would not be sufficient to guarantee that $O_{0,1}(\sigma + \varepsilon) > O_{0,1}$. This would in turn result in a negative value of vega as opposed to the correct postive value of vega. Further-more, even if the value of the calculated vega turns out to be positive, due to sampling errors, one could potentially end up with a discrepancy in the magnitude of vega.

To get around this problem, one can adopt the idea put forth in Observation 2. More precisely, the generated random numbers that were used in the option valuation would be stored and reused with a change in the underlying volatility.

OBSERVATION 4 Doing a Monte Carlo simulation is equivalent to performing a numerical integration of the option payoff with respect to its probability density function.[38] To see this, one would first observe that when using the Monte Carlo simulations in Example 38, the option payoff for each simulated path was initially calculated and then averaged over all the paths. Exhibit 140 illustrates the destinations of all nine simulated paths. as a frequency distribution. These points are in fact simulated points of the distribution of spot exchange rates at time $3\Delta t$. Exhibit 140 also illustrates, with dotted lines, the theoretical distribution of $S_{3\Delta t}$.

As can be seen from Exhibit 140, when the size of the simulated paths increases to a very large number (for example, 10,000) and the horizontal width of each block decreases, the generated frequency distribution will fit the theoretical distribution of $S_{3\Delta t}$ exactly. As before, to calculate the option premiums for these 10,000 paths, one would sum the option payoffs and then present-value the average of the payoffs across the paths. It is important for the reader to note that, by the nature of Exhibit 140, it would be reasonable to expect these 10,000 payoffs to be lumped into categories such that a payoff from any category would be a good proxy for the other payoffs lumped into that category. More precisely, depending on the width of the category, there could be, for example, 2 identical option payoffs belonging to the left-most category of the frequency distribution, 5 identical option payoffs belonging to the second-left-most category of the frequency distribution, 12 identical option payoffs belonging to the third-left-most category of the frequency distribution, and so on. Thus, adding the 10,000 payoffs up and then averaging is equivalent to taking the weighted average of all the payoffs, where each weight (e.g., $\dfrac{2}{10,000}$, $\dfrac{5}{10,000}$, $\dfrac{12}{10,000}$ etc.) would represent the probability of getting the respective payoff.

---

[38] As mentioned in chapter 2, footnote 73, the option premium can be calculated by present-valuing the expected value of the option payoff. In the context of our example, this is $e^{-r_d T}$

$$E_{S_T}[\max(X - S_T, 0)] = e^{-r_d T} \int_0^X (X - S_T) \, g(S_T) \, dS_T,$$ where $g(S_T)$ is defined in Assumption 1 of

the Appendix. This integral can alternatively be calculated using numerical methods that are described in Abramowitz and Stegun (1970) and Burden and Fraires (1985).

EXHIBIT 140   Distribution of the Simulated Rates in Example 38

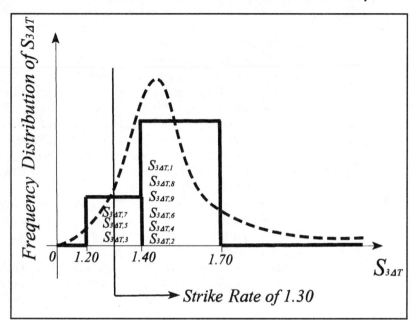

To arrive at the option premium, one can alternatively first divide the frequency distribution by 10,000 (the total of the frequencies) to end up with a probability distribution of $S_{3\Delta t}$. The product of the probability obtained from the probability distribution of $S_{3\Delta t}$ with its corresponding option payoff across all the categories would then be summed and present-valued to arrive at the required option premium. This is the calculation of the expectations of the option payoff, which was discussed earlier.[39]

OBSERVATION 5 Although the fluctuation of the option premium obtained using a Monte Carlo simulation can be reduced by increasing the number of simulated paths, two other variance-reduction methods are also employed:

A. **Antithetic variable technique.** To ensure that the variance of sampling from the standard normal distribution is reduced and the average of the samples drawn is 0[40], for every random number sampled, the negative of the random

---

[39] See footnote 38.

[40] Since the sampling is done from a standard normal distribution whose mean is 0, we would need the drawn samples to average out to 0.

number is also used[41]. As a result, for every path generated, a "mirror" path would be generated. This mirror path would contain the negative of all the random numbers that were generated and used in the first path.

As an illustration, consider Path 1 on page 293. To generate this path, I used the random numbers $z_{1,1} = -1.2569$, $z_{2,1} = 1.8482$, and $z_{3,1} = 0.9912$ and generated an exchange-rate path of [1.3000, 1.1399, 1.4620, 1.6883]. In using the antithetical variable technique, one would generate a mirror path (labeled Path 1A) of Path 1 using the random numbers $z_{1A,1} = 1.2569$, $z_{2A,1} = -1.8482$ and $z_{3A,1} = -0.9912$. This would give rise to a mirror path of [1.3000, 1.5508, 1.2648, 1.1457].

B. **Control variate technique.** This variance-reduction technique hinges on the fact that to value an option, one should be able to analytically value a closely related option. As a result, the methodology is useful only if one can find a related derivative[42] that can be analytically valued. Once this related derivative is identified, the required option premium can be obtained using the following relationship:

Required option premium = Simulated premium of required option − Simulated premium of related derivative + Exact premium of related derivative

To apply the control-variate technique in the context of Example 38 and value the European-style put option, one can choose as a related derivative the *sale* of a currency forward contract. Since the value of a forward contract is simply the future expectation of the spot exchange rate, this can

---

[41] To understand why this reduces the variance, consider two random normal numbers, z_1 and z_2. The variance of $z_1 + z_2$, denoted by $Var(z_1 + z_2)$ is calculated using the formula $Var(z_1) + Var(z_2) + 2Cov(z_1,z_2)$, where $Cov(z_1,z_2)$ represents the covariance between z_1 and z_2. Since this covariance is of the form $Corr(z_1,z_2) \cdot \sqrt{Var(z_1)} \cdot \sqrt{Var(z_2)}$, where $Corr(z_1,z_2)$ represents the correlation between z_1 and z_2, the covariance is at its greatest when z_1 and z_2 are perfectly postitively correlated (i.e., $z_1 = z_2$) and smallest when z_1 and z_2 are perfectly negatively correlated (i.e., $z_1 = -z_2$). Furthermore, since $Var(z_1 + z_2)$ is minimized when the covariance between z_1 and z_2 is at its smallest, $z_1 = -z_2$ would minimize the variance.

[42] Because of the relationship "Required option premium (ROP) = Simulated premium of required option (SPRO) − Simulated premium of related derivative (SPRD) + Exact premium of related derivative. (EPRD)" and the fact that EPRD is a constant,

$Var(ROP) = Var(SPRO) + Var(SPRD) - 2\ Corr(SPRO,SPRD)\ \sqrt{Var(SPRO)}\ \sqrt{Var(SPRD)}$.

Since $Var(ROP)$ is reduced when $Corr(SPRO,SPRD)$ is 1, to minimize the variance, one would want to choose a related derivative that is as highly postively correlated as possible to the option payoff that is being valued.

be calculated using the formula $S_0e^{(r_d - r_f)T}$.[43] Thus, the variance-reducing relationship required for the Monte Carlo simulations becomes

Put option premium = Simulated option premium a path – (– Simulated forward premium using same path) + $(-S_0e^{(r_d - r_f)T})$

where the negative sign indicates the sale of the forward contract. It is important for the reader to note that if one had instead used the fact that the forward contract was purchased, the correlation between the put option payoff and the payoff arising from the purchase of the forward contract would be perfectly positively correlated. This would in turn lead to a higher variance in the estimation, which is what we are trying to minimize.

Valuing Mid-Atlantic and American-Style Vanilla Options

Since there is no early exercise provision in a European-style option, using Monte Carlo simulations to value such an option resulted in present-valuing the average of the option payoffs on the option maturity date across all the simulated paths. Once the notion of early exercise is introduced into the option, as was shown in Example 25, it is possible for the option to be exercised early. As a result, to calculate the payoff associated with any one path, one would have to incorporate the fact that there may be early exercise associated with some of the paths. This implies that for these paths, the payoffs contributing to the calculation of the option premium must be computed at the times of exercise, which can only be done if the exchange rate threshold value that needs to be breached before an exercise can take place is known in advance. Thus, by calculating the expected optimal exercise boundary associated with the option, one can monitor the time at which a simulated path breaches the optimal exercise boundary.[44] This in turn would allow for the easy calculation of the intrinsic value of the option at the time of exercise. Furthermore, if a simulated path does not breach the optimal exercise boundary, a value of zero is assigned to the path. Exhibits 141 and 142 illustrate the optimal exercise boundaries and samples of the simulated paths for the call

---

[43] The value of the forward contract is calculated using the formula $E_{S_T}[S_T]$ when the probability density function of S_T is given by Assumption 1 in the Appendix. This can be evaluated using Relationship 7 of the Appendix and setting $n = 1, \mu_1 = \ln S_0 + \left(r_d - r_f - \dfrac{\sigma^2}{2}\right)T, \sigma_1 = \sigma\sqrt{T}, A_1 = 1$.

[44] The expected optimal exercise boundaries for both the call and put options with early exercise features were discussed on page 52 and illustrated in Exhibit 26.

EXHIBIT 141   Breaching of Call Option's Optimal Exercise Boundary

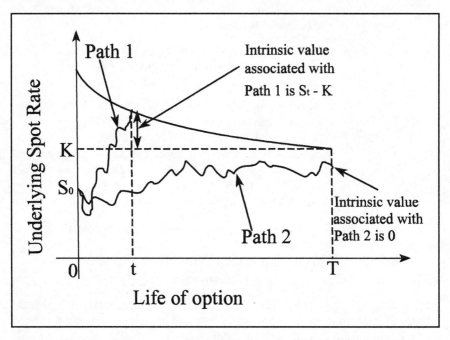

EXHIBIT 142   Breaching of Put Option's Optimal Exercise Boundary

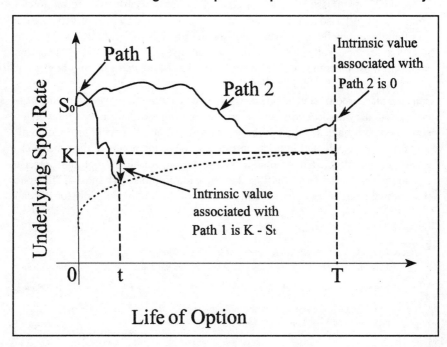

option and the put option, respectively, where Path 1 represents a simulated path that leads to an exercise and Path 2 represents a simulated path with no exercise.

As can be seen from Exhibits 141 and 142, once the optimal exercise boundary associated with the option is established, the calculation of the option payoff associated with the simulated path is trivial. Instead of employing other methods or extra simulations to independently estimate the expected optimal exercise boundary, Tilley in his 1993 paper provided an ingenious way of estimating the boundary using only the simulated paths that are used in the calculation of the option payoffs. This method, which was summarized in Ravindran (1996b), is stated in Methodology 7 in a modified form.

METHODOLOGY 7   Using the Monte Carlo Method to Value Mid-Atlantic Style and American-Style Vanilla Options

---

Stage 1

Determine S_0, X, r_d, r_f, σ, T, t_y (where t_y represents the time of the yth exercise, y = 1, . . ., q and $t_q = T$), h (where h represents the total number of paths), b (where b represents the number of bundles and $\dfrac{h}{b}$ is an integer) and calculate Δt using the formula $\Delta t = \dfrac{T}{n}$ (where n is chosen such that $n \geq q$ and t_y is an integral multiple of Δt for y = 1, . . ., q).

Stage 2

For j = 1, 2, . . ., h, generate $z_{i,j}$, a random number sampled from the standard normal distribution, and calculate $S_{i\Delta t,j}$ using the formula

$$S_{i\Delta t,j} = S_{(i-1)\Delta t,j} \bullet e^{(r_d - r_f - \frac{1}{2}\sigma^2)\Delta t} \bullet e^{\sigma z_{i,j}\sqrt{\Delta t}}$$

where i = 1, 2, . . ., n and $S_{0,j} = S_0$.

Stage 3

a) For y = 1, 2, . . ., q compute the intrinsic value using the formula $IV_{t_y,j} = (S_{t_y,j} - K) \bullet I$, where j = 1, 2, . . ., h and I is defined in Stage 4i) of Methodology 1.

b) Rank these values in an ascending order. Label these ranked values $IV^*_{t_y,1}$, $IV^*_{t_y,2}$, . . . , $IV^*_{t_y,h}$.

c) At time t_q (i.e., $n\Delta t$), find the intrinsic value using b) and set the expected optimal exercise intrinsic boundary value, B_{t_q} equal to 0.[45]

---

45 This stems from the fact that if an American or Mid-Atlantic style option has not been exercised prior to the maturity of the option, the option is no different from a European-style option. As a result, the exercise boundary (or more precisely, the exercise point) at this time is the same as the strike rate of the option, which is reaffirmed in Exhibits 141 and 142. This would imply that the intrinsic boundary value at this time is zero.

METHODOLOGY 7   Using the Monte Carlo Method to Value Mid-Atlantic Style and American-Style Vanilla Options (Continued)

d) At time t_y (for $y = q-1, q-2, \ldots, 1$),

  i) Partition the h ranked intrinsic values obtained in b) into b equalized bundles, with each bundle having $\dfrac{h}{b}$ paths as shown below

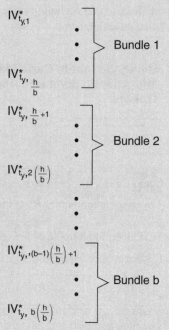

$IV^*_{t_y,1}$

Bundle 1

$IV^*_{t_y, \frac{h}{b}}$

$IV^*_{t_y, \frac{h}{b}+1}$

Bundle 2

$IV^*_{t_y, 2\left(\frac{h}{b}\right)}$

$IV^*_{t_y, (b-1)\left(\frac{h}{b}\right)+1}$

Bundle b

$IV^*_{t_y, b\left(\frac{h}{b}\right)}$

   and for each path j (where $j = (z-1)\left(\dfrac{h}{b}\right)+1, \ldots, z\left(\dfrac{h}{b}\right)$) in bundle z (where $z = 1, \ldots, b$)

   A) Calculate the holding value on any path in bundle z by present-valuing the average of the expected values realized by all the paths in the bundle at the next exercisable time t_{y+1}.

   B) Check with the intrinsic value $IV^*_{t_y,j}$, calculated in b), to see if an exercise should be made.

   C) Compute the higher of the values obtained in A) and B) and set this value to $O_{t_y,j}$.

  ii) Calculate the number of exercises, e_y, made at time t_y in C) and find the e_yth largest intrinsic value using b).

  iii) Set the expected optimal exercise intrinsic boundary value, B_{t_y} equal to the value obtained in ii).

METHODOLOGY 7   Using the Monte Carlo Method to Value Mid-Atlantic Style and American-Style Vanilla Options (Continued)

Stage 4

For each j = 1, 2, ... h, using a), find t* and compute $I_{t^*,j}$, the intrinsic value at this time such that t* is the time where the simulated path *first* breaches the optimal exercise intrinsic boundary (i.e., greater than B_t^*). Furthermore, if the simulated path does not breach the optimal exercise intrinsic boundary by the time the option matures, assign a zero value to $I_{t^*,j}$

Stage 5

The optimum premium is given by the formula $\dfrac{1}{h} [\sum\limits_{j=1}^{h} I_{t^*,j} \bullet e^{-r_d t^*}]$

The use of a Monte Carlo method to value Mid-Atlantic Style option is illustrated in Example 39.

EXAMPLE 39   Valuing a Vanilla American-Style Currency Option Using the Monte Carlo Simulations

The Canadian dollar is currently trading at 1.3000 Cad/US. An investor wants to buy a 4½-year put option on the U.S. dollar that is struck at 1.3000 Cad/US. The current continuously compounded risk-free rates of interest in the United States and Canada are 6 percent and 8 percent respectively. Using an exchange-rate volatility of 10 percent and dividing the 4½-year period into three equal subintervals, we want to value an American-style put option when only nine exchange-rate paths are generated, three bundles are used, and exercise is only permissable at times 1.5 years, 3 years, and 4.5 years.

Stage 1

$S_0 = 1.3000$, $X = 1.3000$, $r_d = 0.08$, $r_f = 0.06$, $\sigma = 0.1$, $T = 4.5$, $t_1 = 1.5$, $t_2 = 3$, $t_3 = 4.5$, $h = 9$, $b = 3$, $n = 3$, $q = 3$, and $\Delta t = 1.5$

Stage 2

The reader is referred to Example 38 for the calculation of these simulated rates.

EXAMPLE 39 Valuing a Vanilla American-Style Currency Option Using the Monte Carlo Simulations (Continued)

Paths	Time			
	0	Δt	$2\Delta t$	$3\Delta t$
1	$S_{0,1} = 1.3000$	$S_{\Delta t,1} = 1.1399$	$S_{2\Delta t,1} = 1.4620$	$S_{3\Delta t,1} = 1.6883$
2	$S_{0,2} = 1.3000$	$S_{\Delta t,2} = 1.2343$	$S_{2\Delta t,2} = 1.3932$	$S_{3\Delta t,2} = 1.5353$
3	$S_{0,3} = 1.3000$	$S_{\Delta t,3} = 1.2681$	$S_{2\Delta t,3} = 1.3354$	$S_{3\Delta t,3} = 1.2380$
4	$S_{0,4} = 1.3000$	$S_{\Delta t,4} = 1.2284$	$S_{2\Delta t,4} = 1.2777$	$S_{3\Delta t,4} = 1.6134$
5	$S_{0,5} = 1.3000$	$S_{\Delta t,5} = 1.2586$	$S_{2\Delta t,5} = 1.3180$	$S_{3\Delta t,5} = 1.2468$
6	$S_{0,6} = 1.3000$	$S_{\Delta t,6} = 1.2852$	$S_{2\Delta t,6} = 1.2090$	$S_{3\Delta t,6} = 1.6362$
7	$S_{0,7} = 1.3000$	$S_{\Delta t,7} = 1.1645$	$S_{2\Delta t,7} = 1.4500$	$S_{3\Delta t,7} = 1.3982$
8	$S_{0,8} = 1.3000$	$S_{\Delta t,8} = 1.3537$	$S_{2\Delta t,8} = 1.5047$	$S_{3\Delta t,8} = 1.6778$
9	$S_{0,9} = 1.3000$	$S_{\Delta t,9} = 1.3127$	$S_{2\Delta t,9} = 1.2915$	$S_{3\Delta t,9} = 1.6498$

Stage 3a

Intrinsic Values at Exercise Times

Exercise Time t_1	Exercise Time t_2	Exercise Time t_3
$IV_{t_1,1} = 1.3 - S_{\Delta t,1} = 0.1601$	$IV_{t_2,1} = 1.3 - S_{2\Delta t,1} = -0.1620$	$IV_{t_3,1} = 1.3 - S_{3\Delta t,1} = -0.3883$
$IV_{t_1,2} = 1.3 - S_{\Delta t,2} = 0.0657$	$IV_{t_2,2} = 1.3 - S_{2\Delta t,2} = -0.0932$	$IV_{t_3,2} = 1.3 - S_{3\Delta t,2} = -0.2353$
$IV_{t_1,3} = 1.3 - S_{\Delta t,3} = 0.0319$	$IV_{t_2,3} = 1.3 - S_{2\Delta t,3} = -0.0354$	$IV_{t_3,3} = 1.3 - S_{3\Delta t,3} = 0.0620$
$IV_{t_1,4} = 1.3 - S_{\Delta t,4} = 0.0716$	$IV_{t_2,4} = 1.3 - S_{2\Delta t,4} = 0.0223$	$IV_{t_3,4} = 1.3 - S_{3\Delta t,4} = -0.3134$
$IV_{t_1,5} = 1.3 - S_{\Delta t,5} = 0.0414$	$IV_{t_2,5} = 1.3 - S_{2\Delta t,5} = -0.0180$	$IV_{t_3,5} = 1.3 - S_{3\Delta t,5} = 0.0532$
$IV_{t_1,6} = 1.3 - S_{\Delta t,6} = 0.0148$	$IV_{t_2,6} = 1.3 - S_{2\Delta t,6} = 0.0910$	$IV_{t_3,6} = 1.3 - S_{3\Delta t,6} = -0.3362$
$IV_{t_1,7} = 1.3 - S_{\Delta t,7} = 0.1355$	$IV_{t_2,7} = 1.3 - S_{2\Delta t,7} = -0.1500$	$IV_{t_3,7} = 1.3 - S_{3\Delta t,7} = -0.0982$
$IV_{t_1,8} = 1.3 - S_{\Delta t,8} = -0.0537$	$IV_{t_2,8} = 1.3 - S_{2\Delta t,8} = -0.2047$	$IV_{t_3,8} = 1.3 - S_{3\Delta t,8} = -0.3778$
$IV_{t_1,9} = 1.3 - S_{\Delta t,9} = -0.0127$	$IV_{t_2,9} = 1.3 - S_{2\Delta t,9} = 0.0085$	$IV_{t_3,9} = 1.3 - S_{3\Delta t,9} = -0.3498$

Stage 3b

Ranked Intrinsic Values at Exercise Times

Exercise Time t_1	Exercise Time t_2	Exercise Time t_3
$IV^*_{t_1,1} = IV_{t_1,8} = -0.0537$	$IV^*_{t_2,1} = IV_{t_2,8} = -0.2047$	$IV^*_{t_3,1} = IV_{t_3,1} = -0.3883$
$IV^*_{t_1,2} = IV_{t_1,9} = -0.0127$	$IV^*_{t_2,2} = IV_{t_2,1} = -0.1620$	$IV^*_{t_3,2} = IV_{t_3,8} = -0.3778$

EXAMPLE 39 Valuing a Vanilla American-Style Currency Option Using the Monte Carlo Simulations (Continued)

$IV^*_{t_1,3} = IV_{t_1,6} = 0.0148$	$IV^*_{t_2,3} = IV_{t_2,7} = -0.1500$	$IV^*_{t_3,3} = IV_{t_3,9} = -0.3498$
$IV^*_{t_1,4} = IV_{t_1,3} = 0.0319$	$IV^*_{t_2,4} = IV_{t_2,2} = -0.0932$	$IV^*_{t_3,4} = IV_{t_3,6} = -0.3362$
$IV^*_{t_1,5} = IV_{t_1,5} = 0.0414$	$IV^*_{t_2,5} = IV_{t_2,3} = -0.0354$	$IV^*_{t_3,5} = IV_{t_3,4} = -0.3134$
$IV^*_{t_1,6} = IV_{t_1,2} = 0.0657$	$IV^*_{t_2,6} = IV_{t_2,5} = -0.0180$	$IV^*_{t_3,6} = IV_{t_3,2} = -0.2353$
$IV^*_{t_1,7} = IV_{t_1,4} = 0.0716$	$IV^*_{t_2,7} = IV_{t_2,9} = 0.0085$	$IV^*_{t_3,7} = IV_{t_3,7} = -0.0982$
$IV^*_{t_1,8} = IV_{t_1,7} = 0.1355$	$IV^*_{t_2,8} = IV_{t_2,4} = 0.0223$	$IV^*_{t_3,8} = IV_{t_3,5} = 0.0532$
$IV^*_{t_1,9} = IV_{t_1,1} = 0.1601$	$IV^*_{t_2,9} = IV_{t_2,6} = 0.0910$	$IV^*_{t_3,9} = IV_{t_3,3} = 0.0620$

Stage 3c

At time t_3

Summary of Option Payoffs at Exercise Time t_3

$O_{t_3,1} = \max[IV^*_{t_3,1}, 0] = 0.0000$

$O_{t_3,2} = \max[IV^*_{t_3,2}, 0] = 0.0000$

$O_{t_3,3} = \max[IV^*_{t_3,3}, 0] = 0.0000$

$O_{t_3,4} = \max[IV^*_{t_3,4}, 0] = 0.0000$

$O_{t_3,5} = \max[IV^*_{t_3,5}, 0] = 0.0000$

$O_{t_3,6} = \max[IV^*_{t_3,6}, 0] = 0.0000$

$O_{t_3,7} = \max[IV^*_{t_3,7}, 0] = 0.0000$

$O_{t_3,8} = \max[IV^*_{t_3,8}, 0] = 0.0532$

$O_{t_3,9} = \max[IV^*_{t_3,9}, 0] = 0.0620$

The optimal exercise intrinsic boundary value, $B_{t_3} = 0$.

Stage 3d

At time t_2

i) From Stage 3b one can see that the following three bundles can be formed using the ranked exchange rates

$$\text{Bundle 1} = [IV^*_{t_2,1}, IV^*_{t_2,2}, IV^*_{t_2,3}]$$
$$\text{Bundle 2} = [IV^*_{t_2,4}, IV^*_{t_2,5}, IV^*_{t_2,6}]$$
$$\text{Bundle 3} = [IV^*_{t_2,7}, IV^*_{t_2,8}, IV^*_{t_2,9}]$$

For ranked intrinsic value $IV^*_{t_2,1}$

A) Since the intrinsic values in this bundle are Paths 8, 1, and 7, the option values associated with these paths at time t_3, can be

EXAMPLE 39 Valuing a Vanilla American-Style Currency Option Using the Monte Carlo Simulations (Continued)

obtained using the summary table of option premiums at time t_3. It can thus be seen that Paths 8, 1, and 7 all lead to an option value of zero. Since the average of these three values is zero, the holding value associated with Bundle 1, or more precisely $IV_{t_2,1}^*$, is zero.

B) The intrinsic value[46] associated with $IV_{t_2,1}^*$ is –0.2047. Since the holding value is greater than the intrinsic value, one will not exercise the option.

C) $O_{t_2,1} = \max[-0.2047,0] = 0.0000$.

For ranked intrinsic value $IV_{t_2,2}^*$

A) Since the intrinsic values in this bundle are Paths 8, 1, and 7, the holding value is equal to zero.

B) The intrinsic value associated with $IV_{t_2,2}^*$ is –0.1620. Since the holding value is greater than the intrinsic value, one will not exercise this option.

C) $O_{t_2,2} = \max[-0.1620,0] = 0.0000$.

For ranked intrinsic value $IV_{t_2,3}^*$

A) The holding value associated with the ranked value $IV_{t_2,3}^*$ is also zero.

B) The intrinsic value associated with $IV_{t_2,3}^*$ is –0.1500. Since the holding value is greater than the intrinsic value, one will not exercise the option.

C) $O_{t_2,3} = \max[-0.1500,0] = 0.0000$.

For ranked intrinsic value $IV_{t_2,4}^*$

A) Since the intrinsic values in this bundle are Paths 2, 3, and 5, the option values associated with these paths at time t_3, can be obtained using the summary table of option premiums at time t_3. It can thus be seen that while Path 2 leads to an option value of 0, Paths 3 and 5 lead to option value of 0.062 and 0.0532, respectively. Since the average of these three values is 0.0384, the holding value associated with Bundle 2, or more precisely $IV_{t_2,4}^*$, is given by $e^{-0.08(1.5)} \cdot 0.0384$, the present value of 0.0384. This simplifies to a value of 0.0341.

B) The intrinsic value associated with $IV_{t_2,4}^*$ is –0.0932. Since the holding value is greater as the intrinsic value, one will not exercise the option.

C) $O_{t_2,4} = \max[-0.0932,0.0341] = 0.0341$.

For ranked intrinsic value $IV_{t_2,5}^*$

A) Since this ranked intrinsic value comes from the same bundle as $IV_{t_2,4}^*$, the holding value is also 0.0341.

---

[46] Strictly speaking, the intrinsic value associated with $IV_{t_2,1}^*$ is zero. This is by virtue of the fact that a payoff is always defined to be a non-negative number. See also page 51.

EXAMPLE 39 Valuing a Vanilla American-Style Currency Option Using the Monte Carlo Simulations (Continued)

B) The intrinsic value associated with $IV^*_{t_2,5}$ is −0.0354. Since the holding value is greater than the intrinsic value, one will not exercise the option.

C) $O_{t_2,5} = \max[-0.0354, 0.0341] = 0.0341$.

For ranked intrinsic value $IV^*_{t_2,6}$

A) Like $IV^*_{t_2,4}$ and $IV^*_{t_2,5}$, the holding value is also 0.0341.

B) The intrinsic value associated with $IV^*_{t_2,6}$ is −0.0180. Since the holding value is greater than the intrinsic value, one will not exercise the option.

C) $O_{t_2,6} = \max[-0.0180, 0.0341] = 0.0341$.

For ranked intrinsic value $IV^*_{t_2,7}$

A) Since the intrinsic value in this bundle are Paths 9, 4, and 6, the option values associated with these paths at time t_3 can be obtained using the summary table of option premiums at time t_3. It can thus be seen that Paths 4, 6, and 9 all lead to an option value of zero. Since the average of these three values is zero, the holding value associated with Bundle 3, or more precisely $IV^*_{t_2,7}$, is zero.

B) The intrinsic value associated with $IV^*_{t_2,7}$ is 0.0085. Since the holding value is less than the intrinsic value, one will exercise the option.

C) $O_{t_2,7} = \max[0.0085, 0] = 0.0085$.

For ranked intrinsic value $IV^*_{t_2,8}$

A) Since this ranked intrinsic value comes from the same bundle as $IV^*_{t_2,7}$, the holding value is zero.

B) The intrinsic value associated with $IV^*_{t_2,8}$, is 0.0223. Since the holding value is less than the intrinsic value, one will exercise the option.

C) $O_{t_2,8} = \max[0.0223, 0] = 0.0223$.

For ranked intrinsic value $IV^*_{t_2,9}$

A) Like $IV^*_{t_2,7}$ and $IV^*_{t_2,8}$, the holding value associated with the ranked intrinsic value $IV^*_{t_2,9}$ is zero.

B) The intrinsic value associated with $IV^*_{t_2,9}$ is 0.0910. Since the holding value is less than the intrinsic value, one will exercise the option.

C) $O_{t_2,9} = \max[0.0910, 0] = 0.0910$

Summary of Option Values at Exercise Time t_2

Ranked Intrinsic Value	Option Payoff	Action
$IV^*_{t_2,1} = IV_{t_2,8} = -0.2047$	$O_{t_2,1} = \max[-0.2047, 0] = 0.0000$	No Exercise
$IV^*_{t_2,2} = IV_{t_2,1} = -0.1620$	$O_{t_2,2} = \max[-0.1620, 0] = 0.0000$	No Exercise

EXAMPLE 39   Valuing a Vanilla American-Style Currency Option
Using the Monte Carlo Simulations (Continued)

$IV_{t_2,3}^* = IV_{t_2,7} = -0.1500$	$O_{t_2,3} = \max[-0.1500,0] = 0.0000$	No Exercise
$IV_{t_2,4}^* = IV_{t_2,2} = -0.0932$	$O_{t_2,4} = \max[-0.0932,0.0341] = 0.0341$	No Exercise
$IV_{t_2,5}^* = IV_{t_2,3} = -0.0354$	$O_{t_2,5} = \max[-0.0354,0.0341] = 0.0341$	No Exercise
$IV_{t_2,6}^* = IV_{t_2,5} = -0.0180$	$O_{t_2,6} = \max[-0.0180,0.0341] = 0.0341$	No Exercise
$IV_{t_2,7}^* = IV_{t_2,9} = 0.0085$	$O_{t_2,7} = \max[0.0085,0] = 0.0085$	Exercise
$IV_{t_2,8}^* = IV_{t_2,4} = 0.0223$	$O_{t_2,8} = \max[0.0223,0] = 0.0223$	Exercise
$IV_{t_2,9}^* = IV_{t_2,6} = 0.0910$	$O_{t_2,9} = \max[0.0910,0] = 0.0910$	Exercise

ii) As can be seen from the above summary, a total of three exercises have been made. The third largest intrinsic value from the table in Stage 3b (or, alternatively, the above table) can be seen to be 0.0085.

iii) The expected optimal exercise intrinsic boundary, B_{t_2}, is 0.0085.

At time t_1

i) From Stage 3b we can see that the following three bundles can be formed using the ranked intrinsic values

$$\text{Bundle } 1 = [IV_{t_1,1}^*, IV_{t_1,2}^*, IV_{t_1,3}^*]$$
$$\text{Bundle } 2 = [IV_{t_1,4}^*, IV_{t_1,5}^*, IV_{t_1,6}^*]$$
$$\text{Bundle } 3 = [IV_{t_1,7}^*, IV_{t_1,8}^*, IV_{t_1,9}^*]$$

For ranked intrinsic value $IV_{t_1,1}^*$

A) Since the intrinsic values in this bundle are Paths 8, 9, and 6, the option values associated with these paths at time t_2 can be obtained using the summary table of option premiums at time t_2. It can thus be seen that Paths 8, 9, and 6 lead to option values of 0, 0.0085 and 0.0910, respectively. Since the average of these three values is 0.0332, the holding value associated with Bundle 1, is given by $e^{-0.08(1.5)} \bullet 0.0332$, the present value of 0.0332. This simplifies to a value of 0.0294.

B) The intrinsic value associated with $IV_{t_1,1}^*$ is -0.0537. Since the holding value is the greater than the intrinsic value, one will not exercise the option.

C) $O_{t_1,1} = \max[-0.0537,0.0294] = 0.0294$

For ranked intrinsic value $IV_{t_1,2}^*$

A) Since the intrinsic values in this bundle are obtained using Paths 8, 9, and 6, the holding value is equal to 0.0294.

B) The intrinsic value associated with $IV_{t_1,2}^*$ is -0.0127. Since the holding value is greater than the intrinsic value, one will not exercise the option.

C) $O_{t_1,2} = \max[-0.0127,0.0294] = 0.0294$

EXAMPLE 39   Valuing a Vanilla American-Style Currency Option Using the Monte Carlo Simulations (Continued)

For ranked intrinsic value $IV^*_{t_1,3}$

A) The holding value associated with this ranked intrinsic value is also 0.0294.
B) The intrinsic value associated with $IV^*_{t_1,3}$ is 0.0148. Since the holding value is greater than the intrinsic value, one will not exercise the option.
C) $O_{t_1,3} = \max[0.0148, 0.0294] = 0.0294$.

For ranked intrinsic value $IV^*_{t_1,4}$

A) Since the intrinsic values in this bundle are Paths 3, 5, and 2, the option values associated with these paths at time t_2 can be obtained using the summary table of option premiums at time t_2. It can thus be seen that all three paths lead to an option value of 0.0341. Since the average of these three values is also 0.0341, the holding value associated with Bundle 2 is given by $e^{-0.08(1.5)} \cdot 0.0341$, the present value of 0.0341. This simplifies to a value of 0.0302.
B) The intrinsic value associated with $IV^*_{t_1,4}$ is 0.0319. Since the holding value is smaller than the intrinsic value, one will exercise the option.
C) $O_{t_1,4} = \max[0.0319, 0.0302] = 0.0319$.

For ranked intrinsic value $IV^*_{t_1,5}$

A) Since this ranked intrinsic value rate comes from the same bundle as $IV^*_{t_1,4}$, the holding value is also 0.0302.
B) The intrinsic value associated with $IV^*_{t_1,5}$ is 0.0414. Since the holding value is lesser than the intrinsic value, one will exercise the option.
C) $O_{t_1,5} = \max[0.0414, 0.0302] = 0.0414$.

For ranked intrinsic value $IV^*_{t_1,6}$

A) As with $IV^*_{t_1,4}$ and $IV^*_{t_1,5}$, the holding value associated with this ranked intrinsic value is also 0.0302.
B) The intrinsic value associated with $IV^*_{t_1,6}$ is 0.0657. Since the holding value is lesser than the intrinsic value, one will exercise the option.
C) $O_{t_1,6} = \max[0.0657, 0.0302] = 0.0657$.

For ranked intrinsic value $IV^*_{t_1,7}$

A) Since the intrinsic values in this bundle are Paths 4, 7, and 1, the option values associated with these paths at time t_2 can be obtained using the summary table of option premiums at time t_2. It can thus be seen that Paths 4, 7, and 1 lead to option values of 0.0223, zero, and zero respectively. Since the average of these three values is 0.0074, the holding value associated with Bundle 3, is given by $e^{-0.08(1.5)} \cdot 0.0074$, the present value of 0.0074. This simplifies to a value of 0.0066.
B) The intrinsic value associated with $IV^*_{t_1,7}$ is 0.0716. Since the holding value is less than the intrinsic value, one will exercise the option.
C) $O_{t_1,7} = \max[0.0716, 0.0066] = 0.0716$.

EXAMPLE 39 Valuing a Vanilla American-Style Currency Option
Using the Monte Carlo Simulations (Continued)

For ranked intrinsic value $IV^*_{t_1,8}$

A) Since this ranked intrinsic value comes from the same bundle as $IV^*_{t_1,7}$, the holding value is also 0.0066.

B) The intrinsic value associated with $IV^*_{t_1,8}$ is 0.1355. Since the holding value is less than the intrinsic value, one will exercise the option.

C) $O_{t_1,8} = \max[0.1355, 0.0066] = 0.1355$.

For ranked intrinsic value $IV^*_{t_1,9}$

A) Like $IV^*_{t_1,7}$ and $IV^*_{t_1,8}$, the holding value is also 0.0066.

B) The intrinsic value associated with $IV^*_{t_1,9}$ is 0.1601. Since the holding value is lesser than the intrinsic value, one will exercise the option.

C) $O_{t_1,9} = \max[0.1601, 0.0066] = 0.1601$.

Summary of Option Values at Exercise Time t_1

Ranked Intrinsic Value	Option Payoff	Action
$IV^*_{t_1,1} = IV_{t_1,8} = -0.0537$	$O_{t_1,1} = \max[-0.0537, 0.0294] = 0.0294$	No Exercise
$IV^*_{t_1,2} = IV_{t_1,9} = -0.0127$	$O_{t_1,2} = \max[-0.0127, 0.0294] = 0.0294$	No Exercise
$IV^*_{t_1,3} = IV_{t_1,6} = 0.0148$	$O_{t_1,3} = \max[0.0148, 0.0294] = 0.0294$	No Exercise
$IV^*_{t_1,4} = IV_{t_1,3} = 0.0319$	$O_{t_1,4} = \max[0.0319, 0.0302] = 0.0319$	Exercise
$IV^*_{t_1,5} = IV_{t_1,5} = 0.0414$	$O_{t_1,5} = \max[0.0414, 0.0302] = 0.0414$	Exercise
$IV^*_{t_1,6} = IV_{t_1,2} = 0.0657$	$O_{t_1,6} = \max[0.0657, 0.0302] = 0.0657$	Exercise
$IV^*_{t_1,7} = IV_{t_1,4} = 0.0716$	$O_{t_1,7} = \max[0.0716, 0.0066] = 0.0716$	Exercise
$IV^*_{t_1,8} = IV_{t_1,7} = 0.1355$	$O_{t_1,8} = \max[0.1355, 0.0066] = 0.1355$	Exercise
$IV^*_{t_1,9} = IV_{t_1,1} = 0.1601$	$O_{t_1,9} = \max[0.1601, 0.0066] = 0.1601$	Exercise

ii) As can be seen from the above summary, a total of six exercises have been made. The sixth largest intrinsic value from the table in Stage 3b (or alternatively the above table) can be seen to be 0.0319.

iii) The expected optimal exercise intrinsic boundary, B_{t_1}, is 0.0319.

Stage 4

As can be seen from Stage 3, the expected optimal exercise intrinsic boundaries at times 1.5 years, 3 years, and 4.5 years are 0.0319, 0.0085, and 0, respectively.

From the table in Stage 3a, it can be seen that

Paths 1, 2, 3, 4, 5, and 7 get exercised at 1.5 years, resulting in intrinsic values of 0.1601, 0.0657, 0.0319, 0.0716, 0.0414, and 0.1355, respectively since all these intrinsic values are no lesser than 0.0319.

Paths 6 and 9 get exercised at 3 years, resulting in intrinsic values of 0.0910 and 0.0085 respectively, since the intrinsic values at time 1.5 years

EXAMPLE 39 Valuing a Vanilla American-Style Currency Option Using the Monte Carlo Simulations (Continued)

are lesser than 0.0319 and the intrinsic values at time 3 years are no lesser than 0.0085.

Path 8 never gets exercised, resulting in intrinsic value of zero.

Stage 5

The put option premium is given by the formula

$$\frac{1}{9}\,[e^{-0.08(1.5)}(0.1601+0.0657+0.0319+0.0716+0.0414+0.1355) +$$

$$e^{-0.08(3)}(0.0910 + 0.0085)]$$

which simplifies to 0.0586.

It is important for the reader to make the following three observations about Example 39.

OBSERVATION 1 By reducing the value of Δt, increasing the value of h, and allowing for continuous exercise, one can arrive at an option premium of 0.0634 Cad/US.

OBSERVATION 2 In the context of Example 39, I bundled the nine paths into three bundles of three paths each. As the number of paths increases, there can be more than one way of bundling the paths. Suppose, for example, that one is simulating 100 paths. These paths could be bundled into 2 bundles, comprising 50 paths each; 4 bundles comprising 25 paths each; 10 bundles comprising 10 paths each; or 25 bundles comprising 4 paths each. Furthermore, the higher the number of bundles, the lower the number of paths in a bundle; and the lower the number of bundles, the higher the number of paths in a bundle. While both extremes lead to poor convergence, I find that in practice reasonable results can be obtained for h paths by setting both the number of paths in a bundle and the number of bundles to approximately $\sqrt{h}$.

OBSERVATION 3 In order to apply the control-variate method to reduce the variance of the simulations, one can use a European-style option when valuing either a Mid-Atlantic-style option or an American-style option. More precisely, if one is valuing a call (put) option with early exercise features, a European-style call (put) option can be used as a control variate.

Valuing Exotic Options

Like the binomial method discussed earlier, the valuation of exotic options using the Monte Carlo method can similarly be partitioned, as demonstrated in Exhibit 131. Furthermore, as was illustrated in Examples 38 and 39, unlike the binomial method, the methodology employed to value European-style options and options that permit early exercise are remotely similar in that the latter required the ranking of intrinsic values and the bundling of paths at all exerciseable times. Despite their dissimilarity, once the methodologies underlying the valuation of European-style exotic options are understood, it is easy to finesse the mechanics presented in Methodology 7 to value exotic options permitting early exercise. Furthermore, as most of the exotic options that trade in the marketplace are European-style in nature, I will henceforth only state the algorithms used for valuing European-style exotic options across all four categories.

Domestic-Currency-Denominated Option on A Single Domestic-Currency-Denominated Asset

The methodology required to value these type of options is very similar to that in Methodology 6 and is presented as Methodology 8.

METHODOLOGY 8   Using the Monte Carlo Method to Value a European-Style Domestic Option on a Single Domestic-Currency-Denominated Asset

---

Stage 1

Determine S_0, X, r_d, r_f, σ, T, n, h (where h represents the total number of paths), and other necessary parameters[47] and calculate Δt using the formula $\Delta t = \dfrac{T}{n}$

Stage 2

For j = 1, 2, . . . , h, generate $z_{i,j}$, a random number sampled from the standard normal distribution and calculate $S_{i\Delta t,j}$ using the formula

$$S_{i\Delta t,j} = S_{(i-1)\Delta t,j} \bullet e^{(r_d - r_f - 1/2\sigma^2)\Delta t} \bullet e^{\sigma z_{i,j}\sqrt{\Delta t}}$$

where i = 1, 2, . . . , n and $S_{0,j} = S_0$.

Stage 3

For j = 1, 2, . . . , h, compute $\max[I_{n\Delta t,j}, 0]$ the intrinsic value of the option at time $n\Delta t$[48] along path j and let

$$O_j = \max[I_{n\Delta t,j}, 0]$$

Stage 4

The optimum premium is given by the formula $e^{-r_d T}\left[\dfrac{1}{h}\displaystyle\sum_{j=1}^{h} O_j\right]$

---

47 See footnote 18.

48 The only exceptions occur when one is computing premiums for both the choice option and compound option. In these instances, the valuation can be done using a two-stage Monte-Carlo simulation process, as demonstrated in Examples 42 and 43. The intrinsic values in these instances are calculated at the time of choice and the time of the second optional payment, respectively.

The use of a Monte Carlo method to value a European-Style average rate put option is illustrated in Example 40.

EXAMPLE 40 Valuing an Average Currency Option Using the Monte Carlo Simulations

The Canadian dollar is currently trading at 1.3000 Cad/US. An investor wants to buy a continuously averaged 4½-year Category II European-style put option (i.e., the in-the-money option payoff on the maturity date is the strike rate minus the arithmetically averaged rate) on the U.S. dollar that is struck at 1.3000 Cad/US. The current continuously compounded risk-free rates of interest in the United States and Canada are 6 percent and 8 percent, respectively. Using an exchange-rate volatility of 10 percent and dividing the 4½-year period into three equal subintervals, I want to value this put option using nine exchange-rate simulated paths.

Stage 1

$$S_0 = 1.3000, X = 1.3000, r_d = 0.08, r_f = 0.06,$$
$$\sigma = 0.1, T = 4.5, n = 4, h = 3, \text{ and } \Delta t = 1.5$$

Stage 2

The reader is referred to Example 38 for the calculation of these simulated rates.

	Time			
Paths	**0**	**Δt**	**$2\Delta t$**	**$3\Delta t$**
1	$S_{0,1} = 1.3000$	$S_{\Delta t,1} = 1.1399$	$S_{2\Delta t,1} = 1.4620$	$S_{3\Delta t,1} = 1.6883$
2	$S_{0,2} = 1.3000$	$S_{\Delta t,2} = 1.2343$	$S_{2\Delta t,2} = 1.3932$	$S_{3\Delta t,2} = 1.5353$
3	$S_{0,3} = 1.3000$	$S_{\Delta t,3} = 1.2681$	$S_{2\Delta t,3} = 1.3354$	$S_{3\Delta t,3} = 1.2380$
4	$S_{0,4} = 1.3000$	$S_{\Delta t,4} = 1.2284$	$S_{2\Delta t,4} = 1.2777$	$S_{3\Delta t,4} = 1.6134$
5	$S_{0,5} = 1.3000$	$S_{\Delta t,5} = 1.2586$	$S_{2\Delta t,5} = 1.3180$	$S_{3\Delta t,5} = 1.2468$
6	$S_{0,6} = 1.3000$	$S_{\Delta t,6} = 1.2852$	$S_{2\Delta t,6} = 1.2090$	$S_{3\Delta t,6} = 1.6362$
7	$S_{0,7} = 1.3000$	$S_{\Delta t,7} = 1.1645$	$S_{2\Delta t,7} = 1.4500$	$S_{3\Delta t,7} = 1.3982$
8	$S_{0,8} = 1.3000$	$S_{\Delta t,8} = 1.3537$	$S_{2\Delta t,8} = 1.5047$	$S_{3\Delta t,8} = 1.6778$
9	$S_{0,9} = 1.3000$	$S_{\Delta t,9} = 1.3127$	$S_{2\Delta t,9} = 1.2915$	$S_{3\Delta t,9} = 1.6498$

EXAMPLE 40 Valuing an Average Currency Option Using the Monte Carlo Simulations (Continued)

Stage 3

Path	Average Exchange Rate at time $3\Delta t$	Option Payoff
1	$\frac{1}{4}(S_{0,1} + S_{\Delta t,1} + S_{2\Delta t,1} + S_{3\Delta t,1}) = 1.3976$	$O_1 = \max[1.3 - 1.3976, 0] = 0.0000$
2	$\frac{1}{4}(S_{0,2} + S_{\Delta t,2} + S_{2\Delta t,2} + S_{3\Delta t,2}) = 1.3657$	$O_2 = \max[1.3 - 1.3657, 0] = 0.0000$
3	$\frac{1}{4}(S_{0,3} + S_{\Delta t,3} + S_{2\Delta t,3} + S_{3\Delta t,3}) = 1.2854$	$O_3 = \max[1.3 - 1.2854, 0] = 0.0146$
4	$\frac{1}{4}(S_{0,4} + S_{\Delta t,4} + S_{2\Delta t,4} + S_{3\Delta t,4}) = 1.3549$	$O_4 = \max[1.3 - 1.3549, 0] = 0.0000$
5	$\frac{1}{4}(S_{0,5} + S_{\Delta t,5} + S_{2\Delta t,5} + S_{3\Delta t,5}) = 1.2809$	$O_5 = \max[1.3 - 1.2809, 0] = 0.0191$
6	$\frac{1}{4}(S_{0,6} + S_{\Delta t,6} + S_{2\Delta t,6} + S_{3\Delta t,6}) = 1.3576$	$O_6 = \max[1.3 - 1.3576, 0] = 0.0000$
7	$\frac{1}{4}(S_{0,7} + S_{\Delta t,7} + S_{2\Delta t,7} + S_{3\Delta t,7}) = 1.3282$	$O_7 = \max[1.3 - 1.3282, 0] = 0.0000$
8	$\frac{1}{4}(S_{0,8} + S_{\Delta t,8} + S_{2\Delta t,8} + S_{3\Delta t,8}) = 1.4591$	$O_8 = \max[1.3 - 1.4591, 0] = 0.0000$
9	$\frac{1}{4}(S_{0,9} + S_{\Delta t,9} + S_{2\Delta t,9} + S_{3\Delta t,9}) = 1.3885$	$O_9 = \max[1.3 - 1.3885, 0] = 0.0000$

Stage 4

The option premium is given by $e^{-0.08(4.5)} \left[\dfrac{O_1 + O_2 + O_{3+} \ldots + O_9}{9} \right] = 0.0026$ Cad/US.

It is important for the reader to make the following four observations about Example 40.

OBSERVATION 1 To obtain a more accurate value for the continuously sampled European-style average rate option, one would have to reduce the value of Δt and increase h the number of simulated paths.[49] Doing this results in a premium of about 0.0279 Cad/US for a continuously averaged rate option.

OBSERVATION 2 As in Observation 4 accompanying Example 26, the underlying average rate can be simulated using the Monte Carlo method. More precisely, by using the modified expressions for both r_f and σ that are given in that observation, starting with the current spot rate S_0, one can use the algorithm outlined in Methodology 6. This follows from the fact that since one is now modeling the average rate process, the simulated value at time $n\Delta t$ will be a continuously averaged rate of the underlying exchange rate. Consequently, one only needs to calculate the intrinsic value using this simulated average rate and the strike rate along each path as in a vanilla European-style option. This philosophy can also be used to value geometrically averaged rate options using the appropriate modifications that are also presented in Observation 4 accompanying Example 26.

OBSERVATION 3 Unlike Observation 5 accompanying Example 26, valuing Category I and III European-style average options can be quite easily done using the Monte Carlo method. This follows from the observations that the fixed strike rate of the option can be thought of as being replaced by the value of the exchange rate at time $n\Delta t$ and that the intrinsic value along each simulated path can be easily calculated.

OBSERVATION 4 To reduce the number of simulated runs, in addition to using the antithetic-variable technique, one can use the control-variate technique. Since a closed-form solution to value geometric average options can be easily developed, a geometric average option would serve as a good control variate.

The use of a Monte Carlo method to value a European-Style cash-or-nothing put option is illustrated in Example 41.

It is important for the reader to make the following two observations about Example 41 on page 318.

OBSERVATION 1 To obtain a more accurate value for the European-style cash-or-nothing option, one would have to reduce the value of Δt and increase h, the number of simulated paths. Doing this results in a premium of about Cad$ 261.75.

OBSERVATION 2 Unlike Observations 1 and 2 accompanying Example 27, in using a Monte Carlo method, one does not have to worry about the problems of both the converging premium and a

---

[49] See Observation 1 accompanying Example 38 on a rule-of-thumb number for Δt and h.

EXAMPLE 41 Valuing a Cash-or-Nothing Currency Option Using the Monte Carlo Simulations

The Canadian dollar is currently trading at 1.3000 Cad/US. An investor wants to buy a 4½-year cash-or-nothing put option on the U.S. dollar that is struck at 1.3000 Cad/US and pays a bet payoff of Cad$ 1,000. The current continuously compounded risk-free rates of interest in the U.S. and Canada are 6 percent and 8 percent, respectively. Using an exchange-rate volatility of 10 percent and dividing the 4½-year period into three equal subintervals, I want to value a European-style cash-or-nothing put option using nine exchange-rate simulated paths.

Stage 1

$S_0 = 1.3000$, $X = 1.3000$, $B = 1000$, $r_d = 0.08$, $r_f = 0.06$, $\sigma = 0.1$, $T = 4.5$, $n = 3$, $h = 9$ and $\Delta t = 1.5$

Stage 2

Since the exchange-rate paths are no different from those presented in Example 40, the reader is referred to Example 40 for the calculation of these simulated rates.

Stage 3

Path	Exchange Rate at Time 3Δt	Option Payoff
1	$S_{3\Delta t,1} = 1.6883$	$O_1 = 0.0000$
2	$S_{3\Delta t,2} = 1.5353$	$O_2 = 0.0000$
3	$S_{3\Delta t,3} = 1.2380$	$O_3 = 1000$
4	$S_{3\Delta t,4} = 1.6134$	$O_4 = 0.0000$
5	$S_{3\Delta t,5} = 1.2468$	$O_5 = 1000$
6	$S_{3\Delta t,6} = 1.6362$	$O_6 = 0.0000$
7	$S_{3\Delta t,7} = 1.3982$	$O_7 = 0.0000$
8	$S_{3\Delta t,8} = 1.6778$	$O_8 = 0.0000$
9	$S_{3\Delta t,9} = 1.6498$	$O_9 = 0.0000$

Stage 4

The option premium is given by $e^{-0.08(4.5)} \left[\dfrac{O_1+O_2+O_3+\ldots+O_9}{9} \right] = 155.0392$ Cad/US.

simulated value being identical to the strike value. The only form of convergence that a user has to worry about would involve that of Observation 1 of Example 41.

The use of a Monte Carlo method to value a European-Style choice option is illustrated in Example 42.

EXAMPLE 42   Valuing a Choice Currency Option Using the Monte Carlo Simulations

The Canadian dollar is currently trading at 1.3000 Cad/US. An investor wants to buy a 4½-year choice option that would allow him to choose in 1.5 years between a U.S. dollar call and a U.S. dollar put, both of which are struck at 1.3000 Cad/US and expire three years after the choice time. The current continuously compounded risk-free rates of interest in the United States and Canada are 6 percent and 8 percent, respectively. Using an exchange-rate volatility of 10 percent and dividing the 1½-year period into one subinterval, I want to value this European-style choice option using nine exchange-rate simulated paths.

Stage 1

$S_0 = 1.3000$, $X = 1.3000$, $r_d = 0.08$, $r_f = 0.06$, $\sigma = 0.1$, $t = 1.5$, $T = 4.5$, $n = 1$,[50] $h = 9$ and $\Delta t = 1.5$

Stage 2

Since the exchange-rate paths are no different from those presented in Example 40, the reader is referred to Example 40 for the calculation of these simulated rates.

Stage 3

Path	Exchange Rate at Time Δt	Call Option Premium[51]	Put Option Premium[52]	Option Payoff
1	$S_{\Delta t,1} = 1.1399$	0.0386	0.1091	$O_1 = \max[0.0386, 0.1091] = 0.1091$
2	$S_{\Delta t,2} = 1.2343$	0.0751	0.0668	$O_2 = \max[0.0751, 0.0668] = 0.0751$
3	$S_{\Delta t,3} = 1.2681$	0.0916	0.0550	$O_3 = \max[0.0916, 0.0550] = 0.0916$
4	$S_{\Delta t,4} = 1.2284$	0.0724	0.0690	$O_4 = \max[0.0724, 0.0690] = 0.0724$

50 As mentioned in footnote 48, n here is chosen such that the time interval from today to t (the time the choice is made) is partitioned into exactly n subintervals. This is contrary to many of the other examples where the entire option life T is partitioned into exactly n subintervals.

51 For j = 1, 2, . . . , 9, the vanilla call option premium is calculated using the method prescribed in Methodology 6 when $S_0 = S_{\Delta t,j}$, $r_d = 0.08$, $r_f = 0.06$. $\sigma = 0.1$, $X = 1.3$ and $T = 3$.

52 For j = 1, 2, . . . , 9, the vanilla put option premium is calculated using the method prescribed in Methodology 6 when $S_0 = S_{\Delta t,j}$, $r_d = 0.08$, $r_f = 0.06$. $\sigma = 0.1$, $X = 1.3$ and $T = 3$.

EXAMPLE 42   Valuing a Choice Currency Option Using the Monte Carlo Simulations (Continued)

5	$S_{\Delta t,5} = 1.2856$	0.0868	0.0581	$O_5 = \max[0.0868, 0.0581] = 0.0868$
6	$S_{\Delta t,6} = 1.2852$	0.1006	0.0497	$O_6 = \max[0.1006, 0.0497] = 0.1006$
7	$S_{\Delta t,7} = 1.1645$	0.0467	0.0967	$O_7 = \max[0.0467, 0.0967] = 0.0967$
8	$S_{\Delta t,8} = 1.3537$	0.1405	0.0324	$O_8 = \max[0.1405, 0.0324] = 0.1405$
9	$S_{\Delta t,9} = 1.3127$	0.1159	0.0420	$O_9 = \max[0.1159, 0.0420] = 0.1159$

Stage 4

The option premium is given by $e^{-0.08(1.5)} \left[\dfrac{O_1 + O_2 + O_3 + \ldots + O_9}{9} \right] = 0.0876$ Cad/US.

It is important for the reader to make the following two observations about Example 42.

OBSERVATION 1 To obtain a more accurate value for the European-style choice option, one would have to reduce the value of Δt and increase h, the number of simulated paths. Doing this results in a premium of about 0.146 Cad/US.

OBSERVATION 2 To value the option in Example 42, upon simulating a rate at time Δt, I used this simulated rate as an initial exchange-rate value and performed another set of Monte Carlo simulations for a remaining option life of three years so as to obtain both the vanilla call and put option premiums at time Δt. Instead of performing a set of Monte Carlo simulations for each simulated rate, I could have alternatively used the idea underlying Methodology 7 and first found the expected optimal exercise intrinsic boundary (or point) at time Δt. As in Methodology 7, once this expected optimal exercise point is determined, the simulated paths can be used to obtain the in-the-money payoff and hence the premium for the choice option.

The use of a Monte Carlo method to value a European-Style call-on-put option is illustrated in Exhibit 43 on page 321.

It is important for the reader to make the following two observations about Example 43.

OBSERVATION 1 To obtain a more accurate value for the European-style compound option, one would have to reduce the value of Δt and increase h, the number of simulated paths. Doing this results in a premium of about 0.0403 Cad/US.

EXAMPLE 43   Valuing a Compound Currency Option Using the Monte Carlo Simulations

The Canadian dollar is currently trading at 1.3000 Cad/US. An investor wants to buy a 4½-year call-on-put option that would allow him to pay in 1.5 years 0.0050 Cad/US for a U.S. dollar put that is struck at 1.3000 Cad/US and expiring three years after the second installment date. The current continuously compounded risk-free rates of interest in the United States and Canada are 6 percent and 8 percent respectively. Using an exchange-rate volatility of 10 percent and dividing the 1½-year period into one subinterval, I want to value this European-style compound option using nine exchange-rate simulated paths.

Stage 1

$S_0 = 1.3000$, $X_1 = 0.005$, $X_2 = 1.3000$, $r_d = 0.08$, $r_f = 0.06$, $\sigma = 0.1$, $t = 1.5$, $T = 4.5$, $n = 1,$[53] $h = 9$, and $\Delta t = 1.5$

Stage 2

Since the exchange-rate paths are no different from those presented in Example 40, the reader is referred to Example 40 for the calculation of these simulated rates.

Stage 3

Path	Exchange Rate at Time Δt	Put Option Premium[54]	Option Payoff
1	$S_{\Delta t,1} = 1.1399$	0.1091	$O_1 = \max[0.1091-0.0050,0] = 0.1041$
2	$S_{\Delta t,2} = 1.2343$	0.0668	$O_2 = \max[0.0668-0.0050,0] = 0.0618$
3	$S_{\Delta t,3} = 1.2681$	0.0550	$O_3 = \max[0.0550-0.0050,0] = 0.0500$
4	$S_{\Delta t,4} = 1.2284$	0.0690	$O_4 = \max[0.0690-0.0050,0] = 0.0640$
5	$S_{\Delta t,5} = 1.2856$	0.0581	$O_5 = \max[0.0581-0.0050,0] = 0.0531$
6	$S_{\Delta t,6} = 1.2852$	0.0497	$O_6 = \max[0.0497-0.0050,0] = 0.0447$
7	$S_{\Delta t,7} = 1.1645$	0.0967	$O_7 = \max[0.0967-0.0050,0] = 0.0917$
8	$S_{\Delta t,8} = 1.3537$	0.0324	$O_8 = \max[0.0324-0.0050,0] = 0.0274$
9	$S_{\Delta t,9} = 1.3127$	0.0420	$O_9 = \max[0.0420-0.0050,0] = 0.0370$

Stage 4

The option premium is given by $e^{-0.08(1.5)}\left[\dfrac{O_1+O_2+O_3+\ldots+O_9}{9}\right] = 0.0526$ Cad/US.

---

53 See footnote 50.

54 See footnote 52.

OBSERVATION 2 As in Example 42, instead of using Monte Carlo simulations to simulate the put option premium for each simulated exchange rate at time Δt, the technique described in Methodology 7 can be used to value these type of options. Since it is possible for the number of installments to be greater than two (as many as 11^{55}, instead of using the technique illustrated in this example, one would be better off using Methodology 7 to value these early exercise options.

The use of a Monte Carlo method to value a European-Style Deferred-Strike option is illustrated in Example 44.

EXAMPLE 44 Valuing a Deferred-Strike Currency Option Using the Monte Carlo Simulations

The Canadian dollar is currently trading at 1.3000 Cad/US. An investor wants to buy a 4½-year deferred-strike put option on the U.S. dollar whose strike rate will be set in exactly 1.5 years. The current continuously compounded risk-free rates of interest in the United States and Canada are 6 percent and 8 percent, respectively. Using an exchange-rate volatility of 10 percent and dividing the 4½-year period into three equal subintervals, I want to value this European-style deferred-strike option using nine exchange-rate simulated paths.

Stage 1

$S_0 = 1.3000$, $r_d = 0.08$, $r_f = 0.06$, $\sigma = 0.1$, $t = 1.5$, $T = 4.5$, $n = 3$, $h = 9$ and $\Delta t = 1.5$

Stage 2

Since the exchange-rate paths are no different from those presented in Example 40, the reader is referred to Example 40 for the calculation of these simulated rates.

Stage 3

Path	Exchange Rate at Time Δt	Exchange Rate at Time $3\Delta t$	Option Payoff
1	$S_{\Delta t,1} = 1.1399$	$S_{3\Delta t,1} = 1.6883$	$O_1 = \max[1.1399 - 1.6883, 0] = 0.0000$
2	$S_{\Delta t,2} = 1.2343$	$S_{3\Delta t,2} = 1.5353$	$O_2 = \max[1.2343 - 1.5353, 0] = 0.0000$
3	$S_{\Delta t,3} = 1.2681$	$S_{3\Delta t,3} = 1.2380$	$O_3 = \max[1.2681 - 1.2380, 0] = 0.0301$

---

[55] An example would be the purchase of a quarterly reset three-year cap, floor, or collar in which the premium is paid in 11 installments (1 compulsory and 10 optional).

EXAMPLE 44   Valuing a Deferred-Strike Currency Option Using the Monte Carlo Simulations (Continued)

4	$S_{\Delta t,4} = 1.2284$	$S_{3\Delta t,4} = 1.6134$	$O_4 = \max[1.2284{-}1.6134,0] = 0.0000$
5	$S_{\Delta t,5} = 1.2856$	$S_{3\Delta t,5} = 1.2468$	$O_5 = \max[1.2586{-}1.2468,0] = 0.0118$
6	$S_{\Delta t,6} = 1.2852$	$S_{3\Delta t,6} = 1.6362$	$O_6 = \max[1.2852{-}1.6362,0] = 0.0000$
7	$S_{\Delta t,7} = 1.1645$	$S_{3\Delta t,7} = 1.3982$	$O_7 = \max[1.1645{-}1.3982,0] = 0.0000$
8	$S_{\Delta t,8} = 1.3537$	$S_{3\Delta t,8} = 1.6778$	$O_8 = \max[1.3537{-}1.6778,0] = 0.0000$
9	$S_{\Delta t,9} = 1.3127$	$S_{3\Delta t,9} = 1.6498$	$O_9 = \max[1.3127{-}1.6498,0] = 0.0000$

Stage 4

The option premium is given by $e^{-0.08(4.5)}\left[\dfrac{O_1+O_2+O_3+ \ldots +O_9}{9}\right] = 0.0032$
Cad/US.

It is important for the reader to make the following observation about Example 44.

OBSERVATION To obtain a more accurate value for the European-style option, one would have to reduce the value of Δt and increase h, the number of simulated paths. Doing this results in a premium of about 0.0415 Cad/US.

The use of a Monte Carlo method to value a look-back option is illustrated in Example 45.

EXAMPLE 45   Valuing a Lookback Currency Option Using the Monte Carlo Simulations

The Canadian dollar is currently trading at 1.3000 Cad/US. An investor wants to buy a continuously sampled 4½-year Category IV lookback put option (i.e., the in-the-money option payoff on the maturity date is calculated by subtracting the lowest sampled rate from the strike rate) on the U.S. dollar that is struck at 1.3000 Cad/US. The current continuously compounded risk-free rates of interest in the United States and Canada are 6 percent and 8 percent, respectively. Using an exchange-rate volatility of 10 percent and dividing the 4½-year period into three equal subintervals, I want to value this European-style lookback option using nine exchange-rate simulated paths.

Stage 1

$S_0 = 1.3000$, $X = 1.3000$, $r_d = 0.08$, $r_f = 0.06$, $\sigma = 0.1$, $T = 4.5$, $n = 3$, $h = 9$ and $\Delta t = 1.5$

EXAMPLE 45   Valuing a Lookback Currency Option Using the Monte Carlo Simulations (Continued)

Stage 2

Since the exchange-rate paths are no different from those presented in Example 40, the reader is referred to Example 40 for the calculation of these simulated rates.

Stage 3

Path	Minimum Realized Exchange Rate by Time $3\Delta t$	Option Payoff
1	$\min[S_{0,1}, S_{\Delta t,1}, S_{2\Delta t,1}, S_{3\Delta t,1}] = 1.1399$	$O_1 = \max[1.3 - 1.1399, 0] = 0.1601$
2	$\min[S_{0,2}, S_{\Delta t,2}, S_{2\Delta t,2}, S_{3\Delta t,2}] = 1.2343$	$O_2 = \max[1.3 - 1.2343, 0] = 0.0657$
3	$\min[S_{0,3}, S_{\Delta t,3}, S_{2\Delta t,3}, S_{3\Delta t,3}] = 1.2380$	$O_3 = \max[1.3 - 1.2380, 0] = 0.0620$
4	$\min[S_{0,4}, S_{\Delta t,4}, S_{2\Delta t,4}, S_{3\Delta t,4}] = 1.2284$	$O_4 = \max[1.3 - 1.2284, 0] = 0.0716$
5	$\min[S_{0,5}, S_{\Delta t,5}, S_{2\Delta t,5}, S_{3\Delta t,5}] = 1.2468$	$O_5 = \max[1.3 - 1.2468, 0] = 0.0532$
6	$\min[S_{0,6}, S_{\Delta t,6}, S_{2\Delta t,6}, S_{3\Delta t,6}] = 1.2090$	$O_6 = \max[1.3 - 1.2090, 0] = 0.0910$
7	$\min[S_{0,7}, S_{\Delta t,7}, S_{2\Delta t,7}, S_{3\Delta t,7}] = 1.1645$	$O_7 = \max[1.3 - 1.1645, 0] = 0.1355$
8	$\min[S_{0,8}, S_{\Delta t,8}, S_{2\Delta t,8}, S_{3\Delta t,8}] = 1.3000$	$O_8 = \max[1.3 - 1.3, 0] = 0.0000$
9	$\min[S_{0,9}, S_{\Delta t,9}, S_{2\Delta t,19}, S_{3\Delta t,9}] = 1.2915$	$O_9 = \max[1.3 - 1.2915, 0] = 0.0085$

Stage 4

The option premium is given by $e^{-0.08(4.5)} \left[\dfrac{O_1 + O_2 + O_3 + \ldots + O_9}{9} \right] = 0.0502$ Cad/US.

It is important for the reader to make the following observation Example 45.

OBSERVATION To obtain a more accurate value for the European-style option, one would have to reduce the value of Δt and increase h. Doing this would yield a premium of 0.1124 Cad/US for a continuously sampled lookback option discussed in Example 45.

The use of a Monte Carlo method to value a nonlinear put option is illustrated in Example 46 on page 325.

It is important for the reader to make the following observation about Example 46.

OBSERVATION To obtain a more accurate value for the European-style option, one would have to reduce the value of Δt and increase h. Doing this would yield a premium of 0.1264 Cad/US for a nonlinear payoff option.

EXAMPLE 46 Valuing a Nonlinear Currency Option Using the Monte Carlo Simulations

The Canadian dollar is currently trading at 1.3000 Cad/US. An investor wants to buy a 4½-year nonlinear payoff put option on the U.S. dollar that is struck at 1.3000^2 Cad/US. The current continuously compounded risk-free rates of interest in the United States and Canada are 6 percent and 8 percent respectively. Using an exchange-rate volatility of 10 percent and dividing the 4½-year period into three equal subintervals, I want to value this European-style nonlinear payoff option using nine exchange-rate simulated paths.

Stage 1

$S_0 = 1.3000$, $X = 1.3000^2$, $r_d = 0.08$, $r_f = 0.06$, $\sigma = 0.1$, $T = 4.5$, $n = 3$, $h = 9$ and $\Delta t = 1.5$

Stage 2

Since the exchange-rate paths are no different from those presented in Example 40, the reader is referred to Example 40 for the calculation of these simulated rates.

Stage 3

Path	Exchange Rate at Time $3\Delta t$	Option Payoff
1	$S_{3\Delta t,1} = 1.6883$	$O_1 = \max[1.3^2 - 1.6883^2] = 0.0000$
2	$S_{3\Delta t,2} = 1.5353$	$O_2 = \max[1.3^2 - 1.5353^2] = 0.0000$
3	$S_{3\Delta t,3} = 1.2380$	$O_3 = \max[1.3^2 - 1.2380^2] = 0.1574$
4	$S_{3\Delta t,4} = 1.6134$	$O_4 = \max[1.3^2 - 1.6134^2] = 0.0000$
5	$S_{3\Delta t,5} = 1.2468$	$O_5 = \max[1.3^2 - 1.2468^2] = 0.1355$
6	$S_{3\Delta t,6} = 1.6362$	$O_6 = \max[1.3^2 - 1.6362^2] = 0.0000$
7	$S_{3\Delta t,7} = 1.3982$	$O_7 = \max[1.3^2 - 1.3982^2] = 0.0000$
8	$S_{3\Delta t,8} = 1.6778$	$O_8 = \max[1.3^2 - 1.6778^2] = 0.0000$
9	$S_{3\Delta t,9} = 1.6498$	$O_9 = \max[1.3^2 - 1.6498^2] = 0.0000$

Stage 4

The option premium is given by $e^{-0.08(4.5)} \left[\dfrac{O_1 + O_2 + O_3 + \ldots + O_9}{9} \right] = 0.0227$ Cad/US.

The use of a Monte Carlo method to value a European-Style knockout put option is illustrated in Example 47.

EXAMPLE 47   Valuing a Knock-Out Currency Option Using the Monte Carlo Simulations

The Canadian dollar is currently trading at 1.3000 Cad/US. An investor wants to buy a continuously monitored 4½-year knock-out put option on the U.S. dollar that is struck at 1.3000 Cad/US. The current continuously compounded risk-free rates of interest in the United States and Canada are 6 percent and 8 percent respectively. Using an exchange-rate volatility of 10 percent, a barrier level of 1.1500 Cad/US, and dividing the 4½-year period into three equal subintervals, I want to value this European-style knock out option using nine exchange-rate simulated paths.

Stage 1

$S_0 = 1.3000$, $X = 1.3000$, $H = 1.1500$, $r_d = 0.08$, $r_f = 0.06$, $\sigma = 0.1$, $T = 4.5$, $n = 3$, $h = 9$ and $\Delta t = 1.5$

Stage 2

Since the exchange-rate paths are no different from those presented in Example 40, the reader is referred to Example 40 for the calculation of these simulated rates.

Stage 3

Path	Exchange Rate at Time $3\Delta t$[56]	Option Payoff
1	KO	$O_1 = 0.0000$
2	$S_{3\Delta t,2} = 1.5353$	$O_2 = \max[1.3 - 1.5353, 0] = 0.0000$
3	$S_{3\Delta t,3} = 1.2380$	$O_3 = \max[1.3 - 1.2380, 0] = 0.0620$
4	$S_{3\Delta t,4} = 1.6134$	$O_4 = \max[1.3 - 1.6134, 0] = 0.0000$
5	$S_{3\Delta t,5} = 1.2468$	$O_5 = \max[1.3 - 1.2468, 0] = 0.0532$
6	$S_{3\Delta t,6} = 1.6362$	$O_6 = \max[1.3 - 1.6362, 0] = 0.0000$
7	$S_{3\Delta t,7} = 1.3982$	$O_7 = \max[1.3 - 1.3982] = 0.0000$
8	$S_{3\Delta t,8} = 1.6778$	$O_8 = \max[1.3 - 1.6778, 0] = 0.0000$
9	$S_{3\Delta t,9} = 1.6498$	$O_9 = \max[1.3 - 1.6498, 0] = 0.0000$

Stage 4

The option premium is given by $e^{-0.08(4.5)} \left[\dfrac{O_1 + O_2 + O_3 + \ldots + O_9}{9} \right] = 0.0089$ Cad/US.

---

56 For Path 1, the label KO depicts the fact that the barrier has been breached by the paths prior to the time $3\Delta t$. More precisely, the barrier is breached as long as any path goes below a level of 1.15. This would imply that Path 1 breaches the barrier at time Δt, resulting in no contribution to the option premium.

It is important for the reader to make the following observation about Example 47.

OBSERVATION To obtain a more accurate value for the European-style knock-out option, one would have to reduce the value of Δt and increase h. Doing this would yield an option premium of 0.0019 Cad/US.

Domestic-Currency-Denominated Option on Multiple Domestic-Currency-Denominated Assets

The methodology required to value these type of options is presented as Methodology 9.

METHODOLOGY 9 **Using the Monte Carlo Method to Value a European-Style Domestic-Currency-Denominated Option on Multiple Domestic-Currency-Denominated Assets**

Stage 1

Determine $S_{k,0}$, X, r_d, $r_{k,f}$, σ_k, T, n, h (where h represents the total number of paths; k, l = 1, . . . , m and l > k), and other necessary parameters[57], and calculate Δt using the formula $\Delta t = \dfrac{T}{n}$

Stage 2

For j = 1, 2, . . . , h and k = 1, 2, . . ., m, generate $z_{k,i,j}$, a random number sampled from the standard normal distribution, and calculate $S_{k,i\Delta tj}$ using the formulae[58]

$$\omega_{1,i,j} = z_{1,i,j}$$

$$\omega_{2,i,j} = \rho_{1,2}\omega_{1,i,j} + \sqrt{1 - \rho_{1,2}^2}\, z_{2,i,j}$$

$$\vdots$$

$$\omega_{k,i,j} = \hat{\Sigma}_{21,1,k-1}\, \hat{\Sigma}_{11,k-1,k-1}^{-1}\, \tilde{\omega}_{k-1} + \sqrt{1 - \hat{\Sigma}_{21,1,k-1}\, \hat{\Sigma}_{11,k-1,k-1}^{-1}\, \hat{\Sigma}_{12,k-1,1}}\, z_{k,i,j}$$

$$\vdots$$

$$\omega_{m,i,j} = \hat{\Sigma}_{21,1,m-1}\, \hat{\Sigma}_{11,m-1,m-1}^{-1}\, \tilde{\omega}_{m-1} + \sqrt{1 - \hat{\Sigma}_{21,1,m-1}\, \hat{\Sigma}_{11,m-1,m-1}^{-1}\, \hat{\Sigma}_{12,m-1,1}}\, z_{m,i,j}$$

---

57 See footnote 18.

58 $S_{k,i\Delta tj}$ is the value of the kth asset at time $i\Delta t$ on Path j and $\tilde{\omega}_{k-1}$ is the transpose of the matrix, $[\omega_{1,i,j}, \omega_{2,i,j}, \ldots, \omega_{k-1,i,j}]$, where the transpose of the matrix is defined in footnote 9 of the Appendix and $\hat{\Sigma}_{12,k-1,1}$, $\hat{\Sigma}_{21,1,k-1}$, $\hat{\Sigma}_{11,k-1,k-1}$, have been defined on the page of notations.

METHODOLOGY 9 Using the Monte Carlo Method to Value a European-Style Domestic-Currency-Denominated Option on Multiple Domestic-Currency Denominated Assets (Continued)

$$S_{k,i\Delta t,j} = S_{k,(i-1)\Delta t,j} \cdot e^{(r_d - r_{k,f} - 1/2\sigma_k^2)\Delta t} \cdot e^{\sigma_k \omega_{k,i,j}\sqrt{\Delta t}}$$

where $i = 1, 2, \ldots, n$ and $S_{k,0,j} = S_{k,0}$[59]

Stage 3

For $j = 1, 2, \ldots, h$, compute $I_{n\Delta t,j}$, the intrinsic value[60] of the option at time $n\Delta t$ along path j and let

$$O_j = \max[I_{n\Delta t,j}, 0]$$

Stage 4

The option premium is given by the formula $e^{-r_d T}\left[\dfrac{1}{h}\displaystyle\sum_{j=1}^{h} O_j\right]$.

---

59 Suppose, for example, there are n assets. If instead of modeling the n assets and trying to determine their values at time n∆t, one is interested in modeling one asset at n different times or, more precisely, at times ∆t, 2∆t, … , n∆t, then it can be shown that correlation $\rho_{i,j}$ or the autocorrelation between continuously compounded returns at any two points i∆t and j∆t (where i < j) is given by the expression $\sqrt{\dfrac{i}{j}}$. See Relationship 6i of the Appendix. In such an instance, it can be shown that $\omega_{k,i,j} = \dfrac{1}{\sqrt{k}}\displaystyle\sum_{a=1}^{k} z_{a,i,j}$ for k = 1, 2, …, m. This property becomes useful when one is attempting to simulate the yield curve using forward rates.

60 The intrinsic value at any time will be a function of the k asset values.

The use of a Monte Carlo method to value a European-Style basket option is illustrated in Example 48.

EXAMPLE 48 Valuing a Basket Currency Option Using the Monte Carlo Simulations

The Canadian dollar is currently trading at 1.3000 Cad/US and 2.2000 Cad/£. A hedger wants to buy a 4½-year European-style call option on the Canadian dollar basket that is struck at Cad$ 480 mm when the notional amounts on the US$ and £ are 200 mm and 100 mm, respectively. More precisely, the payoff on the option maturity date is $\max[480 - (200 \cdot S_{1,T}) - (100 \cdot S_{2,T}), 0]$, where $S_{1,T}$ represents the Cad/US rate on option maturity and $S_{2,T}$ represents the Cad/£ rate on option maturity. The current continuously compounded risk-free rates of interest in the United States, Canada, and the United Kingdom are 6 percent, 8 percent, and 9 percent, respectively. Using an exchange-rate volatility of 10 percent for the Cad/US exchange rate, a volatility of 17 percent for the Cad/£ exchange rate, a correlation of 60 percent between the continuously compounded returns of these exchange rates, and dividing the 4½-year period into three

EXAMPLE 48   Valuing a Basket Currency Option Using the Monte Carlo Simulations (Continued)

equal subintervals, I want to value this put option using only four exchange-rate simulated paths.

Stage 1

$S_{1,0} = 1.3000$, $S_{2,0} = 2.2000$, $N_1 = 200$, $N_2 = 100$, $X = 480$, $r_d = 0.08$, $r_{1,f} = 0.06$, $r_{2,f} = 0.09$, $\sigma_1 = 0.1$, $\sigma_2 = 0.17$, $\rho_{1,2} = 0.6$, $T = 4.5$, $n = 3$, $h = 4$, $\Delta t = 1.5$

Stage 2[61]

Path	0	Time		
		Δt	$2\Delta t$	$3\Delta t$
1	$S_{1,0,1} = 1.3000$ $S_{2,0,1} = 2.2000$	$z_{1,1,1} = -1.2569$ $z_{2,1,1} = -0.3553$ $\omega_{1,1,1} = -1.2569$ $\omega_{2,1,1} = -1.0384$ $S_{1,\Delta t,1} = 1.1399$ $S_{2,\Delta t,1} = 1.7084$	$z_{1,2,1} = 1.8482$ $z_{2,2,1} = 0.4250$ $\omega_{1,2,1} = 1.8482$ $\omega_{2,2,1} = 1.4489$ $S_{1,2\Delta t,1} = 1.4620$ $S_{2,2\Delta t,1} = 2.2268$	$z_{1,3,1} = 0.9912$ $z_{2,3,1} = -0.8790$ $\omega_{1,3,1} = 0.9912$ $\omega_{2,3,1} = -0.1085$ $S_{1,3\Delta t,1} = 1.6883$ $S_{2,3\Delta t,1} = 2.0987$
2	$S_{1,0,2} = 1.3000$ $S_{2,0,2} = 2.2000$	$z_{1,1,2} = -0.6072$ $z_{2,1,2} = 0.9866$ $\omega_{1,1,2} = -0.6072$ $\omega_{2,1,2} = 0.4250$ $S_{1,\Delta t,2} = 1.2343$ $S_{2,\Delta t,2} = 2.3170$	$z_{1,2,2} = 0.8052$ $z_{2,2,2} = -1.4481$ $\omega_{1,2,2} = 0.8052$ $\omega_{2,2,2} = -0.6754$ $S_{1,2\Delta t,2} = 1.3932$ $S_{2,2\Delta t,2} = 1.9406$	$z_{1,3,2} = 0.6095$ $z_{2,3,2} = 2.0101$ $\omega_{1,3,2} = 0.6095$ $\omega_{2,3,2} = 1.9738$ $S_{1,3\Delta t,2} = 1.5353$ $S_{2,3\Delta t,2} = 2.8215$
3	$S_{1,0,3} = 1.3000$ $S_{2,0,3} = 2.2000$	$z_{1,1,3} = -0.3867$ $z_{2,1,3} = -1.2306$ $\omega_{1,1,3} = -0.3867$ $\omega_{2,1,3} = -1.2165$ $S_{1,\Delta t,3} = 1.2681$ $S_{2,\Delta t,3} = 1.6462$	$z_{1,2,3} = 0.2388$ $z_{2,2,3} = -2.7401$ $\omega_{1,2,3} = 0.2388$ $\omega_{2,2,3} = -2.0488$ $S_{1,2\Delta t,3} = 1.3354$ $S_{2,2\Delta t,3} = 1.0358$	$z_{1,3,3} = -0.8018$ $z_{2,3,3} = -0.3323$ $\omega_{1,3,3} = -0.8018$ $\omega_{2,3,3} = -0.7469$ $S_{1,3\Delta t,3} = 1.2380$ $S_{2,3\Delta t,3} = 0.8547$
4	$S_{1,0,4} = 1.3000$ $S_{2,0,4} = 2.2000$	$z_{1,1,4} = -0.6464$ $z_{2,1,4} = -1.0228$ $\omega_{1,1,4} = -0.6464$ $\omega_{2,1,4} = -1.2061$ $S_{1,\Delta t,4} = 1.2284$ $S_{2,\Delta t,4} = 1.6498$	$z_{1,2,4} = 0.1376$ $z_{2,2,4} = 1.2632$ $\omega_{1,2,4} = 0.1376$ $\omega_{2,2,4} = 1.0931$ $S_{1,2\Delta t,4} = 1.2777$ $S_{2,2\Delta t,4} = 1.9968$	$z_{1,3,4} = 1.7210$ $z_{2,3,4} = -1.2301$ $\omega_{1,3,4} = 1.7210$ $\omega_{2,3,4} = 0.0485$ $S_{1,3\Delta t,4} = 1.6134$ $S_{2,3\Delta t,4} = 1.9444$

61 To calculate the underlying exchange rates, the formulae $\omega_{1,i,j} = z_{1,i,j}$ and $\omega_{2,i,j} = (0.6 \cdot \omega_{1,i,j}) + (\sqrt{1 - 0.6^2} \cdot z_{2,i,j})$ were used to correlate the two exchange rates, which were then calculated using the recursive relation for $S_{k,i\Delta t,j}$ in Methodology 9.

EXAMPLE 48 Valuing a Basket Currency Option Using the Monte Carlo Simulations (Continued)

Stage 3

Path	Exchange Rates at Time $3\Delta t$	Option Payoff
1	$(S_{1,3\Delta t,1}, S_{2,3\Delta t,1}) = (1.6883, 2.0987)$	$\max[480 - (200 \bullet 1.6883) - (100 \bullet 2.0987), 0] = 0.0000$
2	$(S_{1,3\Delta t,2}, S_{2,3\Delta t,2}) = (1.5353, 2.8215)$	$\max[480 - (200 \bullet 1.5353) - (100 \bullet 2.8215), 0] = 0.0000$
3	$(S_{1,3\Delta t,3}, S_{2,3\Delta t,3}) = (1.2380, 0.8547)$	$\max[480 - (200 \bullet 1.2380) - (100 \bullet 0.8547), 0] = 146.93$
4	$(S_{1,3\Delta t,4}, S_{2,3\Delta t,4}) = (1.6134, 1.9444)$	$\max[480 - (200 \bullet 1.6134) - (100 \bullet 1.9444), 0] = 0.0000$

Stage 4

The option premium is given by $e^{-0.08(4.5)} \left[\dfrac{O_1 + O_2 + O_3 + O_4}{4} \right] = 25.6274$ Cad/US.

It is important for the reader to make the following two observations about Example 48.

OBSERVATION 1 To obtain a more accurate value for the European-style basket option, one would have to reduce the value of Δt and increase h. Doing this would yield an option premium of Cad\$ 29.36 mm.

OBSERVATION 2 As in Observation 4 accompanying Example 34, one could have modeled the basket as an asset instead of resorting to a multivariate Monte Carlo method. To model the basket as an asset, however, the dividend and volatility parameters have to be adjusted.[62] This adjustment is no different from those given in the same observation.

The use of a Monte Carlo method to value a European-Style spread option is illustrated in Example 49 on page 331.

It is important for the reader to make the following two observations about Example 49.

OBSERVATION 1 To obtain a more accurate value for the European-style spread option, one would have to reduce the value of Δt and

---

[62] This is analogous to using the Monte Carlo method to simulate the average as opposed to the underlying exchange rate. See Observation 2 accompanying Example 40.

EXAMPLE 49 Valuing a Spread Currency Option Using the Monte Carlo Simulations

The Canadian dollar is currently trading at 1.3000 Cad/US and 2.2000 Cad/£. A hedger wants to buy a 4½-year European-style at-the-money call option on the spread between the Cad/US exchange rate and the Cad/£ exchange rate. More precisely, the payoff on maturity is max $[S_{2,T} - S_{1,T} - 0.9, 0]$, which can be rewritten as max $[-S_{1,T} + S_{2,T} - 0.9, 0]$, where $S_{1,T}$ represents the Cad/US rate on option maturity and $S_{2,T}$ represents the Cad/£ rate on option maturity. The current continuously compounded risk-free rates of interest in the United States, Canada, and the United Kingdom are 6 percent, 8 percent and, 9 percent, respectively. Using an exchange-rate volatility of 10 percent for the Cad/US exchange rate, a volatility of 17 percent for the Cad/£ exchange rate, a correlation of 60 percent between the continuously compounded returns of these exchange rates, and dividing the 4½-year period into three equal subintervals, I want to value this put option using four exchange-rate simulated paths.

Stage 1

$S_{1,0} = 1.3000$, $S_{2,0} = 2.2000$, $N_1 = -1$, $N_2 = 1$, $X = -0.9$, $r_d = 0.08$, $r_{1,f} = 0.06$, $r_{2,f} = 0.09$, $\sigma_1 = 0.1$, $\sigma_2 = 0.17$, $\rho_{1,2} = 0.6$, $T = 4.5$, $n = 3$, $h = 4$, $\Delta t = 1.5$

Stage 2

The reader is referred to Example 48 for the calculation of these simulated rates.

Stage 3

Path	Exchange Rates of Assets at Time $3\Delta t$	Option Payoff
1	$(S_{1,3\Delta t,1}, S_{2,3\Delta t,1}) = (1.6883, 2.0987)$	max$[-1.6883 + 2.0987 - 0.9, 0] = 0.0000$
2	$(S_{1,3\Delta t,2}, S_{2,3\Delta t,2}) = (1.5353, 2.8215)$	max$[-1.5353 + 2.8215 - 0.9, 0] = 0.3862$
3	$(S_{1,3\Delta t,3}, S_{2,3\Delta t,3}) = (1.2380, 0.8547)$	max$[-1.2380 + 0.8547 - 0.9, 0] = 0.0000$
4	$(S_{1,3\Delta t,4}, S_{2,3\Delta t,4}) = (1.6134, 1.9444)$	max$[-1.6134 + 1.9444 - 0.9, 0] = 0.0000$

Stage 4

The option premium is given by $e^{-0.08(4.5)} \left[\dfrac{O_1 + O_2 + O_3 + O_4}{4} \right] = 0.0674$ Cad/US.

increase h. Doing this would yield an option premium of Cad$ 0.1169.

OBSERVATION 2 As in Observation 2 accompanying Example 35, one could have modeled the spread as an asset instead. To do this, however, one would have to first reexamine the implications of the distribution of a spread when it is modeled as an asset.

As stated on page 278, the implication of this assumption is that given the current spread between two asset values, the change in spread is assumed to be normally distributed. With this assumption, and the notation used on page 278, one can show that the spread in the future has a mean of

$$\mu_* = aS_{1,0}e^{(r_d - r_1, f)\Delta t} - bS_{2,0}e^{(r_d - r_2, f)\Delta t} - D_0$$

and a variance of

$$\sigma_*^2 = (a^2\sigma_1^2 S_{1,0}^2 - 2ab\rho_{1,2}\sigma_1\sigma_2 S_{1,0}S_{2,0} - b^2\sigma_2^2 S_{2,0}^2)\Delta t$$

In this instance, the recursive formula would be of the form

$$D_{i\Delta t} = D_{(i-1)\Delta t} + \mu_* + \sigma_* z_i$$

where $i = 1, 2, \ldots, n$, and D_0 as defined on page 278. With this ability to now simulate a spread, in order to value a spread option, one has to only compute the intrinsic value of the option on the maturity date across all the simulated spread paths and then discount the average of the option values.

Domestic-Currency-Denominated Option on a Single Foreign-Currency-Denominated Asset

The methodology required to value these type of options is presented as Methodology 10.

METHODOLOGY 10   Using the Monte Carlo Method to a Value European-Style Domestic-Currency-Denominated Option on a Single Foreign-Currency-Denominated Asset

Stage 1
Determine r_d, r_f, σ_s, σ_F, $\rho_{FX,S}$ and calculate $q^* = r_d - r_f + q + \rho_{FX,S}\sigma_S\sigma_F$

Stage 2
Set $r_f = q^*$ and follow Methodology 8.

The use of a Monte Carlo method to value a European-Style product option on a single asset is illustrated in Example 50 on page 333.

It is important for the reader to make the following observation about Example 50.

OBSERVATION 1 To obtain a more accurate value for the option, one would have to reduce the value of Δt and increase h. Doing this would yield an option premium of Cad\$ 3.0229.

EXAMPLE 50   Valuing a Category II Product Equity Option Using the Monte Carlo Simulations

A U.S. stock is currently trading at $US 20. A Canadian investor wants to buy a 4½-year European-style put option on the stock that is struck at $US 20. The current continuously compounded risk -free rates of interest in the United States and Canada are 6 percent and 8 percent, respectively, the volatility of the stock is 30 percent, the continuously compounded dividend rate of the stock is 3 percent, and the correlation between the continuously compounded return of the stock and the Cad/US exchange rate is 10 percent. Using a volatility of 10 percent for the exchange rate, dividing the 4½-year period into three equal subintervals, and using nine simulated paths, I want to value this Category II product put option (i.e., the in-the-money option payoff on the option maturity date is the product of the guaranteed exchange rate and the difference between the strike value and the stock value on the option maturity date) when the guaranteed exchange rate used in the payoff is 1 Cad/US.

Stage 1

$r_d = 0.08$, $r_f = 0.06$, $q = 0.03$, $\rho = 0.1$, $\sigma = 0.3$, $\sigma_F = 0.1$ and
$q^* = r_d - r_f + q + \rho\sigma\sigma_F = 0.053$

Stage 2

$S_0 = 20$, $X = 20$, $\hat{F} = 1$, $r_d = 0.08$, $r_f = q^* = 0.053$, $\sigma = 0.3$, $T = 4.5$ $n = 3$, $h = 9$, $\Delta t = 1.5$

Stage 3

Path	0	Time		
		Δt	$2\Delta t$	$3\Delta t$
1	$S_{1,0} = 20$	$z_{1,1} = -1.2569$ $S_{1,\Delta t} = 12.2671$	$z_{1,2} = 1.8482$ $S_{1,2\Delta t} = 23.5469$	$z_{1,3} = 0.9912$ $S_{1,3\Delta t} = 32.9893$
2	$S_{2,0} = 20$	$z_{2,1} = -0.6072$ $S_{2,\Delta t} = 15.5745$	$z_{2,2} = 0.8052$ $S_{2,2\Delta t} = 20.3786$	$z_{2,3} = 0.6095$ $S_{2,3\Delta t} = 24.8145$
3	$S_{3,0} = 20$	$z_{3,1} = -0.3867$ $S_{3,\Delta t} = 16.8888$	$z_{3,2} = 0.2388$ $S_{3,2\Delta t} = 17.9464$	$z_{3,3} = -0.8018$ $S_{2,3\Delta t} = 13.0109$
4	$S_{4,0} = 20$	$z_{4,1} = -0.6464$ $S_{4,\Delta t} = 15.3518$	$z_{4,2} = 0.1376$ $S_{4,2\Delta t} = 15.7177$	$z_{4,3} = 1.7210$ $S_{4,3\Delta t} = 28.7927$
5	$S_{5,0} = 20$	$z_{5,1} = -0.4478$ $S_{5,\Delta t} = 16.5139$	$z_{5,2} = 0.1930$ $S_{5,2\Delta t} = 17.2552$	$z_{5,3} = -0.6371$ $S_{5,3\Delta t} = 13.2902$

EXAMPLE 50 Valuing a Category II Product Equity Option Using the Monte Carlo Simulations (Continued)

6	$S_{6,0} = 20$	$z_{6,1} = -0.2770$ $S_{6,\Delta t} = 17.5834$	$z_{6,2} = -0.6825$ $S_{6,2\Delta t} = 13.3190$	$z_{6,3} = 2.2871$ $S_{6,3\Delta t} = 30.0399$
7	$S_{7,0} = 20$	$z_{7,1} = -1.0825$ $S_{7,\Delta t} = 13.0788$	$z_{7,2} = 1.6066$ $S_{7,2\Delta t} = 22.9724$	$z_{7,3} = -0.4808$ $S_{7,3\Delta t} = 18.7396$
8	$S_{8,0} = 20$	$z_{8,1} = 0.1469$ $S_{8,\Delta t} = 20.5468$	$z_{8,2} = 0.6798$ $S_{8,2\Delta t} = 25.6740$	$z_{8,3} = 0.7055$ $S_{8,3\Delta t} = 32.3850$
9	$S_{9,0} = 20$	$z_{9,1} = -0.1044$ $S_{9,\Delta t} = 18.7346$	$z_{9,2} = -0.3169$ $S_{9,2\Delta t} = 16.2312$	$z_{9,3} = 1.8157$ $S_{9,3\Delta t} = 30.7862$

Stage 3

Path	Stock Price at Time $3\Delta t$	Option Payoff
1	$S_{1,3\Delta t} = 32.9893$	$\max[(20 - 32.9893) \bullet 1,0] = 0.0000$
2	$S_{2,3\Delta t} = 24.8145$	$\max[(20 - 24.8145) \bullet 1,0] = 0.0000$
3	$S_{3,3\Delta t} = 13.0109$	$\max[(20 - 13.0109) \bullet 1,0] = 6.9891$
4	$S_{4,3\Delta t} = 28.7927$	$\max[(20 - 28.7927) \bullet 1,0] = 0.0000$
5	$S_{5,3\Delta t} = 13.2902$	$\max[(20 - 13.2902) \bullet 1,0] = 6.7098$
6	$S_{6,3\Delta t} = 30.0399$	$\max[(20 - 30.0399) \bullet 1,0] = 0.0000$
7	$S_{7,3\Delta t} = 18.7396$	$\max[(20 - 18.7396) \bullet 1,0] = 1.2604$
8	$S_{8,3\Delta t} = 32.3850$	$\max[(20 - 32.3850) \bullet 1,0] = 0.0000$
9	$S_{9,3\Delta t} = 30.7862$	$\max[(20 - 30.7862) \bullet 1,0] = 0.0000$

Stage 4

The option premium is given by $e^{-0.08(4.5)} \left[\dfrac{O_1 + O_2 + O_3 + \ldots + O_9}{9} \right] = 1.1596$ Cad/US.

Domestic-Currency-Denominated Option on Multiple Foreign-Currency-Denominated Assets

The methodology required to value these type of options is presented as Methodology 11.

The use of a Monte Carlo method to value a European-Style product option on multiple assets is illustrated in Example 51 on page 335.

METHODOLOGY 11 Using the Monte Carlo Method to Value a European-Style Domestic-Currency-Denominated Option on Multiple Foreign-Currency-Denominated Assets

Stage 1

Suppose there are m_1 foreign currency denominated assets that are converted by their respective m_1 exchange rates into the domestic currency and there are an additional m_2 domestic assets such that $m_1 + m_1 + m_2 = m$. Arrange the m assets such that the first m_1 assets are the exchange rates, the next m_1 assets are the foreign-currency denominated assets, and the last m_2 assets are the domestic-currency denominated assets. Furthermore, the m_1 foreign-currency denominated assets are arranged such that the $(m_1 + k)$th foreign asset gets converted into the domestic currency using the kth exchange rate where $k = 1, 2, \ldots, m_1$.

Stage 2

For $k = 1, 2, \ldots, m_1$, determine $r_d, r_{k,f}, q_{k+m_1}, \rho_{k,k+m_1}, \sigma_k, \sigma_{k+m_1}$ and calculate $q^*_{k+m_1} = r_d - r_{k,f} + q_{k+m_1} + \rho_{k,k+m_1} \sigma_k \sigma_{k+m_1}$.

Stage 3

For $k = 1, 2, \ldots, m_1$, set $r_{k+m_1,f} = q^*_{k+m_1}$ and follow Methodology 9.

EXAMPLE 51 Valuing a Category I Product Equity Option Using the Monte Carlo Simulations

A U.S. stock is currently trading at $US 20 and the current Cad/US exchange-rate level is at 1.3000 Cad/US. A Canadian investor wants to buy a 4½-year European-style put option on the stock that is struck at $US 20. The current continuously compounded risk-free rates of interest in the United States and Canada are 6 percent and 8 percent respectively. The volatility of the stock is 30 percent, the continuously compounded dividend rate of the stock is 3 percent, and the correlation between the continuously compounded return of the stock and the Cad/US exchange rate is 10 percent. Using a volatility of 10 percent for the exchange rate, dividing the 4½-year period into three equal subintervals and using four simulated paths, I want to value this Category I product put option (i.e., the in-the-money option payoff on the option maturity date is the product of the exchange rate on the option maturity date and the difference between the strike price and the stock price on the option maturity date).

Stage 1

$m_1 = 1, m_2 = 0, m = 2$.

Thus first asset is the foreign exchange rate that is denominated in Cad/US, and the second asset is the U.S. stock that is denominated in U.S. dollars.

EXAMPLE 51 Valuing a Category I Product Equity Option Using the Monte Carlo Simulations (Continued)

Stage 2

$r_d = 0.08$, $r_{1,f} = 0.06$, $q_2 = 0.037$, $\rho_{1,2} = 0.1$, $\sigma_1 = 0.1$, $\sigma_2 = 0.3$ and
$q_2^* = r_d - r_{1,f} + q_2 + \rho_{1,2}\sigma_1\sigma_2 = 0.053$.

Stage 3

$S_{1,0} = 1.3000$, $S_{2,0} = 20$, $X = 20$, $r_d = 0.08$, $r_{1,f} = 0.06$, $r_{2,f} = q_2^* = 0.053$,
$\sigma_1 = 0.1$, $\sigma_2 = 0.3$, $\rho_{1,2} = 0.1$, $T = 4.5$, $n = 3$, $h = 9$, $\Delta t = 1.5$

Stage 4[63]

Path	0	Time		
		Δt	$2\Delta t$	$3\Delta t$
1	$S_{1,0,1} = 1.3000$ $S_{2,0,1} = 20$	$z_{1,1,1} = -1.2569$ $z_{2,1,1} = -0.3553$ $\omega_{1,1,1} = -1.2569$ $\omega_{2,1,1} = -0.4792$ $S_{1,\Delta t,1} = 1.1399$ $S_{2,\Delta t,1} = 16.3244$	$z_{1,2,1} = 1.8482$ $z_{2,2,1} = 0.4250$ $\omega_{1,2,1} = 1.8482$ $\omega_{2,2,1} = 0.6077$ $S_{1,2\Delta t,1} = 1.4620$ $S_{2,2\Delta t,1} = 19.8647$	$z_{1,3,1} = 0.9912$ $z_{2,3,1} = -0.8790$ $\omega_{1,3,1} = 0.9912$ $\omega_{2,3,1} = -0.7755$ $S_{1,3\Delta t,1} = 1.6883$ $S_{2,3\Delta t,1} = 14.5415$
2	$S_{1,0,2} = 1.3000$ $S_{2,0,2} = 20$	$z_{1,1,2} = -0.6072$ $z_{2,1,2} = 0.9866$ $\omega_{1,1,2} = -0.6072$ $\omega_{2,1,2} = 0.9209$ $S_{1,\Delta t,2} = 1.2343$ $S_{2,\Delta t,2} = 27.3056$	$z_{1,2,2} = 0.8052$ $z_{2,2,2} = -1.4481$ $\omega_{1,2,2} = 0.8052$ $\omega_{2,2,2} = -1.3603$ $S_{1,2\Delta t,2} = 1.3932$ $S_{2,2\Delta t,2} = 16.1236$	$z_{1,3,2} = 0.6095$ $z_{2,3,2} = 2.0101$ $\omega_{1,3,2} = 0.6095$ $\omega_{2,3,2} = 2.0610$ $S_{1,3\Delta t,2} = 1.5353$ $S_{2,3\Delta t,2} = 33.4665$
3	$S_{1,0,3} = 1.3000$ $S_{2,0,3} = 20$	$z_{1,1,3} = -0.3867$ $z_{2,1,3} = -1.2306$ $\omega_{1,1,3} = -0.3867$ $\omega_{2,1,3} = -1.2631$ $S_{1,\Delta t,3} = 1.2681$ $S_{2,\Delta t,3} = 12.2391$	$z_{1,2,3} = 0.2388$ $z_{2,2,3} = -2.7401$ $\omega_{1,2,3} = 0.2388$ $\omega_{2,2,3} = -2.7025$ $S_{1,2\Delta t,3} = 1.3354$ $S_{2,2\Delta t,3} = 4.4135$	$z_{1,3,3} = -0.8018$ $z_{2,3,3} = -0.3323$ $\omega_{1,3,3} = -0.8018$ $\omega_{2,3,3} = -0.4108$ $S_{1,3\Delta t,3} = 1.2380$ $S_{2,3\Delta t,3} = 3.6941$
4	$S_{1,0,4} = 1.3000$ $S_{2,0,4} = 20$	$z_{1,1,4} = -0.6464$ $z_{2,1,4} = -1.0228$ $\omega_{1,1,4} = -0.6464$ $\omega_{2,1,4} = -1.0823$ $S_{1,\Delta t,4} = 1.2284$ $S_{2,\Delta t,4} = 13.0798$	$z_{1,2,4} = 0.1376$ $z_{2,2,4} = 1.2632$ $\omega_{1,2,4} = 0.1376$ $\omega_{2,2,4} = 1.2706$ $S_{1,2\Delta t,4} = 1.2777$ $S_{2,2\Delta t,4} = 20.3060$	$z_{1,3,4} = 1.7210$ $z_{2,3,4} = -1.2301$ $\omega_{1,3,4} = 1.7210$ $\omega_{2,3,4} = -1.0518$ $S_{1,3\Delta t,4} = 1.6134$ $S_{2,3\Delta t,4} = 13.4296$

63 To calculate the underlying exchange rates, the formulae, $\omega_{1,i,j} = z_{1,i,j}$ and $\omega_{2,i,j} = (0.1 \cdot \omega_{1,i,j}) + (\sqrt{1-0.1^2} \cdot z_{2,i,j})$ were used to correlate the two exchange rates, which were then calculated using the recursive relation for $S_{k,i\Delta t,j}$ in Methodology 9.

EXAMPLE 51 Valuing a Category I Product Equity Option Using the Monte Carlo Simulations (Continued)

Stage 5

Path	Exchange Rate and Stock Price at Time $3\Delta t$	Option Payoff
1	$(S_{1,3\Delta t,1}, S_{2,3\Delta t,1})$ $= (1.6883, 14.5415)$	$\max[(20 - 14.5415) \bullet 1.6883, 0]$ $= 9.2156$
2	$(S_{1,3\Delta t,2}, S_{2,3\Delta t,2})$ $= (1.5353, 33.4665)$	$\max[(20 - 33.4665) \bullet 1.5353, 0]$ $= 0.0000$
3	$(S_{1,3\Delta t,3}, S_{2,3\Delta t,3})$ $= (1.2380, 3.6941)$	$\max[(20 - 3.6941) \bullet 1.2380, 0]$ $= 20.1867$
4	$(S_{1,3\Delta t,4}, S_{2,3\Delta t,4})$ $= (1.6134, 13.4296)$	$\max[(20 - 13.4296) \bullet 1.6134, 0]$ $= 10.6007$

Stage 6

The option premium is given by $e^{-0.08(4.5)} \left[\dfrac{O_1 + O_2 + O_3 + O_4}{4} \right] = 6.9773$ Cad/US.

It is important for the reader to make the following observation about Example 51.

OBSERVATION To obtain a more accurate value for the European-style Category I product option, one would have to reduce the value of Δt and increase h. Doing this would yield an option premium of Cad$ 5.1150.

CONCLUSION

In Chapters 2 and 3 of this book, I partitioned the gamut of derivatives to its core option building blocks and provided the applications of each. In the process, I also provided the intuition underpinning the effect of all the relevant variables that would affect the price and risk-characteristics of each building block. In order to mathematically quantify all the risks inherent in each building block and support the intuition developed in earlier chapters, I provided two intuitively powerful methods: the binomial method and the Monte Carlo method. To ensure that anyone can easily apply these methodologies, I have provided recipes in a step-by-step fashion with a lot of insight into the philosophy underlying each methodology. In the process, I have tried not to concern myself with the efficiency of these algorithms.

At the beginning of this chapter, I commented that to be able to value a derivative one has to first model the underlying asset behavior and then be able to use the model to value the derivative of interest. While the discussion in this chapter has been focused on the use of a lognormal or the geometric brownian motion assumption, in the interest-rate and commodity markets practitioners also sometimes use the other more sophisticated term *structure models*. I have found that in the pursuit of more sophisticated and complex models, the simplicity and, more importantly, the ability to combine the intuition with the model is lost. The Black–Scholes 1973 model and Black's 1976 models have been around for at least two decades, not because there is a lack of more sophisticated models today, but because the simplicity associated with these models enables them to withstand the test of time. Instead of simply resorting to more sophisticated models, the ingenuity of a trader or a financial engineer lies in the art of successfully adopting or "tricking" the Black–Scholes or even Black's model to value the derivatives of interest.

However, if it is necessary to use models built from a nongeometric brownian motion assumption, the Monte Carlo method can still be easily used to model the process for the underlying asset value, rate, or price. Furthermore, with the availability of cheap and fast computer chips, the Monte Carlo method is coming back as a popular valuation tool. In addition to its versatility and robustness, the ability to value early-exercise options using this method via Tilley's algorithm has increased the attractiveness of the method.

Since most nontraditional customized derivatives that are used and traded by both the end users and market makers are essentially European-style in nature, my personal bias has been and will continue to be to first see if a closed-form or even a quasi-closed form solution can be found. If I do not succeed in this pursuit, I will end up settling for a methodology that is driven by either a numerical integration technique or a Monte Carlo method.

⑥ ASSUMPTIONS AND USEFUL MATHEMATICAL RELATIONSHIPS

In this section of the book, I state the frequently used geometric brownian motion assumption that is necessary in the derivation of the option pricing formulae. Using this assumption, I additionally provide without proof commonly used mathematical relationships and identities that are needed for valuing many of the vanilla and exotic derivatives encountered in practice across any asset class.

A. DEFINITIONS[1]

Definition 1

A stochastic process $\{X(t), t \geq 0\}$ is said to be a Brownian motion process with drift coefficient μ and variance parameter σ^2 if

A. $X(0) = 0$

B. $\{X(t), t \geq 0\}$ has stationary and independent increments

C. for every $t > 0$, $X(t)$ is normally distributed with mean μt and variance $\sigma^2 t$.

When $\mu = 0$ and $\sigma = 1$, this type of process is also called a standard Brownian motion process.

Definition 2

A stochastic process $\{Y(t), t \geq 0\}$ is said to be a geometric Brownian motion process if $\{X(t), t \geq 0\}$ is a Brownian motion with drift coefficient μ and variance parameter σ^2 and $Y(t) = e^{X(t)}$.

---

[1] See Ross (1993) for more details.

B. ASSUMPTIONS

Assumption 1

When the ith underlying spot contract[2] for (i = 1,2, . . ., n) has a current spot value[3] of $S_{i,0}$, a continuously compounded risk-free rate of r_d, a continuously compounded foreign risk-free (or dividend) rate of $r_{i,f}$, and an annualized volatility[4] of σ_i, the value of this ith spot contract at some time T in the future (i.e., $S_{i,T}$) is assumed to be lognormally distributed. More precisely,

$\ln S_{i,T}$ is normally distributed with mean $\ln S_{i,0} + \left(r_d - r_{i,f} - \dfrac{\sigma_i^2}{2} \right) T$ and

variance $\sigma_i^2 T$, where $\rho_{i,j}$ is the correlation[5] between $\ln S_{i,T}$ and $\ln S_{j,T}$ and $\rho_{i,j} = \rho_{j,i}$ for all $i \neq j$ and $i,j = 1,2,\ldots,n$.

   In particular, when there is only one underlying spot contract (i.e., n = 1), the value of the spot contract at some time T in the future (i.e., $S_{1,T}$) is assumed to be lognormally distributed. Thus,

$\ln S_{1,T}$ is normally distributed with mean $\ln S_{1,0} + \left(r_d - r_{1,f} - \dfrac{\sigma_1^2}{2} \right) T$ and variance $\sigma_1^2 T$.

Assumption 2

When the ith underlying forward/futures[6] contract (for i = 1,2, . . .,n) has a current forward/futures value[7] of $F_{i,0}$ and an annualized volatility of σ_i, the value of this ith forward/futures contract at some time T in the future (i.e., $F_{i,T}$) is assumed to be lognormally distributed. More precisely,

$\ln F_{i,T}$ is normally distributed with mean $\ln F_{i,0} - \dfrac{\sigma_i^2}{2} T$ and variance $\sigma_i^2 T$,

where $\rho_{i,j}$ is the correlation between $\ln F_{i,T}$ and $\ln F_{j,T}$ and $\rho_{i,j} = \rho_{j,i}$ for all $i \neq j$ and $i, j = 1,2, \ldots,n$.

---

[2] This assumption is used when modeling assets that do not trade as forward or futures contracts (e.g., stock prices, spot equity index values).

[3] This value may be denominated as rate, points, or price.

[4] The volatility of a spot contract is defined as the standard deviation of the natural logarithm of the return of the spot contract. See Relationship 18 for the formula used to calculate the historical volatility.

[5] Although, statistically speaking, this definition is correct, it is more exact to think of $\rho_{i,j}$ as the correlation between the continuously compounded returns of the ith spot contract and the jth spot contract. See Relationship 18 for the formula used to calculate the historical correlation.

[6] This assumption is used when modeling assets that trade as either a forward contract or a futures contract (e.g., interest rates, commodity prices, currency forwards).

[7] See footnote 2.

In particular, when there is only one underlying forward/futures contract (i.e., n = 1), the value of the forward/futures contract at some time T in the future (i.e., $F_{1,T}$) is assumed to be lognormally distributed. Thus,

$\ln F_{1,T}$ is normally distributed with mean $\ln F_{1,0} - \dfrac{\sigma_1^2}{2}T$ and variance $\sigma_1^2 T$.

C. RELATIONSHIPS

Relationship 1

If $a_1, a_2, \ldots, a_n$ represent any n real numbers (or variables), the following properties hold true:

$$\max[a_1, a_2, \ldots, a_n] = -\min[-a_1, -a_2, \ldots, -a_n]$$

In particular,

$$\max[a_1, a_2] = a_1 + \max[a_2 - a_1, 0] = a_2 + \max[a_1 - a_2, 0]$$
$$\min[a_1, a_2] = a_1 - \max[a_1 - a_2, 0] = a_2 - \max[a_2 - a_1, 0]$$

Relationship 2

If $\ln H_{i,T}$ (for $i = 1, \ldots, n$) is normally distributed with mean μ_i, variance σ_i^2, correlation between $\ln H_{i,T}$ and $\ln H_{j,T}$ being $\rho_{i,j}$ (for all $i,j = 1, \ldots, n$ and $i \neq j$), and $g_{H_{1,T}, \ldots, H_{n,T}}(h_1, \ldots, h_n)$ represents the joint probability density function[8] of $H_{1,T}, \ldots, H_{n,T}$, then $g_{H_{1,T}, \ldots, H_{n,T}}(h_1, \ldots, h_n)$ has the following form:

$$g_{H_{1,T} \ldots, H_{n,T}}(h_1, \ldots, h_n) = \frac{|\Sigma_{n,n}|^{-1/2}}{(\sqrt{2\Pi})^n \prod\limits_{i=1}^{n} h_i} e^{-1/2(H-\mu)' \Sigma_{n,n}^{-1}(H-\mu)}$$

where $H' = [h_1, h_2, \ldots, h_n]$ and $\mu' = [\mu_1, \mu_2, \ldots, \mu_n]$ represent the transpose[9] of the matrices H and μ respectively, $\Sigma_{n,n}$ is defined in the notation section, $h_i > 0$ $\rho_{i,j} = \rho_{j,i}$ and $|\Sigma_{n,n}| > 0$.[10]

In particular,

A. When n = 1, $\ln H_{1,T}$ is normally distributed with mean μ_1, variance of σ_1^2 and $g_{H_{1,T}}(h_1)$ would have the following form:

$$g_{H_{1,T}}(h_1) = \frac{1}{\sigma_1 h_1 \sqrt{2\Pi}} e^{-1/2\left[\frac{\ln h_1 - \mu_1}{\sigma_1}\right]^2} \text{ where } h_1 > 0.$$

B. When n = 2, $\ln H_{1,T}$ and $\ln H_{2,T}$ are bivariate normally distributed with

---

[8] This is sometimes called the multivariate lognormal density function.

[9] If A represents the matrix $\begin{bmatrix} a & b & c \\ d & e & f \end{bmatrix}$, the transpose of A is given by the matrix $\begin{bmatrix} a & d \\ b & e \\ c & f \end{bmatrix}$. See, for example, Anton and Rorres (1987) and Nicholson (1986).

[10] $\Sigma_{n,n}$ is also known as the variance-covariance matrix and $|\Sigma_{n,n}|$ is defined as the determinant of the matrix $\Sigma_{n,n}$. See Anton and Rorres (1987) and Nicholson (1986) for the definition of matrix determinants.

means μ_1 and μ_2, respectively, variances σ_1^2 and σ_2^2, respectively, and correlation coefficient $\rho_{1,2}$. Furthermore, $g_{H_{1,T},H_{2,T}}(h_1,h_2)$ would have the following form:

$$g_{H_{1,T},H_{2,T}}(h_1,h_2) = \frac{1}{\sigma_1\sigma_2\sqrt{1-\rho_{1,2}^2}h_1h_2(\sqrt{2\Pi})^2}e^{-\frac{Q}{2(1-\rho_{1,2}^2)}}$$

where $Q = \left[\dfrac{\ln h_1 - \mu_1}{\sigma_1}\right]^2 - 2\rho_{1,2}\left[\dfrac{\ln h_1 - \mu_1}{\sigma_1}\right]\left[\dfrac{\ln h_2 - \mu_2}{\sigma_2}\right] + \left[\dfrac{\ln h_2 - \mu_2}{\sigma_2}\right]^2$

and $h_1, h_2 > 0$.

Relationship 3

If N[a] represents the probability that Z, the standard normal variate, is less than any real number a, then

$$N[a] = Pr\,(Z \le a) = \int_{-\infty}^{a} \frac{1}{\sqrt{2\Pi}}\,e^{-\frac{z^2}{2}}\,dz.$$

By the nature of the definition, it can be shown that $N[a] = 1 - N[-a]$. From this, it readily follows that $N[0] = 0.5$, $N[\infty] = 1$ and $N[-\infty] = 0$

Furthermore[11]

A. When $a > 0$, N[a] can be approximated, to an accuracy of 1×10^{-5}, using the expression $1 - e^{-\frac{1}{2}a^2}\left[\dfrac{c_1}{\alpha} + \dfrac{c_2}{\alpha^2} + \dfrac{c_3}{\alpha^3}\right]$, where $\alpha = \dfrac{1}{1 + 0.33267a}$, $c_1 = 0.4361836$, $c_2 = -0.1201676$ and $c_3 = 0.9372980$.[12]

B. When $0 < N[a] \le 0.5$, a can be approximated, to an accuracy of 4.5×10^{-4}, using the expression $\alpha - \dfrac{c_1 + c_2\alpha + c_3\alpha^2}{1 + c_4\alpha + c_5\alpha^2 + c_6\alpha^3}$, where $\alpha = \sqrt{-2\ln p}$, $c_1 = 2.515517$, $c_2 = 0.802853$, $c_3 = 0.010328$, $c_4 = 1.432788$, $c_5 = 0.189269$ and $c_6 = 0.001308$.[13]

Relationship 4

If $BN[a_1,a_2,\rho]$ represents the probability that Z_1, the first standard normal variate, is less than a_1 and Z_2, the second standard normal variate, is less than a_2 where both the standard normal variates are correlated with a correlation coefficient ρ

---

[11] These and other forms of approximations are given in Abramowitz and Stegun (1970).

[12] When $a < 0$, $-a > 0$. Consequently, when a is negative, N[a] can be computed by first calculating N[−a] and then using the relationship $N[a] = 1 - N[-a]$.

[13] When $1 > N[a] > 0.5$, from the relationship $N[-a] = 1 - N[a]$ it can be seen that $0 < N[-a] < 0.5$. To compute a, one has to first calculate −a from the value of N[−a]. As an example, consider the calculation of a such that $N[a] = 0.8$. Since $N[-a] = 1 - 0.8 = 0.2$, we can use the approximating formula to find −a such that $N[-a] = 0.2$. This would result in −a being −0.84162, which would imply that $a = 0.84162$.

and both a_1 and a_2 represent any two real numbers, then

$$BN[a_1,a_2,\rho] = \Pr (Z_1 \le a_1, Z_2 \le a_2)$$

$$= \int_{-\infty}^{a_1} \int_{-\infty}^{a_2} \frac{1}{2\Pi\sqrt{1-\rho^2}} \, e^{-\frac{1}{2(1-\rho^2)}[z_1{}^2 - 2\rho z_1 z_2 + z_2{}^2]} dz_2 dz_1.$$

By the nature of the definition,

A. $BN[a_1,a_2,\rho] + BN[-a_1,a_2,-\rho] = N[a_2]$

B. $BN[a_1,a_2,\rho] - BN[-a_1,-a_2,\rho] = N[a_1] + N[a_2] - 1$

C. $BN[a_1,a_2,\rho] = \begin{cases} \left[N\left[\dfrac{a_2 - \rho a_1}{\sqrt{1-\rho^2}} \right] \bullet N[a_1] \right] + BN\left[-\dfrac{a_2 - \rho a_1}{\sqrt{1-\rho^2}}, a_2, -\sqrt{1-\rho^2} \right] \\ \quad \text{when } \rho \ge 0 \\[2em] \left[N\left[\dfrac{a_2 - \rho a_1}{\sqrt{1-\rho^2}} \right] \bullet N[a_1] \right] - BN\left[\dfrac{a_2 - \rho a_1}{\sqrt{1-\rho^2}}, -a_2, -\sqrt{1-\rho^2} \right] \\ \quad \text{when } \rho \ge 0 \end{cases}$

D. $BN[a_1,a_2,\rho] = BN[a_2,a_1,\rho]$

In particular,

A. $BN[a_1,a_2,0] = N[a_1] \bullet N[a_2]$

B. $BN[a_1,a_2,1] = \begin{cases} N[a_1] \text{ when } a_1 - a_2 \le 0 \\ N[a_2] \text{ when } a_1 - a_2 \ge 0 \end{cases}$

C. $BN[a_1,a_2,-1] = \begin{cases} 0 \qquad\qquad \text{when } a_1 + a_2 \le 0 \\ N[a_1] - N[-a_2] \text{ when } a_1 + a_2 \ge 0 \end{cases}$

D. $BN[0,0,\rho] = \dfrac{1}{4} + \dfrac{\sin^{-1}(\rho)}{2\Pi}$

E. $BN[\infty,a_2,\rho] = N[a_2]$

F. $BN[a_1,\infty,\rho] = N[a_1]$

G. $BN[-\infty,a_2,\rho] = BN[a_1,-\infty,\rho] = 0$

H. $BN[\infty,\infty,\rho] = 1$

Relationship 5

If $\ln H_{i,T}$ is normally distributed with mean μ_i and variance σ_i^2 (for $i = 1,2$) and the correlation between $\ln H_{1,T}$ and $\ln H_{2,T}$ is $\rho_{1,2}$; then

$$E_{H_{1,T} H_{2,T}}[\max(A H_{1,T}^B - C H_{2,T}^D, 0)] = A e^{\mu_1 B + 1/2\sigma_1^2 B^2} N[f(B\rho_{1,2}\sigma_1\sigma_2) + \alpha] -$$
$$C e^{\mu_2 D + 1/2\sigma_2^2 D^2} N[f(D\sigma_2^2)]$$

where A, B, C, and D are any real numbers with A having the same sign as

C, $\alpha = \dfrac{\sigma_1^2(1 - \rho_{1,2}^2)}{\sqrt{\sigma_1^2 - 2D\rho_{1,2}\sigma_1\sigma_2 + D^2\sigma_2^2}}$ and the function f(m) defined as

$$\dfrac{-\left(D - \dfrac{\rho_{1,2}\sigma_1}{\sigma_2}\right)(\mu_2 + m) + \mu_1 - \ln\left(\dfrac{C}{A}\right) - \dfrac{\rho_{1,2}\sigma_1\mu_2}{\sigma_2}}{\sqrt{\sigma_1^2 - 2D\rho_{1,2}\sigma_1\sigma_2 + D^2\sigma_2^2}}.^{14}$$

In particular,

A. When $A = B = C = D = 1$, $\mu_i = \ln H_{i,0} + \left(r_d - r_{i,f} - \dfrac{\sigma_{*,i}^2}{2}\right)T$ and $\sigma_i = \sigma_{*,i}\sqrt{T}$ (for $i = 1, 2$),

$$E_{H_{1,T}H_{2,T}}[\max(H_{1,T} - H_{2,T}, 0)] = H_{1,0}\, e^{(r_d - r_{1,f})T}N[d_1] -$$
$$H_{2,0}e^{(r_d - r_{2,f})T}N[d_1 - \sigma\sqrt{T}\,]$$

where

$$\sigma = \sqrt{\sigma_{*,1}^2 - 2\rho_{1,2}\sigma_{*,1}\sigma_{*,2} + \sigma_{*,2}^2} \text{ and } d_1 = \dfrac{\ln\left(\dfrac{H_{1,0}}{H_{2,0}}\right) + \left(r_{2,f} - r_{1,f} + \dfrac{\sigma^2}{2}\right)T}{\sigma\sqrt{T}}.^{15}$$

B. When $A = B = 1$, $C = K$, $D = 0$, $\mu_1 = \ln H_{1,0} + \left(r_d - r_{1,f} - \dfrac{\sigma_{*,1}^2}{2}\right)T$, $\sigma_1 = \sigma_{*,1}\sqrt{T}$,

$$E_{H_{1,T}H_{2,T}}[\max(H_{1,T} - K, 0)] = H_{1,0}e^{(r_d - r_{1,f})T}N[d_1] - KN[d_1 - \sigma_{*,1}\sqrt{T}]$$

where $d_1 = \dfrac{\ln\left(\dfrac{H_{1,0}}{K}\right) + \left(r_d - r_{1,f} + \dfrac{\sigma_{*,1}^2}{2}\right)T}{\sigma_{*,1}\sqrt{T}}.^{16}$

C. When $A = K$, $B = 0$, $C = D = 1$, $\mu_2 = \ln H_{2,0} + \left(r_d - r_{2,f} - \dfrac{\sigma_{*,2}^2}{2}\right)T$, $\sigma_2 = \sigma_{*,2}\sqrt{T}$,

$$E_{H_{1,T}H_{2,T}}[\max(K - H_{2,T}, 0)] = -H_{2,0}e^{(r_d - r_{2,f})T}N[-d_1] +$$
$$KN[-(d_1 - \sigma_{*,2}\sqrt{T})]$$

where $d_1 = \dfrac{\ln\left(\dfrac{H_{2,0}}{K}\right) + \left(r_d - r_{2,f} + \dfrac{\sigma_{*,2}^2}{2}\right)T}{\sigma_{*,2}\sqrt{T}}.^{17}$

---

[14] The cumulative probability function $N[.]$ is defined in Relationship 3.

[15] Multiplying this expected payoff by a $e^{-r_d T}$ results in the option pricing formula that can be used to value the exchange or Margrabe option.

[16] Multiplying this expected payoff by a $e^{-r_d T}$ results in the option pricing formula that can be used to value the vanilla call option.

Relationship 6

If $\ln H_{i,T}$ is normally distributed with mean μ_i and variance σ_i^2 for $(i = 1,2)$ and the correlation between $\ln H_{1,T}$ and $\ln H_{2,T}$ is $\rho_{1,2}$; then the correlation[18] between $H_{1,T}$ and $H_{2,T}$ is not necessarily equal to $\rho_{1,2}$. More precisely, the correlation between $H_{1,T}$ and $H_{2,T}$ is given by the formula

$$\frac{e^{\rho_{1,2}\sigma_1\sigma_2} - 1}{\sqrt{e^{\sigma_1^2} - 1}\ \sqrt{e^{\sigma_2^2} - 1}}$$

In particular, when $H_{2,T} = H_{1,t}$, $\mu_2 = \ln H_0 + \left(r_d - r_f - \dfrac{\sigma^2}{2}\right)t$, $\sigma_2 = \sigma\sqrt{t}$, $\mu_1 = \ln H_0$ $+ \left(r_d - r_f - \dfrac{\sigma^2}{2}\right)T$, $\sigma_1 = \sigma\sqrt{T}$ and $t \le T$,

A. the correlation between $\ln H_{1,t}$ and $\ln H_{1,T}$ is $\sqrt{\dfrac{t}{T}}$.

B. the correlation between $H_{1,t}$ and $H_{1,T}$ is given by $\dfrac{\sqrt{e^{\sigma^2 t} - 1}}{\sqrt{e^{\sigma^2 T} - 1}}$.

Relationship 7

If $\ln H_{i,T}$ is normally distributed with mean μ_i and variance σ_i^2 (for $i = 1,2, \ldots,n$), where $\rho_{i,j}$ is the correlation between $\ln H_{i,T}$ and $\ln H_{j,T}$ and $\rho_{i,j} = \rho_{j,i}$ (for all $i \neq j$ and $i, j = 1,2, \ldots,n$) then

$$E_{H_{1,T}\ldots H_{n,T}}[H_{1,T}^{A_1} \ldots H_{n,T}^{A_n}] = e^{\sum_{i=1}^{n} [A_i\mu_i + \frac{\sigma_i^2 A_i^2}{2}] + \sum_{i=1}^{n-1}\sum_{j=i+1}^{n} \rho_{i,j}A_iA_j\sigma_i\sigma_j}$$

where $A_1, \ldots A_n$ are any arbitrary real numbers.[19]
In particular, when $n = 2$,

$$E_{H_{1,T}H_{2,T}}[H_{1,T}^{A_1}H_{2,T}^{A_2}] = e^{A_1\mu_1 + A_2\mu_2 + \frac{1}{2}A_1^2\sigma_1^2 + \frac{1}{2}A_2^2\sigma_2^2 + \rho_{1,2}A_1A_2\sigma_1\sigma_2}$$

---

[17] Multiplying this expected payoff by a $e^{-r_d T}$ results in the option pricing formula that can be used to value the vanilla put option.

[18] This represents the correlation between the proportionate change in asset 1 and proportionate change in asset 2. It is important for the reader to note that this definition of correlation is different from the usual definition of correlation that is given in footnote 5. See footnote 30 for the formula that is used to calculate this type of correlation.

[19] When $n = 1$, $\mu_1 = \ln H_0 + \left(r_d - r_f - \dfrac{\sigma^2}{2}\right)T$ and $\sigma_1 = \sigma\sqrt{T}$, the variance of $H_{1,T}$ which is calculated using the formula $E_{H_{1,T}}[H_{1,T}^2] - \{E_{H_{1,T}}[H_{1,T}]\}^2$ simplifies to $H_0^2 e^{2(r_d - r_f)T}[e^{\sigma^2 T} - 1]$. This implies that the standard deviation of $H_{1,T}$ is $H_0 e^{(r_d - r_f)T}\sqrt{e^{\sigma^2 T} - 1}$ which is different from σ, the volatility of $H_{1,T}$. Furthermore, the standard deviation of $H_{1,T}$ is an increasing function of σ.

Relationship 8

If $\ln H_{i,T}$ is normally distributed with mean μ_i and variance σ_i^2 for ($i = 1,2$) and the correlation between $\ln H_{1,T}$ and $\ln H_{2,T}$ is $\rho_{1,2}$, then

    A. $\ln(H_{1,T}H_{2,T})$ is normally distributed with mean $\mu_1 + \mu_2$ and variance $\sigma_1^2 + \sigma_2^2 + 2\rho_{1,2}\sigma_1\sigma_2$

    B. $\ln\left(\dfrac{H_{1,T}}{H_{2,T}}\right)$ is normally distributed with mean $\mu_1 - \mu_2$ and variance $\sigma_1^2 + \sigma_2^2 - 2\rho_{1,2}\sigma_1\sigma_2$

Furthermore, both $\ln(H_{1,T} + H_{2,T})$ and $\ln(H_{1,T} - H_{2,T})$ will not be normally distributed unlike $\ln(H_{1,T}H_{2,T})$ and $\ln\left(\dfrac{H_{1,T}}{H_{2,T}}\right)$, as illustrated above.[20]

Relationship 9

If $\ln(R)$ is normally distributed with mean μ and variance σ^2, when A, B > 0 and C, D and E are any real numbers,

$$\int_A^B R^C N[D\ln R + E] \frac{1}{\sigma R\sqrt{2\Pi}} e^{-1/2\left[\frac{\ln R - \mu}{\sigma}\right]^2} dR =$$

$$e^{\mu C + 1/2\sigma^2 C^2} [BN[\alpha,\beta,Y] - BN[\theta,\beta,Y]]$$

where $\alpha = \dfrac{\ln B - \mu}{\sigma} - C\sigma$, $\beta = \dfrac{CD\sigma^2 + D\mu + E}{\sqrt{1 + D^2\sigma^2}}$, $Y = -\dfrac{D\sigma}{\sqrt{1 + D^2\sigma^2}}$,

$\theta = \dfrac{\ln A - \mu}{\sigma} - C\sigma$.[21]

---

[20] To overcome the constraint that $\ln(H_{1,T} + H_{2,T})$ is not normally distributed, it is common in practice to make the assumption that $\ln(H_{1,T} + H_{2,T})$ has a normal distribution with a mean μ and variance σ^2. Using this assumption, one would then estimate μ and σ^2 using the results in Relationship 7.

    To overcome the constraint that $\ln(H_{1,T} - H_{2,T})$ is not normally distributed, it is common in practice to make the assumption that $H_{1,T} - H_{2,T}$ has a normal distribution with a mean μ and variance σ^2. Using this assumption, one would then estimate μ and σ^2 using the results in Relationship 7. It is important for the reader to note that since $H_{1,T} - H_{2,T}$ can be negative, unlike $\ln(H_{1,T} + H_{2,T})$, it does not make sense to assume that $\ln(H_{1,T} - H_{2,T})$ is normally distributed.

[21] The bivariate cumulative probability function BN[.,.,...] is defined in Relationship 4.

Relationship 10

For any nonnegative random variable R, when both A, B > 0, C, D and E are any real numbers.

$$\int_A^B R^C N[D\ln(R) + E]\, dR =$$

$$\frac{1}{C+1}\{B^{1+C}N[\alpha] - A^{1+C}N[\beta] - e^{\frac{(1+C)(1+C-2DE)}{2D^2}}[N[\alpha - \frac{1+C}{D}] - N[\beta - \frac{1+C}{D}]]\}$$

where $\alpha = D\ln(B) + E$, $\beta = D\ln(A) + E$.

Relationship 11

For any nonrandom variable R, when both $A_1, B_1 > 0$, $H_1 \in [-1,1]$, C_1, D_1, E_1 and F_1 are any real numbers.

$$\int_{A_1}^{B_1} R^{C_1} BN[D_1\ln R + E_1, F_1\ln R + G_1, H_1]\, dR = \frac{1}{C_1+1}\{B_1^{C_1+1}BN[\alpha,\beta,H_1]$$

$$- A_1^{C_1+1}BN[Y,\theta,H_1] - Integral_1 - Integral_2\}$$

where $\alpha = D_1\ln B_1 + E_1$, $\beta = F_1\ln B_1 + G_1$, $Y = D_1\ln A_1 + E_1$, $\theta = F_1\ln A_1 + G_1$[22,23]

Relationship 12

If $\ln H_u$ is normally distributed with mean $\ln H_0 + Au$ and variance $\sigma^2 u$ (for $u \in [0,T]$), then

A. $\Pr(H_T \le a, M_{0,T} \le b) = N\left[\dfrac{\ln\left(\dfrac{a}{H_0}\right) - AT}{\sigma\sqrt{T}}\right] -$

$$\left(\frac{b}{H_0}\right)^{\frac{2A}{\sigma^2}} N\left[\frac{\ln\left(\dfrac{a}{H_0}\right) - 2\ln\left(\dfrac{b}{H_0}\right) - AT}{\sigma\sqrt{T}}\right]$$

---

[22] Integral$_1$ is the integral given in Relationship 9 with $A = A_1$, $B = B_1$, $C = C_1 + 1$, $D = \dfrac{F_1 - D_1 H_1}{\sqrt{1 - H_1^2}}$,

$E = \dfrac{G_1 - E_1 H_1}{\sqrt{1 - H_1^2}}$, $\mu = -\dfrac{E_1}{D_1}$, $\sigma = \dfrac{1}{D_1}$.

[23] Integral$_2$ is the integral given in Relationship 9 with $A = A_1$, $B = B_1$, $C = C_1 + 1$, $D = \dfrac{D_1 - F_1 H_1}{\sqrt{1 - H_1^2}}$,

$E = \dfrac{E_1 - G_1 H_1}{\sqrt{1 - H_1^2}}$, $\mu = -\dfrac{G_1}{F_1}$, $\sigma = \dfrac{1}{F_1}$.

B. $\Pr(H_T \ge a,\ m_{0,T} \ge c) = N\left[\dfrac{-\ln\left(\dfrac{a}{H_0}\right) + AT}{\sigma\sqrt{T}}\right] -$

$$\left(\dfrac{c}{H_0}\right)^{\frac{2A}{\sigma^2}} N\left[\dfrac{-\ln\left(\dfrac{a}{H_0}\right) + 2\ln\left(\dfrac{c}{H_0}\right) + AT}{\sigma\sqrt{T}}\right]$$

C. $\Pr(a + \delta a \ge H_T \ge a,\ b \ge M_{0,T} > m_{0,T} \ge c) = \displaystyle\sum_{n=-\infty}^{\infty} \dfrac{1}{a} K_n(a)\delta a$

where A is a constant that is independent of H_0 and u, $M_{0,T}$ and $m_{0,T}$ represent the max (H_u) and min (H_u), respectively, for $u \in [0,T]$, $0 \le c \le a \le b < \infty$,

$$\phi(x) = \dfrac{1}{\sqrt{2\Pi}} e^{-\frac{x^2}{2}}, \text{ and}$$

$$K_n(a) = \dfrac{1}{\sigma\sqrt{T}}\left[\left(\dfrac{b}{c}\right)^{n\left(\frac{2A}{\sigma^2} - 1\right)} \phi\left(\dfrac{\ln a - \ln H_0 - 2n\ln\left(\dfrac{b}{c}\right) - \left(A - \dfrac{\sigma^2}{2}\right)T}{\sigma\sqrt{T}}\right)\right.$$

$$\left. - \left(\dfrac{c^{n+1}}{H_0 b^n}\right)^{2\left(\frac{A}{\sigma^2} - 1\right)} \phi\left(\dfrac{\ln a + \ln H_0 - 2\ln c - 2n\ln\left(\dfrac{c}{b}\right) - \left(A - \dfrac{\sigma^2}{2}\right)T}{\sigma\sqrt{T}}\right)\right]. [24]$$

In particular,

A. $\Pr(M_{0,T} \le b) = N\left[\dfrac{\ln\left(\dfrac{b}{H_0}\right) - AT}{\sigma\sqrt{T}}\right] - \left(\dfrac{b}{H_0}\right)^{\frac{2A}{\sigma^2}}\left[\dfrac{-\ln\left(\dfrac{b}{H_0}\right) - AT}{\sigma\sqrt{T}}\right]$

B. $\Pr(m_{0,T} \le c) = N\left[\dfrac{\ln\left(\dfrac{c}{H_0}\right) - AT}{\sigma\sqrt{T}}\right] + \left(\dfrac{c}{H_0}\right)^{\frac{2A}{\sigma^2}}\left[\dfrac{\ln\left(\dfrac{c}{H_0}\right) + AT}{\sigma\sqrt{T}}\right]$

C. $g_{M0,T}(b) = \begin{cases} \dfrac{2}{b\sigma\sqrt{T}\sqrt{2\Pi}} e^{-1/2\left[\frac{\ln(b/H_0) - AT}{\sigma\sqrt{T}}\right]^2} - \\[2em] \dfrac{2A}{b\sigma^2}\left(\dfrac{b}{H_0}\right)^{\frac{2A}{\sigma^2}} N\left[\dfrac{-\ln\left(\dfrac{b}{H_0}\right) - AT}{\sigma\sqrt{T}}\right] & \text{if } b > 0 \\[2em] 0 & \text{otherwise} \end{cases}$

---

[24] This result is extracted from Kumitomo and Ikeda (1992).

$$
\text{D. } g_{m_{0,T}}(c) = \begin{cases} \dfrac{2}{c\sigma\sqrt{T}\sqrt{2\Pi}}\, e^{-1/2\left[\frac{\ln(c/H_0)-AT}{\sigma\sqrt{T}}\right]^2} + \\[2ex] \dfrac{2A}{c\sigma^2}\left(\dfrac{c}{H_0}\right)^{\frac{2A}{\sigma^2}} N\left[\dfrac{\ln\left(\dfrac{c}{H_0}\right)+AT}{\sigma\sqrt{T}}\right] & \text{if } c > 0 \\[3ex] 0 & \text{otherwise} \end{cases}
$$

$$
\text{E. } g_{1st}(v) = \begin{cases} -\eta \bullet \dfrac{\ln(H/H_0)}{\sigma v\sqrt{v}\sqrt{2\Pi}}\, e^{-1/2\left[\frac{\ln(H/H_0)-Av}{\sigma\sqrt{v}}\right]^2} & \text{if } 0 < v < T \\[3ex] 0 & \text{otherwise} \end{cases}
$$

where $g_{M_{0,T}}(b)$, $g_{m_{0,T}}(c)$, $g_{1st}(v)$ represent the probability density functions of $M_{0,T}$, $m_{0,T}$ and the time taken for a geometric brownian motion process with drift A starting at H_0 to reach a level of H (also known as the first passage time), respectively. Furthermore, in the probability density function of $g_{1st}(v)$, η is 1 if $H_0 > H$ and -1 otherwise.[25]

Relationship 13

If R_1 and R_2 are any two random variables, then

$$
\Pr(R_1 > a_1, R_2 > a_2) = 1 - \Pr(R_1 \le a_1) - \Pr(R_2 \le a_2) + \Pr(R_1 \le a_1, R_2 \le a_2).
$$

Furthermore, if R_1 and R_2 are both continuously differentiable, then

$$
g_{R_1,R_2}(a_1,a_2) = \frac{\delta^2}{\delta a_1 \delta a_2}[\Pr(R_1 \le a_1, R_2 \le a_2)]
$$

where $g_{R_1,R_2}(a_1, a_2)$ represents the joint probability density function of R_1 and R_2. In general, if $R_1, \ldots, R_n$ (for $n \ge 1$) are continuously differentiable, then

$$
g_{R_1,\ldots,R_n}(a_1, \ldots, a_n) = \frac{\delta^n}{\delta a_1 \ldots \delta a_n}[\Pr(R_1 \le a_1, \ldots, R_n \le a_n)]
$$

where $g_{R_1,\ldots,R_n}(a_1, \ldots, a_n)$ represents the joint probability density function of $R_1, \ldots, R_n$.

---

[25] While $g_{M_{0,T}}(b)$ and $g_{m_{0,T}}(c)$ can be used to value derivatives with continuous look-back features, $g_{1st}(v)$ can be used to value the derivatives with continuous knock-in or knock-out features.

Relationship 14

If $f(m)$ is a continuously differentiable function in the region $m \in (a,b)$ and both functions $q(m,w)$ and $\dfrac{\delta}{\delta m}[q(m,w)]$ are continuous in the region $w \in (-\infty, f(m))$ and $m \in (a,b)$, then in this region,

$$\frac{\delta}{\delta m}\left[\int_{-\infty}^{f(m)} q(m,w)\, dw\right] = \left\{q(m,f(m)) \frac{\delta}{\delta m}[f(m)]\right\} + \int_{-\infty}^{f(m)} \frac{\delta}{\delta m}[q(m,w)]\, dw.$$

In particular, if $q(m,w)$ is $q_1(w)$ (i.e., only a function of w), then

$$\frac{\delta}{\delta m}\left[\int_{-\infty}^{f(m)} q_1(w)\, dw\right] = q_1(f(m)) \frac{\delta}{\delta m}[f(m)]$$

Relationship 15

Suppose that $q(m,w)$ and all of its partial derivatives of order less than or equal to $n + 1$ are continuous in region R that is bounded by $m \in (a,b)$ and $w \in (c,d)$. Suppose further that m_0 and w_0 are two points in R. For every m and w in R, $q(m,w)$ can be approximated by the nth degree polynomial.[26]

$$q(m_0,w_0) + \left[(m - m_0)\frac{\delta q}{\delta m}(m_0,w_0) + (w - w_0)\frac{\delta q}{\delta w}(m_0,w_0)\right]$$

$$+ \left[\frac{(m - m_0)^2}{2} \frac{\delta^2 q}{\delta m^2}(m_0,w_0) + m - m_0)(w - w_0)\frac{\delta^2 q}{\delta w \delta m}(m_0,w_0)\right.$$

$$\left. + \frac{(w - w_0)^2}{2} \frac{\delta^2 q}{\delta w^2}(m_0,w_0)\right] + \ldots$$

$$+ \left[\frac{1}{n!} \sum_{j=0}^{n} \binom{n}{j}(m - m_0)^{n-j}(w - w_0)^j \frac{\delta^n q}{\delta m^{n-j}\delta w^j}(m_0,w_0)\right]$$

In particular, if $q(m,w)$ is $q_1(w)$ (i.e., only a function of w) and this function in conjunction with its $n + 1$ derivatives is continuous in the region $w \in (c,d)$. Suppose further that w_0 is a point in the interval (c,d). For every w in the interval, $q_1(w)$ can be approximated by the nth degree polynomial.[27]

$$q_1(w_0) + (w - w_0)\frac{\delta q_1}{\delta w}(w_0) + \frac{(w - w_0)^2}{2} \frac{\delta^2 q_1}{\delta w^2}(w_0) + \ldots + \frac{1}{n!}(w - w_0)^n \frac{\delta^n q_1}{\delta w^n}(w_0)$$

---

[26] This is also known as the Taylor polynomial (or series) of degree n in two variables. See Burden and Fraires (1985).

[27] This is also known as the Taylor polynomial (or series) of degree n in one variable. See Burden and Fraires (1985). When $w_0 = 0$, this approximating polynomial is also called a Maclaurin polynomial (or series).

Relationship 16

If Y_i (for $i = 1, \ldots, n$) is normally distributed with mean μ_i and variance σ_i^2, where the correlation between Y_i and Y_j (for $i \neq j$) is ρ_{ij}, then the joint density function of $Y_1, \ldots, Y_n$ is

$$f_{Y_1, \ldots, Y_n}(y_1, \ldots, y_n) = \frac{|\Sigma_{n,n}|^{-\frac{1}{2}}}{(\sqrt{2\Pi})^n} e^{-\frac{1}{2}(Y - \mu)' \Sigma_{n,n}^{-1}(Y - \mu)}$$

where $Y' = [y_1, y_2, \ldots, y_n]$, and $\mu' = [\mu_1, \mu_2, \ldots, \mu_n]$ represent the transpose of the matrices Y and μ, respectively, $\Sigma_{n,n}$ is defined in the notation section, $y_i > 0$ $\rho_{i,j} = \rho_{j,i}$ and $|\Sigma_{n,n}| > 0$.

A. If we partition the matrices Y, μ, $\Sigma_{n,n}$ into $\begin{bmatrix} Y_{(1,\ldots,r)} \\ \hline Y_{(r+1,\ldots,n)} \end{bmatrix}$, $\begin{bmatrix} \mu_{(1,\ldots,r)} \\ \hline \mu_{(r+1,\ldots,n)} \end{bmatrix}$,

$\begin{bmatrix} \Sigma_{11,r,r} & \Sigma_{12,r,n-r} \\ \hline \Sigma_{21,n-r,r} & \Sigma_{22,n-r,n-r} \end{bmatrix}$ respectively, where $Y_{(1,\ldots,r)}$ represents the

transpose of the matrix $[Y_1, \ldots, Y_r]$, $Y_{(r+1,\ldots,n)}$ represents the transpose of the matrix $[Y_{r+1}, \ldots, Y_n]$, $\mu_{(1,\ldots,r)}$ represents the transpose of the matrix $[\mu_1, \ldots, \mu_r]$, $\mu_{(r+1,\ldots,n)}$ represents the transpose of the matrix $[\mu_{r+1}, \ldots, \mu_n]$, $\Sigma_{11,r,r}$, $\Sigma_{12,r,n-r}$, $\Sigma_{21,n-r,r}$ and $\Sigma_{22,n-r,n-r}$ are defined in the notation section.

Then the conditional distribution of $Y_{(1,\ldots,r)}$ given $Y_{(r+1,\ldots,n)}$ will also be normally distributed with mean $\mu_{(1,\ldots,r)} + \Sigma_{12,r,n-r}\Sigma_{22,n-r,n-r}^{-1}$ $[Y_{(r+1,\ldots,n)} - \mu_{(r+1,\ldots,n)}]$ and variance $\Sigma_{11,r,r} - \Sigma_{12,r,n-r}\Sigma_{22,n-r,n-r}^{-1}\Sigma_{21,n-r,r}$.

In particular, when $r = 1$ and $n = 2$, this implies that $Y = \begin{bmatrix} Y_1 \\ Y_2 \end{bmatrix}$,

$\mu = \begin{bmatrix} \mu_1 \\ \mu_2 \end{bmatrix}$, $\Sigma_{2,2} = \begin{bmatrix} \sigma_1^2 & \rho_{1,2}\sigma_1\sigma_2 \\ \rho_{1,2}\sigma_1\sigma_2 & \sigma_2^2 \end{bmatrix}$, and that $Y_{(1)}$ given $Y_{(2)}$

will also be normally distributed with mean $\mu_1 + \dfrac{\rho_{1,2}\sigma_1}{\sigma_2}[Y_2 - \mu_2]$ and variance $\sigma_1^2(1 - \rho_{1,2}^2)$.[28]

B. Since the vector Y has a multivariate normal distribution with mean μ and variance $\Sigma_{n,n}$, the vector $(\Sigma_{n,n}^{1/2})^{-1} Y$ has a multivariate normal distribution with mean $(\Sigma_{n,n}^{1/2})^{-1} \mu$ and variance I, where $\Sigma_{n,n}^{1/2}$ is a symmetric matrix such that $\Sigma_{n,n} = \Sigma_{n,n}^{1/2}\Sigma_{n,n}^{1/2}$ and I is a $(n \times n)$ identity matrix.

Furthermore, $(\Sigma_{n,n}^{1/2})^{-1}[Y - \mu]$ has a multivariate normal distribution with mean $\underline{0}$ and variance I, where $\underline{0}$ represents the $(n \times 1)$ zero vector.[29]

---

[28] Σ_{11} is σ_1^2, Σ_{12} and Σ_{21} are both $\rho_{1,2}\sigma_1\sigma_2$, Σ_{22} is σ_2^2.

[29] This is sometimes called a null vector. See Anton and Rorres (1987) and Nicholson (1985).

Relationship 17

If R_i (for $i = 1, \ldots, n$) has a multivariate joint density function $g_{1,R_1,\ldots,R_n}(r_1, \ldots, r_n)$, then

$$g_{1,R_1,\ldots,R_n}(r_1, \ldots, r_n) = g_{2,R_1,\ldots,R_i \mid R_{i+1},\ldots,R_n}(r_1, \ldots, r_n) \, g_{3,R_{i+1},\ldots,R_n}(r_{i+1}, \ldots, r_n)$$

where $g_{2,R_1,\ldots,R_r \mid R_{r+1},\ldots,R_n}(r_1, \ldots, r_n)$ represents the conditional multivariate joint density function of $R_1, \ldots, R_i$ given $R_{i+1}, \ldots, R_n$, $g_{3,R_{i+1},\ldots,R_n}(r_{i+1}, \ldots, r_n)$ represents the multivariate joint density function of $R_{i+1}, \ldots, R_n$, and $1 \leq r \leq n$. Furthermore,

$$E_{R_1,\ldots,R_n}[f(R_1, \ldots, R_n)] = E_{R_{i+1},\ldots,R_n}\{E_{R_1,\ldots,R_i \mid R_{i+1},\ldots,R_n}[f(R_1, \ldots, R_n)]\}$$

where $f(R_1, \ldots, R_n)$ is a function of $R_1, \ldots, R_n$, and $E_{R_1,\ldots,R_i \mid R_{i+1},\ldots,R_n}[f(R_1, \ldots, R_n)]$ is the expectation of the function $f(R_1, \ldots, R_n)$ taken with respect to the variables $R_1, \ldots, R_i$ when $R_{i+1}, \ldots, R_n$ are given.

Relationship 18

Let the historical prices of an asset collected over every r-day period be $P_0, P_1, \ldots, P_n$. Then under Assumptions 1 and 2, the historical annualized volatility, σ_H, of the asset price as defined in these assumptions is calculated using the formula

$$\sigma_H = \frac{\sqrt{\lambda}}{\sqrt{(n-1)r}} \left\{ \sum_{i=1}^{n} \alpha_i^2 - \frac{\left[\sum_{i=1}^{n} \alpha_i \right]^2}{n} \right\}^{\frac{1}{2}}$$

where $\alpha_i = \ln\left(\dfrac{P_i}{P_{i-1}}\right)$ and λ would typically represent 252, the number of trading days per annum.

Furthermore, if the historical prices of a second asset over the same period of time are $Q_0, Q_1, \ldots, Q_n$, then under the same set of assumptions, the historical correlation, ρ, between the continuously compounded returns in the asset prices as defined in these assumptions is calculated using the formula

$$\rho = \cfrac{\sum\limits_{i=1}^{n} \alpha_i \beta_i - \cfrac{\left[\sum\limits_{i=1}^{n} \alpha_i\right]\left[\sum\limits_{i=1}^{n} \beta_i\right]}{n}}{\sqrt{\left\{\left[\sum\limits_{i=1}^{n} \alpha_i^2 - \cfrac{\left[\sum\limits_{i=1}^{n} \alpha_i\right]^2}{n}\right]\left[\sum\limits_{i=1}^{n} \beta_i^2 - \cfrac{\left[\sum\limits_{i=1}^{n} \beta_i\right]^2}{n}\right]\right\}}}$$

where $\beta_i = \ln\left(\cfrac{Q_i}{Q_{i-1}}\right)$.[30]

---

[30] The correlation calculated using this method is the correlation between the natural logarithm of the proportionate changes in the two assets. See footnote 4.

To calculate the correlation defined in footnote 18, one would have to define $\alpha_i = \cfrac{P_i}{P_{i-1}}$ and $\beta_i = \cfrac{Q_i}{Q_{i-1}}$ before applying the formula.

⑥   GLOSSARY*

accreting cap   A cap where the notional principal amount applied to each underlying caplet increases during the life of the cap. This type of cap is the opposite of an amortizing cap.

accreting collar   A collar where the notional principal amount applied to each underlying caplet and floorlet increases during the life of the collar. This type of collar is the opposite of an amortizing collar.

accreting floor   A floor where the notional principal amount applied to each underlying floorlet increases during the life of the floor. This type of floor is the opposite of an amortizing floor.

accreting principal swap   See **accreting swap**.

accreting swap   A swap in which payments are exchanged on a notional principal amount that increases during the life of a swap. This type of swap, which is also known as accreting principal swap, accumulating swap, accumulation swap, construction loan swap, drawdown swap, escalating principal swap, escalating swap, and staged drawdown swap, is the opposite of an amortizing swap.

accrual chooser swap   This swap is a special case of an as-you-like-it swap and a generalized version of the binary chooser swap. In this type of swap, an investor could, for example, enter into a quarterly reset interest-rate swap. The investor would then choose once every quarter the daily trading range of the underlying interest-rate index (e.g., LIBOR, BA, CMT yield) for the next three months. He would receive the daily interest on the floating-rate index plus a spread only if the index sets within the selected range each day. On any day that the index falls outside the selected range, the investor would not receive any interest. In return, the investor would pay interest on a floating-rate index, which need not necessarily be the same index that is used to monitor the breaching of the barrier. This swap is less risky than a binary chooser swap.

---

*This chapter focuses on the description of derivatives instruments that trade in the marketplace. For a description of these and other financial terms, the reader is referred to *The Chase/Risk Magazine* (1996) and Gastineau (1992). Although many of the terms have been extracted from these two references, I have attempted to give my explanations for most of them.

accreting swaption   An option whose underlying asset is an accreting swap.

accumulating swap   See **accreting swap**.

accumulation swap   See **accreting swap**.

adjustable-rate instrument   Any instrument that yields the investor a return (principal plus interest) that is indexed to a standard floating reference rate(s) (e.g., three-month LIBOR, S&P 100).

adjustable-rate note   See **floating-rate note**.

adjustment swap   See **off-market swap**.

advance guarantee   See **call option**.

all-or-nothing option   See **binary option**.

alligator spread   See **butterfly spread**.

alternative currency option   A currency option that allows the purchaser to exercise into any one of the currencies of choice. For any chosen currency, there would be an appropriate strike rate associated with it. As an example, consider the purchase of an alternative currency call option on four underlying currencies. Ignoring the cost of the premium paid at the inception of the contract, the buyer would receive at option maturity an in-the-money payoff that is the maximum of [$Currency_1 - Strike_1$, $Currency_2 - Strike_2$, $Currency_3 - Strike_3$, $Currency_4 - Strike_4$]. This option is an example of a choice option.

   When there are only two currencies, an alternative currency option is also known as a dual currency option. Furthermore, in the special case when the strikes are all equal, an alternative currency option is the currency version of an alternative option.

alternative option   An option that has an in-the-money payoff that is given by the difference between the highest (or the lowest) value of the underlying assets and the strike value for a call (put) option upon exercise. This option, which is also known as an extrema option, multi-factor option, and multi-index option, can be created using the choice option.

   When there are only two underlying assets and the in-the-money payoff is of the form [max(Asset Value 1, Asset Value 2) − Strike Value], an alternative option is also known as a better-of-the-two-assets option. Furthermore, when the in-the-money payoff is of the form [Strike Value − min(Asset Value 1, Asset Value 2)], an alternative option is also known as a worse-of-two-assets option.

American option   An option that allows the purchaser to buy or sell the asset underlying the option at a prespecified price anytime during the life of the option up to and including its expiration date. This type of option, which is also known as an American-style option, cannot be cheaper than a Mid-Atlantic option.

American-Style option   See **American option**.

amortizing cap   A cap where the notional principal amount applied to each underlying caplet decreases during the life of the cap. See also **accreting cap**.

amortizing collar   A collar where the notional principal amount applied to each underlying caplet and floorlet decreases during the life of the collar. See also **accreting collar**.

amortizing floor   A floor where the notional principal amount applied to each underlying floorlet decreases during the life of the floor. See also **accreting floor.**

amortizing principal swap   See **amortizing swap**.

amortizing swap   A swap in which payments are exchanged on a notional principal amount that decreases during the life of a swap. This type of swap, which is also known as an amortizing principal swap, is the opposite of an accreting swap.

amortizing swaption   An option whose underlying asset is an amortizing swap.

annuity bond An ordinary bond-like instrument that pays the holder a fixed coupon amount at regular intervals during the life of the bond. However, unlike the bond, this fixed coupon amount contains both the principal and interest.

annuity swap Any swap in which a series of irregular cash flows are exchanged for a series of regular cash flows yielding the same present value. This type of swap is also known as a level payment swap.

anti-crash warrant A call (put) warrant whose strike value is set to a level that is prevailing at a predetermined time in the future. The level is chosen to be the maximum (minimum) of the index value at the time of issue and the index value at the predetermined time. This type of a warrant, which is also known as a partial look-back warrant, can be categorized under the look-back option building block.

arrears swap See **in-arrears swap**.

as-you-like-it option An option that allows the purchaser a choice at some prespecified time in the future between a call option with a prespecified strike and expiry date and a put option with another prespecified strike and expiry date, where both the strikes and expiry dates need not necessarily be the same. This structure, which is known as a call-or-put option, chooser option, and you-choose option, is philosophically identical to the as-you-like-it warrant.

as-you-like-it swap These interest-rate swaps are typically used by investors to achieve an above-market return by taking a view on the trading range of short-term rates. The as-you-like-it swap, which is also known as a chooser swap and you-choose swap, is a generic name that is used to describe a binary chooser swap, knock-out chooser swap, and accrual chooser swap.

as-you-like-it warrant A warrant that allows the purchaser a choice between a call warrant and a put warrant for a prespecified time. See also **as-you-like-it option**.

Asian option An option that pays the purchaser an in-the-money payoff that is the difference between the average value of the underlying variable that is calculated on predetermined dates and a prespecified strike value upon exercise, when the option finishes in-the-money. This type of option, which is also known as an average option, average price option, and averaging option, is a building block that is discussed in Chapter 3. See also **average rate option**.

asset-based swap See **asset swap**.

asset-or-nothing option An option that pays out the asset or the underlying value of the asset to the holder as long as the option finishes in-the-money on the option maturity date. This instrument is an example of a binary option. See also **cash-or-nothing option**.

asset swap A swap where the returns from one asset are exchanged for a stream of cash flows indexed to another floating reference rate and possibly denominated in a different currency. This type of swap is also known as an asset-based swap.

at-the-money (ATM) forward option An option whose strike value and time to maturity are set equal to the value of the forward contract of the asset underlying the option and the maturity of the forward contract, respectively. In an upward-sloping yield-curve environment, an ATM forward call (put) option is less expensive (more expensive) than an ATM spot call (put) option that expires at the same time, provided the asset value is an increasing function of the yield. In the event that the asset value is a bond price[1], in an upward-sloping yield curve, the forward bond price will be lower than the spot bond price.

---

[1] The price of a bond is inversely related to that of its yield.

This would in turn make an ATM forward call (put) option more expensive (less expensive) than an ATM spot call (put) option.

at-the-money (ATM) spot option   An option whose strike value is set equal to the spot value of the asset underlying the option. See also **at-the-money forward option**.

Atlantic option   See **Mid-Atlantic option**.

average cap   A collection of average caplets, which is also known as an average rate cap.

average caplet   A caplet that pays the purchaser the difference between the average of the interest rates (e.g., three-month LIBOR) over a prespecified period and a preset strike rate if the option finishes in-the-money. This caplet is an interest-rate call option variation of an Asian option.

average floor   A collection of average floorlets, which is also known as an average rate floor.

average floorlet   A floorlet that pays the purchaser the difference between a preset strike rate and the average of the interest rates (e.g., three-month LIBOR) over a prespecified period if the option finishes in-the-money. This floorlet is an interest-rate put option variation of an Asian put option.

average option   See **Asian option**.

average price option   See **Asian option**.

average rate cap   See **average cap**.

average rate floor   See **average floor**.

average rate option   An example of the Asian option when the asset underlying the option is currency. This type of option is also called a currency average rate option.

average strike option   A variation of the Asian option, in which the purchaser is paid the difference between the final value of the asset on exercise date and a strike value, which is obtained by calculating the average value of the underlying on predetermined fixing dates when the option finishes in-the-money. This option is also known as an average strike price option and floating strike option. See also **Asian option** and **average strike rate option**.

average strike price option   See **average strike option**.

average strike rate option   An example of an average strike option when the asset underlying the option is currency.

averaging option   See **Asian option**.

back bond   A bond, which in addition to being the asset underlying the option is also physically delivered upon the exercise of the option. See also **bond option**.

back contract   A futures contract that has the longest term to expiry among all the contracts currently trading.

back spread   An option strategy where the purchaser would buy and sell the same type of European-style options expiring on the same day. In this strategy, the number of options purchased would outnumber the options sold, where typically the purchased options will all be struck at one level and the sold options will all be struck at another level. Exhibit A1 illustrates the buyer's profit profile when only call options are used. Exhibit A2 illustrates the buyer's profit profile when only put options are used.[2] The seller of this strategy is also known as the purchaser of a front spread.

---

[2]   The label "Buy at a lower strike" in both these exhibits implies that a greater number of options were bought at a lower strike level. Similarly, the label "Buy at a higher strike" indicates the fact that a greater number of options were purchased at a higher strike level.

EXHIBIT A1   Call Back Spread

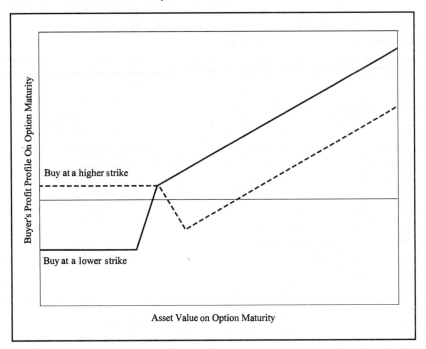

EXHIBIT A2   Put Back Spread

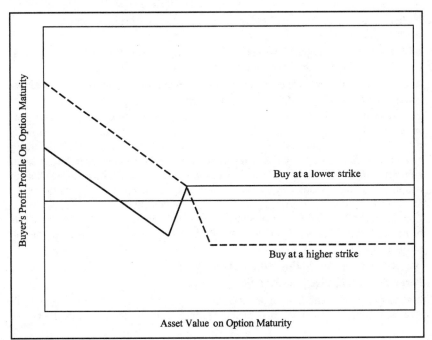

back-to-back swap A swap that is used or overlaid on an existing swap to reverse the cash flow pattern of the underlying swap in both size and timing. This type of swap is also known as a matching swap, mirror swap, reversal, and reverse.

back end set swap See **in-arrears swap**.

barrier floater A floating rate note in which either the coupon and/or the principal gets knocked out or in if the reference index underlying the note breaches a prespecified barrier level.

barrier option A vanilla option that may either come into existence or cease to exist when an asset value (not necessarily the same as the asset underlying the option contract) breaches a prespecified barrier during a prespecified time. Sometimes a rebate may be given to the purchaser of the barrier option when the underlying vanilla option does not come into existence or ceases to exist. This option, which is also called a limit option, stoption and trigger option, is an example of a sudden birth/sudden death option.

barrier-style swap See **trigger swap**.

baseball option A variation on the barrier option theme, whereby the prespecified barrier has to be breached three times during a prespecified time interval before the underlying option can cease to exist. Since the barrier has to be breached thrice before the option is extinguished, it is intuitively reasonable to expect a baseball knock-out option to be more expensive than a traditional knock-out option.

basis-rate swap See **basis swap**.

basis swap A swap in which cash flow exchanges between two parties are based on any two distinct floating-rate indexes (e.g., average prime versus LIBOR). This type of swap is also called a basis rate swap, floating-floating swap, and index swap. See also **coupon swap**.

basket A synthetic index whose value is created by bundling together a group of assets (e.g., a basket of bonds, basket of currencies, basket of stocks, basket of commodities).

basket swap A swap in which at least one of the payment streams is indexed to the total return or price return of the underlying basket.

basket option An option whose underlying asset is a basket. This option, which is discussed in Chapter 3, is also known as a portfolio option.

bear floater A floating rate note that benefits the investor as the rate underlying the note increases. This note is the opposite of a bull floater.

bear spread The purchaser of this option strategy would effectively buy a European-style call option at a higher strike and sell a European-style call option at a lower strike for the same notional amount, where both the options expire on the same day. This strategy can also be replicated by buying a European-style put option at a higher strike and selling a European-style put option at a lower strike on the same notional amount, where both the options expire on the same day. A bear spread, which is the opposite of a bull spread, is also known as floored put, limited put, put spread, and vertical bear spread. As can be seen from Exhibit A3, the more option contracts are bought and sold, the greater the resemblance of the resulting position to that of a purchase of a put option version of a cash-or-nothing option.

Bermuda option See **Mid-Atlantic option**.

Bermudan option See **Mid-Atlantic option**.

best-buy option A call (put) option that allows the purchaser the right to buy (sell) the asset underlying option at a prespecified time in the future for the lowest (highest) value

EXHIBIT A3   Bear Spread

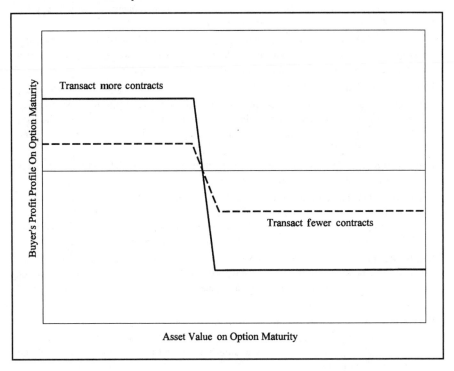

the asset realizes during a prespecified time interval, which may be a subset of the life of the option. This type of option can be categorized into either a look-back option or a partial look-back option.

bet option   See **binary option**.

better-of-two-assets option   A special case of an alternative option when there are only two underlying assets. In this type of option, the purchaser of a call option would receive an in-the-money payoff that is the difference between the maximum of the underlying asset values and a prespecified strike value upon exercise. This option, which is also known as outperformance option, can be categorized under the umbrella of a rainbow option.

binary chooser swap   This swap is a special case of an accrual chooser swap in that after selecting the trading range for the next period, the investor would receive a payoff at the end of that period that is contingent only on the interest-rate level at the end of the period. This type of swap is much riskier than an accrual chooser swap.

binary option   An option that pays out a prespecified amount of asset or cash (or both) to the purchaser as long as the option finishes in-the-money on the option maturity date. The amount paid out is independent of the in-the-moneyness of the option. This option is also known as a all-or-nothing option, asset-or-nothing option, bet option, cash-or-nothing option, digital option, and supershares option.

blended interest-rate swap   An interest-rate swap that combines at least two distinct but characteristically similar interest-rate swaps to produce a more attractive overall blended swap rate. Here, the meaning of characteristically similar implies that if one swap was a DM$ LIBOR fixed-floating rate swap, then the blended rate concept can only be applied to a pool of DM$ LIBOR fixed-floating rate swaps.

bond   A traditional debt instrument that repays interest in the form of coupons at regular intervals and principal on the maturity of the bond. This debt instrument, which is also known as a coupon bond, has a shorter duration than a bullet maturity.

bond futures   A futures contract on either a bond or a basket of bonds.

bond index swap   A swap in which the cash flows paid by one counterparty of the transaction are pegged to the total return value of the underlying bond index, while the cash flows received by the same counterparty could be pegged to either a fixed or a floating rate (e.g., three-month LIBOR).

bond option   An option whose underlying instrument is a bond. This type of option is also called a bondtion and an option-on-a-bond.

bond-over-stock (BOS) warrant   A warrant that gives its purchaser a payoff that is based on the difference between the price of a bond and the price of a prespecified quantity of stocks. This warrant can be alternatively viewed as an instrument that allows the purchaser to exchange a quantity of stocks for the bond underlying the warrant.

bond warrant   The purchaser of this warrant has the right to purchase the debt of the issuer (that may be in the form of either an equity or a bond) at some time in the future for an agreed-upon price. This is also known as a debt warrant.

bondtion   See **bond option**.

borrower's option   A call option on an interest-rate index (e.g., three-month LIBOR). This option, which is also known as a caplet, is an example of an interest-rate guarantee where the purchaser of the interest-rate guarantee has paid for the right-to-pay a fixed rate during the period of interest.

Boston option   See **break forward**.

bottom straddle   The purchaser of this strategy has bought a straddle. See also **top straddle**.

bottom vertical combination   The purchaser of this strategy has bought a strangle. See also **top vertical combination**.

box   The purchaser of this strategy would effectively be long a bull spread by purchasing and selling call options and be long a bear spread by purchasing and selling put options. The lower and upper strike levels in both the bull and bear spreads are identical and all four transacted European-style options expire at the same time. This type of strategy is also known as a box spread and time box.

box spread   See **box**.

break forward   The purchase of a vanilla currency call option that is financed by the sale of an off-the-market FX forward. This option, which is also known as a Boston option, cancellable forward, cancellable option, forward break, and forward with optional exit (FOX), has the buyer's profit profile illustrated in Exhibits A4 and A5.[3]

---

[3]   In Exhibit A4, Strategy 2 illustrates the purchase of an at-the-money call option and the sale of an FX forward, while Strategy 1 illustrates the purchase of the same option that is financed by the sale of an off-the market FX forward. Similarly, in Exhibit A5, Strategy 2 illustrates the purchase of an at-the-money put option and the purchase of an FX forward, while Strategy 1 illustrates the purchase of the same option that is financed by the purchase of an off-the market FX forward.

EXHIBIT A4 Break Forward Using a Call Option

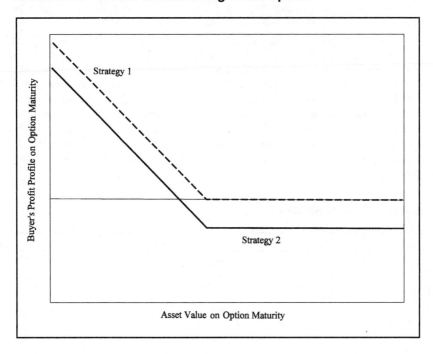

EXHIBIT A5 Break Forward Using a Put Option

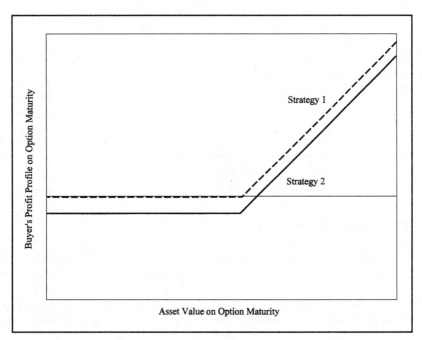

bull floater   A floating rate note that benefits the investor as the rate underlying the note decreases. See also **bear floater**. This type of note is also called an inverse floater, maximum rate note, reverse floater, and reverse floating rate note.

bull spread   The purchaser of this option strategy would effectively sell a European-style call option at a higher strike and buy a European-style call option at a lower strike for the same notional amount, where both the options expire on the same day. This strategy can also be replicated by buying a European-style put option at a lower strike and selling a European-style put option at a higher strike on the same notional amount, where both the options expire on the same day. A bull spread, which is also known as a call spread and vertical bull spread, is shown in Exhibit A6. From the exhibit it can be seen that, like the bear spread, the greater the number of transacted option contracts in a bull spread, the more the profit profile resemblance to that of a purchase of a call option version of a cash-or-nothing option.

EXHIBIT A6   Bull Spread

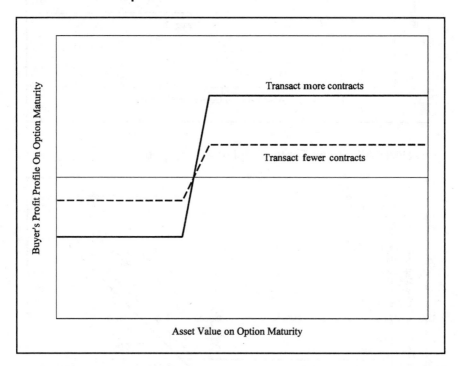

bullet maturity   See **zero-coupon bond**.

bullet swap   See **zero-coupon swap**.

bunny bond   A coupon bearing bond that allows the purchaser the right to receive the coupon payments in either cash or additional bonds that are identical to the purchased bond. This bond is also known as a guaranteed coupon reinvestment bond.

butterfly spread   The purchaser of this option strategy would effectively buy two call options struck at varying levels and sell another two call options. Both the written call options would be struck at a level that is the midpoint of the purchased options' strike levels. All the four transacted options are European-style in nature and expire simultaneously. This option strategy, which is also known as an alligator spread and a sandwich spread, is illustrated in Exhibit A7 and can alternatively be replicated using the put options.

EXHIBIT A7 Butterfly Spread

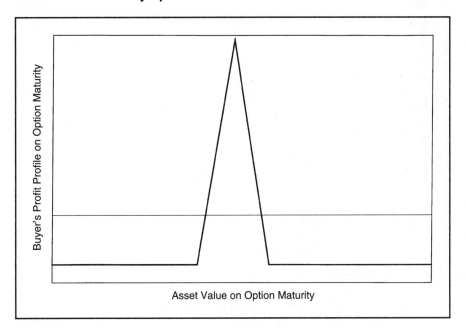

Buyer's Profit Profile on Option Maturity

Asset Value on Option Maturity

buy-write See **covered-call**.

calendar spread The purchaser of a bullish (bearish) form of this strategy would buy a European-style call option and sell another European-style call option that is struck at the same level but expiring earlier than the former option. The strike level for this strategy is chosen such that the option is in-the-money (out-of-the-money). This type of strategy, which is also known as a horizontal spread and a time spread, is illustrated in Exhibit A8 and can be replicated using put options.

call option An option that gives the purchaser the right to buy the asset underlying the option at a prespecified time(s) in the future for either a prespecified price or some function of the future asset price. For this right, the purchaser pays a premium at the inception of the contract. This type of contract is also known as an advance guarantee. See also **put option**.

call or put (COP) option See **as-you-like-it option**.

call spread See **bull spread**.

callable bond The issuer of this type of instrument has the right to repurchase the bond from the holder for a prespecified price at prespecified times in the future. See also **puttable bond**.

EXHIBIT A8   Calendar Spread

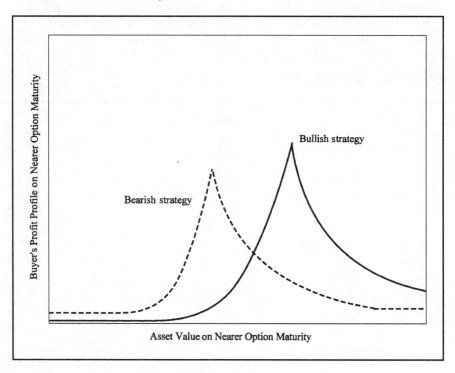

callable swap **callable swap**   A swap that allows the fixed-rate receiver the right to terminate the swap contract at prespecified times in the future. This swap is a special case of a cancelable swap. See also **puttable swap**.

cancelable forward   See **break forward**.

cancelable option   See **break forward**.

cancelable swap   A swap that allows at least one counterparty in a swap to terminate the swap at prespecified times during the life of the swap. This swap, which is also known as a retractable swap and terminable swap, is the interest-rate version of a Mid-Atlantic option whose underlying asset is a swap with a fixed maturity date. Special cases of the swap include both the callable swap and puttable swap. See also **extendable swap**.

cap   A collection of caplets that is also known as a ceiling.

cap/floor collar   See **collar**.

capital guarantee notes   A special case of an adjustable rate note where the purchaser of the note is guaranteed the full principal on maturity.

capitalized option   See **contingent premium option**.

caplet   See **borrower option**.

capped call   A long call position that caps off the holder's payoff. Provided this structure is European-style in nature and has no path-dependent features, it can be replicated by purchasing a bull spread.

capped put   A long put position that caps off the holder's payoff. Provided this structure is European-style in nature and has no path-dependent features, it can be replicated by purchasing a bear spread.

capped floater   See **capped floating-rate note**.

capped floating-rate note   A note whose coupon and/or principal is linked to the value of the index underlying the note. Despite the possibility of unlimited favorable movements in the underlying index, the investor's maximum return is capped in this type of note for a higher level of guaranteed return. This type of note is also called a capped floater.

capped index option (CAP)   This is the exchange-traded version and variation of the capped call (put) whose underlying assets are the S&P 100 and 500 indexes. Each contract comprised of two strike prices and the purchaser of a single call (put) CAP contract would effectively receive the maximum payoff as long as the upper (lower) strike level is breached during the life of the option. In the event this level is not breached prior to option maturity, the CAP would settle like a regular bull (bear) spread. Thus, a call (put) CAP contract can be viewed as a rebate paying knock-out option whose barrier level is set at the upper (lower) strike level.

capped look-back option   A look-back option that limits the buyer's upside payoff at the maturity of the option. Due to the limitation of the potential upside, this type of option will be cheaper than a look-back option.

capped option   Any option that limits the holder's upside payoff.

capped swap   Any swap whose floating-rate index (indexes) value(s) is (are) capped.

caption   An option to either purchase or sell a cap at a prespecified price during a prespecified time in the future. This product, which is an interest-rate call option variation of the compound option, is also known as an option-on-a-cap.

cash-and-carry arbitrage   A strategy in which a futures contract is sold and the asset underlying the futures contract is purchased. This strategy is used when the implied repo rate from the sale of the futures contract is greater than the market repo rate. See also **reverse cash-and-carry arbitrage**.

cash-or-nothing option   An option that pays out a fixed amount of money to the holder as long as the option finishes in-the-money. The fixed amount received by the investor would be independent of the in-the-moneyness of the option. This type of option is an example of a binary option and is a building block discussed in Chapter 3.

cash-settled option   Any option that allows the purchaser to receive cash, instead of taking delivery of the underlying asset, upon exercise.

cash flow swap   Any swap that has irregular cash flows.

ceiling   See **cap**.

choice option   An option that has in-the-money payoff such that the holder gets to choose from a predefined range of payoffs/instruments, either the best or the worst (or some combination thereof), at the time of choice. This building block is discussed in Chapter 3.

chooser option   See **as-you-like-it option**.

chooser swap   See **as-you-like-it swap**.

Christmas tree   The purchaser of this option strategy actually purchases a type of front spread, in which the options that are sold are struck at least two different levels. Exhibit A9 illustrates the buyer's profit profile when only call options are bought and sold using this

EXHIBIT A9 Call Christmas Tree

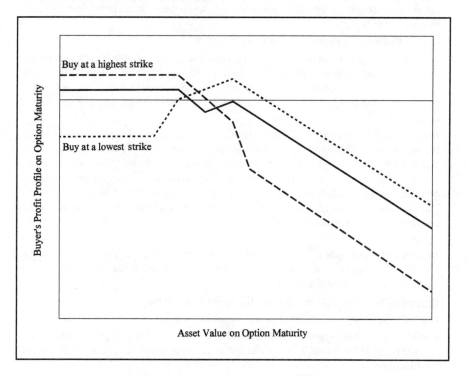

strategy. Exhibit A10 illustrates the buyer's profit profile when only put options are purchased and sold using this strategy.[4].

circus swap A simple form of a cocktail swap in which interest payments in two currencies are linked via a cross-currency basis swap and a currency swap. Although the end result is a currency swap, liquidity constraints in the underlying currency could make it uneconomical for one to directly transact into a currency swap.

cliquet option See **ratchet option**.

constant maturity treasury (CMT) – linked FRN A floating rate note (FRN) whose coupon and/or principal payments are linked to the yield of the then-prevailing on-the-run underlying treasury.

collateralized mortgage obligation (CMO) swap A swap whose amortization schedule of the notional principal is linked to the prepayment rate in a mortgage pool or tranche.

cocktail swap Any complex swap structure involving several distinct swaps spanning different currencies and counterparties.

---

[4] The label "Buy at a Highest Strike" in both the exhibits represents the fact that the underlying options were bought at the highest strike level and sold at two distinct lower levels. Similarly, the label "Buy at a lowest strike" in both the exhibits represents the fact that the underlying options were bought at the lowest strike level and sold at two distinct higher levels. Finally, the middle line with no label depicts the fact that the underlying options were bought at a level that is between the two strike levels at which the other options were sold.

EXHIBIT A10   Put Christmas Tree

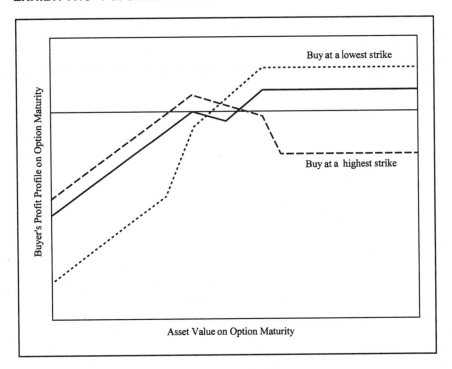

Buy at a lowest strike

Buy at a highest strike

Buyer's Profit Profile on Option Maturity

Asset Value on Option Maturity

COFI swap   Any interest-rate swap whose floating-rate index is linked to the 11th District Cost of Funds Index (COFI).

collar   Purchasing this interest-rate product is equivalent to purchasing a cap and selling a floor. This derivative strategy, which is also known as a cap/floor collar, hedge wrap, and interest-rate collar, is illustrated in Exhibit A11. While the collar also goes under the name interest-rate collar and swaption collar when the assets underlying the strategy involves swaptions, the noninterest-rate variation of this product is called a cylinder. With a floating interest-rate exposure, the purchase of this instrument would result in a net effect that is equivalent to the purchase of a bear spread.

collar swap   Any swap whose floating-rate payment is embedded with a collar and is also known as a floor-ceiling swap.

collared floater   See **collared floating-rate note**.

collared floating-rate note   A floating rate note that is embedded with a collar. This type of note is also called a collared floater.

combination option   Any strategy that involves the purchaser transacting in at least two distinct options. Examples of this type of option include a bull spread, bear spread, and straddle.

commodity futures   A futures contract whose underlying asset is a commodity.

commodity index note   A note whose coupon and/or principal is linked to the performance of the commodity price underlying the note. This type of note is also called a commodity-linked bond or commodity-linked note.

EXHIBIT A11 Collar

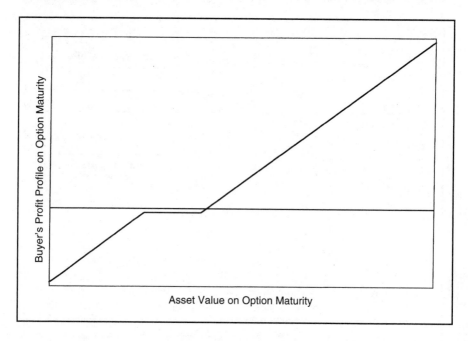

commodity-linked bond See **commodity index note**.

commodity-linked note See **commodity index note**.

commodity option An option whose underlying asset is a commodity (e.g., gold, oil, electricity).

commodity swap A swap in which at least one of the payment streams is indexed to the price of the commodity.

complex option See **exotic option**.

compound average rate option An option that allows the holder to buy or sell an average rate option for a prespecified price during a prespecified time in the future. See also **compound option**.

compound option An option that allows the holder to either buy or sell the underlying vanilla option for a prespecified price during some prespecified time in the future. This option, which is also known as a split-fee option, installment option, option-on-an-option, and pay-as-you-go option, is a building block that is discussed in Chapter 3. See also **caption** and **floortion**.

conditional forward purchase contract The purchaser of this forward agreement has the right to cancel the purchase by paying a fee to the seller on the maturity of the contract. Instead of choosing to possibly pay and cancel the contract, the purchaser could alternatively buy a below-market forward rate, which would allow for the cancellation of the contract of purchase with no cash.

conditional forward sale contract The seller of this forward agreement has the right to cancel the sale by paying a fee to the purchaser on the maturity of the contract. Instead of choosing to possibly pay and cancel the contract, the seller could alternatively sell an above-market forward rate, which would allow for the cancellation of the contract of sale with no cash.

condor The purchaser of this strategy would effectively purchase an out-of-the-money strangle and sell an even further out-of-the-money strangle, where both strangles would expire at the same time (see Exhibit A12).

EXHIBIT A12 Condor

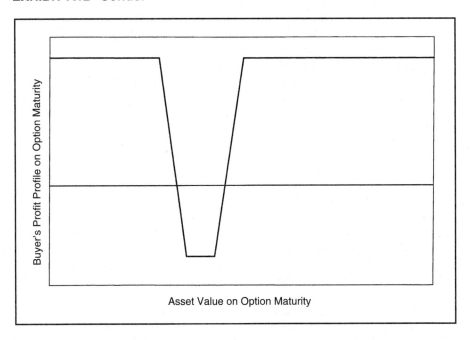

constant maturity swaps (CMS) An interest rate swap in which at least one of the payment streams is indexed to the then-prevailing on-the-run swap rate of a prespecified term. See also **constant maturity treasury swaps**.

constant maturity treasury See **consant maturity treasury swaps**.

constant maturity treasury swaps (CMT) An interest-rate swap in which at least one of the payment streams is indexed to the then-prevailing on-the-run bond yield of a prespecified term. This type of swap is also known as a constant maturity treasury. See also **constant maturity swaps**.

constant maturity treasury (CMT) option A cap (floor) structure that would pay out if the then prevailing on-the-run underlying treasury yield rises above (below) a prespecified strike rate at each option reset date.

construction loan swap See **accreting swap**.

contingent cap Since a cap is a collection of caplets, the purchaser of a contingent cap pays premiums only for the caplets that finish in-the-money. As long as a caplet finishes out-of-the-money, the purchaser does not have to pay any premium. Although it is reasonable to expect these premiums to differ for each caplet due to the yield curve and volatility influences, the market practice is to level off these uneven conditional premiums. Thus, the purchaser could expect to pay the same amount of conditional premium regardless of the maturity of the caplet. This product, which is also known as a pay-later cap, is an interest-rate version of the contingent premium option.

contingent floor   Since a floor is a collection of floorlets, the purchaser of a contingent floor pays premiums only for the floorlet that finish in-the-money. As long as a floorlet finishes out-of-the-money, the purchaser does not have to pay any premium. Although it is reasonable to expect these premiums to differ for each floorlet due to the yield curve and volatility influences, the market practice is to level off these uneven conditional premiums. Thus, the purchaser could expect to pay the same amount of conditional premium regardless of the maturity of the floorlet. This product, which is also known as a pay-later floor, is an interest-rate version of the contingent premium option.

contingent option   See **contingent premium option**.

contingent premium option   An option that does not require the purchaser to pay the premium at the inception of the contract. Instead, the premium is paid on the maturity date only when the option finishes in-the-money. This option is also known as a capitalized option, contingent option, pay-later option, and pay-only-if-you-need option. See also **deferred premium option**.

   The purchaser of this European-style option can equivalently replicate the position by going long a European-style option and shorting a European-style cash-or-nothing option. This option would have a bet payout that is equivalent in size to the conditional premium that needs to be paid if the contingent premium option finished in-the-money.

contingent premium swaption   A contingent premium option that has a swap as the underlying asset. This type of option is also known as a pay-later swaption.

contingent swap   See **trigger swap**.

contingent takedown option   An option that is usually embedded in a bond and allows the holder to purchase another bond of similar coupon for a prespecified price at a prespecified time.

convertible bond   A company-issued bond that allows the purchaser the ability to exchange the bond for the company's shares at a prespecified time(s) in the future for a prespecified price(s).

convertible option contract   A hybrid of a nonrebate-paying knock-out option and a FX forward. In this variation, as the currency rate breaches the barrier during the life of the option, the existing currency option is knocked out and a FX forward expiring on the same date knocks in.

corridor   Purchasing this interest-rate product is equivalent to purchasing a cap and selling another cap that is struck at a different rate but maturing at the same time. This is a cost-reducing hedging strategy that gives interest-rate protection between the two strikes. See also **flooridor**.

costless collar   A collar that costs the purchaser nothing to enter into. This strategy is also called a forward band, free collar, no-cost collar, zero collar, and a zero-cost collar.

costless option   An option strategy that does not cost the purchaser anything to enter into. This strategy, which is also called a no-cost option, premium-free option, and zero-cost option, can only be achieved if the purchaser of the option also sells away part of the upside so as to finance the purchase.

coupon bond   See **bond**.

coupon swap   A traditional interest-rate swap between two counterparties, where only interest cash flows are exchanged on a preagreed notional principal amount at prespecified frequencies. The payment from one party is calculated using a fixed interest rate (also called a swap rate), while the payment from the second party is calculated using a floating interest-rate index during the life of the swap. This swap is also called a fixed-floating swap, interest-rate index swap, and interest-rate swap.

covered call   The purchaser of this strategy would effectively sell a European-style call option on an asset and purchase the asset underlying option. This strategy, which is also known as a buy-write, is illustrated in Exhibit A13. See also **covered put**.

EXHIBIT A13   Covered Call

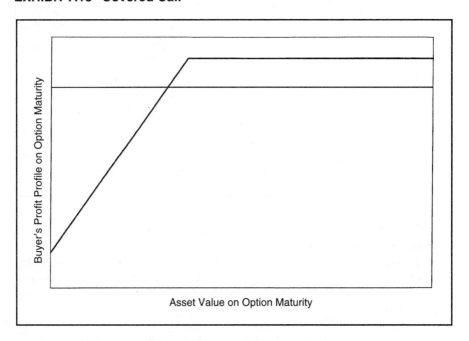

covered put   The purchaser of this strategy would effectively sell a European-style put option and sell the asset underlying the option. This strategy, which is also known as a sell-write, is illustrated in Exhibit A14.

covered write   An option strategy that is no different in outcome than a buy-write strategy. The only philosophical difference between this strategy and the buy-write is that in a covered write strategy, there is a time lag between the sale of the option and the purchase of the underlying asset, in that the former lags the latter. On the other hand, in a buy-write strategy, the underlying asset is purchased at the same time the option is sold and consequently there is no time lag between the two events. This type of strategy is sometimes also known as an overwrite.

cross-currency basis swap   A variation on the traditional currency swap in which the interest payments exchanged are indexed to the two floating rate indexes. As in the traditional currency swap, the notional principals get exchanged both at the inception and the maturity of the swap. See also **circus swap**.

cross-currency cap   See **diff cap**.

EXHIBIT A14 Covered Put

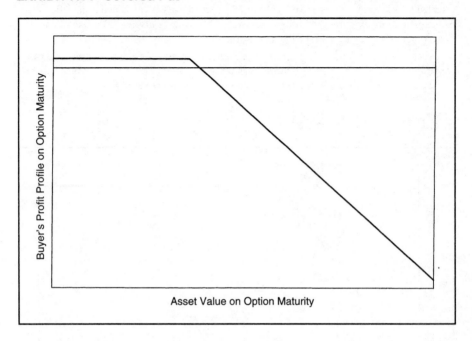

cross-currency coupon swap   See currency swap.

cross-currency floor   See diff floor.

cross-currency option   The purchaser of this option will receive a regular option payoff in a currency that is different from the asset underlying the option. The premium to purchase this protection is denominated in the same currency as the payoff. Examples of this type of option include the diff cap, diff floor, and quanto.

cross-currency swap   See currency swap.

cross-currency swaption   An option whose underlying instrument is a currency swap.

cross-indexed basis (CRIB) swap   See diff swap.

cross-rate option   A currency option whose underlying currency unit does not have a liquid market. For example, the Cad/US exchange rate market is a liquid one, unlike the Cad/Peso exchange rate market. Thus, a currency option on Cad/Peso is an example of cross-rate option.

cross-rate swap   See diff swap.

cumulative cap   In a traditional interest-rate cap, the settlement of the in-the-money payoff is done periodically (e.g., once every quarter). In a cumulative cap, however, the settlement is done once over a collection of periods. Thus, this type of instrument can be thought of as hedging the total interest expense during these specified periods. Due to the nature of cumulation, this type of instrument is cheaper than buying a traditional cap. Furthermore, buying this has an impact that is similar to an average rate cap.

currency average rate option   See average rate option.

currency coupon swap   See currency swap.

currency exchange warrants   A warrant that entitles the holder to purchase units of currency at a prespecified exchange rate on a prespecified date in the future.

currency forward   See **FX forward**.

currency futures   A futures contract whose underlying asset is currency.

currency-linked note   A note whose coupon and/or principal is linked to the performance of the currency underlying the note.

currency option   An option whose underlying asset is currency.

currency protected swap (CUPS)   See **diff swap**.

currency swap   An agreement between two counterparties, where the interest cash flows are exchanged on a preagreed notional principal amounts at prespecified frequencies using either a fixed-fixed rate or a fixed-floating rate. For example, the payment from one party is calculated using a fixed domestic interest rate in domestic currency, while the payment from the second party is calculated using a floating foreign interest-rate index in foreign currency during the life of the swap. The appropriate notional principals are first swapped at the inception of the contract and then swapped back on the maturity of the swap. This type of swap is also called a cross-currency coupon swap, cross-currency swap, currency coupon swap, and currency swap agreement.

   In other variations of the currency swap, it is possible for the principals to be exchanged only on the inception of the swap contract or the maturity of the swap contract. See also **cross-currency basis swap**.

currency swap agreement   See **currency swap**.

currency swap option   An option whose underlying asset is a currency swap. This type of option is also called a currency swaption.

currency swaption   See **currency swap option**.

cylinder   This is the noninterest-rate variation of a collar. This strategy, which is also called a fence, fence spread, flexible forward, forward rate bracket, range forward, and tunnel, is illustrated in Exhibit A11.

debt warrant   See **bond warrant**.

decline guarantee   See **put option**.

deferred-coupon bond   Unlike a traditional bond, this debt instrument does not pay any coupon during the first few years of the bond and then pays high coupons during the rest of the bond life. The principal, as usual, is repaid on the bond maturity date. This type of bond, which can be thought of as an intermediary between a bond and a zero-coupon bond, is also known as a deferred-interest bond.

deferred-coupon swap   Unlike a traditional coupon swap, this does not allow for the exchange of interest payments during the first few years of the swap. Instead the compounding of payments during the early years, in addition to the regular interest cash flow exchanges, is done during the rest of swap. This type of swap, which can also be thought of as an intermediary between a coupon swap and a zero-coupon swap, is also called a deferred swap and is analogous to the deferred bond. This swap is unlike a delayed start swap, in which the entire swap is deferred until a prespecified time in the future.

deferred-interest bond   See **deferred coupon bond**.

deferred-payment American option   An American-style option that upon exercise by the purchaser gets settled on the option maturity date. This type of option is also known as a deferred-payout option.

deferred-payment bond A bond that although purchased today is only paid for by the investor at some time in the future.

deferred-payout option See **deferred payment American option**.

deferred-premium option The purchaser of a deferred premium option would pay the premium for the instrument at the time of option exercise instead of traditionally paying at the inception of the option contract. This type of option is different in philosophy from a contingent premium option, where the purchaser pays the premium on option maturity only if the option finishes in-the-money. Due to the nonconditional nature of the premium paid out by the purchaser for this type of option, it is intuitively reasonable to expect this amount to be lower than that paid out for the purchase of a contingent premium option.

deferred-start option See **deferred-strike option**.

deferred-strike option This option typically has two types of strikes (a floating and a fixed one) attached to the payoff of the option. While the fixed component, if present, is set at the inception of the contract, the floating strike gets set at some prespecified time in the future, prior to option maturity. Furthermore, the mechanism used to set this strike value could be dependent on the path transversed by the asset value prior to the setting date. This type of option is also called a deferred-start option, deferred-strike price option, forward start option, and a moving strike option.

deferred-strike price option See **deferred-strike option**.

deferred swap See **deferred-coupon swap**.

delayed LIBOR reset swap See **in-arrears swap**.

delayed reset swap See **in-arrears swap**.

delayed-start swap Any swap that starts at a prespecified time in the future. This type of swap, which is also known as a forward start swap and forward swap, is unlike the deferred coupon swap, which although starting today, has its coupons compounded and paid out sometime in the future.

deleveraged FRN A floating rate note that only pays out a percentage of the upside. Since this return is usually less than 100 percent, in addition to participating on the upside, the purchaser would either receive a spread above the floating rate index or a higher percentage of guaranteed principal and/or coupons.

derivative Any contractual agreement to exchange cash flows using the future value of underlying assets on a specified notional amount without actually trading the underlying. These can be traded either in the exchange or the over-the-counter market.

detachable warrant Any warrant that although originally issued with a security (e.g., a bond), can be detached and traded separately and independently of the security.

diagonal bear spread The purchaser of this strategy would sell a short-dated European-style call option and buy a long-dated European-style call option at a higher strike. This strategy, which can also be replicated by buying and selling European-style put options, is illustrated in Exhibit A15.[5]

---

[5] Strategy 1 of Exhibit A15 illustrates the fact that a long-dated at-the-money call option was purchased and a shorter-dated out-of-the-money call option was sold by the purchaser of this strategy. Similarly, Strategy 2 illustrates the purchase and the sale of the options when the difference in the strike values is decreased. This indicates that as the spread between the two strikes narrows, the graph under Strategy 1 will converge to that under Strategy 2.

EXHIBIT A15 Diagonal Bear Spread

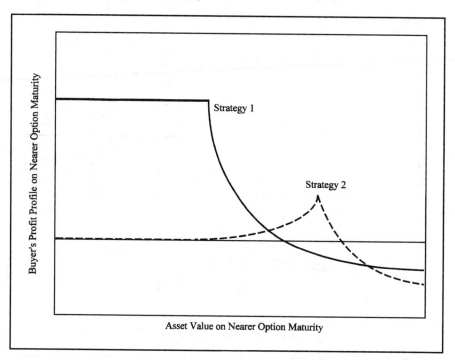

diagonal bull spread   The purchaser of this strategy would sell a short-dated European-style call option and buy a long-dated European-style call option at a lower strike. This strategy, which can also be replicated by buying and selling European-style put options, is illustrated in Exhibit A16.[6]

diff cap   The purchaser of this cap will receive a regular cap in-the-money payoff in a currency that is different from that of the underlying interest-rate index. The premium to purchase this protection is usually denominated in the same currency as the payoff. This cap, which is also known as a cross-currency cap and differential cap, is a special example of a cross-currency option.

diff floor   The purchaser of this floor will receive a regular floor in-the-money payoff in a currency that is different from that of the underlying interest-rate index. The premium to purchase this protection may be denominated in the same currency as the payoff. This floor, which is also known as a cross-currency floor, differential floor, is a special example of a cross-currency option.

diff swap   A variation on the currency swap theme between two counterparties, where the interest cash flows are exchanged on a preagreed notional principal amount at prespecified

---

[6]Strategy 1 of Exhibit A16 illustrates the fact that a long-dated out-of-the-money call option was purchased and a shorter-dated at-the-money call option was sold by the purchaser of this strategy. Similarly, Strategy 2 illustrates the purchase and the sale of the options when the difference in the strike values is decreased. This indicates that as the difference decreases, the graph under Strategy 1 will converge to that under Strategy 2.

EXHIBIT A16 Diagonal Bull Spread

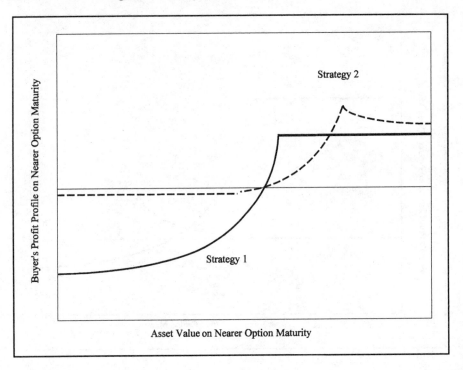

Asset Value on Nearer Option Maturity

(y-axis label: Buyer's Profit Profile on Nearer Option Maturity)

(graph labels: Strategy 2, Strategy 1)

frequencies. The payment from one party is calculated using either a fixed or floating domestic interest-rate in domestic (foreign) currency, while the payment from the second party is calculated using either a fixed or floating foreign interest-rate index in domestic (foreign) currency during the life of the swap. Unlike a traditional currency swap, there is no exchange of notional principal in this swap. This type of swap is also called a cross-indexed basis swap, cross-rate swap, currency protected swap, differential swap, and rate differential swap.

difference option   An option that allows the purchaser to exchange one asset for another asset plus cash. This option, which is also known as a dual option, spread option, and a spreadtion, is a building block discussed in Chapter 3. When the cash element is absent, this type of option is also called an exchange option.

difference swap   See **diff swap**.

differential cap   See **diff cap**.

differential floor   See **diff floor**.

differential swap   See **diff swap**.

digital option   See **biary option**.

discount swap   An example of an off-market swap in which the receiver of the fixed rate gets fixed payments based on a below-market rate. The difference between the market fixed rate and the transacted fixed rate is compounded and paid out to the receiver of the fixed-rate payments on the maturity of the swap.

discrete exercise option   See **Mid-Atlantic option**.

double barrier option   A variation of the barrier option when there are two barriers. In this variation, if the value of an asset (not necessarily the same as the asset underlying the option contract) starts between the barriers, then the underlying vanilla option comes into existence or ceases to exist as soon as one of the barriers is breached. Sometimes, a rebate may be given to the purchaser of a double barrier option when the underlying vanilla option does not come into existence or cease to exist. See also **double knock-in option** and **double knock-out option.**

double knock-in option   A special case of the double barrier option, in which the underlying vanilla option starts to exist as soon as any one of the barriers is breached. Sometimes, a rebate may be given to the purchaser if the option does not come into existence before the prespecified time. See also **double knock-out option.**

double knock-out option   A special case of the double barrier option, in which the underlying vanilla option ceases to exist as soon as any one of the barriers is breached. Sometimes, a rebate may be given to the purchaser at the time the option is knocked out. See also **double knock-in option.**

down-and-in option   An example of a barrier option where the underlying vanilla option comes into existence when the asset (not necessarily the same as the asset underlying the option contract) value has to transverse downwards to breach a prespecified barrier during a prespecified time. In the event the barrier is not breached, the purchaser of the down-and-in option does not receive anything. Sometimes a down-and-in option may be structured in a way that when the barrier is not breached, the purchaser of the option would receive a rebate on the option expiry date.

down-and-out option   An example of a barrier option where the underlying vanilla option ceases to exist when the asset (not necessarily the same as the asset underlying the option contract) value has to transverse downwards to breach a prespecified barrier during a prespecified time. In the event the barrier is not breached, the down-and-out option gets settled like a vanilla option. Sometimes a down-and-out option may be structured in a way that when the barrier is breached, the purchaser of the option would receive a rebate at the time the barrier is breached.

drawdown swap   See **accreting swap.**

drop-lock floating-rate note   A floating-rate note that is converted to a fixed-rate note when the index underlying the note drops to a preset level during a prespecified time.

drop-lock swap   This is a variation of the delayed start swap where the fixed rate of the delayed start swap gets reset by an agreed amount should the fixed rate of an identical swap starting and maturing at the same time change by a prespecified amount during a prespecified time.

dual coupon swap   A coupon swap in which one party of the swap has the option to choose the currency in which the interest payments of the swap get settled on each coupon date. Typically, the choice is made between the base currency and another alternative currency.

dual currency bond   A bond in which the coupon is paid in the base currency of the investor and the principal is paid in the base currency of the issuer. To purchase such a bond, the investor would pay a dollar amount denominated in the issuer's currency, where the base currencies of both the investor and the issuer are different.

dual currency option   An example of an alternative currency option, when there are only two underlying currencies.

dual currency swap   A currency swap (or a variation on the cross-currency coupon swap theme) that is purchased by the issuer to hedge the coupon payments in a dual currency bond back into the currency of the issuer.

dual option   See **exchange option**.

dual option bond   A bond with an embedded option. More precisely, this option allows the purchaser of the bond to receive both the coupons and the principal payment in the currency of choice.

dual strike option   See **exchange option**.

duet bond   A bond whose interest and principal payments are indexed to the value of the exchange rate on the payment dates.

electricity forward agreement   Like a forward rate agreement, this agreement allows a party of the contract to be guaranteed a price for the drawdown of electric power for a pre-specified period in the future up to a maximum capacity.

embedded option   An option that is embedded in a note or debt instrument. This type of option is also known as an embeddo and a latent option.

embeddo   See **embedded option**.

equity index-linked note   A note whose coupon and/or principal is linked to the value of the equity index underlying the note. This type of note is also called an equity index participation note, equity linked note, equity participation note, guaranteed return index participation, index participation certificate, index principal return note, market indexed note, and protected equity note. An equity-linked note can also be alternatively thought of as an equity linked adjustable rate note.

equity index participation note   See **equity index-linked note**.

equity index swap   A swap in which at least one of the payment streams is indexed to the total return or price return of the underlying equity index. This type of swap is also called an equity-linked swap and equity swap.

equity index warrant   A warrant that entitles the holder to purchase shares of the issuing company for a prespecified price at a prespecified time in the future. This type of warrant is also called an equity warrant.

equity-linked foreign exchange option   The purchaser of this currency option would have effectively purchased a foreign equity with a limit on the currency exposure and received an in-the-money option payoff in a currency that is different from that of the asset underlying the option. The premium required to purchase this protection is usually denominated in the same currency as the payoff, and the exchange rate applied for converting the payoff into another currency is the value of the currency (strike rate of the currency option) on the option maturity date if the option finishes out-of-the-money (in-the-money). This is the equity-linked version of the Category V option type that was discussed under the product option building block in Chapter 3.

equity-linked note   See **equity index-linked note**.

equity-linked swap   See **equity index swap**.

equity participation note   See **equity index-linked note**.

equity swap   See **equity index swap**.

equity warrant   See **equity index warrant**.

escalating principal swap   See **accreting swap**.

escalating rate swap   Any swap in which the fixed-rate payments increase over time due to an increasing fixed rate. This type of swap, which is also known as a step-up coupon swap, is the opposite of a step-down coupon swap.

escalating swap See **accreting swap**.

European option An option that allows the purchaser to buy or sell the asset underlying the option at a prespecified price or some related function of the asset price on its expiration date. This type of option, which is also called a European-style option, cannot be more expensive than a Mid-Atlantic option, which in turn cannot be more expensive than an American option.

European-style option See **European option**.

exchange option A special case of a difference option when there is no cash component. More precisely, the purchaser of this option has the right to exchange one asset for another asset on the date of exercise. This type of option is also called a dual option, dual strike option, margrabe option, and switch option.

exchange-rate agreement (ERA) A currency exchange agreement between two parties that is based on the difference in the values between the guaranteed rate at the inception of the contract and the forward rate at the maturity of the contract. The forward rate used in the settlement is the rate applied to the same length of time (i.e., life of ERA).

exotic option Any option with a more complicated payoff than a vanilla option. This type of option is also called a complex option, nonvanilla option, nonstandard option, and second generation option.

extendible swap A swap that allows the fixed-rate payer the right to extend at prespecified times in the future. This swap is the interest-rate version of a Mid-Atlantic option, whose underlying asset is a fixed-tenor swap. See also **cancellable swap**.

extension swap A swap that, when implemented, will start on the day the currently existing swap expires.

extinguishable option An option that ceases to exist only if the price(s) of an asset and/or a combination of assets (not necessarily the same asset underlying the option) satisfies a prespecified condition(s). This type of option, which is also called a sudden death option, out option, and vanishing option, is a building block discussed in Chapter 3. See also **in option**.

extrema option See **alternative option**.

fairway option A variation on the cash-or-nothing option theme in which the option has a settlement value only if the price of the asset underlying the option trades within a range (or the fairway) during a prespecified time. Typically, this settlement value would be a cash amount that would be paid out at the end of the option maturity depending on the proportion of days the asset traded in the fairway.

fence See **cylinder**.

fence spread See **cylinder**.

fixed exchange-rate foreign equity option The purchaser of this option on a foreign equity will receive an option payoff in a currency that is different from that of the asset underlying the option. The premium required to purchase this protection is denominated in the same currency as the payoff. The exchange rate applied for converting the payoff into another currency is prespecified at the inception of the contract, and typically an exchange rate of unity is applied for this conversion. This option is the Category II type product option discussed in Chapter 3. See also **guaranteed exchange-rate option**.

fixed-fixed currency swap A special case of the currency swap, where the payment from the first party is calculated using a fixed rate in domestic currency while the payment from the second party is calculated using another fixed rate in foreign currency during the life of the swap. The appropriate notional principals are first swapped at the inception of the contract and then swapped back on the maturity of the swap.

fixed-floating swap   See **coupon swap**.

flexible cap   The purchaser of a traditional cap would have bought the right to exercise all the underlying caplets. The purchaser of a flexible cap, on the other hand, would have bought the right to exercise only a predefined number of caplets. Because of the ability to exercise only a subset of the caplets, a flexible cap will be cheaper than a traditional cap. Furthermore, if the predefined number of caplets is exactly equal to the total number of the caplets underlying a cap, the value of a flexible cap will be the same as that of a cap. See also **rent-a-cap**.

flexible floor   The purchaser of a traditional floor would have bought the right to exercise all the underlying floorlets. The purchaser of a flexible floor, on the other hand, would have bought the right to exercise only a predefined number of floorlets. Because of the ability to exercise only a subset of the floorlets, a flexible floor will be cheaper than a traditional floor. Furthermore, if the predefined number of floorlets is exactly equal to the total number of the floorlets underlying a floor, the value of a flexible floor will be the same as that of a floor. See also **rent-a-floor**.

flexible forward   See **cylinder**.

floating-floating swap   See **basis swap**.

floating-rate note   A note whose coupon and/or principal is linked to the value of the asset underlying the note. Typically, a percentage of the principal component in such a note is guaranteed at the inception of the contract and is independent of the value of the asset. This type of note is also called an adjustable-rate note.

floating strike option   See **average strike option**.

floor   A collection of floorlets.

floor-ceiling swap   See **collar swap**.

floored put   See **bear spread**.

flooridor   Purchasing this interest-rate product is equivalent to purchasing a floor and selling another floor that is struck at a different level but maturing at the same time. This is a cost-reducing hedging strategy that gives interest-rate protection between the two strikes. See also **corridor**.

floorlet   A put option on an interest-rate index (e.g., LIBOR, BA, PIBOR). This option, which is also known as a lender's option, is a special case of an interest-rate guarantee, where the purchaser has paid for the right to receive a fixed rate.

floortion   An option to either purchase or sell a floor at a prespecified price during a prespecified time in the future. This product, which is an interest-rate put option variation of the compound option, is also known as an option-on-a-floor and a rent-a-floor.

forward currency bond   A variation on the dual currency bond theme, in which both the coupons and the principal of the bond are repaid to the holder in a currency that is different from that used to purchase the bond.

forward   See **FX forward**.

forward band   See **costless collar**.

forward break   See **break forward**.

forward cap   See **periodic cap**.

forward currency swap A hybrid of a currency swap and a delayed start swap. In this variation, the currency swap starts at some prespecified time in the future.

forward exchange agreement A currency exchange agreement between two parties that is based on the difference in the values between the forward rate at the inception of the contract and the spot rate on the maturity of the contract. This type of agreement, which is also called a forward exchange-rate agreement, can be thought of as the currency version of a forward rate agreement. See also **FX forward**.

forward exchange-rate agreement (FXA) See **forward exchange agreement**.

forward floor See **periodic floor**.

forward outright rate See **FX forward**.

forward plus A variation of the cylinder, in which the purchaser of the strategy would effectively purchase and/or sell participating options so as to participate in either/or both the downside and the upside. This type of contract, which is also called a participating range forward, is illustrated in Exhibit A17.[7]

EXHIBIT A17 Forward Plus

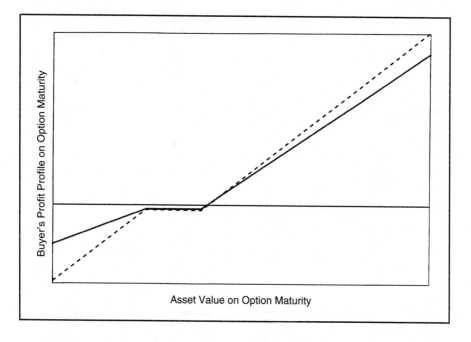

Asset Value on Option Maturity

Buyer's Profit Profile on Option Maturity

forward point agreement A special case of a diff swap in which interest payments are exchanged only once. The forward point agreement, which can alternatively be thought of as a single-period diff swap, is also called a forward spread agreement.

---

[7]The dotted line in Exhibit A17 shows a graph of the buyer's payoff when a cylinder is purchased. The solid line illustrates the fact that the buyer of the strategy has effectively given up a portion of upside for a lower participation of the downside.

forward rate agreement (FRA) A special case of a coupon swap in which interest payments are exchanged only once. The forward rate agreement, which is also known as a future rate agreement, can alternatively be thought of as a single-period coupon swap. Typically, in these type of contracts, the counterparties tend to cash-settle the difference in interest payments on contract maturity dates.

forward rate bracket See **cylinder**.

forward spread agreement See **forward point agreement**.

forward start agreement Any agreement that starts at a prespecified time in the future. Examples of this contract include the forward point agreement and the forward rate agreement.

forward start option See **deferred strike option**.

forward start swap See **delayed start swap**.

forward swap See **delayed start swap**.

forward with optional exit (FOX) See **break forward**.

fration See **interest-rate guarantee**.

free collar See **costless collar**.

front contract The most liquid short-term contract as designated by the members of the futures exchange. As the near-month contract approaches expiry, the next contract will be designated the front contract.

front spread In this strategy, more option contracts are sold than are purchased. The seller of this strategy would be the purchaser of a back spread. This strategy is also known as the ratio vertical spread.

futures contract An obligation to buy or sell a prespecified amount of currency/commodity/interest-rate/index for a prespecified price at a prespecified time in the future in an exchange.

future rate agreement See **forward rate agreement**.

futures option An option whose underlying asset is a futures contract. This type of option is also known as a futures-style option and an option-on-a-future.

futures-style option See **futures option**.

FX forward An agreement that obligates two parties to exchange a specified amount of one currency for another at a prespecified rate on a prespecified date in the future. This type of agreement is also called a currency forward, forward, forward outright rate, outright, and outright forward.

G-hedge A special case of a collar, where the strike rates of both the cap and the floor are symmetrical about the forward rates.

generic swap See **vanilla swap**.

gold-linked note A note whose coupons and/or principal is linked to the price of gold.

gold warrant A warrant that entitles the holder to purchase an ounce of gold for a prespecified price at a prespecified time in the future.

guaranteed coupon reinvestment bond See **bunny bond**.

guaranteed exchange-rate option The purchaser of this option on a foreign instrument (e.g., bond, equity index, commodity) will receive an option payoff in a currency that is different from that of the asset underlying the option. The premium to purchase this protection is denominated in the same currency as the payoff. The exchange rate applied for converting the payoff into another currency is prespecified at the inception of the contract and is usually unity. This type of option, which is described as a Category II product option in Chapter 3, is also an example of a quanto.

When the underlying asset class is equity, this option is also called a fixed exchange-rate foreign equity option.

guaranteed exchange-rate warrant A warrant that entitles the domestic investor to purchase units of foreign equity indexes for a prespecified price at a prespecified time in the future using a guaranteed exchange rate. The rate used in guaranteeing the exchange rate is prespecified at the inception of the contract.

guaranteed investment contract (GIC) A note that is usually issued by insurance companies and banks to the retail market.

guaranteed return index participation See **equity index-linked note**.

guts A special case of a strangle where the call and put option contracts that are purchased are both in-the-money. This strategy, which is also known as a mambo combo, is illustrated in Exhibit A18.

EXHIBIT A18 Guts

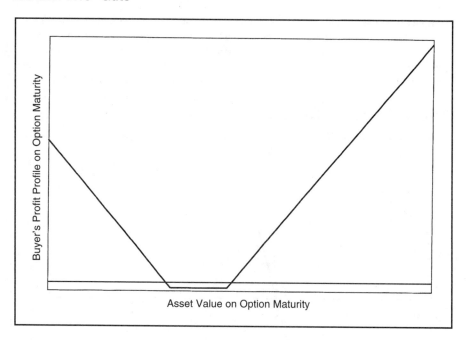

harmless warrant A warrant that has no value to the issuer of the debt. More precisely, when exercised, this warrant never results in more debt to the issuer.

heaven and hell bond A bond in which the principal amount repaid is linked to the value of the exchange rate on the maturity of the bond.

hedge wrap See **collar**.

high-coupon swap   A special case of an off-market swap where the receiver of the fixed rate receives fixed payments based on above-market coupon rates. For receiving these rates, the receiver of the floating-rate payment receives an up-front compensation. See also **discount swap**.

high-low option   The purchaser of this option would receive an in-the-money payoff that is the difference between the range value (i.e., maximum value realized by the asset during the period of interest minus the minimum value realized by the asset during the period of interest) and the strike value. The payoff arising from this option cannot be perfectly replicated by simply purchasing the appropriate call and put look-back options. This type of option is also known as a range option.

hindsight option   See **look-back option**.

horizontal spread   See **calendar spread**.

IMM swap   A money-market interest-rate swap whose cash flow dates match those of the Eurodollar futures contracts that trade on the International Monetary Market (IMM). However, the floating rate for each date is set using market conventions and not the settlement rate of the futures contract, thereby introducing a basis risk. This type of swap is also called a money-market swap.

impact forward   A collared forward, in which the purchaser in addition to buying a FX forward, also buys a European-style put option and sells a European-style call option, both of which are out of the money. The premiums on the two options balance out to arrive at a zero cost structure, and both the options expire on the day the forward gets settled. The upside and the downside is limited to the gap between the strike prices. See Exhibit A19.

EXHIBIT A19   Impact Forward

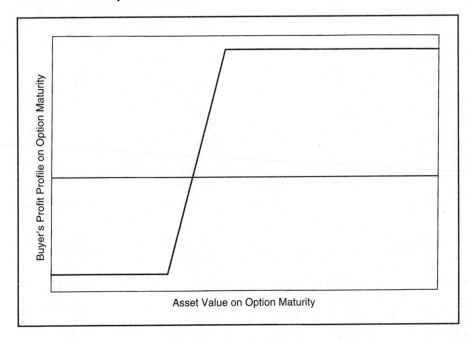

in-advance swap A swap (typically an interest-rate swap) in which the floating-rate reset date is one period in advance of its setting date for a vanilla fixed-floating swap. See also **in-arrears swap**.

in-arrears swap A swap (typically an interest-rate swap) in which there is no time lag between the setting of the floating reference rate and the exchange of payments arising from this setting. This type of swap is also known as an arrears swap, a back-end set swap, delayed LIBOR reset swap, delayed reset swap, reset in-arrears swap, and reset swap. See also **in-advance swap**.

in-option Any option that begins to exist only if the price(s) of an asset and/or a combination of assets (not necessarily the same asset underlying the option) satisfies a prespecified condition(s). This type of option, which is also called a sudden birth option, is a building block discussed in Chapter 3. Special cases of the in-option include the down-and-in option and the up-and-in option. See also **extinguishable option**.

index accreting rate swap A special case of an interest-rate accreting swap in which the notional principal amount is a function of the interest-rate index (e.g., three-month LIBOR). This type of swap is also called an index accreting swap.

index accreting swap See **index accreting rate swap**.

index amortizing rate swap A special case of an interest-rate amortizing swap in which the notional principal amount is a function of the interest-rate index (e.g., three-month LIBOR). This type of swap is also called an index amortizing swap.

index amortizing swap See **index amortizing rate swap**.

index currency option note (ICON) A variation of the dual currency bond in which the principal is also repaid on bond maturity in the currency of the investor. This principal is converted using the exchange rate prevailing on the bond maturity date such that if the exchange rate exceeds a preset level, an amount of the face value (i.e., $100 or $1,000) will be paid out to investor in the domestic currency. If the exchange rate is below another level, which is different from the first level, the investor does not get any principal back. If the exchange rate falls between these two levels, the principal gets converted to an amount using some function of the prevailing exchange rate. Whatever this converted amount, it is always greater than zero and less than the face value.

index participation certificate See **equity index-linked note**.

index principal return note See **equity index-linked note**.

index principal swap An interest-rate swap whose notional principal amount is a function of the interest-rate index. The index accreting rate swap and index amortizing rate swap are special cases of this type of swap.

index swap See **basis swap**.

installment option See **compound option**.

interest-rate collar See **collar**.

interest-rate guarantee (IRG) An interest-rate option whose underlying instrument is a forward rate agreement (FRA). An IRG that allows the purchaser the right-to-pay the strike rate of the option as a fixed rate on the underlying FRA can be thought of as a caplet that is struck at the same rate. Similarly, an IRG that allows the purchaser the right-to-receive the strike rate of the option as a fixed rate on the underlying FRA can be thought of as a floorlet that is struck at the same rate. This type of interest-rate contract is also called a fration.

interest-rate option An option whose underlying asset is an interest-rate index (e.g., three-month LIBOR, one-month BA, 10-year U.S. swap rate).

interest-rate index swap   See **coupon swap**.

interest-rate swap   See **coupon swap**.

international spread option   An example of a difference option, in which the investor can take a view or hedge the relative movements between a point on the domestic yield curve and another point on the foreign yield curve. To do this, the purchaser pays the premium and receives the in-the-money payoff in either the domestic currency or the foreign currency but not both.

inverse floater   See **bull floater**.

inverted curve enhancement swap   A swap in which the receiver of the floating rate puts a floor on the rate. This floor rate has to be prespecified at the inception of the swap contract. In return, the counterparty will receive an extra spread that could either be received as an up-front premium or amortized into the swap.

iron butterfly   The purchaser of this strategy would buy a straddle and sell a strangle. The net effect of this position is equivalent to the selling of a butterfly spread with exactly the same strikes.

jellyroll   The purchaser of this strategy would effectively be long a calendar spread using call options and short a calendar spread using put options, where both the calendar spreads would be struck at the same level. Because the purchase (sale) of a call (put) calendar spread is equivalent to the purchase of a longer (shorter) dated call (put) option and the sale of a shorter (longer) dated call (put) option, this strategy can be collapsed to the purchase of a longer-dated synthetic forward and the sale of a shorter-dated synthetic forward.

joint option   The purchaser of this option on a foreign instrument (e.g., bond, equity index) will receive an in-the-money option payoff in a currency that is different from that of the asset underlying the option. The premium to purchase this protection is usually denominated in the same currency as the payoff. Unlike a guaranteed exchange-rate option, the exchange rate on the maturity of the option (provided it is favorable) is applied for converting the payoff into another currency in this option. This type of option is discussed as a Category V product option in Chapter 3.

When the underlying asset class is an equity, this type of option is also called an equity-linked currency option.

knock-in forward   A FX forward that comes into existence if the underlying exchange rate breaches a prespecified barrier before the expiry of the forward contract. See also **knock-out forward**.

knock-in option   An option that may come into existence when an asset value (not necessarily the same as the asset underlying the option contract) breaches a prespecified barrier during a prespecified time. This option, which is a special case of a barrier option, includes both the down-and-in option and the up-and-in option.

knock-in swap   A swap contract that comes into existence if the asset value underlying the swap contract (or the value of an asset that is correlated to the asset underlying the swap contract) breaches a prespecified barrier before a prespecified time. The swap that is knocked into can either have a fixed tenor or a fixed maturity date. See also **knock-out swap**.

knock-out forward A FX forward that ceases to exist if the underlying exchange rate breaches a prespecified barrier before the expiry of the forward contract. See also **knock-in forward**.

knock-out option An option that may cease to exist when an asset value (not necessarily the same as the asset underlying the option contract) breaches a prespecified barrier during a prespecified time. This option, which is a special case of a barrier option, includes both the down-and-out option and the up-and-out option.

knock-out swap A swap contract that ceases to exist if the asset value underlying the swap contract (or the value of an asset that is correlated to the asset underlying the swap contract) breaches a prespecified barrier before a prespecified time. See also **knock-out swap**.

ladder option See **ratchet option**.

latent option See **embedded option**.

lender's option See **floorlet**.

level-payment swap See **annuity swap**.

leverage reverse floating-rate note A reverse floating-rate note in which the in-the-money payoff to the holder is leveraged and is higher than a regular reverse floating-rate note. This leveraging is achieved by increasing the fixed rate and settling it against a fraction of the floating rate.

liability-based swap A swap that is strictly motivated by the end user's desire to modify the nature of the liabilities.

limit option See **barrier option**.

limited exercise option See **Mid-Atlantic option**.

limited put See **bear spread**.

lock-step option See **ratchet option**.

long-dated forward Any FX forward that has a maturity greater than one year.

long-dated option Any option that has a maturity greater than two years.

look-back option A call (put) option that allows the purchaser the right to buy (sell) an asset at a prespecified time in the future for the lowest (highest) value the asset reaches during the option life. This type of option is also called a hindsight option, look-back strike option, and a no-regret option. This option is discussed as a Category I and II look-back option in Chapter 3. See also **modified look-back option**.

look-back strike option See **look-back option**.

look-back swap Typically an interest-rate swap in which the receiver (payer) of the floating-rate index has the option of receiving (paying) the higher (lower) of the floating-rate index and the floating-rate index set in arrears during the life of the swap, resulting in a higher (lower) fixed rate.

look-forward option A special case of the modified look-back option in which the strike value is set equal to spot price at the inception of the contract.

low-coupon swap A special case of an off-market swap where the receiver of the fixed rate receives fixed payments based on a below-market coupon rates. For receiving these rates, the receiver of the floating-rate payment pays an up-front compensation. The only difference between a low-coupon swap and a discount swap is the timing of this compensation.

macroeconomic swap A swap that is designed to mitigate the risk arising from business seasonal cycles by linking the payments in the swap to a macroeconomic index.

macroeconomic option An option that is designed to mitigate the risk arising from business seasonal cycles by using a macroeconomic index as an underlying asset.

mambo combo See **guts**.

Mandarin collar The purchaser of this strategy would have bought a cylinder, resulting in a bear spread-like profit profile due to an underlying short position, as illustrated in Exhibit A3. The purchaser then additionally sells off two cash-or-nothing options, one of which is struck at a level that is smaller than the lower strike level of a bear spread while the other is struck at a level that is bigger than the higher strike level of a bear spread. Because the purchaser of a Mandarin collar is selling away part of the upside, this strategy generates premium to the user. See Exhibit A20.

EXHIBIT A20 Mandarian Collar

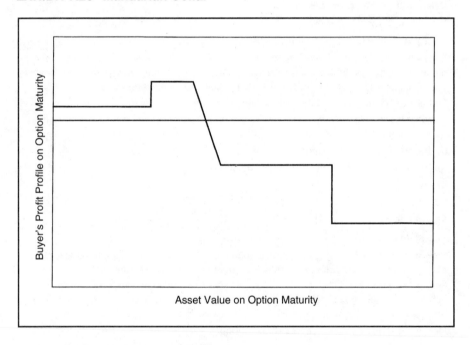

margrabe option See **exchange option**.

market-indexed note See **equity index-linked note**.

matching swap See **back-to-back swap**.

maximum-rate note See **bull floater**.

Mid-Atlantic option An option that allows the purchaser to buy or sell the asset underlying the option at a prespecified price(s) on prespecified dates during the life of the option, inclusive of its expiration date. This option, which is also known as an Atlantic option, a Bermuda option, Bermudan option, limited exercise option, discrete exercise option, and Quasi-American option, cannot be cheaper than a European-style option.

mini-max The purchaser of this strategy would have effectively financed the purchase of an option by selling away another option that is struck at a different level. The purchased and sold options would be both European-style in nature and expire on the same day. By the nature of this strategy, a cylinder is an example of a mini-max.

mini-max floater A floating-rate note that is embedded with a collar.

mini-max strategy Any risk management strategy that minimizes the premium paid for the insurance. An example of this would be the purchase of a cap that is partially funded by the sale of another cap, which could either be a bull spread or a bear spread.

mirror swap See **back-to-back swap**.

mismatched swap In a vanilla swap, there are no timing mismatches in the cash flows that are paid and received by the two parties involved in any settlement period. Unlike this, in a mismatched swap there are timing mismatches in the settlement of cash flows. As a result, both parties involved in the swap are exposed to each other's settlement risk.

modified look-back option A call (put) option that allows the purchaser the right to buy (sell) the highest (lowest) value the asset reaches during the option life for a prespecified price at a prespecified time in the future. This type of option is discussed as a Category III and IV look-back option in Chapter 3. See also **look-back option**.

money-market swap See **IMM swap**.

mortgage over treasury option An example of a yield curve spread option where the two indexes underlying the option are the mortgage yield and the treasury yield.

moving strike option See **deferred strike option**.

multi-factor option See **alternative option**.

multicurrency swap An extension of the currency swap theme, in which there are at least two currencies inherent in the swap.

multi-index option See **alternative option**.

multi-period option Any option whose payout is linked to the values of the underlying index/rate on at least two days. Examples of this type of option are an average rate option and a look-back option.

multiple traded option Any exchange-traded option contract that trades in at least two countries. The Nikkei index option, which trades in both Singapore and Chicago, is an example of this type of option.

municipal swap An interest-rate swap whose floating-rate index is linked to tax-exempt U.S. municipal bonds.

naked option In transacting in this instrument, the buyer is introduced to the market exposure arising from the movements in the value of the asset underlying the option.

naked swap In transacting in this instrument, the buyer is introduced to the market exposure arising from the movements in the value of the asset underlying the swap.

near-month contract An exchange trading futures contract or options contract that has the shortest term to expiry amongst all the contracts that are currently trading. See also **front contract**.

no-cost collar See **costless collar**.

no-cost option See **costless option**.

no-regret option See **look-back option**.

nonlinear payoff option   A vanilla option's payoff upon exercise is a linear function of the in-the-moneyness of the option. A nonlinear payoff option's payoff upon exercise, on the other hand, is a nonlinear function of the in-the-moneyness of the option. This type of option is discussed as a building block in Chapter 3.

nonpar swap   See **off-market swap**.

nonstandard option   See **exotic option**.

nonvanilla option   See **exotic option**.

off-market coupon swap   See **off-market swap**.

off-market swap   A swap in which the payer (receiver) of the fixed rate pays (receives) a rate that is not the market rate. When this rate is below (above) the market rate, this type of swap is also called a discount swap and low-coupon swap (premium swap and high coupon swap). Thus, this type of swap has a non-zero present value at the inception of the contract. This type of swap is also called an adjustment swap, nonpar swap, and off-market coupon swap.

offsetting swap   A swap that mitigates only the market risk of an existing swap. This swap does not completely cancel the existing swap and therefore does not completely mitigate the entire risk of the existing swap.

one-touch option   An example of a sudden birth option, in which the purchaser will receive a prespecified bet amount at the time the prespecified barrier is breached. In the event the barrier is not breached before the expiry of the option, the purchaser does not receive any payoff. This type of option is a hybrid of the barrier option and the cash-or-nothing option.

option   An agreement that allows the purchaser the right, but not the obligation, to buy or sell a function of the underlying asset at a certain price on or before a prespecified date for a premium. This is also called an option contract.

option contract   See **option**.

option-dated forward   A forward exchange-rate agreement where the purchaser has the right to select the date of exchange. If selected, the forward rate, which was agreed upon at the inception of the contract, will be exchanged for the spot rate prevailing on the selection date. This is also called an option-dated forward contract.

option-dated forward contract   See **option-dated forward**.

option-on-a-cap   See **caption**.

option-on-a-floor   See **floortion**.

option-on-an-option   See **compound option**.

option-on-a-future   See **futures option**.

option on a swap   An option whose underlying instrument is a swap. This type of option is also called a swaption.

option on a bond   See **bond option**.

out option   See **extinguishable option**.

outperformance option   See **better-of-two-assets option**.

outright   See **FX forward**.

outright forward   See **FX forward**.

over-and-in option   See **up-and-in option**.

over-and-out option   See **up-and-out option**.

over-and-out warrant A warrant that is philosophically similar to the up-and-out option. This type of warrant is also called an over-the-top warrant.

over-the-top option See **up-and-out option**.

over-the-top warrant See **over-and-out warrant**.

overwrite See **covered write**.

partial average rate option An average rate option whose averaging period is a fraction of the option life.

partial look-back option A look-back option whose look-back period is a fraction of the option life.

partial look-back warrant See **anti-crash warrant**.

participating cap A cap that is usually purchased on a smaller notional principal amount than required by the borrower. As a result, the amount of protection received from the purchase of a participating cap is a fraction of that received from the purchase of a cap.

participating floor A floor that is usually purchased on a smaller notional principal amount than that required by the borrower. As a result, the amount of protection received from the purchase of a participating floor is a fraction of that received from the purchase of a floor.

participating forward An off-market FX forward contract in which the seller, in addition to guaranteeing a floor rate (which is lower than the market rate) of the contract, participates in the upside of the market should the settlement rate exceed the guaranteed rate. This amount of participation is a function of the guaranteed floor rate, and the lower the floor rate, the higher the percentage of participation. This type of contract, which is also called a participating forward contract and a profit-sharing forward is illustrated in Exhibit A21.[8]

participating forward contract See **participating forward**.

participating interest-rate agreement An off-market forward rate agreement in which the purchaser, in addition to capping the interest-rate (which is higher than the market rate) of the contract, participates in the downside of the market should the settlement rate be lower than the guaranteed rate. This amount of participation is a function of the guaranteed cap rate, and the higher the cap rate, the higher the percentage of participation. See Exhibit A22 and also participating forward.[9]

participating option Any call (put) option where the purchaser gets paid a percentage of the in-the-money payoff as long as the value of the asset at maturity exceeds (is below) a prespecified strike level. Typically, this percentage is any amount that is less than 100 percent. A participating cap and a participating floor are capital-market examples of a participating option, which is also called a profit-sharing option.

---

[8]The dotted line in Exhibit A21 illustrates the payoff to the seller of an at-the-market FX forward. The solid line in the exhibit illustrates the fact that an off-market FX forward was sold so as to finance the participation of upside as the asset value on option maturity increases.

[9]The dotted line in Exhibit A22 illustrates the payoff to the buyer of an at-the-market forward-rate agreement. The solid line in the exhibit illustrates the fact that an off-market forward-rate agreement was bought so as to finance the participation of upside as the value of interest rates on option maturity decreases.

EXHIBIT A21 Participating Forward

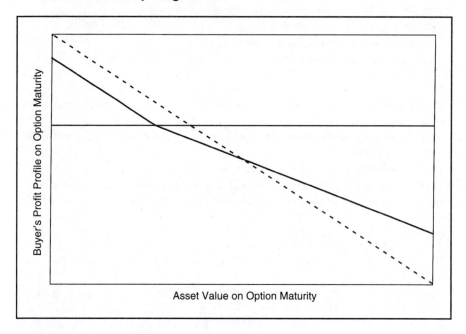

EXHIBIT A22 Participating Interest-Rate Agreement

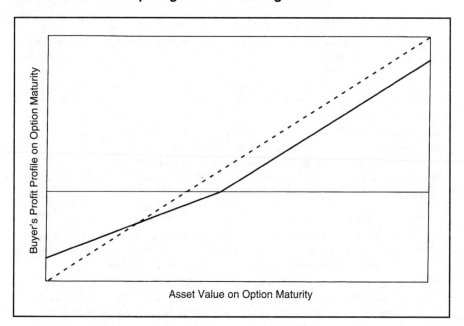

participating range forward See **forward plus**.

participating swap A swap in which the floating-rate component is partially swapped to a fixed rate so that the receiver (payer) of the floating rate can participate in the increase (decrease) in the rates. This type of swap is a sting of participating interest-rate agreements.

path-dependent option Any option whose existence and/or value is dependent on the path transversed by the asset underlying the option during a prespecified time, which may be a subset of the option life.

pay-as-you-go cap See **rent-a-cap**.

pay-as-you-go floor See **rent-a-floor**.

pay-as-you-go option See **compound option**.

pay-later cap See **contingent cap**.

pay-later floor See **contingent floor**.

pay-later option See **contingent premium option**.

pay-later swaption See **contingent swaption**.

pay-only-if-you-need option See **contingent premium option**.

payer's swaption An interest-rate option that allows the purchaser the right-to-pay a fixed rate and receive a floating rate on the underlying swap, upon option maturity.

periodic cap An interest-rate example of a deferred strike option in which the floating strike rate component for each underlying caplet is unknown at the inception of the contract. The strike rate that is applied at the expiry of each caplet is set at a prespecified spread over the value of the index set at the time of the previous option expiry. For the first caplet, however, the strike rate is set at the same prespecified spread above the value of the index taken at the inception of the contract and is thus completely known. This instrument is also known as the forward cap.

periodic floor An interest-rate example of a deferred strike option in which the floating strike rate component for each underlying floorlet is unknown at the inception of the contract. The strike rate that is applied at the expiry of each floorlet is set at a prespecified spread below the value of the index set at the time of the previous option expiry. For the first floorlet, however, the strike rate is set at the same prespecified spread below the value of the index taken at the inception of the contract and is thus completely known. This instrument is also known as the forward floor.

periodic rate-setting swap A swap in which one side of the cash flow is indexed to a floating rate and the other side of the cash flow is indexed to a fixed rate. Instead of applying the floating rate that was set three or six months ago, the effective floating rate would be averaged every day from the time of the last settlement to that of the next settlement. For example, to obtain the value of the cash flow for the first settlement, the floating rates are averaged from the inception of the swap contract to the date of the first cash flow. This type of swap is also known as a periodic resetting swap.

periodic resetting swap See **periodic rate-setting swap**.

perpendicular spread This purchaser of this strategy is a purchaser of either the bear spread or the bull spread, not both.

perpetual floating rate-note A floating rate note that does not have a fixed maturity date.

pop-up option See **up-and-in option**.

portfolio option See **basket option**.

positive cash flow collar   A collar that generates a positive cash flow to the purchaser.

power option   An example of the non-linear payoff option in which the in-the-money payoff to the purchaser at the option expiry is the difference between a power function of the underlying asset price (e.g., the square of the asset price or the cube of the asset price) and a prespecified strike price. These types of options are also called turbo options.

power swap   The floating rate/price component of this swap is calculated using a power function of the underlying rate/price (e.g., the square of the rate/price or the cube of the rate/price).

premium-free option   See **costless option**.

premium swap   An example of an off-market swap in which the receiver of the fixed rate gets fixed payments based on an above-market rate. The difference between the market fixed rate and the transacted fixed rate is compounded and paid out to the payer of the fixed-rate payments on the maturity of the swap. See also **discount swap**.

prepaid swap   A fixed-floating swap in which the fixed side is present-valued and paid at the inception of the contract. The floating side is settled as in the same manner as a vanilla swap.

product option   Any option whose in-the-money payoff is calculated by multiplying the values of at least two different assets. This type of option is discussed as a building block in Chapter 3.

profit-sharing forward   See **participating forward**.

profit-sharing option   See **participating option**.

protected equity notes   See **equity index-linked notes**.

protective call   The purchaser of this option loses money as the value of the underlying asset increases. The call option is purchased to limit the maximum loss that can arise from an increase in the underlying value of the asset.

protective put   The purchaser of this option loses money as the value of the underlying asset decreases. The put option is purchased to limit the maximum loss that can arise from a decrease in the underlying value of the asset.

put option   An option that allows the purchaser the right to sell the asset underlying the option at a prespecified time(s) in the future for either a prespecified price or some function of the future asset price. For this right, the purchaser pays a premium at the inception of the contract. This is also known as a decline guarantee.

put spread   See **bear spread**.

puttable bond   The holder of this instrument has the right to sell the bond back to the issuer for a prespecified price at a prespecified time. See also **callable bond**.

puttable swap   A swap that allows the fixed-rate receiver the right to terminate the swap contract at prespecified times in the future. This swap is a special case of a cancelable swap. See also **callable swap**.

quantity-adjusting option (quanto)   Any option whose underlying asset trades in a foreign country and whose purchaser wants the in-the-money payoff to be denominated in a currency that is different from that in which the underlying asset trades. The payoff on the option maturity date could either be converted to the currency of interest using a guaranteed exchange rate or the spot exchange rate prevailing on the option maturity date. The premium paid for the option is usually also denominated in the same currency as the payoff.

quasi-American option   See **Mid-Atlantic option**.

rainbow option   A special case of the alternative option when there are only two underlying assets. In this variation, the purchaser of an option receives the positive value of the
difference between the highest (or the lowest) value of the underlying two assets and the
strike value for a call (put) option upon exercise. This option, which is also known as a relative performance option, includes both the better-of-two-assets option and the worse-of-
two-assets option.

range forward   See **cylinder**.

range option   See **high-low option**.

ratchet option   An option that allows the buyer to lock in favorable gains realized by the
movements of the underlying asset value during the life of the option. This type of option,
which is also known as a cliquet option, ladder option, lock-step option, and step-lock option, can be replicated by buying and selling barrier options.

rate-differential swap   See **cross-indexed basis swap**.

ratio forward   See **participating forward**.

ratio spread   The purchaser of this strategy would effectively purchase and sell different
amounts of the option contracts. Examples of this strategy, which is also known as a variable spread, include a back spread and a front spread.

ratio vertical spread   See **front spread**.

receiver's swaption   An interest-rate option on a swap that allows the purchaser the right to
receive a fixed rate and pay a floating rate on the underlying swap, upon the option's maturity.

reduced-cost option   An option whose cost is reduced by the purchaser selling away part
of the upside to reduce the premium needed to purchase the insurance. See also **costless
option**.

relative performance option   See **rainbow option**.

rent-a-cap   A variation on the caption theme in which the purchaser of the cap would pay
prespecified prices at prespecified times in the future, where more than two payments are
made to the seller and the premium on each caplet is paid only if it is required. This type
of instrument is also called a pay-as-you-go cap. See **also flexible caps**.

rent-a-floor   A variation on the floortion theme in which the purchaser of the floor would
pay prespecified prices at prespecified times in the future, where more than two payments
are made to the seller and the premium on each floorlet is paid only if it is required. This
type of instrument is also called a pay-as-you-go floor. See also **flexible floors**.

reset in-arrears swap   See **in-arrears swap**.

reset option   A call (put) option whose strike level is decreased (increased) to make the
option more in-the-money should the option become out-of-the-money on the reset date.
This type of option is also called a strike reset option.

reset swap   See **in-arrears swap**.

retractable swap   See **callable swap**.

reversal   See **back-to-back swap**.

reverse   See **back-to-back swap**.

reverse cash-and-carry arbitrage   A strategy in which a futures contract is purchased
and the asset underlying the futures contract is sold. This strategy is used when the market
repo rate is greater than the implied repo rate from the purchase of the futures contract. See
also **cash-and-carry arbitrage**.

reverse dual-currency bond   The purchaser of this bond pays for the bond in the domestic currency that is the currency of the investor. Although the investor receives the

principal on bond maturity in the same currency, the coupons are paid in the currency of the issuer (i.e., foreign currency).

reverse floater See **bull floater**.

reverse floating rate-note See **bull floater**.

reverse interest-rate collar The purchaser of this interest-rate strategy can be thought of as the seller of a collar who also has a floating-rate exposure.

reverse range forward The purchaser of this noninterest-rate strategy can be thought of as the seller of a cylinder who also has a market exposure. This type of strategy is also known as a reverse risk reversal, risk conversion, risk reversal, and spread conversion.

reverse risk reversal See **reverse range forward**.

reversible swap The purchaser of this product would effectively buy an interest-rate swap (e.g., pay fixed and receive floating) and an option on the same swap. This option, if exercised, would allow the purchaser to pay floating and receive fixed on twice the notional amount on the swap, resulting in a net position of receiving a fixed rate and paying a floating rate on the remaining life of the swap.

risk conversion See **reverse range forward**.

risk reversal See **reverse range forward**.

roll-down A strategy where the holder of the option closes the position and purchases another option with a lower strike price. See also **roll up**.

roll-forward A strategy where the holder of the option closes the position and purchases another option with a longer time to expiry.

roll-up A strategy where the holder of the option closes the position and purchases another option with a higher strike price. See also **roll down**.

roller-coaster cap A hybrid of the accreting cap and the amortizing cap where the notional principal underlying each caplet varies across time in a nonincreasing or nondecreasing fashion.

roller-coaster swap A hybrid of the accreting swap and the amortizing swap where the notional principal underlying each settlement varies across time in a nonincreasing or nondecreasing fashion.

rolling over This term describes any one of the roll down, roll forward, and roll up strategies.

Russian option A hybrid of a perpetual American-style vanilla option and a European-style look-back option. In this variation, the look-back option has an infinite life and can be exercised anytime during the life of the option.

safe return certificate An equity linked note whose principal is guaranteed on maturity. See also **equity index-linked note**.

sandwich spread See **butterfly spread**.

seagull A strategy in which the purchaser would buy an at-the-money European-style call option by using the premiums obtained from the sale of an out-of-the-money European-style call and put option. This strategy is illustrated in Exhibit A23.

seasonal swap An interest-rate swap in which the principal is designed to track the seasonal financing needs of a corporate. See also **macroeconomic swap**.

second-generation option See **exotic option**.

sell-write See **covered put**.

EXHIBIT A23 Seagull

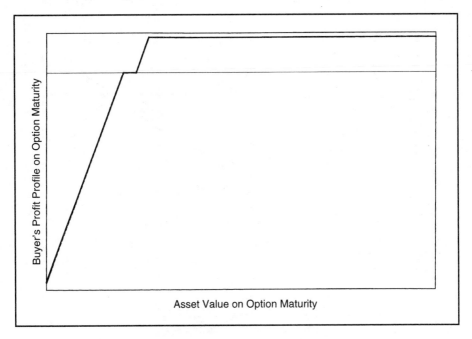

semifixed swap   An interest-rate coupon swap in which the payer of the fixed rate pays one of the two possible prespecified fixed rates. The applied fixed rates will be contingent on the current value of the floating-rate index breaching a prespecified barrier.

shout option   A hybrid of an American-style option and a look-back option. In this variation, the purchaser of the call (put) option upon exercising the option will receive the payoff only on the day the option matures. The payoff received will be the absolute value of the difference between the higher (lower) of the asset values at the time of shout and option maturity and the value of the asset at option maturity. This option is discussed in Chapter 3 under the look-back option building block.

split collar   In a traditional collar, the purchaser buys a cap and sells a floor expiring at the same time. Unlike a traditional collar, in this strategy, the purchaser buys a cap and sells a floor expiring at different times. The noninterest-rate variation of this strategy is called a split cylinder.

split cylinder   Unlike the purchaser of a cylinder, the purchaser of this strategy buys a European-style call option and sells a European-style put option, each of which expire at different times. This strategy is illustrated in Exhibit A24.[10]

split-fee option   See compound option.

split risk reversal   Like a risk reversal, the purchaser of this strategy is the seller of a split cylinder.

---

[10]The solid (dotted) line in Exhibit A24 illustrates the fact that a long-dated (short-dated) call option was purchased and a short-dated (long-dated) put option was sold.

EXHIBIT A24   Split Cylinder

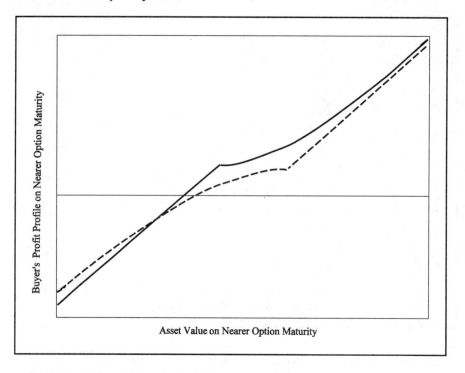

Buyer's Profit Profile on Nearer Option Maturity

Asset Value on Nearer Option Maturity

spraddle   See **strangle**.

spread conversion   See **reverse range forward**.

spread-lock agreement   A contract that allows the purchaser to lock in a prespecified interest-rate swap spread for a finite period of time.

spread-lock option   An option whose underlying asset is a spread-lock agreement.

spread-lock swap   A delayed start swap in the interest-rate market, in which the payer of the fixed rate has purchased a spread-lock agreement. In addition to this, the payer has a choice of fixing the benchmark bond yield before the commencement of the swap. If no fixing of the underlying bond yield is done before the commencement of the swap, the payer is automatically exercised into the bond yield prevailing on the commencement date of the swap. This type of agreement is also called a swap-spread lock.

spread option   See **difference option**.

spreadtion   See **difference option**.

staged drawdown swap   See **accreting swap**.

standard option   Any European-style or American-style option with a prespecified expiry date and prespecified strike price. When exercising such an option, the value of the underlying asset at the time of exercise is the only factor that is crucial for determining whether the option finished in-the-money or out-of-the-money. See also **exotic option**.

step-down coupon note   A note in which the holder receives higher coupons during the initial life of the note and lower coupons during the remaining life of the note. This type of note is the opposite of a step-up coupon note.

step-down coupon swap   Any swap in which the fixed-rate payments decrease over time due to a decreasing fixed rate. This type of swap, which is also known as a step-down swap, has the effect of an amortizing swap.

step-down swap   See **step-down coupon swap**.

step-lock option   See **ratchet option**.

step-up coupon note   A note in which the holder receives lower coupons during the initial life of the note followed by higher coupons during the remaining life of the note. See also **step-down coupon note**.

step-up coupon swap   Any swap in which the fixed-rate payments increase over time due to an increasing fixed rate. This type of swap, which is also known as a step-up swap, has the effect of an accreting swap.

step-up swap   See **step-up coupon swap**.

stock index futures   A futures contract whose underlying asset is an equity or stock index.

stock index option   An option whose underlying asset is an equity or stock index.

stock option   An option whose underlying asset is a stock.

stock-over-bond warrant   A warrant that gives its purchaser a payoff that is based on the difference between the price of a prespecified quantity of stocks and the price of a bond. This warrant can be alternatively viewed as an instrument that allows the purchaser to exchange a bond underlying the warrant for a quantity of stocks. See also **bond-over-stock warrant**.

stoption   See **barrier option**.

straddle   The purchaser of this option strategy would effectively buy a European-style call and put option expiring at the same time and struck at the same level. This strategy, which is illustrated in Exhibit A25, is a special case of a strangle where both the options are struck at the same level.

strangle   The purchaser of this option strategy would effectively buy a European-style call and put option struck at different levels. This type of strategy, which is called a spraddle, surf and turf is illustrated in Exhibit A26.When both the strikes are set at the same level, this strategy is also called a straddle.

strap   The purchaser of this option strategy would effectively buy two European-style call options and one European-style put option all expiring at the same time and struck at the same level. Exhibit A27 illustrates this strategy.[11]

strike reset option   See **reset option**.

strike step option   A vanilla option whose strike levels get reset during the life of the option as the value of the underlying asset trades through or beyond different levels.

strip   The purchaser of this option strategy would effectively buy two European-style put options and one European-style call option, all expiring at the same time and struck at the same level. [12] See Exhibit A28.

---

[11]Strategy 2 illustrates the payoff of the buyer when only one call option and one put option are purchased. Strategy 3 illustrates the payoff when two call options are purchased and two put options are purchased. Strategy One illustrates the buyer's profit profile associated with the purchase of a strap (i.e., two call options and one put option).

[12]Strategy 2 illustrates the payoff of the buyer when only one call option and one put option are purchased. Strategy 3 illustrates the payoff when two call options are purchased and 2 put options are purchased. Strategy 1 illustrates the buyer's profit profile associated with the purchase of a strip (i.e., one call option and two put options).

EXHIBIT A25 Straddle

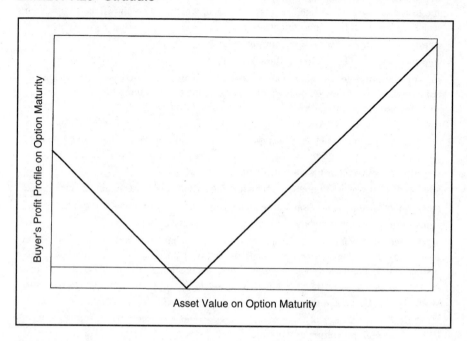

EXHIBIT A26 Spraddle

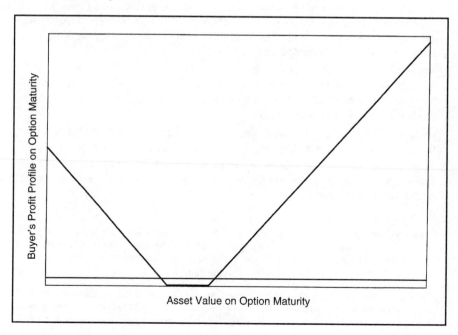

EXHIBIT A27 Strap

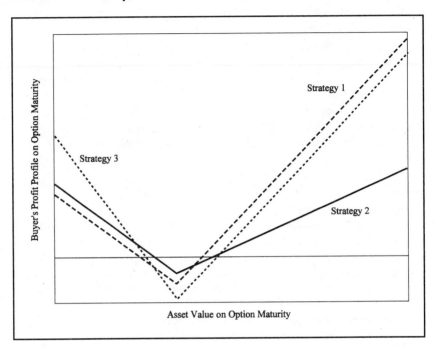

EXHIBIT A28 Strip

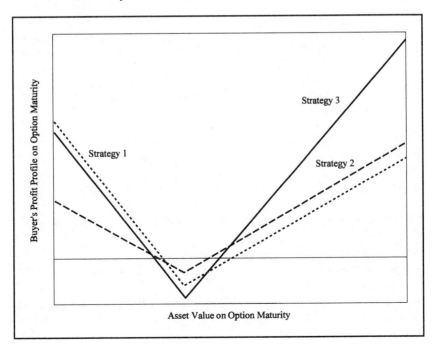

sudden birth option   See **in-option**.

sudden death option   See **extinguishable option**.

supershare option   See **binary option**.

surf and turf   See **strangle**.

swap   A contractual agreement between two parties to exchange cash flows based on values or movements in prespecified indexes. These indexes could belong to any one asset class or a combination of asset classes.

swap option   See **option-on-a-swap**.

swap-rate lock   Any agreement that locks the absolute level of the swap rate on a swap that is starting at some time in the future. A simple example of this type of swap is the delayed start swap.

swap-spread lock   See **spread lock swap**.

swaption   See **option-on-a-swap**.

swaption collar   See **collar**.

switch option   See **exchange option**.

synthetic call   A long position in a European-style call option that can be synthetically created by going long in the underlying forward position and going long a European-style put option. The forward and the put option will expire at the same time as the call option, with both the options being struck at the forward level. See also **synthetic forward** and **synthetic put**.

synthetic forward   A long position in a forward that can be synthetically created by going long a European-style call option and going short a European-style put option. The call option and the put option will expire at the same time as the forward, with both the options being struck at the forward level. See also **synthetic call** and **synthetic put**.

synthetic put   A long position in a European-style put option that can be synthetically created by going short in the underlying forward position and going long a European-style call option. The forward and the call option will expire at the same time as the put option, with both the option struck at the forward level. See also **synthetic call** and **synthetic forward**.

table top   The purchaser of this strategy would have effectively purchased an option by selling the same type of option at two different strike prices. Thus, this strategy can be thought of as a zero-cost version of a Christmas tree strategy, which is illustrated in Exhibits A9 and A10.

tailored swap   Any swap that is customized to mitigate the appropriate market risk exposure of the end user.

tandem option   A sequence of options with nonoverlapping time periods and variable strikes.

tax-exempt swap   An interest-rate swap in which at least one of the indexes is based on a tax-exempt index.

terminable swap   See **callable swap**.

time box   See **box**.

time spread   See **calendar spread**.

top straddle   The purchaser of this strategy has sold a straddle. See also **bottom straddle**.

top vertical combination   The purchaser of this strategy has sold a strangle. See also **bottom vertical combination**.

total rate-of-return swap The floating-rate component of this swap is calculated using the earnings gained by the underlying index, which would also reflect the reinvestment of the dividends that are paid out, appreciation/depreciation of the capital, and so on.

touch option An option that has as its constituents, in the broadest sense, the sudden birth and sudden death options.

trigger option See **barrier option**.

trigger swap A swap that may either come into existence or cease to exist as soon as an asset value (not necessarily the same as the asset underlying the swap contract) breaches a prespecified barrier during a prespecified time interval. This type of swap is also called a barrier-style swap and contingent swap.

tunnel See **cylinder**.

tunnel option An option whose underlying asset is an tunnel.

turbo option See **power option**.

up-and-away option See **up-and-out option**.

up-and-in option An example of a knock-in option where the underlying vanilla option starts to exist when the asset (not necessarily the same as the asset underlying the option contract) value has to transverse upwards to breach a prespecified barrier during a pre-specified time. In the event the barrier is breached, the purchaser of the up-and-in option receives the normal option payoff. This type of option is also known as an over-and-in option.

Sometimes an up-and-in option may be structured in a way that if the barrier is not breached, the purchaser of the option would receive a rebate on the option expiry date.

up-and-out option An example of a knock-out option where the underlying vanilla option ceases to exist when the asset (not necessarily the same as the asset underlying the option contract) value has to transverse upwards to breach a prespecified barrier during a prespecified time. In the event the barrier is not breached, the purchaser of the up-and-out option receives the normal option payoff. This type of option is also known as an over-and-out option and an up-and-away option.

Sometimes an up-and-out option may be structured in a way that if the barrier is breached, the purchaser of the option would receive a rebate at the time of breaching.

vanilla swap Any commodity/currency/equity/interest-rate swap in its simplest form. This type of swap is also called a generic swap.

vanishing option See **extinguishing option**.

variable spread See **ratio spread**.

vertical bear spread See **bear spread**.

vertical bull spread See **bull spread**.

vertical spread An option strategy that includes both the bear and bull spreads.

volatility option An option whose underlying asset is the volatility.

warrant Philosophically, a warrant is no different from an option. The only difference between these instruments is that a warrant has a life that is longer than one year and is often issued in conjunction with a stock or a bond issue.

weighted-average rate option   A variation on the average rate option, where the average of the asset values is calculated using a weighted average, instead of a simple average. An average rate option is simply a weighted-average rate option where the weights are all set equal to each other.

weighted collar   The purchaser of this strategy would buy caps and sell floors in unequal amounts, unlike a traditional collar.

weighted corridor   The purchaser of this strategy would buy caps and sell caps in unequal amounts, unlike a traditional corridor.

weighted flooridor   The purchaser of this strategy would buy floors and sell floors in unequal amounts, unlike a traditional flooridor.

when-issued option   An option whose underlying asset is a when-issued bond or a bond that is to be auctioned.

worse-of-two-assets option   A special case of an alternative option when there are only two underlying assets. In this type of option, the purchaser of a call option is paid out the positive value of the difference between the lowest of the underlying assets and a prespecified strike value upon exercise. This option, which is the opposite of the better-of-two-assets option, falls under the category of a rainbow option.

yield-curve agreement   See **yield-curve swap**.

yield-curve option   See **yield-curve spread option**.

yield-curve spread option   An option that allows an investor to monetize his or her view on the steepening or flattening of the yields between any two points on the yield curve. This type of option is also called a yield curve option.

yield-curve swap   An interest-rate swap with the exchanged cash flows that reflect the floating rates at different points along the yield curve. This type of swap is also called a yield curve agreement.

you-choose option   See **as-you-like-it option**.

you-choose swap   See **as-you-like-it swap**.

zero collar   See **costless collar**.

zero-cost collar   See **no-cost collar**.

zero-cost option   See **costless option**.

zero-coupon bond   A debt instrument that repays both the principal and interest only on maturity of the instrument. This type of instrument is also known as a bullet maturity. See also **bond**.

zero-coupon cross-currency swap   A cross-currency swap whose coupon cash flows are compounded and exchanged only on the maturity of the swap. Like a traditional cross-currency swap, the principals are also exchanged at the inception and the maturity of the swap contract. This type of instrument is also known as a zero-coupon currency swap.

zero-coupon currency swap   See **zero-coupon cross-currency swap**.

zero-coupon swap   An interest-rate swap whose cash flows on one or both sides of the swap are compounded and exchanged only on the maturity of the swap. Like a traditional coupon swap, there is no exchange of principal during the life of the swap. The zero-coupon swap is also known as a bullet swap.

zero-premium option See **costless option**.

zero-premium risk reversal A risk reversal strategy that costs nothing to enter into.

⑥ BIBLIOGRAPHY

Abramowitz, M. and I.A. Stegun. 1972. *Handbook of Mathematical Functions.* New York: Dover Publications.

Anton, H. and C. Rorres. 1987. *Elementary Linear Algebra with Applications.* New York: John Wiley & Sons.

Babbs, S. 1992. "Binomial Valuation of Lookback Options." Working Paper. Midland Global Markets.

Bernard, G.A. 1993. "A Direct Approach to Pricing Death Benefit Guarantees in Variable Annuity Products." *Product Development News*, June. Society of Actuaries.

Black, F. 1976. "The Pricing of Commodity Contracts." *Journal of Financial Economics* 3, pp. 167–79.

Bouaziz, L., E. Briys, and M. Crouhy. 1994. "The Pricing of Forward Starting Asian Options," *Journal of Banking and Finance* 18, pp. 823–39.

Boyle, P.P. 1977. "Options: A Monte Carlo Approach." *Journal of Financial Economics* 4, pp. 323–38.

_____. 1986. "A Lattice Framework for Option Pricing with Two State Variables." *Journal of Financial and Quantitative Analysis* 23, no. 1, pp. 1–12.

Boyle, P.P., J. Evnine, and S. Gibbs. 1989. "Numerical Evaluation of Multivariate Contingent Claims." *Review of Financial Studies* 2, no. 2, pp. 241–50.

Boyle, P.P. and S.H. Lau. 1994. "Bumping up against the Barrier with the Binomial Method." *Journal of Derivatives, Summer* 1, pp. 6–14.

Brotherton-Ratcliffe, R. and B. Iben. 1993. "Yield Curve Applications of Swap Products." *Advanced Strategies in Financial Risk Management*, Chapter 15, pp. 245–66. New York Institute of Finance.

Burden, R.L. and J.D. Faires. 1985. *Numerical Analysis.* Boston: Prindle, Weber & Schmidt.

Chase/Risk Magazine. 1996. *Guide to Risk Management: A Glossary of Terms.* London: Risk Publications.

Chan, S.H.Y. 1996. *Pricing the Partial Lookback Option.* Master's thesis. University of Waterloo.

Conze, A. and R. Viswanathan. 1991. "Path Dependent Options: The Case of Lookback Options." *Journal of Finance* 46, pp. 1893–1907.

Cox, J.C., S.A. Ross, and M. Rubinstein. 1979. "Option Pricing: A Simplified Approach." *Journal of Financial Economics* 7, pp. 229–63.

Das, S. 1995. "Range Floaters." *The Handbook of Derivative Instruments: Products, Pricing, Portfolio Applications, and Risk Management.* Chapter 12. Rev. ed. Burr Ridge, IL: Irwin Professional Publishing, pp. 276–85.

Dattatreya, R.E., R.E.S. Venkatesh, and V.E. Venkatesh. 1994. *Interest Rate and Currency Swaps: The Markets, Products, and Applications.* Chicago: Probus.

Ferguson, T.S. 1989. "Who Solved the Secretary Problem?" *Statistical Science* 4, no. 3, pp. 282–94.

Garman, M. 1989. "Recollection in Tranquility." *Risk*, March.

Gastineau, G.L. 1992. *Swiss Bank Corporation: Dictionary of Financial Risk Management.* Chicago: Probus.

Geske, R. 1979. "The Valuation of Compound Options." *Journal of Financial Economics* 7, pp. 63–81.

Goldman, M.B., H.B. Sosin, and M.A. Gatto. 1979. "Path Dependent Options: Buy at the Low and Sell at the High." *Journal of Finance* 34, pp. 1111–27.

Gootzeit, A., D. Knowling, P. Schuster, and S. Sonlin. 1994. "Guaranteed Minimum Death Benefit Provisions—How Much Variable Risk Do We Want?" *Product Development News*, June. Society of Actuaries.

Group of Thirty Global Derivatives Study Group. 1993. *Derivatives: Practices and Principles.* Washington, D.C.: Group of Thirty.

Heynen, R. and H. Kat. 1994. "Selective Memory," *Risk*, November.

Hogg, R.V., and A.T. Craig. 1989. *Introduction to Mathematical Statistics.* New York: Macmillan.

Hull, J. and A. White. 1993. "Efficient Procedures for Valuing European and American Path-Dependent Options." *Journal of Derivatives*, Fall, pp. 21–31.

Hull, J.C. 1997. *Options, Futures, and Other Derivative Securities.* 3rd Ed. Englewood Cliffs, New Jersey: Prentice Hall.

Huynh, C.B. 1994. "Back to Baskets." *Risk*, May.

Jarrow, R. and S. Turnbull. 1996. *Derivative Securities.* Cincinnati: South-Western College Publishing.

Kemna, A. and A. Vorst. 1990. "A Pricing Method for Options Based on Average Asset Values." *Journal of Banking and Finance* 14, pp. 113–29.

Kolkiewicz, A.W. and K. Ravindran. 1994. "Discussion of H.U. Gerber's and E.S.W. Shiu's 'Option Pricing by Esscher Transforms.'" *Transactions of Society of Actuaries* 46, pp. 157–62.

Kunitomo, N. and M. Ikeda, 1992. "Pricing Options with Curved Boundaries." *Mathematical Finance* 2, no. 4, pp. 275–98.

Levy, E. 1992. "Pricing European Average Rate Currency Options." *Journal of International Money and Finance* 11, pp. 474–91.

Margrabe, W. 1978. "The Value of an Option to Exchange One Asset for Another." *Journal of Finance* 33, pp. 177–86.

Mitchell, G.T. 1994. "Variable Annuity Minimum Death Benefits—A Monte Carlo Pricing Approach." *Product Development News*, February. Society of Actuaries.

Mueller, H. 1992. "Update on Variable Products." *Product Development News*, July. Society of Actuaries.

Nicholson, W.K. 1986. *Elementary Linear Algebra with Applications*. Boston: Prindle, Weber, & Schmidt.

Peng, S.Y. and R.E. Dattareya. 1995. *The Structured Note Market: The Definitive Guide for Investors, Traders, and Issuers*. Chicago: Probus.

Ravindran, K. 1993a. "Option Pricing: An Offspring of the Secretary Problem?" *Mathematica Japonica* 38, pp. 905–12.

_____. 1993b. "Low-Fat Spreads." *Risk*, October.

_____. 1993c. "LIBOR Binary Notes." *Derivatives Week*, December 6.

_____. 1994. "Exotic Options." *Advanced Interest Rate and Currency Swaps*, Chapter 5. Chicago: Probus, pp. 81–169.

_____. 1995. "Effectively Riding the Yield Curve." *Derivatives Use, Trading & Regulation*, 1, no. 3, pp.211–14.

_____. 1995. "Effectively Hedging a Currency Exposure." *Derivatives Use, Trading & Regulation*, 2, no. 2, pp. 301–11.

_____. 1996a. "Monte Carlo Simulations: Part I." *Derivatives Use, Trading & Regulation*, 2. no. 1, pp. 105–12.

_____. 1996b. "Monte Carlo Simulations: Part 2." *Derivatives Use, Trading & Regulation*, 2, no. 2, pp. 200–08.

_____. 1997a. "Valuing Interest Rate Swaps." *Derivatives Use, Trading & Regulation* 2, no. 4, pp. 387–400.

Ravindran, K. and A.W. Edelist. 1996. "Deriving Benefits from Death." *Frontiers in Derivatives: State-of-Art Models, Valuation, Strategies & Products*, Chapter 11. Burr Ridge, IL: Irwin Professional publishing, pp. 259–77.

Reiner, E. 1992. "Quanto Mechanics." *Risk*, March.

Rose, J.S. 1982. "Twenty Years of Secretary Problems: A Survey of Developments in the Theory of Optimal Choice." *Advances in Management Studies* 1, pp. 53–64.

Ross, S.M. 1993. *Introduction to Probability Models*. San Diego: Academic Press, 5th edition.

Rubinstein, M. 1991a. "Options for the Undecided." *Risk*, April.

_____. 1991b. "Double Trouble." *Risk*, December.

_____. 1994. "Return to Oz." *Risk*, November.

Rubinstein, M. and E. Reiner. 1991. "Breaking Down the Barriers." *Risk*, September.

Schwager, J.D. 1983. *A Complete Guide to the Futures Markets: Fundamental Analysis, Technical Analysis, Trading, Spreads and Options*. New York: John Wiley & Sons.

Stoll, H.R. and R.E. Whaley. 1993. *Futures and Options: Theory and Applications*. Cincinnati: South-Western Publishing.

Stulz, R.K. 1982. "Options on the Minimum or the Maximum of Two Risky Assets." *Journal of Financial Economics* 10, pp. 161–85.

Thomas, B. 1993. "Something to Shout About." *Risk*, May.

Tilley, J.A. 1993. "Valuing American Options in a Path Simulation Model." *Transactions of the Society of Actuaries* 45, pp. 499–549.

Vorst, T.C.F. 1996. "Averaging Options." *Handbook of Exotic Options*, Chapter 6. Burr Ridge, IL: Irwin Professional Publishing, pp. 175–99.

Wei J. 1996. "Valuing Derivatives Linked to Foreign Assets." *Frontiers of Derivatives*, Chapter 5. Burr Ridge, IL: Irwin Professional Publishing, pp. 89–126.

Wilmott, P., J. Dewynne, and S. Howison. 1993. *Option Pricing: Mathematical Models and Computation*. Oxford: Oxford Financial Press.

Zhang, P.G. 1995. "Flexible Arithmetic Asian Options." *Journal of Derivatives* 2, no. 3, pp. 53–63.